5th International Symposium on Hearing

The 5th International Symposium on Hearing has been sponsored by the NATO Special Programme Panel on Human Factors.

Organizing Committee

G. van den Brink, Rotterdam, Symposium Director[1]
F.A. Bilsen, Delft, Symposium Director[2]
J.H. ten Kate, Delft
J. Raatgever, Delft
M. Rodenburg, Rotterdam
J. Verschuure, Rotterdam
Miss P. Maters, Rotterdam, Secretary

1. Department of Biological and Medical Physics, Erasmus University, Rotterdam, The Netherlands
2. Applied Physics Department, Delft University of Technology, Delft, The Netherlands

Preceding Symposia on Hearing:

I.   1969: Driebergen, The Netherlands, *Frequency Analysis and Periodicity Detection in Hearing*. (R. Plomp and G.F. Smoorenburg) A.W. Sijthoff, Leiden (1970).
II. 1972: Eindhoven, The Netherlands, *Hearing Theory*. (B.L. Cardozo) IPO, Eindhoven (1972).
III. 1974: Tutzing, Germany, *Facts and Models in Hearing*. (E. Zwicker and E. Terhardt) Springer Verlag, Berlin, Heidelberg, New York (1974).
IV. 1977: Keele, Great Britain, *Psychophysics and Physiology of Hearing*. (E.F. Evans and J.P. Wilson) Academic Press (1977).

Psychophysical, Physiological and Behavioural Studies in Hearing

Proceedings of the 5th International
Symposium on Hearing

Noordwijkerhout, The Netherlands
April, 8-12, 1980

G. van den Brink/F.A. Bilsen/Editors

Delft University Press/1980

Published by
Delft University Press
Mijnbouwplein 11
2628 RT DELFT
The Netherlands

Distributed by
Sijthoff & Noordhoff
International Publishers
P.O. Box 4
2400 MA ALPHEN AAN DEN RIJN
The Netherlands

ISBN 90 286 0780 3

PREFACE

Experimentists in various disciplines, such as anatomy, physics, chemistry, physiology, psychophysics and psychology, have been carrying out their studies in order to increase our knowledge and understanding of sensory perception. To profit maximally from the results, obtained from these different viewpoints each should take the work of the others into account. The need for intensive communication is, therefore, ever present.

In 1969, in the field of auditory research, this need resulted in Plomp's initiative to organizing an international symposium "Frequency analysis and periodicity perception in hearing". Considering the lively discussions and the numerous references in literature to the proceedings of this Driebergen symposium, the meeting clearly fulfilled its need. It was clear at the time that this sort of symposium should be held regularly. This resulted in meetings in 1972 (Eindhoven), 1974 (Tutzing) and 1977 (Keele). At the meeting in Keele it was agreed that the next one should be held in 1980, again in the Netherlands.

With regard to the program, we decided to carry on the – now expanded – tradition of including anatomy, physiology, psychophysics and the development of models in the program, but to pay more attention to the behavioural aspects of hearing at the same time. As a result, some contributions on animal behaviour have been included in the program. One of the great advantages of this sort of symposium is, that one has the opportunity of paying immediate attention to topics that are of current interest at the time.

The interest in the present symposium exceeded our original estimation, as did the number of contributions. We had to make a choice between two alternatives: one that we should refuse a relatively large number of them; the other that we accepted all of them but divide them into regular papers and smaller research messages. We felt that younger scientists, in particular, should not be discouraged, but in fact quite a number of our older colleagues chose to communicate by means of a research message. The difference in the proceedings can be seen only in the lengths of the contributions: up to eight pages for a paper and up to four pages for a research message. The opportunity to comment on a contribution, as allowed during previous meetings, has been adopted unchanged.

We were fortunate in that the NATO Special Programme Panel on Human Factors was willing to sponsor this meeting and are grateful that this panel gave us complete freedom in the organization. Some expenses that according to NATO rules, were not covered by this grant, were paid from additional funds, provided by the University Fund of the Erasmus University Rotterdam and by the Delft University of Technology.

We want to express our gratitude to the organizing committee, consisting of our colleagues ten Kate, Raatgever, Rodenburg, Verschuure and of Miss Maters, who acted as general secretary. Their joint efforts were essential for the organization. Mrs. M. Mulder – van Nouhuys, Mrs. G. Pruymboom-van Aalst, Miss E. Nieuwenhuis and Mrs. J. Middelkoop-Hoek also contributed in a valuable way in the administration. Finally we would like to acknowledge the pleasant and constructive contacts with Mr. P.A.M. Maas of Delft University Press.

G. van den Brink,
F.A. Bilsen.

Rotterdam/Delft, April 1980.

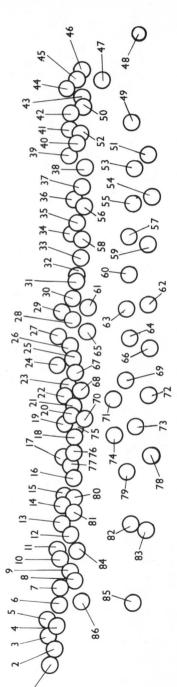

LIST OF PARTICIPANTS   *(Numbers refer to photograph)*

ALLEN, J.B.,Bell Laboratories, Murray Hill, N.J. 07974, USA. *(38)*

BEZEMER, A'., Institute for Perception Research, P.O. Box 513, Eindhoven,
   the Netherlands. *(77)*

BILSEN, F.A., Applied Physics Department, University of Technology,
   Lorentzweg 1, Delft, the Netherlands. *(66)*

BLAUERT, J.P., Ruhr-University Bochum, Universitätsstrasse 150, 4630 Bochum 1,
   Germany. *(44)*

BOER, E. de, Wilhelmina Gasthuis, Fysisch Laboratorium, KNO-kliniek,
   1e Helmersstraat 104, 1054 EG Amsterdam, the Netherlands. *(67)*

BRINK, G. van den, Dept. of Biol. & Med. Physics, Erasmus University Rotterdam,
   P.O. Box 1738, 3000 DR Rotterdam, the Netherlands. *(19)*

BUUNEN, T.J.F., St.Canisius-Wilhelmina Ziekenhuis, St. Annastraat 289, Nijmegen
   the Netherlands. *(23)*

COLBURN, H.S., Massachusetts Institute of Technology, 77 Massachusetts Avenue,
   Cambridge, MA 02139, USA. *(45)*

CORNELIS, J.G., Fysisch Laboratorium, KNO-kliniek, Wilhelmina Gasthuis,
   1e Helmersstraat 104, 1054 EG Amsterdam, the Netherlands. *(20)*

DALLOS, P., Auditory Physiology Laboratory (Audiology), Frances Searle Building,
   North Western University, 2299 Sheridan Road, Evanston, Illinois 60201,
   USA. *(70)*

DRESCHLER, W.A., Vakgroep KNO-Heelkunde en Audiologie, Academisch Ziekenhuis
   der Vrije Universiteit, de Boelelaan 1117, 1007 MB Amsterdam, the
   Netherlands. *(49)*

DUIFHUIS, H., Institute for Perception Research, P.O. Box 513, Eindhoven,
   the Netherlands. *(60)*

EGGERMONT, J.J., Lab. voor Medische Fysica en Biofysica, Geert Grooteplein 21,
   6525 EZ Nijmegen, the Netherlands. *(69)*

EVANS, E.F., Dept. of Communication, University of Keele, Keele, Staffs. ST5
   5BG, Great Britain. *(72)*

FASTL, H., Institute of Electroacoustics, Technical University München,
   D-8000 München 2, Arcisstrasse 21, Germany. *(62)*

FESTEN, J.M., Vakgroep KNO-Heelkunde en Audiologie, Academisch Ziekenhuis der
   Vrije Universiteit, de Boelelaan 1117, 1007 MB Amsterdam, the
   Netherlands. *(51)*

FETH, L., Dept. of Audiology and Speech Sciences, Purdue University, Heavilon
   Hall, West Lafayette, Indiana 47907, USA. *(30)*

FRITZE, W., Allgemeines Krankenhaus der Stadt Wien, II Universitätsklinik für
   Hals-Nasen- und Ohrenkrankheiten, Alserstrasse 4, A-1097 Vienna, Austria.
   (43)

GERLACH, R.E., Drittes Physikalisches Institut, Universität Göttingen,
   Bürgerstrasse 42-44, D-3400 Göttingen, Germany. *(8)*

GOLDSTEIN, J.L., Bioengineering Program, Dept. of Interdisciplinary Studies,
   School of Engineering, Tel-Aviv University, Ramat-Aviv, Tel Aviv, Israel.
   (85)

GREENWOOD, D.D., Division of Audiology and Speech Sciences, University of
   British Columbia, Vancouver, V6T 1W5, Canada. *(76)*

HAFTER, E.R., Dept. of Psychology, University of California, 3210 Tolman Hall, Berkeley, CA 94720, USA. *(42)*

HENNING, G.B., Dept. of Experimental Psychology, South Parks Road, Oxford OX1 3UD, Great Britain. *(57)*

HEUSDEN, E. van, Instituut voor Zintuigfysiologie, Kampweg 5, 3769 DE Soesterberg, the Netherlands. *(11)*

HOEKSTRA, A., Audiologisch Centrum Amersfoort, Zangvogelweg 150, 3815 DP Amersfoort, the Netherlands. *(58)*

HOKE, M., Ear, Nose and Throat Clinic, University of Münster, Kardinal-von-Galen-Ring 10, D-4400 Münster, Germany. *(9)*

HORST, J.W., Audiologisch Instituut, Academisch Ziekenhuis, Oostersingel 59, 9713 EZ Groningen, the Netherlands. *(33)*

HOUTGAST, T., Instituut voor Zintuigfysiologie TNO, Kampweg 5, 3769 DE Soesterberg, the Netherlands. *(41)*

HOUTSMA, A.J., Massachusetts Institute of Technology, 77 Massachusetts Avenue, Cambridge MA 02139, USA. *(3)*

JOHANNESMA, P.I.M., Lab. voor Medische Fysica en Biofysica, Geert Grooteplein Noord 21, 6225 EZ Nijmegen, the Netherlands. *(48)*

JOHNSTONE, J.R., Dept. of Physiology, University of Western Australia, Nedlands 6009, W. Australia. *(75)*

KATE, J.H. ten, Applied Physics Department, University of Technology, Lorentzweg 1, Delft, the Netherlands. *(64)*

KEMP, D.T., Institute of Laryngology and Otology, Gray's Inn Road, London WC1X 8EE, Great Britain. *(4)*

KIM, D.O., Washington University, School of Medicine, Dept. Physiology & Biophysics, 660 South Euclid Avenue, Saint Louis, MO 63110, USA. *(22)*

KLINKE, R., Zentrum der Physiologie, Theodor-Stern-Kai 7, D-6000 Frankfurt am Main 70, Germany. *(18)*

KOHLLÖFFEL, L.U.E., Inst. für Physiologie und Biokybernetik, Universitätsstrasse 17, Erlangen D-8520, Germany. *(14)*

KUWADA, S., Dept. of Neurophysiology, University of Wisconsin, Medical School, Medical Sciences Building, Madison, Wisconsin 53706, USA. *(16)*

LONG, G.L., Central Institute for the Deaf, 818 South Euclid Avenue, Saint Louis, Missouri 63110, USA. *(84)*

MANLEY, G., Inst. für Zoologie der Technische Universität, Arcisstrasse 21, D-8000 München, Germany. *(56)*

McFADDEN, D., Dept. Psychology, University of Texas, Mezes Hall 330, Austin, TX 78712, USA. *(29)*

MOORE, B.C.J. (The Psychological Lab.) Dept. of Experimental Psychology, University of Cambridge, Downing Street, Cambridge CB2 3EB, Great Britain. *(36)*

NARINS, P.M., Dept. of Biology, University of California, Los Angeles, CA 90024, USA. *(46)*

NASSE, H., Drittes Physikalisches Institut, Universität Göttingen, Bürgerstrasse 42-44, 4300 Göttingen, Germany. *(82)*

NELSON, D.A., University of Minnesota, Dept. of Otolaryngology, 2630 University Avenue, SE, Minneapolis, MN 55414, USA. *(24)*

PATTERSON, R.D., MRC Applied Psychology Unit, 15 Chaucer Road, Cambridge, CB2 2EF, Great Britain. *(73)*

PICK, G.F., Dept. of Communication & Neuroscience, University of Keele, Keele, Staffs. ST5 5BG, Great Britain. *(78)*

PICKLES, J.O., Neurocommunications Research Unit, The Medical School, Birmingham University, Birmingham, B15 2TJ, Great Britain. *(1)*

PLOMP, R., Vakgroep KNO-Heelkunde en Audiologie, Academisch Ziekenhuis der Vrije Universiteit, de Boelelaan 1117, 1081 HV Amsterdam, the Netherlands. *(10)*

PRIJS, V.F., Academisch Ziekenhuis Leiden, Afd. KNO, Rijnsburgerweg 10, 2333 AA Leiden, the Netherlands. *(61)*

RAATGEVER, J., Applied Physics Department, University of Technology, Lorentzweg 1, Delft, the Netherlands. *(63)*

RITSMA, R.J., Audiologisch Instituut, Academisch Ziekenhuis, Oostersingel 59, 9713 EZ Groningen, the Netherlands. *(53)*

RODENBURG, M., Afdeling KNO, Erasmus Universiteit, Postbus 1738, 3000 DR Rotterdam, the Netherlands. *(55)*

RUTTEN, W.L.C., Afdeling KNO, Academisch Ziekenhuis Leiden, Rijnsburgerweg 10, 2333 AA Leiden, the Netherlands. *(31)*

SACHS, M.B., The John Hopkins University, Dept. of Biomedical Engineering, Neural Encoding Laboratory, 720 Rutland Avenue, Baltimore, MD 21205, USA. *(81)*

SCHARF, B., Auditory Perception Laboratory, Northeastern University, Boston, Massachusetts 02115, USA. *(52)*

SCHREINER, C., Max-Planck-Institute for Biophysical Chemistry, Am Fassberg Abt. 11, Postbox 968, D-3400 Göttingen, Germany. *(7)*

SCHROEDER, M.R., Drittes Physikalisches Institut, Universität Göttingen, Bürgerstrasse 42-44, D 3400 Göttingen, Germany. *(79)*

SIEBEN, U., Drittes Physikalisches Institut, Universität Göttingen, Bürgerstrasse 42-44, 4300 Göttingen, Germany. *(6)*

SMITH, R.L., Institute for Sensory Research, Syracuse University, Merrill Lane, Syracuse, NY 13210, USA. *(86)*

SMOLDERS, J., Zentrum der Physiologie, Theodor-Stern-Kai 7, D-6000 Frankfurt am Main 70, Germany. *(39)*

SMOORENBURG, G.F., Instituut voor Zintuigfysiologie TNO, Kampweg 5, 3769 DE Soesterberg, the Netherlands. *(12)*

STERN Jr., R.M., Depts Electrical Engineering, Carnegie Mellon University, Pittsburgh PA 15213, USA. *(74)*

STOPP, P.E., Neurocommunications Research Unit, the Medical School, University of Birmingham, Birmingham B15 2TJ. Great Britain. *(50)*

TERHARDT, E., Institute for Electroacoustics, Technical University München, D-8000 München 2, Arcisstrasse 21, Germany. *(5)*

TYLER, R.S., MRC Institute of Hearing Research, The Medical School, University of Nottingham, Nottingham NG7 2UH, Great Britain. *(80)*

VERSCHUURE, J., Afdeling KNO, Erasmus Universiteit, Postbus 1738, 3000 DR Rotterdam, the Netherlands.

VIEMEISTER, N.F., Dept. of Psychology, University of Minnesota, Elliott Hall, 75 East River Road, Minneapolis, Minnesota 55455, USA. *(17)*

VIERGEVER, M.A., Technische Hogeschool Delft, Afdeling Wiskunde, Julianalaan 132, 2628 BL Delft, the Netherlands. *(34)*

VLAMING, M.S.M.G., Applied Physics Department, University of Technology, Lorentzweg 1, Delft, the Netherlands. *(35)*

WEBER, D.L., MRC Applied Psychology Unit, 15 Chaucer Road, Cambridge, CB2 2EF, Great Britain. *(71)*

WHITFIELD, I.C., Neurocommunications Research Unit, the Medical School, University of Birmingham, Birmingham B15 2TJ, Great Britain. *(37)*

WIGHTMAN, F.L., Auditory Research Laboratory (Audiology), Northwestern University, Evanston, Illinois 60201, USA. *(27)*

WILSON, J.P., Department of Communication and Neuroscience, University of Keele, Keele, Staffs. ST5 5BG, Great Britain. *(13)*

WIT, H.P., Audiologisch Instituut, Academisch Ziekenhuis, Oostersingel 59, 9713 EZ Groningen, the Netherlands. *(15)*

YATES, G.K., MRC Institute of Hearing Research, University of Nottingham, Nottingham NG7 2UH, Great Britain. *(21)*

YOST, W.A., Parmly Hearing Institute, Loyola University of Chicago, 6525 Sheridan Road, Chicago, IL 60626, USA. *(28)*

ZANTEN, G.A. van, Lab. voor Experimentele Fysica, Afd. Medische Fysica, Princetonplein 5, 3508 PA Utrecht, the Netherlands. *(59)*

ZWICKER, E., Institute of Electroacoustics, Technical University München, D-8000 München 2, Arcisstrasse 21, Germany. *(26)*

ZWISLOCKI, J.J., Institute for Sensory Research, Syracuse University, Merrill Lane, Syracuse, N.Y. 13210, USA. *(68)*

ADMINISTRATIVE STAFF:

Petra MATERS, general secretary (Rotterdam). *(25)*

Gabriëlle PRUYMBOOM – VAN AALST (Rotterdam). *(65)*

Marjan MULDER – VAN NOUHUYS (Delft). *(2)*

Els NIEUWENHUIS (Rotterdam).

Joyce VAN MIDDELKOOP – HOEK (Delft).

CONTENTS

FIRST AUTHOR INDEX *(Comments in italics)*

Section I
Cochlear Functioning

This section begins with the consideration of cochlear mechanics. Mathematical models rather than measurements have received most attention over the last five years. New proposals for models are presented, the results of which are now being compared much more carefully with experimental data. Mechanisms of neural transduction and the physiology of the organ of Corti are then discussed, as is the possible site of a sharpening mechanism in the frequency domain, the second filter. Stimulated acoustic emissions or cochlear echoes, a recently discovered aspect of cochlear functioning, are dealt with in the second part. Their origin as well as possible relations with known psychoacoustical phenomena appear to be matters of great interest.

1

DIMENSIONALITY OF COCHLEAR WAVES

E. de Boer

*Physics Lab., ENT Clinic, AZUA Wilhelmina Gasthuis,
Amsterdam, The Netherlands*

I. INTRODUCTION

A most important basis for cochlear frequency analysis is mechanical resonance. In the 'classical' type of (linear) cochlea model the basilar membrane
(BM) is described by way of its mechanical impedance $z(x)$ and this is made to
show resonance for each frequency at a frequency-specific location. The impedance $z(x)$ in such a model contains a stiffness component that varies as an
exponential function $\exp(-\alpha x)$ of location x, and a mass component that is constant. As a result, the radial frequency ω_r and the location x_r at which resonance occurs for that frequency are related as $\omega_r \sim \exp(-\alpha x_r/2)$ -- this determines the "cochlear frequency-to-place map".

Wave motion between the cochlear windows and the locus of resonance can be
well understood from a one-dimensional model. The pressure varies as $\exp(-\alpha x/4)$
and the BM velocity as $\exp(\frac{3}{4}\alpha x)$. Near the locus of resonance, however, the
condition for one-dimensionality (the local wavelength should be much larger
than the diameter h of the cochlear channel) is not met any more and models of
higher dimensionality must be studied. Mathematically, this is rather difficult
and useful results can only be obtained when certain simplifications are made.
A two-dimensional model is then found to have a type of response that is
incompatible with experimental results ([SWW,DEEP][x]). Hence it is necessary to study three-dimensional models. This paper presents some typical results from a theoretical study in this direction. To conserve space, all mathematical derivations have been left out, only starting points and results are given. Suffice it to say that the study was focused on resonance phenomena in the cochlea; consequently, the results presented pertain only to the resonance region of the cochlea model.

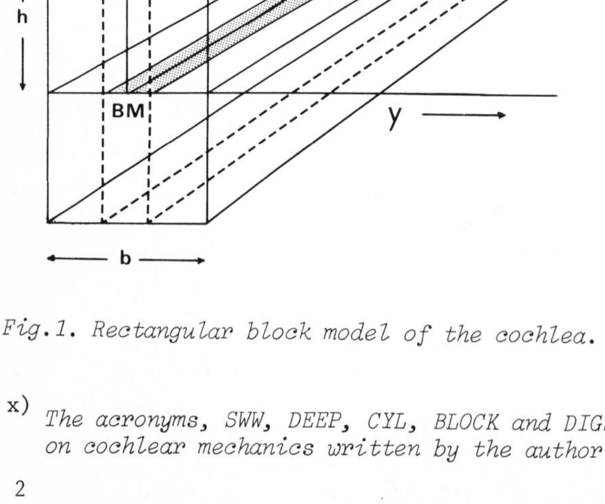

2. MODELING

Fig.1 shows a schematic two-channel model of the cochlea in the form of a rectangular block. The longitudinal dimension (not drawn to scale)

Fig.1. Rectangular block model of the cochlea.

x) *The acronyms, SWW, DEEP, CYL, BLOCK and DIGSOL, refer to a series of papers
on cochlear mechanics written by the author.*

is designated as the x-axis. A fraction - to be called ε - of the width (b) of the cochlear partition is flexible: the basilar membrane (BM); the rest is rigid. The physics of the model is considered in its most simplified form: the fluid is incompressible, inviscid and linear; the BM is linear and assumed to be completely described by its mechanical impedance $z(x)$ (cf. Viergever, 1978).

In the one-dimensional model the kinetic effects of all fluid movements except those in the x-direction are neglected. In a two-dimensional model the influence of fluid movements in the y-direction is neglected. At first sight this assumption seems well justified because the BM is a very narrow strip. However, on closer inspection things turn out differently. The two-dimensional model can be visualised by erecting vertical walls at the edges of the BM, see the dashed lines in Fig.1. Actually, appreciable fluid movements in the y-direction may be expected near the edges and close to the membrane, hence the validity of a two-dimensional model is questionable. It appears, therefore, useful to try to solve a three-dimensional model in such a way that the nature of fluid movements near the BM can be judged. This, then, is the reason for choosing the rectangular block structure for this study.

3. SOLUTION METHOD

The response of the model is the result of the interaction between the basilar membrane (BM) and the fluid. The *fluid load* depends very much on the geometry of the fluid columns; calculating it necessitates the solution of a particular boundary value problem. The latter can be written in the form of an integral equation, the "Siebert equation", see [SWW] for the two-dimensional, and [CYL,BLOCK] for the three-dimensional cases. The equation reads:

$$\frac{1}{z(x)} \int_{-\infty}^{+\infty} W(k)Q(k) \, e^{-ikx}dk = \frac{i}{2\omega\rho} \int_{-\infty}^{+\infty} W(k) \, e^{-ikx}dk \tag{1}$$

where $z(x)$ is the BM impedance, ρ the fluid's density, ω the radial frequency, $W(k)$ the Fourier transform of the BM velocity $w(x)$ and $Q(k)$ is a 'form factor' depending on the geometry. For a two-dimensional model $Q(k)$ is of the form (Siebert, 1974, [SWW])

$$Q(k) = \frac{1}{k \tanh kh} \, , \tag{2}$$

where h is the height of the cochlear channel. For three-dimensional models $Q(k)$ is a more complicated function, see [CYL,BLOCK].

The Siebert equation can be solved in a closed form for certain functions $z(x)$. For this paper we use the following - 'hyperbolic' - approximation to the impedance function:

$$z(x) = i\omega M_o + \frac{C_2}{i\omega(x-x_a)} \tag{3}$$

where M_o, C_2 and x_a are appropriately chosen constants. This approximation is fairly accurate in the region of resonance, cf. [DEEP]. With no great loss of accuracy, $z(x)$ can be made into a *periodic function of x* via use of the z-transform ([DIGSOL]); the corresponding solution for $W(k)$ consists of a discrete series of spectrum values W_n. Then the method of [DIGSOL] for solving eq.(1) can be applied using the $z(x)$ function of eq.(3); the result is a recurrence relation between the components W_n:

$$W_n\left[1 + \frac{Q_n}{M_1 - \frac{1}{2}iC_3}\right] = W_{n-1}\left[1 + \frac{Q_{n-1}}{M_1 + \frac{1}{2}iC_3}\right] \tag{4}$$

M_1 and C_3 are constants derived from those mentioned above: $M_1 = M_o/2\rho$ and

3

$C_3 = C_2/2\omega^2\rho$. Eq.(4) can readily be solved: we assume first $W_n = 0$ for $n \leqslant 0$, (implying there are no waves running to the left), then take $W_1 = 1$ and compute all the other W_n. After introducing damping as outlined in [SWW], the result is Fourier transformed and the desired $w(x)$ is obtained.

4. RESULTS

Fig.2 shows typical response curves for various models, magnitude (a) and phase (b). The abscissa shows the x-region around the locus of resonance (for each frequency considered the coordinate system is chosen so that the BM resonates at x=0; response curves are identical when the fundamental cochlear parameters m_o, α and h are the same). In contrast to the findings reported elsewhere, it is not the spatial derivative but the BM velocity $w(x)$ itself which is plotted. Curves 1 and 2 are shown to provide a frame of reference, they correspond to a one- and a two-dimensional model, respectively. For these curves the damping constant δ is chosen as 0.05. Other parameters are (see the cited papers and Fig.1 for their meaning):

A=0.075; h=b=0.1; α=3.0; ϵ=0.1; m_o=0.05; M_o=2.4 m_o.

The character of the two response curves 1 and 2 is entirely different. In curve 1 the resonance of the BM (x=0) is the most manifest. Curve 2 shows a less pronounced peak, located relatively far away from x=0. This response is better characterised by its steep cut-off slope than by its peak. Note also the excessive phase variations in this case.

The three curves 3-A,B and C show three-dimensional responses, computed for the rectangular block model of Fig.1. The three curves correspond to damping constants (δ) of 0.02, 0.05 and 0.1. Note that the cross-section of each channel is square and that only 0.1 of the width is taken up by the BM. The block model appears to give rise to a well-pronounced response peak, situated between those of curves 1 and 2. This response shows only moderate phase variations in the region of the magnitude maximum.

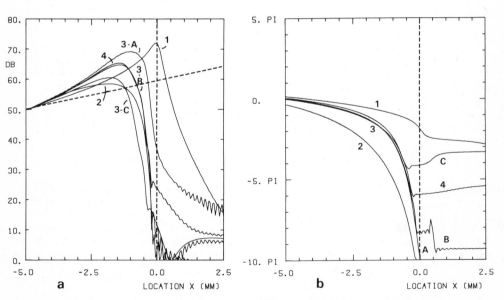

Fig.2. *Response curves in the resonance region. Part (a): magnitude; part (b): phase. Vertical dashed line indicates locus of BM resonance. Sloping dashed line in part (a): asymptotic behaviour for x < -0.5 (cm).*

It should be emphasised that the computed response refers solely to the resonance region. The asymptotic nature of the response in the remaining part of the cochlea (which can be considered as a one-dimensional wave propagation medium) is indicated by the dashed line. This has a slope of 19.5 dB per cm, corresponding to a velocity variation of the form $\exp(\frac{3}{4}\alpha x)$ with $\alpha=3.0$. It is observed that the response peak is well elevated from the dashed line, this is a typical three-dimensional effect, related to the fact that only a small fraction of the cochlear partition is flexible ([CYL,BLOCK]). In fact, the energy flux carried by the fluid must be focused in the direction of the centre line $y=0$, and this is the physical reason behind the peak.

Curve 4 is the response of another type of three-dimensional model, namely one with a cylindrical cross-section ([CYL]), computed for $\delta=0.05$. Its parameters are slightly different ($m_0=0.045$) and the response is seen to be almost the same as curve 3-B. Apparently, this model portrays typical three-dimensional effects in quite an accurate way.

To illustrate the fundamental differences between a two- and a three-dimensional model, we compute at various locations in the x-direction the pressure distribution across the width. Fig.3 presents typical results, the pressure at $z=0$ is plotted as a function of y in the interval from $y=0$ (the centre) to $y=\frac{1}{2}b$ (one of the walls). The labels of the curves correspond to the x-coordinate of the cross-section inspected (see legend). Each of the magnitude curves (upper part) is normalised with respect to its own average across the width, the scale is linear. The phase values are plotted in the lower part of the figure. The figure is computed for the typical damping value: $\delta=0.05$, and corresponds to the situation of curve 3-B of Fig.2.

It is seen that near the response peak of the velocity (which occurs around $x=-1.5$ mm), the pressure magnitude at the centre ($y=0$) of the BM rises to 2-3 times its average value. Phase variations over the width remain moderate. Furthermore, there is a noticeable pressure gradient around the edge ($y=\frac{1}{2}b\varepsilon$) of the BM which means that there are appreciable fluid movements in the y-direction across this edge. This implies that it is not legitimate to replace the three-dimensional structure by a two-dimensional model with vertical walls at the edges of the BM (the dashed lines in Fig.1). It might be possible to construct an equivalent two-dimensional model but then the effects of the pressure enlargement near $y=0$ and the spreading-out of the fluid in the y-direction must certainly be taken into account, with the result that the effective parameters must be altered.

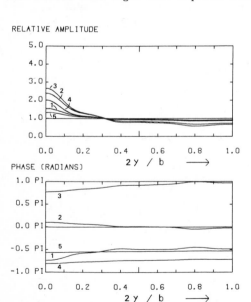

5. DISCUSSION

The results presented in Figs. 2 and 3 confirm that in the region of resonance the response is far better represented by a three- than by a two-dimensional model. From one- as well as two-dimensional models it is known that they do not lead to response forms that agree in all respects with experimental findings (Zweig *et al*,

Fig.3. Pressure distribution across the width. Upper part: relative amplitude of pressure, lower part: phase (scaled between $-\pi$ and $+\pi$). Curves 1 through 5 correspond to $x = -1.0,-1.5,-2.0,-2.5$ and -3.0 (cm), respectively.

1976, [SWW]). In [CYL] it is shown that the form of the response peak in three dimensions agrees in all respects with experimental data. Moreover, this agreement is only possible for a response in three dimensions. In this respect, the present results leave little to be desired.

The type of model that is considered here, belongs to the most simple specimina of mechanical structures that can mimick the mechanics of the cochlea. Despite the simplicity, it is difficult to get much physical insight into what is going on, the reason being that the mathematics is often formidably complex and opaque. Yet it seems certain that more effort should be directed at the evaluation of influences that have mostly been neglected so far, such as: the presence of the tectorial membrane, the structure of the organ of Corti, etc. Furthermore, physiological processes may cause significant feedback effects (Kemp, 1978) and this may lead to completely new developments in the theory of cochlear action.

REFERENCES

Boer, E. de (1979). Short-wave world revisited: Resonance in a two-dimensional
[SWW]   cochlear model. *Hearing Research* 1, 253-281.
Boer, E. de (--). A cylindrical cochlea model - the bridge between two and
[CYL]   three dimensions. *Hearing Research* (submitted for publication)
Boer, E. de (--). "Deep water" waves in the cochlea. *Hearing Research* (submit-
[DEEP]   ted for publication)
Boer, E. de (--). Digital solution of cochlear mechanics problems. *J. Acoust.*
[DIGSOL] *Soc. Amer.* (submitted for publication)
Boer, E. de (--). Short waves in three-dimensional cochlea models. (in prepara-
[BLOCK] tion)
Kemp, D.T. (1978). Stimulated acoustic emissions from within the human auditory
         system. *J. Acoust. Soc. Amer.* 64, 1386-1391.
Siebert, W.M. (1974). Ranke revisited - a simple short-wave cochlear model.
         J. Acoust. Soc. Amer. 56, 594-600.
Viergever, M.A. (1978). On the physical background of the point-impedance
         characterization of the basilar membrane in cochlear mechanics.
         Acustica 39, 292-297.
Zweig, G., Lipes, R. and Pierce, J.R. (1976). The cochlear compromise. *J.
         Acoust. Soc. Amer.* 59, 975-982.

Acknowledgements.

The author is greatly indebted to Max A. Viergever, whose work on the three-dimensional model led to most stimulating discussions on this topic. The study was made possible by the support of the Netherlands Organization for Pure Research (ZWO), The Hague.

AN ACTIVE COCHLEAR MODEL WITH NEGATIVE DAMPING IN THE PARTITION: COMPARISON WITH RHODE'S ANTE- AND POST-MORTEM OBSERVATIONS

D. O. Kim, S. T. Neely, C. E. Molnar,
and J. W. Matthews

Washington University
St. Louis, Missouri 63110, USA

ABSTRACT

Results are presented from a two-dimensional model for cochlear mechanics with active properties represented by the inclusion of negative damping in the impedance of the cochlear partition over a limited region, or with passive properties without negative damping. Model solutions were obtained using both a finite-difference method in the frequency domain and a Green's-function method in the time domain. Results from our active model are similar to Rhode's ante-mortem observations of basilar-membrane motion in the squirrel monkey, and results from our passive model are similar to Rhode's post-mortem observations. We suggest from these results: 1) that an active source of mechanical energy in the cochlear partition may underlie normal cochlear mechanical response; 2) that the loss of this energy source upon death may be responsible for the early post-mortem broadening of tuning and peak shift; and 3) that a later reduction in the stiffness of the cochlear partition may be responsible for further shifts of the amplitude peak and of the phase pattern occurring hours after death.

INTRODUCTION

We present in this paper our recent results from a model for cochlear mechanics where active mechanical behavior is incorporated. A novel feature of our model is the presence of a controlled energy source in the cochlear partition represented by negative values of the damping of the partition impedance over a certain localized region of the partition. Our results demonstrate, in a plausible cochlear mechanical model, a marked influence exerted by the presence of a source of mechanical energy in the cochlear partition upon the sensitivity and sharpness of tuning observed near the peak of the response to a single-tone stimulation. Cochlear-partition motion in our active model shows higher sensitivity and sharper tuning than in a conventional passive model where damping values are assumed to be positive everywhere along the partition. In the following sections of this paper, we describe the assumptions of our model and compare the model cochlear-partition displacement with Rhode's (1973) experimental data from the squirrel monkey. We note close similarity between our active model results and Rhode's ante-mortem observations, and between our passive model results and Rhode's post-mortem observations. In addition, we show profiles of power flux density over the basal and partition boundaries of the model for the active and passive conditions of the model.

MODEL

Two implementations of a cochlear model (Neely, 1978; Matthews, 1979) have been adapted for the present study. Both versions make the same set of assumptions about the cochlea:

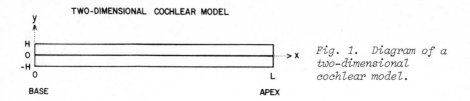

Fig. 1. *Diagram of a two-dimensional cochlear model.*

1) All quantities of the model are constant with respect to the z axis, and the cochlea is represented as a two-dimensional, rectangular chamber filled with fluid and divided into two symmetric halves (scalae) by a partition (Figure 1);

2) The fluid is incompressible, inviscid and satisfies Laplace's equation, $\nabla^2 P(x,y)=0$, where $P(x,y)$ is the pressure at (x,y);

3) The upper and lower walls are rigid;

4) At x=L, corresponding to the apical end, we have $P(L,y) - P(L,-y)=0$, for $0 \leqslant y \leqslant H$, where H is the height of each scala;

5) At x=0, corresponding to the basal end, we have

$$\frac{\partial P(0,y)}{\partial x} = - \frac{\partial P(0,-y)}{\partial x} = \rho A_s \cos(\omega t), \text{ for } 0 \leqslant y \leqslant H,$$

where ρ is the fluid density, A_s is the amplitude of the stapes acceleration, and ω is the angular frequency of excitation;

6) The partition displacement is very small compared with the scala height;

7) There is no longitudinal coupling within the partition;

8) The partition dynamic characteristics are linear, and described in the frequency domain by impedance parameters, $Z(x) = R(x) + j[\omega M(x)-K(x)/\omega]$ where $R(x)$, $M(x)$, and $K(x)$ are the damping, mass and stiffness parameters of the partition.

We have used the following parameter values:

1) cochlear length, L = 2.2 cm;

2) scala height, H = 0.1 cm;

3) fluid density, $\rho = 1.0$ gm·cm^{-3};

4) partition mass, $M(x) = 0.01$ gm·cm^{-2} for all x;

5) partition stiffness, $K(x) = K_o \exp(-4.5x)$ dyne·cm^{-3} where x is distance from the base in cm, and $K_o = 10^9$, or 0.4×10^9;

6) partition damping, $R(x) = 200$ dyne·sec·cm^{-3} for all x, or $R(x) = f_R(x)$.

The two cochlear model implementations of this study use different solution methods: a finite-difference method in the frequency domain (Neely, 1978); and a Green's function method in the time domain (Matthews, 1979). For the conventional case of passive partition characteristics without negative damping, the solutions obtained from the two methods are in excellent agreement. Comparison of the solutions for the active cases will be made in the Discussion section.

RESULTS

In Figure 2-A and -B, model results of amplitude and phase of the ratio of the cochlear-partition displacement to the stapes displacement are shown for one stimulus frequency of 1550Hz versus distance along the cochlea for three conditions: 1. The partition damping $R(x)$ has negative values over a certain region as shown in Figure 3 and the stiffness parameter K_o is equal to 10^9; 2. $R(x)=200$ for all x and $K_o=10^9$; 3. $R(x)=200$ for all x and $K_o=0.4 \times 10^9$. From Figure 2-A, it can be noted that the model response amplitudes for conditions 1 and 2 are similar in the basal region but quite different in the

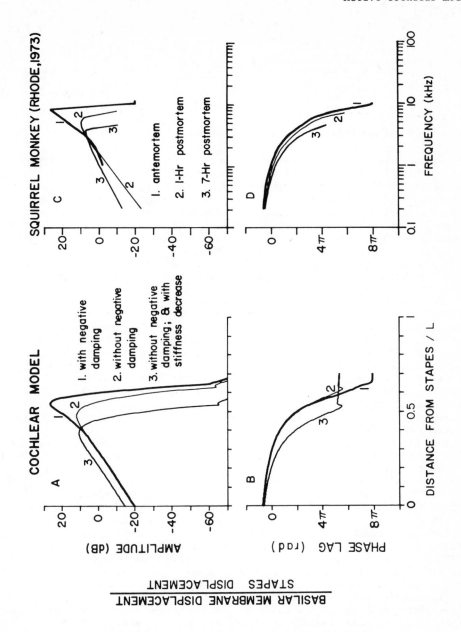

Fig. 2. A and B: Amplitude and phase of cochlear-partition displacement relative to the stapes displacement of the model (frequency-domain solution) for
a stimulus frequency of 1550 Hz versus distance from the stapes. The three
conditions correspond to different parameter values of the partition. For all
three conditions, the x position was represented by 400 points and the y position was represented by 16 points. For the phase, positive senses are the
inward displacement of the stapes, and the displacement of the partition to
the scala tympani. C and D: Amplitude and phase of basilar-membrane displacement relative to the stapes displacement for one position along the basilar
membrane of the squirrel monkey versus a logarithmic scale of stimulus frequency. C and D are redrawn from Fig. 3 of Rhode (1973).

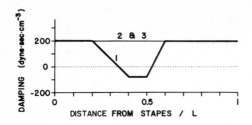

Fig. 3. Damping profiles for the three conditions used for the model results shown in Figure 2-A and -B. The profile of condition 1 is referred to as $f_R(x)$ in the text.

region around the peaks. The response for condition 1 shows a sharper peak which is shifted slightly toward the apex and larger in amplitude than the response for condition 2 where there was no negative damping in the partition. In spite of the marked difference in response amplitudes near the peaks, the response phases for conditions 1 and 2 (Figure 2-B) are quite similar in most of the regions except in the phase plateau region apical to the peaks. In this region, condition 1 shows a larger amount of total phase shift than condition 2. Model responses for conditions 2 and 3 in Figure 2-A and -B show that a decrease in the stiffness coefficient K_o leads to a basal shift of both the amplitude and phase, with little change in the shapes of the response curves.

In Figure 2-C and -D, Rhode's (1973) experimental results of amplitude and phase of the ratio of the basilar-membrane displacement to the stapes displacement are shown for one position along the basilar membrane versus a logarithmic scale of stimulus frequency for three conditions. The antemortem response shows a sharper peak which is shifted slightly to the high-frequency side and larger in amplitude than the postmortem responses. Differences in the response amplitudes for the antemortem and the 1-Hr postmortem conditions are quite prominent in the frequency region near the peaks but are inconspicuous in the frequency region below the peaks. The 7-Hr postmortem response appears to be of similar shape to the 1-Hr postmortem response but shifted to the low-frequency side.

A complication in comparing the model and experimental results shown in Figure 2 is that the horizontal axes of the two cases are different: A linear scale of distance from the stapes for the model results, and a logarithmic scale of stimulus frequency for the experimental results. We do not yet have model results for different stimulus frequencies. However, plots of basilar-membrane displacement on a linear scale of distance along the cochlea for one stimulus frequency are expected to be fairly similar to plots of basilar-membrane displacement on a logarithmic scale of the stimulus frequency for one position of the basilar membrane. This general similarity is expected from the "shift invariance" property observed in experimental results (Bekesy, 1960, p. 461-462; Rhode, 1971, Fig. 8), as well as in cochlear models (e.g., Sondhi, 1978). To the extent that the shift invariance is a reasonable approximation for our comparison of results in Figure 2, we note that the salient features of postmortem changes observed in the animal are fairly well reproduced by the model results in Figure 2-A and -B. Results of this model suggest that the rapid changes in basilar-membrane motion after death may be due to the loss of an internal energy source in the cochlear partition and that the slower changes occurring over several hours from death may be due to a decrease in the stiffness of the partition.

In Figure 4, we show profiles of power flux density, i.e., the time-averaged power per unit area, over the basal and partition boundaries. Here, positive flux densities correspond to flow of energy into the fluid; negative densities to flow of energy from the fluid (into the cochlear partition). For steady state conditions with sinusoidal excitation as we consider here, the x-component of the power flux density, $E_x(0,y)$, over the basal boundary is (de Boer, 1979)

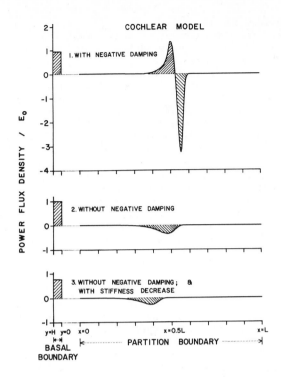

Fig. 4. *Profiles of power flux density normalized with E_o for the three conditions used for the model results shown in Figure 2-A and -B. E_o is equal to 0.43 erg · sec^{-1} · cm^{-2} which corresponds to the power flux density at $x=0$, and $y=H$ for condition 2. For all three conditions, a constant stapes displacement (10^{-6} cm) is applied. Positive values correspond to energy flow into the fluid and the negative values correspond to energy flow from the fluid into the partition.*

$$E_x(0,y) = 0.5 \ P(0,y) \cdot V_x(0,y) \cdot \cos[\theta_1(y)],$$

where $P(0,y)$ and $V_x(0,y)$ are the peak amplitudes of sinusoidal time variation of pressure and x-component of velocity at position $(0,y)$, and $\theta_1(y)$ is the phase difference between $P(0,y)$ and $V_x(0,y)$. Plots in Figure 4 for the basal boundary show $[E_x(0,y) + E_x(0,-y)]$ versus y for $H \geqslant y \geqslant 0$. The left-most cross hatched areas in Figure 4 thus represent total power into the fluid through the basal boundary, i.e., the power into the fluid through the oval window minus the power out of the fluid through the round window.

Similarly, the y-component of the power flux density over the upper surface of the partition is

$$E_y(x,0^+) = 0.5 \ P(x,0^+) \cdot V_y(x,0^+) \cdot \cos[\theta_2(x)],$$

and over the lower surface of the partition

$$E_y(x,0^-) = 0.5 \ P(x,0^-) \cdot V_y(x,0^-) \cdot \cos[\theta_3(x)].$$

Plots in Figure 4 for the partition boundary show $[E_y(x,0^+) - E_y(x,0^-)]$ versus x for $0 \geqslant x \geqslant L$. This represents the total power into the fluid from both sides

11

of the partition at position x. The $E_y(x,0^-)$ part is subtracted from $E_y(x,0^+)$ because the y-component of the power flux at the lower surface is pointing into the partition from the fluid.

The middle cross-hatched area above zero in Figure 4-1 represents the power delivered from the negative-damping region of the partition into the fluid, and the right-most cross-hatched area below zero in Figure 4-1 represents the power dissipated in the positive-damping region of the partition. The lower two panels of Figure 4 show profiles of power flux density for conditions 2 and 3 where the damping is positive everywhere along the partition (Figure 3). The major difference between these conditions and condition 1 is that, for conditions 2 and 3 over the partition boundary, there is only a region of power dissipation and no region of power source. We have verified that, for each condition shown in Figure 4, the total power into the fluid is equal to the total power taken from the fluid, as expected from conservation of energy. It is interesting to note that, for condition 1, the total power delivered from the negative-damping region of the partition (i.e., the middle cross-hatched area of Figure 4-1) is 1.5 times the total power delivered through the basal boundary (i.e., the left-most cross-hatched area of Figure 4-1). This gain in power through the internal energy source of the model underlies the substantial increase in the response near the peak for condition 1 of the model.

DISCUSSION

The hypothesis of active mechanical behavior of the cochlea was suggested by Gold (1948) and Kemp (1979). Strong support for this hypothesis is provided by a form of tinnitus where spontaneously emitted tones can be detected in the ear canals of some human subjects whose thresholds of hearing are in the normal range (Kemp, 1979). Our model results presented in this paper demonstrate specific effects of incorporating a source of mechanical energy into the partition of the model. To the extent that our active and passive model results shown in Figure 2 simulate Rhode's ante- and post-mortem observations, our model results support the hypothesis of active mechanics in a normal cochlea. It is unknown what kind of mechanisms may underlie the hypothesized internal energy source in the cochlear partition. Our conjecture is that energy available through cellular metabolism in the cochlear partition may be somehow transduced into mechanical energy. [Note: The appearance of negative damping in the cochlear-partition point impedance could also conceivably be produced by some form of longitudinal coupling within the cochlear partition. Longitudinal coupling could not, of course, produce spontaneous oscillations in the absence of external energy input through the stapes.]

The hypothesis of active cochlear mechanics is compatible with the hypothesis of bidirectional coupling of electrophysiological and mechanical processes in the cochlea. Bidirectional coupling has been suggested from various observations of physiologically vulnerable behavior: 1) in the ear-canal sound pressure, regarding "echoes" in response to brief transient stimuli (Kemp, 1978; Anderson and Kemp, 1979) and regarding distortion products in response to continuous two-tone stimuli (Kim, 1980); 2) in basilar-membrane motion (Rhode, 1973; Robles, Rhode and Geisler, 1976; Lepage and Johnstone, 1980); and 3) in psychoacoustic (Smoorenburg, 1972) and neural (Siegel, Kim and Molnar, 1977; Kim, Siegel and Molnar, 1979; Kim, Molnar and Matthews, 1980) responses regarding distortion products which are interpreted to be associated with basilar-membrane motion. [For further discussions of bidirectional coupling, see Kim, Molnar and Matthews (1980), and Kim (1980).] The hypotheses of active mechanics and bidirectional coupling in the transduction in the cochlea are consistent with various observations that noxious disturbances reduce sensitivity and frequency selectivity of individual inner hair cells (Sellick and Russell, 1978) and of single cochlear neurons (e.g., Kiang, Moxon and Levine, 1970; Robertson and Manley, 1974; Evans, 1974; Dallos and Harris, 1978; Robertson and Johnstone, 1979).

As stated earlier in this paper, the solutions obtained from the two implementations of the model are in excellent agreement for conditions 2 and 3 which have no negative damping in the partition. For condition 1, which has negative damping in the partition, the time-domain solution was not stable. The time-domain solution of the model to a smoothly-gated sinusoidal stimulus initially approached the pattern obtained with the frequency-domain method, but the model response subsequently entered into irregular, unstable oscillations rather than remaining in a steady-state condition. We have not yet determined whether this instability of the model response is due to an instability of the physical condition modeled, or due to inaccuracies in the model implementation. However, we did observe that, for damping profiles with less pronounced negative values, the time-domain solution was stable and in good agreement with the frequency-domain solution.

In addition to further study of the stability properties of active models and their computational implementations, other extensions of this work are needed. We feel that the most important extension is the incorporation of both active and nonlinear behavior into the same model for cochlear mechanics. This may be helpful in understanding how a damping profile such as that shown in Figure 3 might arise under a particular condition of stimulation. Such an understanding would allow us to examine model response for various stimulus frequencies for a fixed position along the cochlear partition which can be compared with Rhode's observations more directly. In view of the success of nonlinear cochlear models having increases in damping with increasing response for reproducing a wide range of nonlinear phenomena observed (Kim, Molnar and Pfeiffer, 1973; Hubbard and Geisler, 1972; Hall, 1974; Matthews, Cox, Kim and Molnar, 1979), it should be interesting to investigate cochlear models where similar nonlinear behavior is combined with active behavior, for example, with respect to the questions of cochlear mechanical stability and the tendency to spontaneous oscillation.

Acknowledgements

We thank Professor J.R. Cox for helpful discussions and S.J. Eads for typing the manuscript. This study was supported by US-NIH grants NS07498, RR00396, and GM01827. D.O. Kim is a recipient of a US-NIH Research Career Development Award (NS00162).

REFERENCES

Anderson, S.D. and Kemp, D.T. (1979). The evoked cochlear mechanical response in laboratory primates. *Arch. Otorhinolar.* 224, 47-54.
Bekesy, G.v. (1960). *Experiments in Hearing* (McGraw-Hill, New York).
Dallos, P. and Harris, D. (1978). Properties of auditory nerve responses in absence of outer hair cells. *J. Neurophysiol.* 41, 365-383.
de Boer, E. (1979). Short-wave world revisited: resonance in a two-dimensional cochlear model. *Hearing Res.* 1, 253-281.
Evans, E.F. (1974). Auditory frequency selectivity and the cochlear nerve. In *Facts and Models in Hearing*, E. Zwicker and E. Terhardt (Springer-Verlag, New York), pp. 118-129.
Gold, T. (1948). Hearing II. The physical basis of the action of the cochlea. *Proc. Roy. Soc. B.* 135, 492-498.
Hall, J.L. (1974). Two-tone distortion products in a nonlinear model of the basilar membrane. *J. Acoust. Soc. Am.* 56, 1818-1828.
Hubbard, A.E. and Geisler, C.D. (1972). A hybrid computer model of the cochlear partition. *J. Acoust. Soc. Am.* 64, 1386-1391.

Kemp, D.T. (1978). Stimulated acoustic emission from within the human auditory system. *J. Acoust. Soc. Amer. 64:1386-1391.*

Kemp, D.T. (1979). Evidence of mechanical nonlinearity and frequency selective wave amplification in the cochlea. *Arch. Otorhinolar. 224:37-45.*

Kiang, N.Y.S., Moxon, E.C. and Levine, R.A. (1970). Auditory-nerve activity in cats with normal and abnormal cochleas. In: *Sensory Neural Hearing Loss,* G.E.W. Wolstenholme and J. Knight, Eds. (J. & A. Churchill, London), pp. 241-273.

Kim, D.O., Molnar, C.E. and Pfeiffer, R.R. (1973). A system of nonlinear differential equations modeling basilar-membrane motion. *J. Acoust. Soc. Amer. 54:1517-1529.*

Kim, D.O., Siegel, J.H. and Molnar, C.E. (1979). Cochlear nonlinear phenomena in two-tone responses. *Scand. Audiol. Suppl. 9:63-81.*

Kim, D.O. (1980). Cochlear mechanics: implications of electrophysiological and acoustical observations. *Hearing Res. 2:, in press.*

Kim, D.O., Molnar, C.E. and Matthews, J.W. (1980). Cochlear mechanics: nonlinear behavior in two-tone responses as reflected in cochlear-nerve-fiber responses and in ear-canal sound pressure. *J. Acoust. Soc. Amer. 67:, in press.*

Lepage, E. and Johnstone, B. (1980). Non-linearity of basilar membrane motion in the first turn of the guinea pig cochlea. *Hearing Res. 2:, in press.*

Matthews, J.W. (1979). personal communication.

Matthews, J.W., Cox, J.R., Kim, D.O. and Molnar, C.E. (1979). A nonlinear mechanical model of the peripheral auditory system: interpretation of neurally and acoustically observed distortion products $(2f_1-f_2)$ and (f_2-f_1). *J. Acoust. Soc. Amer. 65:S84(A).*

Neely, S.T. (1978). Mathematical models of the mechanics of the cochlea. Engineer's Degree Thesis, California Inst. Tech., Pasadena, California.

Rhode, W.S. (1971). Observations of the vibration of the basilar membrane in squirrel monkeys using the Mössbauer technique. *J. Acoust. Soc. Amer. 49: 1218-1231.*

Rhode, W.S. (1973). An investigation of post-mortem cochlear mechanics using the Mössbauer effect. In, *Basic Mechanisms in Hearing,* A.R. Møller, Ed., pp. 49-67, (Academic Press, New York).

Robertson, D. and Manley, G.A. (1974). Manipulation of frequency analysis in the cochlear ganglion of the guinea pig. *J. Comp. Physiol. 91:363-375.*

Robertson, D. and Johnstone, B.M. (1979). Abberrant tonotopic organization in the inner ear damaged by kanamycin. *J. Acoust. Soc. Amer. 66:466-469.*

Robles, L., Rhode, W.S. and Geisler, C.D. (1976). Transient response of the basilar membrane measured in squirrel monkeys using the Mössbauer effect. *J. Acoust. Soc. Amer. 59:926-939.*

Sellick, P.M. and Russell, I.J. (1978). Intracellular studies of cochlear hair cells. In *Evoked Electrical Activity in the Auditory Nervous System,* R.F. Naunton and C. Fernandez, Eds., pp. 113-139 (Academic Press, New York).

Siegel, J.H., Kim, D.O. and Molnar, C.E. (1977). Cochlear distortion-products: effects of altering the organ of corti. *J. Acoust. Soc. Amer. 61:S2(A).*

Smoorenburg, G.F. (1972). Combination tones and their origin. *J. Acoust. Soc. Amer. 52:615-632.*

Sondhi, M.M. (1978). Method for computing motion in a two-dimensional cochlear model. *J. Acoust. Soc. Amer. 63:1468-1477.*

COMMENT ON: "An active cochlear model with negative damping in the partition: comparison with Rhode's ante- and post-mortem observations". (D.O. Kim, S.T. Neely, C.E. Molnar and J.W. Matthews)

E.F. Evans
Dept. of Communication & Neuroscience, University of Keele, U.K.

Your remarks avoid a continuing inconsistency in the data: that the majority of divert measures of basilar membrane vibration (by Rhode and others) do not indicate nonlinear behaviour of the magnitude you require. Secondly, even Rhode's squirrel monkey data at 7 kHz do not account for the magnitude and time course of the loss of sensitivity and tuning of cochlear fibres in hypoxia (see Evans (1975). Normal and abnormal functioning of the cochlear nerve. In: *Sound Reception in Mammals* (ed. by R.J. Bench, A. Pye & J.D. Pye) pp. 133-165. Academic Press, London).

COMMENT ON "An active cochlear model with negative damping in the partition: comparison with Rhode's ante- and post-mortem observations" (D.O. Kim, S.T. Neely, C.E. Molnar and J.W. Matthews).

J.B. Allen
Bell Laboratories, Murray Hill, New Jersey 07974, U.S.A.

You have indicated (personal communication) that the shape of the damping profile as shown in Fig. 3 was carefully chosen to avoid instable results in the time domain model. In fact the damping values were chosen to give a good fit to Rhode's data with the input being a tone of 1550 Hz. Given this extra degree of freedom, namely $R(x, f_o)$ with the damping a function of both place x and the input frequency f_o, it is not surprising that you were able to fit Rhode's data, given also that the model comes very close without this adjustment. The problem I have is that when many stimulus frequencies are present simultaneously, you will not have this degree of freedom available to you.

REPLY TO COMMENT OF J.B. ALLEN

D.O. Kim
Washington University, St. Louis, Missouri 63110, U.S.A.

The strategy that we have taken in this modeling study is to demonstrate quantitatively specific consequences arising from a specified premise regarding cochlear mechanics. We have demonstrated in this paper that the premise expressed by the damping profile of our Fig.3 leads to interesting consequences.
At the present time, we are not aware of any evidence that rules out our premise. Rather, the observed spontaneous acoustic emissions from the ear, as cited in the paper, partially support the premise. If the premise should turn out to be false, the model should obviously be modified. If the type of premise is generally true, however, it is expected to be possible to find a damping profile appropriate for a particular multi-frequency stimulus. Physiological mechanisms producing the damping profile of Fig.3, if present in the actual cochlea, need to be investigated. Our present model results provide a specific motivation in our search for such a mechanism, implausible as it may appear to some. Until subsequent research in this area clearly demonstrates that such mechanisms are absent or unnecessary to postulate, we feel it worthwhile to continue with this approach.

TWO POSSIBLE MECHANISMS FOR THE
SECOND COCHLEAR FILTER

J. J. Zwislocki

Institute for Sensory Research, Syracuse University,
Syracuse, New York

In the past years the main attention was paid to cochlear macromechanics
in which the basilar membrane and the structures attached to it were considered as a unitary body whose parts vibrated in phase with each other (e.g.
Békésy, 1960; Ranke, 1942; Zwislocki-Moscicki, 1948). Formally, the structure
was represented as a second-order system consisting of a stiffness, a mass, and
a resistance connected in series (e.g. Zwislocki-Moscicki, 1948; Peterson and
Bogert, 1950). Although attempts at considering relative motions within the
organ of Corti were made since the mid-nineteenth century (for review see
Wever, 1949, Békésy, 1960), they do not seem to have provided germinal insights
except for the belief that the cochlear hair cells are excited as a result of
radial bending of stereocilia, a process that must be accompanied by a radial
shear motion between the tectorial membrane and the reticular lamina (e.g.
Békésy, 1960). This belief has been decisively strengthened by recent experiments of Hudspeth and Corey (1977) on the hair cells of the frog's vestibular
system. Of course, if a shear motion takes place between the tectorial membrane and the reticular lamina, the structures attached to the basilar membrane
cannot be considered as a unitary body.
   According to older views (e.g. Békésy, 1960), the tectorial membrane was
supposed to pivot around an axis located at the spiral limbus and be incapable
of performing any radial motion. Under these conditions the shear motion
would be due almost entirely to radial motion of the reticular lamina resulting from the perpendicular vibration of the basilar membrane. Deformations of
the tectorial membrane seen in histological preparations of the cochlea suggest, however, that the tectorial membrane can be easily deformed in the radial
direction and that, at least in the mammals, it is only weakly mechanically
coupled to the limbus. Accordingly, in several preceding articles (Zwislocki,
1979, 1980a,b; Zwislocki and Kletsky, 1979, 1980) we pointed out some possible
consequences of a radial motion of the part of the tectorial membrane overlying the organ of Corti, assuming that its viscoelastic coupling to the organ
was stronger than to the spiral limbus. Such an assumption appears to be consistent with the morphological relations which point to multiple attachments of
the tectorial membrane to the organ of Corti, the strongest appearing to be
through the stereocilia of the outer hair cells (e.g. Lim, 1972). The latter
are probably quite stiff, as can be inferred from the experiments of Flock
(1977) and Hudspeth and Corey (1977). On the assumption that the relevant
part of the tectorial membrane is more strongly coupled to the organ of Corti
than to the limbus, we were able to demonstrate mathematically that the shear
motion between the tectorial membrane and the reticular lamina had to be the
strongest relative to the displacement amplitude of the basilar membrane where
the cochlear wavelength was the shortest and the weakest where the wave length
was the longest (Zwislocki, 1979, Zwislocki and Kletsky, 1979). The mathematical derivations, which can be found in Zwislocki and Kletsky (1979) indicate the
intuitively expected result that, where the wavelength is long, the radial
force exerted on the tectorial membrane by its attachments to the organ of
Corti is oriented in the same direction over a substantial length of the membrane, so that the spatial integral (convolution integral) of this force is
large. In addition, adjacent parts of the tectorial membrane tend to move in

the same direction so that their motion is minimally opposed by the viscoelastic coupling between them. As a result, the tectorial membrane is maximally entrained by the organ of Corti and the radial shear motion is minimized. Where the wavelength is short, adjacent portions of the tectorial membrane tend to be driven in opposite directions and to move in opposite directions so that their motion is strongly opposed by the viscoelastic coupling between them. Consequently, the tectorial membrane is nearly immobilized and the shear motion is maximized. Since the shortest waves occur near the vibration maximum of the basilar membrane (e.g. Rhode, 1971; Kohllöffel, 1972a), the maximum is sharpened in the shear motion. These relationships are schematized in the upper two traces (A,B) of Fig. 1.

Fig. 1. Schematic representation of the wavelength and amplitude of the reticular lamina (solid line) and the tectorial membrane (dashed line) at the location of the outer hair cells, according to two mathematical models. Traces A and B belong to a model (see text) in which the mass of the tectorial membrane is neglected. Trace A holds for frequencies far below CF; trace B, for those near CF.

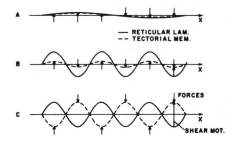

Trace C belongs to a model in which a resonance of the tectorial membrane and its viscoelastic attachments to the organ of Corti is included (see text). The arrows with filled heads indicate the direction of radial elastic forces acting on the tectorial membrane. The arrows with unfilled heads show the magnitude of the shear motion between the tectorial membrane and the reticular lamina.

The mathematical derivations of the shear motion were made under the assumption of a viscoelastic coupling between the tectorial membrane and the organ of Corti, of a coupling with the same phasor angle betwen adjacent portions of the tectorial membrane, and by neglecting the mass of the tectorial membrane. As a consequence, the result showed the tectorial membrane to move approximately in phase with the reticular lamina. It has become increasingly clear, however, that the mass of the tectorial membrane can be substantial (e.g. Zwicker, 1971; Kronester-Frei, 1979) and is not negligible. Such a mass together with its viscoelastic attachments must be capable of resonance if the damping of the system is smaller than aperiodic. That the latter may be true was shown in two preceding articles on the basis of purely morphological considerations and approximately known physical constants (Zwislocki, 1980a,b). On the assumption that the resonance of the tectorial-membrane system took place near the maximum of the basilar-membrane vibration, it was possible to calculate approximately the Q_{10dB} of the system. The obtained values were about 1/2 the values measured by Evans and Wilson (1973) for the guinea-pig neural tuning curves and by Schmiedt (1977) and Schmiedt and Zwislocki (1980) for those of Mongolian gerbils at all characteristic frequencies (CFs). The smaller values do not mean a disagreement since the neural tuning curves include all the mechanisms that may be involved in cochlear frequency analysis. However, it must be noted that the constants entering the calculations are known only approximately, and the assumption that the resonance frequency of the tectorial-membrane system coincides approximately with the maximum of basilar-membrane vibration has not been tested experimentally. If the resonance takes place at the assumed location, it could contribute materially to the sharpening of the frequency analysis in the cochlea. It could occur coincidentally with the wavelength mechanism mentioned above (Zwislocki, 1979; Zwislocki and Kletsky, 1979).

To partially test the hypothesis of a radial resonance of the tectorial-membrane system, I would like to consider some quantitative relationships entering the cochlear mechanisms. These relationships are probably qualitatively similar for all mammals, but their quantitative consideration requires a specific example. Because of the availability of certain relevant data, the human cochlea is chosen, but these data have to be supplemented by inferences from other mammalian cochleas.

It is convenient to begin with the compliance of the basilar membrane. Békésy (1960) measured it in human and several other mammalian species, postmortem. His results indicate that it varies by a factor of about 1 to 1000 from the base to the apex, although in one experiment on a human cochlea a variation of only about 100 was found. The smaller variation is difficult to reconcile with measurements of the travel time and of the location of the maximum of basilar-membrane vibration. As a consequence, the larger variation seems to be more accurate, although I accepted the smaller one in the past because its measurement was described in greater detail (Zwislocki-Moscicki, 1948; Zwislocki, 1953, 1965). It follows from dynamic measurements of Kohllöffel (1972b) and Rhode (1973) that the compliance increases post-mortem by up to an order of magnitude. From neural and CM latencies, it could be calculated that the compliance measured by Békésy (1960) post-mortem was increased by a factor of 4 to 8 (Zwislocki, 1974; Schmiedt and Zwislocki, 1977). Békésy's measurements indicate that the compliance increases approximately exponentially from the cochlear base to the apex. Accordingly, with the more conservative correction by a factor of 4 for postmortem changes, the acoustic compliance measured at the basilar membrane may be expressed approximately by the formula

$$\frac{P}{V} = C_o e^{\beta x} = 1 \cdot 10^{-10} e^{2x} \ ,$$

where P means the pressure amplitude, V--the amplitude of the basilar-membrane volume displacement per centimeter length, C_o--the compliance at the basal end of the basilar membrane, and β--a coefficient reflecting the rate of change of the compliance with distance.

The second essential parameter is the effective acoustic mass measured at the basilar membrane, which is determined for sinusoidal motion by $M_{Ba} = P/\omega^2 V$, where $\omega = 2\pi f$ is the angular frequency and $\omega^2 V$ means the acceleration associated with the volume displacement. It is known in acoustics that the acoustic mass is equal to the mass divided by the square of the area exposed to sound pressure, in symbols, $M_{Ba} = M_{Bm}/b^2$, where M_{Ba} means the acoustic mass per cm length of the basilar membrane, M_{Bm}--the effective mass per unit length and b--the width of the basilar membrane. To calculate the effective mass M_{Bm}, we must know the transversal mode of motion of the basilar membrane. In accordance with the morphological impression, Békésy (1960) observed that this motion resembled that of an elastic beam clamped at the spiral osseous lamina and supported at the spiral ligament. Over the section supporting the major part of the organ of Corti, such a motion can be approximated very roughly by a stiff beam rotating around an axis located at the edge of the spiral lamina (Zwicker, 1971) and marked by 0 in Fig. 2. The approximation cannot be used satisfactorily for all relationships but should be permissible for a rough estimation of the effective mass. The figure shows a drastic simplification of the cochlear structures in cross section, which are essential for our calculations. According to this approximation, the inertia moment per unit length acting on the basilar membrane is equal approximately to

$$M_{BM} = \rho h \frac{\omega U_{B\ max}}{b} \int_0^{kb} z^2 dz = \frac{1}{3} \rho h \omega U_{B\ max} k^3 b^2$$

where M_{BM} means the moment, ρ--the average density of the tissue of the basilar membrane and of the structures attached to it, h--the average height of the organ of Corti, $U_{B\ max}$--the maximum velocity of the basilar membrane assumed to occur roughly at the outer edge of the basilar membrane, b--the width of the basilar membrane, kb--the width occupied by the main mass, and z--the cross-sectional length coordinate. To obtain the effective mass, the moment has to be divided by the average acceleration $\omega U_{B\ max}/2$ and by the associated lever arm b/2, giving $M_{Bm} = (4/3)\rho h k^3 b$. To obtain the acoustic mass in the same frame of reference, we have to divide the latter formula by the width of the basilar membrane squared: $M_{Ba} = (4/3b^2)\rho h k^3 b$. In this expression hkb is the cross-sectional area of the tissue associated with the basilar membrane, which was measured by Wever (1949). According to these measurements the area grows approximately in direct proportion to the width of the basilar membrane. This

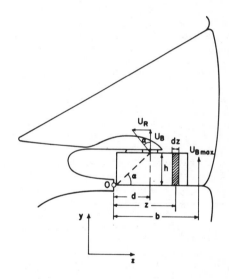

Fig. 2. A highly simplified schematic drawing of a cross section through scala media with some pertinent coordinates. For the limited purpose of calculating the effective mass loading of the basilar membrane, this membrane is assumed to rotate as a stiff beam around the axis 0. U_B means the velocity of the basilar membrane and U_R--the radial velocity of the reticular lamina at the middle row of the outer hair cells. Other symbols should be self-explanatory (also see text).

means that the acoustic mass would grow in inverse proportion to the width of the basilar membrane if k were constant and h did not change with the coordinate z (Fig. 2). Neither is entirely true, and histological sections seem to indicate that the mechanical mass is concentrated increasingly toward the location of maximum displacement of the basilar membrane in the cross section. This would tend to increase the effective mass and, with it, the acoustic mass. As a consequence, to the first order of approximation, the acoustic mass associated with the basilar membrane appears to be independent of the distance from the basal end of the cochlea. For a distance of about 0.7 cm from the basal end, where h is still reasonably constant over the cross section and $k \simeq 1$, Wever gives $b \simeq 1.5 \cdot 10^{-2}$ cm and $hb \simeq 7 \cdot 10^{-5}$ cm^2. Assuming that $\rho \simeq 1.2$ g/cm^3, we obtain $M_{Ba} \simeq 0.5$ g/cm^3.

Using the estimates of C_a and M_{Ba} it is possible to calculate the resonance frequency of the basilar membrane loaded with the organ of Corti and other tightly coupled masses, it is $f_r = 1/2\pi \sqrt{M_{Ba} C_a}$. Its relation to the

19

Fig. 3. Locus of maximum basilar-membrane vibration as measured by Békésy post-mortem (crosses and intermittent line). Locus of maximum basilar-membrane vibration in vivo as inferred from hearing loss and cochlear lesions (circles and solid line). Theoretical locus of basilar-membrane resonance when the effect of the tectorial membrane is neglected (dash-dot line) and when the effect of radial motion of the tectorial membrane is included (vertical cross). C_a*--compliance of the basilar membrane;* M_{Ba}*--*

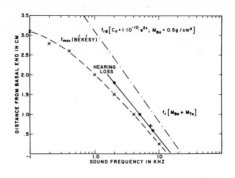

effective acoustic mass of structures directly attached to the basilar membrane; M_{Ta}*--effective acoustic mass loading due to radial motion of the tectorial membrane (further explanation in text).*

location in the cochlea is shown in Fig. 3 by the dash-dot line. For comparison, the crosses and dashed line show the location of the maximum vibration amplitude of the basilar membrane measured by Békésy (1960) post-mortem. The filled circles and solid line indicate the relationship between the frequency of the maximum hearing loss and the location of maximum cochlear damage based on the data of Crowe, Guild, and Polvogt (1934). If it is assumed that the frequency of maximum hearing loss coincides approximately with the maximum of basilar-membrane vibration, these data suggest that the maximum is displaced somewhat *in vivo* toward the cochlear apex by comparison to Békésy's post-mortem observations. Such a displacement is consistent with the findings of Kohllöffel (1972b) and Rhode (1973) on postmortem effects. The figure suggests that the resonance frequency of the basilar membrane is substantially higher than the frequency of its vibration maximum. The following section shows, however, that the difference disappears if the mass load resulting from a possible radial motion of the tectorial membrane is taken into consideration.

The effect of a radial motion of the tectorial membrane, which has been demonstrated qualitatively on mechanical models (Zwislocki, 1980a; Zwislocki and Kletsky, 1980), can be derived with the help of Fig. 2. From the simplified geometry of the organ of Corti it follows that the radial velocity of the reticular lamina at the location of the outer hair cells is $U_R = U_B h/d$, where d is the radial distance of the apical parts of the outer hair cells from the edge of the spiral lamina and h is the height of the organ of Corti. (Allen, 1978). The radical mechanical force per unit length exerted by the tectorial membrane on the reticular lamina is $F_R = Z_{Tm}U_R$, where Z_{Tm} is the mechanical impedance per unit length of the tectorial membrane together with its elastic attachments to the spiral limbus and the organ of Corti. The mechanical moment exerted by this force on the basilar membrane is on the order of $M_{TM} = h.F_R$, and the effective loading of the basilar membrane

$$Z_{Ta} = \frac{4F_R h}{b^3 U_{max}}$$

Expressing the force in terms of Z_{Tm}, U_B, h and d, we obtain

$$Z_{Ta} = \frac{4Z_{Tm}h^2 U_B}{b^3 dU_{max}}$$

From the histological sections it can be estimated that $h \simeq d$, $d \simeq b/2$, and $U_B \simeq U_{max}/2$. Therefore, $Z_{Ta} = Z_{Tm}/b^2$. We are interested in the mass loading of the basilar membrane, and it can be shown that, below the resonance of the tectorial membrane system, this mass loading is $M_{Ta} = qM_{Tm}/b^2$, where M_{Tm} is the effective mass of the tectorial membrane, and $q = 1$ at low frequencies and grows with Q near the resonance frequency according to the formula

$$q = \frac{(X/Q)^2 + (1-X^2)}{(X/Q)^2 + (1-X^2)^2} \ ,$$

with X standing for the ratio between a given frequency and the resonance frequency, f/f_r. Both the length and thickness of the tectorial membrane grow appreciably with distance from the basal end, a fact that has been demonstrated particularly clearly for the domestic pig by Zwicker (1971) but appears to be

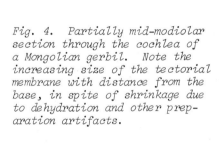

Fig. 4. Partially mid-modiolar section through the cochlea of a Mongolian gerbil. Note the increasing size of the tectorial membrane with distance from the base, in spite of shrinkage due to dehydration and other preparation artifacts.

generally true for the mammalian cochlea. Figure 4 shows this growth in the Mongolian gerbil as an example. We cannot go very wrong by assuming that the tectorial-membrane mass is an approximately constant fraction of the mass associated more directly with the basilar membrane. In primates (e.g. Engström and Angelborg, 1974) and in humans (e.g. Schuhknecht, 1974), the cross-sectional area of the tectorial membrane appears to be about 1/4 of that of the structures associated more directly with the basilar membrane when standard histological procedures are used. According to Kronester-Frei (1979), such procedures reduce the area by a factor of 2.5 to 3.5, so that *in vivo* the area of the tectorial membrane should be at least 1/2 the area of the cell mass associated with the basilar membrane. As already mentioned, the latter is approximately $7 \cdot 10^{-5} cm^2$ for a distance of about 0.7 cm from the basal end, so that we obtain $3.5 \cdot 10^{-5} cm^{-2}$ for the area of the tectorial membrane. The density of the tectorial membrane, which consists to a large extent of proteins should be slightly higher than that of the organ of Corti, say $1.3 g/cm^3$ (previously a slightly larger density was assumed, Zwislocki, 1980a,b). Accordingly, the mass of the tectorial membrane corresponding to the above cross-sectional area should be on the order of $4.5 \cdot 10^{-5} g/cm$ and, with the width of the basilar membrane at the corresponding location being approximately $b \simeq 1 \cdot 5 \cdot 10^{-2} cm$, the effective acoustic mass of the tectorial membrane loading the basilar membrane should amount to $M_{Ta} = q \cdot 0.2 g/cm^4$.

To calculate q, it is necessary to know the resonance frequency and the effective resistance. According to Fig. 3, the resonance frequency should be around 7 kHz for a distance of 0.7 cm. The resistance can be calculated approximately from the hydrodynamics of the gap between the tectorial membrane and the reticular lamina (Allen, 1978; Zwislocki, 1980a, b). It is given by the formula $R = d_g \eta_e / h_g$, where d_g is the gap width, h_g--the gap height and η_e--the coefficient of viscosity. According to previous considerations (Zwislocki, 1980a,b), the follow-approximate numerical values should hold for the given cochlear location: $d_g \simeq 75$ µm, $h_g \simeq 2$ µm and $\eta_e \simeq 1.10^{-2}$ cgs units. With these values we obtain $R \simeq 0.37$ dynes sec/cm^2 and $Q = 2\pi f M_{Tm}/R \simeq 5$. With this Q the maximum q is on the order of 3 and the maximum $M_{Ta} \simeq 0.6 g/cm^4$.

The maximum loading of the basilar membrane by the tectorial membrane should increase the total acoustic mass to $M_a = M_{Ba} + M_{Ta}$ and should change the resonance frequency by a factor of $(M_{Ba}/M_a)^{1/2} \simeq (0.5/1.1)^{1/2} = 0.67$. According to Fig. 3, this would mean a change in resonance frequency from 11 kHz to 7.35 kHz indicated by the vertical cross. Its approximate coincidence with the maximum of basilar-membrane vibration, as inferred from hearing loss and cochlear lesions, suggests that the calculated mass loading by the tectorial membrane is of the right order of magnitude.

For the calculated Q of the tectorial membrane the maximum mass loading occurs just below the resonance frequency of the tectorial membrane system. It is not known if the resonance of this system actually occurs at the correct frequency-location combination. However, the hypothesis that it does is consistent with experimental findings available thus far, as has been brought out in this and three preceding papers.

At the location of maximum mass loading, the tectorial membrane should move with an enhanced amplitude and 180° out of phase with the reticular lamina, thereby contributing to an increased shear motion, as is indicated schematically at the bottom of Fig. 1 (trace C), and to the sharpening of cochlear frequency analysis.

The above derivations show that the suggested resonance of the tectorial-membrane system is consistent with the approximately known values of cochlear constants. However, its existence can be proved only by a direct experiment or, indirectly, by measuring the stiffness of tectorial-membrane attachments to the organ of Corti and the spiral limbus.

REFERENCES

Allen, J.B. (1978). A physical model of basilar membrane dissipation. *J. Acoust. Soc. Am.* 63, S43 (A).

Békésy, G. V. (1960). *Experiments in Hearing*. McGraw Hill, New York.

Crowe, S. J., Guild, S. R. and Polvogt, L. M. (1934). Observations on the pathology of high-tone deafness. *Bull. Johns Hopkins Hosp.*, 54, 315-379 (cit. Wever, 1949).

Engström, H. and Angelborg, C. (1974). Morphology of the walls of the cochlear duct. In: *Facts and Models in Hearing* (E. Zwicker and E. Terhardt, eds). pp 3-17. Springer, Berlin.

Evans, E. F. and Wilson, J. P. (1973). The frequency selectivity of the cochlea. In: *Basic Mechanisms in Hearing* (A.R. Møller, ed). pp 519-551. Academic Press, London.

Flock, Å. (1977). Physiological properties of sensory hairs in the ear. In: *Psychophysics and Physiology of Hearing* (E. F. Evans and J. P. Wilson, eds). pp 15-25. Academic Press, London.

Hudspeth, A. J. and Corey, D. P. (1977). Sensitivity, polarity, and conductance change in the response of vertebrate hair cells to controlled mechanical stimuli. *Proc. Natl. Acad. Sci. U.S.A. (Biophysics)* 74, 2407-2411.

Kohllöffel, L. U. E. (1972a). A study of basilar membrane vibrations. II. The vibratory amplitude and phase pattern along the basilar membrane (post-mortem). *Acustica* 27, 66-81.

Kohllöffel, L. U. E. (1972b). A study of basilar membrane vibrations. III. The basilar membrane frequency response curve in the living guinea pig. *Acustica* 27, 82-89.

Kronester-Frei, A. (1979). Effect of changes in endolymphatic ion concentrations on the tectorial membrane. *Hearing Res.* 1, 81-94.

Lim, D. J. (1972). Fine morphology of the tectorial membrane. *Arch. Otolaryng.* 96, 199-215.

Peterson, L. C. and Bogert, B. P. (1950). A dynamical theory of the cochlea. *J. Acoust. Soc. Am.* 22, 369-381.

Ranke, O. F. (1972). Das Massenverhaltnis zwischen Membran und Flussigkeit in Innenohr. *Akust. Zeits.* 7, 1-11.

Rhode, W. S. (1971). Observation of the basilar membrane in squirrel monkeys using the Mössbauer technique. *J. Acoust. Soc. Am.* 49, 1218-1231.

Rhode, W. S. (1973). An investigation of postmortem cochlear mechanics using the Mössbauer effect. In: *Basic Mechanisms in Hearing* (A. R. Møller, ed). pp 49-67. Academic Press, London.

Schmiedt, R. A. (1977). Single and Two-Tone Effects in Normal and Abnormal Cochleas: A Study of Cochlear Microphonics and Auditory-Nerve Units. P.D. Dissertation, Syracuse University. Special Report, ISR-S-16, Institute for Sensory Research, Syracuse University, Syracuse.

Schmiedt, R. A. and Zwislocki, J. J. (1977). Comparison of sound-transmission and cochlear-microphonic characteristics in Mongolian gerbil and guinea pig. *J. Acoust. Soc. Am.* 61, 133-149.

Schmiedt, R. A. and Zwislocki, J. J. (1980). Effects of hair-cell lesions on responses of cochlear-nerve fibers. I. Lesions, tuning curves, two-tone inhibition, and responses to trapezoidal wave patterns. *J. Neurophysiol.* (in press).

Schuhknecht, H.F. (1974). *Pathology of the Ear*. Harvard University Press, Cambridge.

Zwicker, E. (1971). Die Abmessungen des Innenohrs des Hausschweines. *Acustica* 25, 232-239.

Zwislocki-Moscicki, J. (1948). Theorie der Schmeckenmechanik: Qualitative und quantitative Analyse. *Acta Otolaryng.* Suppl. 72, 1-76.

Zwislocki, J. (1953). Review of recent mathematical theories of cochlear dynamics. *J. Acoust. Soc. Am.* 25, 743-751.

Zwislocki, J. J. (1965). Analysis of some auditory characteristics. In: *Handbook of Mathematical Psychology.* Vol. III. (R. D. Luce, R. R. Bush, and E. Galanter, eds). pp 1-97. Wiley, New York.

Zwislocki, J. J. (1974). Cochlear waves: Interaction between theory and experiments. *J. Acoust. Soc. Am.* 55, 578-583.

Zwislocki, J. J. (1979). Tectorial membrane: A possible sharpening effect on the frequency analysis in the cochlea. *Acta Otolaryng.* 87, 267-269.

Zwislocki, J. J. (1980a). Theory of cochlear mechanics. *Hearing Res.* 2 (in press).

Zwislocki, J. J. (1980b). Five decades of research on cochlear mechanics. *J. Acoust. Soc. Am.* 67 (in press).

Zwislocki, J. J. and Kletsky, E. J. (1979). Tectorial membrane: A possible effect on frequency analysis in the cochlea. *Science* 204, 639-641.

Zwislocki, J. J. and Kletsky, E. J. (1980). Micromechanics in the theory of cochlear mechanics. *Hearing Res.* 2 (in press).

Wever, E. G. (1949). *Theory of Hearing*. Wiley, New York.

Acknowledgements. This research was supported by NIH grant NS-03950.

THE ELECTROPHYSIOLOGICAL PROFILE OF THE ORGAN OF CORTI

G.A. Manley and A. Kronester-Frei

Institute of Electroacoustics, Technical University,
München, Federal Republic of Germany

1. INTRODUCTION

This paper briefly outlines data obtained from electrophysiological recordings in the guinea pig cochlea. A more detailed report is in preparation.
This work was performed in order to more closely investigate the influence,
if any, of the tectorial membrane on the distribution of potentials in scala
media. The tectorial membrane of mammals has been recently shown to consist
of an agglomerate of protofibrils of varying degrees of hydration. In the
mouse, two kinds of protofibrils are distinguishable from their ultrastructure, and are systematically distributed in the tectorial membrane
(Kronester-Frei, 1978). In situ, the marginal zone of the tectorial membrane
is in close contact with the surface of the organ of Corti and appears to
morphologically separate off the subtectorial space from the scala media
proper (Kronester-Frei, 1979a, b).
Conceptions as to the electrical environment of the subtectorial space
have ranged from regarding the whole of the tectorial membrane as at zero
potential, i.e. the same as that of the perilymph space of scala tympani
(Lawrence *et al*, 1974; Lawrence, 1975) to regarding the endocochlear potential as being present in the subtectorial space in direct contact with the
upper surfaces of the hair cells (Davis, 1968; Tanaka *et al*, 1977). The difficulty of obtaining the necessary precision in specifying the location of
the electrode tip led Sohmer *et al* (1971) to conclude that it was not possible to make any detailed association of the recorded electrical events during
a penetration of the organ of Corti with the structures of this organ. This
uncertainty in the localization of the electrode tip at any given point in
time stems from the unknown degree of tissue distortion caused by the penetration itself and the alterations in the tissue caused by the subsequent
histological preparation procedure.
We have described (Manley and Kronester-Frei, 1980) a new technique for
observing the organ of Corti in the living animal, which allows a sufficiently exact quantification of electrode depth and position for determining
potential distributions in the organ of Corti. The tissues and the electrode
are observed through a monocular microscope via a minute, high-quality mirror
which is inserted into scala vestibuli. A micrometer scale in the eyepiece
makes it possible to measure the tissue dimensions in the individual animal,
the exact angle of penetration and the position of the electrode tip as well
as the angle of observation. The electrode tip is thus locatable in two dimensions to an accuracy of at least $\pm$ 2 μ. This method thus made it worthwhile to re-investigate this question with the realistic possibility of obtaining more reliable data.

2. METHODS

The experiments were carried out on coloured guinea pigs (180 - 350 g)
which were anaesthetized according to the technique described by Evans (1979).
The techniques of exposing the cochlea and observing the organ of Corti and
the electrode position have been described elsewhere (Manley and Kronester-

Frei, 1980). A hole is made in the bone of scala tympani through which the basilar membrane of the basal turn of the cochlea is illuminated by a light fibre. The light fibre and the mirror can both be moved by micromanipulators in order to obtain the best illumination and contrast. A recording electrode (glass micropipette) was passed through the basilar membrane from the scala tympani side, having been first visually positioned as seen through the tissues of the organ of Corti. Sometimes a second electrode, for recording and current injection, was passed in the same region of the cochlea through the stria vascularis into scala media. In a few experiments, the chain of middle-ear ossicles and the eardrum with its bony tympanic ring were left intact, to enable acoustic stimulation to be carried out. Thus the changes in phase of the cochlear microphonic during the penetration could be measured. In some cases, the compound action potential evoked by short tone bursts with rapid onset times (0.1 ms) were recorded by a silver-ball electrode on the round window. In most experiments, however, the middle ear was removed to reduce the total preparation time of the observation and recording systems.

In order to establish the various dimensions of the guinea-pig organ of Corti in this region of the basal turn in the unfixed state, the cochlea was removed from the animal and rapidly prepared for observation with Nomarski optics according to the technique of Kronester-Frei (1979a).

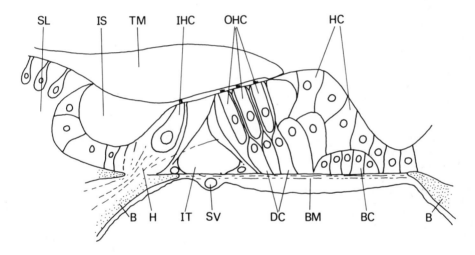

Fig. 1. Scale drawing of the unfixed organ of Corti in the basal region of the guinea-pig cochlea. The basilar membrane is here about 150 μ wide. SL – spiral limbus; IS – inner sulcus; TM – tectorial membrane; IHC – inner hair cell; OHC – outer hair cells; HC – Hensen's cells; B – bone; H – Habenula perforata; IT – inner tunnel; SV – spiral blood vessel; DC – Deiter's cells; BM – basilar membrane; BC – Boettcher's cells.

The drawing in Fig. 1 shows the dimensions of the organ of Corti and tectorial membrane under these conditions. The endolymph and perilymph remain in their normal locations. The basilar membrane in this region is normally about 150 μ wide. This drawing was the basis of the electrode depth comparisons in Figs. 3 and 4.

3. RESULTS

On opening the scala tympani, the compound action potential to a 14 kHz tone with a rise-time of 0.1 ms suffered an average loss of sensitivity of

6 dB. Opening the scala vestibuli produced an additional average loss of 7 dB.
In some cases the loss of sensitivity was also noted at frequencies which excite areas of the cochlea outside the operated area, indicating a general
loss of sensitivity perhaps associated with interference with the cochlear
blood supply or general deterioration in the condition of the animal. An average loss of sensitivity of 13 dB is, however, considering the gravity of the
operation, acceptable.

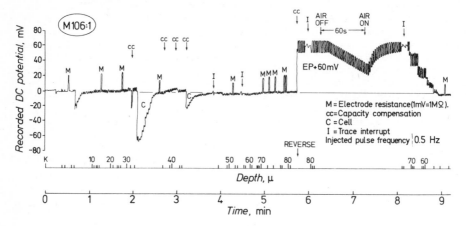

*Fig. 2. Schematic representation of the potentials recorded by an electrode
passing through the organ of Corti in the inner sulcus region, as described
in the text. The trace is interrupted four times, so the time scale is for
reference only. At cc the capacity compensation control on the preamplifier
was turned through its whole range in order to vibrate the electrode tip.*

A schematic representation of the potential changes observed during one
electrode penetration is illustrated in Fig. 2. The electrode was advanced
in 2 μ steps at irregular intervals. Portions of the trace are omitted four
times, during which no essential changes occurred. The electrode resistance
was measured repeatedly. In this case contact with two, or possibly three,
cells was obtained for short periods. No effort was made in this experiment
to hold the cells or to use fine electrodes for this purpose. On other
occasions, cells were held for 5 - 10 min. The capacity-compensation control
of the pre-amplifier was fully turned on several occasions to vibrate the
electrode tip. This led on one occasion to the penetration of a cell and on
the last occasion to the sudden appearance of the endocochlear potential (EP).
It was found that a step-wise movement of the electrode, together with the
use of the capacity-compensation control, facilitated the movement of the
electrode through the tissues with little distortion. Shortly after contact
(K) with the basilar membrane was achieved at the correct location for an
electrode path through the inner sulcus, current pulses of about 3 μA and
repetition rate 0.5 Hz were passed through the second electrode into scala
media. It can be seen that the sudden appearance of the endocochlear potential is accompanied by a ten-fold increase in size of the pulse recorded by
the electrode in the organ of Corti/tectorial membrane complex. A brief
hypoxia was then induced to demonstrate that the electrode was definitely
recording the EP. The EP became smaller in a step-wise fashion upon withdrawal of the electrode through reversing the stepping motor. Apart from
contacts with cells, the potential in the organ of Corti with reference to
that of scala tympani was zero.

After correcting for the angles of penetration with reference to the
organ of Corti, using the data gathered from measurements of the observed

positions of the electrode during the penetration, it was possible to determine accurately the electrode tip location at the point of the first appearance of the EP. Of 16 animals where the penetration was chosen to pass through
the inner sulcus, the EP first appeared in 13 cases upon contact with the un-
der-surface of the tectorial membrane. Six cases of the 13, selected because
they display a wide range of EP values, are illustrated in Fig. 3. The lines

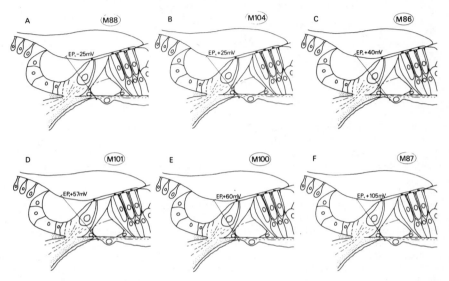

Fig. 3. Schematic drawing of the path of an electrode through the inner
sulcus in six different preparations arranged in order of the magnitude of
the final measured EP. The electrode path through the inner sulcus is drawn
accurately for each case. A crossed line at the end of each path indicates
the point of first contact with the EP.

indicating the paths of the electrodes are drawn exactly for each case from
the measurements taken during the respective penetrations. Even in case A,
where the EP is negative (the animal had died a few minutes previously) the
point of EP contact is the same. The inner sulcus itself was at zero potential. In the remaining three cases (two are shown in Fig. 4), the EP was

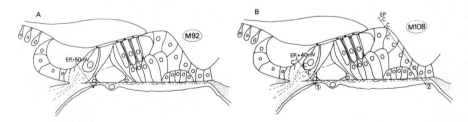

Fig. 4. Schematic representation of two cases where the EP was found as soon
as the electrode penetrated the inner sulcus. In B, a second penetration
was made through Claudius' cells. C - contact with a cell.

found as soon as the electrode entered the inner sulcus. Fig. 4B also shows
a later penetration through the outer region of the organ of Corti.
    In many cases it was possible, using a relatively slow, stepping pene-
tration, to barely contact the EP - that is, to leave the electrode in a

position where partial EP's were recorded. One such case where a continuous record was taken for more than 20 min is illustrated in Fig. 5. This portion of the record shows spontaneous changes in the recorded EP with the electrode

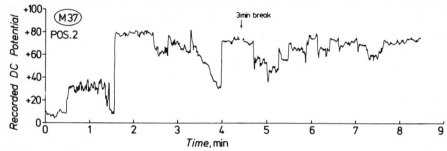

Fig. 5. Part of the record of unstable potentials recorded with the electrode just at the point of contact with EP and not being moved. 'POS. 2' indicates a recording path ending near the top of the inner hair cells. The time scale is for reference only. The potential was stable during the 3 min break indicated.

not being intentionally moved. It is evidently possible to record partial EP's, which are unstable presumably because tiny relative motions of the electrode and tissues cannot be eliminated. At the same time, phase measurements of the cochlear microphonic, with reference to the phase in scala tympani, were recorded by means of a phase meter using long tones of frequency 12 kHz and 1 kHz. Essentially identical data are indicated for another preparation in Fig. 6. The phase shifts back and forth, up to 160 - 180°, according to the momentary value of the recorded EP.

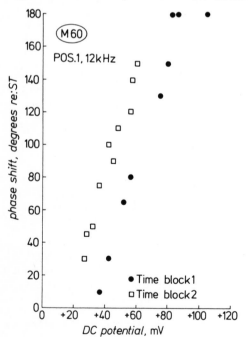

In one case, using the current-injection electrode also as a recording electrode (electrode A in Fig. 7), the rate of the potential changes induced by anoxia was investigated. In the first case (records A1 and B1), the electrode through the organ of Corti (B1) was just touching the underside of the tectorial membrane (depth 69 μ), i.e. contact with the EP had just been obtained (position shown in Fig. 3D). An anoxia of 2 min duration produced a more rapid decline of the EP for the scala media elec-

Fig. 6. Phase of the 12 kHz microphonic with reference to that in the scala tympani as dependent on the magnitude of the recorded EP. Data are from two blocks of time in a long unstable recording similar to that of Fig. 5. 'POS. 1' indicates a penetration through the inner sulcus.

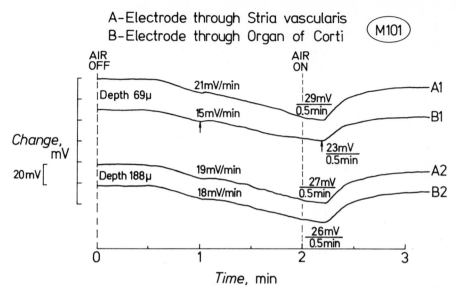

Fig. 7. Differential effect of a 2 min anoxia on the EP recorded from electrodes in the scala media or tectorial membrane, as described in the text. The decay slope is measured between the arrows and the recovery slope during the 0.5 min following the second arrow. The mV scale is a relative one, the traces are staggered for clarity only.

trode (Al, rate of fall berween the arrows 21 mV/min) than for the organ of Corti - tectorial membrane electrode (B1, rate of fall 15 mV/min). The same difference can be noted for the recovery rates. It should be noted that the ordinate scale is a *relative* one in Fig. 7 and the traces have been staggered at the origin for clarity - the initial EP magnitude is the same. The organ of Corti electrode was then pushed deeper, through the tectorial membrane to a depth of 188 µ. A second anoxia gave virtually identical fall and recovery times for the EP at both electrodes (A2 and B2) in this case. The distance between the electrodes in both cases was probably the same, about 4-500 µ.

4. DISCUSSION

An "organ of Corti potential" as reported by various authors was never observed - the only negative potentials could be reasonably attributed to the penetration of cells. They were normally unstable and of short duration and were gained and lost through small movements of the electrode. The "organ of Corti potential" should be regarded as an artifact connected with the mode of electrode motion and perhaps other factors.

Our experience indicated that penetrations can be made with little tissue distortion and small backlash on drive reversal (e.g. the EP is gained and lost at the same depth ± 2 - 4 µ) when small, rapid steps of the electrode are made. The deeper the penetration, the larger the backlash. A single deep penetration destroys the reliability of any additional penetrations. Experiments not reported here, recording from the outer hair cell region of the organ of Corti indicate that tissue distortion during recordings in this area are larger than those encountered with the electrode near the bony inner edge and that it will be more difficult to obtain reliable recordings from the sub-tectorial hair-cell space.

It is, of course, impossible to carry out such radical surgical procedures on the cochlea without damage. Experience allows such damage, reflected
in a loss of sensitivity of the cochlea, to be kept to a minimum, although
less than a 10 dB loss in sensitivity is probably impossible to achieve. The
observation method used, although difficult, brings the one great advantage
that it can be stated with confidence where the electrode tip was located at
a particular time of the recording. Thus it is possible to determine that,
in the region of the inner sulcus, the lower surface of the tectorial membrane is the limit of the EP - space. The three cases where the EP was found
in the inner sulcus, i.e. as soon as the electrode had penetrated the inner
hair cell area (Fig. 4), can reasonably be regarded as aberrant and induced
by surgical damage to the organ of Corti/tectorial membrane region, which
would not necessarily manifest itself in an obviously poor EP. The material
of the tectorial membrane which isolates the subtectorial space from the
scala media proper is probably easily disturbed (Kronester-Frei, 1979a).

The fact that under normal conditions the EP is not present in the inner
sulcus has important implications for models of inner-ear function. It means,
for example, that the tectorial membrane is so constructed that it can form
an electrical barrier. This barrier is at the underside of the tectorial membrane and not, as suggested by Lawrence *et al*, (1974) and Lawrence (1975) at
the upper surface. The upper surface of the tectorial membrane has an open
structure, whereas the lower surface, or basal layer, consists of an approximately 1 μ thick layer of parallel, closely-packed protofibrils (Kronester-
Frei, 1978). It is possible that the charges on these molecules can under
certain conditions inhibit ion movements. The data of Fig. 7 indicate that
an electrode just touching the undersurface of the tectorial membrane reacts
more slowly to potential changes in the EP space than one in the scala media
proper.

The above speculations are limited to the extent that the recordings
only apply to the inner sulcus region. The anatomical data (Kronester-Frei,
1979b) indicates not only that the subtectorial space is morphologically
separated from the scala media proper, but also that the material which makes
up the Hensen's stripe of the fixed tectorial membrane may connect in life
the tectorial membrane to the organ of Corti and thus separate the subtectorial hair-cell space from the inner sulcus. Thus the conditions directly
above the hair cells could also be different, although the basal layer of the
tectorial membrane is continuous through the whole area. The actual ionic
make-up of the fluid in the subtectorial spaces needs to be experimentally
analyzed in the living animal.

This data could be relatively easily obtained from the inner sulcus
with ion-specific electrodes. It will be important to compare such data with
that derived from x-ray microanalysis of rapidly frozen and freeze-dried
cochleas (Ryan *et al*, 1980). A knowledge of the potentials and of the ionic
make-up of the environment of the hair-cell surfaces is important for
theories of hair-cell stimulation.

If the EP is not directly available to the hair cells, the function of
the organ of Corti/tectorial membrane complex can be reconsidered along at
least two lines. Firstly, it is possible that the cilia tips alone are in
contact with the EP through their morphological contact with the tectorial
membrane and that under some conditions ion transfer from the tectorial membrane can occur. Secondly, it is possible that the ionic and potential
milieu of the endolymph space is necessary for the functional integrity of
the tectorial membrane, as originally speculated by Davis (1968). Certainly,
the tectorial membrane is highly sensitive to ionic disturbances in its
milieu (Kronester-Frei, 1979b) and shows irreversible shrinkage on exposure
to perilymph. Such profound structural alterations must be considered to have
been involved in previous results of the exchange *in vivo* of endolymph for
other fluids. Thus, the fact that cobalt ions injected into scala media are

able to produce a sulphurated deposit in the inner sulcus does not necessarily mean that the inner sulcus is continuous with the scala media proper (Tanaka *et al*, 1977). It is likely that 200 mM Cobalt chloride has a dramatic effect on the structure of the tectorial membrane, destroying its normal positional relationships. The Alcian-blue marking data of Tanaka *et al* (1977) show blue spots produced on contact with the EP either at the underside of the tectorial membrane or on the upper surface of the inner sulcus and are thus compatible with the present data.

It is obvious that the tectorial membrane has in the past been underestimated, being viewed as playing only the primitive rôle of a shearing partner for the organ of Corti. We now know enough about its structure to suggest that it probably plays important additional rôles. It is also obvious that more experimental evidence is needed before these functions can be clearly defined.

Acknowledgements

Supported by the Deutsche Forschungsgemeinschaft under the programme of the Sonderforschungsbereich 50, 'Kybernetik'.

REFERENCES

Davis, H. (1968). Mechanisms of the inner ear. *Ann. Otol. Rhinol. Laryngol.* 77, 644-655.
Evans, E.F. (1979). Neuroleptanaesthesia for the guinea pig. *Arch. Otolaryngol.* 105, 185-186.
Kronester-Frei, A. (1978). Ultrastructure of the different zones of the tectorial membrane. *Cell Tiss. Res.* 193, 11-23.
Kronester-Frei, A. (1979a). Localization of the marginal zone of the tectorial membrane *in situ*, unfixed and with *in vivo*-like ionic milieu. *Arch. Otorhinolaryngol.* 224, 3-9.
Kronester-Frei, A. (1979b). The effect of changes in endolymphatic ion concentrations on the tectorial membrane. *Hearing Res.* 81-94.
Lawrence, M. (1975). Resting potentials in the inner sulcus and tunnel of Corti. *Acta Otolaryngol.* 79, 304-309.
Lawrence, M., Nuttall, A.L. and Clapper, M.P. (1974). Electrical potentials and fluid boundaries within the organ of Corti. *J. Acoust. Soc. Am.* 55, 122-138.
Manley, G.A. and Kronester-Frei, A. (1980). Organ of Corti: observation technique in the living animal. *Hearing Res.* 2, 87-91.
Ryan, A.F., Wickham, M.G. and Bone, R.C. (1980). Studies of ionic distribution in the inner ear: scanning electron microscopy and x-ray microanalysis of freeze-dried cochlear specimens. *Hearing Res.* 2, 1-20.
Sohmer, H.S., Peake, W.T. and Weiss, T.F. (1971). Intracochlear potential recorded with micropipets. I. Correlations with electrode location. *J. Acoust. Soc. Am.* 50, 572-586.
Tanaka, Y., Asanuma, A., Yanagisawa, K. and Katsuki, Y. (1977). Electrical potentials of the subtectorial space in the guinea-pig cochlea. *Jap. J. Physiol.* 27, 539-549.

COMMENT

COMMENT ON "The Electrophysiological Profile of the Organ of Corti" (G.A. Manley and A. Kronester-Frei).

Peter Dallos and Åke Flock
Auditory Physiology Laboratory, Northwestern University, Evanston, IL. USA and Department of Physiology II., Karolinska Institutet, Stockholm, Sweden.

We would like to support and amplify two contentions in the above paper. Our information is based on several hundred penetrations of the organ of Corti in guinea pig cochleas with hyperfine microelectrodes. The majority of recordings were obtained from the third turn of the cochlea, but some tracks have been made in the second and fourth turns as well. Detailed results on both extra- and intracellular electrical characteristics will be published soon. We approach the organ of Corti through a fenestra made in the cochlear wall over the stria vascularis. The electrode track is parallel with the plane of the reticular lamina. The figure shows the dc profile of a representative penetration. At a the electrode goes through the stria and records the EP+. At b Hensen's cell is penetrated and the intracellular negativity may be maintained for any desired period. An advance of the electrode brings its tip into the outer tunnel (c) where the potential is zero or very slightly negative. Further advances lead to encountering either Deiters' cells or outer hair cells. At e an outer hair cell is penetrated, between f and g current is injected for the purpose of dye marking. Immediately after, the electrode is withdrawn and it encounters the EP+ at h. Resting potentials within cells ranged up to the following values: Hensen's and pillar cells: -90mV; Deiters' cells: -79mV; outer hair cells: -70mV; inner hair cells: -42mV.

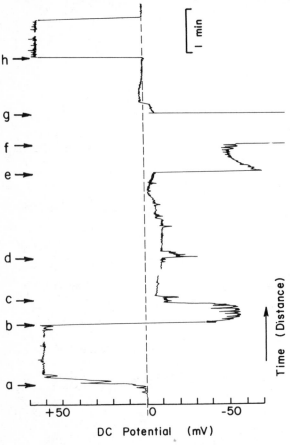

Note that insertion into and withdrawal from the organ of Corti at the Hensen cell-endolymph boundary (points b and h) could be accomplished with regularity with a hysteresis of less than 10 μm. We thus concur that it is possible to penetrate the organ with fine electrodes without unduly distorting it.

The second matter that we wish to comment on is the existence of the so-called organ of Corti potential. We concur that there is no such entity. The large negative voltages that some investigators have measured should be construed as artifacts. This point has been repeatedly made in the literature but the notion still persists.

Supported by NIH, Swedish Medical Research Council, the Guggenheim Foundation.

COMMENT ON "The electrophysiological profile of the organ of Corti"
(G.A. Manley and A. Kronester-Frei).

R. Klinke
Centre of Physiology, J.W. Goethe University, D-6000 Frankfurt, Germany.

I am having difficulties. You tell us that the inner sulcus is at zero potential. Ryan *et al.* (Hearing Res. 2, 1-20, 1980) however report about high potassium concentration in the subtectorial fluid. If that is correct, you would either have to expect a positive (endolymphatic) potential or a negative potassium diffusion potential in the subtectorial space and inner sulcus. Can you resolve this discrepancy? Have you considered the possibility that the three cases where you recorded a positive potential in the inner sulcus represent the normal situation rather than being "aberrant"?

Would a zero potential in the subtectorial space not require either the fluid to be perilymph-like or an additional energy-consuming barrier between the subtectorial space and the endolymphatic space, that is, for your data presented, at the lower surface of the tectorial membrane?

REPLY TO COMMENTS OF P. DALLOS AND A. FLOCK AND OF R. KLINKE

G.A. Manley
Institute of Zoology, Technical University, D-8000 Munich, W. Germany.

The fact that a hysteresis of less than 10 μm is obtainable upon insertion and withdrawal of a fine electrode is possible indicates only that no major *irreversible* distortion was produced by the penetration. It does not, however, allow the conclusion that no reversible distortion is caused by the electrode passage -i.e., that the tissues may be some extent pushed or dragged along by the electrode on penetration and then relax again on withdrawal. I would expect such an effect to be more of a problem in Dallos and Flock's lateral approach to the organ of Corti than in an approach through the basilar membrane. Thus the identifications of structures given in their figure can only be accepted as reliable where deposited dye marks were recovered. Anything further requires an observation technique to control for angles of penetration, distortion and also to allow accurate localization. It remains true, however, that a single deep penetration destroys the value of later penetration due to the production of irreversible distortion. To Klinke's comment, I can only say that I believe the chances are very high that it is not possible to prepare the tectorial membrane for examination by the ion probe technique so as to exclude a high probability of contamination of the underside by endolymph. Our data and that of others indicates that the tectorial membrane is easily disturbed from its normal position. Thus, until measurements of ionic concentrations in the sub-tectorial space are made with double-barreled ion-specific electrodes under visual control, I do not see any point in attempting to assess the need of additional pumping mechanisms. That the three cases found with the positive potential in the inner sulcus could be the 'normals' had, of course, occurred to us. However, since no amount of mental gymnastics could produce a reasonable explanation as to how damage could *exclude* the normally-present ions and/or potential, we adopted the opposite hypothesis as the only reasonable one. To what extent and under what conditions the lower surface of the tectorial membrane forms a barrier to ion transfer remains to be investigated. In the recordings we describe, however, the inner sulcus did not behave like a part of the endolymphatic space.

OBSERVATIONS ON THE GENERATOR MECHANISM OF STIMULUS
FREQUENCY ACOUSTIC EMISSIONS -
TWO TONE SUPPRESSION

D.T. Kemp and R.A. Chum

Institute of Laryngology and Otology
Royal National Throat, Nose and Ear Hospital
Gray's Inn Road, London WC1X 8DA

1. INTRODUCTION

Acoustic excitation of the healthy ear evokes an active mechanical
response within the cochlea which results in the re-emission of sound from
the ear (Kemp, 1978 and 1979, Kemp and Chum, 1980, Anderson and Kemp, 1979, Wit
and Ritsma, 1979 and Wilson, 1980a).   These stimulated acoustic emissions
comprise frequency components present in the stimulus, and also (for complex
stimuli) some distortion products (Kemp, 1979a, Kim, 1980 and Wilson, 1980).
The nature of the evoked cochlear mechanical response, which gives rise to
this phenomenon, is not known but its relationship to and involvement in the
cochlear filtering and transduction process is of considerable interest.
This paper particularly concerns the steady state generation of *stimulus*-
frequency acoustic emissions (SFE) by human ears and the form and significance
of the two tone suppression behaviour exhibited by the generating mechanism.
Input-output functions for acoustic emissions reveal the presence of a
strong, compressive nonlinearity in the generating mechanism.   Suppression
effects, which theoretically must accompany such nonlinearity, have been observed using tone-on-tone (Kemp, 1979), transient-on-transient (Kemp and Chum,
1980) and other paradigms (Wilson, 1980, Wit and Ritsma, 1979).   These data
indicate that, between absorption and re-emission, the stimulus signal has
been separated into its frequency components and then recombined.   The narrow
band channels identified in this way appear, to a first approximation, similar
to those of the known cochlear filter.   Such a relationship is supported by
the parallel vulnerability of the cochlear filter and acoustic emission channels (Kemp, 1978 and Anderson and Kemp, 1979).   The group latency of acoustic
emissions (5-15 ms) is however, somewhat longer than might be expected from
the observed cochlear filter (Anderson, 1980).   Transient suppression experiments have shown that the majority of this latency must have been developed
before the strong nonlinearity is activated (Kemp and Chum, 1980).   Their
model, in which a compressive nonlinearity followed each steep-sloped narrow-
band filter, in an ensemble of such filters, proved useful in accounting for
observed latency and suppression effects but to a first approximation only.
Detailed time domain observations showed an additional nonlinearity which could
only be associated with the filter response itself.   This further similarity
with the cochlear filter, i.e. its inherent nonlinearity, will be explored
further using the frequency domain observations reported here.   The empiri-
cally determined configuration of elements in the acoustic response generator
will be compared with those of the cochlear filtering chain.

2. METHODS

Most of the work that has been performed on stimulated acoustic emissions
has employed stimuli of a duration shorter than the response time of the generating mechanism.   This technique has the advantage of permitting the ident-

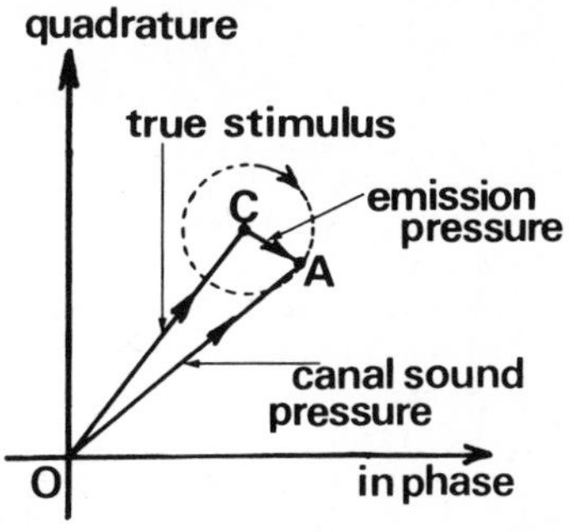

Fig.1. *Vector analysis of the sound pressure in the closed ear canal during continuous tonal stimulation. The 'true stimulus' OC, is defined as the sound pressure in the absence of acoustic emissions, CA. Experimentally, CA rotates rapidly around point C as a function of frequency, see results.*

ification of the acoustic emission or 'cochlear echo' on the basis of its latency. The data thus obtained relates to the transient response of the generating mechanism which, despite the apparent absence of adaptation (Kemp, 1978, Rutten, 1980 and Anderson 1980) can not be used to predict steady-state behaviour, because of the complex nonlinearity involved.

The steady-state generation of stimulus-frequency acoustic emissions (SFE) has previously been observed by Kemp (1979b), Kemp (1980) and Wilson (1980a) via the ripples caused in the intensity-frequency plot of the sound pressure in the closed ear canal when stimulated with a high impedence low level sound source. These ripples are due to the addition of the high latency SFE to the stimulus sound. In this study we fully separated the SFE from the ear canal sound pressure by a vector subtraction technique which exploits the nonlinear properties of the emission generator.

During continuous tonal stimulation the inphase and quadrature components of the closed meatal sound pressure were recorded. A 3 Hz bandwidth, two component BROOKDEAL analyzer was used to acquire the stimulus frequency sound signal. The analyzer was phase locked to the electrical signal driving the acoustic stimulator. For the survey reported in section 3·(i), the stimulus frequency was slowly swept, 8 times, across the frequency range. The digitally averaged inphase and quadrature signals were obtained as a function of frequency. The meatal probe was as described by Kemp (1978) and the noise floor for measurements was -10 dB SPL. Stimulus levels of 40 dB SPL were generally used.

Referring to figure 1 the meatal sound pressure corresponds to vector OA. This sound is the vector sum of the 'true' stimulus sound pressure OC and the acoustic emission, CA. The true stimulus OC was determined from measurements of OA obtained with a stimulus of 70 or 80 dB SPL. At this level the

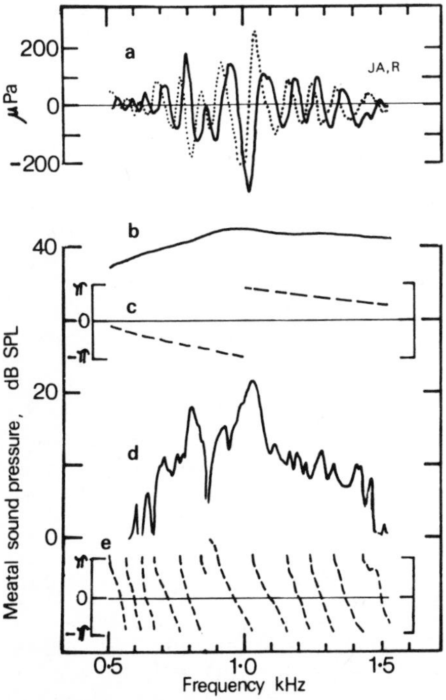

Fig.2. *Acoustic analysis of ear, J.A. right. (a) The inphase (solid line) and quadrature phase components of the SFE sound pressure (CA). (b) The magnitude of the true stimulus (OC). (c) The phase angle of OC with reference to the stimulus source driving voltage. (d) The magnitude of the SFE from (a) and in (e) its phase angle. The 2π discontinuities are for graphical convenience only; the phase variation is contiguous at these frequencies.*

saturating nonlinearity of the emission generator ensures that CA is very small compared to OC. The vector subtraction required to obtain the emission vector CA from OA measured at lower levels, was performed digitally.

Suppression of the SFE by a second tone was studied experimentally by observing with the frequency analyzer, the stimulus frequency component of OA as the intensity of the suppressor tone, M, was logarithmically increased over 10 seconds from 20 dB below the stimulus level to 40 dB above it. The frequencies of both tones, f_s and f_m, remained fixed. For f_m near to f_s, OA changes to approach OC, (the tone stimulus sound pressure), as the emission vector CA reduces due to suppression. Eventually OA attains a steady value equal to OC so that the behaviour of the SFE (CA) with suppressor intensity, can be computed.

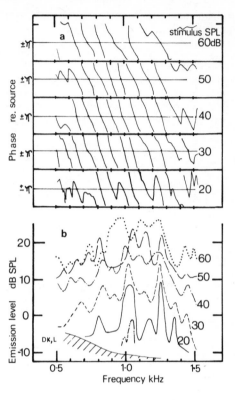

3. RESULTS

(a) Continuous stimulus-frequency emissions (SFE). Eight ears from six normally hearing subjects were examined initially over the restricted frequency range 500 to 1524 Hz. Only one subject did not

Fig.3. (a) The phase of SFE for subject DK left, at various stimulus levels. System noise is the most probable cause of the inflections at 20 dB SPL stimulation. (b) Magnitude of the SFE as a function of stimulus frequency, at various levels.

yield consistent results. This was traced to a non-stationary ear drum impedance and the subject was excluded from the analysis. Figure 2 illustrates the analysis for one normal ear. An SFE intensity of between 10 and 20 dB SPL is found for 40 dB SPL of stimulation. The staggered, oscillatory form of the two phase components of the SFE (2a) as a function of frequency corresponds to the clockwise rotation of the SFE vector CA around C as stimulus frequency is increased. This progressive increase of phase lag with frequency signifies a delay in the SFE with respect to the stimulus, as would be expected from previous transient stimulus investigations.

Transient measurements (cochlear echo technique, Kemp, 1978) typically reveal several natural frequencies of oscillation of the echo generating mechanism, which are characteristic of each ear. These same dominant emission frequencies are strongly present in the SFE at low stimulus levels (e.g. 20 dB SPL) but not at moderate levels (e.g. 60 dB SPL). Figure 3b illustrates this for another ear and also shows the nonlinear growth of SFE with stimulus level. In contrast, the phase of the SFE remains relatively steady with stimulus level (3a).

Figure 4a and b shows data from 6 ears (plus data for a synthesized SFE). With 40 dB SPL stimulation an SFE was found at most frequencies for each ear. The characteristic delayed nature of the SFE is evident both in the two component and phase displays. There is a 3:1 variation in the amplitude of the SFE generated, both with frequency in each ear, and between ears; even those

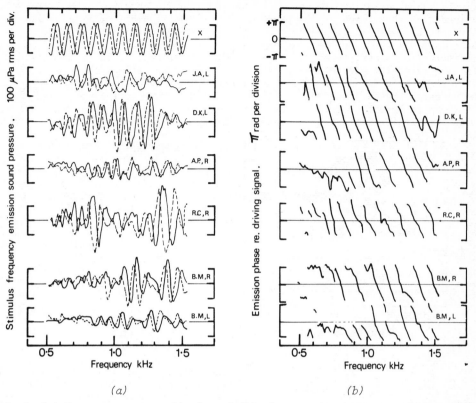

(a)   (b)

Fig.4. (a) Two component amplitude and (b) phase measurement for the SFE from 6 ears, and for the stimulus after transmission through a 10 ms analogue delay line. (x) For the ears, stimulation was 40 dB SPL.

belonging to the same subject. The general level per ear might depend strongly on middle ear admittance. Small differences in impedance were found but strong frequency dependance is not likely to be a middle ear property due to its inherent damping.

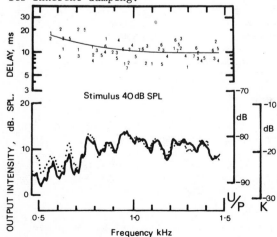

Fig.5 (upper). Latency values for the 7 ears as a function of frequency. Lower (solid line) averaged raw SFE magnitude data for 7 ears with 40 dB SPL stimulation. Dotted line; mean of the ratio of the equivalent SFE volume velocity source at the drum (U), to the stimulus pressure at the drum (P) computed for each subject (cgs units). U/P does not involve the volume of the closed meatus; one source of inter-subject variability. The K-scale represents the estimated ratio of SFE to stimulus signal pressure at the stapes (see Kemp, 1980).

Figure 5 summarises the data collected.   The latency L of the SFE was derived from the slopes of the phase plots for each subject at frequencies wherever the phase $\emptyset$ dropped monotonically with frequency for more than π radians ($L = -d\emptyset/dw$).   The mean latency in this octave frequency range is 10 ms and there is a slight tendency for it to decrease with increasing frequency. Mean SFE intensity was 10 dB SPL, i.e. 30 dB below the stimulation level. After correction for middle ear transmission (Kemp, 1980) the mean ratio, K, of the emission pressure due to the stimulus at the stapes to the cochlear input was found to be 0.1.   This degree of retrograde energy transfer must cause small but significant perturbations of the basilar membrane excitation pattern.

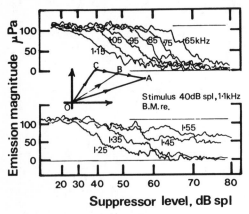

(b) Two tone suppression.   Figure 6 illustrates how the SFE for a fixed stimulus, S, of frequency, f_S, and intensity, P_S, is reduced by the presence of a second tone, M, of frequency f_m and variable intensity, P_m.   Referring to the inset diagram; as the suppressor is increased the total sound pressure vector $\overline{OA}$ is modified through $\overline{OB}$ to equal $\overline{OC}$; the 'true' stimulus level.   The magnitude of the SFE reduces from $\overline{CA}$ through $\overline{CB}$ to zero. From figure 6 it will be noted that suppression develops more sharply for f_m less than f_S (6, upper) than for f_m greater than f_S (lower).   This was observed at all stimulus frequencies and levels employed. Also, suppression occurs at higher levels of M for f_m further from f_S, i.e. the generator of SFE at f_S has a tuned response.

Fig.6. Suppression of the stimulus frequency emission by a suppressor tone. Raw data for ear BM, right at 1 100 Hz, 40 dB SPL stimulation. Suppressor frequency is marked. For inset, see text.

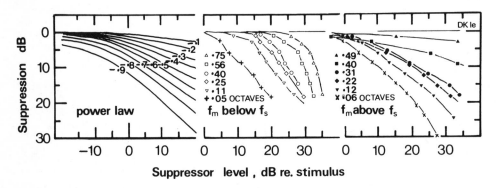

Fig.7. Centre and right; suppression of the SFE at 1 250 Hz, 40 dB SPL stimulation for subject DK left, as a function of suppressor level and for various suppressor frequencies. Left; prediction of two tone suppression for a system with transmission gain G dependent on total input power, P^2 by $G = A(P^2)^C$. (Kemp and Chum, 1980). Values of constant C near −1 correspond to near-saturated nonlinearity, and those near 0, to linearity. C values are marked on the theoretical curves.

In figure 7 (right and centre) data from another subject, has been averaged and replotted on a dB scale so that the asymptotic suppression rate, can be seen. Theoretical curves appear in figure 7 (left). These are based on the experimentally observed power law compressive nonlinearity of the emission generator for click stimulation (Kemp and Chum, 1980). The f_m-above-f_s suppression can clearly be accounted for by this type of model only if the degree of nonlinearity is allowed to be frequency relation dependent. The f_m-below-f_s suppression is greater than one and too sharp to be explained by any simple power low nonlinearity model. It is as though the suppressor suffered relative expansion before interacting with the stimulus in the compressive nonlinearity.

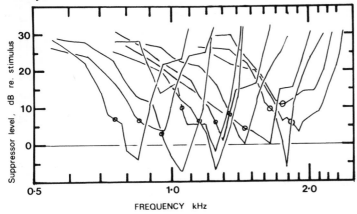

Fig.8. A population of 6 dB suppression contours for subject DK left. The stimulus and observation frequency for each curve is marked with a circle. Straight line segments join data points.

The asymptotic suppression rate is approached at about 10 dB of suppression. Figure 9 (lower) shows how this rate varies with frequency for the two subjects. It drops from 'super-compressive' rates below f_s to near zero nonlinearity for f_m about 0.6 octaves above f_s.

The phase of the SFE was monitored throughout the suppression sequence. No evidence of change was found. Referring again to figure 6, inset; point B was always found to be co-linear with A and C ($\pm$ 10°), i.e. the SFE vector did not rotate during progressive suppression. This contrasts with the rotation caused by stimulus frequency change, 360° per 100 Hz, and the frequency dependance of the nonlinearity.

(c) Generator frequency selectivity. By determining the level of suppressor required to produce a particular degree of SFE suppression, as a function of suppressor frequency, the generator selectivity can be examined (Kemp, 1979b). Figure 8 shows a population of equi-suppression curves for one subject, based on a 6 dB of suppression criterion. These confirm previous reports that a substantial degree of frequency selectivity is possessed by the SFE generator. The mean Q10 dB was 5.1; comparable with cochlear filter measurements.

It appears from figure 8 that for this ear, SFEs for frequencies of 1 050, 1 150 and 1 250 derive much of their strength from a single,frequency selective channel at around 1 250 Hz. A channel at around 1 700 also seems to serve a wide frequency range. Significantly these two frequencies are the dominent frequencies revealed for this ear by click stimulation and also spontaneous cochlear oscillation occurs near these two frequencies (Kemp, 1979a and b). However, at least 5 other distinct channels can be identified, and this indicates that an irregular continuum of channels might exist.

From figure 8 it can be seen that the tip of the suppression curve rarely occurs at the stimulus frequency. Of the 11 stimulus frequencies used, none resulted in an SFE from a channel tuned to a frequency below f_s. The minimum of the 6 dB suppression curve was on average 90 Hz above the stimulus frequency. This statistically significant bias has implications for the structure of the generator channel, discussed later.

Fig.9. Upper. ● Mean 6 dB isosuppression curve from figure 8. ▼ Notional 100% and ▲ 0% suppression curves derived by linear extrapolation from the 50% suppression region of 'figure 6 type' plots for the same subject. □ Mean level for total psychophysical masking of the stimulus by the suppressor. Lower. Solid line and unfilled data points - Suppression rate for the SFE between the 6 and 12 dB suppression levels. Long-dashed line; Comparable suppression rate data computed from Sellick and Russell (1979) from intracellular A.C. receptor potential suppression measurements; guinea pig (f_s=17 Hz). Short-dashed line; Comparable suppression rate data from figure 8 Abbas and Sachs (1976) from single nerve two tone suppression measurement in cat at CF, 17.8 kHz. Here, firing rate was equated to output amplitude.

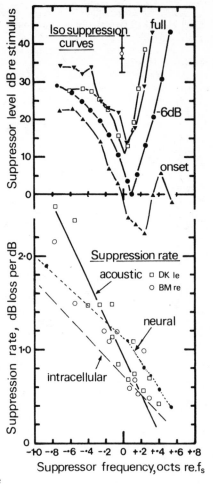

Figure 9 (upper) shows the mean 6 dB equi-suppression curve for ear, DK left. The curve's generality has been confirmed on several other ears. This measure of generator tuning is of course dependent upon the suppression criterion used. The two extreme curves are shown, for '100%' and 'zero' suppression respectively (see figure legend). It is considered highly significant that the '100%' acoustic suppression curve in figure 9 matched closely the mean psychophysical tone-on-tone total masking curve, derived for this ear over the same frequency range. There was a small positive correlation between psychoacoustical and acoustical Q10 dB values. The psychophysical masking curves did not show the irregularities or the off-tune bias of the acoustic curves.

4.   DISCUSSION

This study has supported the proposition that in most healthy humans ears stimulus frequency acoustic emissions are continuously produced during continuous stimulation over a continuum of stimulus frequencies. Because the input output function is nonlinear it is possible to use a suppression technique to explore the tuning of the system responsible for the re-emission of each test frequency. We found almost as many distinct channels as test frequencies used but surprisingly the tips of the tuning curves rarely coincided with the test frequency. An off-tune output could result from the absence of a generator precisely at the test frequency or from the presence of a more efficient generator at a neighbouring frequency. The clustering of curves around 1 250 Hz in figure 8 could be an example of this. However, at stimuli of 850, 950, 1 350 and 1 450 Hz (figure 8) it seems that channels tuned to or slightly below the stimulus are not used whilst more distant channels tuned *above* the stimulus are used.

To interpret this bias we note that the suppression technique reveals only the tuning up to the nonlinearity. If additional filtering follows the nonlinearity then the peak of the transmission curve need not coincide with the tip of the suppression curve. The additional linear filter must be of systematically lower frequency than the first to explain the observed offset bias in emission generator tuning.

The frequency ratio dependance of acoustic emission suppression rate (figure 7 and 9) shows that the transmission nonlinearity is intimately involved with the frequency selective mechanism. This behaviour is also true of the cochlear filter and is theoretically modelable on the basis of nonlinear damping of cochlear mechanics (Kim $et\ al$, 1973). Electrophysiological suppression rate data from Sellick and Russell's (1979) measurements of inner hair cell A.C. component suppression is given in figure 9 (lower) for comparison with the acoustic data. In their work, as in our experiments, narrow band acquisition of the stimulus frequency excitation component allowed the measurement of two-tone suppression into the excitory region. Considering the species and frequency differences, the correspondence between acoustic and hair cell data is good. Abbas and Sachs' (1976) data from single cochlear nerves is also shown and also compares favourably. Therefore, not only is the Q10 dB of emission generators similar to cochlear filter values, but also the inherent nonlinearity has very similar characteristics.

Acknowledgements

This work was supported by a grant from the Medical Research Council. We thank Rita Shoulder (Audiology Dept. ILO) for typing this manuscript.

REFERENCES

Abbas, P.J. and Sachs, M.N. (1976) Two-tone suppression in auditory-nerve fibres. *J.Acoust.Soc.Am.* 59, 112-122.
Anderson, S.D. (1980) Some ECMR properties in relation to other signals from the auditory periphery. *Hearing Research* 2 (in press).
Anderson, S.D. and Kemp, D.T. (1979) The evoked cochlear mechanical response in laboratory primates. *Arch.Otorhinolaryngol.* 224, 47-54.
Boer, E. de (1980) Nonlinear interactions and the 'Kemp Echo'. *Hearing Research* 2 (in press).
Kemp, D.T. (1978) Stimulated acoustic emissions from the human auditory system *J.Acoust.Soc.Am.* 64, 1386-1391.
Kemp, D.T. (1979a) Evidence of mechanical nonlinearity and frequency selective wave amplification in the cochlea. *Arch.Otorhinolaryngol.* 224, 37-45.
Kemp, D.T. (1979b) Evidence for a new element in cochlear mechanics. *Scand. Audiol.* Suppl. 9, 35-47.
Kemp, D.T. (1980) Towards a model for the origin of cochlear echoes. *Hearing Research* 2 (in press).
Kemp, D.T. and Chum, R. (1980) Properties of the generator of stimulated acoustic emissions. *Hearing Research* 2 (in press).
Kim, D.O. (1980) Cochlear mechanics: implications of electrophysiological and acoustic observations. *Hearing Research* 2 (in press).
Kim, D.O., Molnar, C.E. and Pfeiffer, R.R. (1973) A system of nonlinear differential equations modeling basilar membrane motion. *J.Acoust.Soc.Am.* 54. 1517-1529.
Rutten, W.L.C. (1980) Evoked acoustical emissions from within normal and abnormal ears; audiometric and cochleographic findings. *Hearing Res.* 2 (in press)
Sellick, P.M. and Russell, I.J. (1979) Two-tone suppression in cochlear hair cells. *Hearing Research* 1, 227-236.
Wilson, J.P. (1980) Evidence for a cochlear origin for acoustic re-emissions threshold fine structure and tonal tinnitus. *Hearing Res.* 2 (in press).
Wilson, J.P. (1980b) Models for cochlear echoes and tinnitus based on an observed electrical correlate. *Hearing Research* 2 (in press).
Wit. H.P. and Ritsma, R.J. (1979) Stimulated acoustic emissions from the human ear. *J.Acoust.Soc.Am.* 66, 911-913.

COMMENT

COMMENT ON "Observations of the Generator Mechanism of Stimulus Frequency Acoustic Emissions" (D. T. Kemp and R. Chum).

P. Dallos
Auditory Physiology Laboratory, Northwestern University, Evanston, IL. USA

It may be of interest to remember that we demonstrated many years ago that acoustic emissions by the eardrum can be obtained, corresponding to certain distortion components that arise in the cochlea (Dallos, 1966, 1973). The distortion, fractional subharmonic pairs, appears in the sound field and in the cochlear microphonic response. The process is demonstrably related to hydromechanical nonlinearities and is strongly coupled to the drum via the middle ear. This is a high-level phenomenon and probably not directly related to the "Kemp-effect". Yet, its existence has provided an early indication that vibratory events originating in the cochlea can be detected in the sound field .

REFERENCES

Dallos, P. J. (1966). On the generation of odd-fractional subharmonics. *J. Acoust. Soc. Amer.* 40, 1381-1391
Dallos, P. (1973). *The Auditory Periphery. Biophysics and Physiology* (Academic Press, New York) pp. 448-464

THE COMBINATION TONE, $2f_1 - f_2$, IN PSYCHOPHYSICS
AND EAR-CANAL RECORDING

J.P. Wilson

Dept. of Communication & Neuroscience, University of Keele,
Keele, Staffs., U.K.

1. INTRODUCTION

Intermodulation distortion between two primary tones at frequencies f_1 and f_2 produces a cubic difference tone (CDT) at $2f_1 - f_2$ which under suitable conditions is clearly audible as an extra tone, can be matched or cancelled, shows strong dependence on the ratio f_2/f_1, and is relatively constant in level relative to equal-level primaries (Zwicker, 1955, Goldstein, 1967, Smoorenburg, 1972). These properties imply an origin within the frequency-selective part of the auditory system, i.e. within the cochlea. The most popular current model (deriving from Goldstein, 1970, Smoorenburg, 1972) is that the basilar membrane vibrates nonlinearly generating the component $2f_1 - f_2$ over the region where f_1 and f_2 produce large vibration amplitudes. This CDT component then propagates along the basilar membrane as a secondary travelling wave developing maximal amplitude at the place maximally responsive to $2f_1 - f_2$ in a manner indistinguishable from a single tone at this frequency. The stimulus-like nature of this component is emphasized in the work of Goldstein *et al* (1978) which shows that it can act as a primary for interaction with another external tone to produce a secondary CDT. The main difficulty for this model is that direct measures of basilar membrane motion have not revealed the CDT at anywhere near the expected levels (Wilson & Johnstone, 1973, Rhode, 1977). Furthermore, measurements of the CDT phase relative to the primaries shows strong level dependency for the human psychophysical results (Goldstein, 1967, Smoorenburg, 1972, Hall, 1972, Goldstein *et al*, 1978) whereas cochlear nerve fibre recordings in cat show no phase dependency (Goldstein & Kiang, 1968). Recently CDTs have been observed in acoustic ear-canal recordings and thought to be of cochlear origin (Kemp, 1979, Kim *et al*, 1980, Wilson, 1980b). The present report presents a parametric study of psychophysical CDTs using cancellation techniques with corresponding ear-canal recordings in man in order to try and resolve some of these difficulties. Preliminary experiments revealed that CDTs in ear canal measurements appear strongest when $2f_1 - f_2$, rather than f_1 or f_2, lie at the frequency of a strong single tone re-emission. Experiments were therefore performed with $2f_1 - f_2$ held constant at this frequency.

2. PSYCHOACOUSTIC MEASUREMENT OF CDTs BY CANCELLATION

The CDT frequency ($2f_1 - f_2$) was set at 800 Hz, a frequency of strong cochlear re-emission in the subject used. Signal f_1 was generated by a Levell TG 150 oscillator, and $2f_1 - f_2$ by a variable phase oscillator (Feedback Ltd VPO 230). To generate f_2, f_1 was squared and passed to a wide-band quadrature network and $2f_1 - f_2$ passed to a second quadrature network; the in-phase and quadrature outputs of these networks were cross-multiplied and the difference gave the required component, f_2. This was filtered by a B & K 2020 slave filter set at 10 Hz bandwidth to eliminate residuals. The levels of f_1 and f_2 were set equal and the relative level and phase of the $2f_1 - f_2$ component could be adjusted by the subject on the variable phase output

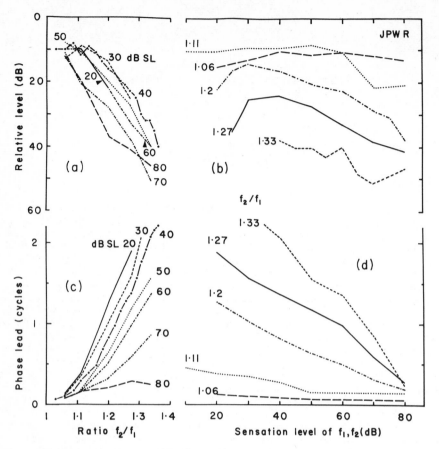

Fig. 1. Psychophysical cancellation of CDT at $2f_1 - f_2 = 800$ Hz
(a)   cancellation level relative to primaries vs. ratio f_2/f_1 with SL of f_1 and f_2 as parameter   (b)   cancellation level vs. SL of f_1 and f_2 with f_2/f_1 as parameter   (c)   phase of CDT (relative to primaries) vs. ratio f_2/f_1 with SL of f_1 and f_2 as parameter   (d)   phase of CDT vs. SL of f_1 and f_2 with f_2/f_1 as parameter.

of the oscillator to obtain cancellation. The reference zero for phase was obtained by applying f_1 and f_2 to a pair of back-to-back diodes: electrical and acoustic phase shifts beyond this point were small at these frequencies. Signals were presented monotically to the right ear over an electrostatic earphone (Wilson, 1968) with a flat response on the ear (+1dB) over the range used (800 Hz - 1.7 kHz). Sensation levels given represent an average value over this range (=2 dB SPL): no attempt was made to allow for audiogram fine-structure which varied by +6 dB .

Fig. 1 shows the relative amplitude levels in (a) and (b) and phases in (c) and (d) of the CDT, which was assumed to be equal and opposite to the cancellation tone; these are plotted in (a) and (c) as a function of frequency (ratio) and in (b) and (d) as a function of sensation level of the stimulus. In (a) the usual strong CDT level dependency upon the ratio f_2/f_1 is observed although not down to the lowest ratios at the lower levels. In general the curves are shifted downwards at the higher levels, although all curves appear to converge on about −10 dB at the lowest ratio of 1.06. The level dependency at each ratio is shown in (b) and is greater at the three higher ratios where the overall level is less.

Fig. 1(c) shows that the CDT phase advance increases with frequency separation of the components and is much greater at lower sensation levels. At f_2/f_1=1.06 there is very little relative phase shift. In Fig. 1(d) it can be seen that the level dependency is much greater for large f_2/f_1 ratios and all the curves appear to converge on a level just above 80 dB SL (say 90 dB SPL).

The amplitude and phase features of these data are consistent with the earlier findings of Goldstein (1967), Smoorenburg (1972), and Hall (1972). The convergence onto small values of phase shift at low f_2/f_1 ratios implies that the CDT is cancelled either at source or, if at the point of reception, with very little delay, and that the nonlinearity is compressive (Schroeder, 1969).

3. EAR-CANAL RECORDED CDTs

Attempts were made to obtain recordings of CDTs from the ear canal of the same subject. The primary components at f_1 and f_2 were produced as in the previous experiment but were fed to the ear canal from two separate B & K 4134 drivers via one half of a divided 5 mm i.d. tube of 3 cm. length. The other half of the tube fed back the signals and any distortion products to a specially-developed sensitive condenser microphone (Wilson, 1980a). The output of the microphone preamplifier was fed to a quadrature pair of Brookdeal 401 Lock-in Amplifiers. The reference for this was the signal being measured which could be f_1, f_2 or $2f_1$-f_2.

a) *Amplitude level characteristics*

The results are plotted in Fig. 2 in a similar manner to Fig. 1 but, because of the lower levels of CDT, the range of possible measurements was more limited. The maximum level was 40 dB below the primaries with a decrease towards *small* f_2/f_1 ratios as well as towards large ratios. Under the most favourable conditions the level of CDT approached closest to the primaries in the region of 20 dB SL. If allowance is made for the strength of a single tone (ST, fig. 2) cochlear re-emission at the $2f_1 - f_2$ frequency, these levels are only about 6 dB below the psychophysical cancellation levels over the range 20 - 50 dB SL. The difference appears greater at 10 dB SL but psychophysical values are subject to uncertainty near threshold for the simple cancellation method used.

In view of the limited range of stimulus parameters possible with this subject further measurements were made in two other subjects selected for strong single-tone cochlear re-emissions (Figs. 3 and 4). In both cases the level of ear-canal CDT was much higher than for the first subject and minimally 12 - 14 dB below ST, i.e., again comparable with accepted levels for cancellation and only 3 dB lower than that for subject JPW-R (but at 1200 Hz frequency rather than 800 Hz). These subjects also demonstrated the tendency for the ear-canal CDT to be strongest near 20 dB SL at least for lower values of f_2/f_1. Thus the level of CDT in the ear canal is approximately what might be expected from psychophysical cancellation levels and the level behaviour for a single tone cochlear re-emission at the CDT frequency. In detail, however, there are discrepancies. In all three subjects the highest levels were not obtained for the lowest f_2/f_1 ratios but for ratios between 1.1 and 1.2. In fact there appears to be a tendency for the negative (and positive) slopes of the function to shift towards higher values of f_2/f_1 for higher SLs. In the psychophysical data, on the other hand, the shift tends to be in the opposite direction, towards lower f_2/f_1 ratios at higher SLs.

The presence of a peak in the ear-canal data is clearest in Fig. 4(a) where measurements have been extended to ratios below unity, if f_2 is defined as the remote frequency (or $2f_2 - f_1$, if f_2 is defined as > f_1). It is also apparent from this figure that levels of $2f_2 - f_1$ are less than for $2f_1 - f_2$

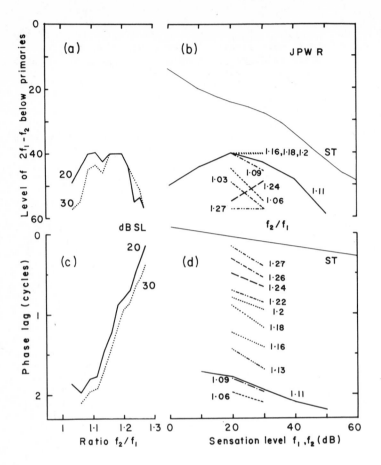

Fig. 2. Ear-canal recorded CDT for same frequency and subject as fig. 1. (a) and (b) levels, and (c) and (d) phases relative to primaries as in fig. 1. The lines ST represent the relative levels and phases of a single tone cochlear re-emission in response to an 8 cycle tone burst as a function of SL.

at comparable frequency separations and that the level of $2f_2 - f_1$ also decreases strongly with frequency separation. Although $2f_2 - f_1$ is not normally heard as a separate tone its influence has been measured by Zurek & Sachs (1979) and the levels reported appear comparable. Pick & Palmer (this vol.) failed to find evidence of response to this component at the cochlear fibre level in cat.

Although many of the measurements have not been extended to higher SLs (Fig. 2-4(b)) those that have appear to decrease quite rapidly. A diagonal line through co-ordinates (0, 0 dB) and (60, 60 dB) (not illustrated) would represent a CDT level corresponding to threshold. Most of the measurements are below such a line and maximum levels are about 10 dB SL. This can be compared with a maximal level for a single tone cochlear re-emission of about 20 dB SPL (Kemp, 1978, Wilson, 1980b). By contrast, Kim et al (1980) report CDT levels approaching 50 dB SPL in cat ear canal for 90 dB SPL stimulation. In view of this apparent discrepancy careful experiments were made with subject GFP-L at levels up to 100 dB SPL and a f_2/f_1 ratio of 1.15, ($2f_1 - f_2 = 1167$ Hz). At the higher levels, measurements were limited by the equipment to -70 dB relative to the primaries. The highest stimulus levels at which CDTs were distinguishable from instrumental limitations were 85 and 75 dB SPL giving -68 and -58 dB relative to the primaries, respectively, i.e. 17 dB SPL. Below this the absolute level decreased whereas the relative level increased. It appears from our results that the maximum level of re-emitted CDT is limited

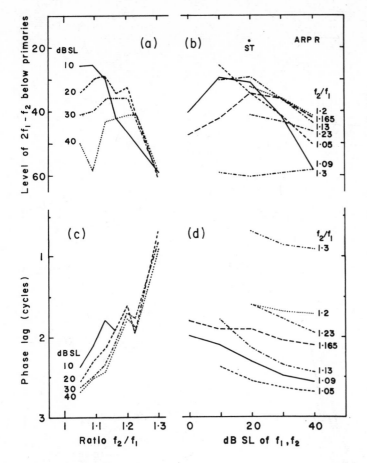

Fig. 3. As Fig. 2
for another subject.

by the same compression mechanism operating for single tone re-emission. Taken with the preliminary observation that CDT re-emission is greatest at frequencies where ST re-emission is strongest it appears likely that CDT re-emission occurs via the $2f_1 - f_2$ site and not directly from the region of interaction.

b) *Phase Characteristics*

The variations in phase with respect to frequency ratio are shown in Figs. 2-4(c).

The phase of the CDT in the ear canal with respect to the primaries can be seen to be strongly dependent upon f_2/f_1 ratio (Figs. 2-4(c)). This dependency appears to be similar at all SLs but shows greater overall phase lag at the higher SLs, i.e. a parallel shift downwards in Figs. 2-4(c). In comparison with the psychophysical cancellation-phase-functions (Fig. 1(c)) the agreement is excellent at 20 dB SL. In detail, however, it is clear that the cancellation data converge onto a single phase value for all SLs at low f_2/f_1 ratios whereas the ear-canal phases do not. This discrepancy is also seen clearly in the phase functions with respect to SL with ratio f_2/f_1 as parameter (Figs. 1-4 (d)). The slopes of these functions are strongly dependent upon f_2/f_1 ratio in the cancellation data and range systematically from -0.01 to -0.44 cycles/10 dB but there is no such tendency for the ear-canal recordings. For the same subject (JPW-R) the mean slope is -0.19 ±0.02 cycles/10 dB and for

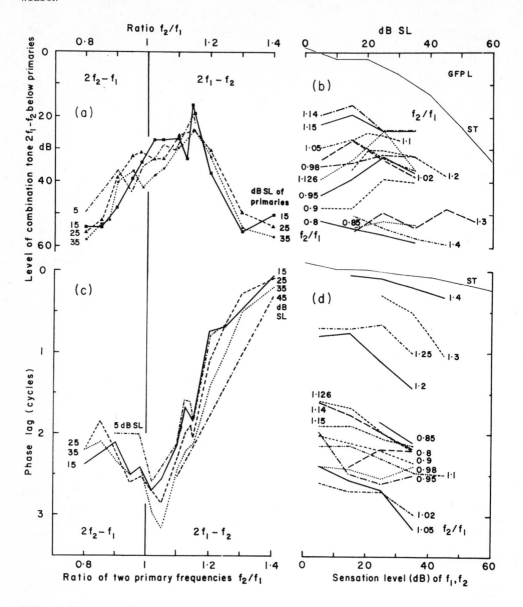

Fig. 4. As figs. 2 and 3 with measurements extending down to $f_2/f_1 < 1$ (or if f_2 defined as $> f_1$, to values representing $2f_2 - f_1$).

the other two −0.125 ±0.02 cycles/10 dB each. These phase/level dependencies can be compared with those for a single tone re-emission which range from −0.02 to −0.15 cycles/10 dB for various subjects and various frequencies but are usually about −0.06 cycles/10 dB (see Figs. 2 and 4 (d)). Thus the level dependency of the CDT phase is probably greater than that for a single tone re-emission. These phase dependencies can also be compared with the psycho-physical data of Goldstein (1978) *et al* at −6° to −10°/dB (=0.17 − 0.28 cycles/10 dB) who do not indicate whether their values depend upon f_2/f_1 ratio and Hall (1972) whose data depend on f_2/f_1 and also on f_1. There is obviously disagreement with the physiological data of Goldstein & Kiang (1968) who find no phase/level dependency in cat cochlear nerve fibre responses to CDTs.

4. DISCUSSION AND CONCLUSIONS

Greenwood (1977) has suggested that cancellation methods may overestimate the CDT level owing to suppression effects. The present experiments, however, indicate that objective levels of CDT may be only of the order of 3 - 6 dB below cancellation levels. The slight discrepancies between cancellation and ear canal CDT properties reported here may nevertheless be explicable as a suppression phenomenon. Taken with the absence of CDTs in basilar membrane vibration (Wilson & Johnstone, 1973, Rhode, 1977) it appears necessary to consider alternative modes of propagation for CDTs. This could either be mechanical via some other structure in the cochlea, e.g. the tectorial membrane, or electrical via current return paths (Wilson, 1977). In the latter case the distortion need not be mechanical but could occur in the first transduction process. This would be consistent with a model for cochlear re-emission based on synchronous hair cell swelling (Wilson, 1980c). This could account for the limited magnitude of cochlear re-emission of about 20 dB SPL for a single tone stimulation (Kemp, 1978, Wilson, 1980b) but would require further assumptions concerning compression mechanisms to account for the "unlimited" magnitude of CDTs observed in cancellation experiments. The most consistent model would appear to be mechanical propagation via a structure other than the basilar membrane. One final, but unlikely, mechanism would appear to be ruled out. The propagation of CDTs via the cochlear re-emission process and internal reflection from the middle ear would limit psychophysical CDTs to about 20 dB SPL and involve large additional phase lags even for small f_2/f_1 ratios.

5. SUMMARY

Psychophysical cancellation level and phase properties of CDTs confirm and extend earlier findings.

Ear-canal CDTs are greatest in subjects with strong single-tone cochlear re-emissions at the CDT frequency. CDT levels can be predicted to a first approximation from psychophysical cancellation levels attenuated and compressed by the cochlear re-emission mechanism, but there are significant discrepancies.

Phase measurements of the ear-canal CDT agree with psychophysical measurements at 20 dB SL, and therefore disagree with cochlear-fibre measurements, but do not show the same level dependency as psychophysics.

The combination tone, $2f_2 - f_1$, has been observed at a lower level than $2f_1 - f_2$ at corresponding primary frequency separations and shows dependence upon f_2/f_1 ratio.

Implications for propagation of CDTs within the cochlea are discussed.

REFERENCES

Goldstein, J.L. (1967). Auditory nonlinearity. *J. Acoust. Soc. Am.* 41, 676-689.

Goldstein, J.L. (1970). Aural combination tones. In: *Frequency Analysis & Periodicity Detection in Hearing* (R. Plomp & G.F. Smoorenburg, eds.). pp 436-444. Sijthoff, Leiden.

Goldstein, J.L., Buchsbaum, G., & Furst, M. (1978). Compatibility between psychophysical and physiological measurements of aural combination tones. *J. Acoust. Soc. Am.* 63, 474-485.

Goldstein, J.L. & Kiang, N.Y.S. (1968). Neural correlates of the aural combination tone, $2f_1 - f_2$. *Proc. IEEE* 56, 981-992.

Greenwood, D.D. (1977). Comment in *Psychophysics & Physiology of Hearing* (E.F. Evans & J.P. Wilson, eds.). p. 40, Academic Press, London.

Hall, J.L. (1972). Auditory distortion products $f_2 - f_1$ and $2f_1 - f_2$. *J. Acoust. Soc. Am.* 51, 1863–1871.

Kemp, D.T. (1978). Stimulated acoustic emissions from within the human auditory system. *J. Acoust. Soc. Am.* 64, 1386–1391.

Kemp, D.T. (1979). Evidence of mechanical nonlinearity and frequency selective wave amplification in the cochlea. *Arch. Oto-Rhino-Laryng.* 224, 37–45.

Kim, D.O., Molnar, C.E., & Matthews, J.W. (1980). Cochlear mechanics: nonlinear behavior in two-tone responses as reflected in cochlear-nerve-fiber responses and in ear-canal sound pressure. *J. Acoust. Soc. Am.* (in press)

Rhode, W.S. (1977). Some observations on two-tone interactions measured with the Mössbauer effect. In: *Psychophysics & Physiology of Hearing* (E.F. Evans & J.P. Wilson, eds.). pp. 27–38. Academic Press, London.

Schroeder, M.R. (1969). Relation between critical bands in hearing and the phase characteristics of cubic difference tones. *J. Acoust. Soc. Am.* 46, 1488–1492.

Smoorenburg, G.F. (1972). Combination tones and their origin. *J. Acoust. Soc. Am.* 52, 615–632.

Wilson, J.P. (1968). High-quality electrostatic headphones. *Wireless World* Dec., 440–443.

Wilson, J.P. (1977). Towards a model for cochlear frequency analysis. In: *Psychophysics & Physiology of Hearing* (E.F. Evans & J.P. Wilson, Eds.). pp. 115–124. Academic Press, London.

Wilson, J.P. (1980a). Recording the Kemp echo and tinnitus from the ear canal without averaging. *J. Physiol.* 298, 8–9P.

Wilson, J.P. (1980b). Evidence for a cochlear origin for acoustic re-emissions, threshold fine-structure and tonal tinnitus. *Hearing Research* (in press).

Wilson, J.P. (1980c). Model for cochlear echoes and tinnitus based on an observed electrical correlate. *Hearing Research* (in press).

Wilson, J.P. & Johnstone, J.R. (1973). Basilar membrane correlates of the combination tone $2f_1 - f_2$. *Nature* 241, 206–207.

Zurek, P.M. & Sachs, R.M. (1979). Combination tones at frequencies greater than the primary tones. *Science* 205, 600–602.

Zwicker, E. (1955). Der ungewöhnliche Amplitudengang der nichtlinearen Verzenrungen des Ohres. *Acustica* 5, 67–74.

Acknowledgements are made to Drs. A.R. Palmer and G.F. Pick who acted as subjects in these experiments and to Dr. Pick for comments on the manuscript.

COMMENT ON: "The combination tone, $2f_1 - f_2$, in psychophysics and ear-canal recording" (J.P. Wilson)

D.O.Kim
Washington University, St. Louis 63110, USA.

From comparisons of the acoustic distortion product ($2f_1 - f_2$) observed in the cat ear canal using an iso-($2f_1 - f_2$) paradigm (Fig. 10 of Kim, 1980) with analogous human acoustic data in panel a) of Figures 2 to 4 of the above paper by Wilson, the following can be noted.
1) As f_2/f_1 increases from near 1.0 to higher values, the general tendency of both sets of the data is that the acoustic ($2f_1 - f_2$) level initially increases. This is in contrast to the psychoacoustic results (Fig. 1-a of Wilson, 1980; Zwicker, 1980), where the ($2f_1 - f_2$) level decreases in this region of f_2/f_1.
2) As in Kim's cat acoustic data, non-monotonic behaviour (i.e. the notches in the curves) is noticeable in Wilson's human acoustic data.
3) The overall maximum value of the relative level of the acoustic ($2f_1 - f_2$) in the cat observed by Kim with primary sound pressure levels of 70 dB is -38 dB. This value is within the range of -40 to -20 dB observed by Wilson from the human with primary sound pressure levels of 12 to 42 dB. More data for higher primary levels are needed to determine the overall maximum of the absolute level of the human acoustic distortion product ($2f_1 - f_2$).

The discrepancy between the ($2f_1 - f_2$) behaviour observed acoustically and psychoacoustically described in 1) above could be due in part to a partial transmission of the ($2f_1 - f_2$) signal from the basal end of the cochlea through the middle ear ossicles into the ear canal and to a partial reflection of the ($2f_1 - f_2$) signal at the basal end back into the cochlea (Matthews, Cox, Kim and Molnar, 1979).

The nonmonotonic behaviour in the acoustic ($2f_1 - f_2$) level obtained with the iso-($2f_1 - f_2$) paradigm may be an indication of interactions between two sources of ($2f_1 - f_2$) signal in the cochlea: one at the primary-frequency region and the other at the distortion-frequency region (Kim, 1980).

REFERENCES

Kim, D.O. (1980). Cochlear mechanics: implications of electrophysiological and acoustical observations. *Hearing Res.* 2, in press.
Matthews, J.W., Cox, J.R., Kim, D.O. and Molnar, C.E. (1979). A nonlinear mechanical model of the peripheral auditory system: interpretation of neurally and acoustically observed distortion products ($2f_1 - f_2$) and ($f_2 - f_1$). *J. Acoust. Soc. Am.* 65 S84(A).
Zwicker, E. (1980). Cubic difference tone level and phase dependence on frequency difference and level of primaries. *This volume.*

ADDITIONAL COMMENT ON: "Model of cochlear function and acoustic re-emission" (J.P. Wilson), and "The combination tone, $2f_1-f_2$, in psychophysics and ear-canal recording" (J.P. Wilson).

D.O. Kim
Washington University, St. Louis 63110, USA.

Wilson suggests that cochlear-echo and distortion-product ($2f_1-f_2$) signals may be mechanically propagated in the cochlea but only "via a structure other than the basilar membrane". As many of us discussed in the "round table" session on cochlear nonlinearity and active behavior during this symposium, a mechanical signal detected in the ear-canal sound pressure, regardless how the signal reached the ear canal, must inevitably have a correlate in the motion of the cochlear partition including the basilar membrane. This correlate in cochlear-partition motion is expected because of the asymmetric coupling of the middle ear to the cochlea with respect to the oval and round windows. Therefore, Wilson's "non-basilar-membrane" propagation hypothesis (absence of $(2f_1-f_2)$ signal in basilar-membrane motion) is contradicted by the presence of cochlear-echo and $(2f_1-f_2)$ signals in the ear canal. Physiological origin in the cochlea for the acoustic $(2f_1-f_2)$ signal is now well established (Kim, 1980; Kemp, 1979; Wilson, 1980). Since the presence of $(2f_1-f_2)$ signal in basilar-membrane motion is a clear indication of a nonlinear behavior, the often-used modeling approach of describing basilar-membrane motion with a linear filter (without "backward" coupling of cochlear-partition nonlinearity) is inconsistent with the experimental evidence. Although further studies of quantitative characterization of nonlinear behavior in cochlear-partition motion with direct mechanical measurements are needed, it is no longer tenable to postulate a strict linear behavior of cochlear-partition motion in a normal cochlea.

REFERENCES

Kemp, D.T. (1979). Evidence of mechanical nonlinearity and frequency selective wave amplification in the cochlea. *Arch. Otorhinolaryngol.* 224, 37-45.
Kim, D.O. (1980). Cochlear mechanics: implications of electrophysiological and acoustical observations. *Hearing Res.* 2, in press.
Wilson, J.P. (1980). Evidence for a cochlear origin for acoustic re-emissions, threshold fine-structure and tonal tinnitus. *Hearing Res.* 2, in press.

REPLY TO COMMENT OF D.O. KIM

J.P. Wilson
Department of Communications & Neuroscience, University of Keele, Keele, Staffs., U.K.

I agree that in principle it would be impossible for there to be *no* $(2f_1-f_2)$ on the basilar membrane. My point is merely that this may not be the primary transmission channel and if so the actual level could be small and make no significant difference to function whether it be doubled in magnitude or halved. Under such conditions the deviations from linearity of the basilar membrane could be small and not important.

ON THE MECHANISM OF THE EVOKED COCHLEAR MECHANICAL RESPONSE

H.P. Wit   and   R.J. Ritsma

Institute of Audiology, University Hospital
Groningen, The Netherlands

1. INTRODUCTION

The existence of emission of acoustical energy from the human auditory system was first demonstrated by Kemp (1978). Shortly afterwards more papers about this subject were published (Anderson and Kemp (1979), Kemp (1979), Wit and Ritsma (1979)). The reader is referred to these articles for details about the evoked cochlear mechanical response (ECMR), as it was called by Kemp.

About 30 years ago Gold (1948) already supposed acoustical energy to be emitted by the auditory system and he proposed an experiment - somewhat different from Kemp's method - to measure it. According to Gold this acoustical energy should be a by-product of positive feedback of an active filter somewhere in the mechanism that transforms acoustical energy into nerve fiber activity in the cochlea. This feedback mechanism was in his opinion responsible for the extra frequency sharpening within the cochlea, nowadays called the "second filter" (Evans and Wilson, 1973).

To explain the observed properties of the ECMR Kemp (1979) proposed a reflection model. In this model mechanical energy is supposed to be conducted through the middle ear to the cochlea, along the basilar membrane to a place of partial travelling wave reflection, then back to the basal end and out through the middle ear.

It is the aim of this paper to show that the ideas of Gold and Kemp can be combined to give a possible explanation for the generation of the cochlear mechanical responses, as was already suggested by Kemp in his first article about the subject (1978). For this purpose two cochlear models were constructed: a simple electrical model (Schroeder, 1973) and a hydromechanical model (Helle, 1974). With these models it could easily be demonstrated that the vibration process in the cochlea can be reversed. Driving the stapes with a vibratory stimulus sets the basilar membrane in motion. When in turn a small area of the basilar membrane is set in motion, the stapes starts to move somewhat later. Although many cochlear models were made in the past and also today such models are used to enlarge the insight into the hydromechanics of the cochlea, this reversion property has in our knowledge never been investigated before. (A good survey of the work done on cochlear models was recently given by De Boer (1979).

One of the properties of the ECMR is the fact that its latency, the time between stimulus onset and response onset, depends on the frequency of the response: The lower the response frequency, the longer its latency. This property supports the idea that the response is generated by a process somewhere on the basilar membrane. However the observed latencies are so large, that they yield travel times for the wave along the basilar membrane that do not correspond to travel times obtained from experiments of other types. This problem will be discussed in the last part of this paper.

2. THE ELECTRICAL MODEL

A simple one-dimensional model of the cochlea was constructed by connecting in series 12 "basilar membrane segments" as given in fig. 1. From "base" towards "apex" the capacity C (membrane compliance) had an increasing value. For practical reasons L had the same value in each segment and L_1 was equal to L. The Q-factor of each RLC-network was made equal to about 1 by giving R the proper value. This chain of 12 basilar membrane sections was connected at the basal end to another RLC-network, representing the middle ear. (A similar, but more complicated, model was a.o. described by Flanagan (1965)).

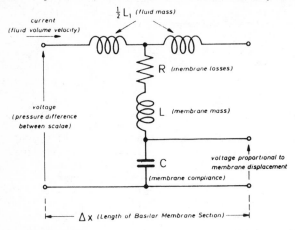

Fig. 1 *Electrical network representing one section of the basilar membrane. From Schroeder (1973).*

By stimulating the model with a short rectangular pulse (50 μs) at its input (equivalent to a sound pressure pulse at the eardrum), the well-known results given in fig. 2a were obtained: The further a membrane section is away from the "stapes", the more the maximum of the signal - representing membrane displacement - is delayed. The results are, apart from a scale factor, similar to those obtained by Tonndorf (1962) with a hydromechanical cochlear model after stimulating this model with a step function stapes displacement.

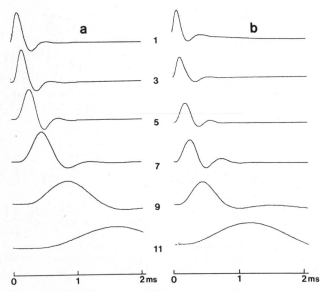

Fig. 2 *Signals measured in the electrical model after stimulation with a short rectangular pulse. a) "membrane displacement" for successive sections (1,3,5,...) after stimulating the "eardrum". b) "stapes displacement" after stimulating the "membrane" in successive sections (for the sake of clarity the vertical scale was chosen equal for all signals).*

If in turn a short pulse is applied to the capacitor in a section, simulating a short displacement of the basilar membrane, the signals given in fig. 2b can be measured at the "stapes" of the model. Speaking in terms of a computational model (Flanagan, 1965) the input and output of it are reversed in this latter case. (We expected that this reversion property of a linear system could mathematically be treated in a simple way; unfortunately this expectation seems to be wrong).

If the capacitor in a section is shortcircuited and a pulse is applied to the input (eardrum) of the model then no voltage can be present across this capacitor. This results in reflection of the signal at that membrane position back towards the input (fig. 3). The total delay of the reflected signal is equal to the delay on the way towards the locus of reflection plus the delay on the way back (fig. 2a and 2b). Similar reflections occur in transmission lines at impedance mismatches.

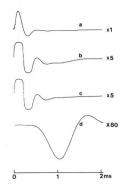

Fig. 3 Reflection of a short pulse applied at the "eardrum" after shortcircuiting a section of the electrical model.
a) signal at "stapes" terminals.
b) the same signal after 5x amplification and clipping. Capacitor at section 8 shortcircuited.
c) same signals as b., no capacitor shortcircuited.
d) signal b minus signal c; vertical scale enlarged by another factor 16. This signal is the result of reflection in section 8.

The result shown in fig. 3 supports Kemp's reflection model for the ECMR. However, the frequency spectrum of the reflected signal (fig. 3d) is much broader than that of the ECMR in many cases. (Evoked cochlear mechanical responses are often tone burst-like signals). This means that reflection alone cannot account for the generation of evoked cochlear mechanical responses.

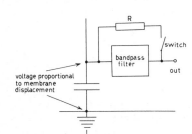

Fig. 4 Detail of membrane section in electrical cochlea model. Active filter with positive feedback coupled to "membrane".

3. POSITIVE FEEDBACK

To simulate the "second filter" the signal across the capacitor in a membrane section was bandpass filtered (fig.4). The frequency selectivity of a filter can be greatly improved by feeding a fraction of its output signal back to the input. (positive feedback). In the circuit of fig. 4 this is done by resistor R. (This resistor and the amplification factor of the filter were given such values that the quality factor of the filter was about 10 with closed switch). Such a positive feedback mechanism was proposed by Gold (1948) to account for the fact that the observed frequency selectivity of the cochlea is much higher than can be expected for "a passive cochlea, where elements are brought into mechanical oscillation solely by means of the incident sound". Fig. 5 shows the frequency selectivity, with and without filter, of the membrane section to which the filter was connected.

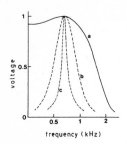

Fig.5 Frequency selectivity of membrane section 7 of the
electrical cochlea model.
a) without filter (see fig. 4).
b) with filter; switch open.
c) with filter; switch closed, positive feedback.
A sine wave of constant amplitude was applied to the input of the model.

As a consequence of this positive feedback part of the output signal of
the filter is present across the capacitor. This signal travels back towards
the input of the circuit, comparable to the results shown in fig. 2b. So if a
click is applied to the input of the model, reflection of a signal with a narrow
frequency band occurs, as fig. 6 shows clearly. Perhaps the ECMR is generated
by a similar mechanism.

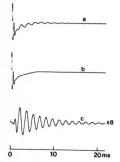

Fig.6 Reflection of signal with narrow frequency band if
positive feedback is present in a section (no.7) of the
electrical model. Short rectangular pulse applied to input of the model. Signal measured at "stapes".
a) switch (see fig.4) closed; positive feedback.
b) switch open; no feedback.
c) signal a minus signal b. Vertical scale enlarged.

4. THE HYDROMECHANICAL MODEL

The advantage of an electrical cochlea model is the fact that signals
can easily be applied to it and easily measured. The electrical model described
above, however, is a crude simplification of the real cochlea. Although a hydromechanical model is still a simplification, it is the physical model that comes
closest to the natural situation.

The hydromechanical model we have built to investigate the reversion property of the cochlea is a copy of the model decribed by Helle (1974). It is
20 times larger than the real human cochlea. The basilar membrane in de model
was made from a latex sheet with a uniform thickness of about 0.3 mm., glued
without tension onto the wedge-shaped slit between scala vestibuli and scala
tympani. The model was filled with a glycerin-water mixture (viscosity 20 cen-
tipoise).

The "oval window" of the model was driven by an electromechanical transducer (Bruel and Kjaer type 4810 "minishaker). A thin stainless steel needle
(0.5 mm) could be placed, through a small hole in scala vestibuli, on top of the
membrane at different positions. Vibrations of the membrane were guided through
this needle to a piezo-electric transducer. (As we were primarily interested
in travel times along the membrane, the extra loading of the membrane by the

needle was no problem). If a short (1 ms) electrical pulse was applied to the driving transducer at the oval window, vibrations of the membrane could be registered after 30 to 110 ms, depending on the position of the needle (fig.7a). Due to imperfections of the model all vibration patterns shown in fig. 7a have about the same central frequency, but clearly can be seen that travel time of the vibration towards a certain place on the membrane is larger, the further this place is away from the windows. (The magnitude of the observed travel times - more than 100 ms for position 4 - excluded direct transportation of the vibration through the fluid or the solid materials of the model as an explanation).

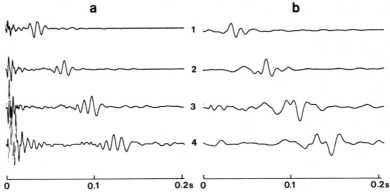

Fig.7 Vibrations in the hydromechanical model after stimulation with a short transient signal at t=o. (Normalized vertical scale).
a) oval window stimulated. Registration of membrane vibrations at 4 different positions, subsequently 24, 34, 44 and 54 cm from the basal end. (total membrane length 66 cm).
b) membrane stimulated at the same 4 different positions. Registration of window vibrations.

If the situation is reversed, which means that the membrane is driven by the needle to which the minishaker is attached and the vibration of a window is registered by the piezo-electric transducer, then the results of fig. 7b are obtained. Conclusion: travel time for transient signals from the oval window towards a certain position on the membrane is about equal to the travel time back from this membrane position towards the windows. (It would be interesting to know whether a two-dimensional mathematical model - e.g. Lesser and Berkley (1972) or Schlichthärle (1978) - yields the same results. In our knowledge such models have only been worked out for the situation that the oval window is driven by a continuous sine wave).

An experiment to detect membrane vibrations with a transducer in which positive feedback is incorporated, was in progress at the time this paper was written.

5. RESPONSE LATENCY

For 9 normal hearing subjects the latency of the acoustical response - the time between stimulus onset and response onset - was measured as a function of response frequency. Several methods were used: click stimulation in those cases where single frequency responses could be registered, stimulation with a transient signal with the same central frequency as the response, masking of a click stimulus with a noise band in order to suppress responses of certain frequencies. Fig. 8 gives the results of these latency measurements. A linear regression line fit yielded $\ln t = 2.41 - 0.83 \ln f$; $R = -0.91$ as the

equation for the straight line in this figure. In some cases it is difficult
to decide on the exact moment of onset of a response, therefore uncertainties
of about one period of the response signal should be taken into account (e.g.
1 ms at 1 kHz).

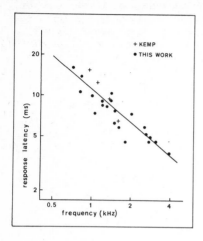

Fig.8 Latency of the evoked cochlear mechanical response as a function of response frequency. Also given are results from Kemp (1978).

If the reflection model is the proper model to account for the observed
response latencies, then the latency of the response of a certain frequency
should be two times the travel time along the basilar membrane towards the
place of reflection plus the time spent in the reflection mechanism itself. Estimations of the total travel time (vice versa), based on values for the velocity of the travelling wave along the cochlear partition as given by several
authors (Eggermont and Odenthal,(1974), Elberling (1974), Parker and Thornton
(1978), Zerlin (1969) give values that are about half the observed response
latencies. Details about this travel time estimation were given in a preceeding
paper (Wit and Ritsma, 1980).

If part of the reflection mechanism indeed would be a filter - with or
without positive feedback - then the delay time due to this filter would have
to be many milliseconds for the lower response frequencies, unless extra time
is spent in other parts of the reflection mechanism. For a filter with a central
frequency of 1 kHz and a bandwidth of 100 Hz the response time is about 10 ms.
However what is meant here by response time, is the time it takes before a
semi-infinite sine wave with a sudden onset reaches its final amplitude. If a
short transient signal, e.g. two full sine waves of 1 kHz, is applied to such
a filter then the total delay of the signal is not more than 1-2 ms, depending
on how this delay is defined.

So we are still left with a discrepancy between the observed response
latency values and the values based on estimations using the reflection model.

6. FREQUENCY SPECTRUM   (preliminary results)

In order to obtain frequency spectra of click evoked acoustical responses, a time window (20 ms) was set between the main amplifier of the microphone signal and the averager. The analogue output signal from the averager
memory was stored on tape and analysed with a real-time spectrum analyser
(Ubiquitous UA-6B). The results for 3 different normal hearing subjects are
given in fig. 9. (For comparison a pure sine wave of 3.00 kHz was analysed under
the same conditions).
These frequency spectra suggest that the ECMR is generated by a bank of very
sharply tuned resonators, 100-200 Hz apart.

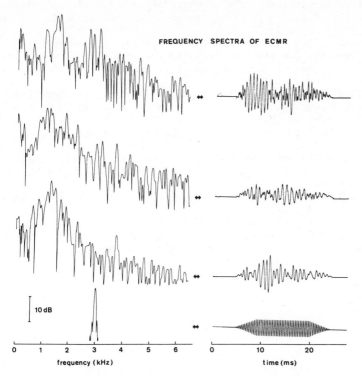

FREQUENCY SPECTRA OF ECMR

10 dB

frequency (kHz)

time (ms)

Fig.9 Frequency spectrum of click evoked ECMR-signal between t=5 and t=25 ms for 3 subjects (stimulus at t=0, rise- and fall-time of the time window 5 ms). The signals are given at the right-hand side of the figure, their frequency spectrum at the left. A calibration signal of 3.00 kHz with its spectrum is also given.

REFERENCES

Anderson, S.D. and Kemp, D.T.(1979). The evoked cochlear mechanical response in laboratory primates. *Arch.Otorhinolaryngol.* 224, 47-54.
De Boer, E.(1979). Short-wave world revisited:resonance in a two-dimensional cochlear model. *Hearing Res.*1, 253-281.
Eggermont, J.J. and Odenthal, D.W. (1974). Frequency selective masking in electrocochleography. *Rev.de Laryngol.* (Bordeaux) 95, 489-496.
Elberling, C.(1974). Action potentials along the cochlear partition recorded from the ear canal in man. *Scand.Audiol.*3, 13-19.
Evans, E.F. and Wilson, J.P. (1973). The frequency selectivity of the cochlea. In: *Basic mechanisms in hearing.* pp. 519-551. Academic Press, New York and London.
Flanagan, J.L. (1965). Speech Analysis, Synthesis and Perception. pp. 91-100, Springer Verlag, Berlin, Heidelberg and New York.
Gold, T. (1948). Hearing II. The physical basis of the action of the cochlea. *Proc.R.Soc.* B 135, 492-498.
Helle, R. (1974). Selektivitätssteigerung in einem hydromechanischen Innenohr modell mit Basilar- und Deckmembran. *Acustica.* 30, 301-312.
Kemp, D.T. (1978). Stimulated acoustic emissions from within the human auditory system. *J.Acoust.Soc.Am.* 64, 1386-1391.

Kemp, D.T. (1979). Evidence of mechanical nonlinearity and frequency selective wave amplification in the cochlea. *Arch.Otorhinolaryngol.* 224, 37-45.

Lesser, M.B. and Berkley, D.A. (1972). Fluid mechanics of the cochlea. Part.1. *J.Fluid.Mech.* 51, 497-512.

Parker, D.J. and Thornton, A.R.D. (1978). Cochlear travelling wave velocities calculated from the derived components of the cochlear nerve and brain-stem evoked responses of the human auditory system. *Scand.Audiol.* 7, 67-70.

Schlichthärle, D. (1978). Anwendung von Methoden der Digitalfiltertheorie auf das Cochlea-leitungsmodell. In:*Fortschritte der Akustik; DAGA'78.* pp. 523-526 VDE-Verlag GmbH, Berlin.

Schroeder, M.R. (1973). An integrable model for the basilar membrane. *J.Acoust. Soc.Am.* 53, 429-434.

Tonndorf, J. (1962). Time/frequency analysis along the partition of cochlear models: A modified place concept. *J.Acoust.Soc.Am.* 34, 1337-1350. (fig. 5 in part.).

Wit, H.P. and Ritsma, R.J.(1979). Stimulated acoustic emissions from the human ear. *J.Acoust.Soc.Am.* 66, 911-913.

Wit, H.P. and Ritsma, R.J. (1980). Evoked acoustical responses from the human ear; some experimental results. Accepted for publication in *Hearing Res.* (Proceedings of the conference on non-linear and active mechanical processes in the cochlea, London, 1979).

Zerlin, S. (1969). Traveling-wave velocity in the human cochlea. *J.Acoust.Soc. Am.* 46, 578-583.

ADDENDUM to: On the mechanism of the evoked cochlear mechanical response

H.P.Wit

Institute of Audiology, University Hospital,
9713 EZ Groningen, The Netherlands.

The mathematical description of the reciprocity property of a linear network – called reversion property in the foregoing paper – is not as complicated as I thought it to be at the time that paper was written.

Consider an m-port network, having m pairs of terminals. The voltage at the j-th pair is given by V_j, the current through this terminal pair by I_j. Then the network can be described by the vector pair $(\underline{V}, \underline{I})$, in which $\underline{V}^T = (V_1, V_2, \ldots\ldots\ldots, V_m)$ and

$$\underline{I}^T = (I_1, I_2, \ldots\ldots, I_m) \qquad \text{(T means "transpose")}$$

If $(\underline{V}_1, \underline{I}_1)$ and $(\underline{V}_2, \underline{I}_2)$ are two pairs belonging to this network, it is called <u>reciprocal</u> if

$$\underline{V}_1^T * \underline{I}_2 = \underline{V}_2^T * \underline{I}_1 \qquad (1)$$

(reciprocity relation in the time domain)

$$(\underline{V}^T * \underline{I} = \int_{-\infty}^{\infty} \underline{V}^T (t - \tau) \, \underline{I} \, (\tau) \, d\tau = \sum_{j=1}^{m} \int_{-\infty}^{\infty} V_j \, (t - \tau) \, I_j \, (\tau) \, d\tau \, ;$$

the convolution of $\underline{V}$ and $\underline{I}$, being both functions of time t)

If in the frequency domain $\underline{V}$ and $\underline{I}$ are connected by means of an admittance matrix Y , $\underline{I} = Y.\underline{V}$, then it can easily be shown that the reciprocity relation is fullfilled if this admittance matrix is symmetrical ($Y = Y^T$). In that case (1) is replaced by

$$\underline{V}_1^T . \underline{I}_2 = \underline{V}_2^T . \underline{I}_1 \qquad (2)$$

(reciprocity relation in frequency domain)

A network consisting of reciprocal elements R,L,C – being 1-port networks – is a reciprocal network.
This means that an R,L,C-network model of the cochlea is reciprocal.

One of the consequences of this property is the following fact:
If a (transient) voltage signal is applied to the input ("eardrum") of the electrical cochlea model and the current is measured in one of the sections (being proportional to basilar membrane velocity), then the same current signal (proportional to eardrum velocity) will be present at the input, if this voltage signal is applied to that particular section.
(This voltage signal is proportional to eardrum pressure in the first experiment and to the pressure at the membrane section in the reverse experiment).

The reciprocity relation can also be proven directly for the cochlea (without transforming it into a network) if it is considered as a closed acoustical system, for which the Laplace equation $\Delta\phi = 0$ holds. (ϕ is the velocity potential).
To do so one should start from Green's reciprocity theorem:

$$\int_S (\phi_1 \frac{\partial\phi_2}{\partial n} - \phi_2 \frac{\partial\phi_1}{\partial n}) \, dS = 0$$

in which ϕ_1 and ϕ_2 are two solutions of the Laplace equation, fulfilling the boundary conditions.
The integral is the surface integral over the boundary.

As $\frac{\partial\phi}{\partial n}$ is the derivative of ϕ in the direction perpendicular to the boundary it is equal to the fluid particle velocity in that direction, which is equal to the velocity of the boundary at that position.

Recently the reciprocity property of the cochlea was also discussed by Sondhi (1979). A more general survey of the acoustical reciprocity relation was given by Ten Wolde (1973), who kept his treatise of reciprocity restricted to the frequency domain.

REFERENCES

M.M. Sondhi,(1979). The acoustical inverse problem for the cochlea, *J.Acoust. Soc.Am.* 66, Suppl. 1, S48.

T.ten Wolde, (1973). On the Validity and Application of Reciprocity in Acousti-cal, Mechano-Acoustical and other Dynamical Systems, *Acustica* 28, 23-32.

Acknowledgement

I wish to thank Prof.Dr.J.C.Willems from the Department of Applied Mathematics of our University for his valuable help.

COMMENT ON : 1) "Observations on the generator mechanism of stimulus frequency acoustic emissions - two tone suppression (D.T. Kemp and R.A. Chum).
2) "On the mechanism of the evoked cochlear mechanical response (H.P. Wit and R.J. Ritsma).

P.I.M. Johannesma
Workgroup Neurophysics, Lab. of Medical Physics and Biophysics, University of Nijmegen, Nijmegen, The Netherlands.

Narrow band filters and active resonators.

The elementary form of a resonator is given by a linear second order dif-ferential equation :

$$A\ddot{y} + B\dot{y} + Cy = x(t) \tag{1}$$

The input to the resonator is given by $x(t)$. The descriptive variable is $y(t)$: displacement for a mechanical system, pressure for a hydrodynamical, voltage for an electrical and concentration for a chemical system.

The behaviour of the resonator is determined by the parameters A, B and C. For a mechanical system A corresponds to mass, B to damping and C to stiffness. Without loss of generality A can be taken equal to one. The value of C determines the resonance frequency; this parameter has to be positive otherwise the system diverges to infinity. The value of damping B determines strength and width of the resonance.

B $\gg$ C : strong damping, weak and wide resonance.

o > B $\ll$ C : weak damping, strong and narrow resonance.

B = o : no damping, infinity strong resonance.

B > o : negative damping, spontaneous oscillations with increasing amplitude.

For the description of a resonator which shows a saturation for large input signals the damping B can be made a function of the system variable y. A polynomial expression including terms up to second degree gives

$$B(y) = b_o + b_1 y + b_2 y^2 \tag{2}$$

In order to ensure stability $B(y)$ should be positive for all y; this is the case if

$$b_o > o, b_1 = o, \ b_2 > o.$$

The equation for the nonlinear resonator reads then :

$$\ddot{y} + (b_o + b_2 y^2)\dot{y} + Cy = x(t) \tag{3}$$

For this system tuning will be sharp if b_o has a small positive value, saturation will be strong for large b_2. This choice of b_2 then also ensures the functional stability of the resonator. A consequence of the nonlinear damping is a decrease in frequency selectivity for an increase in signal amplitude.

In biological systems changes in metabolism may lead to changes of system parameters. The structural stability of a system is given by the changes in its behaviour for small variations of the parameters. A small change in C will induce a small change in the resonance frequency. Likewise a small change in b_2 leads to a small change in saturation and tuning width for large signals. However a small change in b_o may have drastic consequences. A small absolute increase in b_o may relatively be large; because of the small value of b_o this leads to a relatively great change in the sharpness of tuning for small signals. A small decrease of b_o leads to increasing sharpness of tuning but if b_o crosses the zero value a catastrophe occurs. The stable point (0,0) in the $(\ddot{y},\dot{y})$ state-plane becomes unstable.

For negative b_o Eq (3) may be recognized as the Van der Pol equation; it describes a nonlinear or relaxation oscillator characterised by an unstable singular point in the origin and a limit cycle around it. This implies that the system exhibits spontaneous oscillations with a fixed amplitude and frequency determined by the systemparameters b_o, b_2 and C.

The foregoing considerations lead to the conclusion that a narrowly tuned saturating resonator usually will be structurally unstable. The same conclusion holds if the damping B is dependent on velocity $\dot{y}$ instead of displacement y. In this case the resulting relaxation oscillator is described by the Rayleigh equation. Comparable phenomena occur if damping B is dependent on both y and $\dot{y}$ and even when stiffness C is a function of y.

Given the general tuning properties of the peripheral auditory system it can be expected that spontaneous auditory sensations occur. Those sensations will be approximately tonal and have a constant or slowly varying amplitude. If the peripheral auditory system up to the resonators is to some extent reciprocal then the spontaneous relaxation oscillations should not only be subjectively but also objectively detectable.

COCHLEAR MECHANICS AS THE POSSIBLE CAUSE
OF BINAURAL DIPLACUSIS ?

G. van den Brink

*Dept. of Biological & Medical Physics,
Erasmus University Rotterdam, the Netherlands*

1. INTRODUCTION

Over a period of about fifteen years the author has been involved in studies on binaural diplacusis and the perception of pitch of pure tones and complex sounds. The phenomenon of binaural diplacusis has turned out to be a useful aid in studying the relations between the pitch of pure tones and that of the residue, because the fine structure in the relation between diplacusis and frequency provides some sort of a pitch label as a function of the frequency.

The general conclusion from this series of experiments is, that the pitch of a complex sound is determined by the pitches of the individual components under all circumstances, either normal conditions, or with pitch shifts induced by fatigue (van den Brink, 1972) or by partially masking noise (van den Brink, 1975). The components contribute to the pitch of a complex sound with different weights, those around the dominant frequency range having the largest weight. Recently, evidence has been found that this rule may be valid for unfiltered periodic pulse trains too: these signals contain harmonics as well as their fundamental (van den Brink, 1980).

The apparently existing correspondence between binaural diplacusis on one hand and the threshold difference between the left and the right ear on the other hand (van den Brink, 1970) suggest a relation between the two phenomena. In spite of the use that has been made of the phenomenon of binaural diplacusis, no decisive answer has been given yet on the question what causes both, diplacusis and threshold fine structure. It has been assumed that a fine-structure in the mechanical properties of the inner ears might be the origin. In a personal communication, Tonndorf (1974) mentioned the existence of small bloodvessels at the edge between basilar membrane and bony tissue which might possibly cause such a fine-structure. Whatever the cause may be, it is a certainty that the effects are more or less alike for both ears but not identical (van den Brink, 1970, 1980).

Kemp (1978) suggested a connection between echoes or acoustic reflections from within the ear and the fine structure in the auditory sensitivity as a function of the frequency. At the Symposium on "Non-linear and active mechanical processes in the cochlea" in 1979 it has been reported by Wilson (1979) that the occurrence of echoes depends on the position of the body.

The influence of body position on echoes must be due to impedance changes. Impedance differences should result in changes in the threshold fine structure, and different threshold fine—structures might be attended with a change of diplacusis versus frequency. These facts led me to carry out a small experiment wherein the difference between thresholds as well as diplacusis in lying and upright position have been measured.

2. THRESHOLDS IN LYING AND IN UPRIGHT POSITION

The auditory threshold has been measured in exactly the same way as before (van den Brink, 1972), except that they were determined by turns in lying and upright position for each frequency. The threshold curves were very much alike those measured earlier, be it that the high frequency slope was considerably steeper. The difference between the thresholds in both positions is shown in Fig. 1.

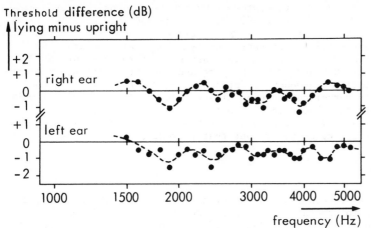

Fig. 1
*Difference be-
tween thresholds
in lying and up-
right position
(subject GB)*

Compared with the effect that had to be measured, the accuracy of the result is relatively bad. The peaks in the separate threshold curves range from a few up to about 8 dB. Since the threshold curves in both positions show a large degree of correspondence, so that the difference between them is relatively small, the effect is hardly to be called significant. The apparent correspondence between the results of the right ear and the left ear were, however, encouraging to draw broken lines through the measuring points. Although a strong effect could hardly be expected, the results indicate that, indeed, the auditory threshold depends on the position of the body.

3. DIPLACUSIS IN LYING AND IN UPRIGHT POSITION

Binaural diplacusis was measured too, according to the method used before (van den Brink, 1972). The relative frequency difference, necessary for equal pitch, was measured as a function of the frequency of the signal in the left ear, for alternating tone bursts of 0.4 s each. The results are shown in Fig. 2.

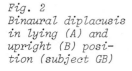

*Fig. 2
Binaural diplacusis
in lying (A) and
upright (B) posi-
tion (subject GB)*

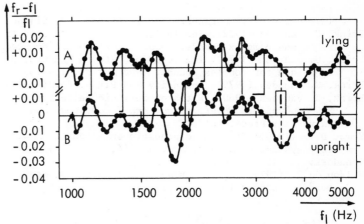

For frequencies up to 2500 Hz the difference between the two curves is not spectacular at all. There seems to be a slight trend of a shift of minima and maxima to higher frequencies for the results in lying position as compared with the results in the upright position. This shift is of the same sort as has been found by changing the intensity in one ear (van den Brink, 1979). Beyond 2500 Hz, however, the effect is very convincing: in some cases, the shift is such that the signs of the extremities are even opposite at the same frequencies. Clear examples exist at 3900 Hz, 4200 Hz and 4600 Hz. The experience that echoes are less clear for low frequencies may, therefore, not be due to the fact that their origin is farther away from the oval window; it is possible that they are less pronounced. The largest difference occurs at 3500 Hz, where diplacusis is 0.0 and −0.02 in lying and upright positions, respectively. Setting a relative frequency difference of −0.01, the signal in the right ear was clearly perceived as being higher than the left ear signal while sitting upright, whereas it sounded distinctly lower while lying down.

It can be concluded that the frequence – pitch relations in either of the ears are not only differing mutually, but that they depend on the position of the body as well.

4. DISCUSSION

Echoes as well as thresholds and the pitches that are being attributed to frequencies all seem to depend upon the position of the body. Although it has been tried only casually, the effect seems to be even stronger in the upside down position. This has only been tried out incidentally.

The discussion on the possible origin of the effects as well as the development of mathematical models are in full progress at the moment by many experimentists. The dependence upon body position seems to make it worthwhile to consider the possibility that fluid pressure and/or blood circulation in the inner ear might be a factor of importance. Day to day changes in binaural diplacusis as well as the role of body position could easily be accounted for in that case. If the pressure changes of the blood circulation penetrate in the inner ear and pressure in the inner ear influences its functioning, it might be worthwhile to measure thresholds and diplacusis with tone pulses that are triggered with a person's cardiogram, using different delays.

A decisive conclusion about the origin of binaural diplacusis may be within reach if the cause of echoes can be traced down.

REFERENCES

Brink, G. van den (1970). Experiments on binaural diplacusis and tone perception. In: *Frequency Analysis and Periodicity Detection in Hearing.* (R.Plomp & G.F.Smoorenburg, eds). pp 362-373, Sijthoff, Leiden.

Brink, G. van den (1972). The influence of fatigue upon the pitch of pure tones and complex sounds. *Proc. Symp. on Hearing Theory.* IPO, Eindhoven.

Brink, G. van den (1975). The relation between binaural diplacusis for pure tones and for complex sounds. *Acustica* 32, 159-165.

Brink, G. van den (1979). Intensity and Pitch. *Acustica* 41, 271-273.

Brink, G. van den (1980). Pitch of periodic pulse trains. *Proc. Symp. on Psychophysical, Physiological and Behavioural Studies in Hearing.* Delft University Press, Delft.

Kemp, D.T. (1978). Stimulated acoustic emissions from within the human auditory system. *J. Acoust. Soc. Am.* 64, 1386-1391.

Tonndorf, J. (1974). Personal communication.

Wilson, J.P. (1979). *Symp.on non-linear and active mechanical processes in the cochlea.* London (proc. in press).

COMMENT ON: "Cochlear mechanics as the possible cause of binaural diplacusis ?"
(G. van den Brink)

J.P. Wilson
Dept. of Communication & Neuroscience, University of Keele, England.

I think that there are some differences in our results on the influence of
body posture on threshold fine-structure. My effect was a systematic disappearance and then reversal of peak position as "more-inverted" postures were taken
up. As these effects occurred only for frequencies below 1 kHz, I interpreted
them as being due to increase in middle ear stiffness, which would be still
espected to have most effect in the frequencies. Your changes at higher frequencies might imply a more direct effect on cochlear properties.

REPLY TO COMMENT OF J.P. WILSON.

G. van den Brink
*Dept. of Biol. & Med. Physics, Erasmus University Rotterdam, Rotterdam, The
Netherlands.*

As long as there is no evidence of the contrary, I am inclined to assume
that a) threshold fine structure, b) binaural diplacusis, c) echoes and d) irregularities in the relation of phase and amplitude of combination tones versus
frequency, are all subject to a common mechanism. I have always been inclined
to seek this mechanism in the mechanics of the cochlea, although von Békésy, in
a personal discussion, mentioned the large number of degrees of freedom in the
middle ear transmission as a possible source of fine structures as a function
of frequency.

The large time constants in echo's, however, provide evidence against the
middle ear as the source of these phenomena. I agree, therefore, that the phenomena I measured are, indeed, likely to be due to cochlear properties.

It is even less clear, what happens at low frequencies. Because diplacusis
reproduces badly below 500 Hz (large day to day differences), I always measured
beyond 500 Hz, where the results are surprisingly consistant over a large period of time. Evidently there is something going on at low frequencies that does
not affect the results at higher frequencies. Could that be due to the middle
ear?

LATENCIES OF STIMULATED ACOUSTIC EMISSIONS
IN NORMAL HUMAN EARS

W.L.C. Rutten

ENT Dept., Univ. Hosp., 10 Rijnsburgerweg,
Leiden, The Netherlands

1. INTRODUCTION

In this paper we intend to explain measured latencies of stimulated acoustic emission ("echoes") by comparison of measured echo-latencies with narrow-band action potential (NAP) latencies and with theoretically calculated echo-latencies. In order to perform these latter calculations it is necessary to work with a model for the generation of echoes. Echo-latencies may be built up out of several parts, for example 1) travelling wave delays along the basilar membrane 2) cochlear filter delays 3) neural delays etc.

Experiments by Kemp (1978) and Rutten(1980) showed that in the echo generating mechanism, neural processes are not involved. This is based on 1) latencies of echoes are almost completely stimulus-intensity-independent 2) the emissive responses follow phase inversion of the stimulus 3) adaptation of the echo responses (i.e. attenuation of the response upon diminishing the inter-stimulus interval) is absent. Therefore, in comparing echo-burst latencies with NAP latencies, one has to correct the latter for the neural synaptic delay, which is about 0.8 ms (Eggermont,1979). Taking this correction into account, one finds (for normals) NAP latencies between 2.5 and 5 ms at 1 kHz in response to 90 dB pe SPL clicks (Eggermont, 1979). These values compare unfavourably to the 1 kHz echo-burst (onset) latencies of about 10 ms (Kemp, 1978; Rutten, 1980) or the 1.4 kHz-latency of 10 ms, reported by Wit and Ritsma (1979). One reason for these large discrepancies might be that a comparison with NAP responses to 90 dB pe SPL clicks (corresponding to 70 dB SL in normals) is not appropriate, since the echo phenomena are essential low-level phenomena. However, NAP latencies at 1 kHz in response to low level 30 dB SL clicks are about 5 ms (see further), which is still a factor of about two smaller than the echo latency. This might already suggest that the echo latency is built up out of more than the sum of travelling wave delay and cochlear filter delay.

It should be noted that experiments show that echo-bursts with a particular frequency f_{echo} do not emerge at a fixed latency. Just as for neural latency data there will be a considerable interindividual spread. However, the amount of available echo-latency data is still limited. The above mentioned discrepancy might thus be due to the unknown interindividual spread in echo latencies. Therefore, we performed echo-experiments in a group of 19 normal human ears. Comparison between echo data and NAP data seems more justified then. A fit of calculated to measured echo latencies, considering various "echo generation pathways" (see also de Boer, 1980) may provide valuable information about the generating mechanism.

2. METHODS

Experimental methods for the detection of emissions up to 2 kHz have been described elsewhere in detail (Rutten, 1980). In order to detect echo bursts with characteristic frequencies higher than 2 kHz we employed an intrameatal assembly of miniature telephone and microphone. This widens the frequency range up to about 6 kHz. The sampling rate of the DATALAB averager was increased to 33 kHz and amplifier passbands were 300-10000 Hz (cf. Rutten, 1980). All subjects were normal

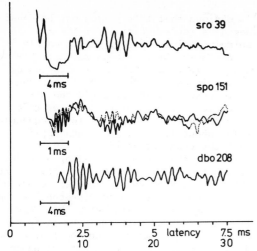

Figure 1. Examples of averaged responses (512 sweeps), containing echo-bursts. The upper trace (subject sro 39) is a response to click stimulation. The middle trace (spo 151) is also a response to click stimulation; it shows a first and a second echo. The dotted trace is a repeated recording, indicating good reproducibility. The lower trace (dbo 208) is a response to toneburst (1050 Hz) stimulation. Four repeated echo bursts can be distinguished.

hearing persons: audiograms within 10 dB from normal (ISO 1964). As stimuli were employed clicks (pulse width 60 µs) and tonebursts (trapezoïdal envelopes 0.1–4–0.1 ms below 2 kHz, or 0.5–1–0.5 ms above 2 kHz).

3. RESULTS

Figure 1 shows three typical response patterns: 1) a response to click stimulation 2) a high-frequency response to click stimulation showing a first and a second echo 3) a low-frequency response to toneburst stimulation, showing four repeated echoes. Below 2 kHz, identification of a response as an echo was performed mainly (but not solely, see Rutten, 1980), on basis of the non-linear input-output behaviour. Above this frequency the non-linearity is no longer a valid criterion because echoes in that frequency-range (with latencies of about 5 ms) show an almost linear input-output behaviour. Moreover, in many ears the acoustic impulse response of outer and middle ear has not yet completely gone to zero at that latency, which makes visual identification of a superimposed echo very difficult and unreliable. Therefore, only in ears with a short acoustic impulse response (< 3 ms) identification of high-frequency echoes was possible, albeit not on basis of non-linearity.

All latency (τ_{echo}) data have been plotted versus frequency (f_{echo}) in figure 2. Data below 17 ms are first echoes, those above 17 ms are second or third echoes. In the following we shall restrict ourselves to first echoes. Latencies of first echoes below 2 kHz seem to lie in the τ–f range, confined by the two dashed lines, the extrapolation of which up to higher frequencies is of course rather arbitrary.

For comparison with NAP data and calculated values it is convenient to express the data between the dashed lines in figure 2 in number-of-periods versus frequency. This has been done in figure 3 (open and closed circles) on a log-log scale. N denotes the number of periods: $N = \tau_{echo} f_{echo}$. Again, the two dashed lines confine the region in the N–f plane in which first-echo-responses occur.

4. DISCUSSION

NAP latency data (responses to 90 dB pe SPL clicks, Eggermont 1979) of normals, converted to number of periods, have been drawn also in figure 3 (shaded area). These data are corrected for neural synaptic delay by subtracting 0.8 ms before conversion. Within the shaded area the latency data of an individual are drawn also (triangles, click 90 dB pe SPL). The other two drawn lines, connecting open and filled squares, are for 50 dB pe SPL (30 dB SL) and 40 dB pe SPL (20 dB SL) clicks respectively, again for the same individual (Rutten, unpublished). It

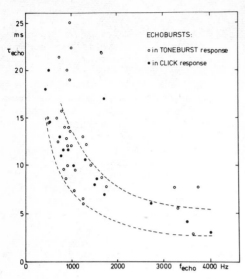

Figure 2. Onset latencies of echo bursts, in response to click- (●) or toneburst (O) stimulation, versus f_{echo}. First echoes lie within the f_{echo} area, confined by the two dashed lines, second or repeated echoes lie outside this area.

is obvious that this person may be considered as representative for the average normal hearing subject. Unfortunately it is not possible to obtain reliable NAP data at 10 or 0 dB SL. Extrapolation of available data to these low levels suggests that even at threshold the NAP latencies are smaller than the average echo latencies, especially for frequencies below about 1.5 kHz. This then implies that the echo latency is built up out of more than the sum of travelling wave delay and cochlear filter response time. On the other hand, average echo-number-of-periods seem to be smaller than twice the low-level NAP data. In its turn, this means that in order to evoke an echo it is not necessary to stimulate the cochlear filter in a retrograde way, at least not again up to the maximum of its impulse response (it is tacitly assumed that at low stimulus intensities the filter impulse response is excited up to its maximum value, about 4 periods, to achieve neural - as well as echo - excitation; see Goldstein *et al.*, 1971).

From the foregoing one may possibly conclude that three latency-parts form together the echo-latency: 1) forthgoing travelling wave delay along the basilar membrane τ_b 2) cochlear filter response time τ_f 3) back going travelling wave delay τ_b. Thus, $\tau_{echo} = \tau_f + 2\tau_b$ or, $N_{echo} = N_f + 2N_b$. Using "Cochlear Filter" theory (tuning-curve-two-segment-approximation; Goldstein *et al.*, 1971; Eggermont, 1979) one is able to calculate N_F:

$$N_F = \frac{\beta}{\pi^2} \left[\frac{(\gamma+1)^2}{\gamma} \frac{6.9}{12} Q_{10dB} - 1 \right] \left[\ln \frac{(\gamma+1)^2}{\gamma} \frac{6.9}{12} Q_{10dB} + 2 \right]$$

(In this theory "Cochlear Filter" refers to the combined action of what we called (basilar membrane) mechanical filter + (haircell second) cochlear filter. Thus, the corresponding delay is $N_F \equiv N_b + N_f$).

Figure 3. Conversion to number of periods N of latencies of echoes and narrow band action potentials (NAP), versus frequency. O and ● : data of fig. 2 (only those between the two dashed lines), converted to N. Shaded area: range of NAP latencies, converted to number of periods for normal hearing subjects (Eggermont, 1979). △ , □ and ■ : NAP-number-of-periods for one normal hearing subject in response to 90 dB pe SPL clicks (△), 50 dB pe SPL clicks (□) and 40 dB pe SPL clicks (■). Drawn lines, labelled "calc. 1" and "calc. 2", connect theoretical N-values, calculated at .5, 1, 2, 4 and 8 kHz.

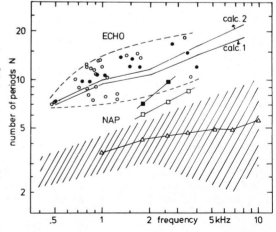

Eggermont (1979) estimates τ_b on basis of data in recruiting ears as:

$$\tau_b = 1.9f^{-0.7} \text{ or } N_b = 1.9f^{+0.3} \text{ (f in kHz).}$$

For β we take $\beta = 1$ (the response time is assumed to be up to the maximum of the impulse response). γ equals the ratio: high frequency slope of the tuning curve/ low frequency slope; $\gamma = 2$ is a reasonable value for normal ears. For Q_{10dB} we take: $Q = 5$ at 500 Hz, 6.5 at 1 kHz, 7 at 2 kHz, 9 at 4 kHz and 11 at 8 kHz (for example, see Vogten, 1978; also: Evans, 1975; Eggermont, 1979). By adding N_F and N_b we obtain N_{echo}. The result of the calculations at these five frequencies is shown in figure 3: the five points are connceted by the drawn line, marked "calc. 1". It is to be noted that these N_{echo} ($= N_F + N_b$) values lie much better in the experimental echo-range than would do $N_{echo} = 2 N_F$ (not drawn for clari- ty, but easily to be checked).

One may object that such a quite direct type of feedback mechanism ("from hair- cell output via a differential wave to the oval window") would lead to "fundamen- tal system instabilities" (cit. de Boer, 1980).

Possibly one circumvents this problem by adding a constant (frequency-indepen- dent) delay between filter output and retrograde wave. Calculation shows that this delay should be about .5 ms, in order to keep the calculated N_{echo} along the "centre line of gravity" of the experimental data-assembly: see drawn line in figure 3, marked "calc. 2".

Resuming, we think to have presented some evidence for a 3-stage echo-latency model, as described above, based upon experimental NAP latency data and theoreti- cally calculated echo-latencies. Physiologically this might imply that an echo is generated when haircells are "vibrating" as a consequence of electrical stimula- tion (in a retrograde way, perhaps by their own electrical output). Possibly contractile proteins (Flock, 1979) play a role in this electro-mechanical trans- formation. This transformation should occur almost instantaneously (i.e. a hypo- thetical filter, representing this transformation should have a low quality factor).

This work was supported by the Heinsius Houbolt Fund. Comments of V.F. Prijs and P. Kuper are gratefully acknowledged.

REFERENCES

de Boer, E.(1980). Non linear interactions and the 'Kemp'-echo. To be published in *Hearing Research*, 1980.

Duifhuis, H.(1973). Consequences of peripheral frequency selectivity for non- simultaneous masking. *J.A.S.A.* 54, 1471-1488.

Eggermont, J.J.(1979). Narrow-band AP latencies in normal and recruiting human ears. *J.A.S.A.* 65, 463-470.

Evans, E.F.(1975). The sharpening of cochlear frequency selectivity in the normal and abnormal cochlea. *Audiology* 14, 419-422.

Flock, A.(1979).Contractile proteins in haircells. Paper, presented at the sympo- sium on non linear and active mechanical processes in the cochlea, Londen.

Goldstein, J.L., Baer, T., and Kiang, N.Y.S.(1971). A theoretical treatment of latency, group delay and tuning characteristics for auditory nerve responses to clicks and tones. In *Physiology of the Auditory System*, edited by M.B. Sachs (National Educational Consultants, Baltimore).

Kemp, D.T.(1978). Stimulated acoustic emissions from within the human auditory system. *J.A.S.A.* 64, 1386-1391.

Rutten, W.L.C.(1980). Evoked acoustic emissions from within normal and abnormal human ears; comparison with audiometric and electrocochleographic findings. To be published in *Hearing Research*, 1980.

Vogten, L.L.M.(1978). Low-level pure tone masking: A comparison of "tuning curves" obtained with simultaenous and forward masking. *J.A.S.A.* 63, 1520-1527.

Wit, H.P. and Ritsma, R.J.(1979). Stimulated acoustic emissions from the human ear. *J.A.S.A.* 66, 911-913.

COMMENT ON "On the mechanism of the evoked cochlear mechanical response"
(H.P. Wit and R.J. Ritsma) AND ON "Latencies of stimulated acoustic
emissions in normal human ears" (W.L.C. Rutten).

J.P. Wilson
*Department of Communications & Neuroscience, University of Keele, Keele,
Staffs., ST5 5BG, U.K.*

"Model of cochlear function and acoustic re-emission"

An active local mechanical feedback onto basilar-membrane (BM) displacement appears to be (i) unlikely, (ii) unsuitable as a sharpening mechanism, and
(iii) unnecessary.
(i) The local feedback would have to be strong in order for the ear-canal-rec-
orded re-emitted SPL to approach that of the stimulus (within 1.7dB, see Wilson,
1980a). As the loss, passing twice through the middle ear, almost certainly
exceeds this value, output must exceed input, and with phase shifts occurring
along the BM, the system is unlikely to be stable. A reverse travelling wave
model could not explain a delayed cochlear microphonic correlate of the acoustic re-emission (Wilson, 1980c).
(ii) As the cochlear re-emission appears to saturate at about 20 dB SPL (Kemp,
1978, Wilson, 1980b, 1980d) sharpening would become negligible at higher sound
levels. Furthermore, thresholds are on average, not lower in frequency regions
of strong re-emission.
(iii) A qualitative model has been proposed (Wilson, 1980c) based on tuned hair
cells with concomitant volume changes. Such volume changes could react on the
middle ear without producing strong local feedback to the BM.
Support for this model has been found on two fronts. (a) Hill *et al.*
(1977) reported changes in crayfish giant axon diameter concurrent with action
potentials. If the electro-chemistry and mechanics of the excitable hair-cell
membrane is analogous to that of the crayfish axon, if the outer hair cell is
assumed to be more sensitive than found by Russell and Sellick (1978) for the
inner hair cell, and if saturation of oscillation is set at about 40 dB SPL
input (20 dB SPL output) by the electrical potential limits, then there is
reasonable quantitative agreement between the magnitudes reported by Hill *et al.*
(1977) and the required volume changes postulated by Wilson (1980c). Fettiplace and Crawford (1978) have provided evidence (in reptile) for electrically tuned hair cells. (b) A further aspect of the model concerns variability
between subjects and variability across frequency within a subject for the strength of the acoustic re-emission. It was postulated (Wilson, 1980c) that this
might be due to irregularities in the "mapping" of hair-cell tuning onto BM
"place". Computer simulations with G.J. Sutton have shown that slight irregularities in mapping slope can lead to enormous increases in summed activity at
these frequencies. The BM response was based on a one-dimensional model of de
Boer (1980) followed by a series of single resonant "second filter" elements
(Q=4) spaced at 0.035mm intervals and the total response of all elements summed.
If a 0.5mm length is tuned to the same frequency, the response is 44 times that
for a uniformly distributed system. The bandwidth of the enhanced summed activity and its phase/frequency characteristics model the observed properties of
cochlear echoes remarkably well. Notably the phase response indicates a long
delay which is not inherent in the individual filter responses or the summed
activity of a uniformly distributed system. It would appear that phase cancellation eliminates the early part of the summed response. Somewhat surprisingly
the frequency and phase characteristics of the response are not strongly dependent upon the extent or degree of the irregularity although, of course, the magnitude is. Similar properties have also been observed in an electrical model
of the BM (24 sections) and second filter (48 sections), but with less delay
(fig. 1.).
Simple-resonant second filters were chosen for simplicity and to model known membrane properties (Mauro *et al.* 1970) but give an unrealistic filter sha-

pe and transient response (Wilson, 1977). The difference signal, either betwe-
en neighbouring segments, or between one channel and the average of its neighb-
ours (on the electrical model), however, gives much more realistic results.
In the cochlea this would imply that neural activity would be determined not
only by a single (inner) hair cell but also by return current paths either from
longitudinally neighbouring hair cells or from radially neighbouring outer hair
cells. This approach then not only accounts for the unusual properties of cochlear echoes, including their long delay, but also for normal cochlear function (and electroreception) in a wide variety of species without recourse to any
radical new mechanisms unsupported by observation.

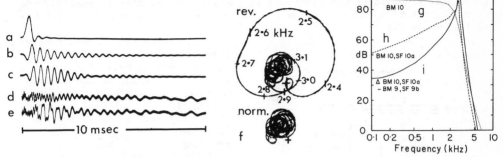

*Fig. 1. Electrical model: (a) BM impulse response at 2.7 kHz place, (b) BM
plus resonant "second filter", (c) difference between 2.7 and 2.95 kHz places,
(d) summed response of all 48 "second filters", (e) as (d) with positions of
2.95 and 2.52 kHz filters reversed - note introduction of delayed waves at
2.7 kHz, (f) Nyquist plots (1 - 11 kHz) of summed responses with and without
filters reversed - note increased radial amplitude and rapid phase shift, encl-
osing origin, with reversal, (g), (h) and (i) frequency response curves for
(a), (b) and (c) respectively.*

REFERENCES

de Boer, E.(1980) *Auditory Physics* (in press).
Fettiplace, R. & Crawford, A.C.(1978). The coding of sound pressure and frequency in cochlear hair cells of the terrapin. *Proc. R. Soc. Lond.* B **203**,
209-218.
Hill, B.C., Schubert, E.D., Nokes, M.A., & Michelson, R.P.(1977). Laser inter-
ferometer measurement of changes in crayfish axon diameter concurrent with
action potential. *Science* **196**, 426-428.
Kemp, D.T.(1978). Stimulated acoustic emissions from within the human auditory
system. *J. Acoust. Soc. Am.* **65**, 1386-1391.
Mauro, A., Conti, F., Dodge, F., & Shor, R.(1970). Subthreshold behavior and
phenomenological impedance of the squid giant axon. *J. gen. Physiol.*
55, 497-523.
Russell, I.J. & Sellick, P.M.(1978). Intracellular studies of hair cells in
the mammalian cochlea. *J. Physiol.* **284**, 261-290.
Wilson, J.P.(1977)(1980b)(1980c) see Wilson(1980d).
Wilson, J.P.(1980a). Subthreshold mechanical activity within the cochlea.
J. Physiol. **298**, 32-33P.
Wilson, J.P.(1980d). The combination tone, $2f_1-f_2$, in psychophysics and ear-
canal recording. In: *Psychophysical, Physiological and Behavioural
Studies in Hearing* (G. van den Brink and F.A. Bilsen, eds.).

COMMENT

REPLY TO COMMENT OF J.P. WILSON

W.L.C. Rutten
ENT Dept., University Hospital, Leiden, the Netherlands.

Contrary to Wilson's suggestion, my paper did not primarily discuss the active aspects of the echo-generation mechanism. The paper is just an attempt to calculate echo latencies on basis of a simple linear filter model, supplemented by experimental (travelling wave) latency data. This does not imply that active and/or nonlinear contributions to the process are absent. Possibly the active contribution comes in after the second filter, as indicated by the arrow labelled A, in Fig. 1.

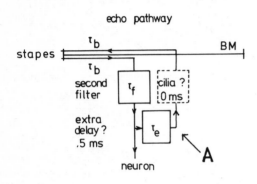

Fig. 1
Echo pathway, as described in Rutten (this volume). The arrow A indicates the place where possibly active processes ("energy") have to be considered in future models. For other symbols, see Rutten (this volume).

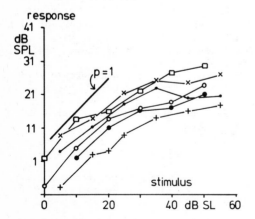

Ad i) and iii): about reverse travelling waves and a haircell-swelling model. Haircells are (strongly) coupled to the basilar membrane, to each other, to the liquid, to the tectorial membrane and to supporting cells. Therefore, it seems highly unlikely that swelling haircells will not interact with the basilar membrane (unless haircells are right in the "center of mass" of the organ of Corti). In other words: haircell-volume changes will influence BM motion and probably cause travelling waves along BM thereby causing ultimately also (as would do our model) instability because of feedback to the input.

Ad ii): about the saturation value of 20 dB SPL. We observed this rather low saturation value of echoes only in about 20% of the number of ears, which showed echoes (see Rutten, 1980). In these ears the input-output behaviour is about linear at low stimulus intensities and *seems* to approach saturation (actually a power law behaviour with p = 1/3 approximates the curves rather well) at about 20 - 30 dB SPL (see Fig. 2).

The remaining 80% of ears shows either higher saturation values (exceeding in some cases 45 dB SPL), or a power-law input-output behaviour, p, (therein varying between 1 and 0 as a function of echo latency (see Rutten, 1980). See also Wit & Ritsma (1979): their data seem to show a trend to saturation above 25-30 dB SPL.

Fig. 2. *Input-output behaviour of echo-burst responses in 20% of the number of echo ears (see Rutten, 1980). Power p=1 indicates linear input-output behaviour. Saturation will be at about 20-30 dB SPL. These are low saturation values, compared to the remaining 80% of echo ears.*

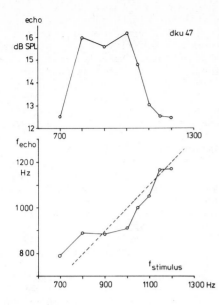

Fig. 3
Frequency and intensity of echo-burst responses versus stimulus-(tone-burst) frequency in a normal human ear.

Ad iii b): about the "mapping" of hair-cells and the computer model. It would be interesting to compare the computer simulation of Wilson with experimental data of Fig. 3. This figure shows the output frequency and -amplitude of an echo-burst versus the input-burst frequency. It shows a rather broad "tuning" (upper half of the figure) and a constant echo frequency in the input-frequency-interval where the echo response is maximal. This might support the idea of irregularities ("clustering") in the mapping density of haircells along BM. A quantitative comparison of these experimental data with Wilson's computer-model results (and -parameters) would be useful.

REFERENCES

Rutten, W.L.C. (1980). Evoked acoustic emissions from within normal and abnormal human ears. *Hearing Res.* 2 (in press).
Wit, H.P. and Ritsma, R.J. (1979). Stimulated acoustic emissions from the human ear. *J. Acoust. Soc. Am.* 66, 911-913.

COMMENT ON "On the mechanism of the evoked cochlear mechanical response" (H.P. Wit and R.J. Ritsma) and on "Latenties of stimulated acoustic emissions in normal human ears" (W.L.C. Rutten), following the comment of Wilson on "Model of cochlear function and acoustic re-emission".

D.T. Kemp

Institute of Laryngology and Otology, Royal National Throat, Nose and Ear Hospital Gray's Inn Road, London WC1X 8DA, Great Britain.

The signifance of acoustic emissions

In their papers, Wit and Ritsma, and Rutten have adopted and developed the suggestion of Kemp (1978) that the mode of propagation of the mechanical disturbance giving rise to stimulated acoustic emissions, is a reverse travelling wave from the site of the evoked cochlear mechanical activity, back to the middle ear. This hypothesis has the advantaged of doubling the contribution of travel time to emission latency, which otherwise presents some problems for modelling. It is also makes minimal assumptions about the primary source.

Wilson has reported that the summation of the contributions from an array of independent elemental tuned emission generators can, under certain circumstances result in group latency values greater than those of the individual elements. This additional source delay is also of value in attempts to model emissions.

COMMENT

A third contribution to latency could be that the elemental generators are each tuned to a frequency sligtly above the basilar membrane resonance for their place, i.e. that the tuned nonlinear mechanical activity is most strongly present on the high frequency slope of the response curve for each point on the basilar membrane. Travel time is greater to there. There is some support for this idea from the new observations of Le Page and Johnstone (1980) and also from the emission generator tuning bias reported by Kemp and Chum (this volume). The latter bias could indicate that the emission energy from sharply tuned generators is transmitted back via a more linear system tuned to a lower frequency i.e. the basilar membrane at place.

The purpose of this comment is not to support any one particular source of extra latency at the exclusion of the others. Clearly they must all be considered in relation to the evidence. However, Wilson would specifically exclude the hypothesis of reverse travelling waves in his assessment of acoustic emissions as purely an epiphenomenon. His argument will be examined.

Wilson postulates synchronous volume changes of the haircell as the primary source of acoustic emissions. This is a useful concept and gains support from Kemp and Chun's observations of very similar nonlinearities in intracellular and acoustic responses. However Wilson then presumes that this motion would not be coupled to the organ of Corti in which the hair cell resides. This implies radially symmetric mechanical loading of the hair cell by the organ of Corti. From anatomical evidence it is extremely unlikely that this specific condition is fulfilled. Therefore direct coupling of this type of motion to the basilar membrane, and therefore the creation of reverse travelling waves would almost certainly occurr in parallel with the compression wave postulated by Wilson. Hence, in the light of acoustic emissions, active mechanical feedback into the basilar membrane is extremely likely. The postuation of cellular swelling does not allow this issue to be bypassed.

This fact undermines Wilson's case against involvement of this mechanical activity in the cochlea filtering process. Such a stand is premature in any case. The primary mechanical source of acoustic emission has yet to be determined experimentally and the particular sharpening mechanism, rejected by Wilson, is in practice only just being tested and developed theoretically (Kim 1980). Other more stable and subtle models should also be considered before the whole idea is rejected.

Of course it is possible that acoustic emissions result from an epiphenomenon of the transduction process. However until the latter process is finally understood we should keep an open mind concerning the implications and possible role of feedback of cochlear filter output back through the organ of Corti onto gross basilar membrane motion. Since the existence of this effect is very strongly indicated by acoustic emissions.

REFERENCES

Le Page, E.L. and Johnstone, B.M. (1980). Basilar membrane mechanics in the guinea pig cochlear. Details of nonlinear frequency response characteristics. *J. Acoust. Soc. Am.* **67**, Suppl. 1 p S45.

Kemp, D.T. (1978). Stimulated acoustic emissions from whether the human auditory system. *J. Acoust. Soc. Am.* **64**, 1386-1391.

Kim, D.O., Neely, C.E., Molnar, C.E. and Matthews, J.W. (1980). An active cochlear model with negative damping in the partition: comparison with Rhode's observations *(this volume)*.

FUNCTIONAL IDENTIFICATION OF AUDITORY NEURONS
BASED ON STIMULUS-EVENT CORRELATION.

P.I.M. Johannesma
Workgroup Neurophysics,
Lab. of Medical Physics and Biophysics,
University of Nijmegen, Nijmegen,
The Netherlands.

1. INTRODUCTION

The neural representation of sound has two complementary aspects: processing and transmission of auditory information. Synaptic, dendritic and somatic potentials reflect information processing inside a neuron; action potentials represent information transmission between neurons. Action potentials of a given neuron do not vary systematically in form, amplitude or duration, they form a sequence of unitary pulses: the neural events. In the mathematical theory of stochastic processes this is known as a point process which is completely specified by the moments of occurrence of the events: t_n, n = 1,N. The activity of a neuron in the interval (o, T) is then written as

$$z(t) = \sum_{n=1}^{N} \delta(t-t_n) \tag{1}$$

where $\delta(t-t_n)$ is the Dirac deltafunction and N is the total number of events in the observation interval (o, T). Since repetition of the experiment will not lead to precisely identical results, z(t) has to be considered as a realisation of a stochastic process. A sensory neuron then forms a stochastic, time invariant nonlinear system.

The correlation procedure has been introduced into sensory neurophysiology by De Boer (1968) under the name reversed or triggered correlation. First and second order correlation functions have been studied for auditory neurons (De Boer and Kuijper, 1968; Johannesma, 1972; Grashuis, 1974; De Boer and De Jongh, 1978; De Jongh, 1978; Aertsen and Johannesma, in preparation). Also for visual neurons the method has been applied (Schellaert and Spekreyse, 1972; Marmarelis and McCann, 1973; Marmarelis, 1978; Von Seelen and Hoffman, 1976, 1979; Gielen, in preparation).

For auditory neurons responding to Gaussian white noise the first order stimulus-event correlation forms a "characteristic stimulus" of the neuron; the second order forms a time-dependent autocorrelation function specifying an ensemble of characteristic stimuli. From this autocorrelation function the spectrotemporal receptive field of the neuron can be derived (Johannesma, 1972; Johannesma and Aertsen, 1979; Aertsen and Johannesma, 1979).

2. STIMULUS-EVENT CORRELATION

The general form of a stimulus-event correlation is

$$R\{\Phi, z\} = \frac{1}{T} \int_{o}^{T} dt \; \Phi(x; \; t-\tau_1, \; \ldots, \; t-\tau_m) \cdot z(t) \tag{2}$$

where Φ is a functional of the stimulus x(t) constructed from the m values of the stimulus at times $t-\tau_1, \ldots, t-\tau_m$. This stimulus functional multiplied with the neural events is integrated over the duration T of the experiment. For the experimental determination of R we make use of Eq(1). Substitution of Eq(1) in Eq(2) leads to

$$R\{\Phi, z\} = \frac{N}{T} \cdot \frac{1}{N} \sum_{n=1}^{N} \Phi(x; \; t_n-\tau_1, \; \ldots, \; t_n-\tau_m) = \frac{N}{T} \cdot < \Phi >_e \tag{3}$$

where N/T is the average firing frequency of the neuron and $< \Phi >_e$ is the average value of the stimulus functional Φ taken over the Pre-Event Stimulus Ensemble (PESE). The PESE is defined as the ensemble of stimuli preceding a neural event (Johannesma, 1972). As such it forms a subensemble of the stimulus Ensemble (SE). Eq(3) leads to the conclusion that correlation of stimulus functional Φ and neural activity is identical in form with the average value of this functional over the PESE.

The general formulation of the correlation given in Eq(2) and Eq(3) can be related to the specific forms of correlation in system theory by

$$\Phi_m = \Phi(x; t-\tau_1, \ldots, t-\tau_m) = \prod_{i=1}^{m} x(t-\tau_i). \tag{4}$$

Also different forms of Φ can be used as base for a correlation. Møller (1973) used instantaneous envelope and frequency of the stimulus, De Boer (1979) took Hermite polynomials as stimulus functionals, Johannesma and Aertsen (1979) used the spectrotemporal intensity density of the stimulus.

These signal characteristics, and more complicated ones such as combinations of amplitude and frequency modulation, can be taken as the functional Φ. Crosscorrelation of this Φ and the neural events $z(t)$ then measures the presence of this feature in the PESE. Comparison of the relative abundance of Φ in PESE and SE forms an indication of the feature selecting properties of the neuron. Different features are represented through corresponding functionals Φ over the stimulus.

3. PROBABILISTIC FORMULATION OF STIMULUS-EVENT CORRELATION.

The stimulus-event correlation defined in Eq(2) is a temporal average of the product of the output-events and functionals of the input-stimulus. As shown in Eq(3) it is, in the case where the output is a series of events, equal to the product of average pulse frequency and the average of the stimulus functional Φ taken over the PESE. These averages are the experimental estimates of the expected values. Averages are the operational counter parts of the conceptual values. Expected value of a variable is the mean value of a stochastic variable with respect to its probability distribution. This leads to a probabilistic approach.

In order to be able to use probabilities instead of probability densities, both time and signal value are made discrete. Time changes its value with small increments Δ; e.g. 10 or 100 µs. The value of the stimulus during a given interval is not specified as a function $x(t)$ but by a finite row of numbers: a vector $\vec{x}$. The Dirac deltafunction $\delta(t)$ transforms into a variable z assuming the value zero if no event occurs and one if an event occurs in the given interval. Finally the stimulus vector assumes only a finite number of discrete values. This procedure as a whole is precisely the one used in analogue-digital conversion.

In this context five probabilities can now be defined:

$f(\vec{x})$ = probability that stimulus $\vec{x}$ occurs in the stimulus ensemble.

$p(\vec{x}, e)$ = probability that stimulus $\vec{x}$ occurs in the SE and that an event occurs immediately following $\vec{x}$.

$\pi(\vec{x}|e)$ = probability that stimulus $\vec{x}$ occurs just preceding a neural event; probability distribution of PESE.

$g(e|\vec{x})$ = neural response function indicating the probability of a neural event given the preceding occurrence of stimulus $\vec{x}$.

$h(e)$ = probability of occurrence of neural event irrespective of stimulus.

The discrete stochastic form of stimulus-event correlation is

$$R\{\Phi, p\} = \sum_{\vec{x}} \sum_{z} \Phi(x) \cdot z \, p(\vec{x}, z). \tag{5}$$

Since z assumes only the values zero and one Eq(5) can be simplified into:

$$R\{\Phi, p\} = \sum_{\vec{x}} \Phi(\vec{x}) \, p(\vec{x}, e). \tag{6}$$

The five probabilities are interrelated by the relation of Bayes for conditional probabilities:

$$f(\vec{x}) \, g(e|\vec{x}) = p(\vec{x}, e) = h(e) \, \pi(\vec{x}|e). \tag{7}$$

Substitution of the righthand side of Eq(7) for p in Eq(6) leads to:

$$R\{h, \Phi, \pi\} = h(e) \cdot \sum_{\vec{x}} \Phi(\vec{x}) \, \pi(\vec{x}|e) \tag{8}$$

which forms the theoretical image of the experiment definition of R given by Eq(3).

A different form emerges from the substitution of the lefthand side of Eq(7) for p in Eq(6):

$$R\{f, \Phi, g\} = \sum_{\vec{x}} f(\vec{x}) \, \Phi(\vec{x}) \, g(e|\vec{x}) \tag{9}$$

Eq(9) states that the stimulus-event correlation is the product of stimulus feature Φ and neural response g for stimulus $\vec{x}$ summated with proper statistical weight f over the stimulus ensemble.

The correlation procedure based on Eq(9) is then as follows:
1. select distribution f of stimulus ensemble.
2. present SE to animal and record events of neuron 1.
3. select stimulus functionals Φ_k, k = 1,K.
4. compute correlations $R_{kl} = R\{f, \Phi_k, g_l\}$ making use of Eq(3).

Two different, rather complementary, ways of application of the correlation approach will now be sketched: the neuro-ethological based on the study of behaviour and the neurophysiological departing from the individual sensory neuron.

4. NEURAL REPRESENTATION OF SENSORY STIMULI.

Ethological studies of animal behaviour supply information on relevant acoustic features of sound. Most animals generate sounds for the purpose of communication and are influenced in their behaviour selectively by sounds from other animals and from the environment. Identification and localisation of sound sources in a complex acoustic environment has a large survival value. Selective adaptation of phonation and audition has taken place in the evolution of the species. The study of acoustic behaviour leads to a description of the bio-acoustic dimensions of the natural acoustic environment (acoustic biotope) of a given animal (Suga, 1972; Scheich, 1977).

For the study of the neural representation of natural sounds a simplification of the acoustic biotope is taken to define the probability distribution f(x) of the stimulus ensemble (Worden and Galambos, 1972; Bullock, 1977 ; Aertsen e.a., 1979; Smolders e.a., 1979). The bio-acoustic dimensions may then be taken as the base for the stimulus functionals Φ_k. Correlation of functionals Φ_k with the activity $z_1(t)$ of neuron 1 leads to the neural feature matrix R_{kl}. This matrix gives the representation of feature set Φ_k; k = 1,K in the neural activity patterns $z_1(t)$; l = 1,L.

The mutual correlations of different stimulus features have to be defined with respect to the stimulus ensemble. An acceptable measure appears to be

$$C_{kk'} = \sum_{\vec{x}} f(\vec{x}) \, \Phi_k(\vec{x}) \, \Phi_{k'}(\vec{x}) \tag{10}$$

where C gives the degree of correlation or the two features. This definition may give a way to investigate the orthogonality of the bio-acoustic dimensions of a biotope. If the stimulus functionals are independent then the matrix elements R_{kl} for different neurons indicate a functional distance of different neurons in this acoustic biotope.

5. FUNCTIONAL IDENTIFICATION OF A SENSORY NEURON.

For the study of the function of a sensory neuron suggestions from system theory can be applied. The distribution of the stimulus ensemble is chosen as vague and wide as possible: Gaussian white noise. The stimulus functionals are the mth order products of the stimulus (the moment functions) or simple combinations of these (the cumulant functions).

The goal of functional identification of a neuron is the determination of the neural response function $g(e|\vec{x})$ for arbitrary stimulus $\vec{x}$. An apparently simple solution for this problem is to use Eq(7) in the form

$$g(e|\vec{x}) = h(e) \; \frac{\pi(\vec{x}|e)}{f(\vec{x})} \; . \qquad (11)$$

For an arbitrary stimulus $\vec{x}$ $\pi(\vec{x}|e)$ and $f(\vec{x})$ can be estimated from the frequency of occurrence of $\vec{x}$ in PESE and SE. However, the number of actually occurring stimuli in an experiment with a duration of e.g. 15 minutes is only a minute fraction of the number of possible stimuli. Use of Eq(11) for general determination of g leads to experiments longer than the lifetime of the observed animal and the observing experimenter.

A second solution is the determination of $g(e|\vec{x})$ from the correlation as given in Eq(9). This implies that Eq(9) has to be inverted or transformed in such a way that

$$g = g\{R, f, \Phi\} \qquad (12)$$

forms an explicit expression for g as function of R, f and Φ. In general this appears impossible. However, for certain classes of neural response functions g it is possible to choose stimulus ensemble f and functionals Φ_k such that the free parameters of g within this functional class can be derived from R. This means that functional correlation determines uniquely the characteristic parameters of the neuron.

As a consequence we come to an adaptive procedure for the functional identification of a sensory neuron:
A. make an initial qualitative functional model of the neuron based on physiological knowledge and aimed at mathematical simplicity: section 6.
B. verify the model qualitatively: section 7.
C. choose stimulus ensemble f and stimulus functionals Φ_k such that the neural response function g can be derived from correlation R_k, k = 1,K and use the correlations R_k to quantify the model: section 8.
D. verify the model quantitatively by confrontation with independent experimental data: section 9.

6. MODEL OF A PRIMARY AUDITORY NEURON.

The approach sketched in sections 3 and 5 is now applied on a primary sensory neuron: a transducer followed by a pulse generator. The transducer transforms the physical variable x of the sensory stimulus, e.g. the pressure variations of sound, into the receptor potential y. The transducer includes linear or nonlinear filtering. This part can be described as a deterministic, time-invariant, continuous, linear or nonlinear system V. The event generator is a probabilistic system: the probability of an event is a continuous, positive and monotonically increasing function of the receptor potential y. Since all temporal integration and filtering of the stimulus is included in the transducer V, the event generator has as argument only the instantaneous value of the receptor potential. Leaving aside adaptation and refractory properties the event probability is taken as an exponential function of the receptor potential (see fig. III-10 in Grashuis, 1974).

The model of a primary sensory neuron is then as represented in fig. 1. The response function of the neuron is

$$g(e|x(s), \; s \le t) = g_o \exp V(x(s), \; s \le t) \qquad (13a)$$

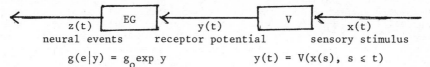

$$g(e|y) = g_0 \exp y \qquad\qquad y(t) = V(x(s), s \leqslant t)$$

Fig. 1: model of a primary sensory neuron.

or in vector notation for sampled signals

$$g(e|\vec{x}) = g_0 \exp V(\vec{x}) \tag{13b}$$

More specifically for a primary auditory neuron (PAN) the transducer V may be thought to consist of a linear band-pass filter followed by a rectifying nonlinearity followed again by a linear low-pass filter (Johannesma, 1971; De Jongh, 1978). This model of the transducer is shown in fig. 2.

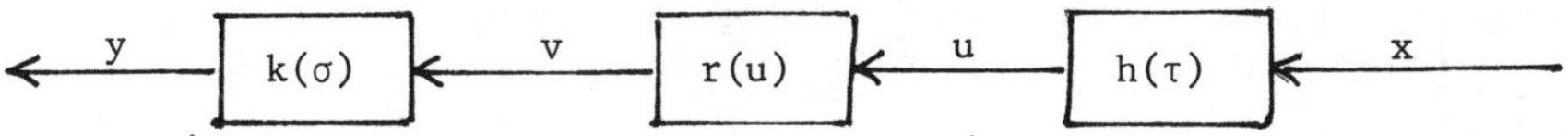

$$y(t) = \int ds\ k(\sigma)\ v(t-\sigma) \qquad\qquad u(t) = \int d\tau\ h(\tau)\ x(t-\tau)$$

$$v = r(u) = r_1 u + r_2 u^2$$

Fig. 2: model of the auditory transducer V.

If the rectifier $r(u)$ is taken as second degree, then this PAN-model may show strong phase-lock for low-frequency choice of h, partial phase-lock for medium frequency and no phase-lock if the spectral content of h is completely above that of k. The generator potential $y(t)$ can be expressed as a second degree functional of the stimulus

$$y(t) = \int ds\ H_1(s)\ x(t-s) + \int ds_1 \int ds_2\ H_2(s_1, s_2)\ x(t-s_1)\ x(t-s_2) \tag{14a}$$

where the kernels H_1 and H_2 are simply related to h, k, r_1 and r_2 of the model. In vector form this reads

$$y = V(\vec{x}) = \vec{c}.\vec{x} + \tfrac{1}{2}\ \vec{x}\ D\ \vec{x} \tag{14b}$$

where $\vec{c}$ is a vector related to the linear response to an impulse and D a matrix related to the quadratic response to pairs of impulses.

Combination of transducer of Eq(14) and event generator of Eq(13) leads to the hypothetical neural response function

$$g(e|\vec{x}) = g_0 \exp(\vec{c}.\vec{x} + \tfrac{1}{2}\ \vec{x}\ D\ \vec{x}) \tag{15}$$

where $\vec{c}$ and D are unknown. Since the dimensionality of $\vec{x}$ is $\simeq 100$ the vector $\vec{c}$ may contain of the order of 100, the matrix D of the order of 10.000 unknown parameters. With Eq(15) a qualitative form of a PAN-model has been formulated.

7. QUALITATIVE VERIFICATION OF THE PAN-MODEL.

The second step is the qualitative verification of the model. This can be based on the following theorem:
  if the response function is $g(e|\vec{x}) = g_0 \exp V(\vec{x})$,
  and the stimulus ensemble is Gaussian,
  then the Pre-Event Stimulus Ensemble is also Gaussian,
  if and only if $V(\vec{x})$ *is first or second degree function of* $\vec{x}$.
The proof of this theorem is based on the fact that a Gaussian distribution of $\vec{x}$ can be written as an exponential function of a second degree functional of $\vec{x}$ and on some algebraic manipulation of the relation of Bayes given by Eq(7).

In recordings made from single units in the cochlear nucleus of the anesthetised cat Gaussian noise, spectrally flat up to 5 kHz, was presented as stimulus (Van Gisbergen, e.a., 1975). For unit 59-5, which showed a primary-

like character and may have been an auditory nerve fiber, the distribution of
stimuli in the PESE has been investigated in detail. The results are presented
in fig. III-1 in Grashuis (1974). The distribution $\pi(\vec{x}|e)$ of stimuli in the
PESE cannot be seen to deviate from Gaussian. As a consequence we take as working hypothesis that a Primary Auditory Neuron in a Gaussian wide band stationary auditory environment may be modelled by a second degree transducer followed by an exponential event generator.

8. PARAMETER ESTIMATION OF THE PAN-MODEL.

For the estimation of the parameter vector $\vec{c}$ and the parameter matrix D
the stimulus ensemble f and stimulus functionals Φ_k have to be selected in
such a way that the parameters can be computed from the correlations R_k. Substitution of the estimated values of $\vec{c}$ and D in Eq(15) then supplies the neu-
ral response function $g(e|\vec{x})$. This function g then may be used for prediction
of PSTH's and for descriptions of the structure of the receptive field.

A possible choice, not necessarily the only one, is given again by a
Gaussian distribution of the stimulus ensemble.

$$f(\vec{x}) = f_o \exp - \tfrac{1}{2}(\vec{x}-\vec{a})\ B^{-1}\ (\vec{x}-\vec{a}) \tag{16a}$$

where

$$\vec{a} = \sum_{\vec{x}} \vec{x}\ f(\vec{x}) \text{ is expected value of SE} \tag{16b}$$

$$B = \sum_{\vec{x}} \vec{x}{\char`^}\vec{x}\ f(\vec{x}) - \vec{a}{\char`^}\vec{a} \text{ is covariance of SE.} \tag{16c}$$

The distribution of the Pre-Event Stimulus Ensemble is also Gaussian

$$p(\vec{x}, e) = p_o \exp - \tfrac{1}{2}(\vec{x}-\vec{m})\ S^{-1}\ (\vec{x}-\vec{m}) \tag{17a}$$

where

$$\vec{m} = \sum_{\vec{x}} \vec{x}\ p(\vec{x}, e) \text{ is expected value of PESE.} \tag{17b}$$

$$S = \sum_{\vec{x}} \vec{x}{\char`^}\vec{x}\ p(\vec{x}, e) - \vec{m}{\char`^}\vec{m} \text{ is covariance of PESE.} \tag{17c}$$

The relation of Bayes gives again the possibility for determination of $\vec{c}$
and D. Combination of Eq(7), (15), (16) and (17) and use of the symmetry of
the covariance matrices B and S leads to

$$\vec{c} = S^{-1}\ \vec{m} - B^{-1}\ \vec{a} \tag{18}$$

for the neural vector, and

$$D = B^{-1} - S^{-1} \tag{19}$$

for the neural matrix.

Eq(18) and (19) give neural vector $\vec{c}$ and matrix D characterising the PAN-
model as function of expected value and covariance of SE and of PESE. Both $\vec{a}$,
B and $\vec{m}$, S are experimentally observable. The expected value $\vec{a}$ of SE will normally be zero, S is the autocorrelation function of the SE. The expected value
$\vec{m}$ of PESE is equal to the first order stimulus-event correlation as defined by
Eq(3) and (4a); the covariance S of the PESE can be derived directly from the
second order stimulus-event correlation defined in Eq(3) and (4b).

Several conclusions can be drawn for the PAN-model defined by Eq(15) in a
Gaussian stimulus environment:
1) *PESE is Gaussian.*
2) *modelparameters $\vec{c}$ and D can be determined completely from first and second*
   order stimulus-event correlation.
3) *neural matrix D is zero if and only if covariance S of PESE is equal to co-*
   variance B of SE.
4) *the expected value $\vec{m}$ of PESE is equal to the convolution of covariance S of*

PESE and neural vector $\vec{c}$.

5) the covariance S of the PESE depends on neural matrix D and covariance B of SE, but not on neural vector $\vec{c}$.

6) the expected value $\vec{m}$ of PESE depends on neural vector $\vec{c}$, covariance B of SE and on neural matrix D.

7) if neural matrix D equals zero, than expected value $\vec{m}$ of PESE is equal to the convolution of covariance B of SE and characteristic vector $\vec{c}$.

9. QUANTITATIVE VERIFICATION BY RESPONSE PREDICTION.

From stimulus-event correlation the neural parameters $\vec{c}$ and D can be derived. Substitution in Eq(15) supplies the response function $g(e|\vec{x})$. This function predicts the neural probability of an event (PSTH) for stationary wideband stimuli.

Verification has been made for 10 units in the cochlear nucleus of the anesthetised cat; long sequences of pseudo-random Gaussian noise with a spectrum flat up to 5 or 15 kHz were presented. Stimulus-event correlation supplied a tentative response function. Independent short pseudo-random noise sequences (5-80 msec) were repeatedly presented and the PSTH of the neuron was constructed. Comparison of predicted and measured response showed a good agreement. The characteristic frequency of the units varied between 800 and 6.000 Hz; they showed different amounts of phaselock. The results are presented in fig. III-11 to III-26 in Grashuis (1974).

The conclusion of these experiments is: for simple auditory units in the cochlear nucleus the response to a wideband stationary stimulus is given by Eq(15) where

$$\vec{c} = a.\vec{m} \tag{20a}$$

and

$$D = b.\{\vec{m}\char`\^\vec{m} + \tilde{\vec{m}}\char`\^\tilde{\vec{m}}\} \tag{20b}$$

In this expression $\tilde{\vec{m}}$ is the Hilbert-transform of $\vec{m}$: a stimulus equal in temporal and spectral envelope but differing 90 degrees in phase for all frequencies.

Narrowband and nonstationary stimuli have been used to investigate the behaviour of the neuron with respect to properties not contained in the model (Van Gisbergen, 1975). With these stimuli a number of neurons demonstrated more complex response functions which could only partly be described in a formal way.

10. DISCUSSION AND CONCLUSIONS.

A model has been presented for a primary auditory neuron consisting of a second degree transducer followed by an exponential event generator. It turns out that first and second order stimulus-event correlation for a Gaussian stimulus ensemble supply sufficient information to determine all parameters of the model. It can be shown that the same conclusion holds, but with different mathematical relations, for a second degree transducer followed by a linear event generator. In this case however a Gaussian SE does not produce a Gaussian PESE.

The approach given here can also be applied on models of secondary auditory neurons. The mathematics becomes more complicated and the number of parameters increases; however, it may give an important contribution to the inpretation of stimulus-event correlations. A combination of model formulation and correlation procedure appears an effective approach to identification of neural function. A qualitative study of the distribution of the PESE gives support for a qualitative model of the neuron, quantitative properties of the PESE as expressed in correlation functions give the parameter estimation.

Verification of the quantitative model has to be made inside the domain of validity (e.g. Gaussian stimuli). Comparison of model and neuron outside this domain (e.g. tones, vocalisations) indicates improvement of the model: higher order nonlinearities, time varying parameters as in adaptation. These

83

considerations suggest an approach starting from global properties based on stimulus-event correlation for a wideband stationary stimulus ensemble and diverging into more specific neural properties investigated with specific stimuli.

REFERENCES

Aertsen, A.M.H.J.; Smolders, J.W.T.; Johannesma, P.I.M. (1979). Neural representation of the acoustic biotope: on the existence of stimulus-event relations for sensory neurons. *Biol. Cybernetics* 32, 175-185.

Aertsen, A.M.H.J.; Johannesma, P.I.M. (1979). Spectrotemporal analysis of auditory neurons in the grassfrog. *Exp. Brain Research Suppl.* II, 87-93.

Boer, E. de; Kuiper, P. (1968). Triggered correlation. *IEEE Tr. on Biomed. Eng.* BME 15, 169-179.

Boer, E. de; Jongh, H.R. de (1978). On cochlear encoding: potentialities and limitations of the reverse-correlation technique. *J. Acoust. Soc. Am.* 63, 115-135.

Boer, E. de (1979). Polynomial correlation. *Proc. IEEE* 67, 317-318.

Bullock, T.H. (ed.; 1977). Recognition of complex acoustic signals. *Life Sciences Res. Rep.*, Vol.5. Springer, Berlin.

Gisbergen, J.A.M. van; Grashuis, J.L.; Johannesma, P.I.M.; Vendrik, A.J.H. (1975). Neurons in the cochlear nucleus investigated with tone and noise stimuli. *Exp. Brain Res.* 23, 387-406.

Grashuis, J.L. (1974). The pre-event stimulus ensemble: analysis of the stimulus-response relation for complex stimuli applied to auditory neurons. Ph. D. thesis, Nijmegen, The Netherlands.

Johannesma, P.I.M. (1972). The pre-response stimulus ensemble of neurons in the cochlear nucleus. In: *Proc. of the IPO symp. on Hearing Theory* (B.L. Cardozo, ed.). Eindhoven, The Netherlands.

Johannesma, P.I.M.; Aertsen, A.M.H.J. (1979). Neural image of sound in the grassfrog. *Exp. Brain Research Suppl.* II, 79-86.

Jongh, H.R. de (1978). Modelling the peripheral auditory system. Ph. D. thesis. Amsterdam, the Netherlands.

Marmarelis, P.Z.; McCann, G.D. (1973). Development and application of white noise modelling techniques for studies of insect visual nervous system. *Kybernetik* 12, 74-89.

Marmarelis, P.Z.; Marmarelis, V.Z. (1978). Analysis of physiological systems. Plenum Press, New York.

Møller, A.R. (1973). Statistical evaluation of the dynamic properties of cochlear nucleus units using stimuli modulated with pseudo random noise. *Brain Res.* 57, 443-456.

Scheich, H. (1977). Central processing of complex sounds and feature analysis. In: Recognition of comple acoustic signals (T.H. Bullock, ed.). *Life Sciences Res. Rep.* 5, 161-182. Springer, Berlin.

Schellaert, N.A.M.; Spekreyse, H. (1972). Dynamic characteristics of retinal ganglion cell responses in goldfish. *J. Gen. Physiol.* 59, 1-21.

Seelen, W. von; Hoffmann, K.P. (1976). Analysis of neuronal networks in the visual system of the cat using statistical signals. *Biol. Cybernetics* 22, 7-20.

Smolders, J.W.T.; Aertsen, A.M.H.J.; Johannesma, P.I.M. (1979). Neural representation of the acoustic biotope: a comparison of the response of auditory neurons to tonal and natural stimuli in the cat. *Biol. Cybernetics* 35, 11-20.

Suga, N. (1972). Analysis of information-bearing elements in complex sounds by auditory neurons of bats. *Audiology* 11, 58-72.

Worden, F.G.; Galambos, R. (eds.; 1972). Auditory processing of biologically significant sounds. *Neurosc. Res. Progr. Bull.* 10.

Acknowledgement This investigation has been supported by the Netherlands Organisation for Advancement of Pure Research (ZWO), the Hague.

A COCHLEAR MICROMECHANIC MODEL OF TRANSDUCTION

J. B. Allen
Bell Laboratories
Murray Hill, New Jersey   07974

1. INTRODUCTION

The cochlea is the organ which converts low level pressure variations into electrical (neural) signals. Its main function is to filter the stapes input signal through a continuum of very narrow, bandpass filters. These narrowband signals are then half-wave rectified and modulate the firing rate of a large number of neurons, which in turn signal the central nerves system.

While this basic outline has long been well documented [Kiang, *et. al.*, (1965); Russell & Sellick, (1978)], certain critical details are as yet unexplained. Existing models of basilar membrane (BM) motion appear to be in reasonable agreement with experimental BM velocity measurements [Allen, (1979), Allen & Sondhi, (1979)]. These models give rise to a low-pass frequency response whose cutoff frequency varies with position along the BM. From observations of the differences between mechanical and neural response, a final transformation from low pass to bandpass appears to take place during the mechanical to neural transduction process at the hair cell level [Evans, E. F. (1977): Hall, J. L., (1977); Allen, J. B. (1977)].

2. THE "SECOND-FILTER"

For introductory purposes, we present in this section results which argue for the validity of modeling the transfer function between mechanical and neural response by a second order spectral zero. In Figs. 1(a-c) we show model calculations which compare model tuning curves with measured neural tuning curves [Kiang & Moxon, (1974)] at different characteristic frequencies (CF's). The model tuning curves were computed using the two-dimensional mechanical model of Allen and Sondhi (1979), followed by a spectral zero systematically located below the CF (and a pole above CF). Our experience has been that any measured neural tuning curve may be closely matched by adjustment of the model spectral zero.

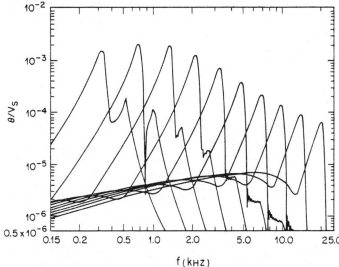

Fig. 1. In this series of figures we make comparisons between cat neural data as measured by Kiang and Moxon(1974) and the mechanical model of Allen and Sondhi (1979) modified to include the transduction filter $H_T(x,s)$: Eq. 1. a) The model neural magnitude response at the transduction filter output.

In Fig. 2 we show (solid line) the cochlear map for model CF values.

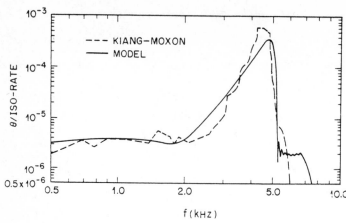

Fig. 1b. *A specific comparison between the model and a neural tuning curve at a CF of 3.5 kHz.*

This curve agrees quite closely with published values of the cochlear map of the cat. The dashed line gives the location of the assumed spectral zero frequency f_z of the model transduction filter used in computing the tuning curves. The curve labeled f_p will be discussed. More specifically we define

x = *positional coordinate along BM* $i = \sqrt{-1}$

f = *stimulus frequency* $s = i\omega$

$\omega = 2\pi f$ $V_{BM}(x,s)$ = *BM velocity*

$\Theta(x,s)$ = *hair cell excitation (tuning)*

$$H_T(x,s) = \frac{s^2 + 2\xi_z(x)s + \omega_z^2(x)}{s^2 + 2\xi_p(x)s + \omega_p^2(x)} \qquad (1)$$

where $H_T(s,x)$ is the *transduction filter* which relates Θ to V_{BM} by the relation

$$\Theta(x,s) = H_T(x,s)V_{BM}(x,s). \qquad (2)$$

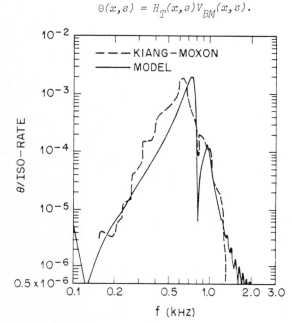

Fig. 1c. *A comparison between the model and a neural tuning curve for a low frequency CF.*

The roots ω_z of the numerator of $H_T(x,s)$ are the zeros of the transduction filter of the model. The damping ratio $\xi_z(x)$ defines the bandwidth (depth or sharpness) of the zeros For Fig. 2, we have assumed $\xi(x) = 0$ in defining the root frequencies $\omega_z(x)$ and $\omega_p(x)$. Since the pole frequency ω_p is above CF and is therefore in the cutoff region, it is a less interesting feature. Thus we will concentrate on the zero for the present.

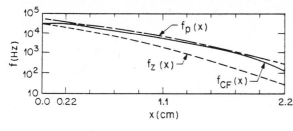

Fig. 2. We compare here the cochlear maps of the zero and pole of the model transduction filter to that of CF.

In Fig. 3 we plot the phase of $\Theta(\omega,x)$ for several model tuning curves. Each curve is for a different place x on the BM. As a result of the transduction filter zero, the phase will jump by as much as π radians (depending on ξ_z) at ω_z. Since we have placed the zero in the left half s plane, the phase slope at $\omega \overset{\simeq}{=} \omega_z$ is positive (with increasing frequency). A zero to the right of the $i\omega$ axis would have caused the phase to decrease across the zero. The phase response to a single frequency tone as a function of place x as found by the model has a very similar shape.

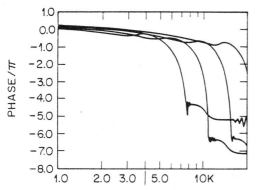

Fig. 3. As with the magnitude response, the phase, whether plotted as a function of log (f) or place x, is quite similar. This figure shows phase as a function of frequency for four different measurement locations.

large number of units in a single animal. neuron's response against the neuron's CF.

In Fig. 4 we reproduce a figure showing phase as found by Kim, Siegel, and Molnar (1979). Using their measurement technique they determined the phase due to a single tone stimulus over a They then plotted the phase of each

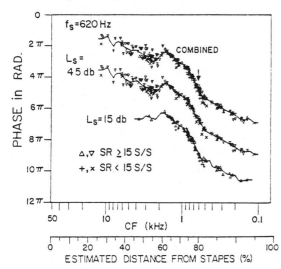

Fig. 4. This figure shows cochlear neural phase response to a single tone of frequency 620 Hz plotted as a function of estimated place along the BM [Kim, Siegel, Molnar, (1979)]. Note the phase jump for CF's of 2 kHz.

In this way they approximately determined the phase of the neural excitation due to the input tone as a function of position along the length of the cochlea, since CF is relatable to the inervation point on the BM by the cochlear map. As may be seen in Fig. 4, Kim *et. al.* found a positive π phase shift (at 2 *kHz*) for CF's above the input stimulus frequency in agreement with the spectral zero model π phase shift (Fig. 3 and Eq. 1).

Thus the second-filter model of a left hand plane spectral zero gives excellent agreement with both the neural tuning magnitude (stapes pressure for threshold neural iso-rate) and phase.

From the above evidence it appears that (a) the transduction filter H_T is required from a modeling point of view; (b) the transduction filter is equivalent to a spectral zero; (c) in some sense the cochlea transduction mechanics acts as a linear system since linear system theory concepts are applicable (e.g., zeros make up the transfer function).

As a result of the cross correlation measurements of deBoer (1973), Evans (1977), Møller, (1977) it appears that the above conclusions are valid at levels well above threshold.

3. A SIMPLE MODEL FOR RADIAL SHEAR

A concept that has been prevalent throughout the recent (last 20 years) history of cochlear modeling is the concept of radial (transverse) shear motion. In the following we present a simplified model of radial shear motion (which we will need later) in order to reveal what we feel are basic principles.

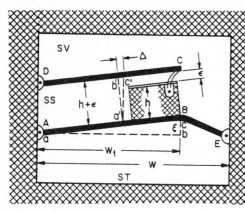

Fig. 5. A cross-section showing the BM displaced. Since AB and DC are equal in length in this simplified model, BC remains parallel to AD after any BM displacement ξ. As a result, triangles abc and a'b'c' are similar, and displacement Δ is proportional to the BM displacement ξ. We define this ratio as the shear gain G, namely G(x) = Δ(x)/ξ(x).

The basic question we ask is the following: assuming that the BM is displaced by an amount ξ, what is the relative shearing displacement between TM and RL. We pick points on TM and RL that are opposite each other in the rest condition and define the distance Δ as their relative radial or transverse (z direction) separation when the BM is displaced by ξ. The displacements of the model are defined in Fig. 5.

A simple analysis of the geometry shows that triangles abc and $a'b'c'$ are similar. For small angles at vertex a we then have the proportionality

$$\frac{\xi}{W_1} = \frac{\Delta}{\varepsilon+h} \tag{3}$$

where ξ = *BM displacement*
 Δ = *radial-shear-displacement* $\qquad \varepsilon$ = *subtectorial dimension*
 W_1 = *length AB $\simeq$ length ab* $\qquad h$ = *organ of corti height.* $\qquad$ (4)

In the following we assume that ε is given by the length of the outer hair cell cilia, since these cilia appear to be firmly fixed to both TM and RL, and that $W_1 \simeq W/2$, where $W(x)$ is the BM width.

We now define a new variable $G(x)$ which we call the *shear gain*:

$$G(x) = \Delta(x)/\xi(x). \qquad (5)$$

For purposes of the present definition we assume here that the TM is rigid, a restriction which we shall later relax. Thus Δ is the displacement between the RL and the rigid TM.

Note that the relation between Δ and ξ is linear (proportional) and instantaneous (frequency independent). It is equivalent to a lever having a displacement gain of G.

Thus according to the above assumptions and Eq.'s (3-5)

$$G(x) \sim \frac{2h(x)}{W(x)} \qquad (6)$$

since $\varepsilon \ll h$.

4. THE RESONANT TECTORIAL MEMBRANE MODEL

(a) *The Physical Model*

In order to introduce a zero into the transfer function between BM motion ξ and TM-RL shear Δ it is necessary that the tectorial membrane move independently and not be locked to BM motion through the radial shear lever gain G, Eq. (5). With this end in mind we introduce an elastic connection between the body of the TM and the scala wall as shown in Fig. 6.

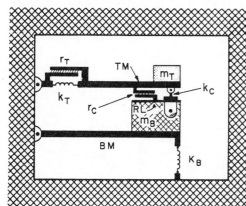

Fig. 6. In this figure we have further abstracted the physical model of Fig. 5. by specifically specifying the BM restoring force K_B, the BM mass m_B, the tectorial mass m_T, the cilia stiffness k_c, and the subtectorial damping r_c. Furthermore we have added the tectorial stiffness and damping k_T and r_T as discussed in the text. By allowing the TM to move independently of BM displacements, with its own resonant frequency as determined by k_T and m_T, it is possible to introduce a zero into the transfer function between TM-RL shear displacements and BM displacement.

The cilia stiffness k_c represents stiffness with respect to radial shear; it may be thought of as a bar clamped at the RL end and pinned at the TM end. Since the space between TM and RL, the subtectorial space, is only 2-6 μm, the equation of motion between these two surfaces must include a viscous force which is shown here as the dashpot labeled r_c. The tectorial membrane mass is labeled m_T, while the elastic connection to the scala wall is k_T. For reasons which will become obvious it is necessary to include a damping loss across k_T labeled r_T.

The basic principle of this model is that the spring-mass system of the TM, namely k_T and m_T, may resonate independently from that of the basilar membrane system of K_B and m_B. When conditions are right the TM can move in phase with the RL producing zero *relative* motion. We will show that this condition will give rise to a spectral zero as assumed in Section 2.

(b) *The Rectilinear Mechanical Model*

In order to analyze the physical model of Fig. 6 it is helpful to redraw it in rectilinear form as shown in Fig. 7. Those not acquainted with this procedure should refer to the book of H. Olson (1958), Chapter 4. The solid lines represent hinged rigid massless rods in the rectilinear circuit, the coils are springs, and the boxes are masses. The radial shear model has been included as a lever having a mechanical advantage of $G(x)$ (see Eq. 5). The mass on the left is the sum of m_B and m_T since vertical BM motion is loaded by both masses, assuming the outer hair cell sterocilia are rigid to vertical forces.

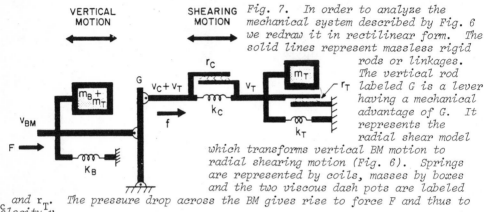

Fig. 7. *In order to analyze the mechanical system described by Fig. 6 we redraw it in rectilinear form. The solid lines represent massless rigid rods or linkages. The vertical rod labeled G is a lever having a mechanical advantage of G. It represents the radial shear model which transforms vertical BM motion to radial shearing motion (Fig. 6). Springs are represented by coils, masses by boxes and the two viscous dash pots are labeled r_c and r_T. The pressure drop across the BM gives rise to force F and thus to velocity v_{BM}.*

(c) *The Electrical Equivalent Circuit*

A straightforward and simple method for finding the electrical equivalent network is to use the mobility method (see Olson, Chapter 14). The mobility equivalent circuit may be drawn by inspection from the rectilinear model. The classical electrical network is then found by forming the dual network (interchange current and voltage, L and C, R and G and parallel with series). After performing these operations we find the classical mechanical analogue circuit shown in Fig. 8.

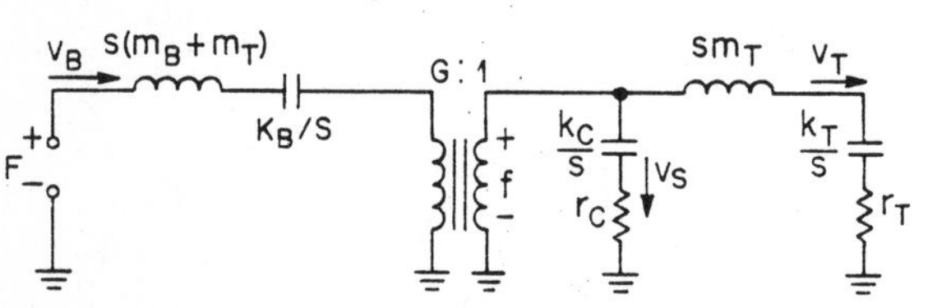

Fig. 8. *The more common form of mechanical-electrical analogue is the force=voltage analogue. The mechanical model of the cochlear duct, as shown in Fig. 6, has thereby been reduced to the electrical circuit of this figure.*

5. ANALYSIS OF THE MODEL

(a) *The Second Filter*

The principle question of interest is: What is the transfer function which relates $V_s(\omega,x)$ to $V_{BM}(\omega,x)$? The quantity V_s is defined as the shear velocity between TM and RL, and it is a quantity that might well drive inner hair cell cilia. According to observations these cilia do not seem to be connected directly to the TM; however, the cilia would be displaced by fluid flow across them (as sea grass bends in a gentle wind).

The transfer function in question may be identified as the second filter, and from the current divider law, can be shown to be

$$H_T(x,s) \triangleq V_s/V_{BM} = G \frac{sm_T + r_T + k_T/s}{sm_T + (r_c + r_T) + (k_c + k_T)/s} \ . \tag{7}$$

As in Section 2 we call $H_T(x,s)$ the *transduction filter*. The transfer function H_T consists of a zero at frequency f_z and a pole at frequency f_p where

$$f_z = \frac{1}{2\pi} \sqrt{k_T/m_T} \qquad f_p = \frac{1}{2\pi} \sqrt{(k_c + k_T)/m_T} \ . \tag{8}$$

Note that $f_p > f_z$ since $k_c + k_T > k_T$.

The significance of this result is that a spectral zero, which is required to account for the difference between the mechanical and neural response, naturally follows from the model. This point is the main result of this paper.

(b) *Basilar Membrane Impedance*

A basic quantity of importance in cochlear macromechanics is the BM impedance, defined as the ratio of pure tone trans-BM pressure to steady state normal velocity.

$$Z_{BM}(s,x) \triangleq \frac{-2P}{V_{BM}} \ . \tag{9}$$

The impedance is usually *assumed* to be of the form

$$Z_{BM} = K_B(x)/s + R(x) + sM_0. \tag{10}$$

All results in this paper have in fact assumed a BM impedance of this form. We hope therefore that the input impedance of the model proposed in Fig. 6 will be in some way consistent with Eq. (10). In a sense this is true, however a rigorous analysis is somewhat difficult (Allen, 1980). If the input impedance to the right of the transformer were real, then Eq. (10) would hold exactly. In fact, according to the model of Fig. 6.

$$Z_{BM}(x,s) = s(m_T + m_B) + \frac{K_B}{s} + G^2(x)\frac{(r_c + k_c/s)(k_T/s + r_T + sm_T)}{(k_c + k_T)/s + (r_c + r_T) + sm_T} \ . \tag{11}$$

Therefore a rigorous analysis of BM motion assuming the model of Fig. 6 is significantly more complicated than previous BM macromechanical models since the time differential equations are fourth order in time rather than second order.

6. A NONLINEAR MICROMECHANICAL MODEL

The nonlinear properties of the cochlea have been well documented in the recent literature. Clearly, for any micromechanical model to be useful it must account for these nonlinear properties, such as combination tone generation, two-tone suppression, and known threshold and Q_{10} variations with input level. Toward this end we propose that the stereocilia stiffness k_c be a decreasing function of signal level (i.e., the cilia become limp with increased SPL). We feel that there are many qualitative justifications for such a proposal: (a) Flock (1977) has pointed out that the outer hair cell stereocilia are composed of the protein actin. Based on the structural composition of the actin filaments Flock has proposed that the cilia bending moment (k_c) could possibly be variable (personal communication), (b) The stereocilia appear to grow limp after strong sound stimulation, (c) Stimulation of the COCB efferent neural system, which terminates at the outer hair cells and thus might effect k_c directly, seems to modify neural tuning in a way which is consistent with decreased k_c in the model, (d) The deep null and π phase shift observed in the rate function reported in Kiang $et.$ $al.$ (1969) (Nelson's notch) for large sound pressure levels is consistent with decreased k_c with SPL (e.g., let k_c go to zero in Eq. 7), (e) The rapid loss of the tip of the tuning curve of the receptor potential curve near CF is also consistent with this hypothesis since as k_c goes to zero the CF appears to decrease toward the zero of H_T, (f) The apparent increase in BM damping might be accounted for by decreased k_c since as k_c decreases r_c is "turned on" in the sense that a greater velocity is allowed across the TM-RL interface (increasing the effective mechanical losses).

The ultimate test of these ideas must await a proper simulation of this model. For technical reasons we have not yet been successful in completing this simulation.

REFERENCES

Allen, J. B. (1977). "Cochlear Micromechanics -- A Mechanism for Transforming Mechanical to Neural Tuning within the Cochlea," *J. Acoust. Soc. Am.* 62, 930-939.

Allen, J. B. (1979). "Cochlea Models 1978," (Symp. on Models of the Auditory System and Related Signal Processing Techniques, Munster, Ger. in *Scandanavian Audiology.*

Allen, J. B., and Sondhi, M. M. (1979). "Cochlear Macromechanics -- Time Domain Solutions," *J. Acoust. Soc. Am.* 66, 123-132.

Allen, J. B. (1980). Unpublished Manuscript.

Békésy, G. von (1953). "Shearing Microphonics Produced by Vibrations Near the Inner and Outter Hair Cells," *J. Acoust. Soc. Am.* 25, 786-790.

deBoer, E. (1973). "On the Principle of Specific Coding," *Dyn. Syst., Measurement & Control (Trans. ASME),* 265-273.

Evans, E. F. (1977). "Frequency Selectivity at High Signal Units in Cochlear Nerve and Nucleus," in *Phycophysics and Physiology of Hearing,* edited by E. F. Evans and J. P. Wilson (Academic Press, London).

Flock, A. (1977). "Physiological Properties of Sensory Hairs," in *Psychophysics and Physiology of Hearing,* edited by E. F. Evans and J. P. Wilson (Academic Press, London).

Hall, J. L. (1977). "Spatial Differentiation as an Auditory Assessment on a Nonlinear Model of the Basilar Membrane," *J. Acoust. Soc. Am.* 61, 520-524.

Kiang, N. Y. S., Watanabe, T., Thomas, E. C., and Clark, L. F. (1965). *Discharge Patterns of Single Fibers in the Cat's Auditory Nerve,* MIT Research Mono. #35, MIT Press Cambridge, Mass.

Kiang, N. Y. S., Boer, T., Marr, E. M. and Demont, D. (1969). "Discharge Rates of Single Auditory-Nerve Fibers as a Function of Tone Level," *J. Acoust. Soc. Am.* 46, p. S106, V6(A).

Kiang, N. Y. S., and Moxon, E. C. (1974). "Tails of Tuning Curves of Auditory-Nerve Fibers," *J. Acoust. Soc. Am.* 55, 620-630.

Kim, D. O., Siegel, J. H., and Molnar, C. E., (1979). "Cochlear nonlinear phenomena in two-tone responses," Symp. on Models of the Auditory System and Related Signal Processing Techniques, Munster, Ger. in *Scandanavian Audiology,* Sup. 9.

Møller, A. R., (1977), "Frequency selectivity of single auditory-nerve fibers in response to broadband noise stimuli," *J. Acoust. Soc. Am.* 62, 135-142.

Olson, H. F., (1958). *Dynamical Analogies,* Van Nostrand, N. Y.

Russell, I. J., and Sellick, P. M. (1978). "Intracellular Studies of Hair Cells in the Mammlian Cochlea," *J. Physiol.* 284, 261-290.

ADDENDUM TO: "A cochlear micromechanical model of transduction"

J.B. Allen
Bell Laboratories, Murray Hill, New Jersey, USA.

I would like to clear up how the zero is introduced into the spectrum, based on simple physical arguments.

The amplitude of the radial mode of TM oscillation is limited only by dashpot r_T. Without this element the resonance would become unbounded. The elements k_c, m_T and k_T, when redrawn in rectilinear form comprise a spring-mass-spring-ground system, with TM element k_T representing the grounded spring and TM mass m_T representing the mass element. When excitation is applied to k_c at RL below the pole resonance frequency, given by $\sqrt{(k_T + k_c)/m_T}$, the mass moves in phase with the excitation. At low frequencies the mass must move by an amount less than the drive point. As the resonance frequency is approached, the mass velocity becomes unbounded. Thus at some point the shear, given by the velocity across k_c, must be exactly zero, in the lossless case.

COMMENT ON: "A cochlear micromechanical model of transduction"
(J.B. Allen)

P. Dallos
Auditory Physiology Laboratory, Northwestern University, Evanston, U.S.A.

One of the critical points of your argument is that the model reproduces
the notch in FTC's at the juncture of the tip and the tail segments that was
shown by Kiang and Moxon (1974) for cat nerve fibers. I would like to point
out that such notches are not seen in Chinchilla FTCs and only rarely in
Guinea pig responses. In my opinion, any model that depends critically on an
idiosyncratic feature seen in the response of a particular species can not
have general validity.

REPLY TO COMMENT OF P. DALLOS

J.B. Allen
Bell Laboratories, Murray Hill, New Jersey 07974, U.S.A.

The notch present in high frequency units in cat can fall below the
middle ear response.
This was, I felt, a clue that a spectral zero might exist. When the zero
moves very close to the $i\omega$ axis in the complex s plane the depth of the notch
in the spectrum is very deep. As the zero moves away from the $i\omega$ axis, the
influence may still be strong on the spectrum, but is not as obvious. For
example in Fig. 1b the zero has the effect of about 30 dB of attenuation at
2 kHz and the notch is not appearent.

COMMENT ON "A cochlear micromechanic model of transduction" (J.B. Allen)

J.J. Zwislocki
Institute for Sensory Research, Syracuse University, Syracuse, New York, U.S.A.

I have three comments that concern the origins of some of the fundamental
ideas used by Allen.
To the best of my knowledge, the model of Fig.6, in which the tectorial
membrane is assumed to be rigid and to rotate around the rim of the spiral limbus, was first proposed by Ter Kuile in 1900 to explain shear motion between
the tectorial membrane and the reticular lamina. A modification of this model,
allowing a radial motion of the tectorial membrane, as shown in Allen's Fig.7,
was proposed by myself at a 1978 meeting of the Acoustical Society of America
over Allen's objections and later published in Acta Otolaryngologica (1979)
and in Science (1979). Some essential consequences of the assumed radial motion
of the tectorial membrane, including a 180° phase shift, were discussed on all
three occasions. Finally, the possibility of a resonance of the tectorial-mem-
brane-stereocilia system was proposed by me at a symposium held at the 50th
anniversary meeting of the Acoustical Society of America, Spring 1979, again
over Allen's strong objections. I quote two summary statements from the text:

"... it seems that local resonance of the stereocilia-tectorial-membrane system is within the realm of possibilities." and "... a significant loading of the basilar membrane by the transversal motion of the stereocilia and associated structures would convert it from the usually assumed second-order system to a fourth-order system." All the papers of that symposium are being published in the May, 1980, issue of the Journal of the Acoustical Society of America. I am glad to learn that the same ideas are now espoused by Allen (Figs. 7, 8 and 9).

REFERENCES

Kuile, E. ter. (1900). Die Uebertragung der Energie von der Grundmembran auf die Haarzellen. *Pflueg.Arch.Ges.Physiol.* 79, 146-157.
Zwislocki, J.J. (1979). Tectorial membrane: A possible sharpening effect on the frequency analysis in the cochlea. *Acta Otolaryng.* 87, 267-269.
Zwislocki, J.J. (1980). Five decades of research on cochlear mechanics. *J.Acoust. Soc.Am.*, (May issue, in Press).
Zwislocki, J.J. and Kletsky, E.J. (1979). Tectorial membrane: A possible effect on frequency analysis in the cochlea. *Science* 204, 639-641.

QUANTITATIVE MODEL ANALYSIS OF BASILAR MEMBRANE MOTION

Max A. Viergever

Dept. of Mathematics, Delft University of Technology, The Netherlands

1. INTRODUCTION

In the operation of the inner ear two stages can be discerned:
I The response of the basilar membrane (BM) to stapes movements,
II The excitation of receptor cells due to membrane motion, followed by the activation of nerve fibers.

Up to now, the theory of cochlear mechanics has mainly concentrated on the first - macromechanical - process. The reasons are obvious: the second process cannot be analysed until the first is sufficiently understood, and validation of models that aim to explain (part of) the second process is as yet not feasible for lack of experimental data.

Although in the last few years much insight has been gained in the mechanisms governing cochlear macromechanics, there are still several important problems to be solved:
a. BM motion is nonlinear in intact cochleae. How is this accounted for ?
b. Which dimensionality is most appropriate in cochlear modelling ?
c. Are exact solution methods necessary, or can we content ourselves with asymptotic techniques ?
d. Is it possible to fit the measured BM vibration data quantitatively ?
In this paper these items will be briefly discussed.

2. NONLINEARITY OF BM MOTION

Whether or not BM motion in living mammals is nonlinear has been a point of discussion for a long time. Rhode's (1971, 1978) measurements with the Mössbauer technique revealed a significant nonlinearity of the saturating type in the mid-frequency region of the living squirrel monkey. In all other experiments, including Rhode's observations in the high frequency regions of the squirrel monkey and guinea pig cochleae, the response of the BM was linear.

Very recently, however, Le Page and Johnstone (1980) reported nonlinear BM behaviour in the basal turn of the guinea pig cochlea. They used a capacitive probe technique in their experiments. The nonlinearity was of the type shown by Rhode in the squirrel monkey; its presence was very much dependent on the physiological integrity of the cochlea, also in conformity with Rhode's (1973) findings. Accordingly, BM nonlinearity is not, as sometimes thought, an artefact of the Mössbauer technique, nor is it species-linked or observable only in limited frequency regions. Very likely, BM motion is essentially nonlinear in properly functioning cochleas, and becomes linear only by the invasiveness of the measuring techniques.

The nonlinearity in BM vibration seemingly necessitates the use of a nonlinear model in the study of cochlear macromechanics. Yet, other recent observations suggest a different approach. Kemp (1978) observed that sound energy is re-emitted by the auditory system, into the outer ear canal, following acoustic stimulation. This phenomenon is almost certainly due to an active, physiologically vulnerable mechanism in the mechano-electrophysiological transduction process. This process takes place in the organ of Corti / tectorial membrane (OC/TM) complex, at or near the point of maximum response of the BM. In order to explain the echo in the auditory canal, there has to be a feedback from the OC via the BM to the outer ear.

The physiological vulnerability of both the mentioned active mechanism and BM nonlinearity, together with the existence of a feedback path from the site of the former to that of the latter, indicates that nonlinearity is not originally present in BM motion, but only as a result of this feedback. Hence I suggest that the inner ear performs a frequency analysis as sketched in Fig. 1. In consequence, when one wants to study the first filter per se (i.e. without information fed back from the OC/TM complex), a linear model approach suffices.

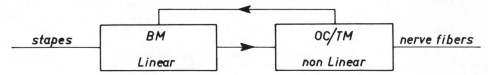

Fig. 1. *Suggested functioning of the cochlea filtering process. The feedback loop changes the character of the BM filter from linear to nonlinear.*
(It should not be ruled out that the feedback mechanism also affects the sharpness of tuning, and increases the low frequency slope of the amplitude curve just before the characteristic frequency. The first filter thus gets the bandpass-like appearance as observed by Rhode).

3. DIMENSIONALITY OF COCHLEAR MODELS

From the position of mathematical modelling, the question of how many dimensions a cochlear model should have is a very crucial one. It is by now well established that one-dimensional (1-D) models are suitable only to illustrate general qualitative features, such as frequency selectivity and travelling wave character of BM motion. For quantitative purposes a multi-dimensional treatment is compulsory, but whether two or three dimensions are required is yet uncertain.

There are two points in favour of 2-D models: The dimension lateral to the BM is the least important for the mechanics of the system, because averaging of fluid pressures in this direction does not essentially alter the loading of the membrane, whereas averaging in the direction perpendicular to the BM changes the driving force of the membrane from a pressure difference across it to a difference of pressure averages. Furthermore, the point-impedance characterization of the BM is the analogue in (1-D and) 2-D models of a visco-elastic plate, and hence has a realistic physical background (Viergever, 1978).

The only comparison of 2-D and 3-D model results has been made by Steele and Taber (1979b). They argue that fluid motion in the cochlea is fully three-dimensional; their numerical calculations show that nevertheless the 2-D approximation estimates the response quite well. Therefore I consider a 2-D approach provisionally the most suitable. For a final conclusion as regards the appropriate dimensionality more research on 3-D models is needed.

4. EXACT VS. ASYMPTOTIC SOLUTION TECHNIQUES

The values of most parameters appearing in cochlea models are known only roughly. This is especially true for the mechanical properties (mass, resistance, and stiffness) of the BM. Consequently, in order to match model results quantitatively with experimental data, extensive parameter variation seems inevitable. Thus we are left with the task of finding a both accurate and fast solution technique for the model equations.

Solution methods can either be exact or asymptotic. By 'exact' I understand all methods that are non-asymptotic; in particular are numerical approximations exact by this standard. Exact methods are intrinsically accurate, but, except for the 1-D model, slow. An accurate solution of the 2-D model requires at least several minutes of computer time.

Asymptotic approximations are computationally fast. As contrasted with exact methods, however, these approaches make use of a priori assumptions about the character of the solution, which entails that the solutions have only a limited validity. This property effectively eliminates long wave and short wave methods as satisfactory solution techniques in quantitative 2-D model analysis of the inner ear. More promising in this respect is the Liouville-Green (LG) approximation, often – but less accurately – called WKB or WKBJ method.

The LG approximation is based on the assumption that the BM wave travels in a medium of which the propagation properties do not vary much within one wavelength. In the cochlea, this requirement is reasonably fulfilled. Steele and Taber (1979a) showed that the accuracy of LG is indeed sufficient, which is corroborated by our results. Computer time involved is an order of magnitude less than that of exact methods. The LG method moreover relates pre-eminently to the physics of the problem, and thus provides excellent insight into the mechanisms whereby the observed behaviour is brought about.

In summary, I conclude that LG is the most appropriate technique for the 2-D cochlear model. The method is discussed in detail in Viergever (1980).

5. QUANTITATIVE MODEL ANALYSIS

The functioning of the cochlea as suggested in Fig. 1 logically implies that, for both qualitative and quantitative analysis of the first filter, the experimental data to be used as reference frame should be linear. In the measurements of Rhode, for instance, the feedback path is at least partially intact, which makes the data "too good" for a study of the BM filter per se. Of the various linear measurement results available, I shall consider in this paper the guinea pig data of Johnstone and Yates (1974, Fig. 3), which were obtained with the Mössbauer technique.

The mathematical model employed in the analysis is, in accordance with the preceding sections, the standard 2-D model as first described by Lesser and Berkley (1972), and the LG approach has been used to solve the model equations. The numerical implementation is simple and straightforward; the program output is directly in the form of the measurement results: frequency is the running variable, and the point of observation on the BM is kept fixed.

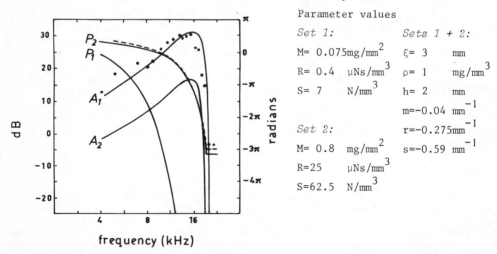

Fig. 2. Model results of BM/stapes transfer ratio with two different parameter sets. A_1 and P_1 are amplitude and phase curves with set 1, A_2 and P_2 with set 2. Measurement results of Johnstone and Yates (1974, Fig. 3) are indicated by dots (amplitude) and dashed line (phase).

The parameters appearing in the equations are: observation point ξ, fluid density ρ, channel height h, BM mass Mexp(mx), BM resistance Rexp(rx), BM stiffness Sexp(sx); x is the coordinate longitudinal to the membrane. Of the nine constants thus introduced, six have been estimated for the data at issue (see Fig. 2 for values), a.o. from Fernandez' (1952) measurements of BM thickness and width in guinea pigs, and from relations between these quantities and the impedance components (Viergever, 1978). The remaining parameters M, R and S were determined by a curve fitting procedure.

Fig. 2 presents the outcome of the curve fitting. The model results conform qualitatively to the experimental data of Johnstone and Yates. The quantitative agreement is poor, however: the amplitude and phase characteristics cannot simultaneously be matched with one set of parameters. A reasonable fit to the amplitude data is obtained with parameter set 1, but the corresponding phase curve is much to steep. Besides, the resonance frequency of the BM, at precisely which frequency the plateaus begin, is too high (21.3 kHz). On the other hand, the measured phase curve is approximated very well with set 2, but then the amplitude is far off. The resonance frequency is in the latter case 19.5 kHz, and the amplitude plateau is at -30 dB. The difference in M, R and S between the two parameter sets cannot substantially be diminished by changes - within acceptable limits - of the parameters m, r, s, h, ρ and ξ.

A previous attempt to fit BM vibration data quantitatively was made by Allen and Sondhi (1979). They tried to cover Rhode's (1971) results, but could not obtain simultaneous matches of amplitude and phase. The present results indicate that this failure should not be ascribed solely to the nonlinear character of Rhode's data.

I conclude with discussing two possible explanations for the discrepancy between model results and measurement results:
a. Inaccuracy of the data. In particular are phase characteristics equivocal, because they have an ambiguity of 2π radians at each input frequency. The Mössbauer technique even has a phase ambiguity of π radians (Rhode, personal communication). Therefore, phase curves may be steeper than usually indicated, especially when the number of input frequencies is small. This might reduce (but probably not remove) the mentioned discrepancy.
b. Incompleteness of the model. The many simplifications leading to the standard 2-D model have been investigated one by one in Viergever (1980). Two of them may have caused significant deviations, viz. omitting the third dimension and not taking into account the OC in the representation of the BM. Inclusion of these effects and of the OC-TM interaction in the model will be the main purposes of the mathematical theory of cochlear mechanics in the coming years.

REFERENCES

Allen, J.B. and Sondhi, M.M. (1979), Cochlear macromechanics: Time domain solutions. *J. Acoust. Soc. Am.* 66, 123 - 132.
Fernandez, C. (1952), Dimensions of the cochlea (guinea pig). *J. Acoust. Soc. Am.* 24, 519 - 523.
Johnstone, B.M. and Yates, G.K. (1974), Basilar membrane tuning curves in the guinea pig. *J. Acoust. Soc. Am.* 55, 584 - 587.
Kemp, D.T. (1978), Stimulated acoustic emissions from within the human auditory system. *J. Acoust. Soc. Am.* 64, 1386 - 1391.
Le Page, E.L. and Johnstone, B.M. (1980), Nonlinear mechanical behaviour of the basilar membrane in the basal turn of the guinea pig cochlea. *Proc. Symp. Nonlinear and active mechanical processes in the cochlea*, to appear in *Hearing Research*.
Lesser, M.B. and Berkley, D.A. (1972), Fluid mechanics of the cochlea. Part I. *J. Fluid Mech.* 51, 497 - 512.

Rhode, W.S. (1971), Observations of the vibration of the basilar membrane in squirrel monkeys using the Mössbauer technique. *J. Acoust. Soc. Am.* 49, 1218 - 1231.

Rhode, W.S. (1973), An investigation of post-mortem cochlear mechanics using the Mössbauer effect. In: *Basic Mechanisms in Hearing* (A.R. Møller, ed.), pp. 49 - 67, Academic Press, New York.

Rhode, W.S. (1978), Some observations on cochlear mechanics. *J. Acoust. Soc. Am.* 64, 158 - 176.

Steele, C.R. and Taber, L.A. (1979a), Comparison of WKB and finite difference calculations for a two-dimensional cochlear model. *J. Acoust. Soc. Am.* 65, 1001 - 1006.

Steele, C.R. and Taber, L.A. (1979b), Comparison of WKB calculations and experimental results for three-dimensional cochlear models. *J. Acoust. Soc. Am.* 65, 1007 - 1018.

Viergever, M.A. (1978), On the physical background of the point-impedance characterization of the basilar membrane in cochlear mechanics. *Acustica* 39, 292 - 297.

Viergever, M.A. (1980), Mechanics of the inner ear; a mathematical approach. In preparation.

PHASE RESPONSE VERSUS BEST FREQUENCY IN CAIMAN AUDITORY NERVE DISCHARGES

J. Smolders and R. Klinke

*Zentrum der Physiologie, J. W. Goethe-Universität
D-6000 Frankfurt, Germany*

1. INTRODUCTION

Comparative investigations of caiman primary auditory fibres (Klinke &
Pause, 1977, 1980) have revealed a number of similarities between these and
mammalian primary afferents. One major difference, however, is that the CF
of caiman fibres shifts downwards with decreasing body temperature (Klinke &
Smolders, 1977). Similar results were reported from the toad (Moffat & Capranica, 1976) and the gecko (Eatock & Manley, 1976). No temperature shift was
found in cat primary fibres (Smolders & Klinke, 1977) nor in psychoacoustic
experiments in humans possessing absolute pitch (Emde & Klinke, 1977). Therefore we wondered if this difference reflects a difference in the basic mechanical properties of the ear of mammalian and sub-mammalian vertebrates. This
hypothesis is supported by Peake & Ling (1979) who doubt the existence of
mechanical tuning in the basilar papilla of the alligator lizard on the basis
of their Mössbauer measurements.

We therefore checked for the existence of a travelling wave in caiman. It
was decided to use the method of Pfeiffer & Kim (1975) and Kim & Molnar (1979).
This method makes use of the phase lock of the neuronal discharges from which
the wave pattern of the basilar membrane motion can be reconstructed. It suf-
fers from the disadvantage that it is an indirect method but offers the advantage that the inner ear need not be disturbed. A second advantage is the
fact that the single fibre data provide information about a large proportion
of a single basilar papilla, quite in contrast to the available mechanical
measurements where data were collected only from single locations.

2. METHODS

The general scheme of the approach was described by Pfeiffer & Kim (1975)
and Kim & Molnar (1979). As many single primary fibres with different CFs as
possible have to be collected from one ear in order to cover a large enough
range of the basilar papilla with sufficient resolution. The test stimulus, a
pure tone of fixed frequency and intensity is identical for each fibre. This
means that in all cases identical vibration patterns of the basilar membrane
are achieved as any phase and amplitude distortions introduced through the
acoustic system and the middle ear are identical for all fibres.

For the present study 3 caiman *(Caiman crocodilus)* were used. The procedure of preparation, acoustic stimulation and data collection is described in
Klinke & Pause (1980). Ten different test stimuli were used: 88, 177, 354, 707
or 1414 Hz at 25 dB or 35 dB attenuation (0 dB attenuation corresponds to 110
dB SPL). Best frequency was determined using iso-intensity-frequency contours
recorded at about 20 dB above threshold. The contours were smoothed using a
hanning window and the maximum was accepted as best frequency (BF $\approx$ CF). Additionally spontaneous rate and click responses were recorded. Period histograms were computed in 256 bins/period and Fourier-transformed. Four response
measures were used: Spontaneous discharge rate (SR), average response rate
(R$\emptyset$), amplitude and phase of the first harmonic of the Fourier transform (R1
and P1). SR, R$\emptyset$ and R1 are measured in spikes/s; P1 in radians. Phase was calculated relative to the positive zero crossing of the electrical signal.

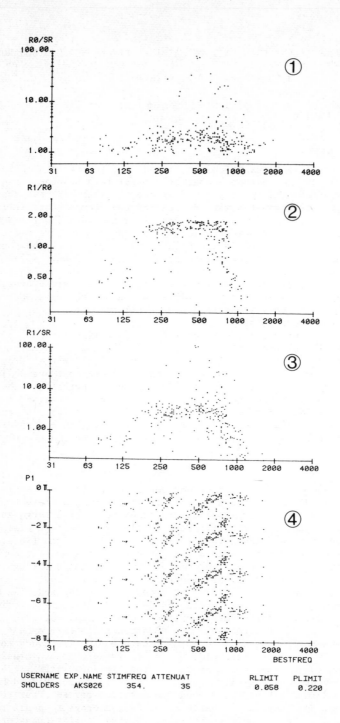

Fig. 1. Amplitude and phase of neuronal responses to a 354 Hz pure tone of a population of caiman primary auditory fibres (see text)

Details are found in Kim & Molnar (1979).

From these four response measures average rate (RØ/SR) and phase locking response measures (R1/SR or R1/RØ) were derived to allow comparison between the different fibres. These response measures were plotted as a function of BF since the spatial distribution of CF on the caiman basilar papilla is unknown. Data point selection depended upon estimates for the standard deviation of amplitude {RLIMIT = $\sqrt{2/N}$} and phase {PLIMIT = 1/A · RLIMIT} were A is the normalized phase locking measure (R1/SR or R1/RØ, see Littlefield, 1973; Pfeiffer & Kim, 1975). Values of RLIMIT accepted were from 0.100 - 0.058 and of PLIMIT between 3.142 - 0.220 rad.

3. RESULTS

The data presented here are based on one of the experiments where 409 neurones (about 7 % of the total population) were recorded from one auditory nerve. Fig. 1 illustrates typical results. The stimulus consisted of a steady pure tone of 354 Hz at 35 dB attenuation. The most restrictive selection criteria were applied. RLIMIT was 0.058 (i.e. period histograms based on less than 600 spikes were discarded). PLIMIT was 0.220 rad (0.035 · 2 π rad = 12.6 deg.). The first panel of fig. 1 (RØ/SR) is the normalized average response rate as a function of the neurones' BF. With the intensity level used nearly all of the fibres were activated. The second panel (R1/RØ) and the third one (R1/SR) give a phase locking measure for the stimulation frequency (remember R1 is the amplitude of the phase locked response in the period histogram and RØ is the average rate). It can be seen that a wide range of the fibres is activated by the stimulus used. In the lowermost panel the phase P1 is plotted. Negative values represent phase lag. As the cumulative phase is unknown the

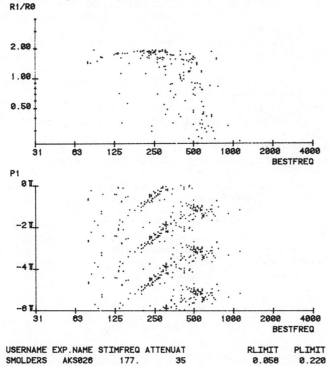

USERNAME	EXP.NAME	STIMFREQ	ATTENUAT	RLIMIT	PLIMIT
SMOLDERS	AKS026	177.	35	0.058	0.220

Fig. 2. Phase data with stimulation of 177 Hz for comparison with figure 1.

points were plotted modulo 2 π. Panel 4 shows that there are significant phase changes in fibres of BF near stimulus frequency where phase lock is high. The phase lag decreases towards higher BFs at about 1.7 π rad/oct.

If stimulation frequencies are lower or higher than the 354 Hz used for fig. 1 it becomes clear that there is hardly a phase change in neurones the BF of which is much lower or much higher than the stimulus frequency. This is illustrated in fig. 2 where stimulation was performed with 177 Hz.

4. CONCLUSIONS

The data do not exclude a travelling wave mechanism in caiman and would rather be compatible with the presence of a travelling wave.

Acknowledgement

This work was supported by the Deutsche Forschungsgemeinschaft (SFB 45).

REFERENCES

Eatock, R.A. & Manley, G.A. (1976). Temperature effects on single auditory nerve fiber responses. *J. Acoust. Soc. Am.* 60, S 80.

Emde, C. & Klinke, R. (1977). Does absolute pitch depend on an internal clock? In: *Inner Ear Biology*, (M. Portmann and J.M. Aran, eds). pp 145 - 146. INSERM, Vol 68, Paris.

Kim, D.O. & Molnar, C.E. (1979). A population study of cochlear nerve fibers: Comparison of spatial distributions of average-rate and phase-locking measures of responses to single tones. *J. Neurophysiol.* 42, 16 - 30.

Klinke, R. & Pause, M. (1977). The performance of a primitive hearing organ of the cochlea type: Primary fibre studies in the caiman. In: *Psychophysics and Physiology of Hearing*. (E.F. Evans and J.P. Wilson, eds). pp 100 - 112. Academic Press, London.

Klinke, R. & Pause, M. (1980). Discharge properties of primary auditory fibres in caiman crocodilus: Comparisons and contrasts to the mammalian auditory nerve. *Exp. Brain Res.* 38, 137 - 150.

Klinke, R. & Smolders, J. (1977). Effect of temperature shift on tuning properties. Addendum to Klinke & Pause (1977).

Littlefield, W.M. (1973). Investigations of the linear range of the peripheral auditory system. *D. Sc. Thesis*, Washington University, St. Louis, Mo.

Moffat, A.J.M. & Capranica, R.R. (1976). Effects of temperature on the response properties of auditory nerve fibers in the American toad (Bufo americanus). *J. Acoust. Soc. Am.* 60, S 80.

Peake, W.T. & Ling, A. (1979). Basilar membrane motion in the alligator lizard: Its relation to tonotopic organization and frequency selectivity. Submitted to *J. Acoust. Soc. Am.*

Pfeiffer, R.R. & Kim, D.O. (1975). Cochlear nerve fiber responses: Distribution along the cochlear partition. *J. Acoust. Soc. Am.* 58, 867 - 869.

Smolders, J. & Klinke, R. (1977). Effect of temperature changes on tuning properties of primary auditory fibres in caiman and cat. In: *Inner Ear Biology*, (M. Portmann and J.M. Aran, eds). pp 125 - 126. INSERM, Vol 68, Paris.

Section II
Frequency and Time Resolution

One of the main functions ascribed to the peripheral part of the auditory system is the performance of frequency analysis on incoming acoustic signals. From direct measurements and calculations on cochlear mechanics (section I) and cochlear nerve phsysiology, the first stage is already evident. Further psychophysical, physiological and behavioural evidence is given in the present section. This information is mainly based on tuning curves obtained with various techniques. Different factors affecting the shape of tuning curves have been studied, like the physiological conditions of the preparation, exposure to intense sounds, the effects of hearing impairment, and of age. Time resolution is coupled with frequency resolution. Temporal aspects, such as cochlear response time, decay of masking, are dealt with in the second part.

THE USE OF PSYCHOPHYSICAL TUNING CURVES TO MEASURE FREQUENCY SELECTIVITY

D.L. Weber, D. Johnson-Davies and R.D. Patterson

MRC Applied Psychology Unit, 15 Chaucer Road, Cambridge, England

1. INTRODUCTION

The traditional physiological tuning curve shows the level that a sinusoid must have to elicit a criterion firing rate in a single fibre of the eighth nerve (e.g. Kiang, 1965). This relation typically has the form of a V, and the point of the V defines the fibre's characteristic frequency. Since the measurement is made in a primary auditory fibre and since the criterion is gross firing rate, it seems reasonable to use the tuning curve as a measure of the frequency selectivity provided by the cochlea. Vogten (1974) and Zwicker (1974) pointed out that it might be possible to obtain an analogous psychophysical measure in humans by presenting a low-level sinusoidal probe with constant frequency and amplitude, and tracing out the locus of the sinusoid with just sufficient power to mask the probe. It was argued that if the probe was near absolute threshold there would be minimal spread of the probe's excitation. In this case, the psychophysical tuning curve would be sufficiently analogous to the physiological tuning curve to justify use of the psychophysical curve as a measure of auditory frequency selectivity. Indeed, the gross characteristics of the two types of tuning curve are quite similar; both exhibit a V-shape and the asymmetry in the slopes of the two branches is the same in both cases. Unfortunately, the analogy breaks down under closer examination because the psychophysical measure reflects not only peripheral but also central processing. There are at least two aspects to this general problem as evidenced by a) the phenomenon of off-frequency listening, and b) the phenomena associated with interactions between the probe and masker. An example of the latter is beats which listeners will use whenever they assist probe detection. This improvement, which alters the shape of the tip of the tuning curve, is presumably based on temporal information in the neural firing pattern -- information that is not represented in the gross firing rate. This paper is primarily concerned with problems arising from masker/probe interactions but we will begin with a brief review of the off-frequency listening issue for perspective.

a) Off-frequency listening

Stated in terms of a simple filter-bank model, this problem with the psychophysical tuning curve arises because the central processor, whose mandate is to maximise performance, uses the information obtained from all of the filters in the bank, not just the one centred on the probe. And whenever the central processor finds it efficient to use different members of the auditory filter-bank in different conditions of the experiment, the analogy between the psychophysical and physiological tuning curve will fail. Johnson-Davies and Patterson (1979) demonstrated that off-frequency listening plays a major role in these experiments by comparing the traditional psychophysical tuning curve with a 'restricted-listening' tuning curve. The latter tuning curve was generated just like the former except that a second, low-level, stationary masker was positioned either 0.2 kHz below or above the probe. The probe was a 2.0-kHz sinusoid presented at about 15 dB SL. The stationary masker alone did not mask the probe. The individual data for two of the listeners have been re-plotted in Fig. 1; the experimental paradigm is presented schematically in the

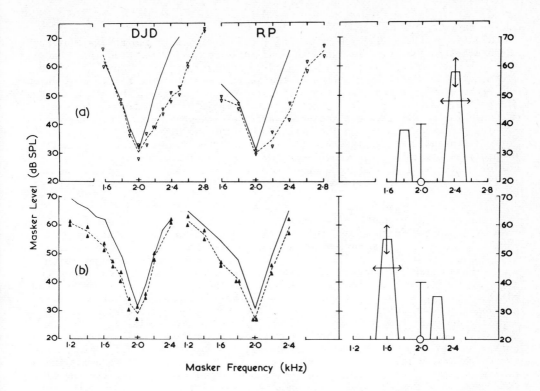

Figure 1. Comparison of traditional and restricted-listening tuning curves (faint solid lines and dashed lines with symbols, respectively). The stationary masker frequency was (a) 1.8 or (b) 2.2 kHz, and its level was either (a) 10 or (b) 15 dB below the corresponding traditional tuning-curve level.

righthand column of the figure -- arrows indicate the experimental variables and the probe is identified by a circle on the baseline. The figure shows that when the primary and stationary maskers were on the same side of the signal, the stationary masker had little effect, as would be expected. But when they were on opposite sides of the probe, the stationary masker depressed the tuning curve dramatically.

Johnson-Davies and Patterson (1979) explained their findings in terms of excitation patterns. Beginning with the traditional psychophysical tuning curve, they argued that the probe has a reasonably wide excitation pattern even when presented at a low level, that when the primary masker is below the probe frequency it swamps the lower portion of the excitation pattern, and thus, that the data on the lower branch of the traditional tuning curve actually reflect activity occurring a significant distance above the probe frequency. The insertion of the stationary masker above the probe restricts the listening region to the area close to the probe with the result that when the primary masker is below the probe frequency, a much lower masker level is required to render the probe inaudible. Similarly, a low-level stationary masker inserted below the probe frequency restricts listening when the primary masker is above the probe, and so depresses the upper branch of the tuning curve. The authors conclude that the data on the two branches of the traditional tuning curve reflect information carried in different populations of neurons, and that, if the psychophysical tuning curve for the probe frequency could be measured in isolation, it would have a rounded tip and be almost twice as wide as the traditional tuning curve.

In terms of the filter-bank analogy, the problem with the traditional psychophysical tuning curve is that when the masker is below the probe frequency, the listener can be expected to use a filter centred somewhat above the probe frequency because it could attenuate the masker more than the filter centred on the probe without attenuating the probe significantly. Thus, the off-frequency filter would provide a better signal-to-noise ratio on which to base a response. And when the masker is above the probe a filter somewhat below the probe would provide the best signal-to-noise ratio. Thus the two branches of the tuning curve represent different groups of filters and the two sets of data cannot properly be joined at the probe frequency. The insertion of the stationary masker on the side of the probe opposite the primary masker eliminates the advantage of off-frequency listening and so restricts the listener to the probe region.

b) Masker/probe interactions

The original psychophysical tuning curves were generated in a simultaneous masking paradigm; in this case the interaction of the signal and masker can give rise to beats, combination tones, and suppression, all of which may influence the shape of the tuning curve. The beats can be eliminated by using a narrow-band noise as masker and/or probe , the combination tones can often be masked with a secondary, low-level masker, and the effects of both can be minimised by using very brief, low-level probes, but suppression cannot be avoided in simultaneous masking. Suppression of the probe does not occur in forward masking; however, forward masking introduces its own difficulties. In particular, threshold changes with probe duration, temporal separation between the masker and probe , and overall masker level, so that a variety of tuning curves can be generated for the same probe frequency. Furthermore, forward-masking tuning curves are still subject to the problem of off-frequency listening (O'Loughlin and Moore, 1979). The same temporal difficulties arise with the pulsation-threshold method. In addition, there is new evidence (Moore, 1980) to indicate that the interpretation of forward masking data is further complicated by the fact that there are pitch changes at the termination of the masker which the listener can use to perform the task in some instances. Thus, until we can evaluate the significance of the effects of the stimulus parameters in forward masking and control the pitch-shift cues, the psychophysical tuning curve will remain an interesting analogy but an impractical method for estimating peripheral frequency selectivity.

In this paper we review two experiments designed to compare the traditional psychophysical tuning curve produced with a sinusoidal masker with the tuning curve generated by a narrow-band noise masker. The first experiment was intended to assess the effect of beats on the shape of the tip of the traditional tuning curve. A simultaneous-masking paradigm was used with a long-duration probe (400 ms). The experiment, reported by Johnson-Davies (1979), also examines the effect of probe level. In the second experiment (Weber, 1980) the effect of beats is further investigated by reducing probe duration to 35 and 5 ms, and the simultaneous tuning curves are then compared with their forward-masking counterparts to assess the role of suppression in these situations.

2. METHOD

The two experiments had similar methods of stimulus generation and similar procedures. As in Johnson-Davies and Patterson (1979), the narrow-band noise masker resulted from the multiplication of low-pass filtered white noise and a sinusoid. The masker bandwidth was twice the -3 dB cutoff of the filtered noise; the frequency of the sinusoid was the centre frequency of the noise masker. Individual programmable attenuators varied the masker level for each observer. The probe was cosine gated with 100-ms (Johnson-Davies) or 5-ms (Weber) rise/fall times. In simultaneous masking, the masker occurred for at least 200-ms before and after the probe presentation. In forward masking, the offset-onset time measured at the half-pressure (6-dB down) values was 5 ms (0 ms between the 0-pressure values).

Thresholds for young normal observers were estimated using an adaptive two-interval forced-choice procedure after Levitt (1971). A typical run required roughly 80 trials and contained 15-20 turnarounds whose average provided the threshold estimate for that run. Each datum reported here is the mean of at least two such estimates per observer averaged across at least four observers.

Johnson-Davies used a 2-kHz sinusoidal probe at 10, 20, and 30 dB SL. The bandwidth of the noise masker in this experiment was 100 Hz. A low-level, low-pass noise prevented the detection of combination tones. Weber used a probe frequency of 1 kHz. The bandwidth of the noise masker was 50 Hz. The 5-ms probe was presented at 38.5 dB SPL (power) for all observers. The 35-ms probe was presented at two levels to provide both equal-energy and equal-power comparisons with the 5-ms probe; the 35-ms probe levels were, therefore, 30.0 and 38.5 dB SPL (power) respectively. These levels ranged from 5 to 16 dB SL for different observers. There were no audible combination tones in this experiment.

3. RESULTS AND DISCUSSION

Probe levels of 10, 20, and 30 dB SL yielded the three tuning-curve comparisons shown in Fig. 2; the noise-masker data are represented by squares and the sinusoidal-masker data by circles. For masker frequencies immediately above and below the 2-kHz probe, noise is a better masker than a sinusoid regardless of probe level. For masker frequencies roughly .8 to .95 times the probe frequency, noise is a better masker at the higher probe levels, but the difference is much smaller at the lowest level. For masker frequencies below .8 times the probe frequency, the difference between the two types of masker actually reverses! No differences are observed for maskers above 1.05 times the probe frequency. A similar pattern appears in the simultaneous-masking tuning curves for a 35-ms probe at approximately 15-20 dB SL (Figs. 3a and 3b). The noise produces more masking than the sinusoid in the region of .8 to 1.15 times the probe frequency, 1 kHz. The reversal in the effectiveness of the two types of maskers for frequencies below .8 times the probe is not, however, so clear. These differences between sinusoidal and noise maskers are in excellent agreement with those present in the classic masking patterns of Egan and Hake (1950) who attribute the difference near the probe frequency to the presence or absence of beating between probe and masker. This hypothesis is further supported by the 5-ms simultaneous-masking data (Fig. 3c) and all of the forward-masking data (Fig. 3d-f) where these differences between the two types of tuning curve do not appear.

Comparisons of tuning curves in simultaneous and forward masking (Wightman et al, 1977; Moore, 1978; Vogten, 1978) have shown that except for maskers near the probe frequency, forward masking requires much higher masker levels than simultaneous masking. This difference is usually attributed to a nonlinear interaction between masker and probe which occurs only when they are simultaneously present and which tends to make probe detection more difficult (Fastl, 1975). One such process is suppression (Houtgast, 1972, 1974), and a simple explanation of the tuning curves is that maskers near the probe frequency mask or swamp the probe, but that other 'maskers' actually suppress the probe. Thus, tuning curves in simultaneous masking confound results from two different processes whereas only one process is represented in forward-masking tuning curves (e.g. Wightman et al, 1977).

Accepting such an explanation, the difference between noise and sinusoidal maskers in the lower branch of the tuning curve would be interpreted as a difference in the amount of suppression they produce. But this hypothesis

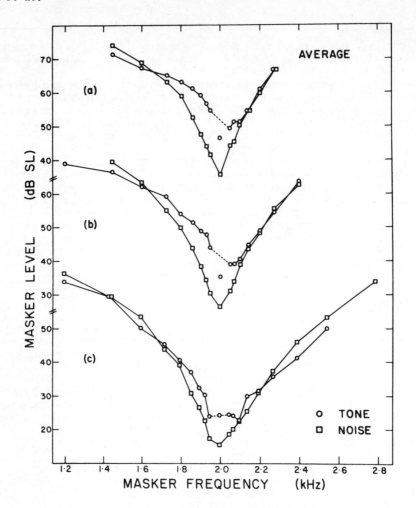

*Figure 2.   Psychophysical tuning curves generated with a sinusoidal masker (0)
or a narrow-band noise masker (□).   The probe was a 2.0-kHz sinusoid at
(a) 30, (b) 20, or (c) 10 dB SL.   The data show the average thresholds for five
listeners.*

encounters two difficulties: First, the relative effectiveness of the two
types of suppressors varies with the frequency difference between masker and
probe. Second, the difference in the effectiveness of the two types of
suppressor disappears at the brief signal duration (Fig. 3c). Although it is
possible that there is an interaction between suppressor variability and
effective suppressor level that could account for the first problem, the
difference in the amount of suppression should also appear with the 5-ms probe
and it does not.

 That the difference in the low-frequency branch appears for the 400- and
35-ms probes but not for the 5-ms probe suggests that the suppression interpretation is invalid - a conclusion that receives further support from the
absence of a difference between the low-frequency branches of the simultaneous-
and forward-masking curves associated with the 5-ms probe (compare Figs. 3c
and 3f). Although the data for the 35-ms probes show the usual difference
between simultaneous and forward masking (for maskers .8 to .95 times the probe

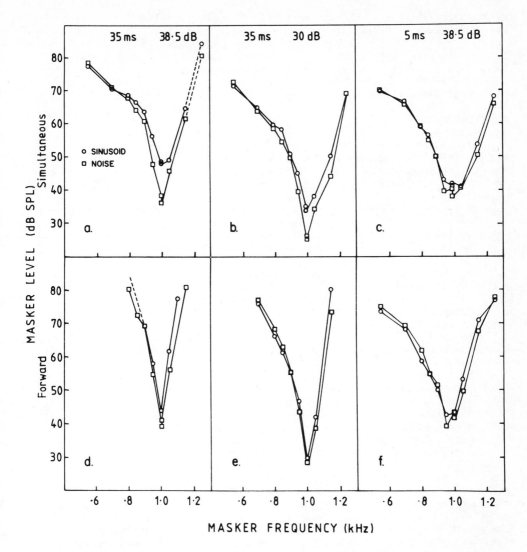

Figure 3. Psychophysical tuning curves generated with a sinusoidal masker (O) or a narrow-band noise masker (□). The probe was a 1.0-kHz sinusoid with a duration of either 35 ms, in which case the probe level was 38.5 or 30 dB SPL (first two columns), or 5 ms, in which case the probe level was 38.5 dB SPL (third column). The data show the average threshold for four listeners. The simultaneous- and forward-masking results are plotted in the upper and lower halves of the figure respectively.

frequency, the average difference is about 6 dB), the 5-ms data show at best a much reduced difference (no difference for maskers in the .8 to .95 range). Wightman et al (1977) used a 10-ms probe and show a small difference; all other experimenters use probes 20 ms or longer, and report data similar to our 35-ms data.

Although Duifhuis (1973) has convincingly summarised psychophysical measures of forward masking, and Harris (1977) has shown parallel behaviour in the eighth nerve response, this information only applies to maskers and probes

of the same frequency. We have very little information about the effect of
parameters such as masker level, probe duration, and offset-onset time for
off-frequency maskers. Thus, it may be that the apparent loss of the suppression effect, i.e., the difference between simultaneous and forward masking, may
be a characteristic of off-frequency forward-masking. But it is difficult to
see how this could account for the disappearance of the difference between
sinusoidal and noise maskers at brief probe durations in simultaneous masking.

4. CONCLUSIONS

The analogy between the physiological tuning curve and the traditional
psychophysical tuning curve is not sufficiently strong to support the use of
the psychophysical tuning curve as a measure of peripheral frequency selectivity. The difficulty is that the psychophysical measure reflects central as well
as peripheral processing. In particular:

1. It is often to the listener's advantage to base decisions concerning the
    presence of the probe on activity in frequency channels below or above the
    nominal probe channel. As a result, off-frequency listening occurs and
    the traditional tuning curve overestimates the frequency selectivity
    available.
2. For some combinations of masker and probe the stimulus contains timing
    information (beats/modulation) that provides the listener with a cue
    that does not exist in the physiological tuning-curve experiment. The
    listener's use of the timing cue raises and narrows the tip of the psycho-
    physical tuning curve artificially.
3. The co-existence of the masker and probe in the traditional paradigm means
    that the swamping and suppression effects of the masker are confounded in
    this case.

The traditional paradigm can be improved by adding a low-level stationary
masker to restrict off-frequency listening, by adding a low background noise to
mask potential combination tones, and by using brief probes and narrow-band
noise maskers to reduce and obscure the beats between the probe and masker.
But the confounding of the suppression and swamping effects of the masker cannot be avoided in simultaneous masking.

Since suppression does not effect the signal in forward masking, it would
appear that if the stimulus parameters are chosen carefully, forward masking
can provide an accurate estimate of masker excitation in isolation (i.e. the
swamping effect without the suppression effect). When the probe is brief and
the masker/probe separation is small, the forward- and simultaneous-masking
paradigms produce essentially the same threshold values (Figs. 3c and 3f) and
the growth of forward masking is very similar to that of simultaneous masking.
Thus we would suggest that the psychophysical tuning curve most analogous to
the physiological tuning curve is the forward-masking, restricted-listening
tuning curve, generated with narrow-band noise maskers and a brief probe that
is separated from the masker by a minimal gap.

ACKNOWLEDGMENTS

*Author DLW was supported by a grant from the National Institutes of Health,
Public Health Service, United States Department of Health Education and
Welfare. Author DJD was supported by a grant from the Science Research Council
of Great Britain.*

REFERENCES

Duifhuis, H.(1973). Consequences of Peripheral Frequency Selectivity for Non-
    Simultaneous Masking. *J. Acoust. Soc. Am.* 54, 1471-1488.

Egan, J.P. and Hake, H.W.(1950). On the masking pattern of a simple auditory stimulus. *J. Acoust. Soc. Am.* 22, 622-630.

Fastl, H.(1975). Pulsation Patterns of Sinusoids vs Critical Band Noise. *Perception and Psychophysics* 18, 95-97.

Harris, D.M.(1977). Forward masking and recovery from short-term adaptation in single auditory nerve fibres. Doctoral dissertation, Northwestern University, Evanston Illinois.

Houtgast, T.(1972). Psychophysical evidence of lateral inhibition in hearing. *J. Acoust. Soc. Am.* 51, 1885-1894.

Houtgast, T.(1974). Lateral suppression in hearing. Doctoral dissertation, University of Amsterdam, The Netherlands.

Johnson-Davies, D. and Patterson, R.D.(1979). Psychophysical tuning curves: Restricting the listening band to the signal region. *J. Acoust. Soc. Am.* 65, 765-770.

Johnson-Davies, D.(1979). Psychophysical tuning-curves obtained with narrow-band noise maskers. Paper presented at a meeting of the British Society of Audiology, Cambridge, England, September 27-28.

Kiang, N. Y.-S., Watanabe, T., Thomas, E.C. and Clark, L.F.(1965). *Discharge Patterns of Single Fibers in the Cat's Auditory Nerve.* MIT Research Monograph No. 35 (Technology, Cambridge, MA).

Levitt, H.(1971). Transformed up-down methods in psychoacoustics. *J. Acoust. Soc. Am.* 49, 467-477.

Moore, B.C.J.(1978). Psychophysical Tuning Curves Measured in Simultaneous and Forward Masking. *J. Acoust. Soc. Am.* 63, 524-532.

Moore, B.C.J.(1980). Detection Cues in Forward Masking. In: *Psychophysical, Physiological and Behavioural Studies in Hearing.* (G. van den Brink and F.A. Bilsen, eds). Delft University Press, Delft.

O'Loughlin, B.J. and Moore, B.C.J.(1979). Restricted-listening tuning-curves in forward masking. Paper presented at a meeting of the British Society of Audiology, Cambridge, England, September 27-28.

Vogten, L.L.M.(1974). Pure-Tone Masking; a New Result from a New Method. In: *Facts and Models in Hearing.* (E. Zwicker and E. Terhardt, eds). pp. 142-155. Springer-Verlag, Berlin.

Vogten, L.L.M.(1978). Simultaneous Pure-Tone Masking: The Dependence of Masking Asymmetries on Intensity. *J. Acoust. Soc. Am.* 63, 1509-1519.

Wightman, F., McGee, T. and Kramer, M.(1977). Factors Influencing Frequency Selectivity in Normal and Hearing Impaired Listeners. In: *Psychophysics and Physiology of Hearing.* (E.F. Evans and J.P. Wilson, eds). pp.295-306. Academic, London.

Weber, D.(1980). The effects of probe duration on tuning curves generated with sinusoidal and narrow-band noise maskers. In preparation.

Zwicker, E.(1974). On a Psychoacoustic Equivalent of Tuning Curves. In: *Facts and Models of Hearing.* (E. Zwicker and E. Terhardt, eds). pp. 132-141. Springer-Verlag, Berlin.

COMMENT

COMMENT ON "The use of psychophysical tuning curves to measure frequency selectivity" (D.L. Weber, D. Johnson-Davies and R.D. Patterson).

J. Verschuure
Dept. of Oto-, Rhino-, Laryngology, Erasmus University Rotterdam,
P.O. Box 1738, Rotterdam, The Netherlands.

Weber *et al.* discuss in their paper the pros and cons of simultaneous masking, postmasking and pulsation; they stick to simultaneous masking for the time being. I discussed the pros and cons of the methods in my thesis (Verschuure, 1978) and came to the conclusion that for studying frequency selectivity pulsation is the best method. The difference in outcome can be explained from the following arguments:

Firstly, Weber *et al.* state that pulsation would suffer from the same problems with regard to temporal conditions as postmasking does. Verschuure *et al.* (1976) explored the existence conditions of the continuity phenomenon. They showed that within certain limits the pulsation pattern does not depend on temporal presentation conditions. Secondly, pitch cues are important in postmasking but not in pulsation (Verschuure and Brocaar, this volume). Thirdly, the problem of off-frequency detection should not be used against postmasking and pulsation. There is evidence of its presence in all three methods. I described a model (Verschuure, 1977, 1978) in which it could be taken into account in a quantitative way. I think this is also possible in postmasking but not in simultaneous masking (Verschuure, 1980).

As last remark a theoretical consideration. In interpreting masking patterns. we use the superposition theorem. In the theorem we assume that the activity of two sine waves (stimulus and probe) is the sum of the activities of the separate sine waves. This cannot be fulfilled in masking because of nonlinear phenomena as suppression and combination tones. The superposition theorem is not needed for interpreting pulsation patterns, because of the alternated presentation of the sine waves.

For clarity I want to stress that I don't want to suggest that simultaneous masking is not a useful method. The choice of method depends largely on the question on which an answer is to be found. I think that simultaneous masking is not a very good method to investigate the frequency resolving power of the auditory system; it can be an excellent method to investigate e.g. loudness summation.

A second point of the comment regards the use of an output method (psychophysical tuning curve) for the measurement of frequency selectivity. This method is often used because of the similarity of its results with neurophysiological tuning curves or frequency threshold curves. We know, however, that the auditory system is nonlinear in many ways, including a change of the slopes of excitation patterns with level (Verschuure, 1977, 1978, 1980): this introduces the possibility of off-frequency detection. The slope-level nonlinearity is apparent in simultaneous masking (e.g. Wegel and Lane, 1924), postmasking (e.g. Gardner, 1947) and pulsation. It will depend upon the detection criteria used in the various methods whether the nonlinearity will actually result in off-frequency detection. I think it cannot be ruled out beforehand. The nonlinearity is governed by the pulsator/masker level. In the determination of output patterns this level is a variable and thus the nonlinearity changes with the variable level; this could lead to strong overestimations of the tuning properties. If we use an input method, one possible source of error is eliminated, although off-frequency detection will still be a complicating matter.

REFERENCES

Gardner, M.B. (1947). Short duration auditory fatigue as a method of classifying hearing impairment. *J. Acoust. Soc. Am.* 19, 178-190.
Verschuure, J. (1977). Pulsation threshold patterns and neurophysiological tuning. In: *Psychophysics and physiology of hearing.* E.F. Evans &

J.P. Wilson Eds, Academic Press, London. pp. 237-245.

Verschuure, J. (1978). Auditory excitation patterns. *Doctoral thesis Erasmus University Rotterdam*, W.D. Meinema B.V., Delft, The Netherlands.

Verschuure, J. (1980). Pulsation patterns and nonlinear auditory tuning. In press: *Hearing Research*, Proc. symposium on nonlinear and active mechanical processes in the cochlea, D.T. Kemp & S.D. Anderson Eds.

Verschuure, J., Rodenburg, M., Maas, A.J.J. (1976). Presentation conditions of the pulsation threshold method. *Acustica* 35, 47-54.

Wegel, R.L., Lane, C.E. (1924) The auditory masking of one pure tone by another and its probable relation to the dynamics of the inner ear. *Phys. Rev.* 23, 266-285.

REPLY TO COMMENT OF J. VERSCHUURE

D.L. Weber and R.D. Patterson.
MRC Applied Psychology Unit, Cambridge, England.

There appears to be some misunderstanding. Verschuure seems to criticize us for advocating the use of simultaneous masking when, in fact, we recommend the use of nonsimultaneous techniques in order to obtain the best analogue to the physiological tuning curve. However, except for this, we interpret his comments as support for the arguments which we have brought together in our paper. Many of these issues have been discussed by others in earlier papers, and we apologize to any who feel that they should have been acknowledged. We regret that Verschuure was unable to attend this meeting since we are confident that our apparent confusions could have been quickly resolved.

Verschuure points out, as most of us would agree, that the appropriate method of measuring frequency selectivity depends on the use to which the attenuation characteristic is to be put. In this paper we have restricted our discussion to the question of how to obtain the tuning curve most analogous to the physiological, single-unit curve and we have decided in favour of non-simultaneous masking. For the sake of completeness we would like, briefly, to mention the other side of the issue, raised by several people at this symposium (Wilson, Zwicker, Pick and Moore).

If the purpose of measuring auditory frequency selectivity is to obtain a frequency weighting function that can subsequently be used to predict masking, then simultaneous methods of measurement are more appropriate because most everyday masking is simultaneous masking. Furthermore, the most appropriate frequency weighting function is probably not the psychophysical tuning curve but rather the "auditory filter shape" as estimated by Patterson and Nimmo-Smith (1980), Houtgast (1977), or Pick, Evans and Wilson (1977).

REFERENCES

Houtgast, T. (1977). Auditory Filter characteristics derived from direct-masking data and pulsation-threshold data with a ripple-noise masker. *J. Acoust. Soc. Am.* 62, 409-415.

Patterson, R.D. and Nimmo-Smith, I. (1980). Off-frequency listening and auditory filter asymmetry. *J. Acoust. Soc. Am.* 67, 229-245.

Pick, G.F., Evans, E.F. and Wilson, J.P. (1977). Frequency resolution in patients with hearing loss of cochlear origin. In: *Psychophysics and Physiology of Hearing*. (E.F. Evans and J.P. Wilson, eds.). pp. 273-282. Academic Press, London.

COMMENT ON: "The use of psychophysical tuning curves to measure frequency
selectivity" (D.L. Weber, D. Johnson-Davies and R.D. Patterson)

D.A. Nelson
Dept. of Otolaryngology, University of Minnesota, Minneapolis, U.S.A.

It has been suggested by Weber, Johnson-Davies and Patterson (1980) and
by Moore (1980) that forward-masked tuning curves are subject to the problem
of off-frequency listening. That problem is particularly evident in forward-
masked tuning curves obtained with high sensation-level probe tones. One such
series of forward-masked tuning curves, obtained at progressively higher
probe-tone levels using the method described by Nelson and Turner (1980), is
shown in Fig. 1. At low probe levels the tuning curve is sharp. As probe level
is increased from 10 dB Sensation Level (SL) to 40 dB SL the tuning curves
become less sharp. More masker level is, of course, required to mask higher
level probe tones. But, since the slope of the growth of forward masking is
more gradual for maskers near the probe in frequency than for maskers remote
from the probe in frequency (Widin and Viemeister, 1979), the rate of increase
in masker level required to mask increased probe levels is much greater for
maskers nearest to the probe frequency.

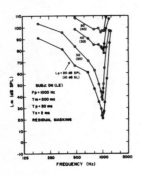

One explanation for broader tuning curves at the
higher probe levels involves the concept of off-frequency listening. At higher probe levels, the spectral
side lobes of the short 20-msec probe tones are well
above detection threshold at their respective frequency
regions. Consequently, the level of the masker must be
increased sufficiently to mask not only the energy at
the probe frequency but also the "splatter" at remote
frequencies.

If this is the case, the introduction of an
appropriate additional masking noise should eliminate
much of the information contained at off frequencies
and should result in a spectrally-restricted
forward-masked tuning curve similar to that obtained
at very low sensation levels in quiet, where the off-
frequency splatter information was well below detection threshold.

*Fig. 1 Forward-masked
tuning curves at four
different probe levels.*

The effects of adding a background noise are
shown in Fig. 2. The continuous white noise was 10 dB
less than the level of white noise required to just mask each probe tone, i.e.,
the probe tones were all at 10 dB sensation level in white noise. Two forward-
masked tuning curves are displayed for each of three probe sound pressure
levels. The top tuning curve in each case was obtained in quiet and the bottom
curve was obtained in background noise. The difference between the two tuning
curves is shaded to show the effect of the additional masking noise.

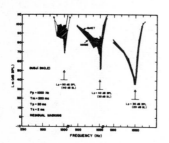

*Fig. 2
Forward-masked tuning curves in quiet (top curves)
and in the presence of background noise (bottom
curves) at a noise level 10 dB below the noise
level that just masks each probe tone. The shaded
area shows the effects of masking the presumed
off-frequency listening cues.*

Presumably, by masking the off-frequency
components of the 20 msec probe tones, the
characteristics of the tuning curves for high-
level probe tones were *nearly* restored to the
sharp characteristics obtained with low sound

pressure level probe tones.

The fact that the restricted-listening tuning curves for high-level probe tones were still characteristically different from the low-level (20 dB SPL) tuning curve obtained in quiet (Fig. 1) is probably due, in part, to the steep rate of the growth of masking produced by maskers at frequencies below the probe frequency (Verschuure, 1979). Furthermore, it should be pointed out that the detection problems posed by the pitch similarity of masker and probe, for maskers nearest to the probe frequency (Moore, 1980), have not been eliminated from these tuning curves; therefore, the tips of the low sensation level forward-masked tuning curves, either in quiet or in background noise, may be excessively sharp.

These results not only support Weber, Johnson-Davies and Patterson's (1980) and Moore's (1980) contention that forward-masked tuning curves are subject to the problems of off-frequency listening, they also raise certain general questions about the growth of forward masking. If the growth of forward masking is calculated for maskers near the probe frequency in Fig. 2, it is seen that the addition of background noise increased the slope of masking. Furthermore, that increase in the slope of forward masking was greater for tonal maskers close to the probe frequency than for tonal maskers remote from the probe frequency. Perhaps some of the nonlinear behaviour of forward masking can also be explained by the concepts of off-frequency listening.

Acknowledgements

The research reported above was supported by grants from NINCDS.

REFERENCES

Moore, B.C.J. (1980). Comment on: Pulsation patterns of two-tone stimuli. (Verschuure and Brocaar). *This volume.*

Nelson, D.A. and Turner, C.W. (1980). Decay of masking and frequency resolution in sensorineural hearing-impaired listeners. *This volume.*

Weber, D.L., Johnson-Davies, D. and Patterson, R.D. (1980). The use of psychophysical tuning curves to measure frequency selectivity. *This volume.*

Widin, G.P. and Viemeister, N.F. (1979). Intensive and temporal effects in pure-tone forward masking. *J. Acoust. Soc. Am.* 66, 388-395.

PSYCHOPHYSICAL FREQUENCY RESOLUTION IN THE
CAT STUDIED WITH FORWARD MASKING

J.O. Pickles

Neurocommunications Research Unit,
Birmingham University, Birmingham, B15 2TJ, England

1. INTRODUCTION

The concept of the critical band was first put forward by Fletcher (Fletcher, 1940) and was later elaborated by Zwicker (e.g. Zwicker, 1954) and
others. It was suggested that the auditory stimulus was subjected to a filtering process early in the auditory system, and that the bandwidths and slopes
of the filters provided the basis for psychophysical frequency resolution over
a wide variety of auditory tasks (Fletcher, 1940; Zwicker, 1970; Scharf,
1970). In a common experiment to measure the critical bandwidth, the subject
detects a signal against a simultaneously-presented masker of complex spectrum, and the signal threshold is measured as the masker spectrum is varied.
Fletcher originally suggested that the critical bandwidth so defined was equal
to the frequency resolution bandwidth of the basilar membrane at the corresponding frequency. In a recent formulation of such a hypothesis, Evans c.s. (1973)
suggested that critical bands were direct analogues of the excitatory tuning
curves of single neurones of the auditory nerve. This implies that the psychophysical critical band filter function should have the same bandwidth and filter shape as the tuning curves of the corresponding primary auditory neurones.
Such hypotheses have however been attacked as a result of the realisation
that when two or more frequency components are simultaneously presented, there
will be interactions due to two-tone suppression in the auditory system (Houtgast, 1972, 1974a,b). It has been suggested that as a result the psychophysical
resolution bandwidths derived from simultaneous masking experiments will be
wider than those of the neural representation (Houtgast, 1974a,b; Vogten,
1978). Non-simultaneous masking techniques such as forward masking are not open
to the same objection, and Houtgast suggested that they would be able to give a
more accurate picture of the neural representation. In agreement with this
view, resolution bandwidths derived from non-simultaneous masking techniques
indicate a bandwidth of frequency resolution about half that shown by simultaneous masking. In support, Pickles (1975, 1979) and Pickles and Comis (1976)
showed in the cat that the effective bandwidths of single fibres of the auditory nerve were one half to one third of the effective bandwidth of the cat's
critical band, measured behaviourally by simultaneous masking techniques in the
same frequency range. In the present experiment, an attempt has been made to
test Houtgast's suggestion more directly, and to see whether non-simultaneous
masking techniques in the cat would give resolution bandwidths closer to those
of auditory nerve fibres.
Psychophysical frequency resolution bandwidths were measured behaviourally in the cat by the method of Zwicker (1954). A narrowband signal was flanked
in frequency by two tonal maskers, and the signal threshold measured as a
function of the frequency separation of the maskers. Resolution bandwidths,
determined by both simultaneous and forward masking, were compared with the
bandwidths of resolution of single fibres of the auditory nerve. The experiments were performed at 1 and 2 kHz, and the maskers were presented at 50 dB
per tone.

2. METHODS

a) *Measurement of thresholds*

Cats were tested free-field by avoidance conditioning in a box with a tiltable grid floor, as described by Pickles (1979). The cats were initially trained to rock the floor of the box on presentation of the warning signal, a 10-sec train of tone pips, in order to avoid a shock given through the floor. Performance was established with 1-kHz tone pips at 90 dB SPL, and once the avoidance response was established, the intensity was gradually reduced. Signals were presented randomly on one third of trials, the others being dummies and used to assess the false positive detection rate.

Thresholds were measured by discrete-trial tracking with a 3-dB step size, and testing was continued until performance had reached equilibrium over 10 trials; that is, until the intensity presented on any trial was within 1 step of the intensity presented 10 trials earlier. After absolute thresholds had been obtained, continuous maskers were introduced, and critical bands were measured by simultaneous masking. The different masker separations were tested in random order, and then retested in the reverse order. Different orders were used for the different cats.

The cats were then transferred to forward masking. The masker was pulsed to appear just before the stimulus pulses, and was at first presented at a very low intensity which was gradually increased over several sessions. Once the performance was established, testing was performed as it had been in simultaneous masking, with however certain differences. Performance tended to be much less reliable with forward than with simultaneous masking. It was found that in order to produce reliable thresholds, the warning period had to be increased from 10 to 12 sec, 2-dB steps had to be used, and testing sessions had to be at intervals of not less than 4 days. Shocks for failure to respond were needed much more often to maintain performance. In order to reduce the possible effects of the shock schedule of the measured bandwidths, the number of shocks per session (overall average 2.5/session) and the points in the threshold run at which they were given, were balanced for masker separations larger and smaller than the critical bandwidth.

b) *Subjects*

Three cats were used. All had at least 3 years' experience of behavioural auditory psychophysics. Their absolute thresholds were similar to those described previously for the cat (Neff and Hind, 1955). Priapus was entirely normal, and Platypus had had its right cochlea destroyed surgically. The right middle ear of Oedipus had been filled with bone cement. In addition, Oedipus had suffered a series of interventions over the years, none of which had affected its masked or absolute thresholds. A cannula had been implanted over the left cochlear nucleus (Pickles, 1976), there was a lesion intended to cover the A1 area of the right auditory cortex, the left superior cervical ganglion and superior sympathetic trunk had been removed, and there was a lesion intended to involve the left superior olivary complex. The sensitivity and psychophysical frequency resolution shown by Oedipus were at least as good as those of the other cats, and it is of importance that these procedures, as yet unconfirmed by histology, did not affect frequency resolution. In one respect, however, Oedipus was inferior to the other animals. Although its performance in forward masking was initially as good as that of the other animals, the performance was not maintained, so that testing could not be completed at 1 kHz. This may have been an effect of the cortical lesion.

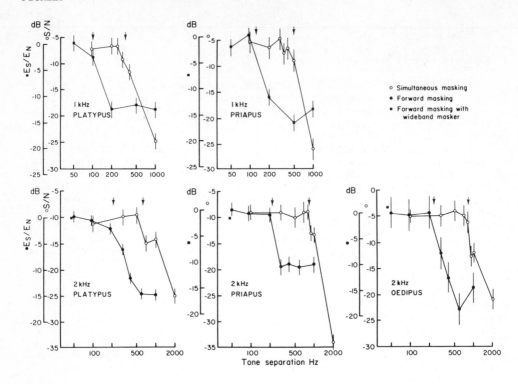

Fig. 1. Forward and simultaneous masked thresholds in the cat, as a function of the frequency separation of the maskers. Arrows mark the point at which the thresholds are 3 dB down. The ordinates are total energy ratios (E_S/E_N, per masker-pulse pair) for forward masking, or power ratios (S/N) for simultaneous masking. 2 trials for each stimulus condition. Bars: ± 1 SEM. Masker intensity: 50 dB SPL/tone.

c) *Stimuli*

The maskers were two tones, derived from separate oscillators. For simultaneous masking they were presented continuously, and for forward masking pulsed at 5/sec (ramps 10 msec, duration 100 msec). In simultaneous masking the signal to be detected was a band of noise 50 Hz wide, produced by multiplying lowpass noise (cutoff 25 Hz at 12 dB/octave) with a sinusoid, and pulsed at 5/sec (ramps 22 msec, duration 150 msec). In forward masking the signal was a pulsed pure tone (ramps 10 msec, no steady portion), each pulse beginning at the end of a masker pulse.

3. RESULTS

a) *Simultaneous masking*

The signal, a band of noise 50 Hz wide, was masked by two continuous tones of variable frequency separation. As the spacing of the masker tones was varied, the signal threshold followed a function similar to that described by Zwicker (1954) at similar intensities, giving a relatively constant threshold for narrow masker spacings, followed by a steep fall as the masker tones were moved outside the critical band (Fig. 1). The bandwidths 3 dB down, which might be taken as indicating the effective bandwidth of the critical band, had a mean

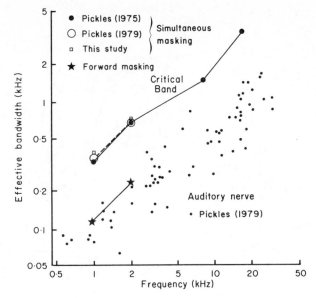

Fig. 2. Effective bandwidths (bandwidths of the equivalent rectangular filter) of the cat's critical band as determined by forward and simultaneous masking, compared with the effective bandwidths of single fibres of the cat's auditory nerve. Auditory nerve effective bandwidths from Pickles (1979).

value of 416 Hz at 1 kHz, and 780 Hz at 2 kHz, in agreement with the values described earlier for the cat by other simultaneous masking methods (Pickles, 1975, 1979). The bandwidths are substantially greater than the effective bandwidths of single fibres of the auditory nerve at the corresponding frequencies (Fig. 2).

b) *Forward masking*

Fig. 1 also shows the forward-masked threshold as a function of the spacing of the masker tones. In this case the signal was a series of brief tone pulses. A tonal signal rather than a narrow-band noise signal was used in order to reduce the temporal variability of the brief signal. The gating of the tone signal spread its spectrum, so that the main spectral peak had a bandwidth very similar to that of the noise used in simultaneous masking. The forward-masked signal threshold showed a function similar to that described for simultaneous masking, but with a decline at narrower bandwidths, and a low-level plateau some 15 dB below the peak. The bandwidths 3 dB down had a mean value of 115 Hz at 1 kHz, and 223 Hz at 2 kHz. These values are some 30% of the values described for simultaneous masking. They are very similar to the effective bandwidths of single fibres of the auditory nerve at the same frequencies (Fig. 2).

The short signal used in forward masking was associated with energy splatter. Spectral analysis indicated that the signal had two side lobes, each 27 dB below and 150 Hz away from the main peak. There was a danger that these lobes would be used in detection, particularly at narrow masker spacings. At 2 kHz, extra sessions were run at the narrowest masker spacings, with added continuous wideband masking noise at an intensity of 0 dB SPL/Hz, which was of sufficient intensity to mask the side lobes. The thresholds were no different, suggesting that these cues had not in fact been used (Fig. 1). At 1 kHz all sessions were run with the wideband masker.

Once the low-level plateau of the masking function had been reached, the forward-masked threshold showed no further tendency to fall as the maskers were separated beyond the critical band found with simultaneous masking. While at 1 kHz it is possible that the plateau was determined by the wideband masker, this cannot be the case at 2 kHz, where there was no such masker at these tonal

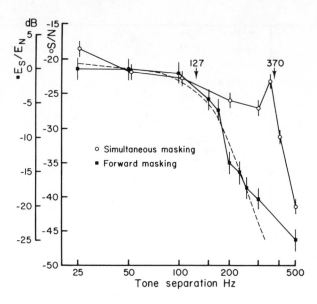

Fig. 3. Forward and simultaneous masked thresholds
in man, as a function of
the frequency separation of
the maskers. Data from one
subject. Arrows: 3-dB bandwidths. The resolution
bandwidth with forward
masking is 35% of the bandwidth with simultaneous
masking. Dotted line: Gaussian filter. Ordinates as
in Fig. 1. Masker intensity
66 dB/tone. 2 trials per
stimulus condition. Bars:
± 1 SEM.

masker separations. This result suggests that during the forward-masking experiments the critical band associated with simultaneous masking was not active in
determining the thresholds.

c) *Simultaneous and forward masking in man*

Resolution bandwidths in man were measured at 2 kHz by the same methods
as in the cat, namely the forward and simultaneous masking of a signal flanked
by two tones of variable frequency separation. The maskers were presented at
66 dB/tone, and in forward masking there was an additional continuous wideband
masker of 16 dB/Hz. Thresholds were determined by discrete-trial tracking with
a 2-dB step size. With simultaneous masking, the threshold function showed a
slope of -7 dB/decade for narrow masker spacings, followed by a notch and then
a sharp fall, similar to the functions described by Nelson (1979) and Patterson and Henning (1977) at similar masker intensities (Fig. 3). Some at least of
these irregularities are thought to be due to the detection of combination
tones between signal and masker. The 3-dB bandwidth was 370 Hz, similar to the
critical bandwidth found by others at 2 kHz (Scharf, 1970). With forward masking the threshold showed a smooth decline with increasing masker separation,
giving a 3-dB bandwidth of 127 Hz. This value is 34% of the value found by simultaneous masking, and parallels the result found in the cat.

4. DISCUSSION

The differences in frequency resolution found with simultaneous and forward masking are similar to the differences found by others in man, although
the ratio of the bandwidths found with the two methods have been reported to be
nearer two-fold than the three-fold of the present study (e.g. Houtgast, 1974a,
b; Moore, 1978). This may be a result of differences in the psychophysical
tasks used. However the one previous study in subjects other than man, in the
chinchilla, did not show any differences at all (McGee *et al*, 1976). Until
there is further information, it might be supposed that this reflects the behavioural difficulty of the forward-masking task.

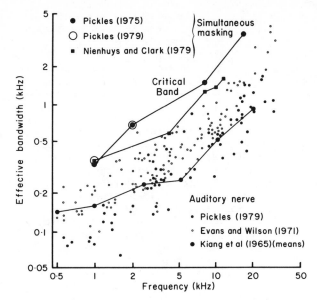

Fig. 4. *Critical bandwidths estimated by simultaneous masking in the cat, after Pickles (1975, 1979) and Nienhuys and Clark (1979), compared with the effective bandwidths of auditory nerve fibres, after Evans and Wilson (1973), Pickles (1979) and Kiang et al (1965). Evans and Wilson estimated their effective bandwidths by integration of the neural tuning curve. Pickles and Comis (1976) found that effective bandwiths, determined by masking the response to a tone by noise of variable bandwidth, were on average 48% of the 10-dB bandwidth. This relation was used by Pickles (1979), and in making estimates from the data of Kiang et al (1965). The data of Kiang et al were averaged over the indicated intervals.*

A conclusion from our earlier studies in the cat was that the effective bandwidth of the critical band as determined by simultaneous masking was significantly wider than the effective bandwidths of single fibres of the cat's auditory nerve (Pickles, 1975, 1979; Pickles and Comis, 1976). It is interesting to compare these results with the results of others in the cat, in view of the different sets of data available. Nienhuys and Clark (1979) measured the critical bandwidth in the cat by simultaneous masking. At 1 kHz, the results are equal to those of Pickles (1975) and at 8 kHz agree to within 20% (Fig.4). In the region in between the discrepancy is rather larger, of the order of 50%, although it does not seriously affect the point to be made here. There is also some variation in the neural data. The auditory-nerve effective bandwidths of Evans and Wilson (1973) are a little larger than those estimated by Pickles (1979) or those calculated from the 10-dB bandwidths of Kiang *et al* (1965), except at the very lowest frequencies. In view of possible variation between animals, perhaps explaining the differences between the different sets of neural data, comparisons should preferably be made in the same animals. This was done by Pickles and Comis (1976) and Pickles (1979), who suggested that the ratio of the psychophysical and neural effective bandwidths was three fold. Nevertheless, if the narrowest of the critical band measures is compared with the broadest of the neural effective bandwidth measures, the psychophysical points lie along the upper boundary of the neural points, rather than following the mean or the minimum values as might otherwise have been expected.

In contrast to the bandwidths determined by simultaneous masking, the resolution bandwidths determined by forward masking lay well within the neural resolution bandwidths (Fig. 2). This result strongly supports the contention of Houtgast (1974a,b) and Vogten (1978) that it is non-simultaneous rather than simultaneous masking techniques that give an accurate measure of the bandwidth of resolution of the auditory system. However, the theoretical justification for that position, that two-tone suppression in the auditory system is responsible for the difference, is open to objection. Firstly, Pickles and Comis

(1976) measured the effective bandwidths of auditory nerve fibres by an analogy of the method that they had used psychophysically, namely the simultaneous masking of the fibre's response to a tone by noise of variable bandwidth. They showed as great a difference between the neural and psychophysical resolution bandwidths as had been shown by the other methods. However, any factor operating in the cochlea, such as suppression, should have affected the two sets of data equally, and therefore cannot be responsible for the difference. While the details of the neural coding of such stimuli need further investigation, there is at the present no reason to suppose that they would explain the large differences observed. The possibility of central factors should therefore be borne in mind (Pickles, 1976).

Secondly, Sachs and Kiang (1968) showed that the neural response to a tone could be much more powerfully suppressed by tones of higher frequency than by tones of lower frequency. However, Nelson (1979) showed that in simultaneous two-tone masking it was the lower tone that was responsible for practically all the masking. This has been taken to suggest that the critical bandwidth is determined by the upwards spread of excitation from the lower tone (e.g., Nelson, 1979). Nevertheless, it is still possible to suggest that suppression plays some role. The tuning curves of auditory nerve fibres are asymmetric, so that as the frequency separation of symmetrically-placed tonal maskers is increased, the upper masker may have passed outside the upper two-tone suppression area before the lower tone has left the lower suppression area. At certain intensities there will then be a range of masker separations in which the response to the signal will be affected only by suppression from the lower tone. It is open to conjecture whether suppression from the lower tone alone is powerful enough to explain the dramatic differences of Figs. 1 and 3.

Therefore, although non-simultaneous masking techniques may indeed give an accurate picture of the neural representation, the neural basis of the critical band as determined by simultaneous masking must be viewed as uncertain. Further detailed electrophysiological analysis of the cues available in the activity of the auditory nerve in response to the complex stimuli used in psychophysical testing is clearly necessary. The electrophysiological information currently available does not lead one to expect a single critical bandwidth, constant over different tasks and over a wide range of intensity. It is also possible that detailed psychophysical analysis of the cues used in psychophysical tasks will point to a similar conclusion, showing different bandwidths of resolution for different tasks and at different intensities (e.g. Scharf and Meiselman, 1977; Nelson, 1979). Moreover the possible influence of central factors should not be overlooked (Pickles, 1976). The similarity between the resolution bandwidths found hitherto with simultaneous masking in the different psychophysical tasks may just be coincidental. Perhaps the concept of a unitary critical band, once so useful, should eventually be abandoned.

5. SUMMARY

Critical bandwidths were measured behaviourally in the cat by both forward and simultaneous masking. The resolution bandwidths found with simultaneous masking were substantially greater than the resolution bandwidths of single fibres of the auditory nerve. However the resolution bandwidths found with forward masking were equal to those of the auditory-nerve fibres. The results suggest that it is non-simultaneous rather than simultaneous masking techniques that give an accurate measure of the neural representation of auditory stimuli.

Acknowledgements

This research was supported by the Medical Research Council of the UK.

REFERENCES

Evans, E.F. and Wilson, J.P.(1973). Frequency selectivity of the cochlea. In: *Basic Mechanisms in Hearing*. (A.R. Møller, ed.). pp. 519-551. Academic Press, New York.

Fletcher, H.(1940). Auditory patterns. *Revs. Modern Phys.* 12, 47-65.

Houtgast, T.(1972). Psychophysical evidence for lateral inhibition in hearing. *J. Acoust. Soc. Amer.* 51, 1885-1894.

Houtgast, T.(1974a). Lateral suppression in hearing. *Ph.D. Thesis*, Institute for Perception TNO, Soesterberg.

Houtgast, T.(1974b). Masking patterns and lateral inhibition. In: *Facts and Models in Hearing*. (E. Zwicker and E. Terhardt, eds). pp 258-265. Springer, Berlin.

Kiang, N.Y.S., Watanabe, T., Thomas, E.C. and Clark, L.F.(1965). *Discharge Patterns of Single Fibers in the Cat's Auditory Nerve*. MIT, Cambridge.

McGee, T., Ryan, A. and Dallos, P.(1976). Psychophysical tuning curves of chinchillas. *J. Acoust. Soc. Amer.* 60, 1146-1150.

Moore, B.C.J.(1978). Psychophysical tuning curves measured in simultaneous and forward masking. *J. Acoust. Soc. Amer.* 63, 524-532.

Neff, W.D. and Hind, J.E.(1955). Auditory thresholds of the cat. *J. Acoust. Soc. Amer.* 27, 480-483.

Nelson, D.A.(1979). Two-tone masking and auditory critical bandwidths. *Audiology* 18, 279-306.

Nienhuys, T.G.W. and Clark, G.M.(1979). Critical bands following the selective destruction of cochlear inner and outer hair cells. *Acta Otolaryngol.* 88, 350-358.

Patterson, R.D. and Henning, G.B.(1977). Stimulus variability and auditory filter shape. *J. Acoust. Soc. Amer.* 62, 649-664.

Pickles, J.O.(1975). Normal critical bands in the cat. *Acta Otolaryngol.* 80, 245-254.

Pickles, J.O.(1976). Role of centrifugal pathways to cochlear nucleus in determination of critical bandwidth. *J. Neurophysiol.* 39, 394-400.

Pickles, J.O.(1977). Neural correlates of the masked threshold. In: *Psychophysics and Physiology of Hearing*. (E.F. Evans and J.P. Wilson, eds). pp 209-218. Academic Press, London.

Pickles, J.O.(1979). Psychophysical frequency resolution in the cat as determined with simultaneous masking, and its relation to auditory-nerve resolution. *J. Acoust. Soc. Amer.* 66, 1725-1732.

Pickles, J.O. and Comis, S.D.(1976). Auditory nerve fiber bandwidths and critical bandwidths in the cat. *J. Acoust. Soc. Amer.* 60, 1151-1156.

Sachs, M.B. and Kiang, N.Y.S.(1968). Two-tone inhibition in auditory-nerve fibers. *J. Acoust. Soc. Amer.* 43, 1120-1128.

Scharf, B.(1970). Critical bands. In: *Foundations of Modern Auditory Theory*, Vol 1. (J.V. Tobias, ed). pp 159-202. Academic Press, New York.

Scharf, B. and Meiselman, C.H.(1977). Critical bandwidth at high intensities. In: *Psychophysics and Physiology of Hearing*. (E.F. Evans and J.P. Wilson, eds). pp 221-232. Academic Press, London.

Vogten, L.L.M.(1978). Low-level pure-tone masking: a comparison of 'tuning curves' obtained with simultaneous and forward masking. *J. Acoust. Soc. Amer.* 63, 1520-1527.

Zwicker, E.(1954). Die Verdeckung von Schmalbandgeräuschen durch Sinustöne. *Acustica* 4, 415-420.

Zwicker, E.(1970). Masking and psychological excitation as consequences of the ear's frequency analysis. In: *Frequency Analysis and Periodicity Detection in Hearing*. (R. Plomp and G.F. Smoorenberg, eds). pp 376-394. Sijthoff, Leiden.

COMMENT

COMMENT ON: "Psychophysical frequency resolution in the cat studied with forward masking" (J.O. Pickles)

E.F. Evans
*Department of Communication & Neuroscience, University of Keele, Keele, Staffs.,
U.K.*

The apparent differences between the effective bandwidths of cat cochlear
fibres in the measurements of Evans and Wilson and in your extrapolation from
the data of Kiang may be accounted for in the following ways: Firstly, our data
in the reference you cite clearly show substantial differences between animals.
The data from our "sharpest" animal match your new behavioural well. Secondly,
Kiang's data have not been corrected for the characteristics of his sound system.
This will have the effect of making the bandwidths of higher CF fibres appear
narrower than they actually are.

COMMENT ON: "Psychophysical frequency resolution in the cat studied with forward masking" (J.O. Pickles).

J.P. Wilson
*Department of Communication & Neuroscience, Univerity of Keele, Keele, Staffs.,
U.K.*

Pickles has demonstrated nicely that non-simultaneous, rather than simultaneous, masking techniques give good agreement with auditory nerve fibre tuning
characteristics. We should, however, avoid any suggestion that these are "the
correct" measures of auditory tuning. In many cases, such as in the analysis +
perception of speech or the detection of wanted signals in the presence of noise,
it will be the simultaneous masking techniques that give the more appropriate
answer. For a full understanding of the system we require both kinds of measurement.

REPLY TO COMMENT OF J.P. WILSON

J.O. Pickles
Neurocommunications Research Unit, Birmingham University, Birmingham, England.

My object in doing these experiments was to see which measure correlated
most closely with auditory nerve resolution. However I agree that most cases
encountered in everyday life correspond to simultaneous rather than forward
masking. It is the mechanism for this condition that seems least understood.

CHRONIC ANOXIA AND AUDITORY NERVE FIBRES

J.R. Johnstone

*Department of Physiology, University of
Western Australia, Nedlands 6009, Western Australia*

The frequency response of an auditory nerve fibre is described by its tuning curve (Fig. 1). This consists of two regions, a low frequency "tail" and a "tip" of reduced thresholds near the characteristic frequency (CF).

The effects of short-term anoxia (5 minutes or less) on tuning curves have been described by Evans (1973) and Robertson and Manley (1974). At all frequencies thresholds are elevated, particularly near the characteristic frequency. The overall result is a reduction or elimination of the tip of the tuning curve leaving a broadly tuned low-pass unit. These changes are partially or completely reversible.

The effects of a more gradual and persistent anoxia have not yet been examined, partly because of the difficulty of holding units for several hours while the respiratory state of the animal is varied.

1. METHODS

Guinea pigs were prepared as described by Wilson and Johnstone (1975) and ganglion cells recorded as described by Johnstone (1977). The animals were anaesthetised, paralyzed and ventilated artificially with carbogen (5% CO_2 in O_2). Anoxia was induced either by slowing the respirator or by replacing the carbogen with a nitrogen-carbogen mixture.

2. RESULTS

Five units from five animals were held for 3-5 hours during which time the animal was made anoxic for $\frac{1}{2}$-$4\frac{1}{2}$ hours then allowed to recover. There are three kinds of response: reversible, pseudo-reversible and irreversible.

(i) *Reversible* (1 unit). This is the change described by Evans (1973), and Robertson and Manley (1974). Threshold increases, particularly at the CF and the tuning curve may end up nearly bandpass with no distinctive CF. Return to full oxygenation returns thresholds. Brief periods of anoxia are fully reversible but more protracted anoxia may also reverse as in Fig. 1 where a unit reverses completely after 1 h on 5% carbogen. The unit also shows the post-anoxic enhancement of threshold noted by Robertson and Manley (1974).

(ii) *Pseudo-reversible* (2 units). Anoxia may cause a decrease in CF. The unit of Fig. 2 changed CF from 21 kHz to 15 kHz (0.5 octave) and its minimum threshold from 41 dB to 67 dB after 15 min anoxia. Eleven minutes after a return to carbogen the threshold had improved to 45 dB but the CF dropped further to 12 kHz, a total shift of 0.8 octave.

A second unit of CF = 18 kHz shifted in threshold from 20 to 48 dB without change of CF. Reoxygenation improved the threshold slightly to 43 dB but the CF dropped to 12 kHz, a change of 0.6 octave.

(iii) *Irreversible* (2 units). Irreversible anoxia caused the shift in CF

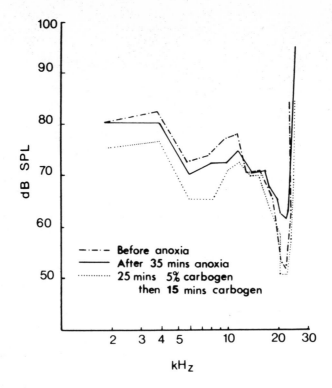

Fig.1. Reversible anoxia

described above but renewed oxygenation fails to restore either CF or threshold. In Fig. 3 the first two tuning curves are duplicates obtained 113 m
apart to indicate the stability possible with this preparation. After 45 m
of anoxia the CF had dropped to 12 kHz and the minimum threshold increased
from 60 to 70 dB. Fifteen minutes oxygenation failed to restore CF (which
further decreased to 10 kHz) or threshold which increased further to 78 dB.
This is a 1.1 octave shift in characteristic frequency. This unit, unlike the
other four units, was initially mistuned slightly (CF = 21 kHz) for its location on the basilar membrane (CF = 27.5 kHz). The final disparity between CF
and location was therefore 1.5 oct.

A second unit of CF = 18 kHz changed threshold from 40 dB to 60 dB
without change of CF during 1 hour's anoxia. Reoxygenation was associated with
a further increase in threshold to 70 dB and the CF decreased to 16 kHz, a
change of 0.17 oct.

3. DISCUSSION

The results extend the original observation by Johnstone (1977) that
units of poor threshold often have a lower CF than their basilar membrane
location would suggest. Units from the first 2.5 mm in particular show this
characteristic, perhaps because they are more readily damaged.

A related observation is that animals with chronically damaged organs
of Corti show similar CF shifts (Robertson & Johnstone, 1979).

The results described here are clear evidence for the existence of two
distinct filters in the cochlea. The first is the travelling wave mechanism

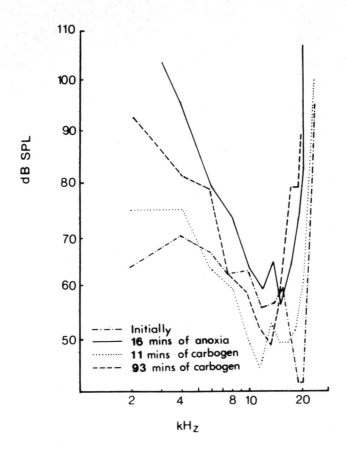

Fig.2. Pseudoreversible anoxia

-- a filter with a 6-12 dB/oct low frequency roll-off and a high pass roll-off of 100 dB/oct for 30 dB followed by a 20 dB/oct roll-off thereafter (Rhode, 1971; Wilson & Johnstone, 1975). It does not resemble the neural tuning curve (Geisler et al, 1974, p. 1169). The second filter is narrow bandpass with slopes of several hundred decibels per octave although the low side extends only as far as 80 dB SPL (e.g., Johnstone, 1977). It is this filter which produces the characteristic shape of the neural tuning curve.

The nature of the second filter is obscure. Since anoxia can cause its centre frequency to change by over an octave it seems most unlikely to be the result of micromechanical tuning in the organ of Corti.

Fettiplace and Crawford (1978) have shown that the second filter in the terrapin cochlea is probably located in the hair cell itself. Injected current pulses cause the membrane potential to ring at a frequency corresponding to the characteristic frequency of adjacent nerve fibres.

If a second filter (and its associated nonlinearity) is located within each hair cell it becomes much simpler to explain many of the troublesome properties of the cochlea, in particular the problem of combination tones. For example, tones of 12 and 13 kHz will produce two travelling waves with their maxima at the 12 and 13 kHz locations. Neurons will fire appropriately at those locations, but also at others, in particular the $2F_1 - F_2 = 11$ kHz location (Goldstein & Kiang, 1968). To explain this kind of result it is not necessary that there be mechanical distortion at the primaries location

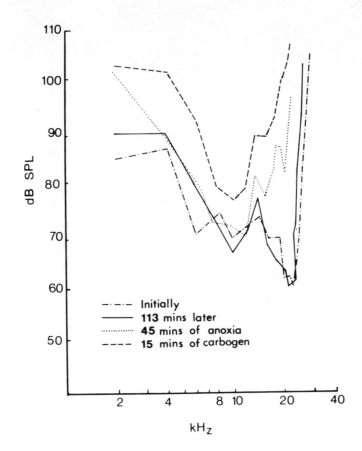

Fig.3. Irreversible anoxia

followed by the propagation of some disturbance along the cochlea to the F_1 – F_2 location as suggested by many researchers, e.g.: Kim *et al* (1979). At the 11 kHz location the amplitudes of the primaries are down 100 $\log_2$ (f/8) dB, i.e., 13 dB and 24 dB. Nonlinearity within a hair cell at the 11 kHz location will produce a family of distortion products one of which ($2F_1$ – F_2 = 11 kHz) can pass through the second filter and cause the nerve fibre to fire.

REFERENCES

Evans, E.F.(1973). The effects of hypoxia on the tuning of single cochlear nerve fibres. *J. Physiol.* 238, 69–70.

Fettiplace, R. and Crawford, A.C.(1978). The coding of sound pressure and frequency in cochlear hair cells of the terrapin. *Proc. R. Soc. Lond. B.* 203, 209–218.

Geisler, C.D., Rhode, W.S. and Kennedy, D.T.(1974). Responses to tonal stimuli of single auditory nerve fibers and their relationship to basilar membrane motion in squirrel monkey. *J. Neurophysiol.* 37, 1156–1172.

Goldstein, J.L. and Kiang, N.Y.S.(1968). Neural correlates of the aural combination tone $2F_1$ – F_2. *Proc. IEEE* 56, 981–992.

Johnstone, J.R.(1977). Properties of ganglion cells from the extreme basal region of guinea pig cochlea. In: *Psychophysics and Physiology of*

Hearing. (E.F. Evans and J.P. Wilson, eds.). pp 89-98. Academic Press, London.

Kim, D.O., Siegel, J.H. and Molnar, C.E.(1979). Cochlear nonlinear phenomena in two-tone responses. In: *Models of the Auditory System and Related Signal Processing Techniques*. (M. Hoke and E. de Boer, eds.). *Scand. Audiol. Suppl.* 9, 63-81.

Rhode, W.S.(1971). Observations on the vibration of the basilar membrane in squirrel monkey using the Mossbauer technique. *J. Acoust. Soc. Am.* 49, 1218-1231.

Robertson, D. and Manley, G.A.(1974). Manipulation of frequency analysis in the cochlear ganglion of the guinea pig. *J. Comp. Physiol.* 91, 363-375.

Robertson, D. and Johnstone, B.M.(1979). Aberrant tonotopic organization in the inner ear damaged by kanamycin. *J. Acoust. Soc. Am.* 66, 466-469.

Wilson, J.P. and Johnstone, J.R. Basilar membrane and middle ear vibration in guinea pig measured by capacitive probe. *J. Acoust. Soc. Am.* 57, 705-723.

COMMENT ON: "Chronic anoxia and auditory nerve fibres" (J.R. Johnstone)

E.F. Evans
Dept. of Communication & Neuroscience, University of Keele, U.K.

Decrease in the CF of cochlear fibre tuning appears to be a general finding in toxic cochlear pathology: in reversible hypoxia (Evans, 1974; Robertson and Manley, 1974) and in reversible cyanide and furosemide poisoning of the cochlea (Evans and Klinke, 1974). Under these conditions, the shift is progressive and small (about 0.2 octave) as the FTC tip threshold is elevated. Eventually, with total loss of the FTC 'tip' segment, the 'tail' segment of the FTC appears only to remain.

SOME PSYCHOPHYSICAL MEASUREMENTS OF FREQUENCY PROCESSING IN THE GREATER HORSESHOE BAT.

Glenis R. Long

*Central Institute for the Deaf
St. Louis, Missouri, U.S.A.**

1. INTRODUCTION

The Greater Horseshoe Bat, *Rhinolophus ferrumequinum*, uses echolocation sounds with a long constant-frequency component (10-100 msec at about 83 kHz). The narrow frequency band from 82-86 kHz containing the biologically relevant signals from moving prey has exceptionally sharp tuning and is over-represented at all levels from the cochlea to the cortex (reviewed in Neuweiler,1980). Long (1977, 1980) found that critical ratio measures from this species also indicate sharp tuning at these frequencies. This report describes two different measures of critical bands from this species and uses these estimates to further investigate the relation of these psychophysical measures to known anatomical and neurophysiological modifications.

2. METHODS

A classically-conditioned response to shock (Long and Schnitzler, 1975) was used to measure:

i) Thresholds of pure tones in bands of noise of decreasing bandwidth and constant energy. The narrow band noises were generated by multiplying a low pass digital noise with a high frequency tone producing noises of twice the bandwidth and skirts of 1000 dB/octave. The widest bandwidth was 19.8 kHz and had a spectrum level of 18 dB SPL.

ii) Thresholds of narrow bands of noise (100 Hz wide) centered between two 50 dB SPL pure tones at varying frequency separations (Δf). Tones and noise were generated by mixing a 50 Hz low-pass noise and a tone of $\frac{1}{2}\Delta f$ and multiplying this by the frequency being measured.

In all conditions the maskers were on continuously and the stimuli were presented as a 7.5 sec train of 50 msec tones (0.5 msec rise and decay) presented 10/sec. This duration was used both because such durations are frequently used by an echolocating animal and because unpublished research by this author found no change in unmasked thresholds at 85 kHz or tones of 50, 30 and 15 msec.

The modified staircase method (Long and Schnitzler, 1975) was used with the mean of the last 6 reversals being used as threshold.

3. RESULTS

Thresholds for a tone in noise of different bandwidths could be fitted by the expected functions, i.e., a line of zero slope within the critical bandwidth and a line of 3 dB/doubling outside the critical bandwidths,for all frequencies except 83.5 kHz (the reference frequency used by these bats while echolocating) and 81.5 kHz. The slopes at these frequencies were greater than 4 suggesting some asymmetry at these frequencies. The shapes of the functions of narrow band noise masked by two tones are also as

---

* *Work completed at the Polytechnic of Central London, London, England*

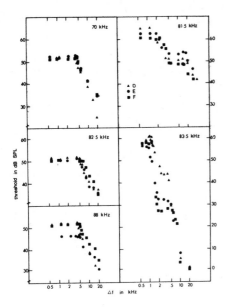

Fig. 1. Thresholds obtained for 100 Hz bands of noise surrounded by two 50 dB SPL tones separated by Δf. Data is presented from 3 different animals, D, E & F at 5 representative frequencies.

Fig. 2. Thresholds for 100 Hz bands of noise surrounded by two tones separated by Δf (filled circles), the lower tone alone (open triangles) and the higher tone alone (open triangles). Data is presented from two animals, E & F, at two frequencies.

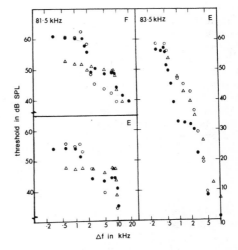

expected except at the same frequencies where the masking decreases in two stages. Fig. 1 shows the data for these frequencies and three other representative frequencies. If the effect of each tone is measured alone (Fig.2) each tone can be seen to be separately responsible for each of the steps at 81.5 kHz but not at 83.5 kHz.

The critical bands determined by the two different methods are shown in Fig. 3 along with critical ratios determined from the broadest noise used. The two methods for measuring critical bands are consistent. At all frequencies below 78 kHz the critical ratios are approximately half as wide as the critical bands at the same frequency, as is found in other animals. Above 78 kHz the relation is not constant; it reaches over 6:1 at 83.5 kHz and the critical bands are narrower than the critical ratios at 81.5 kHz.

4. DISCUSSION

Below 78 kHz, where the cochlea of *Rhinolphus ferrumequinum* is similar to other cochleas, the critical bands and critical ratios have the expected relation to each other and to frequency. Above 80 kHz this is no longer true. These changes can be related to other measures at these frequencies. Long (1980) found that critical ratios at around 81 kHz are broader than the bands of noise used. Bruns (reviewed in Neuweiler, 1980) hypothesizes a discontinuity in the nature of the motion of the basilar membrane around 81 kHz. Neuweiler and Vater (1977) have described 8th nerve fibers that respond to frequencies above and below 81.5 kHz and not to 81.5 kHz. Möller (1978) found cochlear nucleus fibers with characteristic frequencies (CF) from 82-86 kHz that have a gap of inhibition for tones from 78-82 kHz. The above findings suggest that, as well as the auditory "fovea" in the cochlea suggested by Schuller and Pollak (1979), there is a "blind spot" where the basilar membrane changes character. The discovery by Schuller and Pollak of fibers with CF at these frequencies in the inferior colliculus can be explained by reconstruction from responses to neighbouring fibers. The asymmetry of the critical bands at 81.5 kHz could be due to each tone falling in different areas of the cochlea. At 83.5 kHz the asymmetry could be due to changes in the inhibition of one masker by the other.

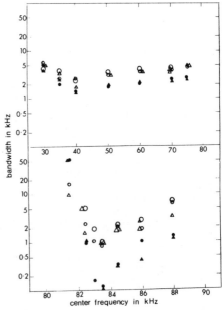

Fig. 3. Critical ratios (solid symbols) and two different measures of critical bands; band narrowing (small open symbols) and two-tone masking of noise (large open symbols) as a function of frequency for two animals (D triangles, E circles).

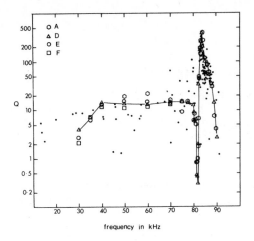

frequency in kHz

Fig. 4. Q_{CR} determined by dividing twice the critical ratio into the center frequency from 4 animals (open symbols) and the Q_{10dB} from cochlear nucleus fibers (Suga et al, 1975).

In order to determine how bandwidths obtained psychophysically relate to neural tuning, Q_{CR} were obtained by dividing twice the critical ratio into the center frequency. These are plotted in Fig. 4 together with Q_{10dB} from cochlea nucleus fibers (Suga *et al*, 1975). With the exception of frequencies between 78–82 kHz the Q_{CR} form an envelope around the Q_{10dB} of the nerve fibers suggesting that below 78 kHz critical ratios, critical bands and nerve fiber tuning are all dependent on the same processes. The discontinuity in the cochlea can account for the discrepancy in the different results around 80 kHz. It is, however, difficult to explain why critical ratios follow the frequency dependency of the nerve fibers better than critical bands at the highest frequencies.

REFERENCES

Long, G.R.(1977). Masked auditory thresholds from the bat, *Rhinolophus ferrumequinum. J. comp. Physiol.* 116, 247–255.
Long, G.R.(1980). Further studies of masking in the Greater Horseshoe Bat, *Rhinolophus ferrumequinum*. In: *Animal Sonar Systems*. (R.-G. Busnel, ed). Plenum Press, New York. In Press.
Long, G.R. and Schnitzler, H.-U.(1975). Behavioral audiograms from the bat, *Rhinolophus ferrumequinum. J. comp. Physiol.* 100, 211–219.
Möller, J.(1978). Response characteristics to pure tones of cochlear nucleus neurons of the awake CF-FM bat, *Rhinolophus ferrumequinum. J. comp. Physiol.* 125, 227–236.
Neuweiler, G.(1980). Auditory processing of echos. Part 1: Peripheral processing. In: *Animal Sonar Systems*. (R.-G. Busnel, ed.). Plenum Press, N.Y. In Press.
Neuweiler, G. and Vater, M. (1977). Response patterns to pure tones of cochlear nucleus units in the CF-FM bat, *Rhinolophus ferrumequinum. J. comp. Physiol.* 115, 119–133.
Schuller, G. and Pollak, G.(1979). Disproportionate frequency representation in the inferior colliculus of doppler-compensating Greater Horseshoe Bats: Evidence for an acoustic fovea. *J. comp. Physiol.* 132, 47–54.

ALTERED PSYCHOPHYSICAL TUNING CURVES FOLLOWING EXPOSURE TO A NOISE BAND WITH STEEP SPECTRAL SKIRTS

Dennis McFadden and Edward G. Pasanen

Department of Psychology, University of Texas
Austin, Texas 78712, U.S.A.

1. BACKGROUND

We have serendipitously observed long-term and short-term changes in the psychophysical tuning curve (PTC) following exposure to a noise band having steep spectral skirts. The planned experiment involved obtaining PTCs both in the presence and the absence of a high-pass noise; the hope was that in the presence of the noise the PTCs would resemble those observed by Wightman *et al.* (1977) using subjects with high-frequency hearing loss. Once the initial practice sessions were completed, the experimental procedure involved interleaving blocks of trials having noise present or not. About three-quarters of the way through the scheduled experiment, it was noticed that performance on some no-noise blocks was different from the baseline data. The remaining noise conditions were then cancelled and no-noise performance was monitored for several months during which some recovery did occur. The implication is that the changes observed were somehow due to the "exposure" to the steep-sided noise band. If correct, this aftereffect is unusual, for unlike common auditory aftereffects, it follows intermittent exposure to a *weak* sound.

2. METHODS

All PTCs were determined using forward masking in conjunction with an adaptive psychophysical technique. The tonal masker was 200 msec in duration. In one of the two observation intervals of a trial the masker was followed immediately by a tonal signal of fixed intensity and 20 msec duration; in the other observation interval no signal occurred. The intensity of the masking tone was adjusted on a trial-by-trial basis for each subject using a "2-up, 1-down" rule. The first four reversals in each 80-trial block were discarded; the remainder were averaged to provide a measure of sensitivity. The signal was typically 35 dB SPL. The rise-decay time for both the signal and tonal masker was 10 msec.

In accord with the original objective of simulating a precipitous high-frequency hearing loss in normal listeners, the high-frequency masker was produced using a multiplier. The noise band obtained was approximately 1000 Hz in width, centered at 3500 Hz, and had attenuation rates of approximately 415 dB/octave beginning at about 3000 Hz and 565 dB/octave beginning at about 4000 Hz. When present, the noise was continuous and approximately 65 dB SPL overall.

Because the original experiment involved rather elaborate counterbalancing of conditions, the daily sessions were quite heterogenous as to the pattern of "exposure"--as few as one or two or as many as four or five consecutive blocks of trials might occur with the steep-sided noise present before a sequence of no-noise blocks was run. Individual blocks were about 4.5 min in length, there were always breaks of about 1 min between blocks, and longer breaks were given after every sixth or seventh block. Thus, while the noise band was continuous when present, the "exposures" were clearly intermittent.

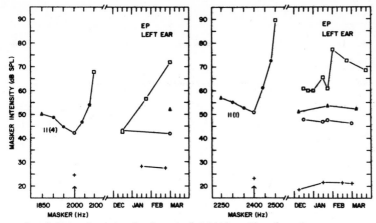

Fig. 1. Earliest possible estimates of PTCs and calendars of recovery for subject EP. Intermittent "exposures" to the steep-sided noise band began mid-October and ended mid-December. In this and following figures, the week and month in which each PTC was determined is indicated --e.g., the fourth week of November is designated 11(4). The low-frequency maskers (triangles), the on-frequency maskers (circles), and absolute sensitivity (plusses) changed little if any, but the high-frequency maskers (squares) dropped sharply in early December. For the 2000-Hz signal recovery was complete within about three months, but not for the 2400-Hz signal. The sensation level (SL) was about 10 dB at 2000 Hz and about 12 dB at 2400 Hz.

3. RESULTS

The two subjects involved did not show identical patterns of change. In Fig. 1 we show data for EP (the second author) at two signal frequencies. The PTC to the left in each panel is based on data taken relatively early in the scheduled experiment, after only a few weeks of intermittent exposure to the high-frequency noise band, and thus, it is our best estimate of initial sensitivity; note, however, that the counterbalanced structure of the planned experiment unfortunately precludes our having data that are literally "pre-exposure." Shown to the right of the PTCs in Fig. 1 is performance across time for three selected tonal maskers, and at the bottom are measures of absolute sensitivity. For the 2000-Hz signal, the low-frequency and the on-frequency masker levels were basically unchanged; however, the high-frequency masker had to be attenuated by about 25 dB initially, with full recovery taking about three months. For the 2400-Hz signal, both the low-frequency and the on-frequency maskers dropped about 5 dB, but the high-frequency masker showed an initial drop of 30 dB, of which 20 dB remained more than three months after the last exposure to the steep-sided noise band. The plus signs at the bottom of Fig. 1 reveal that absolute sensitivity for the 20-msec signals was basically unchanged throughout.

The pattern of change for the second subject was different in several respects. In Fig. 2 are shown pairs of PTCs measured at three different signal frequencies. In each instance, the solid circles represent the earliest reliable estimate of the PTC permitted by the counterbalancing of the original experiment, and the open circles represent data taken after 5-7 weeks of intermittent exposure to the steep-sided noise band (which began in the second week of October). One notable feature of the latter data is that the tips of the PTCs are all shifted downward in frequency, which is reminiscent of an effect discussed by Vogten (1978), but opposite in direction. A second notable feature is that at 1700 and 2000 Hz, the PTCs are generally displaced toward greater masker intensities; that is, this subject was for a time *more* sensitive to the signal after exposure to the steep-sided noise band. The pattern of change at 2200 Hz is clearly different from those at 1700 and 2000 Hz; there is a clear drop in the high-frequency limb of the PTC, much like those

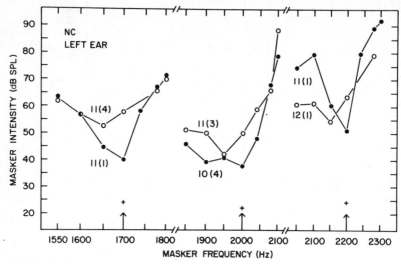

Fig. 2. *Earliest possible estimates (solid circles) and estimates obtained after several weeks of intermittent exposure to the steep-sided noise band (open circles) for subject NC. The SLs were 11, 13, and 11 dB for the 1700-, 2000-, and 2200-Hz signals, respectively.*

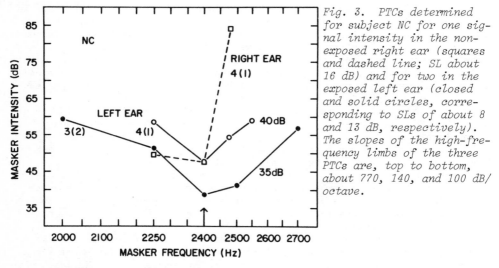

Fig. 3. *PTCs determined for subject NC for one signal intensity in the non-exposed right ear (squares and dashed line; SL about 16 dB) and for two in the exposed left ear (closed and solid circles, corresponding to SLs of about 8 and 13, respectively). The slopes of the high-frequency limbs of the three PTCs are, top to bottom, about 770, 140, and 100 dB/octave.*

shown by EP in Fig. 1. This de-tuning is even more marked at 2400 Hz, as shown in Fig. 3 where data taken from both the exposed left ear (circles) and the non-exposed right ear (squares) of NC are presented. For the left ear, two signal intensities were used, but even the higher intensity did not produce a high-frequency limb as steep as that seen in the right ear. All of these data were collected between 2.5 and 3.5 months after the last experience with the steep-sided noise band, but data taken in December and January (also with a 35-dB signal) are very similar to those marked 3(2) in this figure. Unfortunately, the structure of the planned experiment was such that no data for the 2400-Hz signal were collected until the first week of November, and by that time the PTC was already aberrant. Collected at about the same time was the pre-exposure PTC for 2200 Hz shown in Fig. 2; it also appears aberrant, but to a much lesser degree than that at 2400 Hz.

The changes in acuity seen in Fig. 2 were gradually reversed over the course of several weeks until the PTCs determined at those three frequencies were very similar to the pre-exposure data shown in that figure. In contrast, recovery has apparently ceased at a point short of complete for the 2400-Hz signal.

During the time that the subjects' PTCs were abnormal and recovering, neither subject could report any obvious differences in everyday auditory perception. Performance in the exposed and non-exposed ears has since been compared for a number of different psychophysical tasks, and the sole difference detected is that subject NC shows less lateral suppression (as measured in a forward-masking task) in the exposed ear than in the non-exposed ear.

If the long-term changes seen in these subjects' PTCs were somehow related to their experience with the steep-sided noise band, there is the possibility that a short-term analog could be found. This possibility has been confirmed. In a series of experiments using a number of subjects, we have observed reductions in masker intensity on the high-frequency side of the PTC following controlled exposures to the steep-sided noise. There are apparently large individual differences in susceptibility, and there can be considerable day-to-day variability in the magnitude of the de-tuning. Recovery is typically not complete 0.5 hour post exposure, and typically is complete 24 hours post exposure, but systematic examination of the interim has not been attempted. Some typical reductions in slope of the high-frequency limb are about 160 dB/octave for a 2600-Hz signal and about 75 dB/octave for a 2400-Hz signal (both are two-subject averages) following continuous listening to the noise band for 15 mins at 80 dB SPL overall. There have never been any observable effects on absolute sensitivity for the 20-msec signals presented in the quiet, and a noise band with a less steep spectral edge (about 70 dB/octave) never produced alterations in the PTC even for the longest exposure durations.

A possible explanation of these short-term and long-term aftereffects is that somewhere in the auditory nervous system the steep-sided noise band sets up an "edge" that is somehow different from what is set up by complex sounds with less sharp spectral skirts, and that repeated listening can produce a neural "adaptation" that can last months. Analogous temporary and permanent effects have been reported for the visual system (originally by McCullough, 1965).

REFERENCES

McCullough, C. (1965) Color adaptation of edge-detectors in the human visual system. *Science* 149, 1115-1116.
Vogten, L.L.M. (1978) Low-level pure-tone masking: A comparison of "tuning curves" obtained with simultaneous and forward masking. *J. Acoust. Soc. Amer.* 63, 1520-1527.
Wightman, F., McGee, T., and Kramer, M. (1977) Factors influencing frequency and selectivity in normal and hearing-impaired listeners. In: *Psychophysics and Physiology of Hearing*. (E.F. Evans and J.P. Wilson, eds.). pp. 295-306. Academic Press, New York.

ACKNOWLEDGMENTS

This research was supported by a research grant (NS 08754) from the National Institute of Neurological and Communicative Disorders and Stroke. A preliminary report was given at the 97th meeting of the Acoustical Society of America [*J. Acoust. Soc. Amer.* 65, S118 (1979)].

THE EFFECT OF AGE ON AUDITORY FILTER SHAPE

Roy D. Patterson and Robert Milroy

MRC Applied Psychology Unit, 15 Chaucer Road, Cambridge, England

Experiments involving the detection of a tone in noise show that the masking provided by a given noise component varies inversely with its distance from the tone. Demonstrations of auditory frequency selectivity are typically explained in terms of an auditory filter that is centred at or near the tone frequency to improve signal detection by attenuating off-frequency noise components. Using certain noise spectra it is actually possible to derive the shape or attenuation characteristic of the auditory filter from the experimental data directly; a review of these methods and the filter shapes obtained is presented in Patterson and Nimmo-Smith (1980). Several years ago, in preparation for one such experiment, the filter shapes of three laboratory assistants were measured briefly. Although the data were few it was clear that the filter of one of the assistants, aged 55, was much wider than those of the others who were in their mid-twenties. The experiment (Patterson, 1976) was eventually run on "young normals" like most psychoacoustic studies; in this paper we follow up the serendipitous suggestion provided by the older assistant that the auditory filter broadens with age.

The study was further motivated by demonstrations that patients with sensorineural hearing losses often have poor frequency resolution (de Boer and Bouwmeester, 1974; Pick, Evans, and Wilson, 1977; Zwicker and Schorn, 1978). These results lead to questions concerning 1) the frequency selectivity of normal listeners with comparable ages, 2) the general rate of deterioration of frequency selectivity with age, and 3) the range of individual differences – both across listeners of a given age and between the ears of one listener. This study represents a first attempt to delineate some of the population statistics of frequency selectivity, as represented by the auditory filter.

Our final motivation was to determine whether the auditory filter measure could be used with the population at large. It has often been argued that the basic measure of hearing should not be a measure of absolute sensitivity – the audiogram – but rather a measure of frequency selectivity. Whether fine frequency resolution is a prerequisite for good auditory perception has yet to be demonstrated conclusively. But it seems likely that it is, and in this case it will be important to have a robust, as well as sensitive, measure of frequency selectivity.

1. METHOD

The auditory filters of 16 listeners, whose ages spanned the range 23 to 75 years, were determined at three centre frequencies (0.5, 2.0 and 4.0 kHz) for both ears – a total of 96 filter shapes. The filters were obtained as in Patterson (1976) and Weber (1977) using a sinusoidal signal and a simultaneous, notched-noise masker. The notch was centred on the tone and threshold was measured as a function of notch width. The filter shape is the derivative of the threshold curve. If the distance from the tone, f_o, to the edges of the notch is Δf, then thresholds were measured for values of $\Delta f/f_o$ equal to 0.0, 0.025, 0.05, 0.1, 0.15, 0.2, 0.3 and 0.4.

Thirteen of the sixteen listeners were recruited via a newspaper advertisement that was originally intended to attract young, normal listeners for a completely separate experiment but which, in the event, drew responses from all age groups. Three of these thirteen (CS, WW and JM) participated in a previous psychophysical experiment, the rest were naive. The only further requirements for inclusion were that they could understand speech and were available two hours a day for a four-week period. Two more young listeners (IB and JW) were recruited to increase the age range and the final listener was author RM. Briefly, then, the listeners were a reasonably representative sample of adults with "normal" hearing from a small academic, non-industrial city.

An adaptive, two-interval, forced-choice procedure was used, with a rule of 'signal down after two correct/up after one wrong'. The step size was reduced from 8 to 2 dB after 6 turnarounds and threshold was taken to be the average of all the turnaround-levels beyond the first 6; there were typically 15-20 turnarounds in the 80-trial run. The signal was gated on and off with a 50-ms cosine ramp and its total duration was 400 ms. The noise masker came on 50 ms before and went off 50 ms after the signal; the noise spectrum level outside the notch was 40 dB SPL. Each condition was run twice and if the two estimates of threshold differed by more than 5 dB a third run was performed. The 4.0-kHz conditions proved more variable and so a complete, third replication was included at this signal frequency. The data to be presented are, then, the average of 2 to 4 threshold estimates. The listeners received one hour of practice before the experiment proper began.

2. RESULTS AND DISCUSSION

The listeners were divided into the following four age groups: under 40, 40 to 59, 60 to 71, and 72 to 75 years - a division that yielded four listeners in each group. The rounded-exponential auditory filter described by Patterson and Nimmo-Smith (1980) was fitted to each set of data using a power-spectrum model of masking and the assumption that the filter is symmetric to a first approximation at these stimulus levels. There are threshold curves for both ears of each listener, and so for each of the 12 combinations of signal frequency and age group there are 8 threshold curves. The best and worst curves associated with each combination were selected on the basis of the total range of the curve and the rate of fall in the region below 0.3. The best and worst curves are plotted, separately for each signal frequency, in the upper and lower halves of Fig. 1 respectively. The filter shapes themselves have been omitted for brevity; in general, however, since the curves are basically exponential and the filter shape is the derivative of the threshold curve, the filter has the same shape as the threshold curve that generates it, except that the bends in the filter are more pronounced. When choosing the worst threshold curves, it appeared that a few of them were limited at the wider notch widths by the absolute threshold level. This could produce an artificially low estimate of frequency selectivity and so this analysis was restricted to curves where the threshold for the narrowest notches was at least 20 dB above absolute threshold. The listeners that produced the 11 curves excluded by this criterion are listed in the upper righthand corner of the appropriate sub-figure; their ages are GD 71, AH 72, KP 73 and WC 75.

The data in the upper half of Fig. 1 show the effects of signal frequency: threshold rises at the narrowest notch widths indicating that the absolute width of the auditory filter increases with centre frequency; at the same time, however, the curves become steeper indicating that the relative width of the auditory filter decreases with increasing centre frequency, although the effect is slight between 0.5 and 2.0 kHz. The same effects appear in the lower half of Fig. 1 in the data of the two younger age groups.

The effect of age on the auditory filter is most apparent in the lower half of Fig. 1 where it can be seen that the dashed curves associated with the older groups lie largely above the solid and broken curves associated with the younger groups; this is particularly true for the wider notch widths which, of

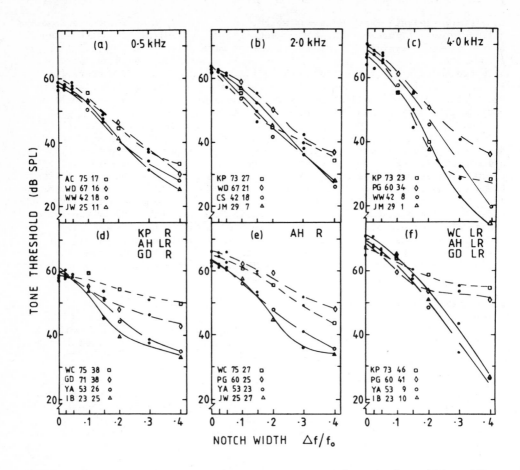

Figure 1.   Tone threshold plotted as a function of the relative width, $\Delta f/f_o$, of the notch in the noise masker. The data are for three signal frequencies, 0.5, 2.0, and 4.0 kHz, and for four age groups, under 40 ———△———, 40-59 ——— ○ ———, 60-71 —— —◇— ——, and 72-75 —□— – – – . The best and worst threshold curves in each age group appear in the upper and lower halves of the figure respectively. The specific listeners, their ages and absolute thresholds are listed in the lower lefthand corner of each sub-figure. Some of the data are plotted as dots to avoid clutter.

course, provide the more sensitive test. The threshold curves of the older groups do not fall as far or as fast as those of the younger groups. The effect of age can also be seen in the upper half of the figure but in this case the effect is considerably smaller; in fact, at the two higher signal frequencies the representative of the oldest age group provides a threshold curve that is comparable with that of the best listener of the youngest group when $\Delta f/f_o < 0.2$.

The within-listener variability is relatively low; the standard deviation for an 80-trial threshold run is about 2.3 dB, and successive runs typically produce threshold estimates less than 5 dB apart for signal frequencies of 0.5 and 2.0 kHz. The data are slightly more variable at 4.0 kHz where the threshold curve is steeper. Thus it would appear that a reliable three-point estimate of frequency selectivity ($\Delta f/f_o$ = 0.0, 0.2, 0.4) could be obtained for a naive listener at three signal frequencies in one two-hour session.

In summary, the experiment indicates that there is a complex but reasonably comprehensible interaction involving age, signal frequency, and individual. For young and middle-aged people (under 60) the relative width of the auditory filter improves with signal frequency and the effects of age and individual are minimal. For these age groups it is the uniformity rather than the variability of the filter shape that is noteworthy -- the differences among the threshold curves of these listeners rise to 10 dB only at the widest notch widths. The filter shape broadens noticeably with age above age 60 but the broadening is not uniform; it is most apparent at 4.0 kHz and least apparent at 2.0 kHz, and there are large individual differences. Some listeners in their mid-70's still resemble young adults when $\Delta f/f_0 < 0.2$ -- the region associated with the passband of the filter; other listeners have lost much of their frequency selectivity by age 70. It should also be noted that, while there would appear to be some correlation between the ears of a young individual, this correlation has disappeared by age 60, and above this age there can be enormous discrepancies between the ears of one individual; for example, listener KP, aged 73, provided both the best and worst threshold curves for the 4.0-kHz column of Fig. 1.

Acknowledgements

The authors would like to express their gratitude to Dan Weber who developed the subject pool and the efficient testing procedure which made this study possible. We would also like to thank Ian Nimmo-Smith for fitting the auditory filter model to these data.

REFERENCES

de Boer, E., and Bouwmeester, J.(1974). "Critical Bands and Sensorineural Hearing Loss," *Audiology* 13, 236-259.

Patterson, R.D. (1976). "Auditory Filter Shapes Derived with Noise Stimuli," *J. Acoust. Soc. Am.* 59, 640-654.

Patterson, R.D., and Nimmo-Smith, I. (1980). "Off-frequency listening and auditory-filter asymmetry. *J. Acoust. Soc. Am.* 67, 229-245.

Pick, G.F., Evans, E.F., and Wilson, J.P.(1977). "Frequency resolution in patients with hearing loss of cochlear origin," In: *Psychophysics and Physiology of Hearing*. (E.F. Evans and J.P. Wilson, eds). pp. 273-282. Academic Press, London.

Weber, D.L.(1977). "Growth of masking and the auditory filter," *J. Acoust. Soc. Am.* 62, 424-429.

Zwicker, E., and Schorn, K.(1978). "Psychoacoustical Tuning Curves in Audiology," *Audiology* 17, 120-140.

COMMENT ON: "The effect of age on auditory filter shape" (R.D. Patterson and R. Milroy)

E.F. Evans
Dept. of Communication & Neuroscience, University of Keele, U.K.

Do your filter bandwidths correlate with elevation of threshold at the corresponding frequencies ? In our own data in patients (published: Pick, Evans and Wilson, 1977 and unpublished), while we find a general relation, we do not find a 1 : 1 relation: some patients have abnormal frequency selectivity without any or any substantial hearing loss at these frequencies.

AUDITORY FILTER BANDWIDTH DERIVED FROM DIRECT MASKING
OF COMPLEX SIGNALS

J.W. Horst   and   R.J. Ritsma

Institute of Audiology, University Hospital
Groningen, The Netherlands

1. INTRODUCTION

Determination of auditory filter bandwidth in masking experiments is usually performed by using a pure tone or a narrow band of noise with fixed bandwidth as test signal, while the masker is varied as to spectral shape. The only experiment to our knowledge in which the test signal bandwidth was systematically varied, was performed by Gässler (1954). He found an auditory filter bandwidth of about 20% of the filter frequency, in good agreement with many of the results that are obtained with a fixed test signal and variable masker. Gässler's signals consisted of evenly spaced components with a flat spectral envelope. For these signals the auditory system appeared to be an integrator with a bandwidth that is now accepted as the *critical bandwidth (CBW)*.
In experiments with complex signals, primarily intended as an investigation of frequency discrimination as a function of the signal-to-noise ratio of complex signals with triangular spectral envelope, it turned out that the masking thresholds could not be described by integration over a critical band (Horst, 1979). Therefore a closer examination of the masking thresholds for complex signals was performed. In our analysis we follow the traditional description of the auditory system by many overlapping filters, each of which is a linear filter. Detection occurs when the signal-to-noise ratio within any of the filters exceeds a certain threshold. By using a peaked signal spectrum the auditory filter centered at the peak will contain maximal signal-to-noise ratio. Thus we expect that this filter will be most effective in the detection task; consequently the masking thresholds will be determined by this same filter.

2. METHOD

As a test signal multitone complexes were used with 20 Hz and 100 Hz fundamental frequency and 2000 Hz central frequency. Their spectral envelope was triangular on a log-log scale, the slope G of the envelope (in dB per octave) was chosen as a variable. The masking noise was obtained by bandpass filtering white noise between 1000 Hz and 4000 Hz (edges 24 dB/oct). The stimuli were presented binaurally through TDH 49 earphones. The masking threshold was determined at a fixed level of the signal of 40 dB SL with a 2IFC procedure. Stimuli consisted of two observation periods of 225 ms each, separated by a pause of 275 ms. In both observation periods a masker burst was presented, while only one period contained a test signal burst. Masker and test signal burst had the same temporal envelope with rise and fall time of 25 ms. The noise level was varied in steps of 1 dB.

3. RESULTS

100 Hz fundamental frequency. Sine phase relation

Results are shown in fig. 1. The masking thresholds in fig. 1a are expressed as signal level L_{CB} within a CB minus noise spectrum level L_n^* at threshold. L_{CB} was calculated from the total signal level by integration of signal energy within a CB centered at 2000 Hz; this CB was taken 400 Hz wide. Fig. 1a shows a clear dependence of $L_{CB} - L_n^*$ on the spectral shape of the

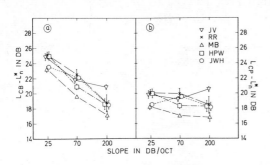

Fig.1 Dependence of the masking threshold on the slope of the spectral envelope for signals with sine phase relation. Fundamental frequency f_o is 100 Hz. Central frequency f_c is 2000 Hz. L_n^* is the noise spectrum level at masking threshold. L_{CB} is the signal level within a critical band (400 Hz wide) at 2000 Hz. L_{CP} is the central component level. Vertical bars indicate standard deviations of the mean.

signals. This means that different distributions of signal energy within a CB yield different masking thresholds.

These results can be translated in an *equivalent rectangular bandwidth (ERBW)* of the auditory filter considerably smaller than the CBW. Fig. 1b presents the results of the same experiment but expressed as the central component level of the signal minus the noise spectrum level. The independence on the slope suggests that only the level of the central component determines the signal's detection in the noise.

100 Hz fundamental frequency. Semi-random phase relation

A difference in spectral shape is inevitably connected with a difference in temporal shape of the signals. One conspicuous difference for the sine phase signals is the strongly peaked temporal envelope of the 25 dB/oct signal as opposed to the nearly flat envelope of the 200 dB/oct signal. Since the possibility of an influence of the temporal envelope on the masking threshold ought not to be excluded, the experiment was repeated with signals with a randomly chosen (though fixed) phase relation and the same power spectrum. Thus the energy was better distributed over the whole fundamental period; consequently the highest temporal peak of the 25 dB/oct signals was 6 dB lower than in the case of the sine phase relation. Yet the same thresholds were found (fig. 2). When this is interpreted in terms of an equivalent rectangular bandfilter, these results yield an ERBW of less than 200 Hz. Optimal positioning of the filter even suggests ERBW < 100 Hz.

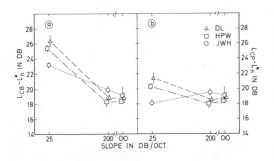

Fig.2 Dependence of the masking threshold on the slope G of the spectral envelope for signals with a semi-random phase relation. $G = \infty$ refers to the 2000 Hz pure tone. For further explanation see fig.1.

20 Hz fundamental frequency. Semi-random phase relation

A fundamental frequency of 20 Hz was used in order to determine the ERBW with more accuracy for these complex signals. Again the signals had a triangular spectral envelope, but the spectrum was limited to a band of 1800 - 2200 Hz. The masking thresholds for the pure tone and the narrow band complex (fig.3)

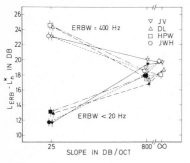

Fig.3 Masking thresholds for f_O = 20 Hz and semi-random phase relation. Open symbols refer to ERBW = 400 Hz.
Filled symbols refer to ERBW < 20 Hz, when only one spectral component is transmitted by the auditory filter. For further explanation see fig. 1 and 2.

show that the central component of the 25 dB/oct complex alone did not contain enough energy to be detected. Thus a spectral peak detector (being unlikely) could be ruled out. The actual ERBW can be deduced from fig. 4 on the assumption that at masking threshold the signal energy within the ERBW is a constant, independent of spectral envelope. Thus fig. 4 yields an ERBW of 80 Hz.

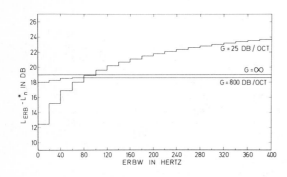

Fig.4 Masking threshold as a function of the ERBW. Only signal energy within a rectangular band around 2000 Hz is taken into account. Threshold levels are obtained by averaging the individual data of fig. 3.
For ERBW = 400 Hz L_{ERB} is equal to the total signal level (open symbols in fig.3); L_{ERB} is for ERBW < 20 Hz equal to the central component level (filled symbols in fig.3).

Fundamental frequency 20 Hz. Flat spectral envelope

Finally, masking thresholds were determined for 400 Hz wide complexes with a flat spectral envelope, 20 Hz fundamental frequency and two different phase relations, one of which was the sine phase relation. These signals resembled those used by Gässler. No difference was found for the two phase relations

Table I Masking thresholds of six observers for the 2000 Hz pure tone and the 20 Hz complex with flat spectral envelope. The last row shows the difference between the pure tone threshold and the average threshold of both complexes. All values are given in dB.

	JV	LE	RR	DL	HPW	JWH	MEAN
Pure tone	19.6±.4	21.4±.6	19.4±.7	18.8±.6	18.1±.5	19.2±.3	19.4±.5
Complex:sine phase	24.0±.6	25.5±.4	25.5±.3	25.4±.3	23.7±1.0	23.4±.4	24.6±.4
semi-random phase	24.9±.5	26.9±.4	25.1±.4	22.9±.3	27.7±.6	22.3±.2	24.9±.9
Complex vs. pure tone	4.8±.5	4.8±.7	5.9±.8	5.3±.8	7.7±.7	3.6±.3	5.4±.6

(table I). However masking thresholds for the complexes were on the average 5 dB higher than for the pure tone. This level difference can be transposed in an ERBW, viz. 80 to 120 Hz. These results are in agreement with the above presented data, although in this case of a flat spectral envelope it is not quite certain that the detection task is limited to the output of the filter tuned to the center of the complex.

4. DISCUSSION

The ERBW found in the present masking experiments is about 4% of the central frequency of the signals. This is much smaller than the traditional value of 15 to 20% for the CBW. ERBW was determined on the assumption that it is constant for all signals used in these experiments. However, masking of a pure tone is known to yield an ERBW equal to the CBW (Houtgast, 1974, Patterson, 1976, Weber, 1978). So we are left with a paradox, for which we have no solution.

Since lateral suppression only shows its influence in nonsimultaneous masking (Houtgast, 1974), it cannot cause this small ERBW.

The auditory bandwidth presented above is about the same as Fletcher (1940) obtained in a rather crude first version of the bandlimiting experiment. It was suggested a.o. by De Boer (1962) that a change of noise bandwidth results in a change of noise variability, which in turn changes the detection criterion. Although some experiments support this view (Hamilton, 1957), it was refuted by other ones (Weber, 1978). It may be that variation of the test signal bandwidth results in a change of the detection criterion. Then it is not clear why Gässler did not find this bandwidth dependence of masking threshold. The differences between Gässler's procedure and ours are: a) Monaural vs. binaural listening, b) Békésy tracking vs. 2IFC, c) uniform masking noise vs. white noise, d) running phase vs. fixed phase relation, e) signal level variation vs. noise level variation.

It does not seem very likely that a), b), c) or e) can explain the measured differences. As for the running phase, although we found no difference for different phase relations, we do not exclude the possibility that the continuously changing timbre of the signal changed the detection criterion.

The present results show that integration of signal energy in the auditory system is not always performed over a complete critical band. ERBW can be reduced to a value 3 to 4 times smaller than the CBW.

REFERENCES

Boer, E. de (1962). Note on the critical bandwidth. *J.Acoust.Soc.Am.*, 34, 985-986.
Fletcher, H. (1940). Auditory Patterns. *Rev.Mod.Phys.*, 12, 47-65.
Gässler, G. (1954). Ueber die Hörschwelle für Schallereignisse mit verschieden breitem Frequenzspektrum. *Acustica* 4, 408-414.
Hamilton, P.M. (1957). Noise masked thresholds as a function of tonal duration and masking noise bandwidth. *J.Acoust.Soc.Am.*, 29, 506-511.
Horst, J.W. (1979). Frequentiediscriminatie en signaal-ruisverhouding. *Ned. Akoestisch Genootschap*, publ.nr. 47, 81-92 (in Dutch).
Houtgast, T. (1974). Lateral suppression in hearing. *Thesis*. (Academische Pers, B.V. Amsterdam).
Patterson, R.D. (1976). Auditory filter shapes derived with noise stimuli. *J.Acoust.Soc.Am.*, 59, 640-654.
Weber, D.L. (1978). Suppression and critical bands in band-limiting experiments. *J.Acoust.Soc.Am.*, 64, 141-150.

Acknowledgements
This research was supported by the Netherlands Organization for the Advancement of Pure Research (Z.W.O.)

COMMENT

COMMENT ON: "Auditory filter bandwidth derived from direct masking of complex signals" (J.W. Horst and R.J. Ritsma).

B.C.J. Moore
Dept. of Experimental Psychology, University of Cambridge, Great Britain.
and
J.W. Horst
Institute of Audiology, University Hospital Groningen, the Netherlands.

Horst and Ritsma analyse their data assuming a critical band with a rectangular shape, and expressing the bandwidth of the auditory filter in terms of equivalent rectangular bandwidth. The discrepancy between their results and other estimates of auditory filter bandwidth is reduced if a more realistic shape is assumed for the auditory filter. Patterson and Nimmo-Smith (1980) estimate that the auditory filter has approximately exponential skirts, a rounded top, and a 3-dB down bandwidth of about 10 percent of the centre frequency.

Consider the results in figures 1(b) and 2(b) of Horst and Ritsma. For a slope of 25 dB/oct the signal components at 1900 and 2100 Hz will be -1.85 and -1.75 dB relative to the component at 2000 Hz. If the auditory filter is centred at 2000 Hz, and is 3 dB down at 1900 and 2100 Hz, then at the output of the filter the components at 1900 and 2100 Hz will be -4.85 and -4.75 dB relative to the central component. Ignoring the small contribution from other components, the total signal output will be +2.2 dB relative to the level of the central component. Thus if threshold is expressed in terms of the level of the central component the threshold should be 2.2 dB lower in the 25 dB/oct condition than in the 200 dB/oct condition. The data reveal no systematic difference for these conditions, so there is a small discrepancy from the predictions of the auditory filter model.

Similar calculations applied to the data shown in figure 3, taking into account all components present, reveal that the total filter output for a signal slope of 25 dB/oct should be approximately +9 dB relative to the level of the central component. This is slightly greater than the difference in threshold between the 25 dB/oct and infinite slope conditions, when threshold is expressed in terms of the level of the central component.

For the signal with a flat spectral envelope and 400 Hz bandwidth, the auditory filter output would be +10 dB relative to the level of the central component, or -3dB relative to the level of the whole complex. Thus the threshold for the complex signal ought to be +3 dB relative to threshold for the pure tone. The difference actually observed is about 5 dB (table I).

In each case the threshold for the complex signal is slightly higher than would be predicted by the auditory filter model of Patterson and Nimmo-Smith. This small discrepancy may indicate that threshold is not determined solely by signal-to-masker ratio at the output of the auditory filter; the exact composition of signal and masker may also play a role (Moore, 1975).

REFERENCES

Moore, B.C.J. (1975). Mechanisms of masking. *J. Acoust. Soc. Am.* <u>57</u>, 391-399.
Patterson, R.D. and Nimmo-Smith (1980). Off-frequency listening and auditory-filter asymmetry. *J. Acoust. Soc. Am.* <u>67</u>, 229-245.

EFFECTS OF NOISE EXPOSURE ON FREQUENCY SELECTIVITY
IN NORMAL AND HEARING-IMPAIRED LISTENERS*

L.L. Feth, E.M. Burns, G. Kidd, Jr., and C.R. Mason

*Dept. Audiology and Speech Sciences, Purdue University,
West Lafayette, Indiana, U.S.A.*

1. INTRODUCTION

Earlier work in our laboratory has demonstrated that psychophysical tuning curves (PTC's) reflect temporary changes in normal ears after brief exposure to moderately intense noise (Balthazor *et al.*, 1976; Feth *et al.*, 1979). Here we will report further work with listeners having normal hearing and some preliminary results on hearing-impaired listeners.

2. METHODS

Pre-exposure PTC's and post-noise-exposure tuning curves (PNPTC's) were obtained using an adaptive 2IFC, forward-masking procedure. The 20-msec probe tone was fixed in frequency (3 kHz) and level (10 dB SL) for the entire experimental run. For a given run the 300-msec masking tone was fixed at one of nine frequencies ranging from 2.4 to 3.6 kHz. Except where noted in the results section, at least four adaptive tracking runs were averaged to produce a point on the psychophysical tuning curve.

For this report we will present the effects of brief (5-min) exposure to a 100 dB SPL octave band (1.2 to 2.4 kHz) of noise. For each listener, the noise exposure was followed by one masked "threshold" determination at 2, 4, 8, 16 and 32 min. At each post-exposure time a different masker frequency was tested so that seven to nine exposures were required to obtain one estimate at each masker frequency and post-exposure time combination. In addition, TTS was measured for both 20-msec and 300-msec 3 kHz tones at the same post-exposure times. In all procedures, a continuous 0 dB spectrum level background noise was presented.

3. RESULTS

Figure 1 contains pre-exposure PTC's and PNPTC's for five listeners. Pre-exposure PTC's are represented by open circles connected by solid lines. For purposes of clarity only two of the five PNPTC's (2 and 32 min post-exposure) are shown for each subject. Generally, the 2 min PNPTC drops below the pre-exposure PTC indicating that the noise exposure has rendered the tonal masker temporarily more effective. PNPTC's obtained from these subjects at 4, 8 and 16 min post-exposure tend to fall between the pre-exposure and the 2 min curves. At 32 min, the post-exposure thresholds approach the pre-exposure values. For subjects 1, 3 and 4 the masked "threshold" levels at frequencies just above the probe frequency remain lower even at 32 min. Subject 2's PNPTC's appear to show little evidence of change due to noise exposure, and, in fact, post-exposure masked "threshold" levels are higher at frequencies just above the probe.

Portions of this material were presented at the 97th Meeting of the Acoustical Society of America, Cambridge, Mass., June 1979.

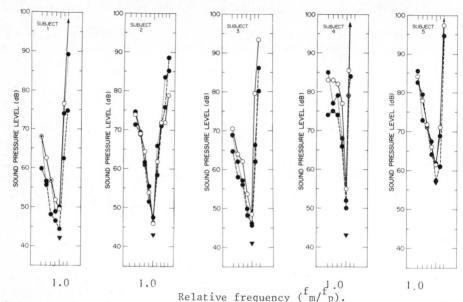

Fig.1. Pre-exposure PTC's (0) and PNPTC's determined at 2 min (---) and 32 min (.....) after a 5 min exposure to a 100-dB octave band (1200 to 2400 Hz) of noise. Each division on the absissia represents a 0.05 change in frequency ratio.

Q_{10dB} Psychophysical Tuning Curves

Subject Number	Pre-Exposure	Post-Exposure					
		2	4	8	16	32	min.
1	7.2	5.8	4.9	5.9	5.7	5.7	
2	10.3	7.9	7.6	10.8	8.4	10.9	
3	9.4	7.4	7.2	9.6	6.3	7.8	
4*	33.0	21.4	15.8	27.2	27.2	30.0	
5*	7.7	9.3	8.5	8.1	7.8	7.4	

Table 1.   Comparison of Q_{10dB} for PNPTC's with those for pre-exposure PTC's.   Subjects 1-4 presented normal audiological thresholds and no evidence of pathology.   Subject 5 has a hearing loss attributable to cochlear pathology.   (*Only two replications per point on PNPTC's.)

Audiometric Data

Frequency	250	500	1000	2000	3000	4000	Hz
Audiometric Threshold (HTL)	70	70	80	60	35	20	dB
Q_{10dB}	–	–	–	3.9	7.7	8.5	

Table 2.   Audiometric data and selectivity indicators for Subject 5.

To assess shape changes in PTC's due to noise exposure, Q_{10dB} was determined for each tuning curve by fitting straight-line segments to the tip portions. All data points above or below the probe frequency were included in the line-segments except for subject 4 where the two lower masker frequencies appeared to be part of a "tail" segment. The datum point at the probe frequency was included in both the upper and lower segment.

Values of Q_{10dB} are given in Table 1. Notice that Q_{10dB} for S4 which is highest for the pre-exposure PTC, is most drastically reduced.

Subjects with hearing losses attributable to cochlear pathologies are also participating in our experiments. Audiometric results for one subject (S5) appear in Table 2. Subject 5 presents a very unusual audiometric configuration. The hearing loss is greatest for low frequencies but approaches normal limits in the 3-4 kHz region. Except for elevated levels, the 3 kHz pre-exposure PTC of subject 5 does not appear to be different from normal. The pre-exposure Q_{10dB} value for S5 is similar to those obtained from three of our four normal-hearing listeners. For S5, the noise exposure had little effect on the low frequency side of the PTC. The post-exposure change is most evident in the drop in masker level at detection "threshold" for masker frequencies at, or just above, the probe frequency.

4. DISCUSSION

The effects of brief noise exposure may be evident in the PNPTC's of our normal listeners in two ways. Except for S2, the masked threshold values for each PNPTC are generally lower than the corresponding pre-exposure curve, and all four normals show post-exposure Q_{10dB} values that represent poorer selectivity than the pre-exposure PTC's. These results, using a forward masking paradigm, agree with those of Balthazor *et al.* (1976), who found similar changes in post-exposure pulsation threshold curves. Our PNPTC's appear to be more sensitive indicators of the temporary effects of noise exposure than are traditional TTS measures, since only S1 showed a substantial post-exposure threshold shift (TTS_2 = 4 dB; TTS_4 = 0 dB for a 300-msec tone).

For three of our four normals, and for our hearing-impaired listener, the brief exposure to moderately intense noise has apparently rendered the tonal maskers more effective. That is, for a given masker, probe threshold is attained with substantially less masker intensity. Because the magnitude of this effect varies with masker frequency, the PNPTC's for three of our four normal listeners show small differences in Q_{10dB} after noise exposure, which may be thought to be indicative of selectivity changes. In Fig. 1, however, S2 shows no apparent downward shift in post-exposure masked threshold levels, yet the changes in Q_{10dB} values for S2 are comparable to those of S1 and S3. Since we have not applied statistical tests to these values, we must be cautious in interpreting such Q_{10dB} differences as indicative of temporary cochlear changes due to noise exposure.

Evans and Wilson (1973) have suggested that the hypothetical second filter contributing to peripheral frequency selectivity may be vulnerable to reversible changes. Our PNPTC's may reflect the temporary changes in that sharpening mechanism brought about by the noise exposure. Wightman *et al.* (1977) suggest that sensorineural hearing loss may result in a permanent change in the sharpening mechanism. We might, then, expect listeners with such losses to show no evidence of post-exposure changes in PTC's. The hearing-impaired listener (S5) presented in this report does show post-exposure changes on the high frequency side of the PNPTC's. Of course, this listener does not represent a "typical" cochlear pathology. Our tuning curves were obtained in the frequency region where the audiogram indicates a transition from 80 dB HTL at 1 kHz to 20 dB HTL at 4 kHz. The severe loss of sensitivity in the low frequency region may contribute to the unexpected sharpness of the pre-exposure PTC and account for the absence of post-exposure changes. On the high frequency side the loss falls just below normal limits and post-exposure masked threshold changes similar to those for normals are evident. There is evidence that tuning curves obtained from pathological ears showing mild sensorineural losses are not distinguishably broader than those obtained at equivalent levels from normal subjects (Dallos *et al.*, 1977).

Acknowledgements

This work was supported by grants from NINCDS and a David Ross Fellowship from the Purdue Research Foundation.

REFERENCES

Balthazor, R.J., Cooper, W.A. Jr. and Feth, L.L. (1976). Effects of noise exposure on pulsation threshold curves. *J. Acoust. Soc. Amer.* <u>59</u>, S3 (Abstract).

Dallos, P., Ryan, A., Harris, D., McGee, T. and Ozdamar, O. (1977). Cochlear frequency selectivity in the presence of hair cell damage. In: *Psychophysics and Physiology of Hearing*. (E.F. Evans and J.P. Wilson, eds), pp 249-259. Academic Press, London.

Evans, E.F. and Wilson, J.P. (1973). The frequency selectivity of the cochlea. In: *Basic Mechanisms in Hearing*. (A.R. Møller, ed), pp519-555. Academic Press, New York.

Feth, L.L., Oesterle, E.C. and Kidd, G. Jr. (1979). Frequency selectivity after noise exposure. *J. Acoust. Soc. Amer.* <u>65</u> S118 (Abstract).

Wightman, F.L., McGee, T. and Kramer, M. (1977). Factors infuencing freuency selectivity in normal and hearing-impaired listeners. In: *Psychophysics and Physiology of Hearing*. (E.F. Evans and J.P. Wilson, eds), pp. 295-306. Academic Press, London.

NARROW-BAND AP STUDIES IN NORMAL AND RECRUITING HUMAN EARS

J.J. Eggermont
Department of Medical Physics and Biophysics,
University of Nijmegen,
Nijmegen, The Netherlands.

1. INTRODUCTION

Narrow-band action potentials (NAP) are compound action potentials from a narrow region of the cochlea and can be derived using a special masking technique (Teas et al.,1962; Elberling, 1974; Eggermont, 1976). NAPs may be regarded as an alternative to single nerve fiber responses (Elberling and Evans, 1979) useful in situations when recording of single nerve fiber activity is impossible (e.g. in humans). For normal human ears NAPs have been derived for 1/2-octave wide regions (2.5 - 3 mm) along the cochlear partition.

The NAP-latency shows as a function of the central frequency, f_{CF}, the same course as does the latency of the dominant peak from PST-histograms or the latency as derived from the cumulative phase of period histograms for single auditory nerve fibers as a function of characteristic frequency (Kiang et al., 1965; Anderson et al., 1971; Eggermont, 1979a). In addition iso-intensity contours for NAP amplitude as evoked by tonebursts in a fixed narrow-band (Eggermont, 1978) follow the same general pattern as the iso-intensity contours for the firing rate of single nerve fibers of fixed CF (Rose et al., 1971).

This leads us to believe that certain parameters of the NAPs (i.e. amplitude and latency) are closely related to firing rate and response latency of single auditory nerve fibers having a characteristic frequency similar to the f_{CF} of the narrow-band. For normal human ears the results will therefore be comparable to data from various animal cochleas and can be tested against theories about cochlear mechanics based mainly upon animal results but extended in applicability to man. In addition it has been our goal to obtain NAP recordings in recruiting human ears and to infer therefrom the changed characteristics of these cochleas (Eggermont, 1978, 1979a, b). Some of these cochleas, however, did show latencies which were considered too short when compared to normal data and calculated delay times of a one-dimensional transmission-line cochlear model (De Boer, 1979). In addition, some recent studies in kanamycin- and noise-damaged animal cochleas (Dallos and Harris, 1978; Salvi et al., 1979) have indicated that single fiber latencies to clicks and tonebursts were - on the average - not different from those obtained in normal ears. Clearly, the results obtained from part of the recruiting human ears are in strong contrast to the single fiber results from animal studies and inadmissible from the point of view of current theory.

In this paper we will present NAP-onset latencies which will be corrected for the f_{CF} independent delay (mainly of synaptic origin) and compare the obtained f_{CF} dependent delay for normal and recruiting human ears with currently available experimental and theoretical evidence for the building up of response latency.

2. METHODS

Recording is performed with a transtympanically placed needle electrode on the promontory with reference to the ipsilateral mastoid. The minute responses were amplified (50.000 x, 10 Hz - 10 kHz), averaged (512 times) and recorded on an XY recorder.

Stimulation was performed by means of a loud speaker, the sound pressure level was monitored at the entrance of the ear canal using a 1/8-inch condensor microphone. Details regarding the methods can be found in Eggermont et al. (1974) and Eggermont (1976).

3. RESULTS

A. *NAP amplitude-intensity function in normal and recruiting human ears.*

For a fixed narrow-band (f_{CF} = 5.2 kHz) we obtained NAPs to tonebursts of varying frequency and intensity in a normal ear as well as in a recruiting human ear (Fig. 1). The NAP amplitude shown as a function of stimulus intensity reveals that the lowest threshold for the normal ear was obtained for a toneburstfrequency of 6 kHz at 20 dB HL. The threshold increased for higher as well as lower toneburstfrequencies. The NAPs were obtained under approximately equal signal-to-noise ratio's i.e. in all cases the high-pass masking noise was filtered out of wide band noise having a level which would just mask the AP response. It is observed that the slope of the amplitude-intensity curves increases gradually with a decreasing toneburstfrequency: the change in slope from 6 kHz to 1.5 kHz is about two-fold; for toneburstfrequencies above the f_{CF} the slope decreases sharply.

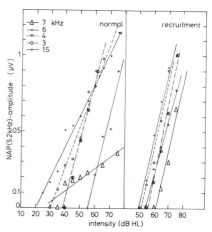

For the recruiting ear, however, an increase in threshold is noted (except at 1.5 kHz) and in addition one observes slopes which are about the same and roughly comparable to those obtained for the normal ear at frequencies well below f_{CF}.

Fig.1. Amplitude-intensity functions for narrow-band action potentials in a normal and a recruiting human ear. The NAPs were derived for a region with f_{CF} = 5.2 kHz for tonebursts having a frequency of 1.5; 3; 4; 6 and 7 kHz. On a linear amplitude scale the input-output functions can be approximated by straight lines. It seems that the slope is related to threshold for frequencies below f_{CF}. The values found in the recruiting ear are about the same as those in the normal ear for the 1.5 kHz toneburst, having the same threshold value.

B. *NAP onset latencies as a function of f_{CF}.*

1. Normal ears

For the NAP latency studies a click stimulus of 90 dB p.e. SPL was used throughout for the normal as well as the recruiting human ears. NAPs were derived for regions from around 10 kHz toward around 425 Hz, thereby representing a substantial part of the human cochlea. For 15 normal human ears the onset latencies are plotted against f_{CF} in the upper part of Fig. 2, it is evident that the latencies increase quite substantially from on average 1.5 ms at 10 kHz to 6 - 7 ms at the more apical end of the cochlea. In the lower part of Fig.2 the estimated frequency-independent part of the delay has been substracted from the NAP-onset latency, a regression line calculated through the data points was estimated as:

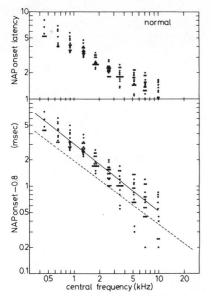

Fig.2. Onset latencies and delay values for click evoked narrow-band action potentials for 15 normal human cochleas as a function of the narrow-band central frequency (f_{CF}) The upper part shows the NAP-onset latencies, the lower part the delays as obtained by subtracting an f_{CF} independent value of 0.8 msec. The drawn line is the calculated regression line, the dashed line is adapted from Anderson et al. (1971) squirrel monkey data.

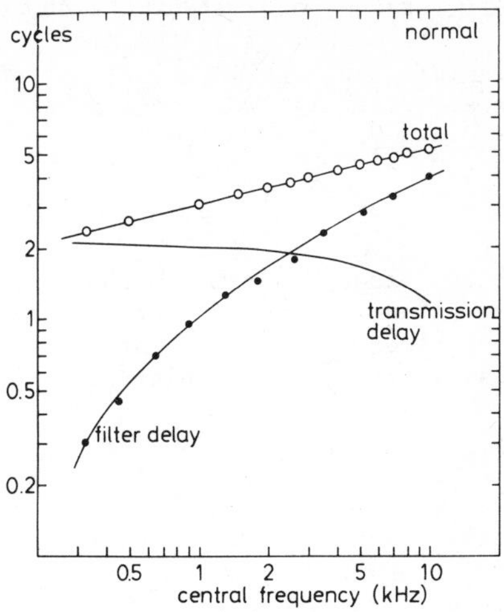

Fig.3. Conversion of delay values for NAPs to number of cycles at the corresponding f_{CF}. The curve marked "total" is obtained by multiplying the values found on the regression line from Fig.2 by f_{CF}. The "transmission-delay" curve is according to calculations by De Boer (1979). The "filter delay" curve represents the difference between both other curves.

$$\tau_{CF} = 3.05\ f_{CF}^{-0.77}\ \text{ms} \quad,\quad f_{CF}\ \text{in kHz.}$$

The dashed line drawn in for reference represents a regression line fit to the Anderson et al. (1971) data obtained for the squirrel monkey:

$$\tau_A = 1.95\ f_{CF}^{-0.725}\ \text{ms.}$$

A few data points at the higher f_{CF} values do show quite small response times of around 2 periods, while others even approach some 10 periods. An uncertainty in the determination of response latency can be estimated at 0.3 ms at most and will be influencing mostly the high f_{CF} values.

The response times can be converted into a number of periods of the f_{CF} by multiplying with f_{CF}. When this is done for the regression line for the normal data one obtains the curve marked "total" in Fig. 3 for which obviously holds:

$$n(f_{CF}) = 3.05\ f_{CF}^{0.23}.$$

For the f_{CF} range under study the number of periods ranges from 2 at the lower end of the f_{CF} toward 5 at the high f_{CF} end. De Boer (1979) calculated for a transmission line cochlear model for the stiffness dominated range a transmission (i.e. travelling wave) delay

$$n'(f_{CF}) = 2.12 \ (1 - \frac{f_{CF}}{22.5})$$

which curve has been drawn in too. Assuming that the frequency dependent total response delay is composed out of a travelling wave delay and a response delay of the cochlear filter, the latter was calculated at distinct f_{CF} points and a curve was fitted by eye. This curve can be reasonably approximated by

$$n''(f_{CF}) = 0.87 \ f_{CF}^{0.72}$$

indicating a sharply increasing function with f_{CF}.

2. Recruiting ears.

For 37 human ears with loudness recruitment for most of the frequencies from 0.5 - 8 kHz, the NAP-onset latencies for 90 dB p.e. SPL clicks - the same intensity as for the normal ears - have been plotted in Fig. 4, upper part. The lower part of the figure shows these values corrected for the frequency independent delay. The shaded area represents the absolute range for the normal ears and the drawn-in curve represents the theoretical transmission delay according to De Boer (1979). One observes quite a number of NAP latencies which are below the normal range and a somewhat smaller number which are also below the theoretical delay for the travelling wave.

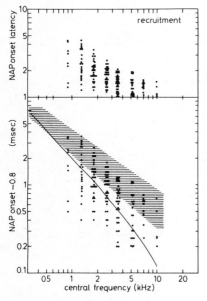

Fig.4. Onset latencies and delay values for click evoked narrow-band action potentials for 37 human ears with sensorineural hearing loss showing loudness recruitment. The format and procedure is analogous to Fig.2. The shaded area represents the range found for normal ears with the exception of the few low-value points at the high f_{CF} end. It is observed that a considerable number of points are below the normal range especially in the 1 - 5 kHz range. In addition a substantial number is below the drawn line, which represents the travelling delay for a transmission line cochlear model (De Boer, 1979). No latencies having larger than normal values have been found.

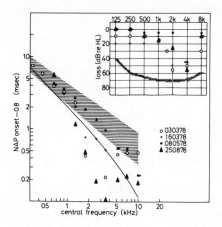

Fig.5. Audiograms and delay values obtained in four humans with a hearing loss restricted to the 2 - 4 kHz range. Three of these ears showed nearly normal hearing at the 8 kHz point. One patient (o) had a history of noise exposure and showed an identical hearing loss at the other ear. Two patients (+, o) had one sided, long existing, hearing losses of unknown origin. The fourth patient (Δ) had a symmetrical bilateral hearing loss, also long existing and of unknown origin. Three out of four patients show a decrease in NAP delay values for decreasing f_{CF} even into the range below the theoretical minimum (drawn curve). The patient with the noise trauma did not show abnormal latency values.

In four human ears where the hearing loss with recruitment was restricted to the 2 - 4 kHz range we had the opportunity to measure the NAP latencies. Fig. 5 (insert) shows the audiograms for these ears together with spectrum of the click stimulus used, the spectrum of the wide band noise was approximately the same. Fig. 5 shows the f_{CF} dependent delay for those four ears together with the range for normal ears as well as the theoretical travelling wave delay. It can be seen that for two ears in particular (Δ and o) the delays decrease initially when f_{CF} is decreased from 10 kHz on, and what is more peculiar they decrease from a value larger than the travelling wave delay to values shorter than this delay. In a third ear (+) the same trend is observed, while in the fourth case (●) the delay merely stays the same in two adjacent narrow-bands. The amount of departure from normal seems to be related to the amount of hearing loss.

These data show that the NAP latencies are normal in the frequency ranges where the hearing is normal and quite dramatically reduced (in 3 out of 4 cases) in the region of the hearing loss.

4. DISCUSSION

A. The NAP amplitude as a function of toneburst level for a particular f_{CF} follows the same pattern across toneburstfrequency as has been reported for the slope of the rate-intensity functions for single nerve fibers (Sachs and Abbas, 1974). Hence, the amplitude of the NAP seems to be related to firing rate.

Any compound action potential can be written as:

$$AP(t) = N \int_{o}^{t} a(t-\tau) \, s(\tau) \, d\tau$$

in which N is the number of newly activated nerve fibers, a(t) is the unit contribution at the recording site, and s(t) is a latency probability density function (Goldstein and Kiang, 1958; Teas et al., 1962). The decomposition of whole nerve action potentials into narrow-band action potentials assumes that

$$AP(t) = \sum_{i=1}^{n} NAP_i(t)$$

in which

$$NAP_i(t) = N_i \int_{o}^{t} a(t-\tau)\, s_i(\tau)\, d\tau.$$

Especially for narrow-bands with high f_{CF} values one assumes that $s_i(t)$ is sharply peaked compared to the duration of a(t) (e.g. Hoke et al., 1979). In that case one may write

$$NAP_i(t) = N_i \cdot a(t) \cdot \int_{o}^{t} s_i(\tau)\, d\tau$$

and the NAP amplitude will be proportional to the number of contributing nerve fibers. For lower f_{CF}-values $s_i(t)$ becomes broader than the a(t) and the NAP amplitude will still be proportional to N_i but not in a simple way.

For a single nerve fiber at place i along the cochlea (to correspond with the center of the ith narrow-band)

$$\int_{o}^{t} s_i(\tau)\, d\tau$$

will be the probability of firing in the interval (o, t).

Since NAPs are related to onset activity of single nerve fibers, the actual number of firings will depend on the onset firing rate of the nerve fiber. As Smith and Zwislocki (1975) have demonstrated the ratio of onset activity to steady state neural activity is constant over a wide intensity range. As firing rate in the determination of rate-intensity functions is dominated by the steady state activity, this leads to the conclusion that NAP amplitude is related to the average firing rate of neurons in the narrow-band.

The steep slopes for the NAP amplitude-intensity functions found in recruiting human ears therefore will reflect the increased slope of the rate-intensity functions observed for single nerve fibers in pathological cochleas (e.g. Evans, 1974), and indicate that loudness recruitment may be a phenomenon that can already take place in a restricted part of the cochlea and does not require the "help" of normal basal regions.

B.   The NAP-onset latency as a function of f_{CF} in normal human ears parallels the delay reported for single nerve fibers in animal studies. Compared to the data of Anderson et al. (1971) in the squirrel monkey the curve for the human ears is shifted toward higher f_{CF} by about 1 octave or alternatively the delay is approximately one period longer at each f_{CF}. At the low f_{CF} end the observed delay can be accounted for nearly completely by travelling wave delay, but at higher f_{CF} values one to three cycles of delay (Fig. 3) have to be added. This may be due to a delay caused by the cochlear filter at the resonance frequency and suggests progressively sharper tuning at the higher f_{CF} values. From a relation between filter delay and Q_{10dB} (Eggermont, 1979a) one expect changes of Q_{10dB} across f_{CF} from about 1 at the low frequency end up to 7 at the high frequency end.

Problems arise when one considers the results obtained in the recruiting ears. It is found that the NAP delays, in some cases, are shorter than the calculated travelling wave delay. In addition shorter than normal single fiber latencies, at the same intensity level, have not been observed in kanamycin- or noise damaged cochleas (Dallos and Harris, 1978; Salvi et al. 1979).

Since it could well be that latency values decrease below normal values but stay above the travelling wave delay limit by a deterioration of the cochlear filter, one is facing two problems. Why has a deterioration of the cochlear filter no appreciable result on the single fiber latencies, and how is it explainable that NAP delays drop below the values calculated for the travelling wave delay?

One obvious reason for the last problem could be that the method of deriving NAP responses, which is likely to be correct for normal ears (e.g. Elberling and Evans, 1979), fails when applied to certain pathological ears. One of the reasons may be that at the CF the thresholds are raised above the effective masking level of the high-pass noise while in the low frequency tail the fibers threshold is normal or even lower than normal (Dallos and Harris, 1978; Kiang et al., 1976). In this case the NAP attributed to a particular narrow-band may actually originate from nerve fibers with a CF approximately 2 - 3 octaves higher. In our experimental situation (see the spectral levels for the click and noise, Fig. 5) this can indeed take place for thresholds elevated above about 50 dB at 8 kHz, and 60 dB at 1.2, and 4 kHz. Calculating the number of ears that would have thresholds in that range (based on Eggermont, 1979a) one arrives at 17 ears qualifying for this criterion at 4 and 8 kHz. These ears would show in particular short latencies in the 1 - 2 kHz range. The actual number of ears having shorter than normal values in this range (about 20) seems to agree with this hypothesis.

This hypothesis, however, is hardly tenable for the ears with hearing loss restricted to the 2 - 4 kHz range. In this particular f_{CF} range the short latency values were found and not 2 octaves below that range, and besides that the thresholds in the 8 kHz range were sufficiently low to assure complete masking of the nerve fibers.

We therefore attempt to suggest another reason why, in particular in the ears with the restricted range of hearing loss, latencies at e.g. 2 kHz can not only be shorter than normal ears but also shorter than found in the same ear at a higher f_{CF}. According to De Boer (1979) the travelling wave delay is proportional to $C(x)^{-1/2}$, where $C(x)$ is the BM stiffness at place x.

From Békésy's (1960) work we know that travelling waves develop from the point where the stiffness is highest and travel to regions with lower stiffness values. One explanation for the paradoxal delays found (Fig. 5) could be that in the 2 - 4 kHz range the stiffness has increased beyond the value at the basal end of the cochlea. This would result in the shortest latency to arise in this range, increasing toward the apical as well as toward the basal end of the cochlea. The travelling wave then starts in the 2 - 4 kHz range. This raises questions about the cause of the hearing loss in these ears. As far as we could investigate there was no history of excessive noise exponse nor to the use of ototoxic drugs, except case 080578 which had a history of noise exponse. The required increase in BM stiffness, however, would be of the order of 10 times, for a decrease in travelling wave delay by a factor 3.

For the large group of recruiting ears with flat hearing losses nearly all the patients suffered from Menière's disease, a status of the inner ear with an enlarged endolymphatic compartment has been suggested therefore. If and how this could influence membrane stiffness remains an open question.

REFERENCES

Anderson, D.J., Rose, J.E., Hind, J.E. and Brugge, J.F. (1971). Temporal position of discharges in single auditory nerve fibers within the cycle of a sine-wave stimulus: Frequency and intensity effects. *J. Acoust. Soc. Am.* <u>49</u> 1131-1139.

Békésy, G. von (1960). *Experiments in Hearing*, McGraw Hill, New York.

Dallos, P. and Harris, D. (1978). Properties of auditory nerve responses in absence of outer hair cells. *J. Neurophysiol.* 41, 365-383.

De Boer, E. (1979). Travelling waves and cochlear resonance. In: *Models of the Auditory System and Related Signal Processing Techniques* (M. Hoke and E. de Boer, eds.). Scand. Audiol. Suppl. 9, 17-33.

Eggermont, J.J. (1976). Analysis of compound action potential responses to tonebursts in the human and guinea pig cochlea. *J. Acoust. Soc. Am.* 60, 1132-1139.

Eggermont, J.J. (1978). Stimulus-response relations for compound action potentials in normal and recruiting ears. In: *Evoked Electrical Activity in the Auditory Nervous System* (R.F. Naunton and C. Fernandez, eds.). Academic Press, New York.

Eggermont, J.J. (1979a). Narrow-band AP latencies in normal and recruiting human ears. *J. Acoust. Soc. Am.* 65, 463-470.

Eggermont, J.J. (1979b). Compound action potentials: tuning curves and delay times. In: *Models of the Auditory System and Related Signal Processing Techniques* (M. Hoke and E. de Boer, eds.). Scand. Audiol. Suppl. 9, 129-139.

Eggermont, J.J., Odenthal, D.W., Schmidt, P.H. and Spoor, A. (1974). *Electrocochleography, Basic Principles and Clinical Application*. Acta Otolaryngol. Suppl. 316, 1-84.

Elberling, C. (1974). Action potentials along the cochlear partition recorded from the ear canal in man. *Scand. Audiol.* 3, 13-19.

Elberling, C. and Evans, E.F. (1979). The validity of high-pass masking of the action potential: experiments in the cat. Paper read at the VIth Symposium of the IERASG, Santa Barbara.

Evans, E.F. (1974). Auditory frequency selectivity and the cochlear nerve. In: *Facts and Models in Hearing* (E. Zwicker and E. Terhardt, eds.). Springer, Berlin.

Goldstein, M. and Kiang, N.Y.-S. (1958). Synchrony of neural activity in electric responses evoked by transient acoustic stimuli. *J. Acoust. Soc. Am.* 30, 107-114.

Hoke, M., Elberling, C., Hieke, D. and Bappert, E. (1979). Deconvolution of compound PST histograms. In: *Models of the Auditory System and Related Signal Processing Techniques* (M. Hoke and E. de Boer, eds.). Scand. Audiol. Suppl. 9, 141-154.

Kiang, N.Y.-S., Watanabe, T., Thomas, E.C. and Clark, L.F. (1965). *Discharge Patterns of Single Fibers in the Cat's Auditory Nerve*. MIT Press, Cambridge U.S.A.

Kiang, N.Y.-S., Liberman, M.C., Levine, R.A. (1976). Auditory nerve activity in cats exposed to ototoxic drugs and high-intensity sounds. *Ann. Otol. Rhinol. Laryngol.* 75, 752-769.

Rose, J.E., Hind, J.E., Anderson, J.E. and Brugge, J.F. (1971). Some effects of stimulus-intensity on response of auditory nerve fibers in the squirrel monkey. *J. Neurophysiol.* 34, 685-699.

Sachs, M.B. and Abbas, P.J. (1974). Rate versus level functions for auditory nerve fibers in cats: toneburst stimuli. *J. Acoust. Soc. Am.* 56, 1835-1847.

Salvi, R.J., Henderson, D. and Hamernik, R.P. (1979). Single auditory nerve fibers and action potential latencies in normal and noise treated chinchilla's. *Hearing Research* 1, 237-251.

Smith, R.L. and Zwislocki, J.J. (1975). Short term adaptation and incremental responses of single auditory nerve fibers. *Biol. Cybernetics* 17, 169-182.

Teas, D.C., Eldredge, D.H. and Davis, H. (1962). Cochlear responses to acoustic transients: an interpretation of whole nerve action potentials. *J. Acoust. Soc. Am.* 34, 1438-1459.

COMMENT ON: "Narrow-band ap studies in normal and recruiting human ears"
(J.J. Eggermont)

D. McFadden
Department of Psychology, University of Texas, Austin, Texas 78712, U.S.A.

I am intrigued by your finding implying alterations in the propagation
velocity of the traveling wave. From the conversation in the halls it is clear
that many of the membrane specialists believe it to be unlikely that the basilar membrane could be altered in its physical characteristics in the ways
necessary to produce such changes in propagation velocity. Nevertheless, I
would like to point out that a long-standing curiousity in the auditory fatigue literature is also in accord with the assumption of alterations in the
physical characteristics of the cochlear partition. Following exposure to an
intense tonal stimulus, it is common to find no change in absolute sensitivity
at that frequency even though there is 20 dB or more of sensitivity loss at
higher frequencies. None of the existing explanations of this effect seem as
parsimonious to me as the presumption that the intense tone causes a temporary,
relatively local alteration in the physical characteristics of the partition
such that the over-stimulated region is now responsive to higher frequencies
than it was prior to the exposure.
Specifically, if the effective stiffness were increased locally or the effective mass decreased locally, one would expect the maximal sensitivity
changes to appear at frequencies higher than the exposure frequency--not because a higher frequency region had been more affected by the intense tone than
its own characteristic region, but because its own region has been temporarily
shifted in its resonance. Permanent changes in the stiffness or mass of the
membrane would, of course, also cause such shifts in resonance, and if the
changes were greater in one local region than in another, one might expect
travel-time anomalies of the sort you report. The idea appears easy to test with
an animal preparation--travel time to some low-frequency region should be
shorter following exposure to an intense high-frequency stimulus than before
exposure.

COMMENT ON: "Narrow-band ap studies in normal and recruiting human ears"
(J.J. Eggermont)

E.F. Evans
Dept. of Communication & Neuroscience, University of Keele, U.K.

Elberling and I found that, in the cat, the NAP method was invalid for
HP maskers less than about 2 kHz. In particular, fibres with the *lowest* rather
than the adjacent CFs were unexpectedly masked out. Could this, I wonder, be
happening for higher frequency HP maskers in your pathological cases thus
preferentially losing lower CF fibres with longer latencies ?

EFFECTS OF ACUTE NOISE TRAUMATA ON
COCHLEAR RESPONSE TIMES IN CATS

E. van Heusden

*Institute for Perception TNO,
Soesterberg, The Netherlands*

INTRODUCTION

In this paper we present preliminary results of a study on the effect of excessive noise stimulation on cochlear response times measured for single cells in the Antero-Ventral Cochlear Nucleus (AVCN).

"Any correlation of auditory physiology with cochlear histology is based on the premise that the best frequency (BF) dimension in the auditory nerve maps in some continuous way onto the longitudinal dimension of the cochlea" (Kiang *et al* , 1976). In the pathological ear there were doubts about this premise because excessive noise and ototoxic agents result in a shift to higher SPLs of the sharply tuned segment of a fiber's frequency tuning curve (FTC), and sometimes fibers become hypersensitive at low frequencies (Kiang *et al.*, 1976; Liberman and Kiang, 1978). Consequently, lower BF values will be assigned to these fibers. Robertson and Johnstone (1979) found this apparent BF shift to lower frequencies in spiral ganglion recordings of kanamycin-damaged guinea pig cochleas. In these animals the normal tonotopic pattern of organization in the cochlea was greatly disrupted.

For neurons whose discharges are phase-locked to the stimulus, timing of discharges with respect to the phase of the stimulus waveform can be measured. The slope of the cumulative phase shift as a function of stimulus frequency approximates a straight line. The slope of this line is a measure of the time delay between stimulus waveform and the corresponding waveform in the period histogram of the discharges (Anderson *et al*, 1971). For AVCN neurons the time delay between stimulus and response measured from the cumulative phase as a function of frequency is a monotonic function of BF (Gibson *et al*, 1977). In the traumatized ear this time delay (cochlear response time) measured in single cells in the AVCN may be a better indicator of the place along the basilar membrane innervated by those cells than the BF is. This hypothesis led us to perform experiments experiments on the cochlear response time before and after inducement of a noise trauma.

METHODS

Young healthy adult cats were anesthetized with sodium pentobarbital. The recording site was the AVCN ipsilateral to the stimulated ear. Stimuli were presented through an electrodynamic transducer (Beyer DT 48) connected to the cat's external meatus. The transducer was calibrated by measuring sound pressure level (SPL) and phase of sinewave stimuli with a calibrated probe tube microphone near the tympanic membrane.

Experiments lasted for about 50 h. Noise traumata were induced halfway through the experiments by exposing the ear for 30 minutes to 105.3 dB SPL pink noise. Such exposure resulted in a threshold shift which remained fairly steady during the experiment.

Cochlear response time is calculated from the phase shift revealed by the period histogram as a function of stimulus frequency and weighted according to firing rate (Goldstein *et al*, 1971).

EXPERIMENTS

Fig. 1 shows tuning curves of unit 760304 before and after inducement of a noise trauma. Frequency selectivity has decreased after inducement of the trauma. The FTC before the trauma at high SPL (higher spike-rate criterion) shows that the decrease in selectivity is not simply an SPL effect, because the tip of this curve is also sharper than the tip of the FTC measure after inducement

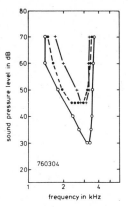

Fig. 1 *FTCs of unit 760304 before (solid curves) and after (dashed curve) inducement of a noise trauma. The curves indicated by open circles and with dots, represent a just-noticeable increase in firing rate above the spontaneous rate (threshold tuning curves). The third curve (+) represents an FTC before the trauma at a higher firing rate such that its tip coincides with the tip of the threshold tuning curve for the traumatized ear.*

of the trauma. Figure 2 shows for unit 760304 the cumulative phase of the discharges with respect to the stimulus waveform as a function of stimulus frequency at two SPLs before and after inducement of the trauma. After inducement of the trauma we see no effect on the degree of phase locking of single cell potentials to the stimulus waveform. The cochlear response times derived from these functions were 2.9 ms before and 3.5 ms after inducement of the trauma.

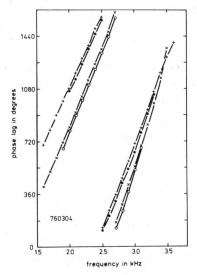

Fig. 2 *Cumulative phase between stimulus waveform and the corresponding waveform in the period histogram of the discharges of unit 760304. The phase is plotted modulo 1560 degrees. The curves before the trauma (+, 60 dB SPL and •, 30 dB SPL) are shallower than the curves of the same unit after inducement of the trauma (×, 60 dB SPL and ○, 45 dB SPL);*

The effect of stimulus SPL on cochlear response time is small. In three more cats, where we succeeded to keep the recording electrode in contact with a unit for the period of time required, we found an increased response time after inducement of the trauma, while frequency selectivity has decreased. The effect of excessive stimulation on the cochlear response time is on the order of the variability in the response times found for different cells with about the same BF and no noise trauma.

Fig. 3 shows tuning curves for unit 780905 before and after inducement of the trauma. The sharply tuned segment of the FTC has shifted markedly to higher SPLs. Furthermore, this unit became hypersensitive at low frequencies. Consequently, the BF seems to shift from 2.4 to 0.7 kHz. The cochlear response time for this unit increased from 2.7 to 3.3 ms after inducement of the trauma.

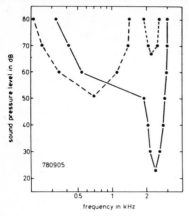

Fig. 3 FTCs of unit 780905 before (solid) and after (dashed) inducement of a noise trauma. The BF seems to shift from 2.4 kHz to 0.7 kHz.

With our angle of approach to the AVCN in each penetration BFs are found in a restricted frequency range in the normal ear. We expect these units to innervate a restricted region on the basilar membrane. Table I shows response time data for four units (unit 780905 included) measured in one penetration of the AVCN. In order to obtain cochlear response time data as a function of BF comparable to our response time data (eardrum to AVCN unit) we adapted travel-time data from Gibson et al (1977) and corrected these data for frequency-independent delays reported by them (1.5 ms) minus their acoustic transmission time estimated by us (0.3 ms). In the normal ear the measured response time for unit 780905 is 2.7 while the response time estimated from the travel-time data is 2.9 ms. The estimated response times of the units presented in Table I are shown in the right column. The measured response times are much lower than the

Table I Response times after inducement of the trauma for units measured in one penetration of the AVCN. BF and response time of unit 780905 before inducement of the trauma were 2.4 kHz and 2.7 ms, respectively. 'Normal' response times were adapted from Gibson et al (1977).

unit nr	BF (kHz)	measured response time (ms)	'normal' response time (ms)
780905	0.7	3.3	4.7
780907	0.4	3.1	5.5
780908	0.36	3.3	5.7
780909	1.1	2.6	4.0

estimated response times based on the assigned BFs. Spikes of unit 780909 are so-called fast negative discharges. Response times of this type of spike were omitted by Gibson et al (1977), since many of these spikes yielded delays at the lower extremes of the distribution. The interpretation given by those authors is that this type of spike represents discharges of presynaptic terminals of auditory nerve fibers and hence might be expected to have time delays less than AVCN neurons by the amount of one synaptic delay. Unit 780909 indeed showed lower response time than other units in this track.

The fact that the units are found in one track and that their response times are similar led us to conclude that they must have had BFs close to 2.4 kHz in the normal ear. An additional indication of a decreased BF after inducement of the trauma is that discharges of units in Table I show phase locking to the stimulus (80 dB SPL) at frequencies higher than 2 kHz. In the normal ear we have seldom found phase locking above 2 kHz for BFs lower than 1.1 kHz. The shift of the BF to lower frequencies in the acoustically traumatized ear is in agreement with the results reported by Robertson and Johnstone (1979) in the kanamycin-damaged ear.

In the traumatized ear response time seems to be a good indicator of a unit's BF, although cochlear response time proves to be increased after inducement of the trauma.

Acknowledgements

The author is indebted to Guido Smoorenburg for his participation in the experiments and discussion of the results and to Nel Blokland and Evert Agterhuis for their assistance. This research was supported by the Netherlands Organization for the Advancement of Pure Research (ZWO).

REFERENCES

Anderson, D.J., Rose, J.E., Hind, J.E. and Brugge, J.F. (1971). Temporal position of discharges in single auditory nerve fibers within the cycle of a sine-wave stimulus: frequency and intensity effects. *J. Acoust. Soc. Amer.* 49, 1131–1139.

Gibson, M.M., Hind, J.E., Kitzes, L.M. and Rose, J.E. (1977). Estimation of traveling wave parameters from the response properties of cat AVCN neurons. In: *Psychophysics and Physiology of Hearing*. (E.F. Evans and J.P. Wilson, eds). pp. 57–68. Academic Press, London.

Goldstein, J.L., Baer, T. and Kiang, N.Y.S. (1971). A theoretical treatment of latency, group delay, and tuning characteristics for auditory-nerve responses to clicks and tones. In: *Physiology of the auditory system*. (M.B. Sachs, ed). pp. 133–142. National Educational Consultants, Inc., Baltimore.

Kiang, N.Y.S., Liberman, M.C. and Levine, R.A. (1976). Auditory-nerve activity in cats exposed to ototoxic drugs and high-intensity sounds. *Ann. Otol. Rhinol. Laryngol.* 75, 752–768.

Liberman, M.C. and Kiang, N.Y.S. (1978). Acoustic trauma in cats: cochlear pathology and auditory-nerve activity. *Acta Oto-Laryng.* Suppl. 358.

Robertson, D. and Johnstone, B.M. (1979). Aberrant tonotopic organization in the inner ear damaged by kanamycin. *J. Acoust. Soc. Amer.* 66, 466–469.

NARROW-BAND ANALYSIS: A LINK BETWEEN SINGLE-FIBRE AND WHOLE-NERVE DATA

V.F. Prijs

*ENT Dept., Academic Hospital, Leiden,
The Netherlands*

1. INTRODUCTION

Since gross electrode experiments are easy to perform and single-fibre measurements are not possible in humans, one has searched for links between single-fibre and whole-nerve data.

Low level tone bursts elicit compound action potentials (AP) coming from a limited group of fibres with CF near the tone frequency. For these APs, change in amplitude should reflect change in the rate in those fibres excited by the tone burst. This principle is used to investigate tuning (Dallos and Cheatham, 1976), two tone suppression (Harris, 1979), and forward masking (Abbas and Gorga, 1979).

However, tone bursts of higher intensity excite a large cochlear area and therefore direct comparison of whole-nerve data and data from a limited group of fibres with approximately the same CF is not possible. Teas *et al.* (1962) proposed a specially designed high-pass noise masking technique to obtain the contributions to the AP from restricted cochlear regions. Elberling (1974) and Eggermont (1976) used this narrow-band analysis successfully to investigate single-fibre like properties, e.g. the latency-frequency relation in the cochlea for high intensities.

In the present study the behaviour of the narrow-band AP (NAP), dependent on intensity, interstimulus interval, level of continuous white-noise masker, and body temperature will be compared to the behaviour of single-fibre responses as reported by others.

2. METHODS

The tone bursts used had a trapezoidal envelope with rise- and fall times of two periods and a frequency of 2 or 4 kHz. The narrow band analysis method and equipment used is described by Eggermont (1976). The animal experimented upon was the guinea pig.

3. RESULTS

a) *Dependence on intensity (I)*

At low tone burst intensities only the regions with central frequencies (f_c) at and just below stimulus frequency respond. With increasing intensity more NAPs come above their threshold, especially for f_c's higher than stimulus frequency (Eggermont, 1976). The increase of the stimulated area on the cochlear partition, is also shown for single fibres by Pfeiffer and Kim (1975).

Amplitude-intensity functions for NAPs show a behaviour identical to that of rate-intensity functions for single fibres: the slope of these NAP input-output curves increases with central frequency but at successively higher threshold levels (Eggermont, 1977; Evans, 1974).

When intensity increases, the onset and peak latency of the NAPs become shorter and the interval between both latencies decreases (fig. 1). PST histo-

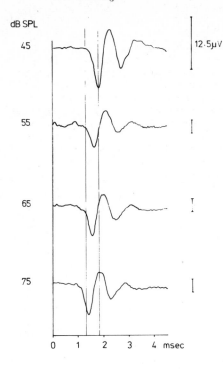

Fig. 1. Narrow-band responses for a central frequency of 4.6 kHz, for several intensities (I) of a 4 kHz tone burst.

grams from single-fibre responses, determined by Özdamar and Dallos (1978) show the same effect for tone-burst stimuli.

b) *Dependence on inter-stimulus interval (ISI)*

When the inter-stimulus interval decreases, the amplitudes of the NAPs decrease (figs. 2 and 3). For single fibres, decrement in discharge rate to the test tone is dependent on the rate to the adapting stimulus (Smith, 1979), Therefore, a

Fig. 2. Narrow-band response amplitudes (A) for several inter-stimulus intervals (ISI) in response to 4 kHz tone-burst stimulation.

Fig. 3. Narrow-band response amplitudes (A) for several inter-stimulus intervals (ISI) in response to 2 kHz tone-burst stimulation.

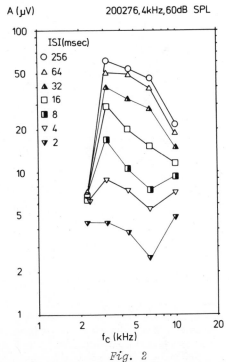

Fig. 2

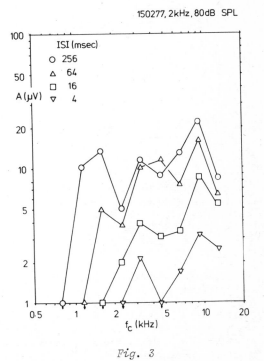

Fig. 3

region that is stimulated more by the tone burst will adapt more; a region
that is stimulated above its saturating level will adapt most. Since the
regions near the stimulus frequency are excited most, these regions show the
largest decrease in NAP amplitude.

c) *Dependence on level of continuous white-noise masker (M)*

The influence of the level of a continuous white-noise masker on amplitudes of NAPs can be described as the effect of decreasing tone-burst intensity
(fig. 4). For single fibres similar results have been found (Evans, 1974).
Since perstimulatory masking with noise can be described according to the same
rules as adaptation (Smith, 1979), the relatively high degree of masking in
the high frequency regions should be caused by more stimulation of those regions by the noise. Figure 5 shows the input-output curves for several NAPs
in response to noise bursts. The relation between these curves and the NAP-
amplitude dependence on noise level underline the single-fibre results of
Smith.

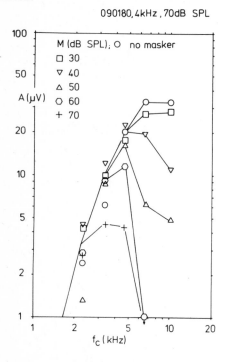

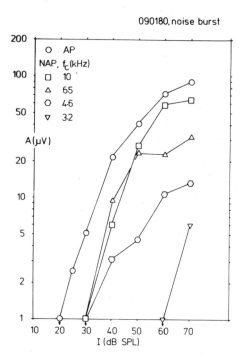

Fig. 4. Narrow-band response amplitu-
des (A) in response to 4 kHz test-tone
burst for several levels of continuous
white-noise masker (M).

Fig. 5. Input-output functions for
whole-nerve and narrow-band action
potentials in response to noise
burst stimulation.

d) *Dependence on body temperature (T)*

When the body temperature of the guinea pig was lowered, the amplitude-
central frequency relations hardly changed, indicating no change of the
Q_{10dB}. Cooling of the animal caused an increase of the NAP onset- and peak-
latency and of the interval between both (fig. 6). This effect is of about
the same size for all NAPs, and is probably caused by the increase of minimum
synaptic delay, desynchronization of firings and broadening of one fibre
response (Katz and Miledi, 1965; Prijs, 1980). From these results the effect

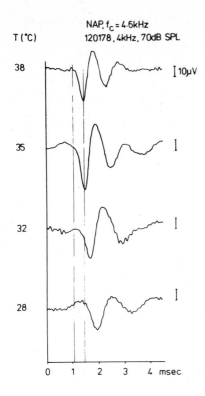

NAP, $f_c = 4.6$ kHz
120178, 4kHz, 70dB SPL
T (°C)

38

10μV

35

32

28

0   1   2   3   4 msec

Fig. 6. Narrow-band responses for a central frequency of 4.6 kHz, in response to 4 kHz tone-burst stimulation at several body temperatures (T).

of cooling upon single-fibre responses can be predicted: the quality of tuning will not change, and the onset of the PST-histograms will be equally delayed for all fibres.

REFERENCES

Abbas, P.J. and Gorga, M.P.(1979). AP responses in forward-masking paradigms and their relationship to responses of auditory-nerve fibres. *J. Acoust. Soc. Am. Suppl.* 1 66, S48–49.

Dallos, P. and Cheatham, M.(1976). Compound action potential (AP) tuning curves. *J. Acoust. Soc. Amer.* 59, 591–597.

Eggermont, J.J.(1976). Analysis of compound action potential responses to tone bursts in the human and guinea pig cochlea. *J. Acoust. Soc. Am.* 60, 1132–1139.

Eggermont, J.J.(1977). Electrocochleography and recruitment. *Ann. of Otol., Rhinol., and Laryngol.* 86 , 138–149.

Elberling, C.(1974). Action potentials along the cochlear partition recorded from the ear canal in man. *Scand. Audiol.* 3, 13–19.

Evans, E.F.(1974). Auditory frequency selectivity and the cochlear nerve. In: *Facts and models in hearing.* (E. Zwicker and E. Terhardt, eds). pp 118–129. Springer-Verlag, Berlin.

Harris, D.M.(1979). Action potential suppression, tuning curves and thresholds: comparison with single fiber data. *Hearing Research* 1, 133–154.

Katz, B. and Miledi, R.(1965). The effect of temperature on the synaptic delay at the neuromuscular junction. *J. Physiol.* 181, 656–670.

Özdamar, Ö. and Dallos, P.(1978). Synchronous responses of the primary auditory fibers to the onset of tone burst and their relation to compound action potentials. *Brain Research* 155, 169–175.

Pfeiffer, R.R. and Kim, D.O.(1975). Cochlear nerve fiber responses: distribution along the cochlear partition. *J. Acoust. Soc. Am.* 58, 867–869.

Prijs, V.F.(1980). On peripheral auditory adaptation II. Comparison of electrically and acoustically evoked APs in the guinea pig. *Acoustica.* To be published.

Smith, R.L.(1979). Adaptation, saturation, and physiological masking in single auditory-fibers. *J. Acoust. Soc. Am.* 65, 166–178.

Teas, D.C., Eldredge, D.H., and Davis, H.(1962). Cochlear responses to acoustic transients: an interpretation of whole-nerve action potentials. *J. Acoust. Soc. Am.* 34, 1438–1489.

COMMENT ON: "Narrow-band analysis: a link between single-fibre and whole-nerve data (V.F. Prijs)

R. Klinke
Centre of Physiology, J.W. Goethe University, D-6000 Frankfurt, Germany.

You conclude from your experiments that cooling of the Guinea pig will not change the quality of tuning of single fibres.

This suggests a phenomenon which again differs from that observed in the behaviour of single fibres to temperature changes in cold blooded animals. Power spectra of REVCOR functions recorded in caiman at different temperatures (Fengler and Klinke, to be published) show that their maximum shifts to higher frequencies with higher body temperature and that the sharpness of tuning deteriorates at the same time.

AP-TUNING CURVE AND NARROW-BAND AP FOLLOWING ACOUSTIC OVERSTIMULATION

J.H. ten Kate

Applied Physics Department, Delft University of Technology, Delft, The Netherlands

1. INTRODUCTION

The N_1 potential in the compound overall action potential (AP) of the nerve fibres on transient sounds is widely used as a measure of cochlear function. It is known from literature that different parts along the basilar membrane contribute differently to the AP, having the smallest portions below 2 kHz.

High pass noise masking technique (Eggermont, 1976) can be used to obtain their weighting factors identifying pathological cochleas (Don and Eggermont, 1978). The AP can even be synthesized with the experimental data.

The determination of AP-tuning curves gives another way of measuring cochlear function. Then a constant reduction of the AP on tonebursts in or after the presence of a masker is used for the determination of the masking level as a function of the frequency (Dallos and Cheatham, 1976, Mitchell, 1976). The shape of the AP-tuning curve at 8 kHz appeared to be only weakly dependent on the intensity level in contrast with psychophysical tuning curves at 1 kHz (Vogten, 1978a). Munson and Gardner, (1950) measuring masking patterns for 1 kHz stimulation obtained maxima at about 1.5 kHz during 100 dB respectively 100-110 phons (see also Ehmer and Ehmer, 1969). Auditory fatigue, temporary threshold shift TTS have maximum effects on the auditory system at $\frac{1}{2}$-1 octave above the frequencies of the stimuli (e.g. Dixon Ward, 1973). Comparable data on reduction of the AP exist for frequencies > 2 kHz, showing a $\frac{1}{2}$-octave shift (Mitchell, 1977). Some preliminary AP results from the cat's cochlea below 2 kHz, presented here, are in agreement with the above described psychophysical data.

2. METHODS

Sound stimulation and physiological techniques used are described elsewhere (Bilsen *et al.*, 1975). The stimulator was provided with a μ-metal shielded TDH 39 Grason Stadler ear phone (characteristics given in Fig.1). Alternating clicks of 100 μs were used during high pass noise masking, testing the reliability of cochleas. The high-pass acoustical noise (flat spectrum below 12 kHz) for the AP-measurements on tone burst was obtained by a filter-bankset (HP 8065A) and by 2 Alison filters (L.F. slope = 60 dB/octave). Microphonics and AP from the round window were amplified 1200 x and averaged 1000 x.

3. RESULTS

a. Narrow band AP and high pass noise masking

N_1 of the narrow band AP on clicks was plotted against central frequencies in the upper part of Fig.1. One cochlea (dotted curve) was classified to be traumatic. The deviation of the dotted curve below the values of the other cochleas in the frequency range below 2 kHz was due to stimulation with pure tones of 560, 889 Hz at 107 dB SPL during several minutes. The origin of the dip at 4.5 kHz could not be determined with certainty. One cochlea (BZB 80) was overstimu-

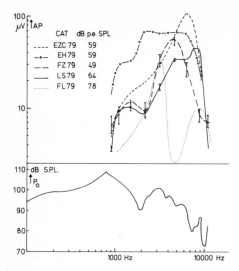

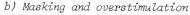

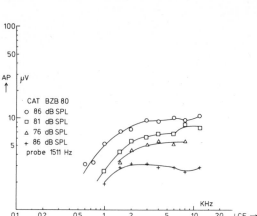

Fig.1. *The upper part of the figure represents the narrow band AP to alternating clicks against the central frequency for five cats. The acoustical characteristic of the stimulator is given in the low Fig.*

Fig.2. *AP values plotted against the low cut-off frequency of the high pass noise. Note the reduction of the curve + with respect to the curve 0.*

lated by a pure "tone" of 1.0 kHz at 130 dB SPL during 20 minutes. Afterwards an overall depression with high pass noise masking was found (Fig.2). The AP is decreased to one third of the original values of N_1. This result indicates a large spread of loss in auditory sensitivity over the frequency range of 10 kHz and is in accordance to data in literature for 1 kHz stimulation at 135-141 dB SPL. (Fig.3, Price, 1979).

b) Masking and overstimulation

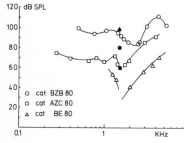

Fig.3. *Simultaneous masker levels for a 30% depression of the AP on the probe are plotted against the frequency. The intensity levels of the probe are indicated by the black triangle, circle and square. Note the frequency shift at the high intensity level.*

Continuous simultaneous masking: A reduction of 30% of the AP was taken as a criterion for the masker level determination during the application of the unlocked tone bursts (1 ms rise and fall time, 10 ms duration) of one frequency together with a continuous tone of another frequency. (Dallos and Cheatham, 1976, Mitchell, 1976). The shape of the AP-tuning curve appeared to be level dependent. A mis-tuning of about ½-octave above the probe frequency was determined at 98 dB SPL for cat BZB 80.

Overstimulation: AP's before and after continuous stimulation with 1 kHz (for a duration of 20 minutes at 112 dB SPL) are measured. The maximum depression was found at 1.5 kHz for two cats. The increase ΔL in intensity level in order to maintain the original N_1 is plotted in the upper part of Fig.4.

Pulsed simultaneous masking: AP-tuning curves were determined in which the probe of 1500 Hz was presented in the midst of a pulsed makser of 80 ms duration (1 ms

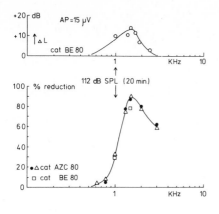

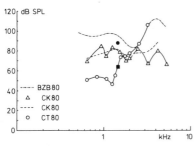

Fig.4. Temporary depression of AP after over-stimulation at 1 kHz is expressed in an increase of intensity in dB to maintain the original AP (upper figure). Maximum reduction is shifted towards 1.5 kHz after overstimulation at 1 kHz (lower figure).

slope). The level of the probe was chosen at 64 dB SPL and at 88 dB SPL respectively for two cats between the values of the intensity levels during continuous masking. A mis-tuning of the AP-tuning curve for cat CT 80 was obtained as a shift to the low frequency region (see Fig.5).

Fig.5. Masker levels in order to reduce the AP by 30% are plotted against frequency in case of pulsed continuous masking. Note the frequency shift of the AP-tuning curve at 64 dB SPL. Black circle and square indicate the levels of the probe.

The high frequency slope showed a deflection and bended in the same way as the curve for continuous masking of cat BZB 80. The frequency selectivity for the other cat CK 80 appeared to be deteriorated at the intensity level of 88 dB SPL. The notches disappeared during the use of forward masking (dashed curve). In the microphonics an evident maximum (see Mitchell, 1977) was found for this cat at 118 dB SPL for 1500 Hz. The cochlea of CK 80 seemed to be more vulnerable to overstimulation than the other examined cochleas. The shape of the tuning curve for cat CK ressembled the tuning curves of eighth nerve fibres in a damaged area (Dallos and Harris, 1978).

Temporal masking effects on the AP: The time-location of the probe in the pulsed masker affected the value of N_1 (Fig.6).

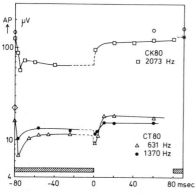

Fig.6. AP-dependence on the location of the burst with respect to the masker. Dashed rectangular areas indicate the presence of the masker. ◇ probe without masker, 64 dB SPL; o probe without masker, 88 dB SPL; ▢ 76 dB SPL.

For cat CT 80 a gradual increase of the AP on the probe during 20 ms was observed after the initial reduction. The AP on the initiation of the masker depressed the AP evoked by the probe. AP on click pairs showed also a reduction of the AP on the second click, if the separation was smaller than 20 ms. The response of the AP from cat CK 80 showed an adaptive course. The value of the AP✱ on the probe after the masker at the end of a 200 ms silent interval was still not the same as the AP without a masker. A resting period of 1 min. appeared to be necessary for obtaining an equal response. Lonsbury-Martin and Meikle (1978) determined comparable adaptation times for single eighth nerve fibres. The growth of the AP after the masking may be related to temporal data of masking in psychophysics (Vogten, 1978b).

4. DISCUSSION

The AP-frequency selectivity at 1.5 kHz and the correlation between PST histograms and AP at low frequencies (Özdamar and Dallos, 1978) are both lost at high level. The AP-reduction after overstimulation and the most sensitive masker frequency correspond in their $\frac{1}{2}$-octave shift. Also the maximum depression on the firing rate of eighth nerve fibres was obtained by Lonsbury-Martin and Meikle (1978) at $\frac{1}{2}$-octave below the characteristic frequency cF. Russell and Sellick (1978) (and Sellick and Russell, 1979) measured the highest saturation values of the DC and AC intensity relations from inner hair cells at about $\frac{1}{2}$-octave below CF. Further experimentation and modelling the AP < 2 kHz are needed for a justification of the comparison between AP and psychophysics.

Acknowledgement

I am grateful to Mrs J.M.W. van Middelkoop-Hoek and Mr. P.G.M. van der Meer for their participation in the experiments.

REFERENCES

Bilsen, F.A., Kate, J.H. ten, Buunen, T.J.F., Raatgever, J. (1975). Responses of single units in the cochlear nucleus of the cat to cosine noise. *J.Acoust.Soc.Am.* 58, 858-866.
Dallos, P. and Cheatham, M.A. (1976). Compound action potential (AP) tuning curves. *J.Acoust.Soc.Am.* 59, 591-597.
Dallos, P. and Harris, D. (1978). Properties of Auditory Nerve Responses in Absence of Outer Hair Cells. *J.Neurophysiol.* 41, 365-383.
Don, M. and Eggermont, J.J. (1978). Analysis of the click-evoked brain stem potentials in man using high-pass noise masking. *J.Acoust.Soc.Am.* 63, 1084-1092.
Dixon Ward, W. (1973). Adaptation and Fatigue. In: *Modern development in Audiology* 2th edition J.Jerger.pp 301-304, Ac.Press Inc., New York.
Eggermont, J.J. (1976). Electrocochleography. In: *Handbook of sensory physiology* V/3 by Keidel W.D. and Neff W.D. (eds), pp 625-705. Springer Verlag, Berlin.
Ehmer, R.H. and Ehmer, B.J. (1969). Frequency Patterns of Residual Masking by Pure Tones measured on the Bekesy Audiometer. *J.Acoust.Soc.Am.* 46, 1445-1448.
Lonsbury-Martin, B.L. and Meikle, M.B. (1978). Neural Correlates of Auditory Fatigue.Frequency-Dependent Changes in Activity of Single Cochlear Nerve Fibers. *J.Neurophysiol.* 41, 987-1006.
Mitchell, C. (1976).Frequency Specificity of the N_1 potential from the cochlear Nerve under various stimulus conditions. *J.Auditory Res.* 16, 247-255.
Mitchell, C. (1977). Frequency Effects of Temporary N_1 Depression Following Acoustic Overload. *Arch.Otolaryngol.* 103, 117-123.
Munson, W.A. and Gardner, M.B. (1950). Loudness Patterns-A New Approach. *J.Acoust.Soc.Am.* 22, 177-190.
Özdamar, Ö and Dallos, P. (1978). Synchronous responses of the primary auditory fibers to the onset of tone burst and their relation to compound action potentials. *Brain Res.* 155, 169-175.
Price, G.R. (1979). Loss of Auditory sensitivity following exposure to spectrally narrow impulses. *J.Acoust.Soc.Am.* 66, 456-465.
Russell, I.J. and Sellick, P.M. (1978). Intercellular studies of hair cells in the guinea pig cochlea. *J.Physiol.* 284, 261-290.
Sellick, P.M. and Russell, I.J. (1979). Two-Tone suppression in cochlear hair cells. *Hearing Res.* 1, 227-236.
Vogten, L.L.M. (1978a). Simultaneous pure-tone masking: The dependence of masking asymmetries on intensity. *J.Acoust.Soc.Am.* 63, 1509-1519.
Vogten, L.L.M. (1978b). Low-level pure tone masking: A Comparison of "tuning curves" obtained with simultaneous and forward masking. *J.Acoust.Soc.Am.* 63, 1520-1527.

DECAY OF MASKING AND FREQUENCY RESOLUTION IN
SENSORINEURAL HEARING—IMPAIRED LISTENERS

D. A. Nelson and C. W. Turner

Departments of Otolaryngology and Communication Disorders
University of Minnesota, Minneapolis, Minnesota

1. INTRODUCTION

Previous investigations of the decay of masking, or forward masking, in
listeners with sensorineural hearing loss have produced equivocal results.
Several investigations have reported that the decay of masking is not extended
in sensorineural ears (Tillman and Rosenblatt, 1975; Cudahy and Elliott, 1975,
1976). A more recent investigation, using an iso-response masking technique
similar to that employed with psychophysical tuning curves (Cudahy, 1977),
found that forward masking did extend over a longer period in sensorineural
ears than in normal ears. The present investigation reexamined the time-
course of forward masking in sensorineural ears using the iso-response masking
technique. It confirmed Cudahy's findings that sensorineural ears do demonstrate abnormal forward masking, and it demonstrated that abnormal forward
masking occurs in conjunction with abnormal frequency resolution as measured
by psychophysical tuning curves (Leshowitz *et al.*, 1975; Carney and Nelson,
1976; Wightman *et al.*, 1977; Thorton and Abbas, 1977; Florentine, 1978;
Zwicker and Schorn, 1978).

2. PROCEDURE

Two types of iso-response forward masking curves, in which the signal or
probe is held constant in level and frequency while the masker is varied to
find masked threshold, were obtained from the same listeners. To obtain temporal masking curves, the frequency of the probe signal (Fp), the frequency of
the masker (Fm), and the level of the probe (Lp) were held constant, while the
level of the masker (Lm) at masked threshold was determined for different temporal separations (Ts) between masker and probe. To obtain forward-masked
psychophysical tuning curves, the frequency of the probe, the level of the
probe, and the temporal separation between masker and probe were held con-
tant, while the masker level at masked threshold was determined for different
masker frequencies. All measurements were made with 1000-Hz probe tones that
were at fixed sound pressure levels.

a) *Stimulus Conditions.*

The stimulus conditions used to obtain both types of forward masking
curves were the same. Masker durations were 200 msec, probe durations were 20
msec, both defined as the time during which the tone-burst envelopes were
greater than 90% of peak amplitude. Maskers and probes were gated with 10-
msec rise and decay times, which were specified as the time between 10% and
90% of peak amplitude of the tone-burst envelopes. Temporal separations between masker and probe were defined as the time between 10% of peak amplitude
during the masker offset to 10% of peak amplitude during probe onset. A temporal separation of 2 msec was used to obtain tuning curves. A masker frequency of 1000 Hz was used to obtain temporal masking curves.

b) *Psychophysical Procedure.*

Masker level thresholds were obtained with a 4AFC adaptive procedure that estimated the masker level corresponding to 71% correct (Levitt, 1971) by averaging the last six out of nine masker-level reversals in an adaptive run. Masker level was varied in 2-dB steps. The temporal masking curves were obtained by testing consecutively longer temporal separations between masker and probe, beginning with a 2-msec condition. The tuning curves were obtained by testing progressively larger frequency separations.

c) *Listeners.*

Both temporal masking curves and tuning curves were obtained from four normal-hearing listeners and from six hearing-impaired listeners. In addition, temporal masking curves alone were obtained from five other listeners with normal sensitivity thresholds at 1000 Hz. "Normal-hearing" listeners demonstrated normal 4AFC sensitivity thresholds for 200-msec tone bursts throughout the entire frequency range. Hearing-impaired listeners were selected according to their audiograms. Listeners were chosen who either demonstrated good sensitivity at the probe frequency and moderate to severe loss at remote frequencies, or who demonstrated poor sensitivity at the probe frequency and good sensitivity at remote frequencies. On the basis of audiologic profiles, listeners who demonstrated evidence of central deficits, conductive loss, or abnormal tone decay were excluded from this investigation.

3. RESULTS

a) *Normal-Hearing Listeners.*

Following conventions used by Vogten (1978), masker levels required to just mask 1000-Hz constant-level probe signals were plotted as a function of the logarithm of temporal separation between masker and probe. Temporal masking curves are shown in the right panel of Fig. 1. The masker levels obtained from listener CT(LE) at four different probe levels are shown by the filled

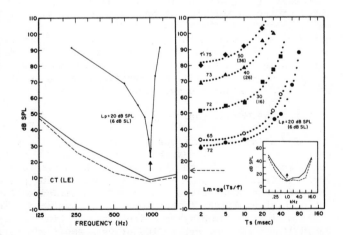

Fig. 1. Temporal masking curves (right panel) and a forward masked tuning curve (left panel) from a normal hearing listener. Sensitivity thresholds for 200-msec tones are shown in the insert: solid lines -- CT(LE), dashed lines -- normal-hearing curve. The tips of the vertical arrows indicate level and frequency of the probe. Time constants (tau) associated with each temporal-masking curve are indicated near the left end of each curve. The equation for those curves is shown in the right panel. The horizontal dashed arrow indicates quiet threshold for the 20-msec probe. Unfilled circles are data replotted from Vogten (1978). The parameter of the temporal masking curves is the level of the probe in SPL and sensation level (SL).

symbols. To provide a single statistic for describing the temporal course of masking, the raw data were fit using a least-squares procedure to the exponential function suggested by Vogten (1978). The equation for that function is included in Fig. 1. The small dotted lines in Fig. 1 indicate the best-fit curve at each probe level. Time constants associated with each curve are labeled (tau). Vogten's equation describes the data quite well. Correlation coefficients obtained by the curve-fitting procedure ranged between .95 and .99 for the curves shown in Fig. 1.

Listener CT(LE) demonstrated temporal masking curves that were typical of those obtained from normal-hearing listeners. His sensitivity thresholds (solid line of insert in Fig. 1) were within 10 dB of the average normal-hearing sensitivity curve (dashed line of insert) at all test frequencies. His time constants ranged from 72 msec for a probe at 20 dB SPL (6 dB Sensation Level - SL) to 75 msec for a probe at 50 dB SPL (36 dB SL). For comparison, Vogten's (1978) data for a probe at 30 dB SPL (15 dB SL) have been replotted as the unfilled circles in Fig. 1. After adjusting Vogten's procedure for specifying temporal separation to correspond with ours, calculations from his data yielded a time constant of 65 msec. Time constants of temporal masking curves from eight other listeners with normal hearing at 1000 Hz ranged between 50 and 100 msec. No effects of probe level on the calculated time constant were evident.

A forward masked psychophysical tuning curve from listener CT(LE) is shown in the left panel of Fig. 1. In this case the probe level was at 20 dB SPL (6 dB SL). The tuning curve had the steep high-frequency slope (358 dB/octave) and the more gradual sloping tail typical of normal tuning curves obtained with similar acoustic conditions. Although the slope of masking on the tail is probably a continuously decreasing function of masker frequency, in this case slopes could be calculated from three segments of the tail of the tuning curve; they were -16, -31, and -167 dB/octave.

b) *Remote Sensitivity Losses.*

Listeners with normal sensitivity or with mild sensitivity loss at the probe frequency, and with sizable sensitivity losses at remote frequencies, appear to have normal temporal masking curves and normal tuning curves. Fig. 2 shows the results from listener MR(LE) who had a severe high-frequency noise-induced hearing loss, with essentially normal sensitivity thresholds at the 1000-Hz probe frequency and below. Her time constants for temporal masking ranged between 78 and 89 msec. They are within what we tentatively call normal limits. The tuning curve at 10 dB SL was also normal. The high-frequency slope was 248 dB/octave and low-frequency slopes were -12, -30, and -57 dB/octave for three segments of the tail of the tuning curve.

Fig. 2. Temporal-masking curves and a forward masked tuning curve for a listener with normal sensitivity thresholds at the probe frequency, and with severe sensitivity losses at higher frequencies.

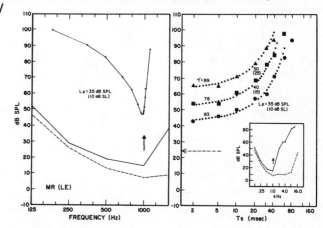

177

The results from listener LS(RE), who presented a mild 20–dB sensitivity loss at 1000 Hz, with moderate to severe sensitivity losses at frequencies both above and below the probe frequency, are shown in Fig. 3. Again, both the temporal masking curves and the tuning curves appear normal. Time constants ranged between 62 and 97 msec for different sensation-level probe tones. Tuning-curve

Fig. 3. Temporal-masking curves and a forward-masked tuning curve for a listener with a mild (20 dB) sensitivity loss at the probe frequency and with moderate to severe sensitivity losses at remote frequencies, both above and below the probe frequency.

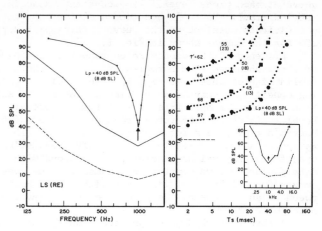

slopes were 172 dB/octave for high frequency maskers and they were –5, –14, –91 dB/octave for three segments of the tail of the tuning curve.

c) *Sensitivity Loss at the Probe Frequency.*

When a moderate or severe sensitivity loss (greater than 30 dB) exists at the probe frequency, both temporal masking curves and tuning curves appear abnormal. The sensitivity curve for the left ear of listener RA, shown by the insert of Fig. 4, documents a severe high-frequency early-onset hearing loss of possible viral origin with a 40 dB sensitivity loss at the probe frequency and normal sensitivity at low frequencies. In this case, the time constants of the temporal masking curves (shown in the right panel of Fig. 4) were between 256 and 333 msec. These time constants are considerably longer than those obtained from the previously-cited two listeners with normal sensitivity at the probe frequency and from the listener with mild sensitivity loss at the probe frequency. The tuning curve (shown in the left panel of Fig. 4) was also abnormal. The high-frequency slope of the tuning curve was 105 dB/octave for the 60 dB SPL probe, which is somewhat reduced from the high-frequency slopes typical of listeners with normal sensitivity at 1000 Hz. The steepest part of the

Fig. 4. Temporal-masking curves and a forward-masked tuning curve for a listener with a 40 dB sensitivity loss at the probe frequency and with normal sensitivity at lower frequencies.

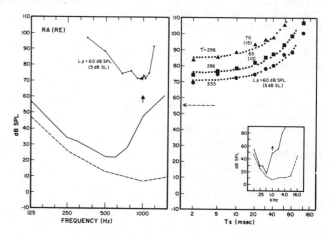

low-frequency tail had a slope of only -24 dB/octave, and the sharp tip region for maskers near the probe frequency was essentially missing.

The results from a second listener with a moderate sensitivity loss at the probe frequency are shown in Fig. 5. Sensitivity loss at 1000 Hz was about 50 dB for this ear and normal sensitivity thresholds existed at lower and at higher frequencies. Again, as with the previous listener, temporal masking curves were extended, with time con-
stants between 286 msec
and 323 msec. The tuning
curve was broad, with a
high-frequency slope of
60 dB/octave and a low-
frequency slope of only
-19 dB/octave.

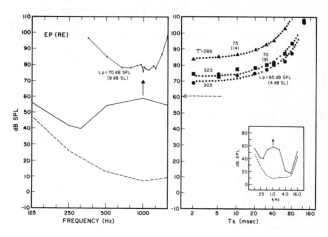

*Fig. 5. Temporal-masking
curves and a forward-
masked tuning curve for a
listener with a 50 dB
sensitivity loss at the
probe frequency and with
normal hearing at both
lower and at higher
frequencies.*

4. DISCUSSION

Results from the four sensorineural hearing-impaired ears displayed in Figs. 2 through 5 suggest several tentative conclusions about the time course of temporal masking, tuning-curve bandwidths and sensitivity loss, conclusions which should be accepted with caution because of the small number of hearing-impaired listeners investigated to date: 1) Temporal masking functions for maskers and probes at the same frequency are essentially normal when sensitivity at the test frequency is normal, or when only mild sensitivity loss exists at the test frequency, even when considerable sensitivity loss exists at frequencies remote from the test frequency. 2) When a moderate to severe sensitivity loss exists at the test frequency, time constants for temporal masking can be on the order of four times as long as for normal-hearing listeners, and forward masked tuning curves are broader.

The first conclusion is consistent with previous results. Time constants derived from iso-response temporal masking curves in normal-hearing listeners are essentially the same as time constants obtained from temporal masking experiments carried out by other investigators using fixed masker levels (Plomp, 1964; Tillman and Rosenblatt, 1975; Widin and Viemeister, 1979; Jesteadt, 1979; Jesteadt and Bacon, 1980). In those experiments, temporal masking lasted for some 200-300 msec or more. However, if a time constant is calculated as the time required for a 37% reduction in masking, time constants between 40 and 100 msec will result that are in the same region as those obtained by the present study. The finding that sensitivity loss at other remote frequencies did not affect the estimate of a time constant at 1000 Hz implies that the forward masking task did not involve processing by remote regions of the cochlea.

The second conclusion is more controversial. The association between abnormal tuning-curve bandwidths and sensitivity loss has been a common finding in recent investigations, but the association between abnormally long time constants and sensitivity loss has not been a common finding. Therefore, the relations between sensitivity threshold, time constants for forward masking, and tuning-curve bandwidths warrant closer examination. Comparisons of time constants from temporal masking curves with sensitivity thresholds for 20-msec probe tones at 1000 Hz are shown in the right panel of Fig. 6. The data demonstrate a positive relation between sensitivity thresholds at the test frequency and time constants for temporal masking. Listeners with normal sensitivity thresholds throughout the audiometric range are indicated by large filled symbols. Their time constants range between 50 msec and 100 msec, our definition of normal time constants. The half filled symbols show the results of listeners who demonstrated normal hearing at the 1000 Hz test frequency, but who also had sensitivity losses at frequencies remote from the test frequency. Time constants for those listeners fell within our normal range. Listeners with sensitivity thresholds at the test frequency of 40 dB SPL or more are indicated by the unfilled symbols. Their time constants, taken from temporal masking curves for low sensation-level probe tones (10-15 dB SL), are all longer than 200 msec. From these comparisons, then, it appears that sensitivity loss at the probe frequency must be at least 30 dB before abnormal time constants for forward masking can be reliably observed.

Fig. 6. Comparison of time constants, sensitivity thresholds, and tuning-curve bandwidths from normal and hearing-impaired listeners. Large filled symbols -- normal sensitivity to all test frequencies. Small filled symbols -- normal sensitivity at the probe frequency, but not necessarily at all frequencies. Half-filled symbols -- nor-

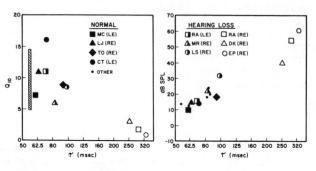

mal sensitivity at the probe frequency with definite sensitivity losses at remote frequencies. Unfilled symbols -- moderate to severe sensitivity loss (greater than 30 dB HL) at the probe frequency. Vertical bar indicates the range of normal tuning-curve bandwidths (Q10) obtained by other investigators (Wightman et al., 1977; McGee, 1978).

Comparisons of tuning-curve bandwidths with temporal-masking time constants are shown in the left panel of Fig. 6. Bandwidth is expressed here as Q10, which is the probe frequency divided by the 10-dB bandwidth of the tuning curve. Tuning-curve bandwidths for listeners with normal hearing throughout the audiometric range (filled symbols) and tuning-curve bandwidths for listeners with normal hearing at the probe frequency, associated with sensitivity loss at remote frequencies (half-filled symbols), were all quite narrow. Q10 values were all above 5. Their time constants were all below 100 msec. The vertical bar includes the range of Q10 values obtained by McGee (1978) and Wightman, et al., (1977) from their normal-hearing listeners, using acoustic conditions similar to those employed in the present investigations. By contrast, the Q10 values from the tuning curves for the three listeners with sensitivity thresholds for 20-msec tone bursts above 40 dB SPL, (sensitivity losses greater than 30 dB) were all low (3.1, 1.8, and 1.1) and the time constants were long (250, 286, and 323 msec). It is worth noting that such a positive relation between bandwidth and time constants is somewhat contrary to what a simple filter model would predict, i.e., wider bandwidths would predict shorter not longer time constants.

Along with abnormal tuning-curve bandwidths and larger time constants, listeners with sensorineural hearing loss also demonstrated an increased amount of forward masking when compared with normal-hearing listeners.

Amount of masking was inferred from masker-probe intensity ratios at masked threshold by assuming that more forward masking had occurred when comparable probes were masked by lower level maskers. That increased amount of masking from sensorineural ears was particularly evident when comparisons were made for probe tones at similar sensation levels for both types of listeners. For example, normal-hearing listener CT required a masker level that was about 19 dB more intense than the probe to forward mask a 6 dB SL probe at a temporal separation of 20 msec. Listener EP, who had a 50 dB sensitivity loss, required a masker level that was only 8 dB above the probe to forward mask a 9 dB SL probe at a temporal separation of 20 msec. At longer temporal separations between masker and probe, and for higher sensation-level probes, the disparity between the amount of masking for normal-hearing and hearing-impaired listeners was even greater. For the hearing-impaired listeners, it appears that the loss of sensitivity was accompanied by an increased susceptibility to forward masking.

In conclusion, these experiments confirmed unpublished reports of abnormal temporal masking curves from sensorineural hearing-impaired listeners. Not only were time constants longer in listeners who had sensitivity losses greater than 30 dB, but tuning curve bandwidths were broader and the inferred amount of forward masking was also greater.

Acknowledgments

This research was supported by research grants from NINCDS.

REFERENCES

Carney, A.E. and Nelson, D.A. (1976). Psychophysical tuning curves in normal and pathological ears. *J. Acoust. Soc. Amer.* 60, S104(A).

Cudahy, E. (1977). Backward and forward masking in normal and hearing-impaired listeners. *J. Acoust. Soc. Amer.* 62, S59(A).

Cudahy, E. and Elliott, L. (1975). Temporal processing in noise by persons with noise-induced and age-related hearing loss. *J. Acoust. Soc. Amer.* 58, S71(A).

Cudahy, E. and Elliott, L. (1976). Temporal masking patterns for hearing-impaired and normal listeners. *J. Acoust. Soc. Amer.* 59, S2(A).

Florentine, M. (1978). Psychoacoustical tuning curves and narrow-band masking in normals and impaired hearing. *J. Acoust. Soc. Amer.* 63, S44(A).

Jesteadt, W. and Bacon, S.P. (1980). Forward masking in noise. *Abstracts of 3rd Midwinter Research Meeting, Association for Research in Otolaryngology.* p. 34.

Jesteadt, W. (1979). Forward masking as a function of frequency. *J. Acoust. Soc. Amer.* 65, 557(A).

Leshowitz, B., Lindstrom, R. and Zurek, P. (1975). Psychophysical tuning curves in normal and impaired ears. *J. Acoust. Soc. Amer.* 58, S71(A).

Levitt, H. (1971). Transformed up-down methods in psychoacoustics. *J. Acoust. Soc. Amer.* 49, 467-477.

McGee, T. (1978). Psychophysical tuning curves from hearing-impaired listeners. Doctoral Dissertation, Northwestern University, Evanston, Illinois.

Plomp, R. (1964). Rate of decay of auditory sensation. *J. Acoust. Soc. Amer.* 36, 277-282.

Tillman, T.W. and Rosenblatt, L. (1975). Forward masking in normal and hearing-impaired listeners. Unpublished paper presented to the Amer. Speech and Hearing Association, Washington, D.C.

Thorton, A.B. and Abbas, P.J. (1977). Low-frequency hearing loss: perception of filtered speech, psychophysical tuning curves, and masking. Unpublished paper presented to the Amer. Speech and Hearing Association.

Vogten, L.L.M. (1978). Low-level pure-tone masking: A comparison of 'tuning curves' obtained with simultaneous and forward masking. *J. Acoust. Soc. Amer.* <u>63</u>, 1520-1527.

Widin, G.P. and Viemeister, N.F. (1979). Intensive and temporal effects in pure-tone forward masking. *J. Acoust. Soc. Amer.* <u>66</u>, 388-395.

Wightman, F., McGee, T. and Kramer, M. (1977). Factors influencing frequency selectivity in normal and hearing-impaired listeners. In: *Psychophysics and Physiology of Hearing* (E.F. Evans and J.P. Wilson, eds). pp. 295-306. Academic, London.

Zwicker, E. and Schorn, K. (1978). Psychoacoustical tuning curves in audiology. *Audiology* <u>17</u>, 120-140.

COMMENT ON: "Decay of masking and frequency resolution in sensorineural hearing-impaired listeners (D.A. Nelson and C.W. Turner)

E.F. Evans
Dept. of Communication & Neuroscience, University of Keele, U.K.

In comparisons (made by Harrison and me) of cochlear fibre PST histograms to tone bursts at CF, between normal and kanamycin damaged guinea pig cochleas, we have not seen obvious differences in rate adaptation. However, there is some evidence of a longer time-course of recovery from post-stimulus suppression in the fibres from pathological cochleas. This needs to be confirmed and examined to see whether it would be adequate to account for your results.

SUPPRESSION IN THE TIME DOMAIN

T. Houtgast and T.M. van Veen

*Institute for Perception TNO,
Soesterberg, The Netherlands*

INTRODUCTION

Adaptation is generally accepted to play a role in auditory perception. Without being specific about the underlying mechanism, adaptation will manifest itself especially when a weaker sound is preceded by a stronger sound, since a high degree of adaptation set by the stronger sound may still be active (at least partly) at the moment the weaker sound is presented. Thus, a weaker sound may appear to be suppressed by a preceding stronger sound.

This notion of suppression in the time domain bears some resemblance to suppression in the frequency domain (lateral suppression): a weak frequency component may be suppressed by an adjacent strong frequency component. This resemblance is emphasised not to suggest a common underlying mechanism, but to indicate the possibility that the difficulties encountered in measuring (psychophysically) the effect of frequency-domain suppression may also apply to time-domain suppression. Effects of frequency-domain suppression are not disclosed by simple direct-masking techniques (which may be understood in terms of a "gain-control" suppression). Likewise, it may well be that other than direct-masking techniques are called for to disclose effects of time-domain suppression. The present paper is concerned with two approaches to this question.

EXPERIMENT 1

This experiment is concerned with broad-band noise of which the intensity is modulated sinusoidally. This stimulus, with an ongoing succession of stronger and weaker parts seems particularly attractive for studying any effect of temporal suppression. Of course, towards high modulation frequencies the "internal" peak-to-valley contrast will decrease progressively, but this contrast might be restored to some degree as a consequence of temporal suppression. The present measurements aim at an estimate of the "valley-depth" as a function of modulation frequency. Type A is a direct-masking experiment (thus, presumably, exclusive any effects of temporal suppression), whereas type B is of a nature which might reveal effects of temporal suppression.

A. Direct masking: Measurement of the masked threshold of a brief pulse coinciding with a valley of the modulated masker. The stimulus is presented schematically in Fig. 1.
Masker. White noise, intensity modulated sinusoidally with a peak-valley level difference of 20 dB, with modulation frequency as the independent variable. For a given modulation frequency, the masker is presented continuously. Two reference conditions with unmodulated noise are included, the level of which corresponds to the level at the peak or at the valley, respectively. The sensation level of the latter noise (corresponding to the valley level) is approximately 45 dB.
Signal. Rectangular pulses (pulse width 0.1 ms), filtered by an octave-band filter with slopes of 48 dB/oct, and 3 kHz center frequency. (All measurements reported in this paper are performed at 3 kHz, this unusually high frequency

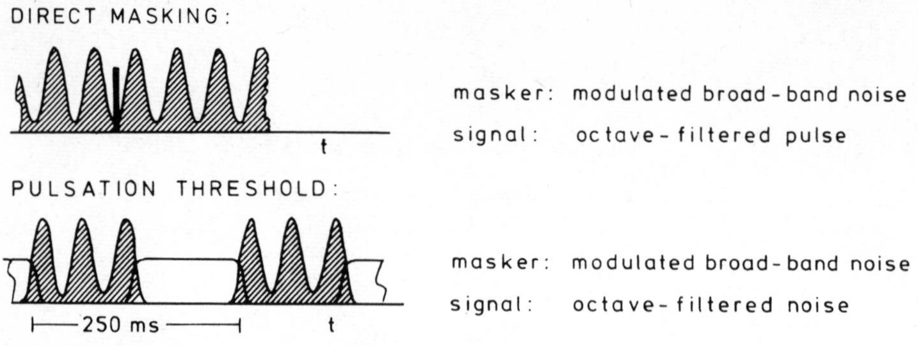

DIRECT MASKING :

masker: modulated broad-band noise

signal: octave-filtered pulse

PULSATION THRESHOLD :

├──── 250 ms ────┤   t

masker: modulated broad-band noise

signal: octave-filtered noise

Fig. 1   Time pattern of the stimuli used in Experiment 1. The data obtained with these two types of measurements are presented in Fig. 2.

being required by the nature of Experiment 2.) Test pulses, always coinciding with a valley in the masker, are presented in pairs (250 ms inter-pulse interval), the pairs being repeated every second. Pulse level is the dependent variable.

Procedure. A Békésy up-down tracking method was used to measure the masked threshold, with a 2-dB level difference between successive pulse pairs. After an initial period, the mean level over the last six turn-over points was taken as the threshold value. Modulation frequency was varied in random order, including the two unmodulated reference noises.

Data. The data for two subjects are presented in Fig. 2, top panel. Each data point is the mean value of six measurements. All values are given relative to the mean threshold obtained for the reference condition with the high-level unmodulated noise.

Result. Fig. 2, top panel represents the "internal" valley depth, as estimated from a direct-masking experiment, as a function of modulation frequency for an intensity-modulated noise with a physical peak-to-valley difference of 20 dB. For high modulation frequencies it approaches a value corresponding to the mean intensity which is, theoretically, about 3 dB below the top-intensity.

B. Pulsation threshold: Measurement of the pulsation threshold of an octave-band noise when alternated with a modulated broad-band noise. The stimulus is presented schematically in Fig. 1. (This experiment was generated by the idea that in this case pulsation threshold is reached when the signal level corresponds to the (internal) valley depth in the modulated masker.)

Masker. The same as used in the previous experiment, but gated periodically, 125 ms on, 125 ms off. Unfortunately, this sets a lower limit to the range of modulation frequencies which can be considered: a minimum of two valleys in each 125-ms masker burst was considered mandatory, requiring a minimum modulation frequency of 20 Hz.

Signal. Octave-band filtered white noise (center frequency 3 kHz, slopes 48 dB/oct), gated in 125-ms bursts which coincide with the silent masker intervals. (That is, in series of three successive bursts, leaving out every fourth signal burst.)

Procedure. As in the previous experiment (Békésy up-down tracking), based on the perceived continuity or pulsation for the series of three successive test-signal bursts.

Data. The data for two subjects are presented in Fig. 2, lower panel (mean values of six individual measurements, with the high-level unmodulated noise as

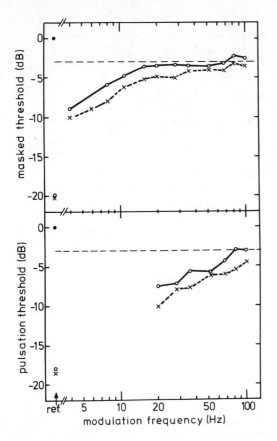

Fig. 2 Data for two subjects
(circles and crosses). Upper panel:
masked threshold of a brief pulse
coinciding with the valley in a
modulated-noise masker. Lower panel: pulsation threshold with a
modulated-noise masker. The maskers intensity is modulated sinusoidally, with a peak-to-valley
ratio of 20 dB. Two reference conditions are included with unmodulated noise of which the level corresponds to the peak and the valley, respectively.

reference condition).

Result. Fig. 2, lower panel, represents the internal valley depth as estimated
from the pulsation-threshold measurements. Also here, towards high modulation
frequencies, the curves approach the level corresponding to the masker's mean
intensity (approximately 3 dB below the top level).

Discussion. The lower panel in Fig. 2 would suggest a considerably higher degree of internal contrast in the modulated-noise masker than that revealed by
the upper panel. Of course, the interpretation of the lower-panel data as representing the internal valley depth totally depends on accepting the hypothesis that pulsation threshold mirrors the *minima* in the modulated-noise masker.
Nevertheless, Fig. 2 is highly suggestive of an interpretation in terms of temporal suppression, the effect of which is not reflected in the upper panel (direct masking), but is so in the lower panel.

EXPERIMENT 2

This experiment is concerned with the interaction between two brief tone
bursts, a masker burst and a test-tone burst (or, in other terms, a suppressor
and a suppressee). Two types of measurements are carried out. Type A is a
detection experiment, the result of which serves as a baseline for the interpretation of the type-B measurements. Type B aims at an estimate of the degree
of suppression of the weaker tone burst by the stronger one, as a function of
temporal and frequency differences between the two bursts.

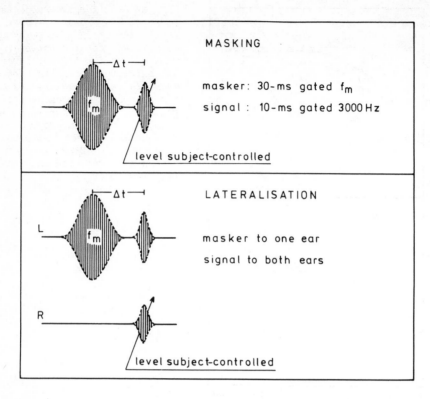

Fig. 3 Time pattern of the stimuli used in Experiment 2. The upper and lower panel refer to the data in the upper and lower panels in Figs. 4 and 5.

A. <u>Masking</u>: Measurement of the detection threshold of a brief tone burst in the presence of a masking tone burst, as a function of temporal and frequency differences between the two bursts. The stimulus is presented schematically in Fig. 3, top panel.

Masker. Tonal burst with a cosine-shaped envelope, with a total duration of 30 ms. The carrier frequency (f_m) and the temporal position relative to the test-tone burst (Δt) are the independent variables. The amplitude is fixed; for a carrier frequency f_m = 3 kHz the sensation level of the masker burst is approximately 65 dB.

Signal. Tonal burst with a cosine-shaped envelope, with a total duration of 10 ms. Carrier frequency is fixed at 3 kHz. The test-tone-burst level is the dependent variable.

Procedure. The masker burst is repeated every 300 ms, whereas the test-tone burst is presented only at every other masker burst. A Békésy up-down tracking method (same details as above) is used to measure the masked threshold of the test-tone bursts.

Data. The data obtained for two subjects are presented in separate figures (Figs. 4 and 5, top panels). Each value represents the mean of three measurements. All values are in dB relative to the absolute, unmasked, threshold of the test-tone burst.

Result. Figs. 4 and 5 (upper panels) represent the amount of masking of the test-tone burst by the masker burst, as a function of their relative "position" in the frequency and time domain (the position of the test-tone burst corresponds with the asterisk, at Δt = 0 and f = 3 kHz). For transparency of the

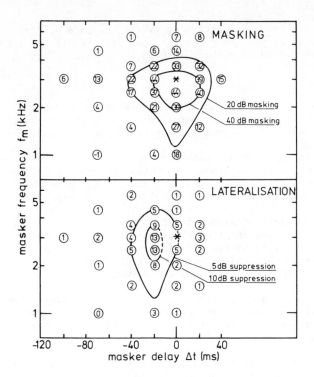

Fig. 4 Data of one subject, referring to the stimuli in Fig. 3. Upper panel: amount of masking (dB) of the 3-kHz signal burst by the masking burst of variable frequency f_m and delay Δt. Lower panel, based on the mid-plane localisation of the binaural signal burst in case of a monaural masking burst: attenuation (dB) to be applied to the contra-lateral ear in order to restore mid-plane localisation, as a function of the maskers frequency f_m and delay Δt.

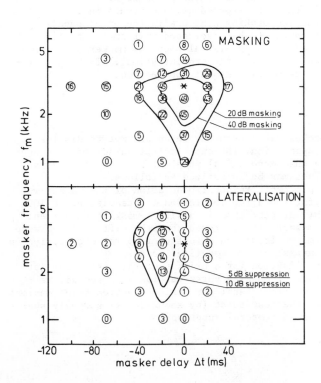

Fig. 5 As Fig. 4, for a second subject.

figure, two iso-masking contours have been fitted by eye to the data points. Broadly speaking, this result is as one would expect: the contours are centered around the asterisk, showing a spread of masking in both the frequency and the time domain.

B. Lateralisation: Measurement of the inter-aural level disparity needed to maintain mid-plane localisation for a brief binaural tone burst, when a masking burst is presented to one ear only. The stimulus is presented schematically in Fig. 3, lower panel.
Masker. Identical to the one in the previous measurements.
Signal. Also similar to the one described above, presented binaurally. For the ear containing the masker burst, the signal level is fixed (50 dB above absolute threshold); the signal level in the contra-lateral ear is the dependent variable.
Procedure. The combination of masker and signal burst as indicated in Fig. 3, lower panel, is repeated every 1.5 sec and the Békésy up-down tracking method is used to measure the level disparity needed for mid-plane localisation of the signal burst. In order to provide the subject with a reference, the signal burst itself, *without* a level disparity, is presented halfway each 1.5-sec interval.
Data. The data for the two subjects are presented in Figs. 4 and 5, lower panels. Each value is the mean obtained for three measurements. The values indicate the attenuation needed in the contra-lateral ear to restore mid-plane localisation of the signal burst.

Discussion. If it is assumed that mid-plane localisation for these high-frequency (3 kHz) signal bursts implies equal internal "effectiveness" of the left-ear and right-ear signal, the present data indicate to what degree the effectiveness of the signal burst is reduced by the presence of the masker burst. The interesting point is that the iso-reduction contours in the lower panels do *not* simply reflect the iso-masking contours in the upper panels, as one would expect if the reduction was to be understood in terms of partial masking. The finding that the reduction is maximal when the masker burst *precedes* the signal burst (by about 20 ms for the present stimuli) is highly suggestive of an interpretation in terms of temporal suppression.

SUMMARY

Two psychophysical approaches are presented, in an attempt to disclose possible effects of temporal suppression. The experimental paradigms were chosen in the light of a possible phenomenological parallel between temporal and lateral suppression. The findings may be summarized as follows.
● In a pulsation-threshold experiment, temporal modulation of the masker was found to reduce the pulsation threshold for modulation frequencies up to 100 Hz. This effect was considerably greater than in a direct-masking experiment with the same modulated-noise masker. It is argued that the difference between these two experimental paradigms reflects the effect of temporal suppression on the internal peak-to-valley contrast of the modulated noise.
● For preserving mid-plane localisation for a brief binaural test burst (at 3 kHz), the addition of an uni-lateral masking burst was found to reduce the required test-burst level in the contra-lateral ear. This reduction being maximal when the masking burst precedes the test burst (by about 20 ms) strongly suggests an interpretation in terms of temporal suppression.

COMMENT ON: "Suppression in the time domain" (T. Houtgast and T.M. van Veen)

J. Blauert
Ruhr-Universität, Bochum, Fed.Rep. of Germany

Looking at the results in the lower panel of each of the diagrams in Fig.5 one recognizes, that the data may represent the precedence effect. This becomes even more elucidated if one considers a cross section through the plots parallel to the delay axis at 3 kHz. The suppression curve that one gets this way is obviously equivalent to the curve of the threshold of equal loudness of an echo, as is typically measured in precedence effect experiments (e.g. Meyer + Schodder, 1952, David + Hanson, 1962, Lochner + Burger, 1958).

REFERENCES

Meyer, E and Schodder, G.R. (1952). *Nachr. Akad. Wiss. in Göttingen Math. Phys.*
    Klasse IIa. Heft 6, 31-46. Vandenhoek und Rupprecht, Göttingen.
David, E.E. and Hanson, R.L. (1962). *Reports 4th ICA* Copenhagen.
Lochner, J.P.A., Burger, J.F. (1958). *Acustica* 8, 1-10.

ADAPTATION OF MASKING

Neal F. Viemeister

*Department of Psychology, University of Minnesota,
Minneapolis, Minnesota 55455, U.S.A.*

1. INTRODUCTION

Several published reports indicate that exposure to stimuli with certain spectral configurations can elicit an audible aftereffect which may persist for several seconds. The "negative afterimage" discovered by Zwicker (1964), later called a "Zwicker tone" by Lummis and Guttman (1972), and also studied by Neelen (1967), is a weak, tone-like perception which decays completely within about ten seconds following exposure to band-reject noise, band-reject pulse trains, lowpass noise, or, less effectively, to highpass noise. The pitch of this aftereffect is rather labile but it is clearly related to the cutoff frequencies of the exposure waveform, and is affected by the intensity of the exposure stimulus. The effect appears to be monaural and can be produced only at low-to-moderate exposure intensities (e.g., noise spectrum levels of 5-30 dB SPL).

An aftereffect which appears to be related to the Zwicker tone was reported by Wilson (1966, 1970). He found that the perception of a white noise which followed exposure to comb-filtered noise was similar to that evoked by comb-filtered noise with a spectrum complementary to that of the exposure stimulus. This "negative afterimage" could be cancelled by presentation of the exposure stimulus at reduced spectral modulation depth. Although some of the properties of these afterimages are similar, the aftereffect described by Wilson is unlike the Zwicker tone in that it can be produced by high intensities.

An effect which appears to be related to that reported by Wilson, and which motivates the present experiments, was observed by D. M. Green in conjunction with his work on multiple-component signals (Green *et al.*, 1959). The effect, essentially, is that the audibility of a given "target" component in a complex of equal-amplitude, harmonically-related sinusoids can be greatly increased by exposure to the complex with the target component suppressed. For example, when a suppressed 1-kHz component in a 200-Hz pulse train is reintroduced, a very distinct 1-kHz tone is heard. The percept decays over several seconds and eventually disappears. Subsequent informal observations of this enhancement effect indicate the following. The effect can be produced over a wide range of stimulus intensities. Contiguous presentation of the complexes is not necessary; indeed, delays of several minutes, perhaps longer can intervene between the presentations. Presentation of white noise after exposure to band-reject noise produces a perception of a narrow-band noise, corresponding to the rejection region of the exposure stimulus, embedded in the white noise. (This effect, of course, is similar to that reported by Wilson.) Exposure to the incomplete harmonic complex for as little as 200-300 msec is sufficient, although both the salience of the target component and its persistence are enhanced by increasing the exposure duration and/or by repeated exposure. Complete recovery from long duration repeated exposures to the incomplete complex may require hours or perhaps days. Recovery does not appear to be expedited by exposure to the complete complex or to the target tone in isolation.

The phenomena discussed above strongly suggest a frequency-specific adaptation process considerably different from more familiar adaptation and fatigue effects in psychoacoustics. In particular, these aftereffects mani-

fest themselves indirectly as an increase in relative sensitivity in the unadapted spectral regions, and, at least in the case of the enhancement effect,
can be demonstrated at exposure levels or recovery intervals for which pure-
tone thresholds are unaffected by the exposure. Although the adaptation
process suggested by these aftereffects may be of fundamental importance in,
for example, intensity coding, the implications of these aftereffects have
not been thoroughly pursued nor has their relationship to other auditory
phenomena been closely examined. This lack of attention may reflect the
difficulties in quantifying the phenomena (e.g. see Lummis and Guttman, 1972)
and in studying them using objective psychophysical techniques.

Viemeister and Green (1972) attempted to study the enhancement effect by
measuring the thresholds for sinusoidal signals masked by incomplete harmonic
maskers which either were continuously present or were gated with the signal.
The enhancement effect can be viewed as a reduction, due to adaptation, of
masking of the target component by the incomplete complex. If this view is
correct, then threshold for detection of the target component should be lower
with a continuous (i.e., adapted) masker than with a brief, pulsed masker.
Considerably lower thresholds were observed with continuous maskers: for
example, the threshold for an 800-Hz, 200-msec signal masked by an equal-
amplitude harmonic complex with a fundamental of 200 Hz and with the 800 Hz
component supressed, is, depending upon signal phase, from 11 to 22 dB lower
when the masker is presented continuously than when it is pulsed. For signals
near 800 Hz, or for random-phase signals, the pulsed-continuous difference is
10-15 dB, depending on the subject. The present experiments extend these
observations and, in general, employ the same strategy of assessing adaptation
as a reduction, due to exposure, of masking effectiveness.

2. PROCEDURE

The maskers used in the experiments were digitally-generated harmonic
complexes with components of equal amplitude and random phase. For a given
condition, the masker waveform was fixed both within and over blocks. Two
modes of masker presentation were used. In the "pulsed" condition the masker
was presented for 100 msec, including 10-msec rise and 10-msec decay times.
In the "continuous" condition the masker was identical to that used in the
pulsed condition but was temporally surrounded by a longer duration version
of the masker. The rise and decay times of the surround stimulus, the "adaptor", were identical to those of the masker. There was a 10-msec delay between the half-amplitude points on the quarter-cycle sinusoids used as the
gating envelopes, i.e., masker onset coincided with adaptor offset. The
maskers were lowpass filtered at 4 kHz and were presented at a nominal level
per component of 43 dB SPL. Distortion products at frequencies corresponding
to suppressed components were at least 70 dB down.

The signals were either sinusoids or narrow-band noise and were generated
by standard analog equipment. The sinusoidal signals were not phase-locked
to the masker. The narrow-band noise was produced by 1-kHz modulation of
lowpass filtered noise. Signal duration was 80 msec: a 10-msec linear-ampli-
tude rise and decay was used for the sinusoidal signals, 5 msec was used for
the noise. The signals began 10 msec after the onset, and terminated 10 msec
before the offset of the masker.

Thresholds were determined using a 2IFC adaptive procedure which provides
an estimate of the signal level necessary for 70.7% correct decisions (Levitt,
1971). The signal level was initially about 10 dB above threshold, and was
adjusted in 1-dB steps after the first two reversals. A block was terminated
after 16 reversals (12 for subject 3) and the mean of the last 14 (10) reversals was designated as threshold. The thresholds to be reported were based
upon the mean of at least three blocks. The standard errors of the threshold estimates were always less than 1.5 dB and typically were about 0.8 dB.

Three experienced subjects, all with normal hearing, participated in the experiments. Subject 3 was the author. The stimuli were presented monaurally via TDH-39 headphones.

3. GENERAL OBSERVATIONS

The thresholds obtained in selected signal and masker conditions are shown in Table 1. Since there are, in certain cases, fairly large differences between subjects, individual data are presented.

Table I. Thresholds (dB SPL) for selected signal and masker conditions. The difference in thresholds obtained with pulsed vs. continuous maskers is also indicated. Entries for conditions C and D are spectrum levels within the 400-Hz passband of the signal.

CONDITION		S1	S2	S3	CONDITION		S1	S2
A. Incomplete harmonic complex, f_0=200 Hz, 1 kHz suppressed. 1-kHz signal.	PULSED	37.6	35.3	36.4	E. One-component masker: 0.8 kHz. 1 kHz-signal.	PULSED	10.0	12.1
	CONT.	26.8	26.6	22.8		CONT.	9.8	13.0
	DIFF.	10.8	8.7	13.6		DIFF.	0.2	-0.9
B. Incomplete harmonic complex, f_0=200 Hz, 3 kHz suppressed. 3-kHz signal.	PULSED	45.4	44.2	45.9	F. Two-component masker: 0.8, 1.2 kHz. 1-kHz signal	PULSED	20.1	26.6
	CONT.	36.3	37.5	35.0		CONT.	19.7	22.0
	DIFF.	9.1	6.7	10.9		DIFF.	0.4	4.6
C. Band-reject noise masker. Bandpass noise signal.	PULSED	25.9	21.9	26.9	G. Three-component masker: 0.8, 1.2, 1.4 kHz. 1-kHz signal.	PULSED	33.4	32.4
	CONT.	15.2	11.5	14.4		CONT.	28.3	26.4
	DIFF.	10.7	10.4	12.5		DIFF.	5.1	6.0
D. Wideband noise masker. Bandpass noise signal.	PULSED	31.4	34.2	34.2	H. Four-component masker: 0.8, 1.2, 1.4, 1.6 kHz. 1-kHz signal.	PULSED	35.2	35.0
	CONT.	31.3	35.6	33.8		CONT.	25.9	25.4
	DIFF.	0.1	-1.4	0.4		DIFF.	9.3	9.6

In condition A, the masker was a 0.2- to 4.0-kHz harmonic complex with a fundamental of 200 Hz and with the 1-kHz component suppressed. Thresholds for the 1-kHz signal obtained with a continuous masker are an average of 11 dB lower than those with a pulsed masker. This pulsed-continuous difference, we presume, reflects adaptation of the masker in the continuous condition. Condition B indicates that this adaptation effect is also observed at 3 kHz. Thresholds are higher for both modes of masker presentation, reflecting a larger critical bandwidth, and the average pulsed-continuous difference is about 2 dB less than that at 1 kHz. In condition C, the masker was a 50-Hz to 4-kHz harmonic complex with a 5-Hz fundamental and with components between 0.8 and 1.2 kHz suppressed. The equivalent spectrum level of this "noise" was 36 dB SPL within the passbands. The signal was a band of noise, 400 Hz wide, centered at 1 kHz. The average pulsed-continuous difference for this condition is 11.2 dB and corresponds closely to that observed in condition A. Condition D is similar to C except that there was no 400-Hz gap in the masker. There is no significant pulsed-continuous difference for this condition, suggesting that the adaptation, if it is occurring, affects both the effective signal and the masker.

Thresholds within 1 dB of those obtained in condition D were obtained with a band-reject adaptor (the masker of condition C) and the "flat" masker of condition D. In this situation, a narrow-band noise, similar to the signal, is heard in *both* observation intervals; the task is more similar to loudness discrimination of narrow-band noise than to detection. The fact that this clearly audible noise band produces no additional masking is consistent with the notion that the unadapted region, nominally the 400-Hz band centered at 1 kHz, is not affected by adaptation. It is also possible, however, that exposure to band-reject noise produces an increase in responsiveness in the unadapted region. If this increase were multiplicative, i.e., an increase in gain, then the effective levels of both the signal and the masker would increase proportionately and, since Weber's law holds, no increase in threshold would be observed. The present experiment does not permit distinction between these rather different views of the effect of adaptation.

Conditions E through H indicate that masker components above the frequency of the signal are responsible for the adaptation effect. A single 800-Hz component (condition E) produces some masking, but no pulsed-continuous difference is observed. The addition of a 1.2-kHz component (condition F) raises the thresholds over those for condition E by about 12 dB. For S1 the thresholds for condition F are within 1 dB of those for a 1.2-kHz masker alone; for S2, however, the thresholds with a single 1.2-kHz masker are 20.4 and 15.3 dB SPL for pulsed and continuous masker presentations, respectively. The pulsed-continuous difference for S2 in condition F thus appears to reflect adaptation of the 1.2-kHz component. The addition of a 1.4-kHz component (condition G) produces a larger increase in the threshold with the pulsed masker than with the continuous masker. An additional masking component at 1.6 kHz (condition H) produces a slight increase in threshold with the pulsed masker, and perhaps a slight decrease in the continuous-masked threshold. Comparison of condition H with A suggests that a further increase in the number of masker components does not appreciably affect either the pulsed- or continuous-masked thresholds. Detailed analysis of the changes in masking produced by adding components is considerably complicated by the masking due to, and possibly the detection of, combination tones. These distortion products almost certainly are affecting performance in conditions A, G, and H, and appear to account for the phase effects discussed in the Introduction. It seems very unlikely that they account for the effect of primary interest here, namely, the reduction in masked threshold with continuous presentation of the masker.

Versions of conditions A and C were run in which the adaptor was presented to the ear contralateral to that for which the masked threshold was measured. The thresholds for both these dichotic conditions were not significantly different from the pulsed thresholds, suggesting that masker adaptation is a monaural effect.

4. TEMPORAL CHARACTERISTICS

a. *Growth*

The development of adaptation over time was investigated by measuring the threshold for a 20-msec, 1-kHz signal temporally centered in a 40-msec masker as a function of the duration of the preceding adaptor. There was a 500-msec silent interval between the end of the masker for the first observation interval and the start of the adaptor for the second; a 2.5-sec silent interval occurred between trials. Except for these differences, the procedure was identical to that previously described. The masker and adaptor were the incomplete harmonic complex used in condition A.

Data for the three subjects are shown in Fig. 1. The points at zero duration correspond to the pulsed condition, those at "infinity" correspond to the continuous condition. The pulsed-continuous difference is about 4 dB smaller than that for the 80-msec signals (condition A in Table I). The curves for subject 2 and 3 suggest that adaptation is essentially complete after 400 msec of exposure. Subject 1 appears to show a more gradual growth of adaptation than the other subjects, but is within 2 dB of his fully adapted threshold after 800 msec of exposure.

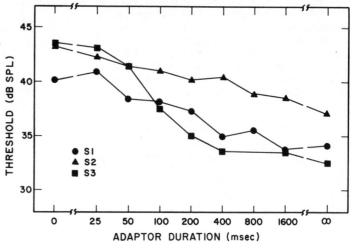

Fig. 1. Masked thresholds for a 20-msec signal as a function of adaptor duration. Thresholds obtained with pulsed and with continuous maskers are plotted at 0 and ∞, respectively.

b. *Recovery*

It was apparent from our informal observations that recovery from moderate-duration exposures was quite protracted and that threshold measurement using the 2IFC tracking task was not practicable. A method of adjustment, with 25% catch trials, was used and the subjects attempted to fix their false alarm rates at approximately 20%. Threshold estimates were based upon the mean of five blocks with 10 reversals per block. The adaptor and the masker were the incomplete harmonic complex used in (a.). The durations of the adaptor, the masker, and the 1-kHz signal were 2400, 100, and 80 msec, respectively. The data shown in Fig. 2 indicate a rather persistent effect of the adaptor. The thresholds measured 6.4 sec after the adaptor range from 1.5 dB to 3.8 dB lower than the unadapted thresholds, and extrapolation of the recovery curve for S3 suggests complete recovery only after approximately 30 sec.

A linear function in the coordinates of Fig. 2, similar to that used to describe the decay of forward masking (Plomp, 1964), describes the data fairly well, although there is some indication of a plateau at short delays. Wilson (1970) indicated that a similar function described his data on the decay of the afterimage. If spectral modulation depth is expressed as a peak-to-trough ratio in dB, then Wilson's data show a decay rate of approximately 2 dB per decade of delay. This compares with rates of 2.7, 4.4, and 3.6 dB/decade shown for S1-S3 respectively. The range of Wilson's decay function is about 5 dB; for the present experiment the average change from zero delay to the pulsed-masked thresholds is 11.8 dB. The possibility, based upon this comparison and upon the decay of forward masking, that the rate of decay increases with the amount of adaptation does not appear correct: Wilson shows recovery by approximately 2 sec; the data of Fig. 2 suggest recovery times larger by about an order of magnitude.

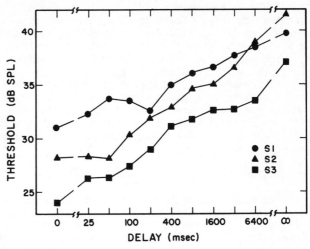

*Fig. 2. Masked thres-
holds for a 80-msec
signal as a function of
the silent interval
following a 2.4-sec
adaptor. Thresholds
obtained with a pulsed
masker are plotted at ∞.*

5. INTENSITY AND FREQUENCY EFFECTS

The effects of masker intensity and of signal frequency were studied using the basic procedure outlined in Section 2. The incomplete harmonic complex used in condition A and in Section 4 was the masker.

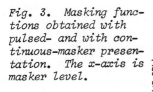

*Fig. 3. Masking func-
tions obtained with
pulsed- and with con-
tinuous-masker presen-
tation. The x-axis is
masker level.*

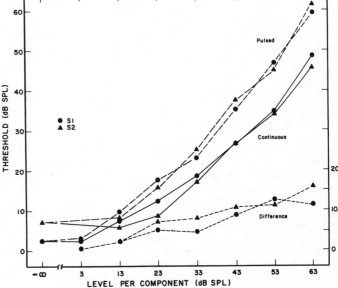

Fig. 3 shows masking functions for a 1-kHz signal obtained with pulsed- and with continuous-masker presentation. These functions appear to be positively accelerated and are not particularly well-described by the typical linear (dB vs dB) masking function. As shown by the lower curves of Fig. 3, the adaptation effect begins once masking is produced and increases gradually with increasing intensity of the masker.

Masking patterns obtained for subjects 2 and 3 with the incomplete harmonic complex at 43 dB per component indicate a clear masking effect by the
800- and 1200-Hz components and a local maximum at 1 kHz, the frequency of
the combination tone. There is no significant pulsed-continuous difference
for signals at 820 or 1160 Hz; the pulsed-continuous difference is largest at
about 1 kHz but is evident over a relatively broad range of frequencies around
1 kHz: the adaptation effect clearly is not limited to signals at the frequency of the suppressed component. Although the magnitude of the pulsed-continuous difference does not appear to be related in any obvious way to the
amount of masking at a given signal frequency, the presence of combination
tones precludes rejection of the hypothesis that the difference is largest
where there is least masking. A similar hypothesis was suggested by Zwicker
(1964) to account for the pitch of the afterimage produced by band-reject
noise.

6. DISCUSSION

It has been assumed in this paper that the pulsed-continuous differences
observed with certain maskers reflect a process of adaptation. It is clear,
however, that a positive pulsed-continuous difference does not, in itself, imply adaptation. In particular, the presence of "off-frequency" cues available
only when the masker is continuous can produce large pulsed-continuous differences in the absence of adaptation. Such off-frequency listening (Leshowitz
and Wightman, 1971) almost certainly does not account for the differences in
masker effectiveness observed in the present experiments: the masker in the
"continuous" condition was, in fact, identically gated to that in the pulsed
condition and, more directly, the data obtained with band-reject noise (condition C), the recovery data (Fig. 2), and the consistency of these data with
those from the other conditions makes an explanation based upon differential
spectral cues extremely unlikely.

Although a process of adaptation appears to underly the pulsed-continuous
differences observed in this experiment, it can be questioned whether this
measure accurately reflects the amount of masker adaptation. As discussed in
section 3, a negligible or small pulsed-continuous difference does not imply
an absence of adaptation. If, for example, both the signal and the masker
were equally attenuated by adaptation then no pulsed-continuous difference
would be observed. The fact that pulsed-continuous differences reported in
other masking situations (e.g., Wier *et al.*, 1977) are small, or even negative, does not exclude the possibility that significant adaptation is occurring. In the present experiments, there is reason to believe that the observed pulsed-continuous differences are underestimating, perhaps considerably, the amount of adaptation. The temporal characteristics discussed in
section 4 suggest a possible cumulation of adaptation over the time course of
a block of trials. The thresholds for the pulsed condition therefore may
have been measured in a state of partial adaptation. This, of course, would
reduce the pulsed-continuous difference; it would also imply that the "true"
recovery function is more protracted than that shown in Fig. 2. Although
certain alterations in procedure may reduce the cumulative effects, there
appears to be no compelling solution to the problem. Particularly disturbing
in this regard is the possibility that the adaptation may persist for days:
the enhancement effect can be observed upon the first presentation of a complete harmonic complex several days, in one case over one week, after the
last exposure to the incomplete complex. Non-sensory factors may, and hopefully do, account for this long persistence. However, the fact that the
effect is not observed when the complete complex is presented to the unexposed
ear and, noting the similarities of this effect to the semi-permanent exposure
effect reported by McFadden and Pasanen (1979), leads to a cautious conclusion
that the persistence is a sensory effect.

In conclusion, the experiments reported largely confirm informal observations of the enhancement effect and indicate that adaptation of masking does occur in a wide variety of conditions. The relationship between the enhancement/adaptation effects and other phenomena and processes in audition is, at present, unclear. Although the properties of masker adaptation are different from those of previously studied adaptation and fatigue phenomena, they may share a common mechanism. Also, there are some similarities between the present experiments, particularly those of section 4, and those on nonsimultaneous masking. While it probably is not useful to consider masker adaptation as nonsimultaneous "masking of the masker", nonsimultaneous masking very likely is involved in the present experiments, except for the recovery experiment with long adaptor-masker delays. Conversely, adaptation of the sort described here may be intimately involved in nonsimultaneous masking.

Acknowledgements

This research was supported by NINCDS and by the center for Research in Human Learning. Presentation of this paper was made possible by support from the Office of International Programs, University of Minnesota. I am grateful to W.D. Ward and S. Bacon for comments on the manuscript.

REFERENCES

Green, D.M., McKey, M.J., and Licklider, J.C.R. (1959). Detection of a pulsed sinusoid in noise as a function of frequency. *J. Acoust. Soc. Amer.* 31, 1146-1452.

Leshowitz, B., and Wightman, F.L. (1971). On-frequency masking with continuous sinusoids. *J. Acoust. Soc. Amer.* 49, 1180-1190.

Levitt, H. (1971). Transformed up-down methods in psychoacoustics. *J. Acoust. Soc. Amer.* 49, 467-477.

Lummis, R.C. and Guttman, N. (1972). Exploratory studies of Zwicker's "Negative Afterimage" in hearing. *J. Acoust. Soc. Amer.* 51, 1930-1944.

McFadden, D. and Pasanen, E.G. (1979). Permanent changes in psychophysical tuning curves following exposure to weak, steep-sided noise. *J. Acoust. Soc. Amer.* 65, S118(A).

Neelen, J.J.M. (1967). Auditory afterimages produced by incomplete line spectra. Inst. Perception Res., Eindhoven, IPO Ann. Prog. Rep. No. 2 Netherlands.

Plomp, R. (1964). Rate of decay of auditory sensation. *J. Acoust. Soc. Amer.* 36, 277-282.

Viemeister, N.F. and Green, D.M. (1972). Detection of a missing harmonic in a continuous or pulsed harmonic complex. *J. Acoust. Soc. Amer.* 52, 142 (A).

Wier, C.C., Green, D.M., Hafter, E.R., and Burkhardt, S. (1977). Detection of a tone burst in continuous- and gated-noise maskers; defects of signal frequency, duration, and masker level. *J. Acoust. Soc. Amer.* 61, 1298-1300.

Wilson, J.P. (1966). Psychoacoustics of obstacle detection using ambient or self-generated noise. In: *Animal Sonar Systems* (R.G. Busnel, ed.). pp. 89-114. Jouy-en-Josas, 1967.

Wilson, J.P. (1970). An auditory afterimage. In: *Frequency Analysis and Psychophysics of Hearing* (R. Plomp and G.F. Smoorenberg, eds). pp. 303-315. Sijthoff, Leiden, Netherlands.

Zwicker, E. (1964). "Negative Afterimage" in Hearing. *J. Acoust. Soc. Amer.* 36, 2413-2415 (L).

ADDENDUM

Neal F. Viemeister

*Department of Psychology, University of Minnesota
Minneapolis, Minnesota 55455, U.S.A.*

The phenomenon I have called the enhancement effect was observed, apparently originally, by Schouten (1940). He mentions it as a method of drawing attention to a particular harmonic, including the fundamental, of a periodic pulse-train. Cardozo (1967a,b) studied "Schouten's artifice" in experiments very similar to those reported in section 4 of my paper. His data show somewhat more rapid growth of adaptation than that shown in Fig. 1, and also show more rapid recovery than that shown in Fig. 2. However, procedural differences between these sets of experiments precludes detailed comparison. Cardozo does not use the term "adaptation" but refers more neutrally to "subsidence of masking" produced by a "conditioning stimulus."

REFERENCES

Cardozo, B.L.(1967a). Ohm's Law and masking. *J. Acoust. Soc. Amer.* <u>42</u>, 1193(A).
Cardozo, B.L.(1967b). Ohm's Law and masking. *IPO Ann. Prog. Rep.* <u>2</u>, 59-64.
Schouten, J.F.(1940). The residue, a new component in subjective sound analysis. *Proc. Kon. Ned. Akad. Wetensch* <u>43</u>, 356-365.

COMMENT ON : "Adaptation of Masking" (N.F. Viemeister)

E. Terhardt
Institute of Electroacoustics, Technical University München, Federal Republic of Germany.

It may be appropriate to notice, that conscious perception of individual spectral components of complex tones in principle is not dependent on the "enhancement effect" mentioned by Dr. Viemeister. Rather, under suitable experimental conditions the spectral pitch of a "target" component can be "heard out" without the aid of suppressing and then re-introducing that component(Plomp, 1964, Plomp & Mimpen, 1968, Stoll, 1980). The limitations of this phenomenon caused by mutual masking, are correctly predictable by assuming that degree of aural frequency resolution which is provided by simultaneous masking patterns of single tones or narrow-band noise (Terhardt, 1979; see Fig. 2, this volume). Nevertheless, as Dr. Viemeister mentions, the re-introduction of a particular component which previously had been removed from the complex tone, increases its audibility to a striking extent. In fact, we use this effect in our laboratory for demonstration purposes.

It appears, however, that only those components can be "enhanced" in this way, which anyhow are detectable in the above-mentioned sense. In the particular case of a complex tone with a flat amplitude spectrum and 200 Hz fundamental frequency as used in Viemeister's experiments, this would apply to the first eight harmonics at best. As Viemeister, in his masking experiments finds a pronounced adaptation effect even for the 15th harmonic (Table I, case B of his paper), it seems that this experimental paradigm does reveal not exactly the same features of the auditory mechanism as the enhancement phenomenon of individual spectral pitches. Of course this does neither reduce the value of that paradigm nor of the data.

With respect to perception of voiced speech elements and musical tones (where the spectral composition of complex tones naturally changes in such a way that some harmonics may be in one moment more or less "suppressed", in the other "re-introduced"), one may speculate that the enhancement effect of spectral pitches will not provide significantly more spectral-pitch information than is already known from the above-mentioned data, since in those signals the fundamental frequency is not constant and the temporal changes of the spectrum are relatively quick in relation to the adaptation time constant. However, if there is an effect, its consequence would be, that individual spectral components are to an even larger extent aurally relevant than has been assumed as yet.

REFERENCES

Plomp, R. (1964). The ear as a frequency analyzer. *J. Acoust. Soc. Am.* 36, 1628-1636.
Plomp, R. and Mimpen, A.M.(1968). The ear as a frequency analyzer II. *J. Acoust. Soc. Am.* 43, 764-767.
Stoll, G. (1980). Psychoakustische Messungen der Spektraltonhöhenmuster von Vokalen. DAGA 80, München.
Terhardt, E. (1979). Calculating virtual pitch. Hearing Research 1, 155-182.

VERY RAPID ADAPTATION IN AUDITORY GANGLION CELLS

Graeme K. Yates
M.R.C. Institute of Hearing Research,
The Medical School, University of Nottingham, U.K.
and
Donald Robertson
Dept. of Physiology, University of W.A.,
Nedlands, 6009, Western Australia

1. INTRODUCTION

From past studies it is well established that at least three forms of adaptation are observable in the auditory nerve. When exposed to very long continuous-tone stimuli, the probability of action potential (AP) generation is initially very high for approximately five to ten milliseconds (ms), then slows over a time course of many tens of ms, and then further reduces over several minutes. The slowest form was described by Kiang *et al* (1965). The midterm adaptation has been extensively studied by Smith (1979) in guinea pigs and Mongolian gerbils. Harris and Dallos (1979) associated forward masking in the auditory nerve with the recovery from this form of adaptation to the masker tone, although their observed time constant is significantly faster than that seen by Smith. Both sets of authors mention a fine structure on the adaptation occurring in the first ten ms and regard this as being immaterial to the masking process; consequently neither has attempted a detailed study of this region of the response. We have made preliminary studies on this very rapid adaptation and find its properties to be different from those of the slower forms.

2. DIFFERENCES

a) *Time constant.* In the guinea pig and Mongolian gerbil Smith found adaptation time constants of about 45 ms, Harris and Dallos report 15 ms for the chinchilla. Both briefly mention a much faster process within the first 5 ms. We have found, by studying this fast process with very fine temporal resolution, that it may be further resolved into two phases. Initially, and at high stimulus intensities, we have found a very high AP probability which is not appropriately described as a firing 'rate' at all. Rather, it appears to be best described as the probability of occurrence of an AP in the first millisecond following the rapid onset of a tone, and the apparent 'rate' is dependent upon the histogram bin width used. This is almost certainly a manifestation of the refractoriness of the nerve, with the steady state AP probability being reduced by the initial near-certainty of occurrence at the tone onset. This initial peak response in the peristimulus time histogram (PSTH) is also approximately exponential in its time course, but decays in the first two or three ms. It is followed by a second phase with more complex properties but having a typical time constant of about ten ms.

b) *Variation of time 'constant' with intensity.* We find the time constant of this second phase not to be independent of stimulus intensity and therefore better referred to as a time parameter. The magnitude of this time parameter, obtained by fitting exponential decay curves to the histograms between 4 and 40 ms post stimulus onset, is a monotonically decreasing function of intensity. At very low intensities it appears to approach a value of about 15 ms, but as stimulus intensity is raised the time parameter falls to a limiting value of

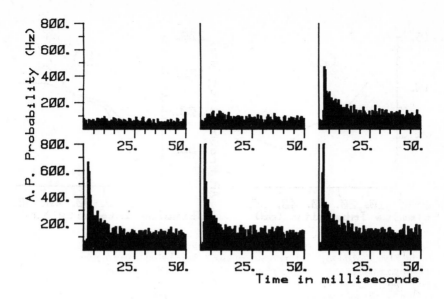

figure 1. PSTH's obtained at intensities of -5, 5, 15, 25, 35 and 45 dB above threshold. Bin width is 0.5 milliseconds.

around 3 ms.

c) *Variation of onset response with intensity.* The response in the first two or three ms is not very prominent at low levels, but grows faster than the steady state response. This is in marked contrast with the midterm adaptation which shows a constant ratio of onset-to-steady-state response (Smith 1979). The second phase of very rapid adaptation also shows a growth of the onset response which is faster than that of the steady state.

3. METHODS

a) *Animals.* Guinea pigs weighing between 200 and 350 grams were anaesthetised using the neuroleptanaestheia technique of Evans (1978). Rectal temperature was maintained at 37.5 C and the animal was artificially respired with a constant pressure respirator (10 cms water) with 5% carbogen. The auditory bulla was opened as described by Sellick and Russell (1979), and a 0.6 mm plastic fibre was introduced to back-illuminate the cochlea. The cochlea was opened with a small hole into scala tympani of the basal turn, placed well away from the spiral ligament and just large enough to allow visualisation of the spiral lamina. Through this hole the thin bone above Rosenthal's canal was punctured using a sharpened needle mounted in a micromanipulator. The subsequent integrity of the cochlea was verified using the gross action potential response to tone bursts of various frequencies.

b) *The sound system* was essentially identical with that of Wilson and Johnstone (1975).

c) *Stimuli* were 50 ms tone bursts at unit centre frequency (10.5 to 14.5 kHz), with rise/fall times of 0.5 ms. They were presented at a rate of 5 per second with intensities randomised over the range specified at the time of data collection.

d) *Electrodes* were glass micropipettes pulled on a Brown-Flaming electrode puller. When filled with 3M KAc they had resistances in the range 70-120 Mohms. They were mounted in a hydraulically driven micromanipulator and advanced into the spiral ganglion through the puncture hole in the bone.

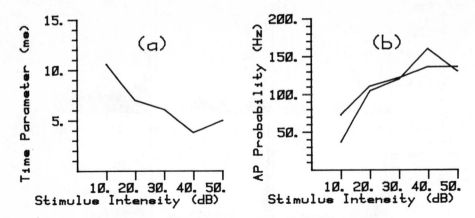

Figure 2. *Variation with stimulus intensity (expressed in dB above threshold) of (a) second phase adaptation time parameter (in milliseconds), and (b) adapted firing rate (flatter curve) and onset response (steeper curve) obtained by extrapolating fitted curves back to 2 msecs and dividing by 3. Data are from the last 4 PSTH's of figure 2.*

e) *Raw data* were acquired in the form of PSTH's, using a small laboratory microcomputer. To obtain the required temporal resolution, histogram bin widths of 0.5 ms were used, requiring the averaging of responses to very many stimuli. Following Smith, intensities have been normalised to unit thresholds, which varied over the range 20 to 60 dB SPL.

4. RESULTS

We aimed at a recording time sufficient to allow a total of 0.25 seconds recording time per bin, requiring 500 stimulus presentations per intensity level. Even so, at low stimulus levels each bin recorded few AP's and the variance was great. This, together with the small degree of adaptation observed at low intensities (figure 1) made fitting of exponentials at these low intensities very inaccurate, so few data are available for this range. Similarly, at very high AP rates, refractory effects become important even beyond the first few ms, and the error bands on the fitted exponentials became relatively larger. However, in no cases were there any data which conflict with our findings below.

a) *Time parameter of very rapid adaptation.* At lower intensities the AP probability adapts exponentially to a steady state with a time parameter of typically ten ms. This is a general figure, being typical of the rate of adaptation at stimulation levels a few dB above threshold (figure 1).

b) *Variation of time parameter with intensity.* Figure 2(a) illustrates the observed variation of the time parameter with intensity, typical of most animals. Some fibres (approximately 20%) showed no such variation, maintaining a fixed time constant of 10 to 15 ms. There did not appear to be a continuum between these two types of behaviour.

c) *Variation of the onset AP probability with intensity.* The response in the first few ms only became prominent at higher stimulation intensities, being indistinguishable from the second phase at lower levels. Hence, its growth is not proportional to the steady state response. Similarly, though less obviously, the growth of the second phase was steeper than that of the steady state (figure 2b).

5. DISCUSSION

Our results reveal a different form of adaptation from that studied by Smith, who found a linear type of adaptation with a fixed time constant of about 50 ms and a fixed ratio between onset and steady state responses. In contrast, the very rapid form of adaptation shows a variation with intensity in both these parameters.

We tentatively associate the first phase of the very rapid adaptation with the refractoriness of the auditory nerve. Its time course extends over two or three ms only, with frequently seen evidence of small oscillations in the number of AP's falling into alternate bins of the PSTH. We have computed hazard functions (Gray 1967) from interval histograms of spontaneous and stimulated AP's and they show a quasi-exponential recovery with a time constant of 2 to 3 ms, in agreement with the time course of the first phase of the response. The oscillation in bin content is to be expected with very narrow bin widths, since a high probability of AP occurrence in one bin will result in a lower probability in the second, but a smaller reduction in the third as the nerve recovers from its absolute refractory period.

We believe the second phase is not a result of refractoriness, however, since its time course is too slow. Our own experiments with an electronic analogue of absolute and relative refractoriness support this contention.

It is possible that the apparent variation of the time parameter of the second phase results from a confusion with the sum of two fixed-period decays, the faster of which grows the more rapidly. Thus, if the second phase of the very rapid adaptation had a time constant of, say, 4 ms and emerged from a midterm adaptation of 40 ms, it may appear as an adaptation with a varying time parameter. We consider this unlikely since the rate of increase of the second phase onset response, relative to the steady state, is much less than the rate of decrease of the time parameter. Another possibility is that the very rapid adaptation, and the various other forms of adaptation described in the literature, are all a single process varying with the logarithm of time, i.e., that if the response to a tone burst were to be plotted against logarithm of time, the various stages of the response would appear as a linear decrease in AP rate. We have plotted our responses on a logarithmic time axis and observe a clear break-point between the first and second, and the second and later, phases. It therefore appears that the very rapid stage of adaptation is a distinct process in the response of auditory nerve fibres.

REFERENCES:-

Evans, E.F. (1978). Neuroleptanaesthesia for the guinea pig: an ideal anaesthetic procedure for physiological studies of the guinea pig. *Arch. Otolaryngol.*, 105,185-186.

Gray, P.R. (1967). Conditional probability analyses of the spike activity of single neurons. *Biophys.J.*, 7,759-777.

Harris, D.M. and Dallos, P. (1979). Forward masking of auditory nerve fibre responses. *J.Neurophysiol.*, 42,1083-1107.

Kiang, N.Y.S. (1965). Discharge patterns of single fibres in the cat's auditory nerve. *Research Monograph* 35, MIT Press, Cambridge, Mass.

Sellick, P.M. and Russell, I.J. (1979). Intracellular studies of the receptor potentials of inner hair cells of the guinea pig cochlea: techniques. In: *Auditory Investigation: The Scientific and Technological Basis.* (H.A. Beagley, ed). pp 368-381. Clarendon Press, Oxford.

Smith, R.L. (1979). Adaptation, saturation, and forward masking in auditory nerve fibres. *J. Acoust. Soc. Am.* 65,166-178.

Wilson, J.P. and Johnstone, J.R. (1975). Basilar membrane and middle ear vibration in guinea pig measured by capacitive probe. *J. Acoust. Soc. Am.* 57,705-723.

COMMENT

COMMENT ON: "Very rapid adaptation in auditory ganglion cells" (G.K. Yates and D. Robertson)

R.L. Smith
Institute for Sensory Research, Syracuse University, Syracuse, U.S.A.

The very rapid adaptation described in the auditory ganglion of guinea pig appears to resemble that seen in the auditory nerve of the gerbil (Brachman and Smith, 1979; Smith and Brachman, 1980a,b). The latter has been observed for both tones and wide-band noise bursts with rise times of 2.5 msec and 10 µsec, respectively, so that it cannot be attributed to frequency splatter at stimulus onset per se. Nevertheless, quantitative investigation with tone bursts may be confounded by rise-time effects, with rise times of less than 1 msec producing considerable frequency splatter, and larger rise times interacting with the rapid adaptation.

A second possible complication occurs because of refractory effects, as noted by the authors. However, this does not reduce the importance of measuring responses during the first millisecond of response. This is so because refractory effects make it unlikely that more than one spike will occur in any one millisecond interval. Hence, firing rates based on one-millisecond intervals are almost always estimates of the probability of occurrence of a spike. There are two additional complications within the first millisecond. First, the refractory limit of one spike per presentation may be approached. Second, the jitter in the location of the first spike within the interval appears to decrease with increasing intensity, producing a mode in the PST (Smith, 1973). The height of the mode should not be confused with firing rate, although it ought not be dismissed as a candidate for conveying information about the stimulus. In any case, when responses are measured over intervals large enough to yield the area under the mode, they appear to reflect the underlying input-output characteristic of the unadapted or onset response (Smith and Brachman, 1980a,b; Brachman and Smith, 1979). The probability of occurrence of spikes in the next few milliseconds is then depressed by refractory effects in addition to the rapid adaptation processes as was noted.

REFERENCES

Brachman, M.L. and Smith, R.L. (1979). Dynamic versus static characteristics of single auditory-nerve fibers. *Neurosci. Abstract* 5, 16.
Smith, R.L. (1973). Short-term adaptation and incremental responses in single auditory nerve fibers. *Ph.D. Dissertation and Special Report LSC-S-11*, Institute for Sensory Research, Syracuse University, Syracuse, N.Y. pp. 168-171.
Smith, R.L. and Brachman, M.L. (1980a). Operating range and maximum response of single auditory-nerve fibers. *Brain Res.* 184, 499-505.
Smith, R.L. and Brachman, M.L. (1980b). Dynamic response of single auditory-nerve fibers: Some effects of intensity and time. *(This volume)*.

COMMENT

REPLY TO COMMENT OF R.L. SMITH.

G.K. Yates
M.R.C. Institute of Hearing Research, The Medical School, University of Nottingham, U.K.

The very rapid adaptation we have described does indeed resemble the very fast process frequently mentioned by Smith for the auditory nerve in the gerbil. However, as we have pointed out, the very rapid adaptation differs from the slower, 40 ms, adaptation in two ways :

a) the time course of the very rapid adaptation is faster and is intensity dependent;
b) the ratio of the onset response to steady state response is also dependent upon intensity.

The rise time of the stimulus does not appear to be a problem for two reasons :

a. The adaptation is not seen in the receptor potential (Russell and Sellick, 1978). Since no other stimulus-frequency selective mechanism is known to follow the receptor potential we can assume that, apart from some possible ringing of the envelope in the first ms or two, frequency splatter should not affect the results. We exclude the first two milliseconds from our exponental curve fitting.
b. We can confirm Smith's observation that very short rise times or the choice of stimulus frequency does not, in experimental fact, affect the form or magnitude of the adaptation.

I agree with the comment on refractory effect, and this is why we have chosen to refer to A.P. probability density rather than to A.P. rate. However, there is a problem with integrating the area under the mode to produce a measure of the unadapted input-output response. This is because the decrease in the adaptation time constant compensates in some degree for the increase in amplitude; the total area does not depend on intensity as much as does the initial amplitude of the (time) exponental adaptation. Hence, we believe that the initial amplitude is a better indicator of the underlying A.P. drive (c.f. the model of Schroeder and Hall, 1974).

REFERENCES

Russell, I.J. and Sellick, P.M. (1978). Intracellular studies of hair cells in the guinea pig cochlea. *J. Physiol.* 284, 261-290.
Schroeder, M.R. and Hall, J.L. (1974). Model for mechanical to neural transduction in the auditory receptor. *J. Acoust. Soc. Am.* 55, 1055-1060.

TEMPORAL MODULATION TRANSFER FUNCTIONS
FOR INTENSITY MODULATED NOISE BANDS

G.A. van Zanten

*Dept. of Medical and Physiological Physics,
State University, Utrecht, The Netherlands*

1. INTRODUCTION

One approach to study how the human auditory system processes periodic changes in noise intensity was called "the system analysis approach". It involved experiments in which modulation thresholds (defined as the lowest modulation index value necessary to make modulated and unmodulated noise distinguishable) were measured at fixed modulation frequency (Pollack, 1951; Rodenburg, 1972, 1977; Viemeister, 1977, 1979). In this approach it is assumed that *(a)* the modulation detector model consists of a (critical) bandfilter followed by a non-linear element (NLE) and a leaky integrator, *(b)* the modulation depth of the integrator output signal is proportional to the modulation depth of the bandfilter input signal, and *(c)* detection occurs if the modulation depth of the integrator output signal surpasses some fixed value. Assumption *(b)* seems to be appropriate for intensity modulation depths up to 80% (Schöne, 1978, 1979). So, the transfer function of the leaky integrator can be measured by psychophysical measurement of the relation between modulation threshold and modulation frequency, which relation is called Temporal Modulation Transfer Function (TMTF).

Following the system analysis approach we describe in this paper experiments designed to provide answers to the following questions: *(1)* How does a TMTF for Intensity Modulated (IM) noise depend on noise bandwidth and noise bandcentre frequency (Exp. I)? *(2)* How does a TMTF depend on the level of a noise that masks excitations (generated by some aural non-linearity) beyond and/or below the stimulus band (Exp. II)?

In the literature there are few experiments, which provide some answers to these questions using IM-noise with a square-wave modulator (SQIM-noise). This study supplements those data and supplies some narrow-band data. The up to now reported TMTF's (e.g. Rodenburg, 1972; Viemeister, 1977, 1979) are mainly measured with Sinusoidally Amplitude Modulated (SAM) noise. A SAM noise threshold m_a can be compared with a SQIM noise threshold m with

$$m = \pi m_a \,/\, (2(1 + (\pi m_a/4)^2) \quad . \tag{1}$$

2. METHOD

A noise generator (based on 25-bit maximum length sequences, $5\frac{1}{2}$ min cycle time) delivered an IM-noise signal, which had a flat spectrum in the audiorange. The modulation frequency f_m was in the 2 to 1000 Hz region and the modulation depth m was variable between 0 and 100%, in steps of 0.5%. The generator signal was filtered by two identical bandpass filters (Krohn-Hite 3342) in series, yielding passband slopes of 96 dB/oct. The noise bandwidth B is defined as the difference between the high and low cut-off frequencies of the filters. The bandcentre frequency f_c is defined as the geometric mean of these cut-off frequencies. The signal was gated and monaurally presented to the subject by headphone (Telephonics TDH 39, NAF-48490-1 earcushion) at a sensation level between 50 and 60 dB.

A trial consisted of two 2.0 sec duration pulses separated by a 0.5 sec duration silent interval. One of the pulses was modulated noise, the other one was unmodulated noise. Subjects had to identify the modulated pulse and got response feedback. For threshold finding an adaptive procedure was used, based on the one described by Cardozo and De Jong (1971), aiming at P(c) = 0.775. Three subjects (GG, TB, and GZ) served in the experiments, all were between 20 and 30 years of age and had normal audiograms, with the exception of TB, who showed a sharp peaked hearingloss of 35 dB at 4 kHz. Effects of this hearing-loss did not show up in the measured thresholds. Intersubject differences in the thresholds were within experimental error except in the f_c = 4.0 kHz, f_m greater than 100 Hz circumstances. Since these differing thresholds formed on-ly a minor part of the data, only the mean of 3 subjects' data is shown in the results of Exp. I.

3. EXPERIMENTS AND RESULTS

Experiment I. For subjects GG, TB, and GZ TMTF's were measured for 10 passbands: B = 0.4, 0.8, and 1.6 kHz around f_c = 0.5, 2.0, and 4.0 kHz, and a 140-4880 Hz broadband covering all other bands. The broadband results are shown in fig. 1. In this figure comparable data from previous investigators are shown too. The vertical pieces of dotted line are Rodenburg's (1972) data. The numbered circles are data from Patterson *et al* (1978). Circles containing numbers 1 and 2 were measured with a broadband AM-noise masked by low-pass noises with cut-off frequencies at 0.4 and 3.2 kHz respectively. The stars are data from Viemeister (1979). Since their data were measured with a SAM-noise stimulus the data of Rodenburg, Viemeister, and Patterson *et al* were recalcu-lated to IM-index with relation (1). The open squares are Pollack's (1951) data. Pollack measured subjects' Difference Limen for Intensity (DLI) between repeated bursts of noise and noise bursts filling the gaps. The IM-index m can be calculated from this DLI with

$$m = (10^{0.1 \ DLI}-1) \ / \ (10^{0.1 \ DLI}+1) \quad . \tag{2}$$

Fig. 2 shows the results for the other 9 bands. The TMTF's for the B = 0.4 kHz bands are the upper three curves. The B = 0.8 and 1.6 kHz bands give the mid-dle and lower sets of TMTF's.

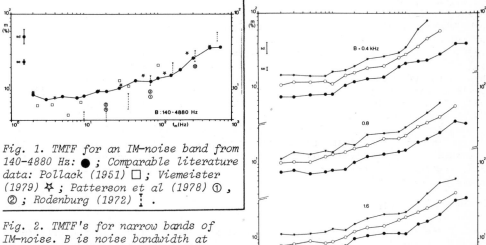

Fig. 1. TMTF for an IM-noise band from 140-4880 Hz: ● *; Comparable literature data: Pollack (1951)* □ *; Viemeister (1979)* ✡ *; Patterson et al (1978)* ① *,* ② *; Rodenburg (1972)* ⋮ *.*

Fig. 2. TMTF's for narrow bands of IM-noise. B is noise bandwidth at centrefrequencies 0.5 kHz ✱ *; 2.0 kHz* ○ *; 4.0 kHz* ● *.*

Experiment II. As a continuous background a "pink" noise was introduced and IM thresholds were measured for subject GZ, with f_c = 2.0 kHz, B = 0.8 kHz, and f_m = 2, 5, 10, 20, 50, 100, and 200 Hz. Fig. 3 shows the results for f_m = 2, 20, and 200 Hz. The results for the other f_m's were similar. In fig. 3 the abscissa is the difference (in dB) of the power spectral densities of the background noise (I_b) and the stimulus (I_s), both measured at f_c. The ordinate is the modulation depth.

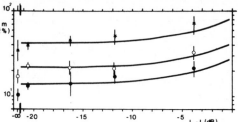

Fig. 3. Intensity modulation thresholds as a function of the difference (in dB) in power spectral densities of a "pink" noise background (I_b) and the stimulus noise band (I_s), B = 0.8 kHz at f_c = 2.0 kHz. Parameter is modulation frequency: 2 Hz ● ; 20 Hz ○ ; 200 Hz ✶ .

4. DISCUSSION

The measured TMTF's all show a low-pass characteristic. They are flat below f_m = 10 Hz and above this frequency they rise with increasing f_m. But the slope cannot be described by a single constant. There are almost flat portions in the broadband TMTF as well as in the narrow band TMTF's. If we assign a single slope to the rising part of the TMTF's, then the slopes are 2 to 3 dB/oct (except for B = 0.4 kHz, f_c = 0.5 kHz). From fig. 1 it is clear that our data are in agreement with most of the previously reported data.

From figs 1 and 2 it appears that the broadband TMTF is the same as the TMTF for the B = 1.6 kHz, f_c = 4.0 kHz band. Apparently the broadband TMTF is governed by the highest frequency region present in the broadband. This effect can be seen in the Patterson *et al* (1978) data too: the high frequency contents of the two stimuli are almost the same and the resulting thresholds (circles numbered 1 and 2) are approximately the same.

Also from fig. 2 it appears that only a limited frequency region from the stimuli is used by the subjects: a TMTF sinks only slightly when B is increased at constant f_c. At constant B, however, a TMTF sinks considerably with increasing f_c.

Let us assume that the NLE of the detector model (see introduction) is a square-law device, then the relative standard deviation in the integrator output signal is proportional to the inverse square root of the bandwidth of the detector's initial filter (Rice, 1954). If we suppose the modulation threshold to be proportional to this relative standard deviation, then the broader the initial bandfilter the lower the threshold will be. If the critical bands (CB's) are the initial filters of a subject's set of detectors, the subject will utilize at threshold level the broadest CB activated by the stimulus. And this is the CB lying in the upper frequency region of the stimulus (because CB-width is proportional to CB-centrefrequency, e.g. Zwicker and Feldtkeller, 1967). So our hypothesis is that the CB that covers the upper frequency region of the modulated noise bands can be viewed as the model's initial filter.

In Exp. II a background noise was added to the stimulus. This caused a reduction in modulation depth in connection with the increase in mean intensity. As thresholds do not depend on the mean intensity at the used SL's (Rodenburg, 1972; Viemeister, 1979), the for stimulus plus noise expected IM-threshold m can be calculated with

$$m = m_s \ (1 + 10^{0.1(I_b - I_s)}) \quad , \tag{3}$$

where m_s is the IM-threshold for the stimulus alone and $I_b - I_s$ is the difference (in dB) between the power spectral densities (at f_c) of the background and stimulus respectively. Relation (3) gives the solid lines in fig. 3. They are fitted by eye through the experimental results. Within error, relation (3) describes the result of Exp. II. This validates the implicit assumption that on-ly stimulus energy in the stimulusband was used by the subject in Exp. I.

5. CONCLUSIONS

TMTF's for narrow band as well as broadband IM-noise show a low-pass characteristic. The constant level portion of the TMTF's extends to a modulation frequency of about 10 Hz. Above this frequency the rising part of the TMTF's has a slope of 2 to 3 dB/oct.

A TMTF for a broadband noise is the same as that for the highest frequency region present in the stimulus. Our hypothesis is that the highest critical band activated by the stimulus governs TMTF height.

For narrow band IM-noise the TMTF's are indeed governed by intensity fluctuations in the stimulus band. No "off-frequency band" detection could be detected.

6. ACKNOWLEDGEMENT

The author is indebted to the Netherlands Organisation for the Advancement of Pure Research (Z.W.O.) for giving financial support for a part of this investigation.

7. REFERENCES

Cardozo, B.L., and De Jong, Th.A. (1971). A note on a sequential up-and-down method of threshold finding. *IPO annual progress report* 6, 125-127.

Patterson, R.D., Johnson-Davies, D., and Milroy, R. (1978). Amplitude-modulated noise: The detection of modulation versus the detection of modulation rate. *J.Acoust.Soc.Am.* 63, 1904-1911.

Pollack, I. (1951). Sensitivity to differences in intensity between repeated bursts of noise. *J.Acoust.Soc.Am.* 23, 650-653.

Rice, S.O. (1954). Mathematical analysis of random noise. In: *Selected papers on noise and stochastic processes.* (Nelson Wax, ed.). pp 114-292. Dover, New York.

Rodenburg, M. (1972). *Sensitivity of the auditory system to differences in intensity.* Thesis, University of Rotterdam.

Rodenburg, M. (1977). Investigation of temporal effects with amplitude modulated signals. In: *Psychophysics and physiology of hearing.* (E.F. Evans and J.P. Wilson, eds). pp 429-439. Academic Press, London.

Schöne, P. (1978). Vergleich dreier Funktionsschemata der akustischen Schwankungsstärke. *Biological Cybernetics* 29, 57-62.

Schöne, P. (1979). Messungen zur Schwankungsstärke von amplitudenmodulierten Sinustönen. *Acustica* 41, 252-257.

Terhardt, E. (1974). Pitch, consonance, and harmony. *J.Acoust.Soc.Am.* 55, 1061-1069.

Viemeister, N.F. (1977). Temporal factors in audition: a system analysis approach. In: *Psychophysics and physiology of hearing.* (E.F. Evans and J.P. Wilson, eds). pp 419-428. Academic Press, London.

Viemeister, N.F. (1979). Temporal modulation transfer functions based on modulation thresholds. *J.Acoust.Soc.Am.* 66, 1364-1380.

Zwicker, E., and Feldtkeller, R. (1967). *Das Ohr als Nachrichtenempfänger.* pp 70-75. Hirzel, Stuttgart.

Section III
Lateral Suppression and Distortion Products

Lateral suppression and distortion products like cubic differ-ence tones are characteristic, and frequently studied, features of the peripheral auditory system in man and animal. Whether these are functional or not is still an open question. The description and analysis of these phenomena contribute to a better understanding of the functioning of the peripheral auditory system. In the first part of the section, the results of two- and three-tone suppression experiments are reported. Their consequences with regard to the in-ternal representation of wide-band signals and to data on periph-eral frequency resolution are also considered. New psychophysical and physiological findings concerning the generation of combination tones are reported in the second part. Both, monaural masking and lateralization paradigms have been used in the psychophysical ex-periments.

A PSYCHOACOUSTICAL APPROACH TO PULSATION THRESHOLD

Christoph Schreiner

Max-Planck-Institut für biophys. Chemie
3400 Göttingen, West-Germany

1. INTRODUCTION

The measurement of the pulsation threshold is a well-established tool for the psychoacoustician (Houtgast,1974a-d;Verschuure,1978;Schreiner,1977). The non-simultaneous presentation condition of the signals ("masker" and "test signal") makes it possible to limit the number of interactions between the stimuli. Thus, we can get a more correct picture of the internal representation of signals with this method than we can get with a simultaneous presentation of the signals, e.g. in direct masking (Houtgast, 1974a).

Indeed, some rules found in neurophysiological experiments could also be demonstrated by this method – at least quantitatively – in psychoacoustics. The most important example is the psychoacoustical equivalent of 'two-tone suppression' (Houtgast, 1974a).However it is not yet known which mechanism of signal processing underlies the continuity effect utilized in the pulsation-threshold method.

Therefore the interpretation of pulsation-threshold data follows in a close relation to electrophysiological results because similar dependencies can be demonstrated in the activities of single nerve cells in the auditory pathway. Such a neurophysiological point of view allows us to get a qualitative description of pulsation-threshold results (Houtgast, 1974a). On the basis of the hypothesis mentioned above,the possibility of a quantitative description is rather vague. To get an understanding of the meaning of pulsation-threshold data for the psychoacoustical approach to signal processing in hearing, it is necessary to have information about the psychoacoustical conditions at the pulsation-threshold itself. The question to be solved is whether or not there exists a quantitative description of pulsation-threshold data in psychoacoustical terms.

A first hint to clarify this question was given by Houtgast (1974a,b), pointing to the connection of "lateral suppression" of a tone in noise and the loudness reduction of a tone in noise. In this paper the meaning of loudness of the signals for the interpretation of pulsation-threshold measurements is described in more detail.

2. METHODS

Two kinds of experiments are performed for this purpose: pulsation-threshold measurements and loudness-matching measurements.

In the left part of fig. 1 the temporal pattern of the pulsation signals is shown. The masker (index M) is perceived as a pulsating sound. The test signal (index T) is perceived as a continuous sound for appropriate masker and test-tone parameters. The pulse duration of the signals is 150 ms, measured at the half-pressure points of the trapezoidal envelope. The ramps have a duration of about 8 ms. There is no gap between offset and onset of the ramp of consecutive pulses. Thus, the choice of the signal parameters is in agreement with the favourable values given in the literature (Verschuure *et al.* 1976, Schreiner *et al.*, (1977).

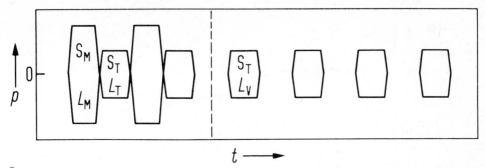

Fig.1. Stimulus paradigm for pulsation-threshold measurements (left) and for loudness evaluation of the test signal.

In the loudness-matching experiments, four pulses of the comparison signal (V) are presented to the subject after four pulses of the test and masker signal, respectively (fig. 1 right). The level of the comparison signal is subject-controlled. The duration of the comparison pulses as well as of the gaps between them is 150 ms.

The level of the signals is referred to the individual hearing threshold of the subjects for a tone of 1.0 kHz and 150 ms duration. The noise evokes equal loudness in each critical band. The noise level is referred to a shift of the hearing threshold: a noise of N=20 dB causes a threshold shift of 20 dB for a 1.0 kHz tone.

The signals are delivered monaurally by earphones to normal hearing subjects. For details of the apparatus see Schreiner *et al.* (1977) and Schreiner (1977).

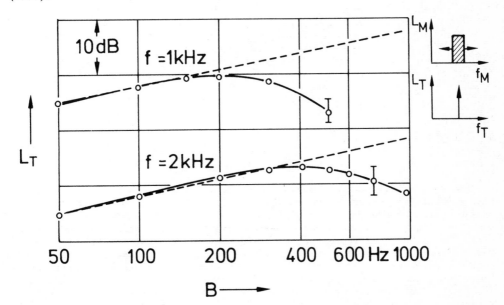

Fig.2. Pulsation threshold of bandpass noise with variable bandwidth B (abscissa). The center-frequency of the noise and the test frequency is 1 kHz and 2 kHz respectively. (Averaged data of three subjects).

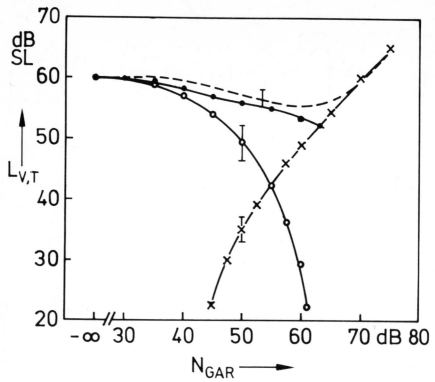

Fig. 3. Loudness-comparison experiments: i) loudness reduction of a tone (1kHz, 60 dB) in noise (circles); ii) loudness reduction of a critical-band noise by a tone (1kHz, 60 dB) centered in the noise (crosses). (The high-frequency slope of the noise excitation is masked by an appropriate signal in order to get an estimation of the loudness in the critical band itself). iii) summation of partial loudness of the tone in noise and of the noise in the critical band around 1 kHz (points). iv) pulsation threshold of a tone-in-noise masker (1kHz, 60 dB; broadband noise) (dashed line). Averaged data of five subjects.

3. RESULTS

a) *Measurements*

Houtgast (1974a) could demonstrate that, given a narrow-band masker and a test tone at the center frequency of the noise, the pulsation threshold decreases for a broadening of the noise, beyond a critical bandwidth value. In fig. 2 this effect is shown for bandpass noises centered around 1+2kHz, respectively. The dashed line represents the intensity of the noises. It turns out that for narrow bandwidths the intensities of masker and test tone are equal at the pulsation threshold. If the bandwidth of the noises exceeds a distinct value, then a decreasing threshold course is observed. The points at which the divergence between intensity and pulsation threshold start correspond quite well to the bandwidth of the 'critical bands' according to the center frequency of the noise (160 Hz and 300 Hz).

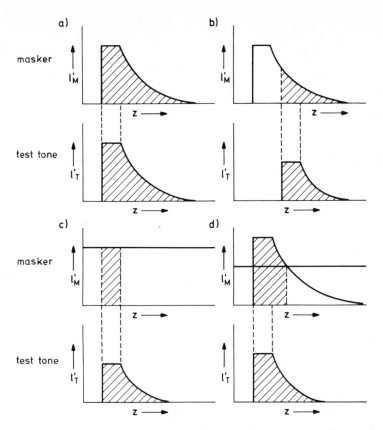

Fig.4. Illustration of the loudness model: The parts of masker and test-tone loudness, which are supposed to be equal at the pulsation-threshold, are shown in the hatched areas. The loudness per critical band l' (ordinate) is plotted versus the tonalness scale z (abscissa). The critical band around the test-tone is marked by dashed lines. Four different masker signals are illustrated: a) pure tone, test and masker signal carry the same frequency; b) pure tone, test and masker tone differ more than one critical band; c) broad-band noise, d) broad-band noise plus pure tone at test frequency.

   This experiment, and others too (Schreiner, 1977), indicates that there exists a close relation between pulsation-threshold and a psychoacoustical quantity, which is connected with the critical bands. A quantity **fulfilling** this condition is the loudness of a signal, which can be calculated from the contribution of the psychoacoustical excitation at each critical band(Zwicker *et al.*,1967).
   To elucidate the difference between the influence of loudness and the influence of intensity on the course of pulsation-thresholds, the following experiments were performed: First, the loudness reduction of a single tone(1kHz, 60 dB) by broad-band noise was measured as a function of the noise level (fig. 3:circles). Then, the loudness reduction of a critical-band noise by a single tone centered in the noise band was measured by comparison with an uninfluenced noise (fig.3:stars). In the next step, the specific loudness in the critical band around 1 kHz (for a signal consisting of a 1 kHz tone and a broad-band noise) was approximated by summing the partial loudness of both components of the signal (fig.3: points). Finally, the pulsation-threshold of a tone-in-noise masker and a test-tone (1 kHz) was measured (fig.3:dashed-line). Both

the loudness of the test-tone in the pulsation-threshold experiment and the tone-in-noise loudness in the critical band around 1 kHz depend in the same way on the level of the masker noise.

With the intention to formulate a useful approach for description and for interpretation of the pulsation-threshold data psychoacoustically, the fol.- lowing conclusions shall be drawn out of these and other (Schreiner, 1977) comparisons of pulsation-thresholds and the loudness of the signals:
(i) At pulsation-threshold the partial loudness of the test signal matches a partial loudness of the masker.
(ii) The partial loudness of the test signal consists of those parts of the signal which are perceived as a continuously represented signal.
(iii) The contributing partial loudness of the masker consists of the critical bands around the frequency region defined by the spectral components of the test signal. Furthermore, the slopes of the corresponding excitation patterns are added to the loudness, if they are not masked by other components of the masker signal.

In fig. 4 some examples for the loudness conditions at the pulsation-threshold are illustrated schematically. The hatched areas in the 'loudness-tonalness pattern' of the masker and the test tone are supposed to be equal at the pulsation-threshold. The four configurations of the masker signal illustrated in fig. 4 are : a),b) pure tone, c) noise, d) pure tone and noise.

b) *Calculations*

A quantitative estimation of threshold values can be given by applying the calculation of loudness (Zwicker *et al.*, 1967) to the interpretation of pulsation-threshold measurements.

In fig. 5 the decrease of pulsation-threshold depending on the bandwidth of bandpass noise (points) is compared to the threshold values, calculated from the loudness model of pulsation-threshold (crosses). The measured data are taken from Houtgast (1974a, fig. 8.2) and are restricted to bandwidths greater than one critical band. The ordinate of fig. 5 is normalized to the absolute maximum of each threshold course. For a bandwidth of one critical band, all parts of the masker's excitation pattern contribute to the threshold determination (vd. fig. 4a). For bandwidths of several critical band without slopes for the masker's contribution to the formation of the threshold (vd. fig. 4c) because all of the slopes of the excitation pattern are masked by other components of the masker noise. In the latter case, the decrease of the pulsation-threshold with growing masker bandwidth becomes more prominent for high noise levels, because of the extended contribution of the excitation slope to loudness .

It turns out that the calculated data fit the decrease of the pulsation-threshold for increasing noise bandwidth very well: the differences between calculations and measurements are less than 1.5 dB.

Some examples of other characteristic behaviours of pulsation-threshold, which can be - at least partially - described by the loudness model are interactions of two (and more) signal components - like summation of pulsation pattern and 'lateral suppression' - as well as the resolution of ripple-noise masker (Schreiner, 1977).

In fig. 6 the differences between a pulsation pattern and a masking pattern are illustrated. The dashed line represents measured data (Houtgast, 1974a). The full line is the difference between an excitation (masking) pattern calculated out of the excitation pattern by aid of the loudenss model. The difference between both patterns is more pronounced at the low-frequency or steep side of the patterns. A very similar difference curve can be demonstrated by eliminating the influence of 'two-tone suppression' from the direct-masking pattern, applying the (nonsimultaneously obtained) estimation of 'lateral

216

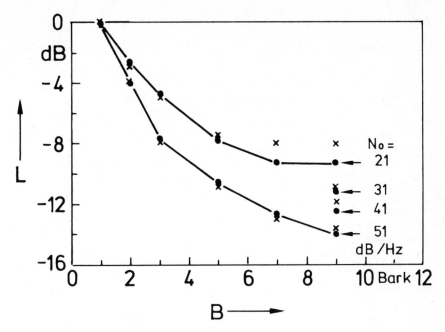

Fig.5. Pulsation threshold of bandpass noise as a function ofbandwidth B. Test signal: 1 kHz. Parameter: noise level.0 dB refers to the threshold values at B=1 Bark. Points: measurements of Houtgast (1974 a,c). Crosses: loudness-model calculations.

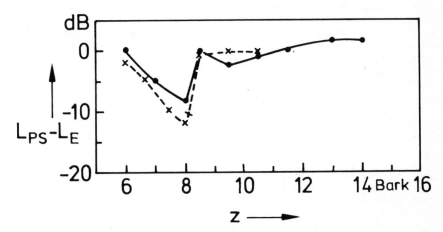

Fig.6. Difference between direct-masking pattern and pulsation pattern(dashed line; measurements by Houtgast (1974d), and difference between excitation pattern (full line).

suppression' given by Houtgast (1974a). Both differences are very similar, indicating that the loudness model seems to be an appropriate approximation for describing the pulsation-threshold including 'two-tone suppression'.

4. DISCUSSION

A psychoacoustical approach to pulsation was suggested, which makes use of the assumption that at pulsation-threshold the loudness of the (pseudo-continuous) test signal and parts of the masker loudness are equal. Most of the known pulsation-threshold data can be described by such a model. As the choices of the filter characteristics and especially the bandwidth of the critical bands play an important role for the threshold calculation, there remains a certain degree of uncertainity in the calculations. One reason is that pulsation-threshold measurements disclose narrower critical bands than other methods (Houtgast, 1974a). For the calculations described above the critical bands given by Zwikker *et al.*, (1967) were used. It turns out that the deviation between calculations with broad and narrow widths of the critical bands seems not to be relevant, except for experiments considering the frequency-resolution power, e.g. ripple-noise resolution (Houtgast, 1974a; Schreiner, 1977).

It might be concluded from the model that the threshold mechanism seems to work at a level of the auditory pathway central to the encoding of loudness. However, the loudness model of the pulsation-threshold makes it possible to describe the threshold course psychoacoustically within certain limits, but still does not elucidate the physiological mechanism underlying the continuity effect. Thus, the problem of the connections between neural and psychoacoustical 'lateral suppression' is shifted to the problem of the relation of single-cell responses to integral quantities, e.g. critical bands and loudness.

In the model, the 'lateral suppression' found in nonsimultaneous experiments is expressed in terms of loudness reduction. The conclusion may be drawn that the instructions for the loudness calculation of the pulsation-threshold involve a quite good quantitative description of the psychoacoustical 'lateral suppression'.

Tietze *et al.* (1978) compared an excitation pattern, which was derived from a pulsation pattern, with a direct-masking pattern and found diverse differences between them, e.g. concerning the slope-nonlinearity. A comparison between a direct-masking pattern and the excitation pattern (calculated from pulsation-threshold data) may give an estimation of the influence of combinationtones, beats etc. on the simultaneous measurement of masking curves (Tietze *et al.*, in prep.). Furthermore, such a comparison can give an estimation of that amount of 'lateral suppression', which is neglected by this quite simple psychoacoustical description of pulsation-threshold.

An electrophysiological study of the responses of single units in the medial geniculate body of guinea pigs to pulsation-threshold signals (Schreiner, 1979 a,b,1980) yielded a close relation of pulsation-threshold data with some temporal features (onset) of the cell activity, with respect to the signal parameters. The threshold of the phasic part of the neural activity seems to correspond with the pulsation-threshold and the threshold of the tonic part of the neural response to pulsation-threshold signals seems to correspond with the (nonsimultaneous) masking threshold of the 'continuous' tone. However, there was no evidence for a 'continuity effect' in the response of single units, except for, at best, one special set of parameters. A further investigation of this problem is indicated.

REFERENCES

Houtgast, T. (1974 a). Lateral suppression in hearing. *Doctoral Thesis,*Free
    University of Amsterdam, Academische Pers,Amsterdam.
Houtgast, T. (1974 b). Lateral suppression and loudness reduction of a tone in
    noise. *Acustica* 8, 214-221.
Houtgast, T. (1974 c). Masking pattern and lateral suppression. In: *Facts and
    models in hearing.* (E. Zwicker and E. Terhardt, eds),pp 258-265. Springer
    Verlag,Berlin.
Houtgast, T. (1974 d). The slopes of masking patterns. In: *Facts and models in
    hearing.*(E. Zwicker and E. Terhardt, eds). pp 269-272. Springer-Verlag,
    Berlin.
Schreiner, Chr. (1977) Monaurale Pulsationsschwelle und Lautheit. *Doctoral The-
    sis,* University of Göttingen.
Schreiner, Chr. (1979 a). Die Darstellung alternierender akustischer Signale in
    der zentralen Hörbahn des Meerschweinchens. *Doctoral Thesis,* University
    of Göttingen.
Schreiner, Chr. (1979 b). Temporal suppression and speech perception. In:
    Hearing mechanisms and speech. (O.Creutzfeldt, H. Scheich and Chr. Schrei-
    ner, eds.)Supplement II to Exp. Brain Res. pp 133-139. Springer-Verlag,
    Berlin.
Schreiner, Chr. (1980). Neuronale Darstellung alternierender Signale. In:*Fort-
    schritte der Akustik.* VDI-Verlag, Düsseldorf.
Schreiner, Chr., Gottlob, D. and Mellert, V. (1977). Influences of the pulsa-
    tion-threshold method on psychoacoustical tuning curves. *Acustica* 37,
    29-36.
Tietze, B., Schreiner, Chr. and Gerlach, R. E. (1978). Bestimmung von Mithör-
    schwellen-Tonheitsmustern mit Hilfe der Pulsationsschwelle. In: *Fort –
    schritte der Akustik.*VDE-Verlag, Berlin.
Verschuure, J. (1978). Auditory excitation pattern. *Doctoral Thesis.*University
    of Rotterdam. W. D. Meinema B.V., Delft.
Verschuure, J., Rodenburg, M. and Maas, A. J.J. (1976). Presentation condi-
    tions of the pulsation-threshold method. *Acustica* 35, 47-54.
Zwicker, E. and Feldtkeller, R. (1967). *Das Ohr als Nachrichtenempfänger.*
    Hirzel-Verlag, Stuttgart.

COMMENT ON "A psychoacoustical approach to pulsation threshold"
(C. Schreiner)

D.M. Harris and P. Dallos
Auditory Physiology Laboratory, Northwestern University, Evanston, Illinois USA

Responses of auditory-nerve fibers of chinchillas were measured under stimulus conditions similar to those used to determine psychophysical pulsation thresholds. A 100 ms tone-burst "signal" at a fiber's CF, 10 dB above response threshold, is repeated 5/sec. A 100 ms tone-burst "masker" is introduced during the interval between signal presentations. Post Stimulus Time (PST) response patterns are collected at each of several masker levels (Fig. 1A).

Human subjects who listen to this stimulus paradigm perceive a pulsating signal at low masker levels. At a certain masker level (pulsation threshold) the perception changes to one of a continuous signal. Verschuure (1977) suggests that "continuity is perceived if the central nervous system cannot detect the signal's absence." Apparently the masker functions to fill the silent interval.

The responses shown in Fig. 1A are typical of those observed from 12 fibers in three animals. They appear to fall into three categories: 1. At low masker levels where the masker-evoked firing rate is less than the signal-evoked rate a pattern indicative of the pulsed signal is obvious. 2. When the masker-evoked rate equals the signal-evoked rate the fiber's response resembles the steady-state response to a continuous tone. 3. At higher masker levels the pattern is dominated by the response to the masker. These three response categories can be identified for any masker frequency within the response area of a fiber.

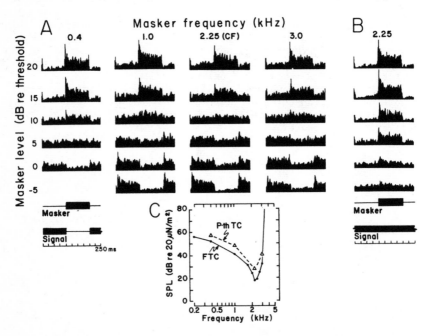

Fig. 1A. PST response patterns evoked in a chinchilla auditory-nerve fiber by a typical pulsation threshold stimulus pattern. Signal: fiber CF (2.25 kHz) 10 dB above threshold (27 dB SPL). Fig. 1B. PST response patterns with masker pulsed and signal continuous. Fig. 1C. This fiber's Frequency Threshold Curve (FTC) compared with the "pulsation threshold" Tuning Curve (P-thTC).

The column of PST histograms shown in Fig. 1B is offered for comparison. In this condition, where the signal actually *is* continuous, the response profiles fall into either category 2 or 3. Since two different stimulus conditions evoke the same PST response pattern in auditory-nerve fibers (disregarding the fine temporal pattern), then the "central processor" is provided with ambiguous information. We may speculate that the auditory illusion associated with pulsation threshold occurs when the observer selects one hypothesis (1B) about the internal representation of the signal when, in fact, another (1A) is true.

If we assume that physiological pulsation threshold is the masker level at which masker-evoked excitation obliterates the gap between signal pulses (i.e., category 2), then the pulsation threshold tuning curve in Fig. 1C (dashed line) can be constructed from the data in Fig. 1A. Such curves represent iso-response curves which, when low-level CF signals are used, approximate a fiber's Frequency Threshold Curve (solid line).

Acknowledgements.

This material has been presented at the 95th meeting of the Acoustical Society of America (1978). We thank Honor O'Malley for her assistance in the collection of this data. This work was supported by grants from NINCDS.

REFERENCES

Verschuure, J. (1977). Pulsation threshold patterns and neurophysiological tuning. In: *Psychophysics and Physiology of Hearing.* (E.F. Evans and J.P. Wilson, eds). pp 237-245. Academic Press, London.

DETECTION CUES IN FORWARD MASKING

Brian C.J. Moore

*Dept. of Experimental Psychology, University
of Cambridge, Cambridge CB2 3EB, U.K.*

1. INTRODUCTION

Houtgast (1972, 1974) has argued that simultaneous masking techniques are not appropriate for revealing the effects of lateral suppression in the auditory system, since if a component f_m in the masker is suppressed by other component(s) in the masker, then a signal in the frequency region of f_m will also be suppressed, leaving the signal-to masker ratio unaltered. Houtgast suggested that non-simultaneous techniques, such as forward masking or the pulsation threshold, should be used. Since that time many different workers have reported suppression "effects" using forward masking.

In this paper we argue that the threshold of a probe signal in forward masking is determined by at least two factors. The first factor is related to the amount of activity evoked by the masker in the channels which are concerned with the detection of the probe (e.g. effective masker level within the critical band around the probe frequency). This may be influenced by lateral suppression. The second factor is related to the presence or absence of qualitative differences between probe and masker. In order for a probe to be detected in forward masking two conditions must be satisfied: (a) the probe must evoke a response of some kind, and (b) the observer must be able to distinguish that response from the response evoked by the masker. Condition (a) will depend primarily on the first factor described above, but condition (b) may depend on the second factor. Whenever there is a difference in subjective quality between probe and masker, distinguishing the probe from the masker will be easier than when they are very similar in quality. In the latter case the response to the signal may be perceived as a continuation of the masker.

It will be shown that two such factors are involved in a number of different stimulus situations, including several which have typically been used to demonstrate suppression. This complicates the interpretation of these demonstrations. In particular the addition of (an) extra component(s) to a masker may introduce a difference in quality between masker and probe, resulting in a reduction in probe threshold unrelated to suppression at a physiological level. For the purpose of discussion in this paper we will call reductions in probe threshold produced by the introduction of quality-differences *cueing*, while reductions in probe threshold produced by physiological suppression will be called *suppression*. Since it may be difficult to distinguish between these two in practice the term *unmasking* will be used to describe the phenomenon of a reduction in probe threshold following the addition of extra components to the masker.

2. EXPERIMENTAL METHODS

a) *Procedure*

Thresholds were determined with an adaptive two-alternative forced-choice procedure which estimates the probe level required for 70.7% correct responses (Levitt, 1971). After two consecutive correct responses the probe level was decreased by 2 dB, and after each incorrect response it was increased by 2 dB. The probe was initially well above threshold. The threshold was usually estimated as the mean of the 26 levels visited after three mistakes had been made. Each point reported in this paper is the mean of at least three such runs. Subjects were given trial-by-trial feedback using lights.

b) *Stimuli*

All stimuli had linear onset and offset ramps. Durations are specified between half-amplitude points. The maskers were of relatively long duration (between 300 and 500 msec), and the interval between the two maskers in a given trial was either 400 msec or 500 msec. Values of rise/fall times and signal duration and delay are given in the description of individual experiments. Sinusoids were generated using Farnell DSG1 synthesized signal generators. Noise bands were generated by multiplying a low-pass filtered noise (cut-off slope 48 dB/oct) with a sinusoid, except in experiment II, where they were generated by conventional band-pass filtering. Stimuli were presented via the left earphone of a Sennheiser HD414X headset.

c) *Subjects*

All subjects had absolute thresholds within 10 dB of the 1964 ISO standard at all frequencies tested. They were given extensive practice prior to the collection of the data reported here, and they were paid for their services.

3. RESULTS AND DISCUSSION

a) *Experiment I: Tonal maskers and suppressors*

In this experiment the masker was a 2-kHz sinusoid at a level of about 60 dB SPL. Probe threshold was measured as a function of probe frequency with and without a second tone at 80 dB SPL added to the masker. The frequency of the second tone was systematically varied. Both masker and probe had 10 msec rise/fall times, the probe had no steady-state portion, and there was no silent interval between masker and probe. Three subjects were tested.

When the frequency of the probe is close to that of the masker the subject may have difficulty in distinguishing the probe from the masker since their pitches will be similar. Adding a second tone to the masker will introduce a pitch difference between masker and signal which might enhance the detectability of the probe (see Terry and Moore, 1977), thus producing unmasking; cueing in this case. However, when the frequency of the probe is moved away from that of the masker, a quality (pitch) difference between masker and probe will be present even for the single tone masker, so that adding the second tone should provide no additional cue. Thus cueing will occur only when the probe frequency is close to that of the masker, independently of the frequency of the second tone. In contrast suppression would be expected to occur in different frequency regions as the frequency of the second tone is altered. (Moore, 1980a).

A subset of the results for one subject is presented in figure 1. Further details can be found in Moore (1980a). The figure shows the *difference* in amount of masking produced by the single tone and two-tone maskers, as a function of probe frequency, for three frequencies of the second tone: 2.1, 2.4 and 2.6 kHz. The shading indicates regions in which the addition of the second tone produced a reduction in probe threshold i.e. unmasking. For all subjects, and for all frequencies of the second tone, the amount of unmasking

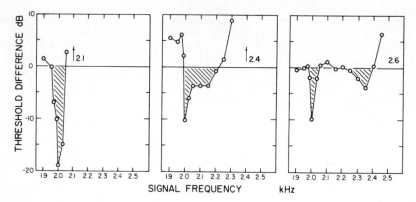

Fig. 1. *Results for one subject showing the change in probe threshold resulting from the addition of a second tone to a 2 kHz masker, as a function of probe frequency. The frequency of the second tone was 2.1, 2.4 or 2.6 kHz.*

shows a local maximum sharply tuned around 2 kHz, as would be expected if the unmasking resulted from cueing. However, as the frequency of the second tone is moved away from 2 kHz the region of unmasking spreads upwards, and for certain frequencies of the second tone (2.6 kHz in fig. 1) there are two distinct frequency regions in which unmasking occurs. The second region of unmasking shifts as the frequency of the second tone is altered, as would be expected if it resulted from suppression, although it cannot be observed when the frequency of the second tone is above about 2.8 kHz. We may conclude that the unmasking has two components - cueing and suppression - but that these components can be separated only for a restricted set of conditions. In the great majority of previous experiments demonstrating two-tone unmasking the probe frequency has been equal to the masker frequency, and the results were almost certainly influenced by cueing.

b) *Experiment II: Comparison of noise and tone maskers*

In this experiment we compared the forward masking of a 1 kHz probe produced by a sinusoid at 1 kHz and a 1/3 octave band of noise centred at 1 kHz. The overall level of the noise was equal to that of the tonal masker, 75 dB SPL. All stimuli had 5 msec rise/fall times. Three temporal relations between masker and probe were used: (i) 5-msec offset-onset, 5-msec probe, (ii) 5-msec offset-onset, 35-msec probe and (iii) 35-msec offset-onset, 5-msec probe. Probe duration was changed by varying the steady-state portion (0 or 30 msec).

If probe threshold depended only on the amount of activity produced by the masker in the channels concerned with detection of the probe, then changing the temporal configuration should not influence the relative effectiveness of the two maskers. The results shown in Table I are not consistent with this.

When there is no silent interval between masker and probe (conditions i and ii) the noise is the more effective masker for the short probe, and the sinusoid is the more effective masker for the long probe. For a fixed offset-offset time (conditions ii and iii) increasing signal duration produces a decrease in threshold following the noise, but an increase (BM and DW) or no change in threshold following the sinusoid. The same effects for a different centre frequency, can be found in Weber and Moore (1980).

Clearly these results cannot be explained by a single factor; once more it is likely that quality differences between masker and probe play a role. The long (35-msec) probe has a well defined tonal quality with a pitch which is similar to that of the sinusoidal masker. This makes discrimination diffi-

*Table I. Probe thresholds for five subjects. The temporal configurations
described in the text are illustrated schematically at the head of each column.*

Observer	(i) Noise	(i) Sin	(ii) Noise	(ii) Sin	(iii) Noise	(iii) Sin
PC	88.5	70.3	43.5	47.7	52.7	46.1
AJ	88.7	62.7	38.7	41.3	48.8	39.3
CL	90.6	67.7	42.4	47.0	48.3	48.4
BM	74.5	64.9	33.9	51.4	45.2	40.9
DW	76.8	66.8	36.8	45.5	47.1	41.3
MEAN	83.8	66.5	39.1	46.6	48.4	43.2
SD	7.5	2.9	4.0	3.7	2.8	3.9

cult. However the noise masker sounds very different from the long probe, so
a quality difference cue is available following the noise but not the sinusoidal masker. The short probe sounds less tonal, and more like the noise, so
that in this case the quality difference cue is available following the sinusoid but not following the noise. The loss of this cue can explain why, for a
fixed offset-offset time, performance can actually *worsen* with increasing probe duration for the sinusoidal masker.

c) *Experiment III. Interactions of noise bandwidth and probe duration*

Weber (1978) measured threshold for a short duration probe as a function
of the bandwidth of a noise centred around the probe frequency and with a
fixed spectrum level. He found that threshold at first increased with increasing bandwidth and then decreased. His results and other similar results (e.
g. Houtgast, 1974; Terry and Moore, 1977; Leshowitz and Lindstrom, 1977) have
been interpreted in terms of an excitatory band in the masker surrounded by
suppression bands. If this interpretation is correct, then the noise bandwidth at which maximum masking occurs should be independent of probe duration.
The next experiment shows that this is not the case.
Probe threshold was measured for a 1 kHz probe following noise maskers
with bandwidths ranging from 50 Hz to 1600 Hz in one octave steps. The spectrum level in the pass band was 40 dB SPL, and the noise was arithmetically
centred at 1 kHz. All stimuli had 5-msec rise-fall times, and there was no
silent interval between masker and probe. Probe durations of 5, 15, 25 and
45 msec were obtained by varying the steady-state portion of the probe (0
msec to 40 msec). A typical set of results is presented in figure 2. Probe
threshold is plotted as a function of masker bandwidth, with probe duration
as parameter. Data for other subjects and other conditions may be found in
Moore (1980b).
It is obvious that the bandwidth at which maximum masking occurs changes
dramatically as a function of probe duration. For a duration of 5 msec threshold is maximum for a bandwidth of 800 Hz, while for a duration of 45 msec
maximum masking occurs for the narrowest bandwidth used, 50 Hz. Again it is
possible to explain these results in terms of the relationship between the
quality of the masker and the quality of the probe. Narrow band noise resembles a sinusoid with fluctuating amplitude. As the bandwidth increases the
fluctuations occur more rapidly and the tonal quality of the noise decreases.
The shortest probe sounds less tonal than the narrowest band of noise: it is

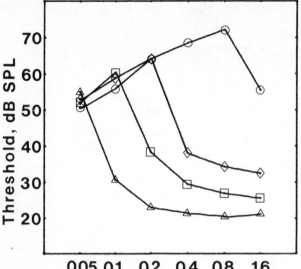

Figure 2. Thresholds for 1-kHz probes in forward masking as a function of masker bandwidth. The noise masker had a spectrum level of 40 dB SPL and a centre frequency of 1 kHz. The parameter is probe duration.

circles	–	*5 msec*
diamonds	–	*15 msec*
squares	–	*25 msec*
triangles	–	*45 msec*

Notice that the noise bandwidth at which maximum masking occurs shifts dramatically with probe duration.

heard as a click or a thud, and is probably detected by "off-frequency liste-ning" to splatter in the energy spectrum of the probe. As the masker bandwidth increases this off-frequency energy is more effectively masked, and the degree of tonality of the noise approaches that of the probe. Hence the probe thres-hold rises. However at the widest noise bandwidth the noise sounds noisy in comparison to the probe. The tonal quality which can be heard at the end of the masker now provides a cue for the presence of the probe and causes a drop in probe threshold. As the probe duration is increased, the bandwidth at which it sounds tonal in comparison to the noise decreases, so that the maxima in the functions occur for narrower bandwidths. For the longest probe duration an increase in bandwidth from 50 to 100 Hz is sufficient to provide this cue and produce a reduction of about 25 dB in probe threshold. It is implausible that this drop in threshold could be produced by noise energy falling in supp-ression bands. Thus we may conclude that the pattern of results revealed in this experiment is more easily explained in terms of the cues used by the ob-server than in terms of interactions between excitation and suppression within the neural representation of masker.

d) *Experiment IV. Unmasking in noise-tone combinations*

We have argued that there is a particular difficulty for the observer when there is no cue to mark where the masker ends and the signal begins. For a sinusoidal masker and probe of the same frequency, the envelope fluctuation associated with switching from masker to probe (or the energy splatter associ-ated with the probe) may provide a cue even though quality differences are mi-nimal, particularly if there is a silent interval between masker and probe. However, if we use a narrow-band noise masker, with a long probe and no silent interval between masker and probe, even this cue can be effectively eliminated, since the masker has "built in" amplitude fluctuations. Under these conditions it is possible to produce very large unmasking effects by adding other compo-nents to the masker, even when the level of those components is so low that it is unlikely that suppression plays a role.

An example is given in Table II, using a noise masker with a bandwidth of 50 Hz, a centre frequency of 1 kHz and a spectrum level of 40 dB SPL. Thres-

hold was measured for two 1 kHz probes, each with 5-msec rise/fall times, one
with a steady state duration of 40 msec, the other with 0 steady state. There
was no silent interval between masker and probe. Thresholds are given in dB
SPL for the noise masker alone, and that masker together with a tone at a level
of 57 dB SPL (i.e. equal to the overall SPL of the noise). The frequency of
the tone in kHz is given at the head of each column.

Table II.	noise alone	noise plus tone					
		1.2	1.4	1.6	1.8	3.0	kHz
5-msec probe	57.5	59.5	58.0	58.4	57.0	57.7	dB
45-msec probe	52.6	36.6	37.4	36.1	36.7	42.0	dB

For the long duration probe there is a large unmasking effect. It is 16
dB for this subject, but others have shown as much as a 30 dB effect. The unmasking is relatively independent of the frequency of the second tone, as would
be expected if it resulted from cueing, although it does decrease when the
frequency of the second tone is very far removed from 1 kHz. For the short
duration probe the addition of the tone to the masker produces either a slight
worsening or no effect.

The effect of the intensity of the tone for the same two probes is given
in Table III, for a tone frequency of 1.2 kHz. The level of the tone is given
in dB SPL at the head of each column.

Table III.	noise alone	noise plus tone				
		57	67	72	77	dB
5-msec probe	57.5	59.5	54.5	50.6	52.0	dB
45-msec probe	52.6	36.6	34.9	32.4	28.0	dB

For both probes increasing the intensity of the tone causes a reduction
in threshold. Presumably this reflects suppression. Notice however that for
the long duration probe this change in threshold is only half that produced
by cueing. Although cueing appears to be negligible for the shortest duration
probe in this particular condition, substantial amounts of cueing can occur
for probes of durations commonly found in experiments designed to demonstrate
suppression. An example is given in Table IV, which shows threshold for a
1-kHz 15-msec probe (10 msec steady-state, 5 msec rise/fall) following a noise
centred at 1 kHz with a bandwidth of 200 Hz and a spectrum level of 40 dB SPL
(63 dB SPL overall level). There was no silent interval between masker and
probe. Threshold is given for the noise alone, and for the noise together
with a tone at 63 dB SPL whose frequency in kHz is given.

Table IV.	noise alone	noise plus tone				
Tone Frequency		1.2	1.4	1.6	1.8	3.0	kHz
Threshold	66.0	49.2	51.5	51.3	49.9	58.0	dB

The unmasking almost certainly arises from cueing, since it is relatively
independent of the frequency of the tone, and occurs for a tone whose level is
not greater than the overall level of the noise. Even for very short probes
cueing can occur. For example the threshold of a 5-msec probe following a
400 Hz bandwidth noise of 40 dB SPL spectrum level (both centred at 1 kHz) can
be reduced by 10 dB by adding a 1.4 kHz tone at 60 dB to the masker. Notice
that in this case the level of the tone is less than the overall level of the
noise (66 dB) and is not very different from the level of the noise in a
"critical band" around 1 kHz.

e) *Experiment V. Unmasking in noise-noise combinations*

In this experiment we again compared thresholds for a short probe (5 msec rise/fall 0 steady-state) and a long probe (5 msec rise/fall, 40 msec steady state) immediately following a 50 Hz band of noise centred at 1 kHz with a spectrum level of 40 dB SPL. Threshold was measured for the noise alone and for that noise together with a second band of noise 1000 Hz wide, also centred at 1 kHz but with a spectrum level of 20 dB SPL. A typical set of results is given in Table V.

Table V.	50 Hz noise alone N_0 = 40 dB	50 Hz noise N_0 = 40 dB plus 1 kHz noise N_0 = 20 dB
5-msec probe	49.2	59.8
45-msec probe	54.5	30.6

The second noise *increases* threshold by about 10 dB for the short probe, but produces about 24 dB of unmasking for the long probe. Notice also that for this subject (and for 3 out of 5 other subjects who were tested for these conditions) threshold is *higher* for the long probe than for the short probe. These results can be explained by assuming that the short probe following the narrow-band noise is detected by "off-frequency listening" to energy splatter. Adding a low-level wide-band noise masks the off-frequency energy and hence raises the threshold for the probe. For the longer probe adding the wide band noise provides the observer with a cue which enables him to determine where the masker ends and the probe begins; when the probe is present activity in the 1 kHz region continues after the activity in other frequency regions has ceased. Thus the unmasking for the long probe can be explained as cueing.

4. CONCLUSIONS

1) Unmasking in forward masking can result both from cueing and from lateral suppression.
2) The importance of cueing will depend upon the stimulus configuration. In particular it will depend upon probe duration, envelope shape, and delay relative to the masker. These factors will interact with the characteristics of the masker such as bandwidth and frequency relative to that of the probe.
3) In general cueing is more likely to occur with long probes than with short ones, but cueing can occur for short probes and energy splatter is more likely to be a problem with short probes.
4) Individual subjects may vary in the extent to which they are sensitive to different cues, and in the extent to which unmasking results from cueing.

REFERENCES

Houtgast, T. (1972). Psychophysical evidence for lateral suppression in hearing. *J. Acoust.Soc.Am.* 51, 1885-1894.
Houtgast, T. (1974). *Lateral Suppression in Hearing*. Ph.D. Thesis, Academische Pers B.V., Amsterdam.
Leshowitz, B. and Lindstrom, R. (1977). Measurement of nonlinearities in listeners with sensorineural hearing loss. In: *Psychophysics and Physiology of Hearing* (E.F. Evans and J.P. Wilson, eds.). Pp. 283-292. Academic, London.
Levitt, H. (1971). Transformed up-down methods in psychoacoustics. *J.Acoust.Soc.Am.* 49, 467-477.

Moore, B.C.J. (1980a). On the mechanism and frequency distribution of two-tone suppression in forward masking. *J. Acoust. Soc. Am.* (in press).

Moore, B.C.J. (1980b). Interactions of masker bandwidth with signal duration and delay in forward masking. Submitted to *J. Acoust. Soc. Am.*

Terry, M. and Moore, B.C.J. (1977). "Suppression" effects in forward masking. *J. Acoust. Soc. Am.* 62, 781-784(L).

Weber, D.L. (1978). Suppression and critical bands in band-limiting experiments. *J. Acoust. Soc. Am.* 64, 141-150.

Weber, D.L. and Moore, B.C.J. (1980). Forward masking by sinusoidal and noise maskers. Submitted to *J. Acoust. Soc. Am.*

Acknowledgements

This work was supported by the Medical Research Council. Experiment II was carried out in collaboration with Daniel L. Weber. I am grateful to the members of the Cambridge "Hearing Group" for their helpful discussion of an earlier version of this manuscript.

COMMENT ON: "Detection cues in forward masking" (B.C.J. Moore).

H. Fastl
Institute of Electroacoustics, Technical University, München, Germany.

The results of experiment II in Moore's paper nicely corroborate our observations about the different post masking effects produced by narrow band noise masker (Fastl, 1977) versus pure tone masker (Fastl, 1979). Moreover, Moore's statement that "for a fixed offset-offset time increasing signal duration produces a decrease in threshold following the noise but an increase following the sinusoid" is correct for identical (center-) frequency of masker and test tone. If, however, test tone frequency differs from masker frequency, a decrease in post masked threshold with increasing test tone duration was found for pure tone maskers, too (Fastl, 1979, Fig. 7). Thus, the somewhat strange effect that masked threshold increases with increasing test tone duration is restricted to test tones with the same frequency as the masker tone. In this case, because of the fixed delay time, the temporal gap between masker tone and test tone is shortened with increasing test tone duration until the test tone follows the masker tone immediately.

Since in such a configuration, the test tone is not easily perceived as a separate event, a higher post masked threshold shows up. In case of different frequencies of masker tone and test tone, however, pitch differences between the two facilitate detection of the test tone. As concerns noise maskers, there exists a difference in timbre between masker and test tone and even if the test tone follows the masker immediately it is easily perceived as a separate event. This interpretation accounts also for the data described by other authors (see Fastl, 1979, p. 287)

REFERENCES
Fastl, H. (1977). Temporal masking effects: II.Critical band noise masker. *Acustica*, 36, 317-331.

Fastl, H. (1979). Temporal masking effects: III.Pure tone masker. *Acustica*, 43, 282-294.

PULSATION PATTERNS OF TWO-TONE STIMULI

J. Verschuure and M.P. Brocaar

*Department of Oto-, Rhino-, Laryngology, Erasmus University
Rotterdam, P.O. Box 1738, Rotterdam, the Netherlands.*

1. INTRODUCTION

Suppression effects have been found in experiments using two-tone stimuli, both in psychophysics (a.o. Houtgast, 1974; Shannon, 1976a, 1976b; Terry & Moore, 1977; Tyler & Small, 1977) and in physiological experiments (a.o. Sachs & Kiang, 1968; Abbas & Sachs, 1976; Abbas, 1978; Javel et al., 1978). These experiments show that the activity at the frequency of a presented sine wave drops if a stronger frequency component (the suppressor) is added. Little is known, however, about the effects of the addition of the suppressor on the distribution of activity of the suppressed component. The distribution can be determined in psychophysics by measuring masking patterns or pulsation patterns. Shannon (1976b) has measured pulsation patterns of two-tone stimuli and Moore (1980) postmasking patterns.

Shannon measured pulsation patterns for a pulsator consisting of two frequency components. The higher of these two served as suppressor. The levels and frequencies of the two components were kept constant. The pulsator was alternated with a single-frequency probe, which is to be heard as a continuous tone. The probe frequency was varied and its pulsation-threshold level was determined. This procedure results in the determination of an input extension pattern (Verschuure, 1977, 1978).

He found little suppression near the summit of the part of the pulsation pattern that can be attributed to the lower component. The amount of suppression increased with increasing frequency of the probe. He concluded that only a part of the lower-frequency pattern is suppressed and that the amount of suppression is determined by the frequency separation of the probe from the suppressor. It was interpreted as a local suppression effect on a part of the pattern.

Moore (1980) measured the same kind of patterns for two-tone stimuli in postmasking. His suppressor was either the higher component or the lower component. He always found maximum suppression near the summit of the part of the pattern attributed to the suppressed component. He concluded that the differences between his patterns and those of Shannon may be caused by pitch cues (Terry & Moore, 1977). The cues can be used as a detection criterion in postmasking but not in pulsation.

Verschuure (1977, 1978) has measured pulsation patterns for single-frequency pulsators. The patterns clearly depended on level. The steep, low-frequency edges of his input-extension patterns got steeper as the pulsator level was raised; the slight, high-frequency edges got less steep. This finding may provide an explanation of the results of Shannon. Suppression of one component by another could result in an excitation pattern with slopes as would be found for a single-frequency pulsator of lower level. The high-frequency edge of the part of the pulsation pattern attributed to the suppressed component would then be steeper: the amount of suppression would seem to increase with increasing frequency separation of the probe from the suppressed frequency component.

It is the purpose of this paper to determine suppression effects in the pulsation patterns of two-tone stimuli and to see whether these effects can be understood as a simple attenuation of the suppressed component if we take the slope-level nonlinearity into account.

2. METHODS

In pulsation an alternation of two stimuli is presented to an observer. We call the stimulus that is to be heard as if it were continuous, the probe. The other stimulus is called the pulsator. We use single-frequency probes.

All frequencies are generated by programmable oscillators KH 4141R. The two sine waves which make up the pulsator are added in a passive circuit. The two signals, pulsator and probe, are gated in a device described by Verschuure *et al.* (1976). The timing is controlled by a programmable clock. We always use a 4 Hz repetition rate in the experiments. The signals are switched on and off with gaussian amplitude transients with a time constant of 3.6 ms. The signals are fed through programmable attenuators GSC 1284 and are again passively mixed. After passing another programmable attenuator they are fed into a TDH 39 headphone. All programmable devices are set from a DEC 8a computer.

For the determination of the shapes of the patterns we have chosen a step-by-step procedure that is sometimes referred to as a modified Békésy procedure. If the probe is continuous, its level is raised by lowering the attenuation of the probe by 0.5 dB. If the probe is pulsating, its level is lowered by 0.5 dB. The pulsation threshold at a certain probe frequency is determined by establishing five reversals of the tracking method. The threshold is defined as the average of the last four reversals. Average results of threshold determinations on five different days are shown in the figures with standard errors. The two authors are the observers.

3. RESULTS

a) Suppressed patterns

We restrict ourselves to the condition where the suppressor has got a higher frequency than the weaker component. We investigate the effect of the higher component on the lower component. We know that suppression effects will appear. Our prime interest is to see whether these effects are limited to an area between the two components or that it can be understood as an attenuation of the lower component, resulting in a pulsation pattern that would fit the single-frequency pattern of a tone presented at the attenuated level.

We first compare the patterns for the 850-Hz condition. Both observers show only little suppression. The patterns of observer JV are shown in Fig. 1. Suppression at 850 Hz itself is 0.7 dB, an insignificant value. The pattern for a single-frequency pulsator is given by plusses for 850 Hz and 60 dB SPL and by crosses for 1500 Hz and 80 dB SPL. The pattern for a pulsator consisting of both components is given by circles. We find only minor differences between the single-component and two-component patterns. There is a small difference at the low-frequency edge of the 1500 Hz pattern, where the pattern for the combined pulsator is a little wider. There is no trace of any suppression in the region between the two frequencies, so no local suppression is found.

In fig. 2 we present the patterns for 1050 Hz in a similar way. Suppression at 1050 Hz is 4.7 dB. The low-frequency edge of the suppressed 1050 Hz pattern gradually merges with the unsuppressed pattern. The high-frequency edge of the suppressed pattern seems to be somewhat steeper, but the difference is not significant. A comparison of this pattern with the single-component pattern for 1050 Hz and 55 dB SPL (not shown) shows no significant difference in the frequency region where the low-frequency edge of the 1500-Hz pattern does not make it impossible to determine the high-frequency edge of the 1050-Hz pattern. The comparison of the low-frequency edge of the 1500-Hz pattern for a single-frequency pulsator and for a two-frequency pulsator shows

Fig. 1
Pulsation patterns for
observer JV at 850 Hz.
Patterns are shown for
single-frequency pulsa-
tors (plusses and
crosses) and for a two-
component pulsator
(circles). Levels and
frequencies are shown
in the plot.

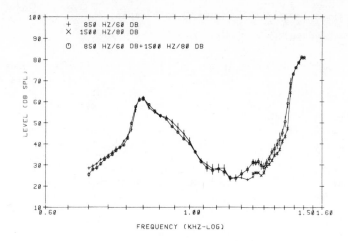

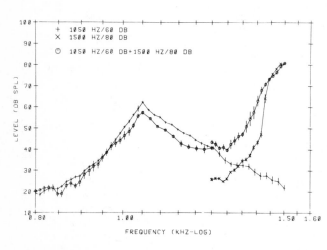

Fig. 2
Pulsation patterns for
observer JV at 1050 Hz.
Single-frequency pat-
terns are shown by
plusses and crosses; the
pattern for the combined
components by circles.

a large difference be-
tween the two. The pat-
tern for the two- fre-
quency pulsator is much
wider. The widening can
be interpreted as en-
hancement, an effect just
contrary to suppression.
We return to this sub-
ject in section 3b.

In Fig. 3 we present the patterns for 1150 Hz. The suppression at 1150 Hz
is 6.1 dB. The widening of the low-frequency edge of the 1500-Hz pattern is
again present and makes a determination of the high-frequency edge of the 1150-
Hz pattern impossible.

The second observer
(MB) shows more suppress-
ion in this condition
(9.8 dB) and a steeper
high-frequency slope of
the lower component. His

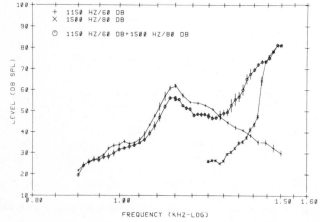

Fig. 3
Pulsation patterns for
observer JV at 1150 Hz.
Single-frequency pat-
terns are given by
plusses and crosses; the
pattern for the combined
components by circles.

results are shown in Fig. 4. Again the single-frequency pattern is represented by plusses for 1150 Hz, and by crosses for 1500 Hz. The circles represent the pattern for the two-component pulsator. The widening of the low-frequency edge of the 1500-Hz pattern is present, but smaller than for observer JV. The suppressed pattern shows suppression over the entire frequency range where it can be interpreted. The amount of suppression increases with decreasing frequency separation of the probe from the suppressor, just as described by Shannon.

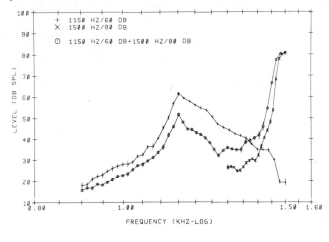

Fig. 4
Pulsation patterns for
observer MB at 1150 Hz.
Single-frequency patterns
are given by plusses and
crosses; the pattern for
the combined components
by circles.

Fig. 5
Comparison of a pulsa-
tion pattern showing
suppression (circles)
and the pattern for a
single-frequency pulsa-
tor of reduced level
(plusses) for observer
MB.

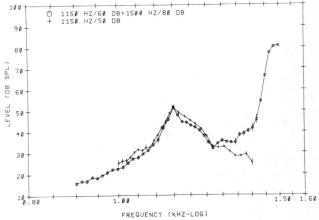

Next we measured the pattern of a 1150-Hz pulsator for the suppressed level (50 dB SPL) in order to see whether simple attenuation takes place or local suppression. The result is shown in Fig. 5, together with the suppressed pattern for the two-component pulsator shown in Fig. 4. It is clear that the suppressed pattern and the pattern for the reduced level coincide well. The small differences can be explained as resulting from a small difference in the measurement of suppression at 1150 Hz and the actual suppression shown by the entire pattern. There is no sign of extra suppression in a region closer to the suppressor.

In no other condition we found any cue for extra suppression in some frequency region near the suppressor, although the observed effects of change of pattern were smaller than those shown in Fig. 4. This was due either to a smaller amount of suppression or to the obscuring widening of the low-frequency edge of the suppressor pattern.

b) Low-frequency edge of suppressor pattern.

In section 3a we have observed a wider low-frequency edge of the 1500-Hz pattern for the two-component pulsator than for the single-component pulsator in some conditions. For a better survey we determined the effect of the second component on the low-frequency edge of the suppressor pattern in a direct experiment.

The suppressor is a 1500 Hz sine wave of 80 dB SPL. The second component has a level of 60 dB SPL. We determine pulsation patterns for frequencies of 850, 950, 1050 and 1150 Hz. The parts of the patterns between the frequencies of the components are shown in Fig. 6, together with the low-frequency edge of a pattern for a single-frequency pulsator of 1500 Hz and 80 dB SPL (crosses).

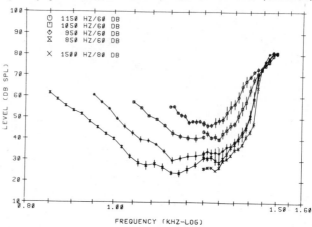

Fig. 6
Pulsation patterns for
observer JV. The pat-
tern for a pulsator
of 1500 Hz and 80 dB
SPL is given by
crosses. All other
patterns are for two-
component stimuli
consisting of a 1500
Hz suppressor of 80
dB SPL and a second
component of 60 dB
SPL at four fre-
quencies given in
the plot.

The change in the low-frequency edge of the part of the patterns attributed to the 1500-Hz component is very clear. Its slope gets less steep if the frequency of the lower component gets higher. This part of the patterns for 850 and 950 Hz almost coincides with the pattern of an undisturbed 1500-Hz component, but it deviates from the undisturbed pattern for the frequencies 1050 and 1150 Hz. The widening of the low-frequency edge of the 1500-Hz pattern makes it impossible to determine the high-frequency edge of the lower-component pattern. The widening effect could be interpreted as an enhancement of activity instead of as a suppression phenomenon as had been expected. This interpretation, however, is based on the assumption that the pulsation threshold at a frequency is a direct measure of the activity present in the auditory system in a channel corresponding to this frequency. Verschuure (1977, 1978) has shown that this assumption is incorrect. His argument is based on the observation that the slopes of pulsation patterns of single-frequency pulsators depend on level of the pulsator. At the steep, low-frequency side of the pattern the slope gets steeper if the level is raised; at the slight, high-frequency side the slope gets less steep. If one now assumes that the probe will be perceived as pulsating if its activity in any auditory channel is noticeably more than the activity of the pulsator in the same channel, pulsation detection is based on a comparison of excitation patterns. These patterns must also show a dependence of their slopes on the level of the exciting sine wave. In Fig. 7 we show how we can construct pulsation patterns from the comparison of excitation patterns. The excitation pattern of the pulsator is represented by dashed lines, those of the probe by dotted lines. At the low-frequency side the slope-level relationship makes it impossible that the summit of the probe's excitation pattern is detected. Detection of pulsation takes place near the threshold, where in Fig. 7 the dotted and dashed lines intersect. This has been called off-frequency detection.

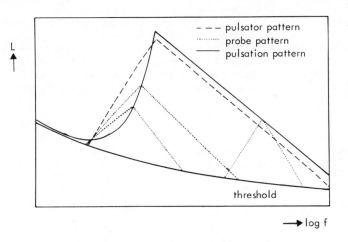

L

- - - pulsator pattern
.... probe pattern
——— pulsation pattern

threshold

⟶ log f

Fig. 7
Theoretical procedure
for the construction
of input extension
patterns in pulsation
(Verschuure, 1978).
The procedure is based
on a comparison of
excitation patterns
(dotted lines for
probe and dashed lines
for pulsator) that
show a slope-level
dependence. Detection
of pulsation at the
low-frequency edge
takes place at the
point of intersection
near the threshold.
The resulting pulsa-
tion pattern is shown
by a solid line.

The resulting pulsation pattern is represented by a solid line. It is clear from Fig. 7 that this pulsation pattern is much steeper than the excitation patterns are. It leads to an overestimation of the tuning properties of the auditory system as far as the low-frequency edge is concerned. Using this nonlinear detection model, the extreme steepness of pulsation patterns could be explained and quantitative relations could be established between patterns for a fixed pulsator level (input extension patterns) and for a fixed probe level (output extension patterns; the latter are sometimes referred to as psychophysical tuning curves).

Returning to our pattern for two-frequency stimuli, we can explain the widening of the low-frequency edge of the suppressor pattern from this model. The high-frequency edge of the lower component intersects with the low-frequency edge of the higher component (suppressor). If this point of intersection is above the threshold of hearing, detection cannot take place near the threshold as shown in Fig. 7; it must shift to the intersection level. The pulsation pattern will go through this (higher) intersection point and will thus be wider. The effect is present for the 1050- and 1150-Hz conditions. The widening effect is only small for the 950- and 850-Hz conditions. We see that in these conditions the high-frequency edge of the low-frequency pattern actually comes very close to the threshold of hearing.

The smaller widening effect of observer MB (Fig. 4) can be understood from his steeper high-frequency edge and the larger amount of suppression; these two facts will shift the intersection point to a lower level.

We conclude that the widening of the low-frequency edge of the suppressor is not caused by enhancement of the activity but by off-frequency detection as described by Verschuure (1977, 1978). Unfortunately, the widening will interfere with the determination of the high-frequency edge of the lower-component pattern.

235

4. DISCUSSION

a) Summary of results

We have described pulsation patterns of two-tone stimuli. The part of the pattern that can be attributed to the higher-frequency suppressor shows a widening of the low-frequency edge. This is not interpreted as enhancement but as being the result of off-frequency detection. Off-frequency detection had been assumed for the explanation of the shape of pulsation patterns of single-tone stimuli. The part that can be attributed to the lower-frequency tone shows suppression. The suppressed pattern is identical to the pattern for a single-tone stimulus of reduced level, if we take the nonlinear slope-level dependence into account.

b) Comparison with other studies

The pulsation patterns reported by Shannon are similar to ours with the exception that Shannon (1976b) states that the patterns of the lower component sometimes show an increasing amount of suppression for increasing probe frequency without any suppression at the summit of that part of the pattern. We did not find such conditions. His figures suggest, in our view, that at least some suppression is present at the summit. If so, the increasing suppression with probe frequency can be understood from the slope-level dependence. The validity of this argument can only be verified in a direct experiment. We found it valid for our two observers. His figures also show the widening of the low-frequency slope of the suppressor. He does not mention it, because it was not his prime interest. The widening is present for all three observers, although its presence is based on only one datum per observer. This fact made us choose for the modified Békésy procedure which yields patterns in more detail.

The postmasking patterns of Moore (1980) show the largest amount of suppression near the frequency of the suppressed tone. Our data, in corroboration with those of Shannon, show the largest amount of suppression in a frequency region between the suppressor and suppressed component, if there is a clear maximum. Otherwise there is a region where suppression is about constant. This region extends from the frequency of the suppressed component to the frequency at which the widening of the low-frequency edge of the suppressor makes a determination of suppression impossible. Moore discussed this essential difference in the results in relation with the data of Shannon. He argues that it is caused by a change of detection criterion in postmaking. Near the frequency of the weaker tone, pitch cues may appear (Terry & Moore, 1977). Such pitch cues cannot be used in pulsation adjustments. This explanation implies that pulsation patterns give a better estimate of the amount of suppression.

Moore (1980) comes to the conclusion that pulsation patterns represent the excitation patterns better than postmasking patterns do (Houtgast, 1974) but he adds that the pulsation method "may be complicated by changes in the shapes of excitation patterns with level and by uncertainty about the frequency region in which the signal is detected". His restriction of this argument to pulsation results, is not justified. His Figs. 3 and 4 (Moore, 1980) show a clear slope-level dependence of postmasking patterns. Because of the steepening of the low-frequency edge this may also lead to off-frequency detection. Whether off-frequency detection is present, depends on the criterion for detection. Gardner (1947) has formulated a clear assumption for detection in postmasking. His formulation explicitly mentioned off-frequency detection. In a recent study Johnson-Davies and Patterson (1979) have shown that off-frequency detection is also important in simultaneous masking. We suggest, therefore, that off-frequency detection is probably of importance to all masking procedures.

As far as we know, enhancement of activity has never been found in physiological studies of two-tone stimuli. If so, it would have appeared as a region of enhancement bordering a region of suppression. The widening can, thus, not be explained as a widening of the excitation pattern. In such conditions the probable alternative explanation is a shift of criterion. Our explanation using off-frequency detection provides such an explanation, but it does not assume that the criterion itself shifts. It assumes that the level at which the detection can take place, shifts. The shift is a very logical one if one thinks in terms of distribution of activity.

Acknowledgements

We thank Dr. M. Rodenburg for his comments on an earlier draft of this paper. Part of the equipment was financed by the Heinsius Houbolt Foundation.

REFERENCES

Abbas, P.J. (1978). Effects of stimulus frequency on two-tone suppression: A comparison of physiological and psychophysical results. *J. Acoust. Soc. Am.* 63, 1878-1886.

Abbas, P.J. and Sachs, M.B. (1976). Two-tone suppression in auditory-nerve fibers: Extension of a stimulus-response relationship. *J. Acoust. Soc. Am.* 59, 112-122.

Gardner, M.B. (1947). Short duration auditory fatigue as a method of classifying hearing impairment. *J. Acoust. Soc. Am.* 19, 178-190.

Houtgast, T. (1974). Lateral suppression in hearing. *Doctoral thesis Free University of Amsterdam*. Ac. Press, Amsterdam.

Javel, E., Geisler, C.D. and Ravindran, A. (1978). Two-tone suppression in auditory nerve of the cat: Rate-intensity and temporal analyses. *J. Acoust. Soc. Am.* 63, 1093-1104.

Johnson-Davies, D. and Patterson, R.D. (1979). Psychophysical tuning curves: Restricting the listening band to the signal region. *J. Acoust. Soc. Am.* 65, 765-770.

Moore, B.C.J. (1980). On the mechanism and frequency distribution of two-tone suppression in forward masking. In press: *J. Acoust. Soc. Am.*

Sachs, M.B. and Kiang, N.Y.S. (1968). Two-tone inhibition in auditory nerve fibres. *J. Acoust. Soc. Am.* 43, 1120-1128.

Shannon, R.V. (1976a). Two-tone unmasking and suppression in a forward-masking situation. *J. Acoust. Soc. Am.* 59, 1460-1470.

Shannon, R.V. (1976b). Suppression in pulsation-threshold patterns. *J. Acoust. Soc. Am.* 60, S 117 (abstract VV7).

Terry, M. and Moore, B.C.J. (1977). "Suppression" effects in forward masking. *J. Acoust. Soc. Am.* 62, 781-784 (L).

Tyler, R.S. and Small, A.M. (1977). Two-tone suppression in backward masking. *J. Acoust. Soc. Am.* 62, 215-218 (L).

Verschuure, J., Rodenburg, M. and Maas, A.J.J. (1976). Presentation conditions of the pulsation threshold method. *Acustica* 35, 47-54.

Verschuure, J. (1977). Pulsation threshold patterns and neurophysiological tuning. In: *Psychophysics and Physiology of Hearing*. E.F. Evans & J.P. Wilson, Eds. Ac. Press, London.

Verschuure, J. (1978). Auditory Excitation Patterns. *Doctoral thesis Erasmus University Rotterdam*. W.D. Meinema B.V., Delft.

COMMENT ON "Pulsation patterns of two-tone stimuli" (J. Verschuure and M.P. Brocaar).

Brian C.J. Moore
Dept. of Experimental Psychology, University of Cambridge, Cambridge CB2 3EB, U.K.

In their paper Verschuure and Brocaar attribute to me the statement that problems associated with changes in the shapes of excitation patterns with level and with uncertainty about the frequency region in which the signal is detected are restricted to the pulsation threshold method. I did not intend to imply any such restriction in my paper (Moore, 1980a), indeed, as I discuss in the paper, I feel that "off-frequency listening" can and does occur in other masking situations. The role of changes in the shape of excitation patterns with level is discussed in relation to forward masking in my 1978 paper, as is the problem of "off-frequency listening". Furthermore, the effects of "off-frequency listening" demonstrated in simultaneous masking by Johnson-Davies and Patterson (1979) can also be found in forward masking (O'Loughlin and Moore, 1979).

The second point of this comment concerns the question of whether the suppression of one component by another can be understood as a simple attenuation of the suppressed component, so that its excitation pattern resembles that of a tone of lower level (the "simple attenuation" hypothesis in Moore, 1980a). The alternative is that suppression is greater in some frequency regions than others (the "distributed attenuation" hypothesis in Moore, 1980a) Verschuure and Brocaar find that for a two-tone complex with the suppressing tone higher in frequency than the suppressed tone, that part of the pulsation pattern that can be attributed to the lower frequency tone resembles the pattern for a tone of lower level. This supports the simple attenuation hypothesis. Some of my data obtained in forward masking show a similar pattern of results. An example is given in figure 1 for four maskers: (1) a 4 kHz tone at 69 dB (squares), (2) a 4 kHz tone at 69 dB plus a 4.6 kHz tone at 81 dB (circles), (3) a 4 kHz tone at 61 dB (triangles), (4) a 4.6 kHz tone at 81 dB (diamonds). All levels are SPL. Maskers (2) and (3) produce similar amounts of masking over quite a wide frequency range, indicating an approximate equivalence of the internal representation of the 4 kHz components. The widening of the low-frequency edge of the suppressor pattern described by Verschuure and Brocaar can just be discerned in this figure, and the masking pattern of the 4 kHz component alone also changes with level in the way described by them [compare maskers 3 (triangles) and 1 (squares)].

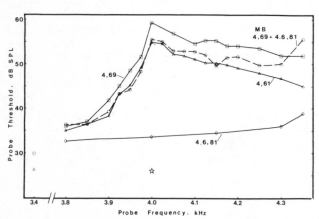

Fig. 1. Probe thresholds as a function of probe frequency for four maskers. For each masker the first figure is the frequency in kHz, and the second is the level in dB SPL. The star indicates the absolute threshold for the probe at 4 kHz. The probe had 10-ms linear rise and fall times, and no steady-state portion. There was no silent interval between masker and probe.

However, not all of the data fit this pattern. An example is given in figure 2, which shows probe threshold as a function of probe frequency for two maskers: (1) a 2 kHz tone at 61 dB (squares) (2) that tone together with a 2.6 kHz tone at 81 dB (triangles). The upper part of the figure shows the difference between the thresholds obtained for the two maskers. It is clear that suppression is observed only over a restricted region of the masking pattern. The maximal amount of suppression is observed around 2 kHz, but this is attributed to a change in the cues used by the observer when the suppressor is added to the masker (see Moore, 1980a, and Moore, this volume). The suppression for probe frequencies from 2.1 kHz to 2.3 kHz cannot be explained in terms of "cueing" and presumably reflects suppression at the physiological level. The lack of suppression for probe frequencies in the range 1.85 to 1.975 kHz means that the results cannot be explained in terms of the simple attenuation hypothesis; the suppression appears to operate locally. Other results showing a local suppression can be found in Moore (1980a) and Moore (this volume).

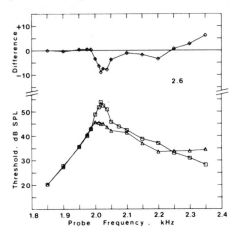

Fig. 2. *The lower part of the figure shows probe threshold as a function of probe frequency for a 2 kHz masker at 61 dB SPL (squares), and for that masker together with a 2.6 kHz tone at 81 db SPL. The upper part of the figure, shows the difference between the two masking patterns; points falling below the solid line indicate suppression. Notice that the suppression occurs only over a restricted region of the masking pattern. The timing of the stimuli is the same as for figure 1.*

Finally, it should be obvious that I do not, as Duifhuis (this volume) states, claim that "cueing" or pattern changes can explain the whole of the suppression which is found in forward masking, nor do I claim that "cueing" plays a role in pulsation threshold measurements.

REFERENCES

Johnson-Davies, J.D. and Patterson, R.D. (1979). Psychophysical tuning curves: Restricting the listening band to the signal region. *J.Acoust. Soc.Am.* 65, 765-770.

Moore, B.C.J. (1978). Psychophysical tuning curves measured in simultaneous and forward masking. *J.Acoust.Soc.Am.* 63, 524-532.

Moore, B.C.J. (1980a). On the mechanism and frequency distribution of two-tone suppression in forward masking. *J.Acoust.Soc.Am.*, in press.

O'Loughlin, B.J. and Moore, B.C.J. (1979). Restricted-listening tuning curves in forward masking. Paper presented at a meeting of the British Society of Audiology, Cambridge, England, September 27-28.

COMMENT

REPLY TO COMMENT OF B.C.J. MOORE.

J. Verschuure
Dept. of Oto-, Rhino-, Laryngology, Erasmus University Rotterdam,
P.O. Box 1738, Rotterdam, The Netherlands.

The major part of Moore's comment deals with the fact that his data are sometimes in line with our data and sometimes are not. The majority of his data shows, in our view, only the suppression area near the frequency of the "suppressed" tone. He argues that a pitch-cue is involved in this area making it impossible to assess the real amount of physiological suppression. In Fig. 2 of the comment he presents a pattern probably showing some real suppression, although its amount will be only 1 or 2 dB. In our view, his argument that local suppression must be present in this case is not correct because he did not verify whether a drop in level of only a few dB would actually result in measurable differences at the low-frequency edge, keeping the slope-level nonlinearity in mind. Verschuure (1978) has presented pulsation data which show only very small differences at these edges (e.g. Fig. 14 and Fig. 15) for differences in level of 20 dB.

We conclude from Moore's comment that the pitch-cue is very important in postmasking. Taking this and the slope-level nonlinearity into account no evidence can be found against what he calls the simple attenuation hypothesis for higher-frequency suppressors. In fact Fig. 1 of his comment supports this hypothesis, possibly because the pitch-cue mechanism does not work anymore for this observer at these high frequencies.

COMMENT ON: "Detection cues in forward masking" (B.C.J. Moore) and "Pulsation patterns of two-tone stimuli" (J. Verschuure and M.P. Brocaar).

D.O. Kim
Washington University, St. Louis, Missouri 63110, U.S.A.
and B.C.J. Moore
Dept. of Experimental Psychology, Cambridge University, U.K.

In distributions of responses of populations of cochlear nerve fibers along the cochlear partition under stimulation by two tones with frequencies f_1 and f_2 (Kim, Siegel and Molnar, 1979; Kim, Molnar and Matthews, 1980), the following are clearly demonstrated.
1) There is mutual suppression of the f_1 and f_2 components: the f_1 component is suppressed by f_2 and the f_2 component is suppressed by f_1; so called "two-tone synchrony suppression".
2) The spatial distribution of this signal suppression does not take the form of an overall reduction but is pronounced only in specific regions of the cochlear partition.
3) The maximum suppression of the component by f_2 occurs at the f_2 place, and the maximum suppression of the f_2 component by f_1 occurs at the f_1 place; i.e. the maximum suppression occurs at the "suppressor place".
Neural results obtained by Young and Sachs (1979) are consistent with the above descriptions. These features of cochlear nerve fiber responses should be helpful in interpretations of the psychoacoustic results related to "two-tone suppression". For example, these neural results are consistent with Moore"s (1980) psychoacoustic results which support the "distributed attenuation" rather than the "simple attenuation" hypothesis. Of course the psychoacoustic paradigm cannot show suppression at or very close to the suppressor frequency, owing to the masking effect of the suppressor.

REFERENCES

Kim, D.O., Siegel, J.H. and Molnar, G.E. (1979). Cochlear nonlinear phenomena in two-tone responses. *Scand.Audiol.* suppl. 9, 63-81.
Kim, D.O., Molnar, C.E. and Matthews, J.W. (1980). Cochlear mechanics: nonlinear behaviour in two-tone responses as reflected in cochlear-nerve-fiber responses and in ear-canal sound pressure. *J.Acoust.Soc.Am.* 67, in press.
Moore, B.C.J. (1980). On the mechanism of two-tone suppression in forward masking. *J.Acoust.Soc.Am.* in press.
Young, E.D. and Sachs, M.B. (1979). Representation of steady-state vowel in the temporal aspects of the discharge patterns of populations of auditory-nerve fibers. *J.Acoust.Soc.Am.* 66, 1381-1403.

TWO-TONE SUPPRESSION AND INTERMODULATION DISTORTION IN THE COCHLEA: EFFECT OF OUTER HAIR CELL LESIONS

P. Dallos, D.M. Harris, E. Relkin and M.A. Cheatham

Auditory Physiology Laboratory, Northwestern University
Evanston, Illinois, USA

1. INTRODUCTION

Two classes of nonlinear phenomena, two-tone suppression (2TS) and combination tone (CT) generation, have been afforded increasing attention during the past fifteen years. The former was first demonstrated as a decrease in the driven firing rate of primary auditory nerve fibers in the presence of an appropriate suppressing tone (Nomoto *et al.*, 1964; Hind *et al.*, 1967;Sachs and Kiang, 1968; Liff and Goldstein, 1970; Arthur *et al.*, 1971). Subsequently this neural two-tone interaction has been studied in copious detail and its analogs have been shown to exist in the compound response of the auditory nerve (Dallos and Cheatham, 1977; Harris, 1979) and in psychophysical measurements (Houtgast, 1972; Shannon, 1976). Some 2TS is apparently notable in basilar membrane displacement (Rhode, 1977) and in intracellular responses from inner hair cells (Sellick and Russell, 1979). A related phenomenon, the interference effect, is measurable in the cochlear microphonic (CM) potential (Black and Covell, 1936; Wever *et al.*, 1940; Legouix *et al.*, 1973; Dallos *et al.*, 1974).

Certain peculiar properties of the psychophysically measured CT, $2f_1-f_2$ (Zwicker, 1955; Goldstein, 1967) prompted investigators to undertake a profusion of studies on the subject, utilizing both psychophysical and electrophysiological methods (e.g., Goldstein and Kiang, 1968; Dallos, 1969; Smoorenburg, 1972; Hall, 1972; Wilson and Johnstone, 1973; Kim *et al.*, 1979). A great deal of effort was also expended on the development of models that could account for either or both of the observed two-tone effects (e.g., Engebretson and Eldredge, 1968; Pfeiffer, 1970; Hall, 1977, Duifhuis, 1976; Kim *et al.*, 1973.

Probably the earliest experiment that linked the nonlinear two-tone effects to the presence of a normal hearing organ was Smoorenburg's (1972) study of the existence of an audible $2f_1-f_2$ component in an ear having a midfrequency threshold elevation. It was noted that the CT could not be heard when f_1 and f_2 were within the elevated threshold region unless they themselves were audible. Conversely, the CT was also inaudible when $2f_1-f_2$ fell within the lesion. A similar experiment was performed on chinchillas that were trained to give behavioral responses to sound (Ryan and Dallos, 1975; data reported in Dallos, 1977). The animals, having high frequency losses induced by ototoxic drugs, did not respond when f_1 and f_2 were within the lesion even though $2f_1-f_2$ fell within the normal hearing range. In these animals the hearing deficit was caused by the destruction of outer hair cells (OHC). Robertson (1976) found that the degree of 2TS that could be seen for guinea pig spiral ganglion neurons was intimately related to the sharpness of the neuron's tuning curve. Both could be reversibly influenced by the removal of perilymph from the scala tympani. Schmiedt and Zwislocki (1977) reported that 2TS was abolished for gerbil auditory nerve fibers when they presumably originated from regions of cochlear hair cell loss. Siegel *et al.* (1977) noted that CTs in chinchilla nerve fibers were abolished when the primaries (f_1 and

f_2) peaked in a region of the cochlea that suffered hair cell damage due to intense sound and that the level of the CT could be influenced by short-term exposure to intense sounds. Leshowitz and Lindstrom (1977) noted that both psychophysical suppression and CT generation were profoundly influenced by the relationship between the primary frequencies and the boundary of the threshold deficit in hearing-impaired listeners. For humans with sensorineural hearing losses Wightman *et al.* (1977) showed that the suppression mechanism did not operate within the elevated threshold segment. On the basis of behavioral and single fiber data from chinchillas, we have intimated before that both the mechanisms of CT generation and 2TS are impaired when there are OHC losses (Dallos, 1977; Dallos and Harris, 1978). We now wish to provide further information on the influence of OHCs on the propensity of the cochlea to produce CTs and 2TS.

2. METHOD

All data reported were obtained from chinchillas, either from normal animals for comparison purposes, or from animals that received kanamycin in order to produce distinct hair cell lesions. Single auditory nerve fiber recording techniques were described in detail before (Dallos and Harris, 1978). We have also provided information previously on the production and monitoring of kanamycin-induced hair cell damage (Ryan and Dallos, 1975; Dallos and Harris, 1978). The progression of hearing loss, from which we infer the extent and nature of the sensory cell loss (Ryan *et al.*, 1979) was monitored by either behavioral means or by testing the compound action potential thresholds across frequency with the aid of a chronically implanted round window electrode (Harris *et al.*, 1979). After the completion of the electrophysiological experiments all abnormal ears were perfused. The organs of Corti were prepared as flat specimens for examination and hair cell counts according to the methods of Engström *et al.* (1966). Cochleograms are provided to indicate the actual extent of hair cell loss.

3. RESULTS

Complete data on 2TS and/or CT thresholds were obtained from 138 fibers in 12 chinchillas having varying degrees of hair cell loss. The majority of units studied had characteristic frequencies (CF) between one octave below the boundary of the lesion and the boundary itself. The boundary frequency was defined as the highest frequency where normal threshold (behavioral or action potential) was measured. Thus, for example, the border frequency is taken as 1.0 kHz in *Oberon* (Fig. 3), 1.4 kHz in *Titania* (Fig. 2) and 4.0 kHz in *Rudolfo* (Fig. 1). A sampling of units was also studied whose CF was clearly either in the normal threshold region or well within the lesion. In addition, data from 191 fibers in 24 normal chinchillas served as the basis for comparison with the material obtained from the pathological ears.

A. *Normal threshold region.* An example of the behavior of a fiber having a CF within the normal threshold segment of the frequency range is shown in Fig. 1. The frequency threshold curve (FTC) of this fiber is entirely normal in configuration. The high and low frequency 2TS areas are shown shaded and these too conform to the pattern seen in chinchilla primary fibers (Harris, 1979). Combination tones, specifically $2f_1-f_2$, were usually obtained by setting the lower primary (f_1) just above the response area of the fiber, so that f_1 itself should not elicit a response at any sound pressure level. The higher frequency primary was then set so that $2f_1-f_2=CF$.* The presence

This procedure results in a f_2/f_1 that depends on the FTC.

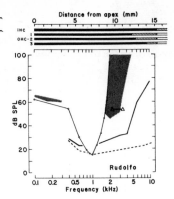

Fig. 1.   *Single fiber tuning curve (FTC), two-tone suppression (2TS) areas (shaded) and thresholds for $2f_1-f_2$ generation (triangles shown at the frequencies of f_1 and f_2 and at the SPL where $2f_1-f_2$ first appears). Normal action potential (AP) threshold is given by the interrupted lines, while the AP threshold of this animal is shown by the heavy lines. At the top of the figure the cochleogram is given. Black bar indicates the spatial extent of greater than 95% retention of hair cells in a given row, stippling indicates retention between 5 and 95%, while open bars correspond to less than 5% of hair cells present. The length is adjusted to correspond with the frequency scale as suggested by Clark and Bohne (1978) but with 11.8% length/octave instead of their figure of 13.6% length/octave. Stimulus tone during 2TS experiments is at CF, its level is +10 dB re fiber threshold. Suppression contours reflect just noticable suppression in PST histograms.*

or absence of a response related to $2f_1-f_2$ was judged by observing post-stimulus-time (PST) histograms while f_1 and f_2 were presented as partially overlapping tone bursts. The frequencies at the lowest SPL of the f_1, f_2 pair that yielded a $2f_1-f_2$ response are marked by triangles in the figure. Above the indicated SPL all pairs of tones at the given frequencies yielded a response. The threshold SPLs seen for this fiber were entirely normal for its CF. We can generalize by noting that fibers whose CFs were at least an octave below the elevated threshold region that were examined by us possessed normal 2TS contours and normal $2f_1-f_2$ thresholds.

B.   *Elevated threshold region.*   Fibers whose CF places them in the elevated segment of the threshold plot possess abnormally-shaped tuning curves. These in some cases represent only the tail segment, in others the entire curve with blunted tip segment, and in slightly over half the cases in our sample the tuning curve has normal tail segment associated with an abbreviated but sharp tip segment (Evans and Harrison, 1976; Kiang *et al.*, 1970; Dallos and Harris, 1978). No matter what the configuration of the FTC may be, it is our observation that when the fibers are judged to originate from a region of the cochlea that is devoid of OHCs, *both 2TS and CT-generation are invariably absent.* It is to be noted that in our material OHC loss in a particular region always implies OHC loss further toward the base of the cochlea. Thus the primaries (f_1;f_2) and the suppressing tone in the 2TS paradigm also correspond to regions where there are no OHCs. An example of this category of fibers is given in Fig. 2. The cochleogram and the threshold pattern both indicate OHC loss corresponding to frequencies above 2.0 kHz, with inner hair cell (IHC) loss corresponding to frequencies above 6.0 kHz. The FTC shown is rather characteristic to the region where the loss is confined to OHCs. The unit did not respond at $2f_1-f_2$ and had

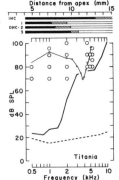

Fig. 2.   *Abnormal FTC within the outer hair cell lesion. All details are as in Fig. 1, except open circles have been added at all frequency-SPL combinations that were tried for eliciting 2TS. None of these yielded any suppression.*

neither high nor low frequency 2TS.

C. Border region. In the transition zone between normal OHC complement and complete elimination of this group of sensory cells there is a narrow spatial extent that probably corresponds to the sloping portion of the threshold curve. Fibers whose CFs are in this vicinity tend to possess widely varying FTCs, ranging from completely normal to entirely distorted (Dallos and Harris, 1978). Here we concentrate on those fibers that have CFs one octave below the transition between normal and elevated threshold regions. The range is arbitrary, but it encompasses units that originate from a cochlear segment where all hair cells are judged to be present. Yet, for these CFs the high frequency suppressor or the primaries for CT production may excite a region where there is OHC destruction and, in most cases, where the IHCs are demonstrably present.

An example is shown in Fig. 3. The FTC for the unit in Fig. 3 has the same configuration as normal units with CF=0.7 kHz. The usual extent of the high frequency 2TS contour is indicated by the dashed line and the actually measured 2TS area is shown shaded. The discrepancy between the normal and the actual 2TS is striking. The threshold for suppression is elevated by some 20 dB and the band of frequencies that are capable of suppressing the response to the CF-tone is severely restricted. We did not attempt to measure low frequency suppression in this fiber. In the majority of cases when such measurement was performed the 2TS area was missing on the low side. We do have examples, however, of fibers for which the high frequency suppression is greatly affected without a change in the low frequency 2TS.

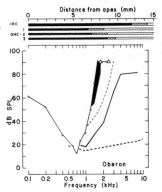

Fig. 3. Normal FTC just below the lesion with abnormal 2TS and CT thresholds. All details are as in Fig. 1, except normal 2TS areas are added (thin dashed line) for comparison.

The thresholds for $2f_1-f_2$ responses are shown for our example by the triangles in Fig. 3. The thresholds are significantly higher than what is seen in normal fibers having similar CFs. In fact, the SPL levels required (90 dB) to produce a $2f_1-f_2$ response are so high that it is likely that the cause for the response is simply distortion introduced by the sound system.

The conclusions that may be drawn from the above example can be amplified with the aid of Fig. 4. In the bottom of the plot of Fig. 4, we show the width (in octave units) of the high frequency 2TS area measured at 80 dB SPL as a function of the units' CF. Only those units with CFs between the highest normal threshold frequency and one octave below that frequency are included. Comparison is made with the width of the 2TS area obtained for normal units. These data are given as medians and interquartile ranges computed for units pooled within one octave frequency bands (according to their CFs) and plotted at the center frequency of the band. It is clear that the majority of 2TS areas lie outside the normal $\pm$ interquartile range and that the trend is toward the reduction in the width of the suppression band. Recall that all these units have CFs within the normal-threshold frequency range.

Thresholds for the generation of $2f_1-f_2$ are plotted in Fig. 4 (middle) where comparison is made between normal and abnormal responses. All thresholds are plotted at the CF of the fiber for the pathological ears, whereas the normal data are pooled within one octave bands and shown as medians and interquartile ranges. It is apparent that an elevation in the $2f_1-f_2$ threshold is a general consequence of the OHC loss caused by kanamycin ototoxicity.

In the top panel of Fig. 4 we show the normal medians and interquartile ranges of the high frequency slopes of the FTCs and individual data points

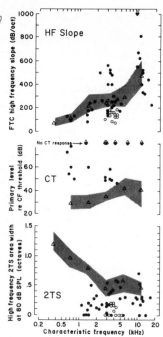

Fig. 4.   Bottom: Widths (in octaves measured at 80 dB SPL) of individual 2TS areas as a function of fiber CF compared to normal median and interquartile range (computed for octave bands of CF). Middle: $2f_1-f_2$ thresholds (expressed in dB re fiber threshold at CF) for individual units as a function of CF compared to normal median and interquartile range. Top: High frequency slopes (db/octave) of FTCs compared to medians and interquartile ranges for normal units. Open circles correspond to data points obtained from one individual whose FTCs had consistently shallow slopes.

for the appropriate tuning curves from abnormal animals. The latter were confined to FTCs whose CF was within the one-octave range below the elevated threshold region. The data are not notably different from the normal, with the exception of a cluster of points around 3 kHz (marked with open circles). All these latter data points were obtained from a single animal. It is not clear why this particular subject differed in this regard from the rest of the group.

4. DISCUSSION

The data reported above are in support of previous indications that nonlinear effects, generated in the cochlea, are highly susceptible to interference with the integrity of this organ. It is possible now to link 2TS and CT-generation to the presence of OHCs in the primary/suppressor region of the cochlea. In this respect it is of interest to consider the response properties of fibers whose CFs are just below the lesion, within the normal-threshold range. The fact that many such fibers possess completely normal FTCs, in other words, normal sharpness of tuning, threshold, and high-frequency slopes probably signifies that their anatomical origin is from a cochlear segment where the interacting hair cell complement is normal. These very fibers, in contrast, tend to have highly abnormal nonlinear response properties. They show greatly reduced or absent 2TS and respond weakly or not at all at $2f_1-f_2$. What is common to these fibers is that the primaries (f_1 and f_2) and the suppressor frequency are tonotopically located in a region of the organ of Corti that is devoid of OHCs or has a reduced OHC population, but where the IHCs are present. We certainly cannot assure the functional integrity of IHCs in this region. However, arguments presented before (Ryan *et al.*, 1979) suggest that their operation may not have been impaired. We have encountered no instance where normal 2TS or CT-generation were observed when OHCs were missing in the suppressor or primary frequency location.

On the basis of CM data we have long maintained that the origin of cochlear distortion processes is to be sought in hair cell mechanisms (Sweetman and Dallos, 1969; Dallos, 1969). It was demonstrated before that CT products are most prominent at the location of the primaries (Dallos and Cheatham, 1974). The original experiments were performed on guinea pigs and we now give some complementary data for chinchillas. In Fig. 5 CM responses are shown as recorded with differential electrodes from the second turn of a chinchilla cochlea. The CM magnitude corresponding to the $2f_1-f_2$ component is given, plotted at the frequency of $2f_1-f_2$. The primaries (f_1 and f_2) were swept across the frequency range with their frequency ratio maintained at $f_2/f_1=1.4$ and their sound pressure levels kept constant. CM plots are given for three primary SPLs: 40, 50, and 60 dB. The best frequency of the elec-

Fig. 5.   Cochlear microphonic measured with differential electrodes and with a 3 Hz narrow-band analyzer from the second cochlear turn of a normal chinchilla. The response corresponding to $2f_1-f_2$ is plotted as a function of the $2f_1-f_2$ frequency. During the experiment the primaries (f_1 and f_2) were always presented at equal SPL (indicated as the parameter) and with an $f_2/f_1=1.4$ ratio. The best frequency of the electrode location is 2.0 kHz as determined from single-tone low-level responses.

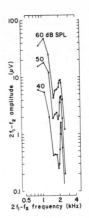

trode pair, determined by obtaining single-frequency iso-SPL CM plots at very low SPLs (0 dB) was 2.0 kHz. The $2f_1-f_2$ plots are bimodal with the dominant response appearing at approximately 1.0 kHz that corresponds to primaries flanking the best frequency location i.e., for $f_2/f_1=1.4$, $(f_1+f_2)/2=2.0$ kHz if $2f_1-f_2=1.0$ kHz. The secondary peak at approximately 2.0 kHz corresponds to a "propagated" distortion component. In all our material this secondary peak is significantly smaller than the primary one; the example illustrates the smallest difference that was encountered. We are uncertain about the origin of the secondary peak. It may be explained by distortion measured in the sound. Of course, it is conceivable that this distortion in the sound is back-radiated by an active process (Gibian and Kim, 1979) but we need more data before this notion can be accepted. Be that as it may, the $2f_1-f_2$ component in the CM is invariably greatest at the location of the primaries and it is quite significant it its magnitude. Since the gross CM primarily reflects the output of OHCs (Dallos and Cheatham, 1976) it is likely that OHC transducer processes are responsible for generating many of the commonly encountered nonlinear phenomena. CM measurements thus appear to be in harmony with the notion that OHC processes are intimately involved in the generation of CTs.

It is conceivable that the bidirectional coupling (Goldstein, 1967; Smoorenburg, 1972) between OHCs and tectorial membrane might be the source of the nonlinearities. One may speculate that the OHCs significantly influence the micromechanics of the organ of Corti through their attachment to the tectorial membrane. The threshold deficit (Ryan and Dallos, 1975) and the elimination of nonlinear effects as demonstrated here, may in part reflect the removal of mechanical coupling between reticular lamina and tectorial membrane in the affected regions of the organ of Corti. The observations (Weiss *et al.*, 1978; Holton, 1980) that 2TS does not exist for fibers that originate in that segment of the alligator lizard's basilar papilla that is devoid of tectorial covering while 2TS does exist for fibers originating in the other half, may be considered as supportive of the notion that tectorial attachment is related to the production, or coupling back to the organ, of nonlinear effects. A similar notion may be entertained on the basis of the result (Moffat and Capranica, 1979) that CTs can be produced in anuran ears that do possess a tectorial covering in spite of the probable lack of a traveling wave type of mechanical frequency analysis. It is thus possible that nonlinear phenomena originate in an interplay of electrical and mechanical processes in the hair cells whose cilia maintain intimate contact with the tectorial membrane. It appears to us that in the mammalian cochlea these cells are the outer hair cells.

This work is supported by grants from the NINCDS. E.R. is an NIH Postdoctoral Fellow. S. Shabica is thanked for her preparation of cochleograms.

REFERENCES

Arthur, R.M., Pfeiffer, R.R. and Suga, N. (1971). Properties of "Two-tone inhibition" in primary auditory neurons. *J. Physiol.* 212, 593-609.

Black, L.J. and Covell, W.P. (1936). A quantitative study of the cochlear response. *Proc. Soc. Exp. Biol Med.* 33, 509–511.

Clark, W.W. and Bohne, B.A. (1978). Animal model for the 4-kHz tonal dip. *Ann. Otol. Rhin. Laryngol.* Suppl. 51.

Dallos, P. (1969). Combination tone $2f_1-f_h$ in microphonic potentials. *J. Acoust. Soc. Am.* 46, 1437–1444.

Dallos, P. and Cheatham, M.A. (1974). Cochlear microphonic correlates of cubic difference tones. In: *Facts and Models in Hearing.* (E. Zwicker and E. Terhardt, eds). pp 312–322. Springer-Verlag, Berlin.

Dallos, P., Cheatham, M.A. and Ferraro, J. (1974). Cochlear mechanics, non-linearities and cochlear potentials. *J. Acoust. Soc. Amer.* 55, 597–605.

Dallos, P. and Cheatham, M.A. (1976). Production of cochlear potentials by inner and outer hair cells. *J. Acoust. Soc. Amer.* 60, 510–512.

Dallos, P. (1977). Comment on "Some observations on two-tone interaction measured with the Mössbauer effect" by W.S. Rhode. In: *Psychophysics and Physiology of Hearing* (E. Evans and J. Wilson, eds) p. 39, Academic, London.

Dallos, P. and Cheatham, M.A. (1977). Analog of two-tone suppression in whole nerve responses. *J. Acoust. Soc. Amer.* 62, 1048–1051.

Dallos, P. and Harris, D. (1978). Properties of auditory nerve responses in the absence of outer hair cells. *J. Neurophysiol.* 41, 365–383.

Duifhuis, H. (1976). Cochlear nonlinearity and second filter: possible mechanisms and implications. *J. Acoust. Soc. Amer.* 59, 408–423.

Engebretson, A.M. and Eldredge, D.H. (1968). Model for the nonlinear characterisitcs of cochlear potentials. *J. Acoust. Soc. Amer.* 44, 548–554.

Engström, H., Ades, H.W. and Andersson, A., (1966). *Structural Pattern of the Organ of Corti.* Williams and Wilkins, Baltimore.

Evans, E. F. and Harrison, R.V. (1976). Correlation between cochlear outer hair cell damage and deterioration of cochlear nerve tuning properties in the guinea pig. *J. Physiol.* 256, 43–44P.

Gibian, G.L. and Kim, D.O. (1979). Cochlear microphonic evidence for mechanical propagation of distortion products (f_2-f_1) and $(2f_1-f_2)$. *J. Acoust. Soc. Amer.* 65, S84.

Goldstein, J.L. (1967). Auditory nonlinearity. *J. Acoust. Soc. Amer.* 41, 676–689.

Goldstein, J.L. and Kiang, N.Y.-s. (1968). Neural correlates of the aural combination tone $2f_1-f_2$. *Proc. IEEE.* 56, 981–992.

Hall, J.L. (1972). Auditory distortion products f_2-f_1 and $2f_1-f_2$. *J. Acoust. Soc. Amer.* 51, 1863–1880.

Hall, J.L. (1977). Two-tone suppression in a nonlinear model of the basilar membrane. *J. Acoust. Soc. Amer.* 61, 802–810.

Harris, D.M. (1979). Action potential suppression, tuning curves and thresholds: comparison with single fiber data. *Hearing Research* 1, 133–154.

Harris, D.M., Geller, H.S., Halpern, L.D. and Koch, D.B. (1979). Chronic N_1 thresholds in chinchilla. *J. Acoust. Soc. Amer.* 65, S141.

Hind, J.E., Anderson, D.J., Brugge, J.F. and Rose, J.E. (1967). Coding of information pertaining to paired low-frequency tones in single auditory nerve fibers of the squirrel monkey. *J. Neurophysiol.* 30, 794–816.

Holton, T. (1980). Relations between frequency selectivity and two-tone suppression in lizard cochlear-nerve fibers. *Hearing Research* 2. 21–38.

Houtgast, T. (1972). Psychophysical evidence for lateral inhibition in hearing. *J. Acoust. Soc. Amer.* 51, 1885–1894.

Kiang, N.Y.-s., Moxon, E.C. and Levine, R.A. (1970). Auditory nerve activity in cats with normal and abnormal cochleas. In: *Sensorineural Hearing Loss.* (G. Wolstenholme and J. Knight, eds). pp 241–268. Churchill, London.

Kim, D. O., Molnar, C.E. and Pfeiffer, R.R. (1973). A system of nonlinear differential equations modeling basilar-membrane motion. *J. Acoust. Soc. Amer.* 54, 1517–1529.

Kim, D.O., Siegel, J.H. and Molnar, C.E. (1979). Cochlear nonlinear phenomena in two-tone responses. *Scand. Audiol.* Suppl. 9, 63–81.

Legouix, J.P., Remond, M.C. and Greenbaum, H.B. (1973). Interference and two-tone inhibition. *J. Acoust. Soc. Amer.* 53, 409-419.

Leshowitz, B. and Lindstrom, R. (1977). Measurement of nonlinearities in listeners with sensorineural hearing loss. In: *Psychophysics and Physiology of Hearing*. (E.F. Evans and J.P. Wilson, eds). pp 283-292. Academic Press, London.

Liff, H.J. and Goldstein, M.H., Jr. (1970). Peripheral inhibition in auditory fibers in the frog. *J. Acoust. Soc. Amer.* 47, 1538-1547.

Moffat, A.J.M. and Capranica, R.R. (1979). Phase cancellation of auditory nerve fiber responses to combination tones, f_2-f_1. *J. Acoust. Soc. Amer.* 65, S82.

Nomoto, M., Suga, N. and Katsuki, Y. (1964). Discharge pattern and inhibition of primary auditory nerve fibers in the monkey. *J. Neurophysiol.* 27, 768-787.

Pfeiffer, R.R. (1970). A model for two-tone inhibition in single cochlear nerve fibers. *J. Acoust. Soc. Amer.* 48, 1373-1378.

Rhode, W.S. (1977). Some observations on two-tone interaction measured with the Mössbauer effect. In: *Psychophysics and Physiology of Hearing*. (E.F. Evans and J.P. Wilson, eds). pp 27-38. Academic Press, London.

Robertson, D. (1976). Correspondence between sharp tuning and two-tone inhibition in primary auditory neurones. *Nature* 259, 477-478.

Ryan, A. and Dallos, P. (1975). Absence of cochlear outer hair cells: Effect on behavioural auditory threshold. *Nature* 253, 44-46.

Ryan, A., Dallos, P. and McGee, T. (1979). Psychophysical tuning curves and auditory thresholds after hair cell damage in the chinchilla. *J. Acoust. Soc. Amer.* 66, 370-378.

Sachs, M.B. and Kiang, N.Y.-s. (1968). Two-tone inhibition in auditory-nerve fibers. *J. Acoust. Soc. Amer.* 43, 1120-1128.

Schmiedt, R.A. and Zwislocki, J.J. (1977). Single-tone and two-tone responses of cochlear nerve fibers: changes after kanamycin and noise treatments. *J. Acoust. Soc. Amer.* 61, S75.

Sellick, P.M. and Russell, I.J. (1979). Two-tone suppression in cochlear hair cells. *Hearing Research* 1, 227-236.

Shannon, R. (1976). Two-tone unmasking and suppression in a forward-masking situation. *J. Acoust. Soc. Amer.* 59, 1460-1470.

Siegel, J.H., Kim, D.E. and Molnar, C.E. (1977). Cochlear distortion products: effects of altering the organ of Corti. *J. Acoust. Soc. Amer.* 61, S2.

Smoorenburg, G.F. (1972). Combination tones and their origin. *J. Acoust. Soc. Amer.* 52. 615-632.

Sweetman, R.H. and Dallos, P. (1969). Distribution pattern of cochlear combination tones. *J. Acoust. Soc. Amer.* 45, 58-71.

Weiss, T.F., Peake, W.T., Ling, A. and Holton, T. (1978). Which structures determine frequency selectivity and tonotopic organization of vertebrate cochlear nerve fibers? Evidence from the alligator lizard. In: *Evoked Electrical Activity in the Auditory Nervous System*. (R.F. Naunton and C. Fernández, eds). pp 91-112. Academic Press, New York.

Wever, E.G., Bray, C.W. and Lawrence, M. (1940). The interference of tones in the cochlea. *J. Acoust. Soc. Amer.* 12, 268-280.

Wightman, F., McGee, T. and Kramer, M. (1977). Factors influencing frequency selectivity in normal and hearing-impaired listeners. In: *Psychophysics and Physiology of Hearing*. (E.F. Evans and J.P. Wilson, eds). pp 296-306. Academic Press, London.

Wilson, J.P. and Johnstone, J.R. (1973). Basilar membrane correlates of the combination tone $2f_1-f_2$. *Nature* 241, 206-207.

Zwicker, E. (1955). Der ungewöhnliche Amplitudengang der Nichtlinearen Verzer-rungen des Ohres. *Acustica* 5, 67-74.

COMMENT ON "Two-tone suppression and intermodulation distortion in the cochlea: effect of outer hair cell lesions" (P. Dallos *et al*).

E.F. Evans
Department of Communication & Neuroscience, University of Keele, Keele, Staffs. ST5 5BG, U.K.

In systematic mappings of the extent of two-tone suppression in single cochlear fibres in cat and guinea pig under various kinds of cochlear pathology, it appears that the two 'side bands' of suppression do not behave identically.

The suppression is mapped using a tone at CF of 80ms duration, on which is superimposed a 50ms tone (5ms rise-fall time) after a 30ms delay. The level and frequency of the second tone is randomized by on-line computer, and the resulting number of discharges analysed and displayed (Evans 1974). Subtracting equal counts from the array demonstrates the extent of suppression at a given criterion as in Figs 1 and 2.

Fig. 1. for comparison, indicates the typical extent of the two suppressive sidebands in a normal guinea pig cochlear fibre of CF 9.0kHz, stimulated by a constant frequency tone at CF, 23 dB above threshold.

In pathology, the high frequency side band of suppression moves upwards approximately with the elevation in CF threshold. The low frequency sideband however, appears to be much more resistant. It has been found to be present relatively unchanged under conditions of elevation in CF threshold by over 40dB (Fig. 2). In this situation, therefore, the low frequency suppression occurs at *lower levels* than the high frequency area (if present), the reverse of the normal situation (Fig. 1).

REFERENCE

Evans, E.F. (1974). Auditory frequency selectivity and the cochlear nerve. In: *Facts and Models in Hearing*. (E. Zwicker & E. Terhardt, eds). pp118-129. Springer, Berlin.

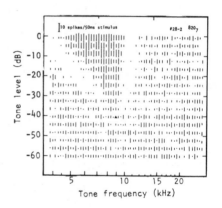

Fig. 1. Response of cochlear fibre to tone of variable frequency and level superimposed on tone at CF (indicated by ▲). Criterion of suppression: 56 % OdB = 96 dB SPL.

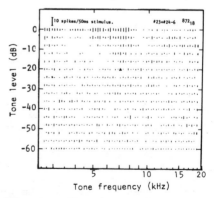

Fig. 2. Fibre in cochlear pathology. CF tone (▲) 10dB above threshold. Criterion of suppression: 25 %. OdB = 110dB SPL.

REPLY TO COMMENT OF E.F. EVANS.

P. Dallos
Auditory Physiology Laboratory, Northwestern University, Evanston, Illinois, U.S.A.

I agree with Evans that under certain circumstances the low and high-frequency suppression bands behave in a different manner. As I indicated in the text, our material contains numerous examples of impaired or absent high-frequency suppression accompanied by normal low frequency 2TS. We have also reported that in normal chinchilla material the low-frequency 2TS is very often not observable (Harris, 1979). It is conceivable that different mechanisms are responsible for the generation of the two bands of 2TS. One of the strongest arguments for this view is our demonstration (Dallos et al., 1974) of the behavior of 2TS in CM. A well-defined, narrow suppression region below the best frequency is never seen in cochlear microphonic responses, while such a region is extremely well defined on the high-frequency side.

REFERENCES

Dallos, P., Cheatham, M.A. and Ferraro, J. (1974). Cochlear mechanics, non-linearities and cochlear potentials. *J.Acoust.Soc.Am.* **55**, 597–605.
Harris, D.M. (1979). Action potential suppression, tuning curves and thresholds: comparison with single fiber data. *Hearing Research* **1**, 133–154.

COMMENT ON: "Two-tone suppression and intermodulation distortion in the cochlea: effect of outer hair cell lesions". (P. Dallos *et al.*)

H.P. Wit
Institute of Audiology, 9713 EZ Groningen, the Netherlands.

In Fig. 5 of the paper by Dallos *et al.* a very sharp secondary peak is present at 2 kHz. Whatever the precise mechanism that produces this peak may be, it must be sharply tuned and it is most probably present at the hair cell level of the cochlear partition.

I consider this finding to be a support for the assumption mentioned in the paper by Ritsma and me, presented at this symposium, that sharply tuned resonators are present in the mammalian cochlea. This assumption was made to explain the shape of frequency spectra of click evoked acoustical responses present in the human ear canal.

A similar idea was put forward by Kemp and Chum who proposed the presence of individual, sharply tuned emission generator channels in specific areas of the organ of Corti.

REFERENCES

Kemp, D.T. and Chum, R.A. (1980). Observations on the generator mechanism of stimulus frequency acoustic emissions - two tone suppression. *This volume*.
Wit, H.P. and Ritsma, R.J. (1980). On the mechanism of the evoked mechanical response. *This volume*.

COMMENT

COMMENT ON: "Two-tone suppression and intermodulation distortion in the cochlea: Effect of outer hair cell lesions". (P. Dallos, D.M. Harris, E. Relkin and M.A. Cheatham).

P.E. Stopp
Neurocommunications Research Unit, University of Birmingham, England.

I would like to re-inforce Dr. Dallos's reservation that the functional integrity of IHCs in Kanamycin-treated animals can be assured, especially when a surface preparation is used as the criterion for assessing hair cell damage.

I myself have completed a study of Kanamycin-intoxicated guinea pigs and have examined the pattern of damage not only by the cochleogram technique, but also by serial section of the same organ of Corti. The results from this study show that it is not a reliable test to go by surface judgments only; I have seen normal-looking areas with quite abnormal-appearing cells (both sensory and supporting) underlying, and even examples of deformed hair cells with very normal-appearing stereocilia. One further disquieting observation, especially for behavioural experimentation: the degree and distribution of damage can be quite dissimilar between the two cochleae of the same animal.

I would therefore suggest that Kanamycin is not a reliable tool for investigating the differences between inner and outer hair cells at least in the guinea pig; other workers, too, have pointed out that rarely does one see all rows of OHCs missing with all IHCs present, but that is quite a different condition.

Dr. Dallos, I am glad to see you have examined at least one Kanamycin-treated tissue in section, but I would like to ask whether you routinely section all cochleae for assessment of damage?

REPLY TO COMMENT OF P.E. STOPP

P. Dallos
Auditory Physiology Laboratory, Northwestern University Evanston, Illinois, U.S.A.

I agree with Dr. Stopp about the difficulties of assessing the integrity of hair cells from surface preparations. We have recently addressed this issue (Ryan et al., 1979) and we feel confident that a combined histological behavioral criterion can be employed to ascertain the functional integrity of remaining inner hair cells. In our experience, Kanamycin functions better for selective hair cell damage than implied by Dr. Stopp; certainly it is a more reliable agent than noise trauma. We do not routinely examine sections, in fact, the pictures that were shown are from the work of Ivan Hunter-Duvar as I have indicated in my talk.

REFERENCES

Ryan, A., Dallos, P. and T. McGee (1979). Psychophysical tuning curves and auditory thresholds after hair cell damage in the chinchilla. *J.Acoust.Soc.Am.* 66, 370–378.

PSYCHOPHYSICAL THREE-TONE SUPPRESSION

H. Duifhuis

*Institute for Perception Research,
Eindhoven, The Netherlands*

1. INTRODUCTION

Lateral suppression in hearing has been the topic of a great number of studies during the last decade. The first order effect, viz. that a suppressor can reduce the response to a suppressee tone to which it is added, is mapped out fairly well both in the neurophysiological and the psychophysical literature (extensive references are given in Duifhuis, 1980). However, details about the underlying mechanism are still largely unknown. This leaves room for quite different interpretations. A closer study of details in suppression hopefully helps to resolve certain issues. A basic issue that will be touched upon here is the hypothesis that psychophysical lateral suppression is a central "attention" effect (pitch cue, pattern change) rather than a peripheral effect (Terry and Moore, 1977; Moore, 1980). It will be argued that the data used to substantiate this hypothesis do not necessarily require such an interpretation. This paper presents data of two suppression experiments. Experiment 1 examines the effect of two suppressors on a single suppressee, and in experiment 2 the effect of suppressing the suppressor is investigated in detail. Though the results are in line with Moore's (1980) experimental data, a different, peripheral, interpretation is drawn.

2. EXPERIMENT 1

The stimulus consisted of a 1-kHz 60-dB suppressee (tone 1) to which two suppressors were added (all levels are in SPL). The one suppressor was below f_1 at $f_2=0.6$ kHz, the other above f_1 at $f_3=1.2$ kHz. Levels of the suppressors (L_2 and L_3) were experimental variables. Suppression was measured with the pulsation threshold method, with the probe fixed at $f_1=1$ kHz. Further experimental details are described in Duifhuis (1980, stimulus mode B). In one experimental series it was verified that the octave relation between f_2 and f_3 had no specific effect on suppression. In general both the 1.2-kHz suppressor and the 0.6-kHz one, when presented at a high enough level, are effective suppressors. Three normal hearing subjects participated in the experiment.

a) *Results*

Figure 1 gives an example of the results for subject FB. The pulsation threshold L_p is plotted as a function of suppressor level. The two thin lines give two-tone suppression results for the 0.6-kHz suppressor (●) and for the 1.2-kHz suppressor (▲). The heavy line (+) gives the results for the combined suppressors, where $L_2=L_3$ is indicated on the abscissa. The 0.6-kHz data show the following behaviour. For L_2 less than 60 dB the suppressor has a negligible effect. Between 60 and 77 dB a clear suppression effect is apparent, and above 77 dB the pulsation threshold is determined by the suppressor becoming excitatory and grows accordingly. The 1.2-kHz suppressor produces a monotonically increasing suppression effect for L_3 greater than 60 dB. It is clear that the combined suppressor data follow the 0.6-kHz suppressor quite closely. This would seem to imply that the low-frequency suppressor is the more

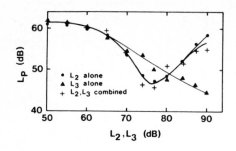

Fig. 1. Pulsation threshold for a 60-dB suppressee at 1 kHz for single and combined suppressors as a function of suppressor level(s). Parameters: f_2=0.6 kHz, f_3= 1.2 kHz. S: FB.

effective one. At any rate, it clearly implies that suppression is not additive. Neither does combined suppression follow the most effective single suppressor. At the highest level the combined effect is much less pronounced than the L_3-alone effect. It was assumed above that the ascending branch of the L_2-alone data reflects the response to L_2 itself. Apparently then L_3 at 90 dB may be an effective suppressor of L_1, but it hardly affects the L_2-response measured at f_p. This was a consistent result.

Results averaged over three subjects are presented in Table 1. The table gives amounts of suppression, defined as L_1-L_p, for two levels of L_2 and L_3 and their combinations. The estimated standard deviation for the data is some 3 to 5 dB. From this limited data the following tentative conclusions may be drawn. For a single suppressor, either at f_2 or f_3, suppression increases as the suppressor level increases from 70 to 80 dB. The effect is stronger for f_2 (< f_1) than for f_3 (> f_1). This is consistent with available literature data (see Duifhuis, 1980). However, for the combined suppressor, no significant effect is apparent. The combined effect is clearly smaller than the sum of the effects if L_2=80 dB. However, for L_2=70 dB there is no significant difference between the sum and the actual data. For L_2=80 dB the combined effect is even smaller than the effect of L_2 alone. If this difference is significant, then it implies a problem for Moore's "pattern change" interpretation. This problem will be worked out in the discussion.

Table 1. Average combined suppression L_1-L_p at 1 kHz for f_2=0.6 and f_3=1.2 kHz (3 subjects).

		L_2 (dB)		
		$-\infty$	70	80
	$-\infty$		5	15
L_3 (dB)	70	4	10	10
	80	9	12	11

3. EXPERIMENT 2

In the second experiment the suppressee was a 50-dB tone at 2 kHz. The first suppressor (f_2, L_2) was at 0.8 kHz. A second suppressor (f_3, L_3) was added at 0.5 kHz at levels that produced suppression at f_2. In other words, the first suppressor was suppressed by the second. The question, first raised by I. Pollack when visiting in 1977, was whether this would cause a release of suppression. A pilot experiment at the time did not show a release effect. This time we returned to the issue asking what changes would be produced in the spectral pulsation threshold pattern. Therefore the probe frequency was now the primary independent variable, and L_2 and L_3 were parameters. The experimental condition with the two suppressor frequencies above f_1 is more complex because combination tones are more pronounced at frequencies around f_1; this will be the subject of further study. Further experimental details are as in experiment 1. Two trained observers participated as subjects.

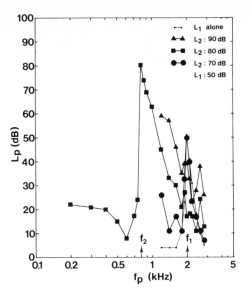

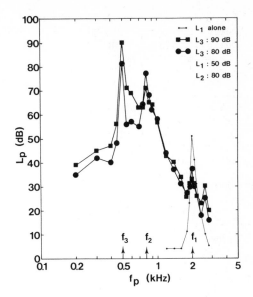

Fig. 2. Two-tone pulsation threshold pattern. The pattern of L_1 alone is suppressed by the 80 and 90-dB 0.8-kHz tone, which at 70 dB has no effect.

Fig. 3. Three-tone pulsation threshold pattern. Increase of L_3 produces some suppression at f_2. This does not reduce the suppression effect at f_1.

a) *Results*

Figures 2 and 3 present results for subject HZ. In the figures the peaked pattern around 2 kHz (thin line) gives the pulsation threshold pattern to the 2-kHz suppressee alone. Figure 2 also gives the effect of the addition of the 0.8-kHz suppressor at three different levels (in the low-frequency range only for L_2=80 dB). It is apparent that the 0.8-kHz tone reduces the 2-kHz excitation pattern before it "covers" it. At L_2=90 dB the pattern at 2 kHz is completely wiped out, even though the excitation level is still under 50 dB. Figure 3 gives three-tone data with L_2 fixed at 80 dB and L_3 at 80 and 90 dB. At these levels L_3 causes only a local effect in a narrow band around 0.8 kHz (at 0.2 and 0.3 kHz one observes combination tones). At 2 kHz there is not much of an effect of L_3. Although L_p is higher than in Fig. 2, which indicates release of suppression, the increase of L_3 from 80 to 90 dB seems to cause an increase of suppression rather than a decrease. Therefore the data are considered to be indecisive. There might be an effect if either L_2 were much lower (but then L_2 would produce insufficient suppression to allow the demonstration of release of suppression), or if L_3 were much higher. The latter would complicate the data by TTS or even PTS effects.

In conclusion, for the condition reported, suppression of the suppressor does not produce a significant release of suppression.

4. DISCUSSION

It should be noted that the focus of this report is on rate suppression, i.e. the reduction of the (r.m.s.) total response, rather than on synchrony suppression, which concerns a single spectral component of the response. Synchrony suppression is a general property of all compressive nonlinear systems. Rate suppression is the more puzzling phenomenon which puts much stronger constraints on theorizing and interpretation.

Lateral rate suppression, both neural and psychophysical, can be interpreted in terms of a BPNL-model (Pfeiffer, 1970) or the hair-cell BPNL-model (Duifhuis, 1976; Duifhuis and Van de Vorst, 1980). In terms of these the above results are readily explained. The interpretation in terms of the 1976-model is outlined briefly below.

A hair cell at position x along the basilar membrane is stimulated effectively at its sensitivity direction only by frequencies close to CF, the tuning frequency associated with x. Suppression can be produced by a frequency far enough off CF driving the hair cell in a less sensitive direction. At x(CF) only frequencies that are effective drivers can be suppressed. Frequencies remote from CF are so inefficient (as exciters) that at the moment they become excitatory they have generated already so much "self-suppression" that an additional suppressor will have little or no suppressing effect. Rather the limited excitatory contributions of the suppressors add, thereby causing a reduction of the apparent two-tone suppression.

In short, the models predict no additivity of suppression. In contrast a possible reduction of suppression produced by a very effective suppressor due to addition of a second suppressor is foreseen. Suppression is confined to a narrow frequency range around CF. Our results at 2 kHz, where the entire excitation pattern is affected, do not contradict this, because the excitation pattern is still confined to a narrow frequency range.

The result that suppression is most prominent around CF was reported by Abbas (1978) in both his neural and psychophysical data. In his psychophysical experiments Abbas used the forward masking technique. Using the same technique Moore (1980) found approximately the same results. However, Moore advocates the pattern change hypothesis to interpret his data. This states that the probe is more easily detected the more its spectral content differs from the (compound) masker stimulus. First of all a central interpretation does not seem a parsimonious solution when the neural data already call for a peripheral one. Secondly, it is hard to reconcile the fact that two suppressors elicit less suppression than a single one in the pattern change model. Thus, although Moore's interpretation cannot yet be ruled out, the evidence brought forward in its support is not in conflict with existing more peripheral interpretations. Therefore I consider it unlikely that the pattern change mechanism plays an important role in lateral suppression. Instead I believe that the major effect originates at the hair cell level, that it is clearly apparent at the hair cell outputs, and because of the mechanical coupling between hair cells and basilar membrane, also, but only weakly, at the membrane level.

REFERENCES (for extensive refences see Duifhuis,1980)

Abbas, P.J.(1978). Effects of stimulus frequency on two-tone suppression: a comparison of physiological and psychophysical results. *J.Acoust.Soc.Am.* 63, 1878-1886.
Duifhuis, H.(1976). Cochlear nonlinearity and second filter: possible mechanism and implications. *J.Acoust.Soc.Am.* 59, 408-423.
Duifhuis, H.(1980). Level effects in psychophysical two-tone suppression. *J.Acoust.Soc.Am.* 67, 914-927.
Duifhuis, H. and van de Vorst, J.J.W.(1980). Mechanics and nonlinearity of hair cell stimulation. Submitted for publication.
Moore, B.J.C.(1980). On the mechanism and frequency distribution of two-tone suppression in forward masking. *J.Acoust.Soc.Am.* 67, in press.
Pfeiffer, R.R.(1970). A model for two-tone inhibition of single cochlear nerve fibers. *J.Acoust.Soc.Am.* 48, 1373-1378.
Terry, M. and Moore, B.J.C.(1977). "Suppression" effects in forward masking. *J.Acoust.Soc.Am.* 62, 215-218(L).

The experimental contributions of F. Brooijmans and H.W. Zelle are gratefully acknowledged.

SOME RESULTS OF A BAND-WIDENING EXPERIMENT OBTAINED WITH A LATERALISATION PARADIGM.

A.W.Bezemer

Institute for Perception Research,
Den Dolech 2, Eindhoven, The Netherlands

1. INTRODUCTION

In 1970 Greenwood and Goldberg found as a result of their physiological experiments that the firing rate measured in neurons of the cochlear nucleus first increases with increasing bandwidth of a noise stimulus and then decreases when the noise bandwidth increases beyond a certain value. In these experiments the noise had a constant spectral power density. Ruggero (1973) obtained a corresponding result from primary auditory nerve fibres.

Several investigators obtained comparable psychophysical results using non-simultaneous measuring methods such as pulsation-threshold (e.g. Houtgast, 1974; Schreiner, 1977) and forward-masking (e.g. Terry and Moore, 1977). In these band-widening experiments the difference found between maximum masking and masking measured at the widest noise band used can be considered a measure of the lateral suppression effect as described by Houtgast (1974).

With experiments carried out with one of the above mentioned threshold-methods, two parameters can be manipulated: masker level and test tone frequency. Test tone level is determined implicitly by the choise of these two parameters. However, it is possible to use the lateralisation phenomenon with partial-masking experiments, which can be done by matching the loudness of a calibration tone presented to one ear to the loudness of the test tone presented together with the masker to the other ear. Practically this means centralising the sound image due to the fusion of the test tone and the calibration tone. With such a paradigm the test tone level can be chosen freely, too. In this paper we explore this possibility and show some results obtained with this method from a band-widening experiment.

2. METHOD

a) *Description of the lateralisation method*

The lateralisation method as described below was used as long as 25 years ago for measuring auditory fatigue or adaptation (e.g. Hood, 1950). More recently a similar method was used for measuring suppression in simultaneous-masking experiments (Houtgast, 1977; Jestaedt and Javel, 1978).

The lateralisation method is based upon the fusion phenomenon that occurs when a pure tone is presented diotically. To one ear of a subject a masker and a test tone are presented and simultaneous with the test tone a calibration tone is presented to the contralateral ear. The calibration tone is equal to the test tone except for its amplitude. The test tone is masked partly by the presence of the masker, but in general the test tone remains well perceptible. The subject's task is to lateralise the sound image due to the fusion of the test tone and the calibration tone by adjusting the level of the calibration tone. The adjusted physical level difference between test tone and calibration tone is a measure of the amount of (partial) masking caused by the masker.

We have performed some experiments both with the lateralisation method and with the classical forward-masking method. After some training subjects preferred experiments to which the lateralisation method was applied over similar experiments that used the threshold paradigm. In general, threshold methods require more concentration and time.

b) *Experimental set-up and procedure*

In all our experiments the masker consisted of bandpass-filtered noise with a variable bandwidth centred around 3 kHz (slope steepness 5 dB/100 Hz). Test tone and calibration tone were pure tones at the centre frequency of the noise band. The time course of the stimulus is shown in fig.1.

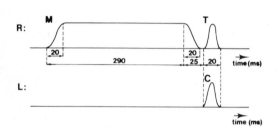

Fig. 1.

Time course of the stimulus with the lateralisation method.
R: stimulus right ear
L: stimulus left ear
M: masker
T: test tone
C: calibration tone

The bandwidth of the noise is the independent variable and can vary from 60 to 2000 Hz. The spectral level of the noise masker and the level of the test tone are independent parameters. All levels are in dB *re* 20 µ Pa.

The subject is asked to set the level of the calibration tone that is required to perceive the fused hearing sensation in the 'middle' of his head by means of the adjustment method.

All conditions are presented three times in a pseudo-random sequence.

3. RESULTS

In a first experiment the influence of masker level on the suppression effect was studied, starting with a fixed test tone level (65 dB). Results of three subjects are shown in fig.2. Because there is no systematic variation ofstandard deviation with noise bandwidth, we computed the mean standard error for each curve. Twice this error is indicated on the left hand side of each curve.

The curves measured at the lowest noise level (10 dB/Hz) show that masking increases with increasing bandwidth. As the noise level increases to 30 dB/Hz, more masking is found for all bandwidths and we observe that for bandwidths over 1200 Hz the curves tend to flatten out. The curves measured at the highest noise level (50 dB/Hz) follow a somewhat different course. Results obtained at this noise level (except for JV) demonstrate lateral suppression: as bandwidth increases, masking effectiveness of the central part of a noise band is reduced by the outer parts. In the results of JV this tendency is present but not significant.

At the lowest noise level lateral suppression has no observable influence. To determine if there is no suppression at all at that level or whether its influence is not measurable with a relatively loud test tone (65 dB), we repeated the experiment with a fixed difference between masker level and test tone level. The results of this experiment for 1 subject are shown in fig.3a.

We observe that in all three conditions masking first increases with increasing bandwidth and then decreases. At all three levels lateral suppression thus has an observable influence. Further we note that least masking is found at the highest noise level. We will discuss this later.

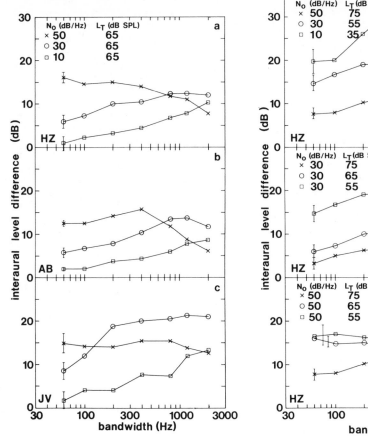

Fig. 2. Masking curves measured for
three subjects.
N_O: spectral noise level

Fig. 3. Masking curves measured for one
subject. Different spectral noise levels.
L_T: test tone level

The set of data collected so far can easily be extended by performing two
series of measurements, one at a masker level of 30 dB/Hz in combination with
a test tone level of 75 dB, and another at a masker level of 50 dB/Hz combined
with a test tone level of 55 dB. Results obtained from these experiments have
been combined with the other results of subject HZ, yielding two sets of
curves measured at fixed noise levels (30 and 50 dB/Hz). These two sets of
curves are shown in fig.3b and 3c respectively.

Both at a noise level of 30 dB/Hz and at a noise level of 50 dB/Hz maximum masking is measured at the lowest test tone level (55 dB) and minimum
masking at the highest test tone level (75 dB). However, at larger bandwidths
the curves approach each other. It is of particular interest to note that the
three curves in each panel do not run parallel to each other.

4.DISCUSSION

The results indicate that the effect of lateral suppression increases with increasing masker level. This agrees with results of Houtgast (1974), Terry and Moore (1977) and Weber (1978). From our results it follows further that if a maximum occurs in the masking curves, it shifts to greater bandwidths with decreasing noise level, especially if we suppose -tentatively- that at the lowest noise level (10 dB/Hz) a maximum will be present at a bandwidth greater than 2000 Hz. Although less pronounced, Houtgast (1974) using the pulsation-threshold method also observed such a shift of the maximum. In results of forward-masking experiments done by Weber (1978) no shift of the maximum is observable.

The results depicted in fig.3a show that when L_T/N_0 is held constant, least masking is found at the highest noise level, in contrast with the results shown in fig.2 where L_T is constant. The question arises to what extent the influence of lateral suppression is responsible for this. It seems justified to suppose that if there were no suppression, more masking would be measured at higher noise levels. However, the assumption that in that case the curves would coincide seems to go too far, because values measured at a bandwidth of 60 Hz differ too much for that to be true, so there must be some other reason to account for the relative positions of these curves.

As mentioned before the curves shown in fig.3b do run not parallel to each other, which we would have expected if the phenomenon of forward masking was caused only by the presented masker. This then cannot be the case.

We observed that suppression has most influence at the lowest test tone level and, as might be expected, most masking is measured at this level too, which can be accounted for by the poorest signal-to-noise-ratio.

Curves measured at a higher masker level (fig.3c) reveal clearly in all cases the influence of lateral suppression. At a low test tone level this influence becomes apparent at a smaller bandwidth than at a higher test tone level, which again can be explained in terms of signal-to-noise-ratio. This is in full agreement with the shift of the maximum as observed in fig.2.

Acknowledgement

This research was supported by the Netherlands Organisation for the Advancement of Pure Research (Z.W.O.).

REFERENCES

Greenwood, D.D. and Goldberg, J.M. (1970). Response of neurons in the cochlear nuclei to variations in noise bandwidth and to tone-noise combinations. *J. Acoust. Soc. Am.* 47, 1022-1040.

Hood, J.D. (1950). Studies in auditory fatigue and adaptation. *Acta-otolaryngol.* Suppl. 92, 1-57.

Houtgast, T. (1974). *Lateral suppression in hearing* , Doctoral dissertation, Free university, Amsterdam.

Houtgast, T. (1977). Phase effects in two-tone suppression investigated with a binaural lateralisation paradigm. In: *Psychophysics and physiology of hearing* (E.F. Evans and J.P. Wilson, eds). pp 165-170. Academic, London.

Jesteadt, W. and Javel, E. (1978). Measurements of suppression in a simultaneous masking paradigm. *J. Acoust. Soc. Am.* 63, S44(A).

Ruggero, M.A. (1973). Response to noise of auditory nerve fibres in the squirrel monkey. *J. Neurophysiol.* 36, 569-587.

Schreiner, C. (1977). *Monorale pulsationsschwelle und lautheit.* Doctoral dissertation, Univ. of Gottingen, W. Germany.

Terry, M., and Moore, B.C.J. (1977). "Suppression" effects in forward masking, *J. Acoust. Soc. Am.* 62, 781-784 (L).

Weber, D.L. (1978). Suppression and critical bands in band-limiting experiments. *J. Acoust. Soc. Am.* 64, 141-150.

COMMENT ON: "Some results of a band-widening experiment obtained with a lateralisation paradigm". (A.W. Bezemer).

B. Scharf
Auditory Perception Lab., Northeastern U., Boston, MA 02115 USA

A striking effect in the data of Bezemer is the large decrease in masking that takes place with increasing signal level despite a constant signal-to-noise ratio. Lateralization of a 3-kHz tone burst is much less affected by a 25-dB weaker (spectrum level) noise masker when the signal is 75 dB than when it is 55 dB and still less when it is 35 dB. A similar finding was noted in the course of our own lateralization experiments, some of which are reported in the paper presented at this symposium by Scharf and Canévet.

In those experiments, the lateralization threshold, i.e. the minimum interaural onset time difference required to lateralize a tone burst toward the leading ear, was measured in the presence of a diotic burst of a different frequency. In the most relevant set of data, onset of a 25-ms masker at 4.160 kHz preceded a 30-ms target at 4 kHz by 15 ms; target level was varied together with masker level so that the target was always 20 dB higher. Table I gives the results for the 4-kHz target under masking and in quiet and also for a 2-kHz target preceded by a 2.008-kHz masker. At both frequencies the masker interferes with lateralization much more at 60-dB target levels than at 90-dB target levels. A similar effect was found at other masker frequencies within one critical band of the target frequency. Accordingly, it is evident that the reduced masking effect at higher target levels noted by Bezemer is not limited to forward masking nor to a noise masker.

Target SPL	Masker SPL	Threshold in μs	
		4 kHz	2 kHz
90 dB	70 dB	365	420
90	quiet	225	350
60	40 dB	2150	530
60	quiet	225	195

Table I. Lateralization threshold, at various target and masker levels. (Masker frequencies were close to the target frequencies of 4 and 2 kHz).

INVESTIGATION OF MONAURAL PHASE EFFECTS BY MEASURING
BINAURAL MASKING THRESHOLDS

H. Nasse and R.E. Gerlach

Drittes Physikalisches Institut
Universität Göttingen, Germany

SUMMARY

Phase effects in octave complexes are investigated in a binaural masking experiment. Typically the right-ear stimulus consists of an octave complex with a strong fundamental and a white-noise masker while the left-ear stimulus contains the octave tone only and the same noise signal. Binaural masking thresholds of the octave tones are measured for the two cases where the fundamental is either present or absent. From these data the effect of the strong fundamental on both the internal level and phase of the weaker harmonic can be estimated because binaural unmasking depends on interaural level and phase differences for the test tones. The patterns of the internal variations of level and phase as a function of the phase relations in the octave complex do not support the theory that the monaural phase effects investigated here are a consequence of vector addition of harmonic distortion products.

1. INTRODUCTION

Interactions of the components of phase-locked two-tone complexes, in particular with a frequency ratio of 1:2, are subject of several psychophysical studies. Clack *et al* (1972) and Terhardt *et al* (1971) found that the threshold of the higher component masked by the fundamental depends on the phase relations in the octave complex. Weber (1977) used an octave complex as a masker in a pulsation threshold experiment and measured a phase dependent pulsation threshold of the octave tone. In contrast to the results of Clack this effect was also observed when the frequency ratio was 2:3. Another type of experiment was performed by Lamoré (1975) who took the level of white noise just sufficient to mask the higher component of an octave complex as a measure of the internal strength of that stimulus. Unlike Clack, he could not explain his results by assuming a vector summation of harmonic distortion products, but on the other hand, he did not exclude it as a possible underlying mechanism.

For the validation of the different hypotheses – aural harmonics or waveform detection – it would be useful to know whether the suppression of the higher (weaker) component is associated with a phase shift. The phase shift can be measured by means of a binaural masking paradigm which is illustrated in the following.

2. METHOD

In a binaural masking experiment with diotic noise and dichotic tone signals of equal frequency, the masked threshold of the tone signals depends on their interaural level difference ΔL and phase difference $\Delta \varphi$. It follows from the "equalization-and-cancellation" model (Durlach, 1972) that in the case where the level L_1 of one of the tone signals is fixed the variable level L_2 is given by the expression

$$L_2 = L_1 - 20 \cdot \lg \left[\cos(\Delta\varphi)/p \pm \sqrt{\cos^2(\Delta\varphi)^2/p^2 - k/p} \right] \tag{1}$$

with

$$k := \frac{2 \cdot 10^{-L_o/10}}{2 \cdot 10^{-L_o/10} - 1} \qquad\qquad p := 2 \cdot 10^{-L_1/10} + k - 2 \cdot 10^{-L_1/10} \cdot k . \qquad (2)$$

The monaural masked threshold ($N_m S_m$-condition) corresponds to a level of 0 dB, L_o is the threshold level in the $N_o S_m$-condition (typically -8 dB). The shape of some curves, calculated from eq. (1), is illustrated in Fig. 1. They are in good agreement with the experimental results. That means that for each subject a set of binaural threshold curves can be predicted from the measurement of the threshold levels in the $N_m S_m$- and $N_o S_m$-condition.

Proceeding the other way round, the unknown level and phase of one tone signal or its change caused by interaction with an added strong component can be derived from the binaural masking threshold.

Two different experimental procedures are used. In the first one (Fig. 2a) a binaural 400-Hz signal, gated synchronously, is masked by diotic noise; the tone level L_1 at the left ear is fixed while L_2 at the binaural masked threshold is determined in a 2-AFC-procedure, where the interaural phase difference is changed in a pseudo-random sequence after each response of the subject. In absence of the 200-Hz component the result is given by the open circles. If the strong fundamental is presented continuously to the left ear (where the level is fixed), the threshold curve is flattened and shifted horizontally according to a lower "internal" level and a phase shift of the 400-Hz signal at the left ear.

The second procedure (Fig. 2b) takes less time and is even more exact. The stimuli are nearly the same as in the first experiment except for a small frequency difference of the 400-Hz signals. This leads to a beating sensation if the level L_2, which is now fixed, is chosen between the minimum and the maximum of its threshold curve (dashed line). It is the subjects task to mark the beginning and the end of the tone sensation by pressing a button. A histogram of the subjects responses (usually 100 in each trial) is plotted in Fig. 2b. If the strong 200-Hz component is added, the interval where the 400-Hz signal is detected in the diotic noise is shortened and shifted (upper histograms) according to a lower "internal" level L_2 and "internal" phase shift. Because the fundamental is now added at the right ear, the theoretical threshold curve (solid line) is not flattened but only shifted horizontally.

The apparatus which is used in both procedures is illustrated in Fig. 4.

3. RESULTS

Individual data of two experienced subjects on the suppression and phase shift of the 400-Hz octave tone caused by interaction with the strong fundamental are shown in Fig. 3. The phase relations in the octave complex are described by $\varphi_{200/400}$ which is the smallest phase angle of the 200-Hz tone at the zero-axis crossing in positive direction of the 400-Hz signal. For each value of $\varphi_{200/400}$ fifteen individual series were run. The variations of the data were 3 dB or 10° respectively, the mean values are plotted in Fig. 3.

The results which were obtained with the methods described above were compared to those measured with a lateralisation paradigm introduced by Houtgast (1977). Both the suppression and phase shift of the octave tone, when measured with these rather different methods, appear to be of the same order, and the shape of the curves looks quite similar, too.

With respect to the two hypotheses mentioned above it can be said that our present results do not support the theory of vector summation of harmonic distortion products as the only reason for the phase dependent sensation of octave complexes. If simple vector summation is the underlying mechanism, points of zero phase shift must correspond to points of minimal or maximal suppression. This is not true for our data.

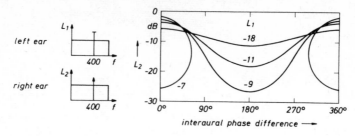

Fig.1. Binaural masking thresholds (N_OS_φ), calculated from eq. (1).

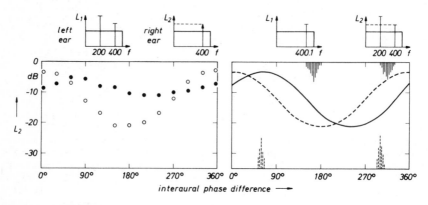

Fig.2. Influence of a strong fundamental on the binaural masking threshold of the octave tones.

a. Measured with a 2-AFC procedure.
   The result in absence of the
   fundamental is represented by
   open circles.

b. Measured with the "binaural-
   beat" procedure. The histograms
   indicate the beginning and the
   end of the tone sensation. The
   result in absence of the fundamental is represented by dashed
   lines.

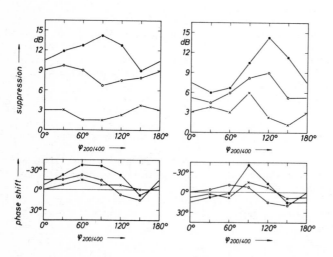

Fig.3. Suppression and
phase shift of the
octave tone (400 Hz,
40 dB SL) as a function
of the phase relations
in the octave complex
measured with a binau-
ral masking paradigm
(individual data of two
subjects). Parameter is
the level of the funda-
mental:
x 50 dB SL, o 55 dB SL,
● 60 dB SL.

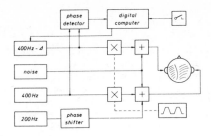

Fig.4. Block diagram of the apparatus.

4. CONCLUSION

The possibility of using binaural masking thresholds for investigation of monaural phase effects has been demonstrated. A welcome property of these thresholds is that quantitative predictions can be derived from the equalization - and - cancellation model so that not all reference values (in absence of the fundamental) need be measured, but can be calculated from a small set of data.

A second important feature of our method is that the probe tone applied to measure the amount of suppression and phase shift is not itself subjected to that suppression. While in other psychoacoustic methods this is achieved by a temporal separation (e.g. pulsation threshold, forward masking) this method uses a *spatial* separation because the probe tone is presented to the contralateral ear. Of course, on a higher level of the auditory system there must be interaural interactions; but if we assume the investigated mechanism to be a peripheral one, the probe tone is not passed through that suppression mechanism.

Nevertheless, the possible influence of the strong component on the contralateral probe tone must be explored. We found that the N_oS_m masking threshold of the probe tone is slightly shifted to higher levels by a strong contralateral tonal signal, dependent on the frequency ratio. If the frequency ratio is 1:2, there is a distinct phase dependence. A second problem is the interaction of noise and tonal signals and the possible reduction of the interaural correlation of the noise signals by the strong sinusoidal signal. Experiments addressing themselves to these questions are still in progress. Early results are reported in the accompanying paper by Sieben *et al*.

REFERENCES

Clack, T.D. *et al*. (1972). Aural Harmonics: The Monaural Phase Effects at 1500 Hz, 2000 Hz, and 2500 Hz Observed in Tone-on-Tone Masking when f_1 = 1000 Hz. *J. Acoust. Soc. Amer.* **52**, 536-541.

Durlach, N.I. (1972). Binaural Signal Detection: Equalization and Cancellation Theory. In: *Foundations of Modern Auditory Theory*. Vol. 2. (J.V. Tobias, ed). pp 369-462. Academic Press, New York.

Houtgast, T. (1977). Phase Effects in Two-Tone Suppression Investigated with a Binaural Lateralization Paradigm. In: *Psychophysics and Physiology of Hearing*. (E.F. Evans and J.P. Wilson, eds). pp 165-170. Academic Press, London.

Lamoré, P.J.J. (1975). Perception of Two-Tone Octave Complexes. *Acustica* **34**, 1-14.

Terhardt, E. and Fastl, H. (1971). Zum Einfluß von Störtönen und Störgeräuschen auf die Tonhöhe von Sinustönen. *Acustica* **25**, 53-61.

Weber, R. (1977). Investigation of Monaural Phase Effects in Two-Tone-Complexes Using the Pulsation Threshold Method. *9th I.C.A., Madrid, Paper H 33.*

Sieben, U. and Gerlach, R.E. (1980). Interaction between Two-Tone Complexes and Masking Noise. *This volume.*

ADDENDUM (H. Nasse and R.E. Gerlach)

Introduction

One of the remaining problems in our paper is a possible influence of the strong component of the complex on the contralateral test tone. This test tone is required to be "independent". On the other hand it is known (Zwislocki, 1970) that the threshold of audibility of a test tone is increased by the simultaneous presentation of a contralateral masker. With a continuous masker this threshold shift is only very small, however, it increases, if there is presented an additional diotic noise (Fig. 1). In the following we describe some additional experiments, conducted over the last weeks to investigate the interaction between a test tone and a contralateral masker in a diotic noise condition.

Experiments

We measured the alteration of the N_oS_m masked threshold caused by the additional presentation of a continuous contralateral masker. Masker and test tone were phase-locked, their frequencies ($f_m < f_t$) had the ratio of small integers. The parameters of the measurements were the level of the noise, the level of the masker, and the relative phase between masker and test tone.

At the frequency ratio of 1 : 2 we obtained the following results:
- For masker levels in a certain range of 15 dB extent the masked threshold is phase-dependent. This dependence reaches a maximum variation of 6 dB (Fig. 2).
- For masker levels below or above this range the masked threshold is flat, however slightly shifted against the N_oS_m-threshold by 1 - 2 or 4 - 5 dB (Fig.2).
- The shape of the phase-dependent masked threshold is nearly constant. Using N_π- instead of N_o-noise results in an exchange of maximum and minimum.
- If the masker is presented ipsilaterally one obtains similar phase-dependent masked thresholds, but 30° - 50° phase shifted.
- At high masker levels there is a phase-dependent lateralization of the test tone, i.e. for certain phase angles the test tone is perceived at the side where the masker is presented (Fig. 3).
- For test tone frequencies greater than 1 kHz there is no phase dependence but only a threshold increase.

For a frequency ratio of 1 : 3 we observed analogous effects, but at higher masker levels and with a weaker lateralization. For a frequency ratio of 2 : 3 we did find no phase dependence of the masked threshold and no lateralization.

Discussion

All phase effects specified above were observed only at harmonic frequency ratios, so that our hypothesis is that the phase effects are due to higher harmonics of the masker generated by nonlinearities. Thus the masked threshold of the test tone measured in diotic noise (N_oS_m-threshold) is actually an internal N_oS_ϕ-threshold, because a higher harmonic of the masker is an iso-frequent signal contralateral to the test tone. The signal level can be estimated to be 15 - 20 dB below the monaural masked threshold (N_mS_m) of the test tone (about 30 - 40 dB below the masker level), if the phase-dependent variation of the masked threshold (Fig. 2) is about 5 dB. This follows from the "Equalization and Cancellation Theory" (Durlach, 1972) and from comparative results of binaural masked thresholds, where the masker is substituted by the first harmonic.

The masked thresholds which are measured with N_π-noise, can be explained in the same way. The binaural unmasking is now a result of binaural summation, rather than of binaural subtraction. On the opposite side, the shape of the masked threshold for the ipsilateral presentation of masker and test tone cannot be explained simply by adding test tone and higher harmonic of the masker. This assumption would result in a threshold with the maximum and minimum at the same phase angles as in the N_π-case. Furthermore the variation of this threshold should keep in a 6 dB range, but for sufficiently high masker levels we measured actually variations, which are considerably larger. Another hint, that the mon-

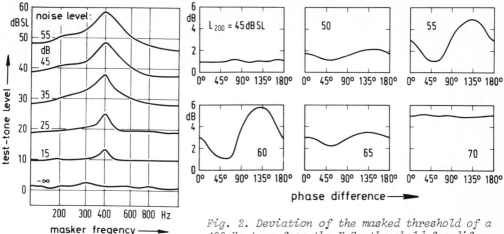

Fig. 2. Deviation of the masked threshold of a 400 Hz tone from the N_oS_m-threshold for different levels and phases of the contralateral masker. (Masker frequency 200 Hz, level of the diotic noise 40 dB)

Fig. 1. Masking of a 400 Hz test tone by a contralateral masker (55 dB SL) under the condition of diotic noise with different levels.

Signal configuration for all experiments

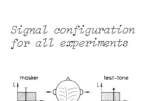

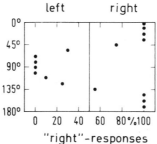

Fig. 3. Lateralization of the 400 Hz signal in dependence on the phase of the contralateral 200 Hz tone. The level of the 400 Hz tone is fixed at 3 dB above the maximum of the masked threshold.

aural phase effects are based on other mechanisms, is the large phase dependence of pitch perception in monaural two-tone complexes. This dependence cannot be observed, if masker and test tone are presented contralaterally.

The increase of the masked threshold, which also occurs in the case of non-harmonic frequency ratios, is caused by an interaction between masker and noise which results in a decrease of the interaural correlation of the noise.

As a result of the experiments described above we arrived at the conclusion that the binaural phase effects are not caused by central interaction between masker and test tone. Nearly all observations can be explained as a result of peripheral nonlinearities and effects of the binaural unmasking. Thus, the existence of the binaural phase effects is no contradiction to the assumption that the contralateral tone is an independent test signal for measuring monaural phase effects.

REFERENCES

Durlach, N.I. (1972). Binaural Signal Detection: Equalization and Cancellation Theory. In: *Foundations of Modern Auditory Theory*. Vol. 2. (J.V. Tobias, ed.) pp. 369–462. Academic Press, New York.

Zwislocki, J.J. (1970). Central Masking and Auditory Frequency Selectivity. In: *Frequency Analysis and Periodicity Detection in Hearing*. (R. Plomp and G.F. Smoorenburg, ed.) pp. 445–454. A.W. Sijthoff, Leiden.

CUBIC DIFFERENCE TONE LEVEL AND PHASE DEPENDENCE
ON FREQUENCY DIFFERENCE AND LEVEL OF PRIMARIES

E. ZWICKER

Institute of Electroacoustics, Technical University
München, Federal Republic of Germany

1. INTRODUCTION

The cubic difference tone with the frequency $2f_1-f_2$ produced within the ear seems to be an important indicator of the nonlinearity in cochlear mechanics. There have been several measurements, psychoacoustically as well as neurophysiologically, of the dependence of level and phase of the $(2f_1-f_2)$-tone on the level of the primaries. Measurements on its dependence on the frequency and frequency separation of the primaries have been undertaken by keeping one of the two frequencies constant. This way the frequency $2f_1-f_2$, i.e. the place of maximal excitation of the difference tones, changes as well. In the case of neurophysiological research it is, however, much better to vary the frequency of both primaries so that the frequency of the cubic difference tone and thereby its excitation along the basilar membrane remains constant. Psychoacoustical data collected for constant frequency of cubic difference tone are reported in this paper. They have been produced using the method (of compensation) and apparatus described earlier (Zwicker 1979a) for a constant $(2f_1-f_2)$-frequency of 1400 Hz. Using the vector-summation method (Zwicker 1980) the cubic difference tones' level and phase have been calculated for the same and similar conditions. Both should be compared with neurophysiological data to be measured.

2. RESULTS OF PSYCHOACOUSTICAL MEASUREMENTS

The level $L_{(2f_1-f_2)}$ and the phase $\varphi_{(2f_1-f_2)}$ of a $(2f_1-f_2)$-tone needed to compensate the cubic difference tone produced in the ear are plotted as a function of the frequency difference f_2-f_1 of the primaries with level L_1 of the lower primary as parameter. Fig's 1 and 2 belong to two different subjects ("A" and "B"). The level of the higher primary is constant ($L_2 = 60$ dB) as is the frequency $2f_1-f_2 = 1400$ Hz. The frequencies f_1 and f_2 of the two primaries are plotted as additional scales on the lower abscissa.

The data show generally decreasing cubic difference tone level $L(2f_1-f_2)$ and increasing phase $\varphi_{(2f_1-f_2)}$ for increasing frequency difference f_2-f_1, as was expected. The detailed structure, however, indicates a nonmonotonic level decrement in several cases, which is accompanied by unusual phase behaviour for that range of f_2-f_1 in which $L_{(2f_1-f_2)}$ drops to a minimum. The more clearly this minimum is marked (see for example Fig. 2 at $f_2-f_1 = 0.65$ with parameter $L_1 = 65$ dB) the more extreme is the change in the corresponding phase. For large f_2-f_1, the phase seems to reach two different values – depending on the parameter L_1 – which differ by almost exactly $360°$. This nonmonotonic behaviour seems to have its counterpart in similar behaviour of the $(2f_1-f_2)$-tone as reported by Helle (1969), Smoorenburg (1972), Weber and Mellert (1975), Hall (1975) and Zwicker (1979a, 1980) under different paradigms.

Differences between the data of the two subjects "A" and "B" (Fig. 1 and Fig. 2) indicate that "A" produces larger values of $L_{(2f_1-f_2)}$ but smoother dependence of $\varphi_{(2f_1-f_2)}$ in relation to the data of "B". The general tendency of the two sets of curves is, however, the same indicating that the composi-

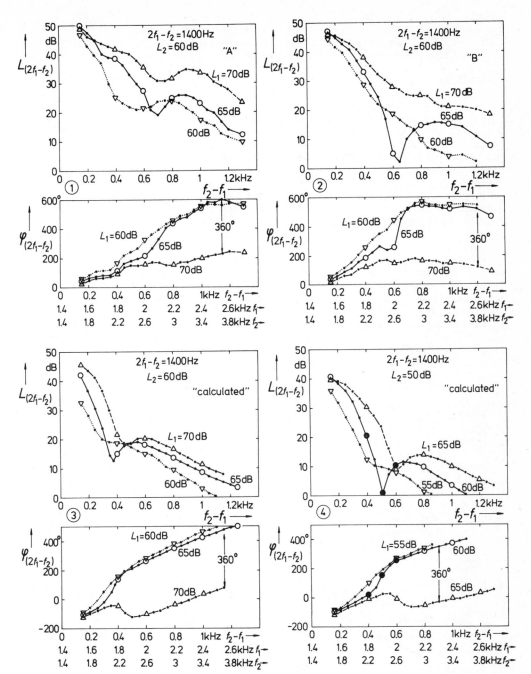

Fig. 1-4. Level $L_{(2f_1-f_2)}$ and phase $\varphi_{(2f_1-f_2)}$ of the cubic difference tone produced by two primaries with level L_1 (parameter) and L_2 as a function of their frequencies f_1 and f_2 and their separation f_2-f_1, respectively. f_1 and f_2 are chosen so that $2f_1-f_2$ = const. = 1400 Hz. Fig. 1 and 2 present psychoacoustical data from two human subjects "A" and "B", respectively. Fig. 3 shows calculated data for the same parameters as used in Fig. 1 and 2, while L_1 and L_2 are somewhat smaller in Fig. 4 as indicated.

tion of the $(2f_1-f_2)$-tone follows the same rules although the individual human ear may differ in the parameters underlying these rules. Additionally, even the data of $(2f_1-f_2)$-level measured acoustically in the outer ear canal of cats (Kim, 1980) show the same tendency.

3. CALCULATED RESULTS

The calculation procedure is based on the assumption that the difference tone to be compensated results from a sum of wavelets of different amplitude and phase (Zwicker, 1979a). Each of them is produced by the excitation time functions at the local spots of the organ of Corti which are composed of the two primaries with level and phase varying locally but producing all the same distortion product $(2f_1-f_2)$ through a nonlinear, symmetrically saturating transfer function with feedback (Zwicker, 1979b).

The wavelets from the many spots have the same frequency but a different distance to travel in order to reach the place of maximal displacement corresponding to that frequency. At that place, the wavelets can be added together.

The calculated data plotted in Fig. 3 are for exactly the same values of the parameters L_1 and L_2 as those used for the psychoacoustically measured data. They show similar behaviour as seen in Fig. 1 or 2 such as decreasing level and increasing phase with increasing frequency difference f_2-f_1. The nonmonotonic decrease of level corresponding with sudden changes in phase is also clearly indicated. Only the values of f_2-f_1 at which these unexpected changes occur are smaller in relation to the corresponding values of the measured data. However, changing the parameters by several dB as indicated in Fig. 4 the minimum appears more clearly and is, for the frequency difference f_2-f_1, comparable to that of the measured data.

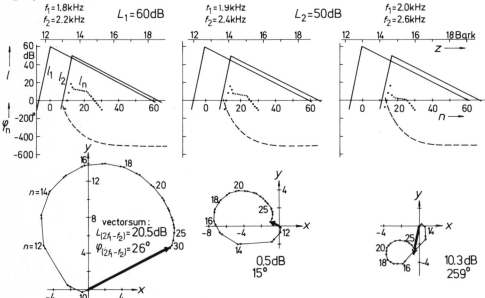

Fig. 5. *Composition of the $(2f_1-f_2)$-tone as a vector sum of many wavelets for three different parameters as indicated (corresp. to shaded symbols of Fig.4). Upper parts: distribution of the excitation level l_1 and l_2 of the two primaries, together with level l_n and phase φ_n of the wavelets produced along the critical band rate z and for whole numbers along the normalized ($z_1 \hat{=} n = 0$; $z = 1$ Bark $\hat{=} \Delta n = 10$) n-scale, respectively. Lower parts: vectorial addition of the many wavelets to the vector sum (level and phase are indicated).*

In order to explain the basis for the unusual behaviour of amplitude as well as phase, the formation of the vector sum is shown in Fig. 5 for the values f_2-f_1 = 0.4, 0.5 and 0.6 with L_1 = 60 dB (corresponding to the values of Fig. 4 indicated by shaded symbols). The upper part of Fig. 5 shows the excitation level l_1 and l_2 of the two primaries as well as the levels l_n of the cubic difference tone of the wavelets and their phase φ_n (determined from the phase of each primary and the traveling phase of the wavelets). These values are plotted along the basilar membrane i.e. as a function of the critical band rate (upper scale). Vectorial summation becomes meaningful only if the phase between neighbouring wavelets is not much larger than 45°. This means that the distance between the local spots creating the wavelets along the basilar membrane has to be much smaller than 1 Bark. Therefore the level l_n of the wavelets is calculated for each tenth of a critical band using a new variable n as indicated by the lower abscissa (n-scale normalized so that z_1 corresponds to n = 0, while Δz = 1 Bark corresponds to Δn = 10). Using the values of l_n and φ_n the wavelets are added vectorially resulting in the strongly marked vector sum as shown for the three conditions in the lower part of Fig. 5. The wavelets are characterized by the value n they belong to.

The angle of the vector sum is, in the case of a minimum, very sensitive against small changes of the wavelets and may rise or fall very quickly as a function of f_2-f_1 depending on whether the vector sum encloses the origin (as in the case of L_1 = 60 dB of Fig. 4) or does not (as in the case of L_1 = 65 dB). This difference creates the phase angle difference of 360° for large values of f_2-f_1. The vectorial summation of the many wavelets – which sometimes ends up near zero – is the reason for the creation of the partly nonmonotonic decrement of the cubic difference tones' level $L(2f_1-f_2)$ and the unusual behaviour of its phase $\varphi(2f_1-f_2)$ as a function of f_2-f_1.

4. CONCLUSION

Psychoacoustically measured data of level and phase of the $(2f_1-f_2)$-tone agree (at least in their pronounced tendencies) with the data calculated on the basis of the saturation-feedback model (Zwicker, 1979b). Since the dependence is nonmonotonic and relatively unusual, this agreement can also be considered as a confirmation of the model.

Acknowledgements. This work was carried out within the "Sonderforschungsbereich 50, Kybernetik", München, which is supported by the "Deutsche Forschungsgemeinschaft".

REFERENCES

Hall, J.L.(1975). Nonmonotonic behavior of distortion product $2f_1-f_2$: Psychophysical observations. *J.Acoust.Soc.Am.* **58**, 1046 – 1050.
Helle, R.(1969). Amplitude und Phase des im Gehör gebildeten Differenztones dritter Ordnung. *Acustica* **22**, 74 – 87.
Kim, D.O.(1980). Cochlear mechanics: Implications of electrophysiological and acoustical observations. *Hearing Research* (in press).
Smoorenburg, G.F.(1972). Combination tones and their origin. *J.Acoust.Soc.Am.* **52**, 615 – 632.
Weber, R. and Mellert, V.(1975). On the nonmonotonic behavior of cubic distortion products in the human ear. *J.Acoust.Soc.Am.* **57**, 207 – 214.
Zwicker, E.(1979a). Different behavior of quadratic and cubic difference tones. *Hearing Research* **1**, 283 – 292.
Zwicker, E.(1979b). A model describing nonlinearities in hearing by active processes with saturation at 40 dB. *Biol. Cyb.* **35**, 243 – 250.
Zwicker, E.(1980). Nonmonotonic behaviour of $(2f_1-f_2)$ explained by a saturation-feedback model. *Hearing Research* (in press).

COMMENT ON "Cubic Difference Tone Level and Phase Dependence on Frequency Difference and Level of Primaries" (E. Zwicker).

T.J.F. Buunen
Biophysics Group, Applied Physics Dept., Delft University of Technology, Delft, The Netherlands.

The behaviour of the CDT's amplitude and phase as psychophysically measured by E. Zwicker can be compared in detail to neurophysiological data obtained with an identical stimulus configuration in both the cochlear nucleus and the VIII-nerve of the cat. Buunen et al. (1977) measured the response of single cells to the CDT in the cochlear nucleus for a two-tone stimulus with increasing frequency separation Δf (= $f_2 - f_1$) while keeping the CDT-frequency constant at f_t, equal to the cell's CF. Fig.1 presents results for three different cells. The ordinate gives the spike rate while the abscis is equivalent to the frequency separation Δf. The solid curve is the response to one pure tone of frequency $f_t + \Delta f$ given for comparison. The dashed curve is the response to the two tones. Fig.2 presents the results for the same stimulus paradigm in the cats' VIII nerve. The data are from a paper by Buunen and Rhode (1978). These electrophysiological data are very much in agreement with the Figs. 1 to 4 of Zwicker's paper.

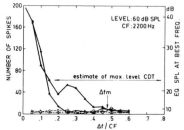

Fig.2. Response of a VIII-nerve fiber to the CDT at frequency CF, as a function of the frequency separation.

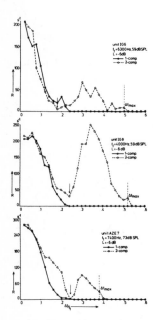

Fig.1. Responses of cochlear nucleus cells to the CDT of frequency f_t, as a function of the frequency separation

The VIII-nerve experiments also produced data about the CDT's phase. This was done by estimation of the orientation in the period histograms. The limited space available for this comment makes it impossible to reproduce the data but they can be found in the paper mentioned before.

The following conclusions from our experiments are in agreement with those of Zwicker;
- the level of the CDT depends non-monotonically on the frequency separation between the stimulus tones,
- abrupt changes in the CDT's phase as a function of the frequency separation occur,
- non-monotonics can be found both psychophysically and electrophysiologically,
- both phase and amplitude data vary very much between subjects.

Several conclusions from the electrophysiological data can be added to the psychophysical in order to check the validity of the model of Zwicker more thoroughly;
- the phase behaviour of the CDT depends (in a cat) very much on the frequency

region of the CDT,(Therefore, the general trends reported by Zwicker are only comparable to the physiological data for the region around 2 kHz.)
- the phase behaviour of the CDT depends (in a cat) strongly upon the level difference between the generating components and not on the overall level,
- on several occasions two non-monotonics were found in the CDT-level as a function of frequency separation.

Up to now no systematic search of the physiological data was made for the phase jump of 360° as reported by Zwicker.

REFERENCES

Buunen, T.J.F., ten Kate, J.H. ten, Raatgever, J. and F.A. Bilsen (1977). "Combined psychophysical and electrophysiological study on the role of combination tones in the perception of phase changes". *J.Acoust.Soc.Am.* 61, 508-519.
Buunen, T.J.F. and W.S. Rhode (1978). "Responses of fibers in the cat's auditory nerve to the cubic difference tone". *J.Acoust.Soc.Am.* 64, 772-781.

RESPONSES OF CAT COCHLEAR NERVE FIBRES TO CUBIC DIFFERENCE TONES

G.F. Pick and A.R. Palmer[1]

*Department of Communication and Neuroscience,
University of Keele, ST5 5BG, England.*

1. INTRODUCTION

When presented with two pure tones (of frequency, f_1 and f_2, $f_1 < f_2$) a subject may hear not only the tones but also distortion products generated within the cochlea. Great interest has been shown in these distortion products and particularly in the behaviour of the cubic difference tones (CDT) since this behaviour puts severe constraints on any proposed mechanism for the nonlinear transformation of sound energy into neural activity. Psychoacoustically, the lower CDT (at frequency $2f_1 - f_2$) is most easily detected, even at relatively low levels of the primary tones, and has received considerable attention (e.g. Zwicker, 1955; Goldstein, 1967 and Smoorenburg, 1972). Many of these psychoacoustic data have been shown to be paralleled by the responses of single units in the auditory periphery of the cat (e.g. Goldstein and Kiang, 1968; Smoorenburg *et al*, 1976 and Buunen and Rhode, 1978). Less attention has been accorded to the upper CDT (of frequency, $2f_2 - f_1$), which should be generated by the nonlinear element at a similar level to the lower CDT, if the transfer characteristic of the nonlinearity can be described by a polynomial function. Goldstein (1967) gave psychoacoustic evidence that the upper CDT was not present at a level similar to the lower CDT and was not masked by the primaries at this level (thus suggesting that the cochlear fibres most sensitive to the upper CDT are not also responding to the primaries). On the other hand, Zureck and Sachs (1979) provided psychophysical evidence to suggest that the upper CDT is present and at a comparable level to that of the lower CDT, at least for a rather limited stimulus set and for one of two subjects. It appears that the upper CDT has received even less attention in neurophysiological studies. Goldstein and Kiang (1968) present results from only one cochlear nerve fibre for which the upper CDT was placed at the characteristic frequency (CF) of the fibre. The response of this fibre is clearly dominated by the response to f_2 at all the levels tested. Littlefield (1973) showed a phase-locked response to the upper CDT, but this occurred only at levels at which the unit was responding to both primaries, and the CDT response matched that expected from a nonlinear neural-spike generator mechanism. In the results of Zureck and Sachs (1979) on the other hand, there was no masking effect of the primaries on the upper CDT.

It would appear therefore that the important question of whether the upper CDT is present at a similar level to that of the lower CDT awaits a definite answer. In this paper we present evidence to suggest that the upper CDT is only generated when both primary tones excite cochlear fibres and thus could result from nonlinearities in the spike generator as suggested by Littlefield. In addition we describe some further properties of the responses to the lower CDT.

2. METHODS

[1] ARP's current address: *National Institute for Medical Research, The Ridgeway, Mill Hill, London NW7 1AA.*

A detailed description of the methods employed will be found in Evans (1979). Briefly, 2.7M KCl-filled micropipettes of 10-20MΩ impedance were inserted under direct vision into the cochlear nerve of cats free of middle ear disease, and anaesthetised with sodium pentobarbitone (30mg/kg). Mean blood pressure, body temperature and end-tidal CO_2 concentration were kept within normal limits. Sound stimuli were applied to the dissected external auditory meatus, under closed bulla conditions, by a closed-field condenser-microphone driver system. Sound levels are expressed in dB SPL at the tympanic membrane as measured by a calibrated probe tube microphone.

The threshold of the gross cochlear action potential in response to short tone pips was measured as a function of tone frequency throughout the experiment, to ensure that the condition of the cochlea was healthy and stable.

The frequencies of two primary tones (50ms duration, 5ms rise/fall, simultaneously presented every 130ms) were selected so that one of the CDT's was situated at the neurone's CF. The level of one primary was kept constant while that of the other (that nearest the CF) was pseudorandomly varied from below the fibre's threshold to about 100dB SPL in 4dB steps by computer, the numbers of discharges evoked by each presentation was stored and the responses to several (8 to 15 depending on stability) repetitions of each level in the pseudorandom sequence were averaged. This procedure was repeated using a number of levels of the fixed tone usually separated by 10dB, and, where possible, at other frequency separations of the primaries. The level of relevant distortion products produced by our sound system was less than -60dB relative to the primaries.

For low frequency fibres, period histograms were obtained from 30s samples of responses to the primaries individually and together. For the histograms the levels of the primaries were within ca. $\pm$ 10dB of the firing-rate threshold for the primaries.

3. RESULTS AND DISCUSSION

The data presented are derived from detailed results obtained from 18 cochlear-nerve fibres in two cats. Figure 1 shows a typical set of results, which were obtained from a single fibre. Fig. 1a and 1c show the discharge rate versus tone level functions for the CF tone and for tones of frequencies f_1 and f_2 as indicated in the Key. Fig. 1b and 1d show the responses when the f_1 and f_2 tones (of Figs. 1a and 1c respectively) were presented simultaneously; the abscissa indicates the level of the tone closest to the CF and the vertical arrows indicate the fixed levels of the second primary tone.

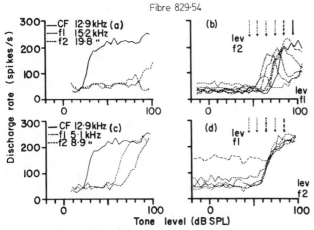

Fig. 1.

a) *Upper CDT at CF*

Figure 1d clearly shows an excitatory response to both primaries. In addition there is some suggestion of two-tone suppression causing lower discharge rates above 70 dB SPL (at least for the dotted and dashed curves). There is, however, no clear indication of a separate response to the CDT.

To determine whether there is indeed a small firing-rate response to the upper CDT, the firing rate for equal level primaries was obtained. From this value the firing rate to the most effective tone (usually f_2) was subtracted. Figure 2 shows a typical example of this measure obtained from 9 fibres with $(f_2 - f_1)/CF=0.2$. Similar results were obtained using a number of primary frequency separations: 0.15 (1 fibre), 0.25 (4 fibres), 0.3 (10 fibres) and 0.35 (2 fibres). A response to the CDT should show up as a firing rate increase but in fact the most noticeable effect is a firing rate decrement presumably reflecting two-tone suppression.

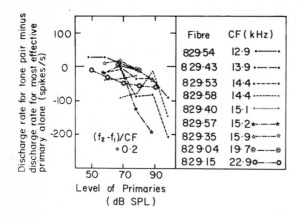

Fibre	CF (kHz)	
829·54	12·9	•———•
8 29·43	13·9	•—·—•
829·53	14·4	•-----•
829·58	14·4	··········
829·40	15·1	············
829·57	15·2	★—·—★
829·35	15·9	☆——☆
829·04	19·7	⊛———⊛
829·15	22·9	o———o

$(f_2-f_1)/CF = 0.2$

Fig. 2.

Three units were investigated for phase-locking to the upper CDT. Figure 3 shows typical period histograms, using equal-level primaries. Figure 3 (upper, middle and lower respectively) show period histograms and for primaries of 70 and 90 dB SPL locked to f_1, f_2 and $2f_2 - f_1$. Typical of all our results, phase-locking to the upper CDT was observed only when there was good phase-locking to both primaries, and might be related to a nonlinear spike-transduction mechanism (Littlefield, 1973).

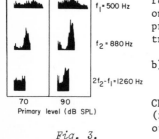

fibre 822·01

Phase-locked to:-
$f_1 = 500$ Hz

$f_2 = 880$ Hz

$2f_2-f_1 = 1260$ Hz

70   90
Primary level (dB SPL)

Fig. 3.

b) *Lower CDT at CF*

Figure 4 shows the effective level of the lower CDT as a function of equal primary levels for $(f_2 - f_1)/CF=0.2$, similar results were obtained for other primary-frequency separations. It shows that the level of the lower CDT increases at a rate lower than that of the primary levels and is typical of other neurophysiological results.

Goldstein (1967) suggested that the level of the lower CDT might be proportional to $a^2b/(a + b)^2$, where a and b represent the amplitudes of f_1 and f_2. This implies that for a fixed b, that the CDT level should be a monotonic function of a. Such monotonic functions were not found psychophysically by Zwicker (1968), Helle (1970) and Smoorenburg (1972). Their **data** were

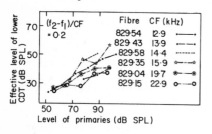

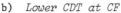

	Fibre	CF (kHz)	
$(f_2-f_1)/CF = 0.2$	829·54	12·9	•———•
	829·43	13·9	•—·—•
	829·35	15·9	★—·—★
	829·04	19·7	★——★
	829·15	22·9	o———o

Level of primaries (dB SPL)

Fig. 4.

similar to the neurophysiological results found in our experiment (Fig. 1b). Smoorenburg observed that the maximum lower CDT occurred at a progressively smaller value of (a-b), as level of f_1 was increased. A similar effect in our data is shown by the progressive deviation of the data in fig. 5 from the 45° line (chain dotted). Smoorenburg suggested that the effect might result from a nonlinear filter mechanism. This explanation would suggest that the effect should become stronger for increased primary-frequency separations, but the converse appears to be the case in our results (Fig. 5).

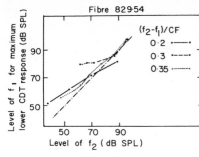

Fibre 82·9·54

$(f_2-f_1)/CF$

0·2 ——·
0·3 - - - -
0·35 ········

Fig. 5.

4. CONCLUSIONS

Our results provide evidence that the upper CDT does not behave in the same way as the lower CDT. The upper CDT is weaker than the lower CDT.

Acknowledgements

We wish to thank Professor E.F. Evans for useful suggestions in planning these experiments and for the use of equipment and computer programs of his design. We are grateful to Ted Evans, Pat Wilson and Graham Sutton for useful suggestions on an earlier draft of this paper. Both authors were supported by the UK Medical Research Council.

REFERENCES

Buunen, T.J.F. and Rhode, W.S. (1978). Responses of fibres in the cat's auditory nerve to the cubic difference tone. *J. Acoust. Soc. Amer.* **64**, 772-781.

Evans, E.F. (1979). Single unit studies of the mammalian auditory nerve. In: *Auditory Investigations: The Scientific and Technological Basis* (H.A. Beagley, ed). pp 324-367. Oxford University Press, Oxford.

Goldstein, J.L. (1967). Auditory nonlinearity. *J. Acoust. Soc. Amer.* **41**, 676-689.

Goldstein, J.L. and Kiang, N.Y-S. (1968). Neural correlates of the aural combination tone $2f_1-f_2$. *Proc. IEEE* **56**, 981-992.

Helle, R. (1970). Amplitude und Phase des im Gehörs gebildeten Differenztones dritter Ordnung. *Acustica* **22**, 74-87.

Littlefield, W.M. (1973). Investigation of the linear range of the peripheral auditory system. D.Sc. Dissertation. Washington University, St. Louis, Mo.

Smoorenburg, G.F. (1972). Combination tones and their origin. *J. Acoust. Soc. Amer.* **52**, 615-632.

Smoorenburg, G.F., Gibson, M.M., Kitzes, L.M., Rose, J.E., and Hind, J.E. (1976). Correlates of combination tones observed in the responses of neurons in the anteroventral cochlear nucleus of the cat. *J. Acoust. Soc. Amer.* **59**, 945-962.

Zureck, P.M., and Sachs, R.M. (1979). Combination tones at frequencies greater than the primary tones. *Science* **205**, 600-602.

Zwicker, E. (1955). Der ungewöhnliche Amplitudengang der nichtlinearen Verzerrungen des Ohres. *Acustica* **5**, 67-74.

Zwicker, E. (1968). Der kubische Differenzton und die Erregung des Gehörs. *Acustica* **20**, 206-209.

PSYCHOPHYSICAL TUNING CURVES FOR THE DIFFERENCE TONES f_2-f_1 AND $2f_1-f_2$

M. Hoke, B. Lütkenhöner and E. Bappert

*Experimental Audiology, Ear, Nose and Throat Clinic,
University of Münster, Federal Republic of Germany*

1. INTRODUCTION

The hypothesis that the nonlinear distortion products f_2-f_1 and $2f_1-f_2$ are generated mechanically and, consequently, propagate mechanically along the cochlear partition, had been controversial for years. More recent findings from Kim *et al* (1979) obtained from auditory nerve fibres revealed that the spatio-temporal distribution patterns of the distortion products f_2-f_1 and $2f_1-f_2$ resemble those generated by a single-tone stimulus of corresponding frequency. A correspondence between psychophysical tuning curves (PTC) for difference tones and single test tones of the same frequency would further support Kim's findings.

PTCs for single test tones have been determined in human observers by several authors (e.g. Houtgast, 1973; Zwicker, 1974; Vogten, 1974; Shannon, 1976; Moore, 1978; Verschuure, 1978; Pickles, 1979; O'Malley and Feth, 1979). They generally resemble the tuning curves obtained from auditory nerve fibres (FTC). PTCs obtained with a simultaneous masking paradigm are less steep than those obtained with any forward masking paradigm (Moore, 1978; Harris and Dallos, 1979), a finding which is attributed to an interaction between masker and test tone in terms of two-tone suppression (Shannon, 1976) and lateral inhibition (Houtgast, 1973), resp. According to O'Malley and Feth (1979) and Moore (1978), the latter PTCs seem to be sharper tuned than FTCs of auditory nerve fibres.

Formby and Sachs (1979) recently reported about investigations of PTCs for a single test tone of 1200 Hz and the difference tones f_2-f_1 and $2f_1-f_2$ of corresponding frequency. They found that the low-frequency slopes of the PTCs were similar under all stimulus conditions, whereas the high-frequency slopes were sometimes contaminated by interactions with the masker.

2. METHOD

This pilot study was done using a simultaneous masking technique. A forward masking paradigm would be more advantageous as it avoids interactions between masker and two-tone stimulus in terms of suppression, as well as the generation of unwanted additional combination tones. Forward masking, however, is not applicable because $\sim$ 30 msec after the termination of the masker signal, the masking drops rapidly whereas the pitch sensation (the only distinctive feature of the difference tone) requires a presentation time of $\sim$ 150 msec. The subjects listened to the stimuli, presented via a TDH 39 earphone, in a sound proof room. Prior to each session we made sure that distortion products for any frequency combination were not present in the acoustic signal.

The higher one of the primary tones and the single test tone, resp., were presented pulsatingly. With respect to frequency, primary tones have been chosen such that the difference tone to be masked was separated as much as possible from the primaries, and that it was the lowest and loudest one (except of those rare conditions where difference tones between masker and one of the primary tones occured). This experimental paradigm made it easier for the subject to listen to the respective aural difference tone. The level of the discrete masker frequencies has been determined using the Békésy up-and-down tracking method (2dB/sec) with recognition of pitch as the decision criterion.

We determined PTCs for single test tones of the frequencies of 750, 1000, 1500 and 2000 Hz, as well as PTCs for aural difference tones both f_2-f_1 and $2f_1-f_2$ of the same frequencies. Three different combinations of the primary frequencies were tested for either difference tone and each difference frequency.

The level of the single test tone was adjusted to 20 dB HL which for the listener equals almost 20 dB SPL for each test frequency. The level of the two-tone stimulus was adjusted to achieve the same sensation level of 20 dB for the difference tone.

3. RESULTS

Fig. 1 shows PTCs for single test tones and difference tones with pitch recognition as the decision criterion. The results exhibit no significant difference for the PTCs of both difference tones. As a general trend, the sharp-

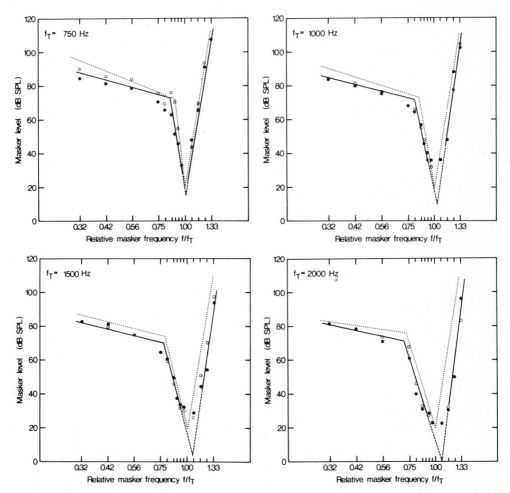

Fig. 1. Psychoacoustic tuning curves for a single test tone (dotted line) and for difference tones (solid lines) of four different frequencies, obtained with a simultaneous masking paradigm. Circles represent mean values for three different frequency combinations to generate $2f_1-f_2$; dots represent the corresponding measures for f_2-f_1. Decision criterion: Recognition of pitch.

ness of tuning *increases* progressively with decreasing test frequency, a feature that could be reproduced in repeated sessions. Compared with the single test tone condition, the PTCs of difference tones show systematic deviations which are more pronounced with increasing test frequency: the tips of the PTCs of difference tones become rounded, whereas the low- and high-frequency slopes of the sharply tuned part are shifted to lower and higher frequencies, resp. In addition, the slope of the high-frequency part seems to become slightly steeper compared to the single test tone condition. Approximating a straight line to the high- and low-frequency slopes of the sharply tuned part, the intersection of both lines is monotonically shifted towards lower level and higher frequency, with increasing difference frequency.

Fig. 2 shows the findings obtained for the four test frequencies in a survey, both for single test tones (left) and difference tones (right).

4. DISCUSSION

a) Tuning of PTCs as a function of test frequency

It is surprising and inconsistent with almost all published data that the tuning increases with decreasing frequency rather than with increasing frequency. Only Moore (1978) published certain similar results showing an increase in tuning of PTCs determined in a forward masking situation, with decreasing the test frequency from 6 to 1 kHz, whereas tuning degrades in a simultaneous masking situation. How can we interpret this phenomenon? The following hypothesis shall be proposed. Unlike the usual decision criterion in the determination of PTCs which is the detection of the test tone, the criterion consistently used throughout this investigation was the recognition of pitch of the test tone, irrespective whether single test tones or difference tones were tested. Recognition of pitch, however, is a performance of higher levels of the auditory system. Prior to the pitch recognition, the acoustic information is subject to an additional filtering. A comparison made between PTCs obtained with either criterion clearly shows a considerable increase in tuning for the pitch criterion.

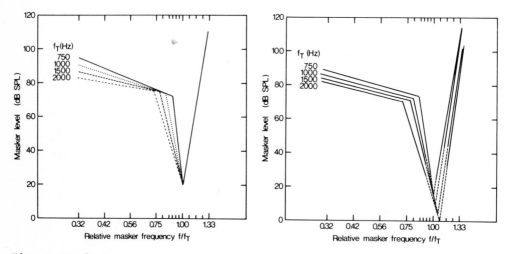

Fig. 2. Psychoacoustic tuning curves (PTC) for single test tones (left) and for the corresponding difference tones (right), taken from fig. 1. The extrapolated tip of the PTCs of difference tones (intersection of the straight lines approximated to the low- and high-frequency slopes) shifts with higher difference frequency towards lower intensity and higher frequency.

280

b) *Shift of the intersection of the straight lines fitted to both slopes*

The shift of the extrapolated tip in direction of lower level and higher frequency is a very consistent finding. The degree of shift increases with increasing difference frequency because the separation between eliciting primary frequencies and difference frequency decreases. This increases the suppression effect of the masker on the primary tones and vice versa, diminishing the difference tone amplitude. Hence, the shape of the resulting PTC is deformed because the increased masker level suppresses the level of the primary tones which reduces the level of the difference tone and shifts the PTC to lower intensity. On the other hand, decreasing the masker level while the masker frequency approaches the test frequency exhibits the opposite effect. This phenomenon cannot be separated by a possible unmasking accompanied with the interaction between primary tone and masker (Houtgast, 1973; O'Malley and Feth, 1979). The shift of the tip of PTCs of single test tones with lower test tone levels to higher frequencies is a well-known finding inherent in simultaneous masking situations (e.g. Vogten, 1973; Moore, 1978). Hence, the described differences in the shape of the PTCs of difference tones can be explained in the same manner.

5. CONCLUSIONS

The results obtained in this pilot study reveal a similar behaviour of single test tones and difference tones when a PTC is determined. Differences found between both stimulus conditions are due to two-tone suppression and unmasking inherent in simultaneous masking techniques. The findings support the above mentioned hypothesis about origin and behaviour of difference tones.

REFERENCES

Formby, C. and Sachs, R.M. (1979). Psychophysical tuning curves for aural combination tones. *J.Acoust.Soc.Am.* 65, S41.

Harris, D.M. and Dallos, P. (1979). Forward masking of auditory nerve fibre responses. *J.Neurophysiol.* 42, 1083-1107.

Houtgast, T. (1972). Psychophysical evidence for lateral inhibition in hearing. *J.Acoust.Soc.Am.* 51, 1885-1894.

Houtgast, T. (1973). Psychophysical experiments on "tuning curves" and "two-tone inhibition". *Acoustica* 29, 168-179.

Kim, D.O., Siegel, J.H. and Molnar, C.E. (1979). Cochlear nonlinear phenomena in two-tone responses. In: *Models of the auditory system and related signal processing techniques* (M. Hoke and E. de Boer, eds.). *Scand.Audiol. Suppl.* 9, 63-82.

Moore, B.C.J. (1978). Psychophysical tuning curves measured in simultaneous and forward masking. *J.Acoust. Soc.Am.* 63, 524-532.

O'Malley, H. and Feth, L.L. (1979). Relationship between psychophysical tuning curves and suppression. *J.Acoust.Soc.Am.* 66, 1075-1087.

Pickles, J.O. (1979). Psychophysical frequency resolution in the cat as determined by simultaneous masking and its relation to auditory-nerve resolution. *J.Acoust.Soc.Am.* 66, 1725-1732.

Shannon, R.V. (1976). Two-tone unmasking and suppression in a forward-masking situation. *J.Acoust.Soc.Am.* 59, 1460-1470.

Verschuure, J. (1978). Auditory excitation patterns. *Doctoral Thesis. Delft.*

Vogten, L.L.M. (1974). Pure-tone masking; a new result from a new method. In: *Facts and models in hearing* (E. Zwicker and E. Terhardt, eds). pp 142-156. Springer, Berlin and New York.

Zwicker, E. (1974). On a psychoacoustical equivalent of tuning curves. In: *Facts and models in hearing* (E. Zwicker and E. Terhardt, eds). pp 132-141. Springer, Berlin and New York.

ADDENDUM: DIFFERENCE OF THE SHAPE OF PSYCHOACOUSTIC TUNING CURVES, DEPENDING ON THE DECISION CRITERION

M. Hoke
Experimental Audiology, Ear, Nose and Throat Clinic, University of Münster, Federal Republic of Germany

As reported in the above paper, a difference exists in the sharpness of psychoacoustic tuning curves (PTC), depending on the decision criterion used in a simultaneous masking paradigm: detection of the test tone or recognition of pitch. The left panel of Fig. 1 demonstrates the findings, obtained for a test tone of 1000 Hz and 20 dB HL, in a normal hearing listener (M.H.). With the recognition of pitch as the decision criterion, the slope of the low-frequency skirt of the sharply tuned part is considerably steeper, whereas there is only a moderate increase in sharpness of the high-frequency slope.

The right panel of Fig. 1 shows the corresponding results obtained from a hearing-impaired listener (J.G.) suffering from a moderate sensory hearing loss. Whereas the PTC, obtained with the detection of the test tone as the decision criterion, shows an almost total deterioration of tuning (cf. Wightman *et al*, 1977; Zwicker and Schorn, 1978), the PTC determined with the recognition of pitch as the decision criterion again shows a considerable increase in tuning, especially of the low-frequency skirt of the sharply tuned part. Note that, in the vicinity of the test tone, even a subthreshold masker can disturb the recognition of pitch.

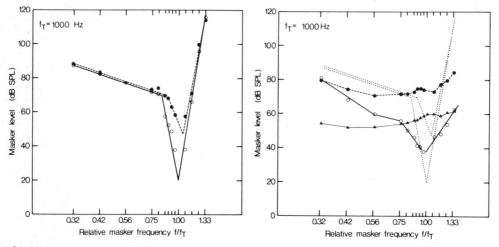

Fig. 1. PTCs for a single test tone of 1000 Hz and 20 dB SL, determined in a normal-hearing (left panel) and a hearing-impaired listener (right panel; dotted: normal measures for comparison; triangles: hearing threshold), with a simultaneous masking paradigm. The symbols represent the means of the data obtained from one listener in three different sessions. Decision criterion was the detection of the test tone (dots) and the recognition of pitch (circles), resp.

REFERENCES

Wightman, F., McGee, T. and Kramer, M. (1977). Factors influencing frequency selectivity in normal and hearing-impaired listeners. In: *Psychophysics and Physiology of Hearing* (E.F. Evans and J.P. Wilson, eds). pp. 295-306. Academic Press, London.
Zwicker, E. and Schorn, K. (1978). Psychoacoustical tuning curves in audiology. *Audiology* 17, 120-140.

Section IV
Intensity Coding and Dynamic Range

An essential and interesting question in auditory research is the neural coding of intensity information. It seems, among other things, to have relevance to the perception of loudness. This topic is all the more intriguing because the statistically determined dynamic range of individual auditory nerve fibres seems to be rather limited. The physiological and psychophysical bases for these matters, such as suppression effects, phase locking of auditory nerve fibres, and the dynamic versus static response of fibres, are discussed. The study of responses to multi-component or wide - band stimuli is particularly provocative in this context, because the widening of neural excitation patterns cannot be used to code intensity, contrary to what is conceivable for narrow-band signals like pure tones.

SUPPRESSION EFFECTS IN THE RESPONSES
OF AUDITORY-NERVE FIBERS TO BROADBAND STIMULI

M. B. Sachs, E. D. Young, T. B. Schalk and C. P. Bernardin

*Department of Biomedical Engineering, Johns Hopkins University
School of Medicine, Baltimore, Maryland 21205 USA*

1.   INTRODUCTION

Two-tone rate suppression refers to a reduction in average discharge rate
to one tone by the simultaneous presentation of a second tone (Sachs and Abbas,
1976); *two-tone synchrony suppression* is a reduction in the phase-locked response to one tone by presentation of another tone (Rose *et al*, 1974).   Properties of two-tone suppression have been related to underlying cochlear mechanisms both by direct measurement (Rhode, 1977; Sellick and Russell, 1979) and
by mathematical models (Hall, 1977).   There has been some uncertainty, however,
as to what role (if any) nonlinear effects such as suppression play in the
shaping of auditory-nerve fiber responses to more complex stimuli (Møller,
1977; Evans, 1978).   In this paper we will present evidence that suppression
does have a very important role in the auditory-nerve encoding of both band-
limited noise and steady-state vowels.

2.   SOME PROPERTIES OF RESPONSES TO ONE- AND TWO-TONE STIMULI

The effects of suppression on responses to complex stimuli will be illustrated best by examining the growth of response (either average rate or some
measure of synchrony) as a function of stimulus level and then comparing that
function with similar functions for two-tone stimuli.   Before discussing results for complex stimuli, we will therefore review some properties of rate
versus level functions and synchrony versus level functions for one- and two-
tone stimuli.

Liberman (1978) and Kim and Molnar (1979) have recently demonstrated that
auditory-nerve fibers may be divided into two or three populations on the
basis of spontaneous rates.   Units with spontaneous rates greater than 18 per
second (high spontaneous group) have low thresholds to characteristic frequency (CF) tones which are within 5 dB of the average high spontaneous threshold in any CF region.   Units with spontaneous rates between .5 and 18 per
second are on the average 10 dB less sensitive than the high spontaneous
units.   Thresholds increase dramatically as spontaneous rate falls below 0.5
spikes per second.   Liberman therefore divides the remaining units into low
(less than .5) and medium (between .5 and 18) spontaneous rate groups.

Discharge rate versus level functions for CF tones are monotonic increasing up to a saturation rate (Sachs and Abbas, 1976).   Figure 1 shows that the
shapes of these functions are related to spontaneous rate (and hence to CF
threshold).   The right column shows typical rate level functions for (from top
to bottom) high, medium and low spontaneous units.   One important measure of
the shapes of these functions is dynamic range, defined as the range, in dB,
over which rate increases from $R_{SP}+.1(R_{SAT}-R_{SP})$ to $R_{SP}+.8(R_{SAT}-R_{SP})$; R_{SP} is
the spontaneous rate and R_{SAT} is the maximum rate produced by a CF tone.   The
dashed lines in Fig. 1 show the dynamic ranges of the three units.   For units
of the same CF (in the same cat) dynamic range is an increasing function of
threshold and consequently a decreasing function of spontaneous rate (Schalk

and Sachs, 1980). This relationship between dynamic range and spontaneous rate is shown on the left in Fig. 1 which contains histograms of dynamic ranges for fibers divided into the three spontaneous groups used by Liberman.

Abbas and Sachs (1976) have studied a two-tone rate suppression situation which is directly relevant to the considerations of this paper. They presented an excitatory tone at fiber CF and a suppression tone at a frequency either above or below CF; the suppressing-tone level was fixed relative to the CF tone level and slightly higher. Rate was measured as a function of the overall sound level of the two-tone stimulus. This condition

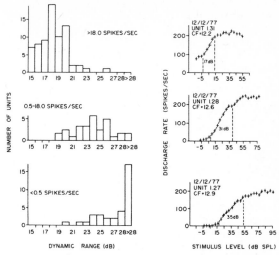

Fig. 1. *Histograms of dynamic ranges for CF tones grouped by spontaneous rates and a typical rate-level function for each group.*

is qualitatively similar to that in which the overall level of a spectrally complex stimulus is varied while spectral shape is kept constant. Figure 2 shows examples of the behavior seen with two tones. Rate to CF tones presented alone (circles) and rate to a two-tone stimulus (triangles) are plotted versus stimulus level. The abscissa gives the level of the CF tone (top line) as well as the level of the suppressing tone (bottom line; always a fixed number of dB more intense than the CF tone). For suppressing tones above CF (right side of Fig. 2) the rate-level function for the two-tone stimulus is similar to the functions for the CF tone alone, but is shifted to the right. The slope is slightly less for the two-tone case; at high levels a two-tone stimulus produces the same saturation rate as the CF tone presented alone. Thus, the amount of suppression, as measured by the difference in evoked rate for one- and two-tone stimuli, decreases as overall level increases in this case. The situation is quite different for suppressors below CF (Fig. 2, left) where the two-tone curves are frequently nonmonotonic. As the levels of the two components are raised together, rate first increases along the same curve as the rate to CF tone alone; at levels about 30 dB above threshold, the two-tone rate decreases. It is clear from Fig. 2 that effects of two-tone suppression for the suppressor below CF become stronger as sound level is increased. These differences between the functions for high- and low-frequency suppressors will be useful in identifying suppression effects with broadband stimuli.

Two-tone synchrony suppression has been studied by a number of investigators (Rose *et al*, 1974; Johnson, 1974; Arthur, 1976). In this paper we shall characterize the synchrony of a unit to any component of a multicomponent periodic stimulus in terms of the period histogram of the unit's response to that stimulus. The *synchronized rate* to a given component is defined as the amplitude

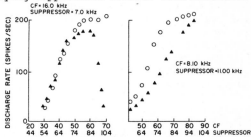

Fig. 2. *Rate-level functions for one- (o's) and two- (▲'s) tone stimuli.*

of that component in the discrete
Fourier transform of the period
histogram. This number has the
dimensions of spikes/second; it
reflects both the degree of phase
locking to the component and the
average discharge rate of the unit
(Kim and Molnar, 1979; Young and
Sachs, 1979).

Figure 3 shows an example of
the dependence of synchronized rate
to each component of a two-tone
stimulus on the overall level of
that stimulus. As in Fig. 2., one
tone is at fiber CF; the suppressing tone frequency is less than CF
and its level is fixed relative to
the CF tone level (suppressor 15 dB
greater). Synchronized rate to the
CF alone is shown by X's, to the CF

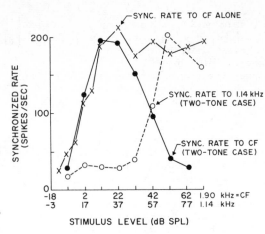

Fig. 3. *Synchronized rate versus level
functions.*

in the two-tone combination by closed circles and to the suppressor by open
circles. At low overall levels of the two-tone stimulus, the synchronized
rate to the CF tone approximates the value for the CF presented alone. At
about the level where synchronized rate to the suppressor begins to increase,
the rate locked to the CF in the two-tone stimulus begins to decline. As
level is increased further, synchronized rate to the CF ultimately decreases
to the noise level of the measurements. At high levels, this unit's response
is dominated by the low frequency suppressor. The nonmonotonic behavior of
synchronized responses to CF tones in the presence of lower frequency suppressors will prove to be a key sign of two-tone synchrony suppression effects in
responses to vowels.

3. RATE SUPPRESSION IN RESPONSES TO BANDLIMITED NOISE

In Section 2 we have seen that
there are strong differences in the
characteristics of two-tone rate
suppression for suppressing frequencies above and below fiber CF. In
order to relate these differences
between high- and low-frequency suppressors to responses to noise, we
have measured rate-level functions
for bands of noise which are either
centered above CF and have their
low-frequency cutoff at CF or are
centered below CF and have their
high frequency cutoff at CF.

Figure 4 shows rate-level functions for broadband noise centered
above CF (Δ's). The low-cutoff frequencies are set at fiber CF and the
bandwidths are equal to unit CF.
Data are illustrated for four fibers
from one cat with CFs in the range
9.5 to 10.5 kHz. CF rate level functions are also shown (+'s) and are

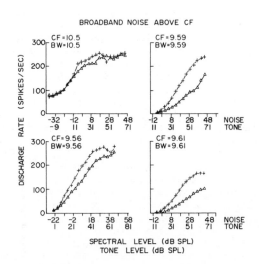

Fig. 4. *Rate-level functions for
broadband noise above CF.*

arbitrarily placed on the abscissa as though their energy were spread over a 200 Hz band, with a spectral level given by the noise abscissa. (The sound pressure level of the tone is thus always 23 dB greater than the noise spectral level.) The upper left graph shows a typical high spontaneous unit response; the lower left graph shows a medium spontaneous unit; the two right graphs are from low spontaneous units. For all but the high spontaneous unit, the noise rate-level functions are considerably less steep than the tone functions. For the high spontaneous unit, the noise function deviates from that for the tones at levels greater than 10-15 dB above threshold. The dynamic range of the noise functions are all greater than those for tones. Clearly the differences between

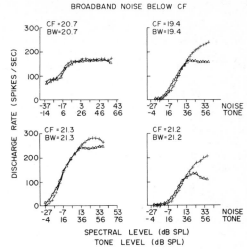

Fig. 5. Rate-level functions for broadband noise below CF.

dynamic ranges for noise and tones are greatest for low spontaneous units and least for high spontaneous units. It is not clear from the data in Fig. 4 whether the noise produces a saturation rate as great as that produced by the CF tone. However, when we have been able to drive a low spontaneous unit into saturation with broadband noise, the saturation rates to the noise and tones have been equal (Schalk and Sachs, 1980).

Rate-level functions for broadband noise centered below CF are shown in Fig. 5 (Δ's). The high-cutoff frequencies are set at fiber CF and the bandwidths are equal to CF. An example of a high spontaneous unit response is shown in the upper left plot. The noise rate-level function is virtually indistinguishable from the CF tone response (+'s). This is typical of high spontaneous units when noise is centered below CF. The dynamic range for noise below CF is approximately the same as that for CF tones. In the lower left plot an example from a medium spontaneous rate unit is shown. Two examples from low spontaneous rate units are shown at the right. At low to moderate levels the curves are quite similar. However, at spectral levels above about 13 dB the noise functions appear either to plateau at rates less than the saturation rate produced by the CF tone or to decrease with increasing spectral level.

It has been shown elsewhere that for large bandwidths, discharge rate is a decreasing function of bandwidth if spectral level is held constant (Ruggero, 1973; Schalk and Sachs, 1980). Thus, addition of energy in bands farther from CF suppresses the responses to energy in bands near CF. The properties of this suppression are strikingly similar to those of two-tone suppression. In particular, the differences in rate-level functions for suppressing tones above and below CF are reflected in differences in rate-level functions for noise centered above and below CF. As in the two-tone case with suppressors above CF, rate-level functions for noise centered above CF increase monotonically toward the same saturation rate as that produced by CF tones (Fig. 4). For bands of noise centered below CF, on the other hand, rate-level functions for low and medium spontaneous units can either plateau at rates less than the CF saturation rate or they can be nonmonotonic (Fig. 5). The similarities of the properties of rate-level functions for noise and two-tone stimuli leads us to conclude that the mechanisms underlying suppression in the two cases are the same.

    In all of our plots which compare noise and CF tone rate-level functions, the amount by which the rate to noise is less than that to CF tones at any spectral level gives an indication of the strength of the suppression mechanism. From Figs. 4 and 5 the apparent effects of suppression are strongest in the low spontaneous units and weakest in the high spontaneous units. We must be careful in interpreting this result, however. Notice in Fig. 5, for example, that the effects of suppression (the plateau in the noise functions) begin at a spectral level of about 13 dB for the medium and low spontaneous units. The high spontaneous unit, on the other hand, saturates at a spectral level of -7 dB. It may well be that this saturation obscures the underlying suppression for these high spontaneous, low threshold units. Indeed, our noise data are well fit by a simple extension of the phenomenological model we have published previously (Sachs and Abbas, 1976). In this model, the input to the final saturating stage is attenuated by a factor which accounts for the suppression. The dependencies on spontaneous rate (or threshold) shown in Figs. 1, 4 and 5 are well accounted for by assuming that the attenuation factor (suppression) is the same for all units of the same CF; only the excitatory threshold of the saturating nonlinearity need vary from unit to unit. Because low threshold, high spontaneous units are well into saturation at levels where the attenuation (suppression) becomes important, they are not affected by it.

4. RATE SUPPRESSION IN RESPONSES TO STEADY-STATE VOWELS

    One simple notion of how vowels are encoded at the level of the auditory nerve is that formant peaks in the acoustic spectrum of the vowel would result in peaks in a profile of discharge rate versus CF across the population of auditory-nerve fibers. These peaks would occur at places on the basilar membrane where CF corresponds to formant frequencies of the vowel. We refer to this as the "place-rate" scheme. We have shown that the shapes of such rate-versus-CF profiles are determined by a number of factors including auditory-nerve tuning, rate saturation and two-tone suppression (Sachs and Young, 1979). In this section we will illustrate the role played by two-tone suppression. Figure 6A shows the spectrum of a synthesized steady-state vowel /ε/, compensated to account for the transfer function of the human external ear (principally a resonance near 3 kHz). The first 3 formants of the vowel are .512, 1.792 and 2.432 kHz and the spectrum shown was measured at the eardrum of the cat. Figure 6B shows the average value of normalized rate in response to this vowel, plotted versus characteristic frequency for the sample of 269 units recorded in this cat. Normalized rate is obtained by subtracting spontaneous rate from the total rate and dividing by saturation rate minus spontaneous rate. The average curves shown are the result

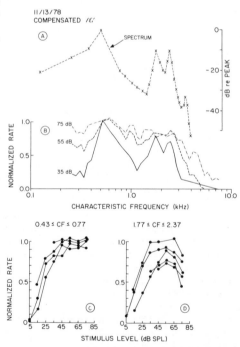

Fig. 6. Spectrum (A) and rate profiles (B) for compensated /ε/. (C) and (D): Sample rate-level functions from which (B) was calculated.

of a moving window average of data from units over a CF range of 0.25 octaves; a triangular window was used. Plots are shown for three levels of the vowel. The rate profile for 35 dB shows clear peaks in the region of the first three formants of /ε/. At 55 dB, peaks can still be distinguished at the first formant frequency and in the region of the second and third formants. At this level the peak near the first formant has reached saturation (normalized rate equal to about 1.0). This saturation is shown in rate versus level plots for individual units with CFs near the first formant in Fig. 6C. As level is increased, those units with CFs between the first and second formants begin to respond with greater rates (compare the 35, 55 and 75 dB curves in the frequency region between the first and second formants in Fig. 6B). As these intermediate units increase their discharge rates between 35 and 55 dB, units in the second/third formant peaks show only a slight increase in rate. Between 55 and 75 dB the height of the second/third formant peaks actually declines slightly, while rates of units with CFs between the formants continue to grow. The result is the disappearance of formant peaks at this level. Rate-versus-level functions for many units with CFs in the region of the second and third formants (Fig. 6D) are nonmonotonic. That is, rate increases with level up to about 55 dB SPL and then declines. This rate-level behavior is strikingly like that observed in *two-tone suppression* for suppressing tones below CF (Fig. 2) and for noise bands centered below CF (Fig. 5). Units with CFs between the first and second formant frequencies do not appear to show this nonmonotonic behavior (see Sachs and Young, 1979). The result of the nonmonotonic behavior of rate functions in the second and third formant region is that average rate at those frequencies is greater than average rate in the region between the second and third formants at low levels, whereas the opposite is true at high levels. In an earlier paper (Sachs and Young, 1979) we concluded that the mechanism of two-tone suppression is the same as the mechanism underlying the nonmonotonic rate-level functions of units in the second/third formant peak. This conclusion was based on the qualitative and quantitative similarities between two-tone rate plots (Fig. 2) and vowel rate plots (Fig. 6D). Thus, in terms of the place-rate scheme, the effect of two-tone suppression is not to sharpen the formant-related peaks as had been suggested (e.g., Houtgast, 1974), but rather to hasten the loss of a separate peak in the second/third formant region.

5. SYNCHRONY SUPPRESSION IN RESPONSES TO STEADY-STATE VOWELS

The loss of formant peaks in rate profiles led us to examine how spectral information about vowels might be encoded in fine temporal properties of auditory-nerve fiber responses rather than in average rate. We have previously discussed in great detail how the phase-locked responses to vowels, as measured by period histograms, are distributed across populations of auditory-nerve fibers (Young and Sachs, 1979). Period histograms for responses to

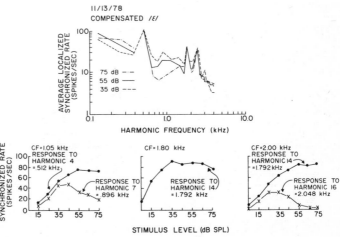

Fig. 7. Average localized synchronized rate vs. CF and typical synchronized rate vs. level functions.

vowels were computed for a large population of fibers in the same cat. From
Fourier transforms of these histograms, synchronized rate was extracted for
each component of the stimulus. The vowels used had a pitch period of 128 Hz,
so that all components were harmonics of 128 Hz. The top of Fig. 7 summarizes
the population response for the compensated /ε/ used on 11/13/78. The plots
show the synchronized rate to each harmonic of the stimulus averaged over
units with CFs within +0.5 octave of the harmonic's frequency. This *averaged
localized synchronized rate* is plotted as a function of the harmonic frequency
in Fig. 7. In these plots, presumed distortion products have been removed
according to an algorithm given previously (see Young and Sachs, 1979). The
plots show the average synchronized response at a particular harmonic of the
stimulus in the region of the cochlea where response to that frequency is expected to be maximal. As such, they reflect a combination of rate (the higher
the average rate, the higher the synchronized rate in spikes/sec), place (only
those units with CFs near the harmonic are averaged) and periodicity information.

The similarity of these plots to the spectrum of this vowel is clear.
Notice particularly peaks at the first three vowel formants remain prominent
even at the highest level; at this level there are no peaks in the rate profile (Fig. 6). Close examination of Fig. 7 reveals that suppression of responses to harmonics which are not related to the formants is crucial in maintaining the formant peaks in this neural representation of the vowel. The
average localized synchronized rate to these harmonics is less at 75 dB than it
is at 35 dB. The suppression of responses to these harmonics allows the main-
tenance of local maxima at the formant frequencies. The suppression is shown
at the single unit level in the lower three graphs of Fig. 7. The unit on the
left has a CF near the seventh harmonic of the vowel. The response of this
unit to harmonic seven contributes to the seventh harmonic point in the average localized synchronized rate plot. Its seventh harmonic response (X's)
grows with level to about 45 dB SPL and then decreases at higher levels. The
response of this unit is dominated by the lower frequency fourth harmonic
(first formant frequency) shown by the filled circles. The unit in the center
graph has a CF near harmonic 14 (second formant frequency); its response to
harmonic 14 (filled circles) increases with level up to about 35 dB SPL and
remains approximately constant at higher levels. The unit in the right graph
has a CF near harmonic 16, midway between the second and third formants. Its
response to harmonic 16 contributes to the harmonic 16 (2.048 kHz) point in
the upper graph; this response (X's) increases up to 25 dB SPL and decreases
with level above 35 dB SPL. The response of this unit is dominated by responses to the second formant (harmonic 14) shown by the filled circles. If
the growth of the responses to harmonics seven and 16 (and other non-formant
harmonics) seen at low levels were to continue at high levels, their responses
would become comparable to the responses to the formants and obliterate the
formant peaks shown so clearly in the top graph.

Synchrony grows monotonically with sound level for single-tone stimuli
(Fig. 3; Arthur, 1976; Johnson, 1974; Rose *et al*, 1974). Thus, the nonmonotonic growth of synchronization to harmonics not related to formants in Fig.
7 must reflect suppression by formant frequency energy. This nonmonotonic
growth of responses to near-CF frequencies in the presence of lower-frequency
tones is strikingly similar to the behavior seen in similar two-tone synchrony
suppression situations (Fig. 3).

6. CONCLUSIONS

Our results show that for both bandlimited noise and periodic vowels,
cochlear frequency analysis at high sound levels is highly nonlinear. Effects
similar to two-tone rate suppression and two-tone synchrony suppression play

a major role in shaping the responses to these stimuli.

Supported by a grant from the National Institute of Neurological and Communicative Disorders and Stroke

REFERENCES

Abbas, P. J. and Sachs, M. B. (1976). Two-tone suppression in auditory-nerve fibers; extension of a stimulus-response relationship. *J. Acoust. Soc. Am.* 59, 112-122.

Arthur, R. M. (1976). Harmonic analysis of two-tone discharge patterns in cochlear nerve fibers. *Biol. Cybernetics* 22, 21-31.

Evans, E. F. (1978). Place- and time coding of frequency in the peripheral auditory system: some physiological pros and cons. *Audiology* 17, 369-420.

Hall, J. L. (1977). Two-tone suppression in a nonlinear model of the basilar membrane. *J. Acoust. Soc. Am.* 61, 802-810.

Houtgast, R. (1974). Auditory analysis of vowel-like sounds. *Acustica* 31, 320-324.

Johnson, D. H. (1974). *The Response of Single Auditory-nerve Fibers in the Cat to Single Tones: Synchrony and Average Discharge Rate* (Thesis, M.I.T., Cambridge, Mass.)

Kim, D. O. and Molnar, C. E. (1979). A population study of cochlear nerve fibers: comparison of spatial distributions of average-rate and phase-locking measures of responses to single tones. *J. Neurophysiol.* 42, 16-30.

Liberman, M. C. (1978). Auditory-nerve response from cats raised in a low-noise chamber. *J. Acoust. Soc. Am.* 63, 442-455.

Møller, A. R. (1977). Frequency selectivity of single auditory-nerve fibers in response to broadband noise stimuli. *J. Acoust. Soc. Am.* 62, 135-142.

Rhode, W. S. (1977). Some observations on two-tone interaction measured with the Mossbauer effect. In: *Psychophysics and Physiology of Hearing* (E. F. Evans and J. P. Wilson, eds), Academic Press, London.

Rose, J. E., Kitzes, L. M., Gibson, M. M. and Hind, J. E. (1974). Observations on phase-sensitive neurons of anteroventral cochlear nucleus of the cat: nonlinearity of cochlear output. *J. Neurophysiol.* 37, 218-253.

Ruggero, M. A. (1973). Responses to noise of auditory-nerve fibers in the squirrel monkey. *J. Neurophysiol.* 36, 569-587.

Sachs, M. B. and Abbas, P. J. (1976). Phenomenological model for two-tone suppression. *J. Acoust. Soc. Am.* 60, 1157-1163.

Sachs, M. B. and Young, E. D. (1979). Encoding of steady-state vowels in the auditory nerve: representation in terms of discharge rate. *J. Acoust. Soc. Am.* 66, 470-479.

Schalk, T. B. and Sachs, M. B. (1980). Nonlinearities in auditory-nerve fiber responses to bandlimited noise. *J. Acoust. Soc. Am.* 67, 903-913.

Sellick, P. M. and Russell, F. J. (1979). Two-tone suppression in cochlear haircells. *Hearing Res.* 1, 227-236.

Young, E. D. and Sachs, M. B. (1979). Representation of steady-state vowels in the temporal aspects of the discharge patterns of populations of auditory-nerve fibers. *J. Acoust. Soc. Am.* 66, 1381-1403.

COMMENT ON: "Suppression effects in the responses of auditory-nerve fibers to broadband stimuli" (M.B. Sachs, E.D. Young, T.B. Schalk and C.P. Bernardin)

R.S. Tyler

M.R.C. Institute of Hearing Research,
University Park, University of Nottingham.

We have observed a psychophysical nonmonotonic growth of masking that is remarkably similar to the physiological nonmonotonic growth of synchronization described by Sachs *et al.*   We used vowel maskers and tonal signals to determine vowel masking patterns with simultaneous masking (SM) and pulsation-threshold (PT) techniques (Tyler and Lindblom, 1980).   In one parametric manipulation of vowel level, the vowel /e/ (F_0 = 120 Hz, F_1 = 375 Hz, F_2 = 2060 Hz, F_3 = 2560 Hz, F_4 = 3400 Hz) was presented at 55.5, 70.5 and 85.5 dB SPL.   The signal thresholds in the region of the higher formants as a function of frequency (in Bark) are shown in Figures 1 and 2 for the SM and PT techniques.   The formants appear more clearly defined in the PT patterns than in the SM patterns.   Note the striking nonlinear increase in signal thresholds in the PT patterns when the vowel level is increased.   This may be a manifestation of the suppression of the F_2 - F_4 region by the more intense F_1 formant, and the interaction of suppression and excitation effects among the higher formants.   However, until we learn more about the PT technique and its interpretation, we must be cautious about comparing pyschophysical and physiological data.

Tyler, R.S., and Lindblom, B. (1980).   Simultaneous - masking and pulsation-threshold patterns of vowels; *in preparation.*

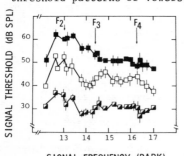

Fig. 1.   Simultaneous masking patterns of the vowel /e/.   Vowel levels were 55.5 (◼), 70.5 (◻), and 85.5 (◾) dB SPL. An average of 5 estimates were obtained per data point, and the height of the vertical line represents 2 standard deviations.   Results from 1 subject.

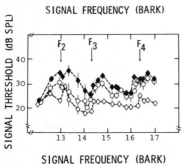

Fig. 2.   Pulsation-threshold pattern of /e/.   Vowel levels were 55.5 (◊), 70.5 (○) and 85.5 (◆) dB SPL.

ON THE SIGNAL PROCESSING POTENTIAL OF
HIGH THRESHOLD AUDITORY NERVE FIBERS

J.L. Goldstein

Bioengineering Program, School of Engineering,
Tel-Aviv University, Ramat-Aviv, Israel

INTRODUCTION

Siebert (1968, 1970) discovered that neural time synchrony found in the auditory nerve for low frequency stimulus tones potentially offers far more precision in measuring stimulus frequencies than average rate responses (i.e., spike counts). In our preceeding meeting at Keele, I reported that optimum processing of interspike interval times from single auditory-nerve fibers correctly predicts the dependencies of psychophysical frequency measurement upon frequency and duration (Goldstein and Srulovicz, 1977). This basic finding constitutes quantitative evidence in support of monaural processing of neural timing information. Qualitative evidence for the same conclusion had previously been drawn from the saturation of average neural rate for sound levels 20-40 dB above threshold and the preservation of complex spectra by neural timing (Kiang, 1965; 1968; Rose, *et al*, 1967; 1971). This qualitative evidence, suggesting the necessity for the use of neural timing, has been challenged by the recent discovery of auditory-nerve fibers with low spontaneous activity and a broad scatter of high thresholds (Kiang, Liberman and Levine, 1976; Liberman and Kiang, 1978; Liberman, 1978; Kim and Molnar, 1979). On the other hand, the quantitative predictions in support of monaural use of neural timing are essentially unaffected by the new findings.

Sachs and Young have recently provided a direct physiological demonstration of the relative superiority of timing information for representing complex spectra, in support of earlier theoretical conclusions (Sachs and Young, 1979; Young and Sachs, 1979). Still lacking, however, is the quantification of the signal processing capability offered by the high threshold fibers when average rate alone is used as the measure of response. Towards this end, I have modified Siebert's 1968 model of auditory-nerve rate processing to incorporate salient aspects of the new data on high threshold fibers.

1. IDEALIZED RATE MODEL OF AUDITORY PROCESSING

Figure 1 presents an idealized model of auditory processing based upon average rate, which includes fibers with saturating rate functions having high and low thresholds. Beyond nonlinear saturating rate functions operating on the root mean square (RMS) response of the filters, no attempt was made to incorporate known aspects of cochlear nonlinearity. The bandpass filters are linear, time-invariant approximations to auditory-nerve timing curves with transfer functions of the form given in eq. 1 (e.g., Goldstein, Baer and Kiang, 1971; Goldstein, 1974).

$$H(f_c,f) = A_0(f/f_c)^{S_1} \quad , \quad f \leq f_c$$
$$= A_0(f_c/f)^{S_2} \quad , \quad f > f_c \, , \tag{1}$$

where f_c = characteristic frequency of the fiber, $A_0 = 8.75$ µbar^{-1}, $S_1 = 10$

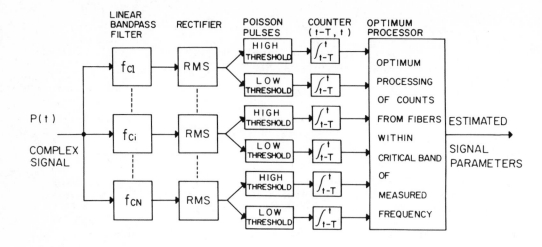

Fig. 1. *Average rate model of auditory processing including high and low threshold fibers.*

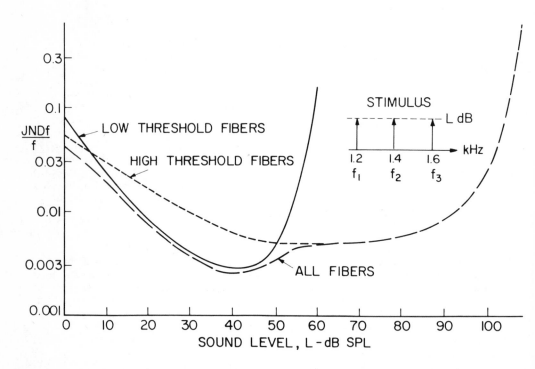

Fig. 2. *Precision in frequency measurement of a component tone (f₂) in a complex tone predicted by rate model with high and low threshold fibers.*

and $S_2 = 30$.

The response of the RMS rectifier at the characteristic frequency f_c to a complex tone signal is taken to be the time invariant form given in eq. 2.

$$RMS(f_c) = \sqrt{\sum_i [a_i \, H(f_c, f_i)]^2} \tag{2}$$

where A_i and f_i are the amplitude and frequency respectively of a component tone in the complex signal.

A single function with a variable threshold parameter is used to characterize the expected rate response of the Poisson pulse generators, as given in eq. 3 (Goldstein, 1974).

$$R(f_c) = (r_m - r_s)\{1 - \exp{-\alpha \cdot RMS(f_c)}\} + r_s , \tag{3}$$

where r_m and r_s are the maximum and spontaneous rates respectively and α is a threshold parameter distributed between 0 and 1. A rate function typical for low threshold fibers is obtained with the parameter values $r_m = 200$ pulses/sec, $r_s = 65$ pulses/sec and $\alpha = 1$. These parameter values were used for all low threshold fibers.

Insufficient data are available in published reports to describe a typical rate function for high threshold fibers. Therefore, I have taken the conservative position of erring in favor of rate processing by using the rate function in eq. 3. The parameter values for the high threshold fibers are $r_m = 125$ pulses/sec, $r_s = 0$ and α is distributed uniformly with $\log\alpha$ over the range $2 \leq 1/\alpha \leq 256$. Thus, the thresholds of the high threshold fibers are 6 to 48 dB higher than those of the low threshold fibers (Liberman, 1979).

The total fiber population is taken as 30,000 units (Rasmussen 1940), distributed uniformly with the logarithm of characteristic frequency between 20 and 20,000 Hz. Three quarters of this total comprise the low threshold population, and the remainder comprise the high threshold population (Liberman 1978; Kim and Molnar, 1979).

Finally, ideal counters with limited memory time T collect the Poisson pulses and supply the optimum central processor with the whole fiber array. A form of central critical band constraint is imposed on the central processor by restricting its information processing to fibers having characteristic frequencies within a critical band of a measured frequency. The parameter values used for the memory and critical band are 100 ms and $0.15 \cdot f$ (15%) respectively. Except for the central critical band and the high threshold fiber population, the model is essentially the same as introduced by Siebert (1968).

2. PRECISION IN FREQUENCY MEASUREMENT OF A COMPONENT TONE

Predictions by the model with complex tone signals were investigated. Figure 2 gives the prediction on precision of frequency measurement (same for discrimination or estimation) as a function of sound level for the center component of a three-tone signal The contribution of the high threshold population of fibers is dramatic in overcoming the limitation of saturation. Beyond about 50 dB SPL the predicted precision is dominated by the high threshold fibers, while the low threshold fibers become ineffective. The large contribution of the minority population results from their very low spontaneous rate.

The critical band constraint on the central processor has essentially no effect on this prediction. Allowing the central processor to gather information from all auditory nerve fibers provides no significant improvement of the precision in frequency measurement of the center tone. This is because the lower (1.2 kHz) and higher (1.6 kHz) frequency tones mask the response to the center tone at characteristic frequencies below and above the center tone frequency of 1.4 kHz. On the other hand, the critical band

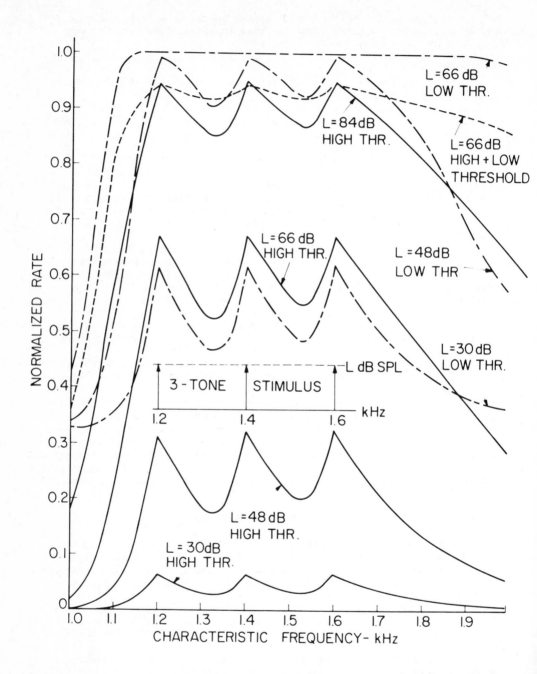

Fig. 3. Expected rate response profiles for high and low threshold fiber populations.

constraint has a significant influence on predictions for frequency discrimination of the lower and higher frequency tones, because the lower and higher edges of the response profile can provide useful information from the low threshold fibers at all sound levels, as shown by Siebert (1968). With the critical band constraint however, the predicted frequency discrimination for the "edge" tones is only very slightly better than for the center tone.

3. RESPONSE PROFILES FOR LOW AND HIGH THRESHOLD POPULATIONS

Expected rate as a function of characteristic frequency for populations of nerve fibers were calculated for the same three-tone stimulus at various sound levels. These expected response profiles, shown normalized relative to maximum rate in Fig. 3, qualitatively demonstrate that the high threshold population preserves spectral detail over a much broader range of sound levels than the low threshold population. For example, at 66 dB SPL the latter is useless for conveying spectral detail.

Since the maximum total rate of the low threshold population is nearly five times greater than that of the high threshold population, summing the rates of the two populations greatly degrades the spectral detail available from the high threshold population. This is illustrated by the normalized summed response profile for 66 dB SPL. Of course the summed response is not optimal for preserving stimulus information available from individual fibers. To preserve stimulus information optimally, only responses from fibers with similar thresholds may be added. Thus the response profile for the low threshold population is an optimal representation, but this is not true of the high spontaneous population. (In reality even the former departs somewhat from optimality, because neither the spontaneous rate nor threshold is uniform within the population — in contrast with the model approximation.)

Independently of optimality, the basic limitation on detecting spectral detail in experimentally measured reponse profiles is the random fluctuation of the fiber responses. Since the variance of a Poisson count is equal to its mean, one can in principle extend the observation time as well as integrate across characteristic frequency to achieve any desired precision. For example, we might require that the expected peak-to-minimum be twice the standard deviation of the measured response profile, so that detection of the two percent expected fluctuation in the summed response profile would require an integrated count of about 10,000.

4. FREQUENCY DISCRIMINATION VS. DURATION AND FREQUENCY

The key to evaluating the relevance of processing neural rate or neural timing is the predicted behavior as a function of signal parameters, as these predictions can be compared with psychophysical data. Based upon calculations already presented by Siebert in 1968, one can show that the predicted frequency discrimination approximately obeys the proportionality given by eq.4.

$$\frac{JNDf}{f} \sim K \Big/ \sqrt{\tau(r_m - r_s)(S_1 + S_2)} \quad , \tag{4}$$

where the duration τ equals the counting time T of the ideal counter when signal duration exceeds T, otherwise τ is the signal duration. The remaining parameters are defined in eqs. 1-3 and their dependence upon frequency is documented (Liberman, 1978; Goldstein, Baer and Kiang, 1971). In contrast with optimum processing of interspike interval time, optimum processing of rate does not predict known trends of psychophysical frequency measurement as a function of frequency and duration (Goldstein and Srulovicz, 1977).

5. DISCUSSION

The conclusion I draw from this study of the potential contribution of high threshold fibers to neural processing of average rate is that it is very difficult if not impossible to prove the negative conclusion that neural rate processing is untenable because of saturation. Obviously, if the high threshold population did not exist at all, then the model presented here would fail completely at high sound levels. However, that negative finding would force one to consider the details of cochlear nonlinearity (e.g. Sachs and Young, 1979). Short of that one could argue that the high threshold population has been too generously endowed in the model, particularly with a rate function that has a similar dynamic range as low threshold fibers. Yet if the inadequacy of neural rate processing under optimum conditions can be proved, the present study indicates that the failure would be marginal. Cognizant of intra-species differences (Liberman, 1978) as well as inter-species differences (Furst and Goldstein, 1980), a marginal failure would appear ambiguous. Therefore in my judgement the case for monaural processing of neural timing is argued by the positive evidence for it, namely the superiority of timing information in representing auditory signals (Siebert, 1970; Sachs and Young, 1979; Young and Sachs, 1979), and the success of optimum processing of interspike intervals in accounting for parameter dependence in human psychophysics of frequency measurement (Goldstein and Srulovicz, 1977). Our further studies at Tel-Aviv, which must be detailed elsewhere, add to this positive evidence (Nudel, 1977; Srulovicz, 1979).

6. SUMMARY

A model of monaural neural processing based on average rate that incorporates recent data on high threshold fibers is presented. This model provides baseline predictions for evaluating the potential benefits of the high threshold units for overcoming the limitations of average rate saturation in individual nerve fibers. The model successfully overcomes the limitations of rate saturation and provides the signal information required by human frequency measurement. In contrast with processing of neural timing however, the model provides no direct account of the dependence of human frequency measurement on signal frequency and duration. It is concluded that human frequency measurement is served by monaural processing of neural timing, while rate may serve some other functions (e.g. Goldstein, 1974; Teich and Lachs, 1979).

REFERENCES

Furst, M. and Goldstein, J.L. (1980). Differences of CT($2f_1-f_2$) phase in psychophysical and physiological experiments. *Hearing Research 2* (in press).
Goldstein, J.L. (1974). Is the power law simply related to the driven spike response rate from the whole auditory nerve? *Sensation and Measurement.* (H.R. Moskowitz *et al*, eds). pp 223-229. D. Reidel, Dordrecht, Holland.
Goldstein, J.L., Baer, T. and Kiang, N.Y.S. (1971). A theoretical treatment of latency, group delay and timing characteristics for auditory-nerve responses to clicks and tones. *Physiology of the Auditory System.* (M.R. Sachs, ed). pp 133-141. National Educational Consultants, Maryland.
Goldstein, J.L. and Srulovicz, P. (1977). Auditory-nerve spike intervals as an adequate basis for aural spectrum analysis. *Psychophysics and Physiology of Hearing.* (E.F. Evans and J.P. Wilson, eds). pp 337-345. Academic Press, London.
Kiang, N.Y.S., Watanobe, T., Thomas, E.C. and Clark, F. (1965). Discharge Patterns of Single Fibers in the Cat's Auditory Nerve. MIT Press, Cambridge.
Kiang, N.Y.S. (1968). A survey of recent developments in the study of auditory physiology. *Ann. Otol. Rhinol. Laryngol. 77*, 656-675.

Kiang, N.Y.S., Liberman, M.C. and Levine, R.A. (1976). Auditory nerve activity in cats exposed to otoxic drugs and high intensity sound. *Ann. Otol. Rhinol. Laryngol.* 85, 752-768.

Kim, D.O. and Molnar,C.E.(1979).A population study of cochlear nerve fibers: comparison of spatial distributions of average-rate and phase locking measures of response to single tones. *J. Neurophysiol.* 42, 16-30.

Liberman, M.C. (1978). Auditory-nerve response from cats raised in a low-noise chamber. *J. Acoust. Soc. Am.* 63, 442-455.

Liberman, M.C. and Kiang, N.Y.S. (1978). Acoustic Trauma in cats. *Acta Oto-Laryngol.* Suppl. 358.

Nudel, B. (1977). Human frequency discrimination of simple tones-experiment and theory. M.Sc. Thesis, School of Engineering, Tel-Aviv University, Supervised by J.L. Goldstein.

Rasmussen, A.T. (1940). Studies of the eighth cranial nerve of man. *Laryngoscope* 50, 67-83.

Rose, J.E., Brugge, J.F., Anderson, D.J. and Hind, J.E. (1967). Phase locked responses to low-frequency tones in single auditory nerve fibers of the squirrel monkey. *J. Neurophysiol.* 30, 769-793.

Rose, J.E., Hind, J.E., Anderson, D.J. and Brugge, J.F. (1971). Some effects of stimulus intensity on response of auditory-nerve fibers in the squirrel monkey. *J. Neurophysiol.* 34, 685-699.

Sachs, M.B. and Young, E.D. (1979). Encoding of steady-state vowels in the auditory nerve: representation in terms of discharge rate. *J. Acoust. Soc. Am.* 66, 470-479.

Siebert, W.M. (1968). Stimulus transformations in the peripheral auditory system. *Recognizing Patterns.* (P.A. Kohlers and M. Eden, eds). pp 104-133 MIT Press, Cambridge.

Siebert, W.M. (1970). Frequency discrimination in the auditory system: place or periodicity mechanisms? *Proc. IEEE* 58, 723-730.

Srulovicz, P. (1979). Neural timing as the physiological basis for aural representation of frequency spectrum: the central spectrum. Ph.D. Thesis, School of Engineering, Tel-Aviv University, Supervised by J.L. Goldstein.

Teich, M.C. and Lachs, G. (1979). A neural-counting model incorporating refractoriness and spread of excitation. I. Application to intensity discrimination. *J. Acoust. Soc. Am.* 66, 1738-1749.

Young, E.D. and Sachs, M.B. (1979). Representation of steady-state vowels in the temporal aspects of the discharge patterns of populations of auditory nerve fibers. *J. Acoust. Soc. Am.* 66, 1381-1403.

ACKNOWLEDGEMENT

This study was previously presented in an invited (unpublished) paper at the meeting of the Association for Research in Otolaryngology, St. Petersburg, Florida, 22-24 January 1979. This reasearch was supported in part by the U.S.-Israel Binational Science Foundation, grant no. 1286/78.

'PHASE-LOCKING' OF COCHLEAR FIBRES AND THE PROBLEM OF DYNAMIC RANGE

E.F. Evans

Department of Communication & Neuroscience, University of Keele, Keele, Staffs. ST5 5BG, U.K.

1. INTRODUCTION

How the peripheral auditory system encodes the level of individual and multiple stimulus components over the ear's substantial dynamic range remains a serious problem (Kiang 1968; Evans, 1975, 1977ab, 1978ab). For the great majority of fibres in the cochlear nerve, the distribution of their thresholds and their dynamic ranges (in terms of mean discharge rate between spontaneous and saturated activity) are restricted to some 20dB and 30-60dB respectively at any given characteristic frequency (CF). Various solutions to this problem have been proposed.

(a) For single component stimuli, it has been assumed that the wide psychophysical dynamic range is accommodated by the spread of neural activity to unsaturated fibres of adjacent CF (e.g. Allanson & Whitfield 1956). This scheme could not account for the intensity coding of multiple component signals of high level. Furthermore, the fact that the level of stimuli can be discriminated over a wide dynamic range in the presence of simultaneous low and high pass masking (Viemeister, 1974; Hellman, 1974; Moore & Raab 1975; Pick, to be published) strongly suggests that spread of neural activity is not a *necessary* condition for the discrimination of the level of single components. Under the latter conditions, Evans & Palmer (1975) found units in the dorsal cochlear nucleus capable of signalling, by substantial changes in their mean discharge rate, differences in the level of a signal over a very wide dynamic range. This occurs by virtue of the lateral inhibition, characteristic of these cells, 'biassing' their discharge rate below saturation, in a manner similar to that found in the retina (Werblin, 1972). The nature of the input to these cells, however, is not clear. Under the same conditions, cochlear fibres have a restricted dynamic range or exhibit very slight changes in mean discharge rate as a result of lateral ('two-tone') suppressive effects (Palmer & Evans to be published). Similarly extended and restricted dynamic ranges for comb-filtered noise stimuli, have been found in dorsal cochlear nucleus (Evans, 1977b) and cochlear nerve respectively (Evans 1977b, see also Narins & Evans, this volume).

(b) Not all of the cochlear fibres, however, may be saturated at high stimulus levels. In the first place, some fibres are encountered in apparently normal cochleas with thresholds substantially higher than the generally restricted distribution (Evans, 1972; Liberman, 1978). In the former study at least, however, these fibres showed, in their broad tuning, evidence of cochlear pathology. Such fibres therefore could not easily serve to convey information on the level of closely separated stimulus components. In the second place, fibres with normal thresholds but with dynamic ranges in excess of 60dB have been reported (Sachs & Abbas 1974). However, the proportion of such fibres in our own material is small; being 10% having dynamic ranges in excess of 60dB and 5% in excess of 70dB (Palmer & Evans, 1979). Furthermore, the change in spike rate per dB of stimulus level change for these fibres above 60dB SPL, was less than one quarter that near threshold. Interestingly, the majority of these fibres have spontaneous discharge rates below 15sp/s, and there is an inverse relationship between spontaneous rate and dynamic range (Evans & Palmer, 1980b).

(c) Dynamic range measured with steady tones may not be representative of that for rapid changes in level (Yates 1978). In cat cochlear fibres, we have not found this to be the case, at least comparing the dynamic range for signalling amplitude modulation above 100c/s, with that for 100ms steady tones (Evans & Palmer 1980a). (For tones as long as tens of seconds, however, the dynamic ranges can be more restricted than those for shorter tones, see results below). (d) The information on the level of (low frequency) stimuli could be conveyed in the degree of synchronization ('phase-locking') of spikes to the stimulus waveform (e.g. as suggested by Moore, 1977). It is known that the 'threshold' of a cochlear fibre's 'phase-locking' response to a low frequency tone can be at least 13dB below that of its mean discharge rate (Rose *et al*, 1967). However, what data hve been available on the degree of phase-locking as a function of level (e.g. Rose *et al* 1971) did not support the suggestion that this parameter exhibited an extended dynamic range (Evans, 1978a, fig. 8). The present study specifically examines this question, using three measures of the degree of phase-locking.

2. METHODS

The activity of single fibres in the cochlear nerve of pentobarbitone anaesthetized cats was recorded with micropipettes using methods of physiological and stimulus control, and response analysis, detailed in Evans (1979). Stimuli were presented by Bruel & Kjaer 4134 microphone used as a driver (with compensation for distortion) in a closed system with bulla intact but vented. The sound pressure level was monitored by probe tube microphone at the tympanic membrane.

Period histograms were constructed from three consecutive 10s periods (with 5s intervals) of continuous stimulation with tones at the CF of each fibre, using a Datalab DL 4000 computer and bin widths ranging from 10µs to 250µs. Period histograms were obtained at successively higher stimulus levels, at 10dB intervals.

The coefficient of synchronization (Rose *et al* 1967) and vector strength (Goldberg & Brown 1969; Buunen & Rhode, 1978), were computed from the period histograms. Absence of synchronization yields values of 50% and 0 respectively; 100% sinusoidal modulation of discharge rate, values of 81.8% and 0.5; half-wave rectified sinusoidal modulation, 100% and 0.79, and perfect, 'jitterless' synchronization, 100% and 1 respectively. The amplitude of the fundamental Fourier (CF) component of the period histogram was also computed (from the vector strength and mean discharge rate).

Interspike interval histograms were computed on the same data used for the period histograms, and therefore represent histograms in response to a total of 30s stimulation at the CF. Bin widths were 40µs.

Rate-level functions for shorter duration (100ms; 5ms rise and fall; 3/s) CF tones were also determined using a randomised sequence of stimulus levels at 2-4dB intervals, and averaging the results from 16 samples at each tone level (as in Palmer & Evans, 1979). A Hamming window of 16dB was employed to construct a smoothed function (continuous line) through the data points (open circles) in Figs. 1-3.

3. RESULTS

Data were obtained on single fibres with CFs ranging from 0.157-3.01kHz. Fig. 1 shows the variation of the three indices of synchronization, with stimulus level, together with the discharge rate to long-term duration (3 x 10s) and short duration (100ms) tones, at CF, for a fibre with intermediate CF of 1.96 kHz. Figs. 2 and 3 represent data from the extremes of CF, for CFs of 0.157 and 3.01kHz and at low and high spontaneous rates, respectively. The interspike interval histograms corresponding to the period histograms of Fig. 1 are shown in Fig. 4.

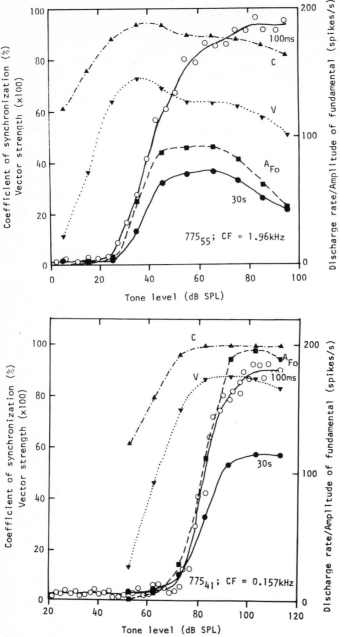

Fig. 1. *Various measures of degree of phase-locking, and mean discharge rate, versus tone level at the CF of a cochlear fibre (1.96 kHz).*
Dashed dotted line, C, coefficient of synchronization. Dotted line, V, vector strength. Dashed line, A_{Fo}, amplitude of fundamental Fourier component. Continuous line through solid circles (30s): mean discharge rate for 3 x 10 s tone bursts. Continuous line through open circles (100 ms). Mean discharge rate (smoothed with Hamming window) for 100 ms tone bursts using sequence of randomised levels. See methods for details.

Fig. 2. *As Fig. 1, for fibre with CF of 0.157 kHz.*

(a) *Discharge periodicity and stimulus level.* The following generalizations can be made:-
(i) The 'threshold' for significant phase-locking in all spontaneously active fibres occurred at a significantly lower sound level than the mean discharge rate threshold. The difference ranged from 5-20dB. Providing the spontaneous discharge rate was sufficient to allow the phase-locking 'threshold' to be discerned, the difference did not appear to be related to the magnitude of the spontaneous discharge rate. Thus, the difference between phase-locking and mean

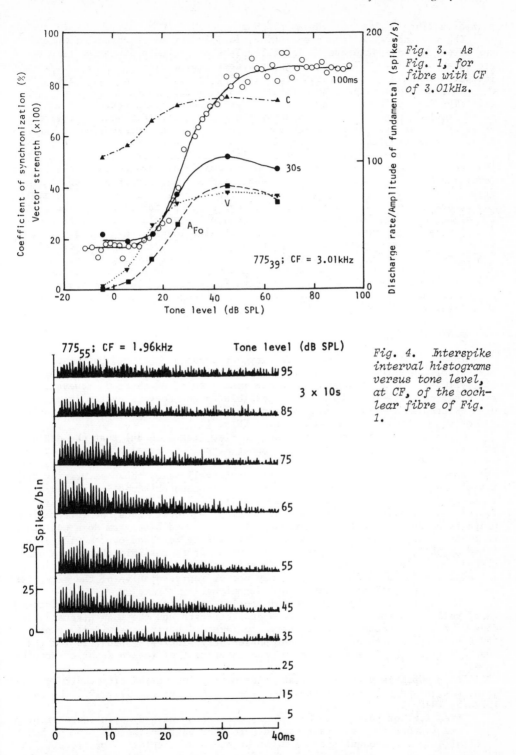

Fig. 3. As Fig. 1, for fibre with CF of 3.01kHz.

Fig. 4. Interspike interval histograms versus tone level, at CF, of the cochlear fibre of Fig. 1.

rate thresholds is larger for the fibre of Fig. 1 (spontaneous rate of 2/s) than

that of a fibre with a spontaneous discharge rate of 60/s (difference of 10dB).
(ii) The two indices of synchronization, coefficient of synchronization and vector strength, both saturate at lower levels than the mean discharge rate under
the same conditions. In some cases, the degree of phase-locking saturated within 10dB of discharge rate threshold (e.g. Fig. 1) and 20-30dB below the level at
which the mean discharge rate saturated (Figs. 1,2,3).
(iii) The interspike interval histograms do not show clear periodicity until
sound levels are reached 10-20dB above the rate threshold. No parameter of
these histograms is evident which would serve to convey information on the
level of the stimulus above saturation of the mean discharge rate.

(b) *Mean discharge rate, stimulus level and duration.* It is of interest
to note that there is, in many cases, a systematic difference between the rate-
level functions for long (3x10s) and short (100ms) duration tones (continuous
lines through the solid and open circles respectively in Fig. 1-3). In most
cases, adaptation and 'order effects' become apparent for the 10s stimuli at
the higher stimulus levels, so that non-monotonic rate level functions occur,
i.e: having a 'turn-over' of the function at high levels, (e.g. Figs. 1,3).
These have not been seen when the functions were determined using short duration
(<<1s) stimuli, using randomisation of the sequence of levels. These effects
of long duration tones are accompanied in some cases by reduction in the dynamic range compared with that for short duration tones and random sequence of
presentation, as in Figs. 1,2 and 3. The difference can amount to as much as
30dB (Fig. 1).

5. DISCUSSION

In principle, discharge periodicity, at least as measured by the period
histogram, can extend the dynamic range of cochlear fibre response to substantially lower levels of stimuli than the mean rate of discharge. However, it is
not clear how such periodicity is accessible to the nervous system, compared
with interspike intervals which appear surprisingly unpromising as a means of
conveying information on stimulus level (Fig. 4).

Certainly, these results confirm the view (Evans 1978a) that the degree of
synchronization of spike discharges cannot signal the level of a stimulus above
saturation of the mean discharge rate. In fact, in most fibres the degree of
synchronization reaches its maximum at levels well below those saturating the
fibre's mean discharge rate. This finding, although obtained independently,
is consistent with the report of McGee, Walsh, & Javel (1979) in cochlear
fibres and cells in the anteroventral cochlear nucleus. Thus the information
which is accessible to the investigator in the period histogram does not appear
to be the solution to the problem of how intensity is coded over a wide dynamic
range at the cochlear nerve level. Of course, it is possible that these data,
obtained with long duration continuous stimulation for reasons of convenience
in computing the period histograms, may not be representative of the situation
at the more appropriate, short, tonal durations.

The amplitude of the fundamental fourier component of the period histogram,
being related to the product of the vector strength and the mean discharge rate,
does of course represent the discharge 'parameter' having the widest dynamic
range: the appearance of significant phase-locking being responsible for the
lower limit of the dynamic range and the saturation of mean discharge rate, the
upper.

It is possible that other statistics of impulse periodicity could be utilized, e.g. as suggested elsewhere (Goldstein & Srulovicz, 1977, 1978, Evans
1977a,b, 1978a).

Three further points may be made in connection with dynamic range problem.
The first is that the results reported here bear only on the question of how the
level of *single* component stimuli might be coded at cochlear nerve level. It
is possible, and seems implicit in the data of Young & Sachs (1979), that the
level of components in a multicomponent stimulus *relative to one another* could

be signalled by the *relative* amplitudes of the appropriate phase-locking parameter.

Secondly, it is becoming increasingly evident that a small proportion of
cochlear fibres, particularly those with low spontaneous discharge rates, not
only tend to have somewhat higher thresholds than the majority (Kiang *et al.*
1965; Kiang *et al* 1970, 1976), but have wider dynamic ranges (Evans & Palmer
1980b) and exhibit more vigorous 'two-tone' (lateral) suppression effects (Sachs
& Young, 1979) making them possible, if infrequent (about 10%), candidates for
signalling, even in their mean discharge rate, the level of signal components,
particularly the relative level of components in a resolveable multicomponent
complex.

Thirdly, it may be necessary to qualify the extent of the psychophysical
dynamic range with which the physiological data are being compared. Caution
may be required in comparing conclusions drawn from psychophysical measurements
on awake human subjects with intact middle ear and efferent neural systems
against those from experiments on anaesthetized animals, where the effects of
the descending control systems are eliminated. In fact there is evidence that
the dynamic range for multicomponent stimuli, such as speech, may be more restricted than at first sight appears. While experiments indicated that speech
could be understood with little loss in intelligibility at levels in excess of
90dB above the threshold for the speech (Fletcher, 1953; Pollack & Pickett,
1958), some deterioration does occur at very high levels (95-105dB SPL) at
least in the discrimination of features of synthetic vowels (Danaher *et al* 1973)
and this may relate to the observations of deterioration in frequency selectivity at levels of about 70dB SPL, as shown psychophysically (Scharf & Meiselman,
1977; Pick, 1977, 1980) and physiologically (Evans 1977b; Møller, 1977). In
patients lacking normal middle-ear protective mechanisms, moreover, deterioration in speech intelligibility has been reported to occur at levels above about
80dB SPL (Borg & Zakrisson, 1973; Jerger and associates, personal communication,
1979).

Acknowledgments

*The work reported was supported in part by grants from the Medical Research
Council. I am grateful to A.R. Palmer and G.F. Pick for their help towards the
programming of the computations performed on the period histograms.*

REFERENCES

Allanson, J.T. & Whitfield, I.C. (1956). The cochlear nucleus and its relation
to theories of hearing. In: *3rd London Symp. on Information Theory.*
(Cherry, ed.) pp.269-284. Butterworths, London.
Borg, E. & Zakrisson, J.-E. (1973). Stapedius reflex and speech features. *J.
Acoust. Soc. Am.* 54, 525-527.
Buunen, T.J.F. & Rhode, W.S. (1978). Responses of fibres in the cat's auditory
nerve to the cubic difference tone. *J. Acoust. Soc. Am.* 64, 772-781.
Danaher, E.M., Osberger, M.J. & Pickett, J.M. (1973). Discrimination of form-
ant frequency transitions in synthetic vowels. *Hearing Res.* 16, 439-451.
Evans, E.F. (1972). The frequency response and other properties of single
fibres in the guinea pig cochlear nerve. *J. Physiol., Lond.* 226, 263-287.
Evans, E.F. (1975). The cochlear nerve and cochlear nucleus. In: *Handbook of
Sensory Physiology.* Vol. V/2, Chapt. 1. (W.D. Keidel and W.D. Neff, eds).
pp. 1-109. Springer, Heidelberg.
Evans, E.F. (1977a). Some interactions between physiology and psychophysics in
acoustics. *Proc. 9th Int. Congr. on Acoustics;* volume of invited review
lectures. pp.55-65. Spanish Acoustical Society, Madrid.
Evans, E.F. (1977b). Frequency selectivity at high signal levels of single
units in cochlear nerve and nucleus. In: *Psychophysics & Physiology of
Hearing.* (E.F. Evans & J.P. Wilson, eds), pp185-192. Acad. Press, London.

Evans, E.F. (1978a). Place and time coding of frequency in the peripheral auditory system: some physiological pros and cons. *Audiol.* 17, 369-420.

Evans, E.F. (1978b). Peripheral auditory processing in normal and abnormal ears physiological considerations for attempts to compensate for auditory deficits by acoustic and electrical prostheses. In: *Sensorineural hearing impairment and hearing aids.* (C. Ludvigsen & J. Barfod, eds). pp 9-47, *Scand. Audiol.* 6, suppl.

Evans, E.F. (1979). Single unit studies of the mammalian auditory nerve. In: *Auditory Investigations: The Scientific and Technological Basis.* (H.A. Beagley, ed). chapt. 15, pp324-367. Oxford University Press, Oxford.

Evans, E.F. & Palmer, A.R. (1975). Responses of units in the cochlear nerve and nucleus of the cat to signals in the presence of bandstop noise. *J. Physiol., Lond.* 252, 60-62P.

Evans, E.F. & Palmer, A.R. (1980a). Dynamic range of cochlear nerve fibres to amplitude modulated tones. *J. Physiol.* 298, 33-34P.

Evans, E.F. & Palmer, A.R. (1980b). Relationship between the dynamic range of cochlear nerve fibres and their spontaneous activity. *Exp. Br. Res.* In Press.

Fletcher, H. (1953). *Speech and Hearing in Communication.* Van Nostrand, N.Y., London, Toronto.

Goldberg, J.M. & Brown, P.B. (1969). Response of binaural neurons of dog superior olivary complex to dichotic tonal stimuli: some physiological mechanisms of sound localization. *J. Neurophysiol.* 32, 613-636.

Goldstein, J.L. & Srulovicz, P. (1977). Auditory-nerve spike intervals as an adequate basis for aural frequency measurement. In: *Psychophysics and Physiology of Hearing.* (E.F. Evans and J.P. Wilson, eds). pp337-346. Academic Press, London.

Goldstein, J.L. (1978). Mechanisms of signal analysis and pattern perception in periodicity pitch. *Audiol.* 17, 421-445.

Hellman, R.P. (1974). Effect of spread of excitation on the loudness function at 250Hz. In: *Sensation and measurement.* (Moskowitz, et al. eds.) pp. 241-249. Reidel, Dordrecht.

Kiang, N.Y.-s. (1968). A survey of recent developments in the study of auditory physiology. *Ann. Otol. Rhinol. Lar.* 77, 656-676.

Kiang, N.Y.-s, Watenabe, T., Thomas, E.C. and Clark, L.F. (1965). *Discharge patterns of single fibres in the cat's auditory nerve.* MIT Press, Cambridge.

Kiang, N.Y-s., Moxon, E.C. and Levine, R.A. (1970). Auditory-nerve activity in cats with normal and abnormal cochleas. In: *Sensorineural Hearing Loss.* (Wolstenholme & Knight, eds). pp241-268. Churchill, London.

Kiang, N.Y-s., Liberman, M.C., & Levine, R.A. (1976). Auditory-nerve activity in cats exposed to ototoxic drugs and high-intensity sounds. *Annal. Otol. Rhinol. Laryngol.* (St. Louis) 75, 752-769.

Liberman, M.C. (1978). Auditory nerve responses from cats raised in a low-noise chamber. *J. Acoust. Soc. Am.* 63, 442-455.

McGee, J-A., Walsh, E.J. & Javel, E. (1979). Discharge synchronization in auditory nerve and AVCN neurons. *J. Acoust. Soc. Am.* 65, Suppl 1, S83.

Møller, A.R. (1977). Frequency selectivity of single auditory nerve fibres in response to broadband noise stimuli. *J. Acoust. Soc. Am.* 62, 135-142.

Moore, B.C.J. (1977). An introduction to the Psychology of Hearing. MacMillan, London.

Moore, B.C.J. & Raab, D.H. (1975). Intensity discrimination for noise bursts in the presence of a continuous, bandstop background: effects of level, width of the bandstop, and duration. *J. Acoust. Soc. Am.* 57, 400-405.

Palmer, A.R. & Evans, E.F. (1979). On the peripheral coding of the level of individual frequency components of complex sounds at high sound levels. *Exp. Br. Res. Suppl II*, 19-26.

Pick, G.F. (1977). Comment on paper by Scharf & Meiselman. In: *Psychophysics & Physiology of Hearing*. (E.F. Evans & J.P. Wilson, eds). pp233-234 Academic Press, London.

Pick, G.F. (1980). Level dependence of psychophysical frequency resolution and auditory filter shape. *J. Acoust. Soc. Am.* In Press.

Pollack, I. & Pickett, J.M. (1958). Masking of speech by noise at high levels. *J. Acoust. Soc. Am.* 30, 127-130.

Rose, J.E. Brugge, J.F., Anderson, D.J. & Hind, J.E. (1967). Phase-locked response to low frequency tones in single auditory nerve fibres of the squirrel monkey. *J. Neurophysiol.* 30, 769-793.

Rose, J.E., Hind, J.E., Anderson, D.J. & Brugge, J.F. (1971). Some effects of stimulus intensity on response of auditory nerve fibers in the squirrel monkey. *J. Neurophysiol.* 34, 685-699.

Sachs, M.B. & Abbas, P.J. (1974). Rate versus level functions for auditory-nerve fibers in cats: tone-burst stimuli. *J. Acoust. Soc. Am.* 56, 1835-1847.

Sachs, M.B. & Young, E.D. (1979). Encoding of steady-state vowels in the auditory nerve: representation in terms of discharge rate. *J. Acoust. Soc. Am.* 66, 470-479.

Scharf, B. & Meiselman, C.H. (1977). Critical bandwidth at high intensities. In: *Psychophysics & Physiology of Hearing*. (E.F. Evans & J.P. Wilson, eds) pp221-232. Academic Press, London.

Viemeister, N.F. (1974). Intensity discrimination of noise in the presence of band reject noise. *J. Acoust. Soc. Am.* 56, 1594-1600.

Werblin, F. (1972). Functional organization of the retina: sharpening up in space and intensity. *Ann. N.Y. Acad. Sci.* 193, 75-85.

Yates, G. (1978). Fast adaptation in the auditory nerve. Paper to *Brit. Soc. Audiol. Keele Meeting*.

Young, E.D. & Sachs, M.B., (1979). Representation of steady-state vowels in the temporal aspects of the discharge patterns of populations of auditory-nerve fibers. *J. Acoust. Soc. Am.* 66, 1381-1403.

ADDENDUM TO 'Phase-locking' of cochlear fibres and the problem of dynamic range.

E.F. Evans
Department of Communication & Neuroscience, University of Keele, Keele, Staffs. ST5 5BG, U.K.

The above findings indicated that the degree of phase-locking of a single cochlear fibre saturated at a too low level for it to code for stimulus level. However, the suggestion was made that the coding of the level of components in a multicomponent stimulus *relative to one another* might not be subject to the same limitations of saturation. This has been tested by examining the responses of cat cochlear fibres, with CFs ranging from 0.43-3.8kHz, to ten-component harmonic complexes.

The complexes contained the second to eleventh harmonics, at equal levels, of a fundamental (75-400Hz) chosen so that the fibre's CF lay approximately at the arithmetic mean of the frequencies of the components. The complexes were generated numerically on-line to the experiment with sampling rate of 10kHz and LP filtering at 4-6kHz (48dB/oct). The complexes were presented for 3 consecutive 10s periods (with 5s intervals) at each level, in ascending and descending series of 10-20dB steps with interleaving of levels. The vector strength as a function of level for each harmonic, and the mean discharge rate, were computed off-line from tape recorded data, using period histograms with approx. 100 bins.

Fig. 1 shows the complex relation between the vector strength of a fibre's phase locked response to each of 5 selected harmonics of a cosine phase mixed complex having a 200Hz fundamental. The mean discharge rate of the fibre in response to the complex is indicated by the continuous line and solid circles. For harmonics above the CF (>1.4kHz), the vector strength decreases as the level of the complex is increased beyond some 20dB above discharge rate threshold. Lower harmonics on the other hand, (e.g. 1.2kHz) became dominant at the highest levels.

Fig. 2 replots the same data to compare the degree to which the components are separated by the fibre's filter action, at the different levels. The solid contour, taken at about 10dB above rate threshold, qualitatively matches the FTC of the fibre. At higher levels, however, the functions become sharper, predominantly by progressive suppression of the phase-locked response to harmonics above the CF in a manner analogous to the 'synchrony suppression' described by Rose *et al* (1974) and others for two-tones, and by

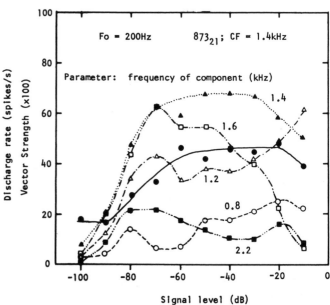

Fig. 1. Mean discharge rate (continuous line) and vector strengths (interrupted lines) versus level of a 10 component harmonic complex. 0dB = 106 dB SPL.

Young & Sachs (1979) for vowels. At the highest level (-10dB), the sensitivity shifted towards lower frequencies, as found in reverse correlation analyses (Evans, 1977b). It is clear that a fibre's phase-locking retains and even improves its selectivity with level; saturation of the mean discharge rate does not destroy its ability to code the *relative* level of the components within the limits set by that selectivity.

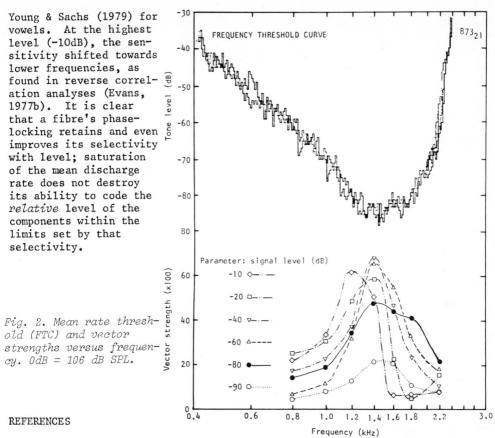

Fig. 2. Mean rate threshold (FTC) and vector strengths versus frequency. 0dB = 106 dB SPL.

REFERENCES

Evans, E.F. (1977). Frequency selectivity at high signal levels of single units in cochlear nerve and nucleus. In: *Psychophysics and Physiology of Hearing*. (E.F. Evans & J.P. Wilson, eds). pp185-192. Acad. Press, London.

Rose, J.E., Kitzes, L.M., Gibson, M.M. and Hind, J.E. (1974). Observations on phase-sensitive neurons of anteroventral cochlear nucleus of the cat: nonlinearity of cochlear output. *J. Neurophysiol. 37*, 218-253.

Young, E.D. & Sachs, M.B. (1979). Representation of steady-state vowels in the temporal aspects of the discharge patterns of populations of auditory nerve fibers. *J. Acoust. Soc. Am. 66*, 1381-1403.

COMMENT ON: "Phase-locking of cochlear fibres and the problem of dynamic range" (E.F. Evans).

I.C. Whitfield
Neurocommunications Research Unit, Medical School, University of Birmingham, England.

As you suggest, there can be no doubt that the olivo-cochlear bundle

(O.C.B.), is deeply involved in the problem. You mentioned that you were unwilling to stimulate your wide dynamic range fibres above 100 dB SPL for fear of damage, and certainly there is evidence for example, that hair cells are more readily damaged in the anaesthetized than in the normal state (Stopp, 1980). When Allanson and I produced our hypothesis about the auditory transfer function so long ago (Allanson & Whitfield, 1956), we envisaged that there would need to be some form of control to keep the input on the working point of the transfer function curve, although it was not then known what form that control might take. The O.C.B. subsequently became an obvious candidate. The action of this pathway is, of course, seriously disrupted, if not entirely suppressed, under the conditions of anaesthesia used in auditory nerve studies.

An apparently crucial objection to the O.C.B. as a candidate for the role of expanding the dynamic range lay in your observation (Evans and Palmer, 1975) that cochlear nucleus units still exhibited a wide dynamic range under conditions where the O.C.B. activity might be expected to be ineffective. However your subsequent observation of fibres with a wide dynamic range (Palmer and Evans, 1979) albeit only a few, makes that objection less insurmountable.

The most obvious way in which the O.C.B. could work would be simply to use diffuse feedback to keep the mean level of activity within the working range (Fig. 1a); however an alternative arrangement would be to feed back inhibitory activity only to the edges of the signal array, thereby creating stop-bands between adjacent signals (Whitfield, 1978). The latter hypothesis is difficult to test physiologically and we are at present trying to tackle it by looking at the anatomical distribution of the fibres.

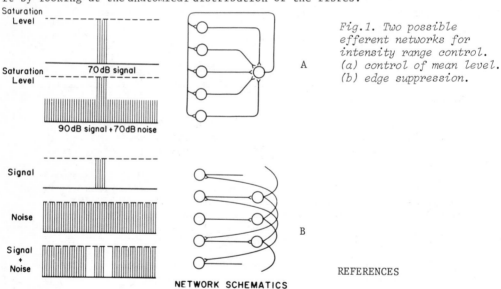

Fig.1. Two possible efferent networks for intensity range control. (a) control of mean level. (b) edge suppression.

REFERENCES

Allanson, J.T. & Whitfield, I.C. (1956). The cochlear nucleus and its relation to theories of hearing. In : *3rd London symp. on Information Theory.* (Cherry, ed.) pp.269-284. Butterworth, London.

Evans, E.F. & Palmer, A.R. (1975). Responses of units in the cochlear nerve and nucleus of the cat to signals in the presence of bandstop noise. *J. Physiol., Lond.* 252. 60-62P.

Palmer, A.R. & Evans, E.F. (1979). On the peripheral coding of the level of individual frequency components of complex sounds at high sound levels. *Exp. Br. Res. Suppl. II,* 19-26.

Stopp, P.E. (1980), to be published.

Whitfield, I.C. (1978). The Neural Code. In : *Handbook* of Perception Vol. IV (Carterette & Friedmann, eds.). Academic Press, New York.

COMMENT ON: ""Phase-locking" of cochlear fibres and the problem of dynamic range" (E.F. Evans).

H.S. Colburn
Research Laboratory of Electronics, Massachusetts Institute of Technology, Cambridge, Mass. 02139 U.S.A.

I would like to take this opportunity to comment on some of the issues that must be considered when physiological results are interpreted in terms of the behavior of the total organism. These issues are not particularly ignored in Dr. Evans' paper, but are worthy of emphasis in my opinion.

First, it is important to keep in mind that the information available from any particular aspect of the response is determined as much by the statistical reliability (or variability) of the result as by the mean values; that is, the random nature of the physiological responses must be incorporated into any evaluation of the information provided by the responses. Thus, if we take the average-rate information as an example, we must consider not only the change in the mean number of responses (for a change in the stimulus parameter of interest), but also the variance of the number of responses during a stimulus presentation in the behavioral situation. An evaluation of the total information provided by a particular aspect of the response is quite difficult, of course, and requires not only the specification of the statistics for a single fiber (as just noted) but also an integration of the information from all the individual fibers or cells in the population under consideration.

Second, it is important to be as explicit as possible about the parameters postulated as a source of information and about the nature of the system interpreting this information. For examples a nonmonotic rate-intensity function can provide as much information in a region with a negative slope as in a region with a positive slope. The complexity of the system required to make use of all available information may be great and simpler, suboptimum systems may be more attractive. For example, instead of postulating optimum use of the number of firings from each fiber, one could postulate a decision based on total count in the whole population of fibers.

When one makes explicit postulates about the parameters providing information to the brain and specifies the statistics of these parameters, then one can calculate the performance that is possible from the use of these parameters by an optimum or any specific suboptimum detector. An example of an explicit, quantitative evaluation of this type has been provided in this Symposium by Goldstein (1980). Other examples can be found in Siebert (1968, 1970) and Colburn (1973, 1977).

REPLY TO COMMENT OF H.S. COLBURN

E.F. Evans
Department of Communication & Neuroscience, University of Keele, Keele, Staffs., U.K.

Generally, physiologists have tacit assumptions on what a biologically "significant" response is. For them, what is most obvious to the eye, and what seems most parsimonious is likely to be most relevant to a biological system. In other words, informal intuition is used and this approach has clearly been valuable. Intuition has to be aided and informed by modelling, in the sensory neurosciences, obviously, it has weaknesses and one will reach a point when the territory is adequately charted that these assumptions need to be made precise in order to make quantitative comparisons between predicted performance of the system hypothesized and the observed behavior. But before that point is reached, "look and see" type physiological experiments are still needed to explore the sifnificant features of the system and to eliminate hypothesized mechanisms of coding. I doubt the cost-effectiveness of extensive modelling of a system before the crucial assumptions are tested.

DYNAMIC RESPONSE OF SINGLE AUDITORY-NERVE FIBERS:
SOME EFFECTS OF INTENSITY AND TIME

R. L. Smith and M. L. Brachman

Institute for Sensory Research, Syracuse University
Syracuse, New York, U.S.A.

1. INTRODUCTION

A characteristic property of auditory-nerve responses is the well-known shape of the PST histograms produced by tone-burst stimulation (Kiang *et al*, 1965). Firing rate is maximum at stimulus onset and then adapts down to a steady-state level. The dynamic response, in this case the higher rate at on-set, could provide a feature for emphasizing changes in sound intensity. How-ever, the magnitude of the effects of intensity on the dynamic response depend to some extent on the experimental paradigm employed. Three situations which illustrate this dependency are discussed below. The first situation, in which stimuli with short rise times are applied and responses are averaged over fairly large time intervals, has been discussed in detail previously (Smith and Zwislocki, 1975; Smith, 1979a) and is reviewed briefly. In the second situation, the stimulus rise time is increased so that slower changes in in-tensity occur. In the third, smaller time intervals are used to measure re-sponses to rapid changes in intensity, either at stimulus onset or during amp-litude modulation by sinusoids. In the latter two situations, dynamic respon-ses are revealed which have operating ranges that are significantly greater than that measured in the first situation, namely, that of the steady-state response. The data come from single auditory-nerve fibers of anesthetized Mongolian ger-bils using standard techniques that are described elsewhere (Smith, 1977, 1979a).

2. SHORT VERSUS LONG RISE TIMES

According to our previous results, onset and steady-state rate-intensity functions are proportional to one another (Smith and Zwislocki, 1975; Smith, 1979a). Consequently, the operating range, i.e. the range of sound intensities between threshold and saturation, is the same for both responses, and the gen-eral shape of response PST histograms is independent of sound intensity. This is illustrated in the PSTs in the left-hand column of Fig. 1, which are typical of those produced by stimuli with short rise times, e.g. 2.5 msec or less. Intensity increases from the top to the bottom of the figure and the higher two intensities can be seen to produce saturation of both the onset and steady-state responses. In contrast, onset responses to stimuli with long rise times (e.g. 25 msec) show systematic changes over a wider range of intensities (Rigden *et al*, 1978; Smith, 1979b). Some examples are shown in the right-hand column of Fig. 1, where the intensities are the same as those on the left. As intensity increases, the maximum response increases and occurs earlier in time. These changes continue to occur even though the steady-state response has saturated, so that the dynamic response has an increased operating range rela-tive to the steady state.

Rate-intensity functions for the long rise-time stimulus are shown in Fig. 2, and further illustrate the increase in operating range. Each symbol cor-responds to a different time interval in the stimulus envelope, as is indica-ted schematically at the top of the figure. For the later intervals, the

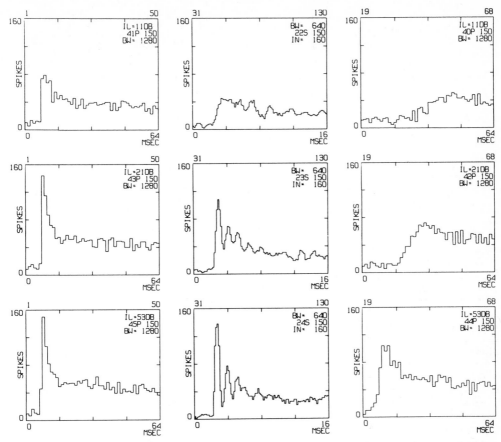

Fig. 1. PST histograms illustrating some effects of sound intensity on the time course of auditory-nerve responses. In this example, stimuli were wide-band noise bursts, but similar results were obtained with CF tone bursts. Intensity level equals 11, 21, and 53 dB re threshold for the top, middle, and bottom rows respectively. Left column: Responses to stimuli with short rise times (nominally 10 μsec). Histogram bin width equals 1.28 msec. Middle column: Smoothed PST histograms (see footnote 1) for the onset portions of the respon- ses to the left. Bin width equals 640 μsec and each bin is advanced 160 μsec from the preceding bin. Right column: Responses to stimuli with long rise times (nominally 25 msec). Unit Ge-55-11; CF = 10.4 kHz.

rate-intensity functions resemble the unit's steady-state function (not shown). They increase monotonically and reach saturation within about 25 dB of thresh- old. During the rising portion of the envelope, successively earlier intervals have lower sound intensities so that their rate-intensity functions are shifted along the intensity axis. In addition, they have a nonmonotonic shape and a maximum firing rate that increases as the time delay to the interval decreases. Consequently, the maximum firing rate continues to increase over the full in- tensity range that is illustrated and has an operating range at least 30 dB greater than that of the steady-state response (Smith and Brachman, 1980a).

The increased operating range might appear to contradict our previously described phenomenological model in which a static nonlinearity preceded an additive adaptation process in the chain of peripheral auditory signal pro- cessing (e.g. Smith and Zwislocki, 1975). If saturation occurred first in the

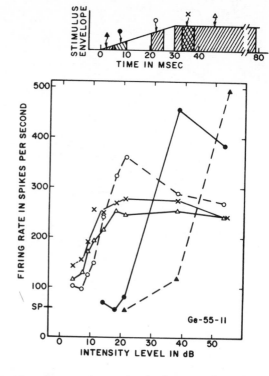

Fig. 2. Rate-intensity functions for a stimulus with a long rise time. Firing rates were obtained for the various time intervals indicated schematically at the top of the figure. Each interval was 5.12 msec long, with the exception of the long interval designated by the unfilled triangle. Same unit as Fig. 1.

spatial sequence of events, how could the dynamic response show less effects of saturation than the steady-state response did? Nevertheless, the answer appears to be consistent with the model and involves the interaction between the long rise time, saturation, and adaptation. According to this explanation, for sufficiently high overall intensity, saturation is reached during the rising portion of the stimulus envelope. Consequently, as intensity increases further, saturation occurs at progressively earlier intervals, i.e. the effective rise time decreases. However, the earlier the interval, the less adaptation from prior stimulation so that the maximum firing rate increases. In other words, in the temporal sequence of events adaptation occurs before saturation is reached, and the amount of adaptation is intensity dependent.

A simulation of these effects is shown in Figs. 3 and 4, which were obtained using a saturation-adaptation model similar to that described previously (Smith and Zwislocki, 1975; Smith 1979b). In the model, the stimulus envelope is the input to a saturating nonlinearity which has the shape of the average rate-intensity function (Zwislocki, 1973, 1976). The output of the nonlinearity serves as the input to the second, adaptation, stage. This stage is effectively a linear filter with a step response, i.e. the response to a unit increase in input, that matches the actual PSTs produced by stimuli with short rise times. Simulated response versus time functions for the long rise-time stimulus and several intensity levels are shown in Fig. 3. These results closely resemble the measured PST histograms in the right-hand column of Fig. 1. The simulated rate-intensity functions in Fig. 4 are similarly comparable to the measured functions of Fig. 2. Notice that in both Figs. 3 and 4 the maximum response continues to grow even though the steady-state response has saturated. Hence, the interaction between the slowly rising stimulus envelope and a static nonlinearity followed by additive adaptation is sufficient to account for a dynamic response with an increased operating range.

The nonmonotonicities illustrated in Fig. 2 also appear in the simulation and consequently may have a similar interpretation to that of the increased operating range. Consider a given time interval during the rising portion of the envelope. When the intensity during the interval is sufficient to produce saturation, a further increase in intensity will have no direct effect on the response during that interval. However, it will produce an increased response in prior intervals, resulting in more adaptation and thus a decrease in response during the observation interval. It may be of interest to note that

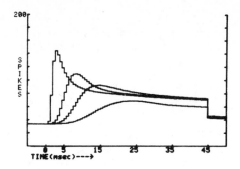

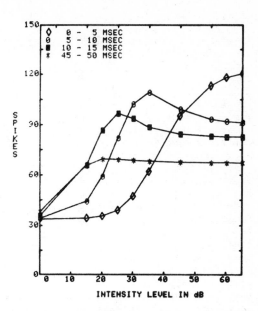

Fig. 3. Simulated responses based
on the hypothesized interaction
between a long stimulus rise time
and a static saturation followed
by additive adaptation (see text).
The curves show the time course of
responses for four input intensity
levels for comparison with the right-
hand PSTs in Fig. 1. The relative
levels of the inputs correspond to
approximately 15, 25, 40, and 60 dB
re threshold. Rise time was nominally 25 msec with a stimulus envelope resembling that of the Grason
Stadler 829 electronic switch.

Fig. 4. Rate-intensity functions for
the simulation of Fig. 3. Firing rates
were computed during the time intervals
indicated by the key in the upper
left.

these interactions can be combined with two-tone suppression producing a somewhat unexpected result. A suppressor above CF causes a change in the shape of
a PST histogram similar to that caused by a decrease in sound intensity (Smith,
1979b). Thus the suppressor does not appear to directly influence response
dynamics but rather to act as a simple stimulus attenuator, as has been demonstrated previously by the shift in the average rate-intensity function (Javel
et al, 1978). The rate-intensity functions in Fig. 5 illustrate that a similar
shift occurs for responses during the rising portion of the stimulus envelope.
It can also be seen that in the nonmonotonic portions of the rate-intensity
functions, two-tone suppression consequently causes an increase in the firing
rate. In terms of the present interpretation, the increase occurs because
suppression effectively reduces the prior intensity, resulting in a decrease
in adaptation.

3. ONSET RESPONSE USING SMALL TIME WINDOWS

In the above illustrations, results were consistent with the assumption
that a static nonlinearity produces saturation and limits the direct effects
of further increases in sound intensity. However, firing rates were always
measured over intervals of several milliseconds or more. Several lines of
evidence suggest that additional dynamic processes are present which are not
subject to the limitations of the static saturation (e.g. Rose et al, 1971;
Schroeder and Hall, 1974; Brachman and Smith, 1979). An example occurs when
the stimulus rise time is small, and the maximum onset response is measured
using small time intervals of two milliseconds or less (Smith and Brachman,
1980a). Under these conditions, at low sound intensities both the onset and
steady-state responses grow in proportion to one another. However, at sufficiently high sound intensities, the onset rate often grows more rapidly with
intensity than does the steady-state rate. If this occurs in the region

315

Fig. 5. *Rate-intensity functions for a long stimulus rise time, in the presence and absence of two-tone suppression. Results are shown for two intervals during the rising portion of the excitor envelope, as indicated schematically below each set of curves. Suppressor onset coincided with excitor onset but the suppressor had a short rise time (2.5 msec). Excitor frequency = 5.73 kHz (CF); suppressor frequency = 7.81 kHz; suppressor intensity = 59 dB SPL.*

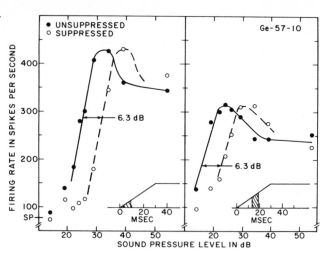

where the steady-state rate has saturated, the onset rate exhibits an increased operating range. An example is shown in Fig. 1 where the smoothed PST histograms (SPSTs)[1] in the middle column come from the initial portion of the same data as the PSTs to their left and provide a more detailed view of the onset response. As can be seen, the maximum response continues to grow at the higher two intensities in spite of the steady-state saturation.

Onset effects can also be demonstrated by comparing rate-intensity functions, such as those in Fig. 6. The rate-intensity function in Fig. 6A is for the steady-state response. That in Fig. 6B is for the onset response, i.e. the maximum response measured using a small time interval. As can be seen, the onset response continues to grow even though the steady-state rate has saturated. Another example is given in Figs. 7A and 7B. In general, auditory-nerve units exhibit a continuum of effects (Smith and Brachman, 1980a), and in an estimated 20% of the units, the onset rate increases in proportion to the steady-state rate over the full intensity range studied, while at least 40% of the units exhibit a substantial increase in the operating range at onset as in Figs. 6 and 7. In the units showing this increase, the effect appears to be over within the first few milliseconds of response even though the firing rate is still several times larger than the steady-state rate. Consequently, firing rates measured after this interval, or averaged over intervals of 10 msec or more, exhibit rate-intensity functions that are proportional to the steady-state rate-intensity function over their full intensity range, in agreement with previous descriptions (e.g. Smith, 1979a).

---

[1]SPSTs differ from PSTs in that consecutive time bins overlap (Parker and Mundie, 1967). In this case the PST histograms on the left have an interval between bins equal to their bin width, 1280 μsec. The SPSTs in the middle column have a smaller bin width, 640 μsec, and the interval between bins is only 160 μsec. A PST histogram with the same bin width would contain every fourth bin of the SPST. The maximum response corresponding to a fixed bin width can be accurately obtained from an SPST, while a PST with the same bin width may miss some important bins. It is possible that this sliding or smoothing operation is more closely related to the kind of processing the nervous system might perform, that is, a running time average with no fixed synchronization signal, than is the collection of a PST histogram in which there is no overlap between bins.

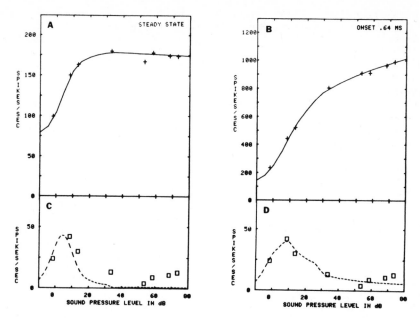

Fig. 6. Comparison of rate-intensity functions and response modulation (RM). Steady-state and onset rate-intensity functions are shown in A and B respectively, where the onset rate was measured using a 640-µsec time interval. RM was produced by amplitude modulation of a CF tone burst by a sinusoid with a 35% modulation index and 150-Hz modulation frequency. The dashed curves are theoretical response modulation functions derived from the corresponding rate-intensity functions (see text). Unit MB-26-2; CF = 1.57 kHz.

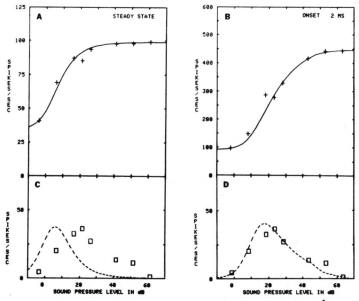

Fig. 7. Comparison of rate-intensity functions and response modulation similar to Fig. 6. Unit MB-17-3; CF = 1.94 kHz.

Several phenomena probably contribute to the increased operating range of the onset response. It may in part reflect an interaction between rise time and adaptation similar to that described above for long rise times, but on a smaller time scale. In addition, increasing the sound intensity increases the synchronization between the onset of the stimulus and the first spike of the response, and this can produce an increase in the first peak of a PST histogram. This increased synchronization, combined with neural refractoriness, is likely to account for the oscillations or ringing frequently observed at stimulus onset, e.g. the middle column of Fig. 1 (Smith and Brachman, 1980a). However, these explanations cannot account for the responses produced by amplitude modulation (AM), which are reviewed next.

4. AMPLITUDE MODULATION

The methods and results of the AM experiments are described in detail elsewhere (Smith and Brachman, 1980b) and can be summarized as follows. Characteristic frequency tone bursts were amplitude modulated by sinusoids which began 150 msec after tone onset in order to allow short-term adaptation to be complete. Response modulation was obtained from the estimated amplitude of period histograms synchronized to the modulating sinusoids. When percent modulation was held constant and average intensity increased from threshold, response modulation was observed to follow a nonmonotonic function, first increasing and then decreasing with further increases in intensity. Attempts were made to quantitatively predict the shape of the response modulation function by taking appropriate increments along the steady-state rate-intensity function. The predictions were systematically in error with maximum response modulation generally occurring at higher average intensities and response modulation occurring over a greater range of intensities than predicted. Examples are given in Figs. 6C and 7C, where the squares show the measured response modulation and the dashed curves, the steady-state predictions. In contrast, predictions obtained in a similar way from increments along the onset rate-intensity function provide a much better fit to the data (Brachman and Smith, 1979) as can be seen in Figs. 6D and 7D. A simple explanation for this agreement is that the same underlying dynamic process is reflected in two aspects of dynamic response--the onset response and response modulation. If this dynamic process were rapidly adapting and not limited by the static saturation, it could effectively be added to or superimposed upon short-term adaptation. It would then be available to respond to rapid changes in intensity but have little effect on average responses measured over sufficiently large time windows.

5. CONCLUSION

The above illustrations are offered as evidence of the importance of dynamic properties in describing the responses of auditory-nerve fibers. In each example the appropriate stimulus-response paradigm reveals a dynamic operating range exceeding that determined from steady-state or average characteristics. Many questions remain about these effects (Smith and Brachman, 1980a,b) and they are not as striking as some reported in the cochlear nucleus (e.g. Møller, 1976). However, for the present, we conclude that the dynamic response components in auditory-nerve fibers are important candidates for conveying information to the central nervous system about changes in the intensity of auditory stimulation.

REFERENCES

Brachman, M. L. and Smith, R. L. (1979). Dynamic versus static characteristics of single auditory-nerve fibers. *Neurosci. Abstr.* <u>5</u>, 16.

Javel, E., Geisler, C. D., and Ravindran, A. (1978). Two-tone suppression in auditory nerve of the cat: Rate-intensity and temporal analyses. *J. Acoust. Soc. Am.* <u>63</u>, 1093-1104.

Kiang, N. Y. S., Watanabe, T., Thomas, E. C., and Clark, L. F. (1965). *Discharge Patterns of Single Fibers in the Cat's Auditory Nerve*. Res. Monograph <u>35</u>, M.I.T. Press, Cambridge, Mass.

Rose, J. E., Hind, J. E., Anderson, D. J., and Brugge, J. F. (1971). Some effects of stimulus intensity on response of auditory-nerve fibers in the squirrel monkey. *J. Neurophysiol.* <u>34</u>, 685-699.

Møller, A. R. (1976). Dynamic properties of primary auditory fibers compared with cells in the cochlear nucleus. *Acta Physiol. Scand.* <u>98</u>, 157-167.

Parker, D. E. and Mundie, J. R. (1967). Neural sensitivity changes following stimulation with transient sound bursts. *J. Aud. Res.* <u>7</u>, 287-301.

Ridgen, M. C., Kim, D. O., and Molnar, C. E. (1978). Average-rate, fundamental and harmonic distortion components of responses of cochlear nerve fibers to single frequency tone bursts: Comparison with an exponential model. *J. Acoust. Soc. Am.* <u>63</u>, S77(A).

Schroeder, M. R. and Hall, J. L. (1974). Model for mechanical to neural transduction in the auditory receptor. *J. Acoust. Soc. Am.* <u>55</u>, 1055-1060.

Smith, R. L. (1977). Short-term adaptation in single auditory nerve fibers: Some poststimulatory effects. *J. Neurophysiol.* <u>40</u>, 1098-1112.

Smith, R. L. (1979a). Adaptation, saturation, and physiological masking in single auditory-nerve fibers. *J. Acoust. Soc. Am.* <u>65</u>, 166-178.

Smith, R. L. (1979b). Some effects of stimulus rise time on responses of auditory-nerve fibers. *J. Acoust. Soc. Am.* <u>65</u>, S83(A).

Smith, R. L. and Brachman, M. L. (1980a). Operating range and maximum response of single auditory-nerve fibers. *Brain Res.* <u>183</u> (in press).

Smith, R. L. and Brachman, M. L. (1980b). Response modulation of auditory-nerve fibers by AM stimuli: Effects of average intensity. *Hearing Res.* <u>2</u> (in press).

Smith, R. L. and Zwislocki, J. J. (1975). Short-term adaptation and incremental responses in single auditory-nerve fibers. *Biol. Cyber.* <u>17</u>, 169-182.

Zwislocki, J. J. (1973). On intensity characteristics of sensory receptors: A generalized function. *Kybernetik (Biol. Cyber.)* <u>12</u>, 169-183.

Zwislocki, J. J. (1976). Intensity characteristics of auditory-nerve fibers: A preliminary analysis. *J. Acoust. Soc. Am.* <u>56</u>, S45(A).

Acknowledgements.

We thank Joseph M. Schmitt for the help he provided in the simulation studies. The research was supported by NSF grant BNS76-14354, NIH grant NS03950, and an NIH Research Career Development Award held by R. L. Smith.

SPECTRAL RESOLUTION OF COMB-FILTERED NOISE BY COCHLEAR FIBERS IN THE CAT:
PRELIMINARY RESULTS OF COMPARISONS WITH THEIR RATE-LEVEL FUNCTIONS

P.M. Narins and E.F. Evans

*Dept. of Biology, University of California
at Los Angeles, Los Angeles, CA.90024, USA
and
Dept. of Communication and Neuroscience,
University of Keele, Keele, Staffs., ST5 5BG, U.K.*

1. INTRODUCTION

Most auditory fibers in the mammalian cochlear nerve are able to signal
changes in stimulus intensity over a dynamic range, between spontaneous discharge and saturation threshold, limited to 30-60 dB (Kiang, 1968; Palmer and
Evans, 1979). There are a small number of fibers with a wide dynamic range:
see Evans, this volume. In the dorsal cochlear nucleus (DCN), however, there
are many cells which under certain conditions exhibit a much wider dynamic
range. The latter result has been demonstrated by examining the response of
single cells in the DCN to CF tones in band-stop noise (Evans and Palmer, 1975).
These workers showed that the cells in the DCN that responded to tones in a
band-stop noise masker over a very wide range of signal intensities exhibited
prominent inhibitory side-bands. It was suggested, therefore, that the bandstop noise "biased" the discharge rate below saturation, thus increasing the
dynamic range of the cell. However, the dynamic range of single cochlear fibers
measured under the same conditions was limited.

Consistent with these results is the observation that cells in the DCN
with lateral inhibitory sidebands are also capable of resolving spectral peaks
of comb-filtered noise (CFN), in terms of their discharge rate, over a wide
range of noise levels (Evans, 1977; Bilsen and ten Kate, 1977), whereas the
ability of cochlear fibers was found to be limited (Evans, 1977). It is of
interest, therefore, to compare the dynamic range over which single cochlear
fibers are able to reflect, in their discharge rates, the spectral envelope of
the CFN stimulus, with that of their rate-level (R-L) functions for broad-band
noise. This experiment, with preliminary computer simulation to provide a
comparison with the CFN data, is the subject of this provisional report. Some
of these results have been reported previously (Narins and Evans, 1978).

2. METHODS

a) Physiology

Recordings were made from 22 single fibers in the cochlear nerve of pentobarbitone anaesthetized adult cats which were artificially respired and maintained at a body temperature between 36°-38°C. In addition, blood pressure and
end tidal CO_2 were monitored to ensure physiological stability. For further
detail see Evans (1972, 1979).

After encountering and isolating a single fiber we determined: a) the FTC
using a threshold following paradigm (Evans, 1979); b) the rate-level (R-L)
function for broad-band noise bursts (0-40 kHz) using a pseudo-random intensity
schedule, and durations indicated in Figs. 2 and 3; and c) the response to continuous comb-filtered noise with systematically decreasing peak spacing

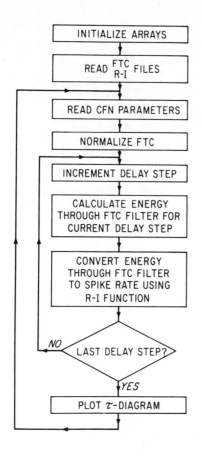

INITIALIZE ARRAYS

READ $^{FTC}_{R-I}$ FILES

READ CFN PARAMETERS

NORMALIZE FTC

INCREMENT DELAY STEP

CALCULATE ENERGY THROUGH FTC FILTER FOR CURRENT DELAY STEP

CONVERT ENERGY THROUGH FTC FILTER TO SPIKE RATE USING R-I FUNCTION

NO LAST DELAY STEP?

YES

PLOT τ-DIAGRAM

Fig. 1. Simplified flow chart for the CFN simulation program.

CFN with a peak-to-valley ratio of 35 dB was generated by adding two identical pseudo-random waveforms with a delay, τ, which could be externally controlled by a computer (Narins *et al*, 1979). After presenting a sequence of CFN stimuli at progressively decreasing mean levels, the R-L function for broad-band noise was redetermined to check for adaptation effects; the mean level of the CFN was then increased in discrete steps, after which the R-L function was once more determined. For each level of CFN, the spike rate of the fiber is plotted as a function of the delay, τ, which is inversely proportional to the spacing between adjacent peaks of the CFN stimulus. Both the resulting "τ-diagrams" and the R-L functions were smoothed using an Hamming window of appropriate width.

b) Simulation

The simulation of the CFN experiments was carried out on a CA alpha LSI - 2/20 minicomputer.

The simulation made the simplest assumptions: (1) that the FTC represents a linear filter attenuation function (as successfully assumed by Evans and Wilson, 1973, for low-level CFN stimulation), therefore the CFN spectrum corresponding to each delay can be linearly filtered by the FTC 'filter'; (2) the filtered CFN energy can be applied to the observed R-L function to predict the fiber's discharge rate. A simplified flow chart of the simulation program is given in Fig. 1. No attempt was made to include non-linear phenomena such as two-tone suppression effects, or to compensate for the effects of adaptation, which produced systematic differences, for example, between the saturated discharge rates under CFN and under broadband stimulation for the R-L functions (Figs. 2 and 3).

At this preliminary stage, unfortunately, the conversion of FTC filtered CFN energy was carried out in such a way that the rates can only be identified with relative, not absolute, CFN levels. This introduces a complicating factor in comparing the dynamic ranges in simulated and observed responses to different levels of CFN: because the biological noise apparent in the physiological data (Figs. 2 and 3) is not present in the simulations (Figs. 4 and 5), its contribution to the limitation of the dynamic range of the former cannot be easily assessed. The comparisons, therefore, must be regarded as provisional at this stage.

3. RESULTS AND DISCUSSION

a) Physiology

A 'by eye' comparison was first made between the dynamic range over which a cochlear fiber could signal spectral peaks of CFN and that exhibited by its rate-level function for broad-band noise. The results for fiber 730_{13} with a CF of 2.87 kHz are shown in Fig. 2. Fig. 2a shows the FTC (solid line) corrected for the sound system frequency response. Fig. 2b illustrates, for different levels of CFN, the variations in firing rate as the delay of the CFN was systematically increased from $\tau = 0$, to $\tau = 2.0$ ms in steps small enough to ensure adequate resolution, e.g., 15 steps per peak. Each of these curves (τ-diagrams) represents the smoothed average of four separate sweeps of delay.

The peak-to-valley ratio for these τ-diagrams decreases nearly monotonically with increasing τ, for all levels of CFN, consistent with the filtering

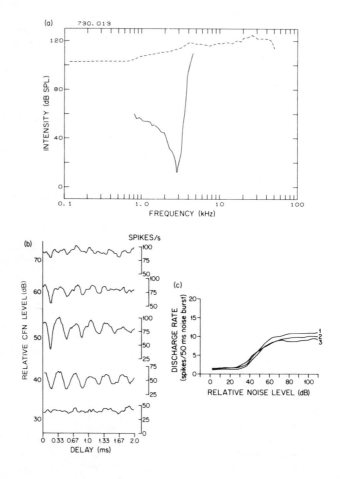

Fig. 2. a) FTC (solid line) for cochlear fiber 730_{13} corrected for sound system and probe tube characteristics (dashed line). b) Variations in discharge rate as the delay of the CFN was increased, for different levels of CFN. c) Rate-level   functions determined with broad-band noise.

characteristics (i.e. finite bandwidth) of the filter. This fiber is able to
follow the spectral peaks in the CFN stimulus over a dynamic range of 30 dB -
40 dB. This is consistent with the dynamic range shown by the fiber's response
to broad-band noise, as illustrated in Fig. 2c. The three R-L functions shown
in Fig. 2c were obtained (1) before the CFN sequence, (2) midway through the
CFN sequence and (3) after the CFN sequence. The small changes in the firing
rate at saturation after exposure to the CFN stimulus are indicative of long-
term adaptation of the cochlear fiber.

The FTC, τ-diagrams and R-L functions for another fiber, 740_{23}, with a
CF = 5.36 kHz are shown in Fig. 3. The response of this fiber is similar to
that shown in Fig. 2, in that the dynamic range using the CFN stimulus paradigm appeared consistent with the R-L function for broad-band noise.

In only one fiber did these methods yield obviously disparate values;
namely, the dynamic range indicated by the CFN paradigm was 20 dB *less* than

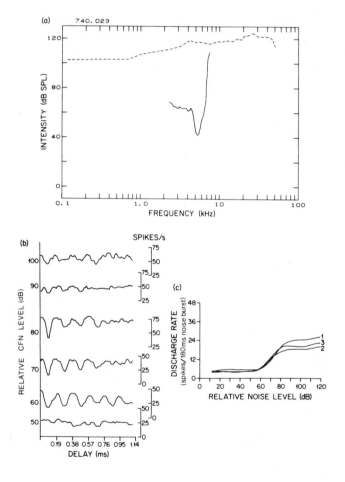

Fig. 3.   Same as Fig. 2 for cochlear fiber 740_{23}

that indicated by the R-L function.

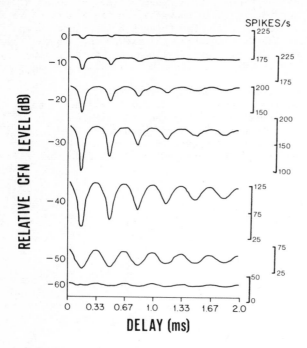

Fig. 4. τ-Diagrams for fiber 730_{13} predicted by the CFN simulation program.

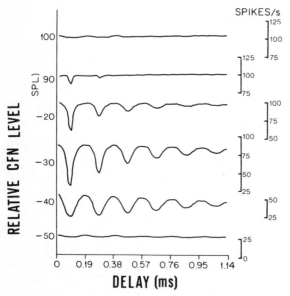

Fig. 5. τ-Diagrams for fiber 740_{23} predicted by the CFN simulation program.

b) Simulation

The τ-diagrams obtained from the simulation program using the digitized FTC's and R-L functions for fibers 730_{13} and 740_{23} are shown in Figs. 4 and 5 respectively. Since adaptation was not incorporated in the simulation program, the spike rates predicted for the higher levels of CFN stimulation were substantially greater than those actually observed.

With this anticipated exception, the simulation adequately models several aspects of cochlear fiber response to CFN:
a) monotonic decrease in peak-to-valley ratio of discharge rate with increasing delay;
b) a 'threshold' level below which the fiber cannot follow the spectral peaks and valleys of the CFN stimulus;
c) a decrease in the peak-to-valley ratio as the fiber approaches saturation, and
d) a first valley which is most resistant to high stimulus levels.

As far as the dynamic range is concerned, for six fibers, the simulation more or less successfully predicted the observed dynamic range (Fig. 5), with the qualifications made explicit under 2 b) above. However, for two fibers, the simulation over-estimated the dynamic range over which a fiber could follow spectral peaks and valleys of the CFN stimulus (Fig. 4).

Both the experimental data and the simulation results in this provisional form indicate that cochlear fibers are capable of representing the spectral structure of a complex sound only over a dynamic range at least limited by their rate-level functions.

Acknowledgements

This research was supported by an N.I.H. postdoctoral fellowship to P.M.N. and several grants from the M.R.C. to E.F.E. The physiological recordings were made at Keele, and we are grateful to Mr. J.S. Corbett for technical assistance. The computer simulations were carried out in U.C.L.A., and for which we are grateful to R. Peoples for assistance. We wish to thank R. Zelick and D. Hurley for helpful comments on the manuscript.

REFERENCES

Bilsen, F.A. and ten Kate, J.H. (1977). Preservation of the internal spectrum of complex signals at high intensities. In: *Psychophysics and Physiology of Hearing.* (E.F. Evans and J.P. Wilson, eds). pp193-195. Academic Press, London.

Evans, E.F. (1972). The frequency response and other properties of single fibers in the guinea-pig cochlear nerve. *J. Physiol.* 226, 263-287.

Evans, E.F. (1977). Frequency selectivity at high signal levels of single units in cochlear nerve and nucleus. In: *Psychophysics and Physiology of Hearing.* (E.F. Evans and J.P. Wilson, eds). pp.185-195. Academic Press, London.

Evans, E.F. (1979). Single unit studies of the mammalian auditory nerve. In: *Auditory Investigations: The Scientific and Technological Basis.* (H.A. Beagley, ed). Chapt. 15, pp.324-367. Oxford University Press, Oxford.

Evans, E.F. and Palmer, A.R. (1975). Responses of units in the cochlear nerve and nucleus of the cat to signals in the presence of bandstop noise. *J. Physiol.* 252, 60-62P.

Evans, E.F. and Wilson, J.P. (1973). Frequency selectivity of the cochlea. In: *Basic Mechanisms in Hearing* (A.R. Møller, ed) pp519-551, Academic Press, N.Y.

Kiang, N.Y.-s. (1968). A survey of recent developments in the study of auditory physiology. *Ann. Otol. Rhinol. Laryngol.* 77, 656-675.

Narins, P.M. and Evans, E.F. (1978). The dynamic range of responses of single cochlear fibers in the cat to individual spectral components of comb-filtered noise. *J. Acoust. Soc. Amer.* 64, S135 (A).

Narins, P.M., Evans, E.F., Pick, G.F. and Wilson, J.P. (1979). A comb-filtered noise generator for use in auditory neurophysiological and psychophysical experiments. *IEEE Trans. Biomed. Engr.* BME-26, 43-47.

Palmer, A.R. and Evans, E.F. (1979). On the peripheral coding of the level of individual frequency components of complex sounds at high sound levels. *Exp. Br. Res. Suppl. II.* 19-26.

COMMENT ON: "Spectral resolution of comb-filtered noise by cochlear fibers in the cat: preliminary results of comparisons with their rate-level functions" (P.M. Narins and E.F. Evans).

J.H. ten Kate
Biophysics Group, Applied Physics Dept., Delft University of Technolgoy, Delft, The Netherlands.

One conclusion of Narins and Evans, that the range of the experimental τ-diagrams "are successfully predicted" by the dynamic range of stimulated τ-diagrams only can be qualitatively accepted with the restriction in so far the peaks and the valleys to the cosine noise are drowned in increasing spike-noise at high levels of intensity (their Figs. 2b and 3b). The stimulated τ-diagrams (their Figs. 4 and 5) in contrast to the experimental ones demonstrate no noise at high level. Moreover the difference between the spike rates in fig. 2b and 2c (etc.) should be due to adaptation. The authors did also mention some adaptation effects but they did not attempt to avoid these effects in their recording by an appropriate choice of a duty cycle for their acoustical stimulation. Adaptation effects of cochlear fibres may be considerably large (Harris and Dallos, 1979, Smith, 1979). Bilsen *et al* (1975) required a constant level in the number of spikes on the bursts of noise during recording-time, to which could be obeyed by the choice of 100 ms bursts with silent intervals of 400 ms (see Fig.1). Under these conditions no adaptation effects were found in the

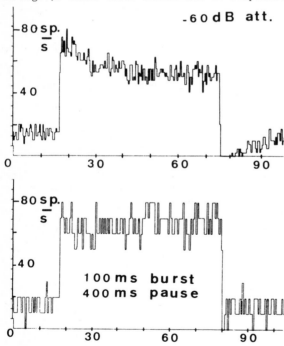

Fig.1. Upper figure: Response of a DCN neuron to a step in continuous noise. Lower figure: Spike counts per 100 ms burst during recording of interrupted noise. Note the absence of adaptation and the increase in stochastic variation in the same recording period.

neural τ-diagrams. Another way of avoiding effects on the recording of τ-diagrams was to adapt the cochlear nucleus neuron completely to the level of the continuous noise. Afterwards the τ-diagrams on comb-filtered noise with small modulation depths were recorded. The spectral resolution of comb-filtered noise is discernible between g = 20-25 dB or modulation depths M = 1.7-0.9 dB (Bilsen *et al*, 1975) (see Fig.2). The thresholds for detection of peaks and valleys are comparable to psychophysical thresholds for repetition pitch. It is not evident from the data of Narins and Evans, whether or not the discharge rate of the cochlear fibre is capable of resolving the spectra of comb-filtered noise with small modulation depths. On the basis of the presented data I conclude that this resolution is an open question.

Evans (1977) determined the filtering characteristics of cochlear fibres

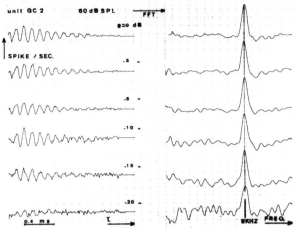

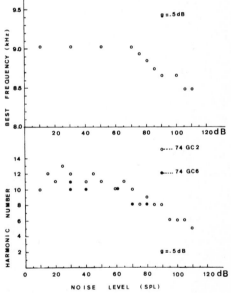

Fig.2. Left part of the figure: The six traces are smoothed τ-diagrams of unit 74 GC2. Note that only five peaks are discernible in the noisy bottom trace, for which the cosine noise has M = 1.7 dB (=g=-20 dB). Right part of the figure: The six traces are obtained with Fast Fourier Transformation from the six left τ-diagrams. The best frequencies appear to be equal for the different modulation depths at this noise level L_n=60 dB SPL.

at different noise levels with the reversed correlation technique. Two types of filtering characteristics of cochlear fibres were encountered, one with and one without frequency shift of the CF (Characteristic Frequency). A same trend was found in the cochlear nucleus data of τ-diagrams presented by Bilsen and ten Kate, 1977. A change in periodicity in the delay was determined with Fourier transformation (see Figs. 2 and 3).

Fig.3. Upper plot: The best frequencies of unit 74 GC2 (determined from τ-diagrams) are plotted against the noise level in dB SPL. Lower plot: The harmonic number (= number of peaks counted for the delay time τ>0) discernible in the smoothed τ-diagrams of unit 74 GC2 and 74 GC6 are plotted against the noise levels in dB SPL. Note the mutual decrease of both plots with increasing noise levels.

In these data above 70 dB SPL the best frequency shifted to lower frequencies and at the same time the harmonic number decreased. At the level of 70 dB SPL the CF of the cochlear nerve-fibre-data of Evans (1977) also started to shift to lower frequencies. The presented data of τ-diagrams (Figs. 2,3, Narins and Evans) are not analysed in this respect of the frequency shift. The discharge rate of the fibres may still transport information about the frequency shift at high level towards the cochlear nucleus.

In the present stage of knowledge the coding of intensity in a number of cochlear nerve fibres with different thresholds cannot be excluded, (even when the dynamic range of one fibre is restricted), because Kiang *et al* (1976) determined a variation of thresholds over a range of 80 dB for normal cats.

REFERENCES

Bilsen, F.A., Kate, J.H. ten, Buunen, T.J.F., Raatgever, J. (1975). Responses of single units in the cochlear nucleus of the cat to cosine noise. *J.Acoust.Soc.Am.* <u>58</u>, 858-866.

COMMENT

Bilsen, F.A., Kate, J.H. ten. (1977). Preservation of the internal spectrum of complex signals at high intensities. In: *Psychophysics and Physiology of Hearing*. E.F. Evans and J.P. Wilson (Eds), pp 193-195. Ac. Press, London.

Evans, E.F. (1977). Frequency selectivity at high signal levels of single units in cochlear nerve and nucleus. In: *Psychophysics and Physiology of hearing*. E.F. Evans and J.P. Wilson (Eds), pp 185-192. Ac. Press, London.

Harris, D.M. and Dallos, P. (1979), Forward masking of auditory nerve fibre responses. *J.Neurophysiol.* 42, 1083-1107.

Kiang, N.Y.S., Liberman, M.C., Levine, R.A. (1976). Auditory nerve activity in cats exposed to ototoxic drugs and high-intensity sounds. *Annals of Otol, Rhinol. and Laryngol.* 75, 752-768.

Smith, R.L. (1979). Adaptation, saturation and forward masking in auditory nerve fibres. *J.Acoust.Soc.Am.* 65, 166-178.

REPLY TO COMMENT OF J.H. TEN KATE

P.M. Narins
Dept. of Biology, University of California at Los Angeles, Los Angeles, CA, U.S.A.

Dependence of discharge rate modulation on CFN peak-to-valley ratio: prediction from simulation.

Bilsen *et al* (1975) measured τ-diagrams for cells in the cochlear nucleus of the cat for changing modulation depths of the stimulus. In his comment, ten Kate observes that the analogous experiment has not been done in the auditory nerve. Using a computer simulation of the auditory nerve experiment (Narins and Evans, this Volume) a prediction of the first three τ-diagram peak-to-valley ratios (P/V) as a function of stimulus P/V for unit 730_{13} was made. According to the simulation (done at 40 dB above the units threshold), the first P/V is most sensitive to a reduction of the stimulus P/V, whereas the second and third P/V of the τ-diagram are relatively insensitive to changes in the stimulus P/V over about a 15 dB range. Stimulus peak-to-valley ratios of less than 15 dB should affect the first three peak-to-valley ratios of the τ-diagram.

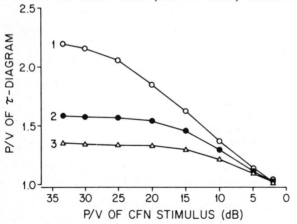

Predicted dependence of the first three τ-diagram peak-to-valley ratios on the peak-to-valley ratio of a comb-filtered noise stimulus in the auditory nerve.

REFERENCES

Bilsen, F.A., ten Kate, J.H., Buunen, T.J.F. and Raatgever, J. (1975). Responses of single units in the cochlear nucleus of the cat to cosine noise. *J.Acoust.Soc.Am.* 58, 858-866.

LOUDNESS OF NOISE IN THE PRESENCE OF TONES:
MEASUREMENTS AND NONLINEAR MODEL RESULTS

J.L. Hall and M.R. Schroeder

*Bell Laboratories, Murray Hill, NJ, USA, and
Drittes Physik. Inst., Universität Göttingen, Germany*

1. INTRODUCTION

As one part of a program to obtain an objective measure of the quality of speech coding systems (Schroeder, Atal, and Hall, 1979), we have measured the loudness of critical-band noise bursts in the presence of pure-tone maskers of various frequencies and intensities. The result can be summarized as follows: If the frequency of the masking tone is below the center frequency of the noise burst, loudness drops off sharply as intensity of the masking tone increases. If the frequency of the masking tone is above the center frequency of the noise burst, loudness drops off less sharply. These results are directly parallel to some aspects of two-tone suppression in primary auditory fibers of the cat (Abbas and Sachs, 1976). In addition, these results can be successfully reproduced by a nonlinear transmission-line model for motion of the basilar membrane (Hall, 1977). We present a heuristic explanation for these results in terms of place of nonlinear interaction on the model membrane.

2. LOUDNESS MEASUREMENTS

a) Methods

The loudness of the masked noise burst was measured by means of a matching paradigm, as shown in Fig. 1. Noise bursts were presented at a uniform rate. The masking tone alternated on for three bursts and off for three bursts. The subjects adjusted the intensity of the unmasked noise bursts until he was satisfied that the masked and unmasked noise bursts were equally loud, then he pushed a button. The intensity of the matching unmasked noise burst was recorded and the next stimulus configuration was presented.

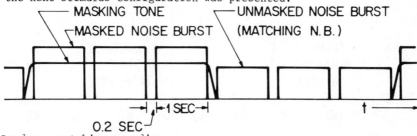

Fig.1. *Loudness matching paradigm.*

The spectrum of the noise bursts was flat over the frequency range 923 to 1083 Hz (one critical band wide, geometric mean 1 kHz). The noise bursts had sinusoidal rise and decay times of 100 msec, and the masking tone had sinusoidal rise and decay times of 200 msec. Stimuli were presented monaurally through Sennheiser HD-414 earphones to subjects seated in a double-walled IAC soundproof booth. Similar results were obtained from the two subjects who participated in the experiment. Stimuli were presented and the experiment was controlled by a data General Eclipse computer.

b) Results

Loudness measurements as a function of intensity of the masked noise burst, with the intensity of the masking tone held constant at 80 dB SPL, are given in Schroeder, Atal, and Hall (1979), Fig. 2. When the frequency of the masking tone is equal to 1 kHz, the matching intensity of the unmasked noise burst decreases with a slope of 3 dB per 1 dB decrease of intensity of the masked noise burst.

In order to get results more directly comparable to existing electrophysiological data, we ran a second series of measurements in which the intensity of the masked noise burst was held constant at 50 dB SPL and the intensity of the masking tone was varied. Results from this second series of measurements are shown in Fig. 2.

If the frequency of the masking tone is less than 1 kHz, the matching intensity of the unmasked noise burst drops off sharply as intensity of the masking tone is increased. A decrease of the frequency of the masking tone, say from 960 Hz to 840 Hz, shifts the curve to the right but has little effect on the slope. The masking tone has to be more intense to have any influence on the loudness of the masked noise burst, but the decrease in frequency can be compensated for by an increase of intensity.

The situation is different when the frequency of the masking tone is greater than 1 kHz. The slope of the curve relating intensity of the unmasked noise burst to intensity of the masking tone decreases with increasing frequency of the masking tone, but the intensity at which the masking tone first starts to influence the loudness of the masked noise burst does not appear to change.

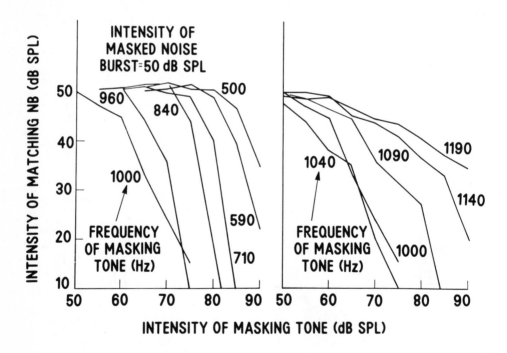

Fig.2. *Loudness of noise as a function of masker intensity.*
Parameter: frequency of masking tone.

3. COMPARISON WITH ELECTROPHYSIOLOGICAL RESULTS

Results directly parallel to those seen in Fig. 2 are shown in Fig. 8 of Abbas and Sachs (1976). They plot "fractional response" (a normalized measure of suppressed firing rate) of a primary auditory fiber in the cat as a function of intensity of the suppressing tone, with frequency of the suppressing tone as a parameter. Decreasing the frequency of the suppressing tone below fiber CF (frequency of exciting tone = CF) resulted in a shift of the fractional response curve to the right, with no change of slope. Increasing the frequency of the suppressing tone above CF decreased the slope. This parallel between electrophysiology and psychophysics has also been noted by Duifhuis (1977) for the case of tone-on-tone masking with the frequency of the masking tone greater than the frequency of the masked tone.

4. COMPARISON WITH MODEL RESULTS

This effect can be reproduced qualitatively in a one-dimensional transmission-line model for motion of the basilar membrane in which damping increases nonlinearly with membrane displacement (Hall, 1977). Fig. 3 shows a measurement of the model response to a fixed-intensity exciting tone at 1 kHz (the characteristic frequency of the place being observed) in the presence of a suppressing tone at frequency f_s and intensity A_s. Results are similar to those we have already seen from psychophysics and electrophysiology. Decreasing the frequency of the masking tone from 615 Hz to 385 Hz shifts the curve to higher suppressing-tone intensities, while increasing the frequency of the masking tone from 1038 Hz to 1077 Hz decreases the slope.

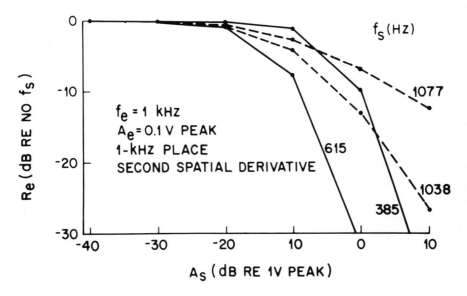

Fig.3. Nonlinear-model results. Response of 1-kHz place to 1-kHz tone as a function of suppressor intensity.
Parameter: frequency of suppressing tone.

5. DISCUSSION

The parallel between results from psychophysics, primary-fiber activity, and the model suggests that all three are mediated by a common nonlinear effect. Consideration of the structure of the model suggests the following heuristic explanation in terms of place of nonlinear interaction: First, we note that each shunt branch in the transmission-line model is a series RLC circuit. At the place of maximum response to a given frequency the RLC circuit is at resonance, so the shunt impedance is dominated by the resistive term. Basal to the place of maximum response, the impedance becomes more and more dominated by the capacitive term.

If the frequency of the suppressing tone is less than the frequency of the exciting tone, then there is a substantial component of suppressing-tone response at the exciting-tone place. The suppressing tone increases membrane damping at the exciting-tone place, and since the shunt impedance for the exciting tone at the exciting-tone place is dominated by the resistive term a given increase in damping produces a large decrease in exciting-tone response.

A decrease in frequency of the suppressing tone can be compensated for by an increase in suppressing-tone intensity. A lower frequency suppressing tone still increases damping at the exciting-tone place, but it has to be more intense because the exciting-tone place is further away from the suppressing-tone place.

If the frequency of the suppressing tone is greater than the frequency of the exciting tone, nonlinear interaction occurs not at the exciting-tone place but at the suppressing-tone place, because of the sharp apical dropoff of suppressing tone response. The suppressing tone no longer reduces the exciting-tone response directly by increasing damping at the exciting-tone place but indirectly by increasing losses in the transmission between base and exciting-tone place.

As the frequency of the suppressing tone increases, the nonlinear interactions occurs in shunt branches that, for the exciting-tone frequency, are more dominated by the capacitive term and less by the resistive term. A given increase of suppressing-tone intensity produces a given increase of resistance regardless of suppressing-tone frequency, but if the suppressing-tone frequency is high this given increase of resistance will produce only a small change in impedance at the exciting-tone frequency, and therefore only a small reduction of exciting-tone response.

REFERENCES

Abbas, P.J., and Sachs, M.B. (1976). Two-tone suppression in auditory-nerve fibers: Extension of a stimulus-response relationship. *J. Acoust. Soc. Am.* 59, 112-122.

Duiffuis, H. (1977). Cochlear nonlinearity and second filter – A psychophysical evaluation. In: *Psychophysics and Physiology of Hearing*. (E. F. Evans and J. P. Wilson, eds). pp 153-163. Academic Press, London.

Hall, J.L. (1977). Two-tone suppression in a nonlinear model of the basilar membrane. *J. Acoust. Soc. Am.* 61, 802-810.

Schroeder, M.R., Atal, B.S., and Hall, J.L. (1979). Objective measure of certain speech signal degradations based on masking properties of human auditory perception. In: *Frontiers of Speech Communication Research*. (B. Lindblom and S. Ohman, eds). pp. 217-229. Academic Press, London.

Section V
Pitch Perception

The general concept that pitch of complex sounds is derived, in one way or another, from the internal spectrum by the auditory system seems to be firmly established now. The position and the height of maxima of excitation in the internal spectrum appear to be important parameters. Suggestions and experimental results as presented in this section contribute to a quantitative evaluation of current pitch theories. Various aspects like the build-up and strength of pitch, its saliency, and induced pitch shifts have been investigated and are reported in this section. The relation to musical sounds was involved in the discussion as well. The fundamental question of whether and how temporal information is carried by the internally resolved spectral components in the processing of pitch information, is discussed.

333

H. Fastl

*Institute of Electroacoustics, Technical University,
München, Federal Republic of Germany*

1. INTRODUCTION

Low-pass noise may elicit pitch sensations which can be determined by matching experiments. A pure tone with the same pitch as the low-pass noise generally shows a frequency near the noise's cut-off frequency (Small and Daniloff, 1967, Rakowski, 1968). With steep low-pass filters, the pitch is more easily identified than with flat filters (Fastl, 1971), i.e. pitch strength of low-pass noise is more pronounced for steep filter slopes. While qualitative or indirect descriptions of pitch strength of various types of sound are quite common (Zwicker, 1975, Yost and Hill, 1978), recently quantitative scalings of pitch strength became available for low-pass noise, too (Fastl and Stoll, 1979). It was found that even a low-pass noise with a very steep filter slope of -192 dB/oct elicits only a pitch strength which is more than a factor of five smaller than the pitch strength of a pure tone at the cut-off frequency. However, quantitative data concerning pitch strength of low-pass noises with flatter filter slopes are still lacking.

Therefore, pitch strength of low-pass noise was scaled as a function of filter slope at two cut-off frequencies. A model is proposed, correlating the pitch strength of low-pass noise with the slope of its masking pattern.

2. EXPERIMENTS

Eight normally hearing observers took part in the experiments on pitch strength, while only one highly experienced observer performed the masking experiments. In a sound-isolated booth, sounds were presented monaurally through an electrodynamic earphone (Beyer DT 48) with a free-field equalizer (Zwicker and Feldtkeller, 1967, p. 40). White noise with 16 kHz bandwidth was either applied directly or filtered by one of a set of seven low-pass filters at each cut-off frequency. The attenuation curves of the filter sets as measured by a spectrum analyzer (HP 3580 A) are shown in Fig. 1. The lower abscissa indicates the frequency response of low-pass filters at 250 Hz cut-off frequency, while the upper abscissa corresponds to 1000 Hz cut-off. Filter slopes between 0 dB/oct (white noise) and -144 dB/oct were used. Throughout the experiments a constant loudness N = 8 sone (GF) of all

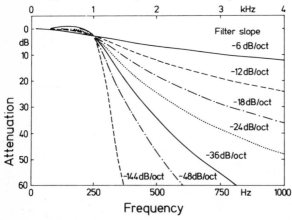

Fig. 1. Attenuation characteristics of filters

noises was maintained and measured by a loudness analyzer for temporally variable sounds (Zwicker, 1977). In Table I, the different sound pressure levels of the low-pass noises necessary for one and the same loudness are listed.

Table I. SPL of low-pass noises for same loudness N = 8 sone (GF)

	Filter slope	0	-6	-12	-18	-24	-36	-48	-144 dB/oct
SPL of low-pass	250 Hz	57	58.5	65.5	68	68.5	69	69	69 dB
noise at	1000 Hz	57	57.5	59	61	62.5	63	63	63 dB

For the experiments on pitch strength, a method of magnitude estimation was applied. The following time pattern was realized: 1 sec reference sound, 0.8 sec interval, 1 sec comparison sound, 1.5 sec interval, then two replicae of this sound pair followed by a pause of 4 sec for the observer's response. The reference sound was assigned a numerical value (e.g. 100) indicating the magnitude of its pitch strength. Relative to this value, the pitch strength of the respective comparison sound had to be scaled by the observer (e.g. 20 for a decrease in pitch strength by a factor of five). At both cut-off frequencies (250 Hz and 1000 Hz), two sets of experiments were performed: in one series a low-pass noise of relatively large pitch strength (filter slope -144 dB/oct) served as reference sound and was assigned the number 100. In the other series, a low-pass noise with small pitch strength (filter slope -12 dB/oct) was chosen as reference sound and assigned the number 10. For each comparison sound, each of the eight observers performed six scalings of pitch strength. Thus, in Fig. 2 and Fig. 4 medians with interquartile ranges are given, each derived from 48 data points.

For the masking experiments, a method of tracking was applied. Continuous low-pass noises with N = 8 sone (GF) loudness and spectral distributions as shown in Fig. 1 served as maskers. Test tones had a duration of 500 msec, were separated by 600 msec intervals and switched on and off by Gaussian-shaped gating signals with 50 msec rise-fall time. For each low-pass masker at each test frequency two threshold values were determined in random succession; their arithmetic mean is indicated in Fig. 3 by dots.

3. RESULTS AND DISCUSSION

a) Pitch strength of low-pass noises

In Fig. 2, the relative pitch strength of several low-pass noises is depicted as a function of filter slope. Fig. 2a shows the results for low-pass noises with 250 Hz cut-off frequency, Fig. 2b for 1000 Hz cut-off. Circles represent data for a low-pass noise with -144 dB/oct filter slope as reference sound, assigned the number 100 (filled circle). Squares refer to data for a reference sound with -12 dB/oct filter slope (assigned the number 10), which however were transformed as follows: in order to get comparable results from both sets of experiments, values of pitch strength were made to coincide at the reference sound -12 dB/oct (filled square), i.e. all medians and interquartiles resulting from the respective second set of experiments and enlarged by a factor of 2.5. Interestingly, this procedure leads for both cut-off frequencies to exact coincidence of pitch strength values at the other reference sound (-144 dB/oct), indicating rather little dependence of these pitch strength scalings on reference sound. Accordingly, the agreement between re-

335

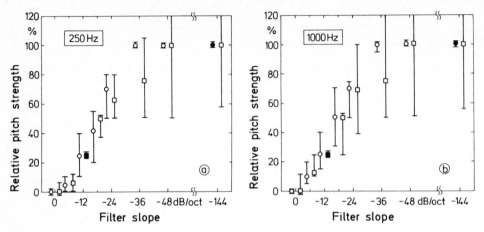

Fig. 2. Relative pitch strength of low-pass noise as a function of filter slope. Loudness of noises N = 8 sone (GF)
circles: reference sound with -144 dB/oct filter slope
squares: reference sound with -12 dB/oct filter slope

lative pitch strength values derived from both sets of experiments (circles vs. squares) is rather good at all filter slopes except at -36 dB/oct where, however, the interquartiles overlap, too. Generally, observers gave reproducible scalings with intraindividual differences of corresponding pitch strength values less than ± 10; moreover, no dramatic interindividual differences could be noticed. When evaluating the interquartile ranges connected with the squares, their enlargement by a factor of 2.5 has to be taken into account.

Results plotted in Fig. 2 suggest an increase in pitch strength of low-pass noise with increasing filter slope, however with saturation for slopes steeper than about -36 dB/oct. This means that extremely steep filters are *not* necessary to produce the maximally possible pitch strength of low-pass noise which is - in comparison to the pitch strength of a pure tone - rather small. Already low-pass filters with slopes of only about -18 dB/oct elicit half of the maximal pitch strength and the widespread filter sets with slopes of -36 dB/oct or -48 dB/oct can be used to produce low-pass noises with almost maximal pitch strength at comfortable listening levels. For first order filters (-6 dB/oct), pitch strength is very small. However, the difference in pitch strength between white noise (0 dB/oct) and low-pass noise with -6 dB/oct filter slope seems to be significant. Results plotted in Fig. 2a and Fig. 2b show quite similar dependence on filter slope, almost independent of cut-off frequency.

b) Masking patterns of low-pass noises

Fig. 3 shows masking patterns of low-pass noises with different filter slopes and cut-off frequencies of 250 Hz (Fig. 3a) and 1000 Hz (Fig. 3b), respectively. The sound pressure level of the test tone at masked threshold is plotted as a function of its critical band rate (lower abscissa) as well as frequency (upper abscissa). Dots represent arithmetic means of two threshold values, which generally deviated by not more than ± 1 dB from each other.

The masking patterns displayed in Fig. 3a and Fig. 3b, respectively, show similar trends, but distinct quantitative differences. The spectral shape of the corresponding low-pass maskers, however, is identical (cf. Fig. 1). In the following, some reasons for the differences in masking patterns will be discussed. First, for filter slopes < -36 dB/oct the patterns at 250 Hz lie

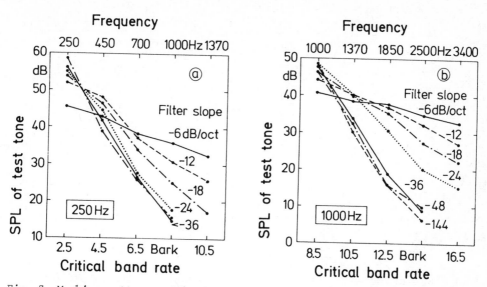

Fig. 3. Masking patterns of low-pass noises with different filter slopes. Loudness of noises N = 8 sone (GF), duration of test tone 500 msec.

about 10 dB higher than the patterns at 1000 Hz. From Table I becomes clear that the overall SPL of the noises at 250 Hz vs. 1000 Hz can account only for a difference of 6 dB. However, calculating the levels L_{CB} within the critical band around the respective cut-off frequency yields a difference of 10 dB as follows:

250 Hz: L_{CB} = 69 dB + 10 lg (100 Hz/250 Hz) dB = 65 dB
1000 Hz: L_{CB} = 63 dB + 10 lg (160 Hz/1000 Hz) dB = 55 dB

Second, for filter slopes ≥ -24 dB/oct the masking patterns of low-pass noises at 250 Hz show steeper slopes than the patterns at 1000 Hz. Above all, this effect is due to the nonlinear relation between frequency and critical band rate, leading to different attenuation characteristics of the filters at 250 Hz vs. 1000 Hz when plotted as a function of critical band rate, but identical characteristics when plotted as a function of frequency (Fig. 1).

For example, the attenuation showing up 6 critical bands above the cut-off of two low-pass filters with -18 dB/oct filter slope is compared:

cut-off frequency	test frequency	attenuation
250 Hz	1000 Hz	36 dB
1000 Hz	2500 Hz	24 dB

As a rule, for identical filter slope in dB/oct, the filter slope in dB/Bark is steeper at 250 Hz than at 1000 Hz. Thus, despite the larger SPL of the low-pass noises at 250 Hz in comparison to the noises at 1000 Hz, the masking patterns of the former show steeper slopes when plotted as a function of critical band rate.

c) Model for pitch strength of low-pass noise

In this section, a model is proposed describing the pitch strength of low-pass noises on the basis of their masking patterns. More specifically, it is suggested that pitch strength of a low-pass noise is correlated to the slope of its masking pattern. To illustrate the predictions of the model, the dependence of pitch strength on the slope of the masking pattern is plotted in Fig. 4. For each filter slope indicated at the upper abscissa of Fig. 4,

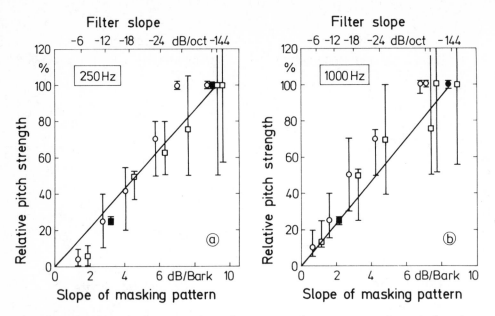

Fig. 4. Relative pitch strength of low-pass noise as a function of the slope of its masking pattern.
Symbols indicate measured data as in Fig. 2, heavy lines results from model.

the corresponding slope of the masking pattern (lower abscissa) was calculated from the data shown in Fig. 3 as follows: for each masking pattern, the level differences between the threshold value at the cut-off and the threshold value lying 2 Bark or 4 Bark above the cut-off were determined. These level differences (in dB) were divided by 2 Bark or 4 Bark, respectively, and the arithmetic mean of the resulting two values was taken as a measure of the slope of the masking pattern, expressed in dB/Bark. Thus, having established correlations between filter slope and slope of masking pattern, the pitch scalings shown in Fig. 2 as a function of filter slope could be rearranged and plotted in Fig. 4 as a function of the slope of the masking pattern. For filter slopes up to -18 dB/oct, the slopes of the masking patterns at 250 Hz are about 50 % steeper than the slopes of the patterns at 1000 Hz. However, the maximal value of the slope of the masking pattern at both frequencies differs only by 9 %.

The heavy line in Fig. 4a and Fig. 4b, respectively, indicates a linear relation between the slope of the masking pattern and pitch strength of low-pass noise. Generally, fair agreement between pitch strength predicted by the model and measured pitch strength values can be noticed. Moreover, at each slope of the masking pattern, the arithmetic mean of the pitch strength values stemming from the two sets of experiments (circles and squares) was calculated and compared to the value predicted by the model. On the average, the deviations between model and data amount to only 4.14 % at 250 Hz and 7.86 % at 1000 Hz. Realizing that the pitch strength scalings were performed by eight observers while the masking patterns stem from only one of those observers, the correlation between data and model has to be considered as rather good. Thus, at present a linear relation between slope of masking pattern and pitch strength of low-pass noise is proposed. Nevertheless, at specific cut-off frequencies power functions with exponents different from one might produce slightly higher correlation, which, however, has to be evaluated in view of the accuracy of measurement.

4. SUMMARY AND CONCLUSION

Pitch strength of low-pass noise increases with filter slope, reaching a maximal value for slopes steeper than -36 dB/oct. Even with very steep filters (-144 dB/oct) low-pass noise produces a pitch strength which is more than a factor of five smaller than the pitch strength produced by a pure tone. A model is proposed, suggesting a linear relation between the slope of the masking pattern and the pitch strength of low-pass noise. Data predicted by the model are in good agreement with measured values.

While in this paper *pitch strength* of low-pass noise is correlated with its masking pattern, *pitch* and masking patterns of low-pass noises can be related, too. In particular, the pitch of low-pass noise with large pitch strength (steep filters) was found to be correlated with an abrupt drop in the masking pattern (Fastl, 1978, Fig. 4). Thus, not only pitch of sounds with line spectra can be traced back to spectral clues (Terhardt, 1974), but also pitch of sounds with continuous spectra as low-pass noise. In addition, pitch strength of low-pass noise is eastly described on the basis of spectral features.

Acknowledgements. Dipl.-Ing. G. Stoll helped collect the pitch strength data at 250 Hz. Professor Dr.-Ing. E. Zwicker and Professor Dr.-Ing. E. Terhardt made valuable comments on the draft. The study was supported by Deutsche Forschungsgemeinschaft, SFB 50 "Kybernetik", München.

REFERENCES

Fastl, H. (1971). Über Tonhöhenempfindungen bei Rauschen. *Acustica* 25, 350 - 354.

Fastl, H. (1978). Mithörschwellen-Muster und Hörempfindungen. In: *Fortschritte der Akustik*. DAGA '78, VDE-Verlag, Berlin, 103 - 111.

Fastl, H. and Stoll, G. (1979). Scaling of pitch strength. *Hearing Research* 1, 293 - 301.

Rakowski, A. (1968). Pitch of filtered noise. *6. ICA Tokyo*, A 105.

Small, A.M. and Daniloff, R.G. (1967). Pitch of noise bands. *J. Acoust. Soc. Am.* 41, 506 - 512.

Terhardt, E. (1974). Pitch, consonance and harmony. *J. Acoust. Soc. Am.* 55, 1061 - 1069.

Yost, W.A. and Hill, R. (1978). Strength of the pitches associated with ripple noise. *J. Acoust. Soc. Am.* 64, 485 - 492.

Zwicker, E. (1975). Scaling. In: *Handbook of Sensory Physiology*. Vol. V, 2 (W. Keidel and W. Neff, eds.), Springer, Heidelberg, 401 - 448.

Zwicker, E. (1977). Procedure for calculating loudness of temporally variable sounds. *J. Acoust. Soc. Am.* 62, 675 - 682.

Zwicker, E. and Feldtkeller, R. (1967). *Das Ohr als Nachrichtenempfänger*. 2. erw. Aufl., Hirzel-Verlag, Stuttgart.

COMMENT ON: "Pitch strength and masking patterns of low-pass noise" (H. Fastl)

R.S. Tyler
M.R.C. Institute of Hearing Research,
University Park, University of Nottingham, U.K.

The pitch of a low-pass noise might be related to an enhancement of the excitation pattern near the spectral edge due to effects akin to lateral suppression. Simultaneous masking patterns of low-pass noise do not show increased masking near the spectral edge (Rainbolt and Small, 1972; Small, 1975), whereas non-simultaneous patterns do (Houtgast, 1972; 1974). Houtgast used low-pass noise with 96 dB/octave and virtually infinite filter slopes. I attempted to replicate the increase in masking near the spectral edge of a low-pass noise using forward masking and a slope of 48 dB/ octave, but was unsuccessful. The increase in non-simultaneous masking near the spectral edge may depend on the filter slope in the same fashion that pitch strength is related to filter slope.

Houtgast, T. (1972). Psychophysical evidence for lateral inhibition in hearing, *J Acoust. Soc. Am.* 51, 1885 - 1894.

Houtgast, T. (1974). *Lateral suppression in hearing.* Doctoral dissertation. University of Amsterdam.

Rainbolt, H. R., and Small, A.M. (1972). Mach bands in auditory masking: an attempted replication. *J. Acoust Soc Am.* 51, 567-574.

Small, A.M. (1975). Mach bands in auditory masking revisited, *J. Acoust. Soc. Am.* 57, 251-252.

INFLUENCE OF MASKING NOISE ON THE PITCH OF COMPLEX TONES

A. J. M. Houtsma

Research Laboratory of Electronics, Massachusetts Institute of Technology, Cambridge, Mass. 02139

INTRODUCTION

This study deals with a specific feature of the pitch of a complex sound comprising only upper harmonics. The pure tone pitch of each harmonic is known to depend on factors such as tone intensity (Terhardt, 1974a), the presence of other tones or noise (Terhardt and Fastl, 1971), auditory fatigue (van den Brink, 1972) and diplacusis effects (van den Brink, 1970). According to one school of thought (Terhardt, 1972a,b) such pure tone pitch shift effects are reflected in the complex tone pitch evoked by two or more pure tone harmonics. This idea has been supported by experimental evidence involving natural and induced binaural diplacusis (van den Brink, 1975).

One of the most consistent pure tone pitch shift effects is probably that caused by lowpass noise with cutoff frequency slightly below the tone frequency (Terhardt and Fastl, 1971; van den Brink, 1975). We performed monotic and dichotic pitch matching experiments with pure tones and harmonic two-tone complexes under lowpass noise conditions and examined whether, as far as fundamental pitch perception is concerned, noise-induced pitch shifts in the harmonics are equivalent to simple frequency shifts in those harmonics in the absence of noise. Our results do not agree with those obtained by van den Brink (1975) and do not support the general concept of the virtual pitch theory (Terhardt, 1972b, 1974b).

PROCEDURE

Subjects were given an alternating sequence of sounds, A, B, A, B, etc., where both A and B had durations of 500 msec and were separated by 300 msec of quiet. A was the test stimulus whose pitch was to be measured, and B the comparison stimulus which was a periodic train of 100 μsec pulses at 50 dB SPL whose fundamental frequency or rate was controlled by the subject. Subjects were instructed to match the pitch of B to the pitch of A. When a match was completed, a signal given by the subject terminated the sequence, recorded relevant parameters, and started a new sequence. The fundamental of signal B was assumed to indicate the pitch of sound A after completion of a match.

Test sounds in the main experiment consisted of a single pure tone or a two-tone complex, each partially masked by lowpass noise. Signal presentation was either monotic or dichotic. In the monotic case, two test frequencies at 600 and 800 Hz and 60 dB SPL were used, both separately and as a two-tone pair, and all stimuli were presented to the left ear. The lowpass noise had a cutoff frequency at 600 Hz and a rolloff slope of 48 dB/octave. In the dichotic case, tones ranged from the second to the eighth harmonic of 200 Hz (400 – 1600 Hz), where odd harmonics were always in the left and even harmonics in the right ear. Harmonics were tested individually and in dichotic pairs of successive order. The masking noise in each ear was derived from the same noise source and filtered separately for each ear at cutoff frequencies approximately ten percent below the tone frequency and rolloffs of 48 dB/octave. The tones were at 60 dB SPL and the comparison stimulus was binaural.

The noise intensity, varying between 30 and 70 dB SPL in ten equal steps, was the experimental variable. The amount of pitch change, both for the single tones and the two-tone complexes, was measured as a function of noise intensity. Matches were performed in runs of ten for the ten different noise intensities which were taken in random order. For the loudest noise (70dB) the tone was barely audible, whereas for the lowest noise intensity (30 dB) the presence of the noise was barely noticeable. For each new matching sequence a random offset of up to ten percent was introduced between the pulse rate and the control dial in order to insure that successive pitch matches were independent. Subjects were instructed to "bracket," i.e., to make sure that the target pitch was approached from both the high and the low direction.

In addition to the main experiment a control experiment was performed to compare the effects of noise-induced pitch changes in pure tones and simple frequency changes on the sensation of central, fundamental pitch. This experiment, which was done both monotically and dichotically, involved a test signal of merely two tones in quiet and with a frequency shift derived from the previous pure tone pitch matching results. For example, if owing to a certain noise level, the pitch of a 600 Hz tone appears to be 610 Hz and the pitch of an 800 Hz tone 815 Hz for a given subject, the control experiment would use a monotic or dichotic two-tone test signal of 610 and 815 Hz in quiet and ask the subject to match this to the periodic pulse signal B.

Three subjects participated. One (R.F.) was a professional musician and had absolute pitch. The other two had considerable musical training and experience.

RESULTS

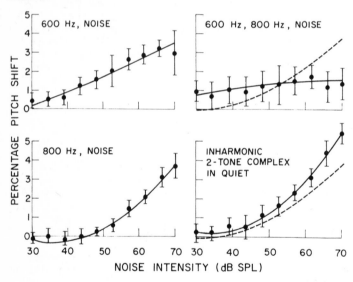

Fig. 1. *Monotic pitch matching results for subject A.H. Left: means and standard deviations for partially masked pure tones. Right top: means and standard deviations for missing fundamental of two-tone complex. Right bottom: means and standard deviations for unmasked two-tone complexes with frequency shifts given by figures on the left. Solid curves: best second order fits to means. Dashed curves: average of solid curves in left column.*

The results of monotic pitch matches by two subjects, including the control experiment, are shown in Figs. 1 and 2. The graphs on the left show noise-induced pitch changes for a 600 Hz and 800 Hz tone, and the graphs on the right show pitch changes in the (missing) fundamental of the two-tone complex (200 Hz) induced by masking noise (top) and frequency shift (bottom). Pitch changes are expressed in percents, defined as $100(f_p-f_t)/f_t$, where

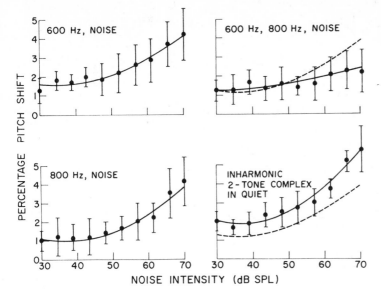

*Fig. 2. Monotic
pitch matches for
subject J.S. Same
conditions as in
Fig. 1.*

f_p is the fundamental of the pulse signal B and f_t is either the pure tone
frequency (600 or 800 Hz) or the missing fundamental (200 Hz). Each data
point represents the mean of ten matches, with standard deviation bars also
shown. A second order curve was fit to the experimental means using a maximum likelihood procedure (solid curves). The dashed curves indicate the
pitches one would expect if complex tone pitch were derived by a minimum
square error estimate from the pure tone pitches shown on the left hand side
of the figures.

In contrast to subject A.H., subject J.S. shows a consistent tendency to
tune everything between one and two percent sharp. Both subjects show a considerably smaller pitch shift effect with the partially masked two-tone complexes than with the single tones, and a somewhat larger effect with the frequency shifted two-tone complexes. Direct comparison of the solid graphs on
the right in each figure shows quite clearly that noise-induced and frequency
shift-induced changes in the perceived pitches of harmonics have a very different effect on the perceived fundamental pitch of the complex.

A valid question one could raise about the monotic results is whether or
not the smaller noise-induced pitch effects observed in the two-tone case are
caused by additional pure tone pitch shifts that the tones may induce upon one
another. Such shifts may go in opposite directions as those caused by the
noise, resulting in an overall cancellation of the observed effect (Terhardt
and Fastl, 1971). For this reason a dichotic version of the experiment was
executed which eliminated possible tone-induced pitch shift effects. This
experiment has the additional advantages of eliminating possibly confounding
effects of aural combination tones and allowing more effective masking of the
higher stimulus harmonic. A disadvantage was the higher amount of pitch ambiguity caused by analytic pitch cues, which made the pitch matching task more
difficult and sometimes necessitated the presentation of a target signal at
the beginning of a match to prevent the subject from zeroing in on the wrong
pitch cue (Houtsma, 1979).

Some typical dichotic matching results are shown in Fig. 3. Again, all
data points are the means of ten matches, and are fit with straight lines
which allows the amount of pitch shift in each case to be expressed in "percent

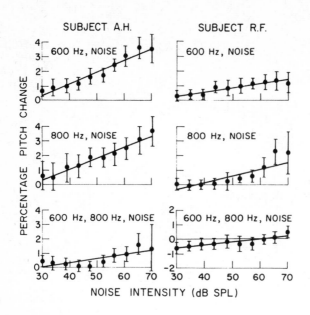

Fig. 3. Dichotic pitch matching results for **two subjects.** Data points are means of ten matches with standard deviations also shown. Solid curves are best first order fits through data points.

pitch change per dB," the slope of the straight line functions. The results are reasonably similar to the monotic ones. Pitch shift slopes for the partially masked two-tone complexes are less than those observed for the partially masked individual harmonics. The second subject (R.F.) also shows substantially smaller induced pitch shift effects than subject A.H. A possible reason for this will be discussed later.

Results similar to those shown in Fig. 3 were obtained for all other harmonics between 400 and 1600 Hz. These results, expressed in percent pitch change per dB, are shown in Fig. 4. They include matches for partially masked individual harmonics, partially masked dichotic two-tone complexes, and frequency shifted dichotic two-tone complexes in quiet (control experiment). In

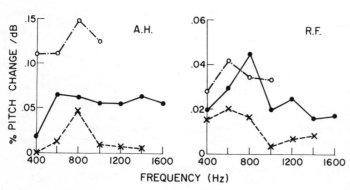

Fig. 4. Comprehensive dichotic pitch matching results. Data points represent slopes of matching functions like those shown in Fig. 3. Solid curve: results for single tones in noise. Dashed curve results for two-tone complexes in noise. Dash-dotted curve: results for frequency shifted two-tone complexes in quiet.

the first case the abscissa represents the pure tone frequency, in the second case the frequency of the lower harmonic, and in the third case the frequency of the lower harmonic before the introduction of frequency shift. The data points, representing the slopes of the actual matching functions, show considerable variation from one frequency to the next. This is probably because no attempt had been made to determine the precise noise cutoff frequency for each tone frequency that would result in comparable masking effects. The chief purpose of the experiment was to compare at each test frequency the single tone results with the two-tone results. In every instance, for both subjects, the pitch shift slope for the complex tone is considerably less than the matching slope for either harmonic by itself. Averaging the slopes over all test frequencies, one finds for subject A.H. values of .064 and .024, and for subject R.F. values of .018 and .009 for the individual tone and the two-tone conditions respectively. The dichotic control experiment was carried out only up to the 6th harmonic. The results show that the observed two-tone pitch shift effect is much stronger than the average effect of the single tones for subject A.H., which was also observed to a lesser extent in the monotic experiment. For subject R.F. the results of the frequency shifted two-tone complexes are of the same magnitude as the individual tone results.

DISCUSSION

The most important finding of this study is that the amount of pitch change in a two-tone complex, induced by lowpass noise, is substantially less than the amount of shift induced by the same lowpass noise in its individual harmonics. Moreover, it was shown directly that a pure tone in lowpass noise and a pure tone of different frequency in quiet may appear to have the same pitch when matched to a common third stimulus, but may be far from equivalent when used as harmonic components of a complex tone. This suggests that complex tone pitch is not obtained through a serial operation in which a processor operates on tone pitches rather than tone frequencies (Terhardt, 1972b; van den Brink, 1974), but rather through an independent process parallel to the pure tone pitch mechanism.

Our findings are qualitatively in agreement with those of Walliser (1969) who found generally smaller shift effects induced in the pitch of a filtered pulse train (harmonics 6-15) than in the pitch of the lower stimulus partial (6th harmonic). The partial masker here was white noise. Our results are very different, however, from those of van den Brink (1975) who obtained pitch matches between a partially masked three-tone complex in one ear and a three-tone complex of the same harmonics in quiet in the other ear. He found that the pitch shift induced by the noise in the three-tone complex was exactly given by the average of the induced binaural pitch shift functions measured for the three individual harmonics. He concluded that "the neural excitation pattern that is characteristic of the perception of a certain residue pitch is determined by the neural excitation patterns induced by the separate components of a complex sound which are already representative of their separate pure tone pitches." The discrepancies between our data and those of van den Brink might be explained by the differences in experimental paradigm. One important difference seems to be that in our experiments all test sounds were matched to the same comparison sound, a periodic narrow pulse, whereas in van den Brink's experiment subjects matched single tones to single tones and a three-tone test complex in one ear to a three-tone comparison complex of exactly the same harmonic order in the other ear. In the latter paradigm, subjects may subconsciously have matched individual single tone pitches between the ears instead of residues, in which case the apparent agreement between complex tone pitch shift and single tone pitch shift would be entirely artifactual. This hypothesis is strengthened by the fact that van den Brink's test matches were usually accurate to within 0.1%, while in his control checks where harmonic complexes of unequal rank orders were matched, a criterion of "a few percent error" was used to decide that the subject was matching residues and not partials. The much greater accuracy in the test matches may indicate that some other cues may have been used besides residue matching. Our experiments, of course, are in principle subject to the same criticism. Subjects could have matched components of the test sounds to component pitches of the periodic pulse. In our case, however, the data do not support that hypothesis.

Standard deviations found in our experiments were typically around 0.5% as can be seen in Figs. 1 through 3, and were generally somewhat larger for the higher masking levels. This is consistent with the observation that just noticeable differences in pure tone frequency increase with masking noise intensity (Harris, 1947; Henning, 1967). Variances were also found to increase on the average with increasing harmonic number in the dichotic two-tone experiments, reaching values of around 1.5% for the highest harmonic pair tested (harmonics 7 and 8). This may reflect the increased ambiguity of two-tone pairs of high harmonic order.

The amount of noise-induced shift in the pitch of pure or complex tones varies between subjects. Similar intersubjective differences in behavior were observed by Terhardt and Fastl (1971) for single tones in lowpass noise. This observation may have a physiological basis. Furthermore, the smaller pitch shifts observed in subject R.F. may also reflect her absolute pitch ability which, if used, could have had an equalizing effect on her pitch matching performance.

Our empirical finding that induced pure tone pitch changes are not reflected to the same extent in complex tone pitch is also consistent with musical experience. Some of these pure tone pitch shift effects have been shown to be as large as a full semitone (Terhardt and Fastl, 1971; Terhardt, 1974a). If similar pitch changes were found in tone complexes comprising such pure tones, musicians would probably complain more often about pitch instability depending on dynamic levels and general musical texture. Our finding may also be interpreted to mean that certain hearing pathologies, e.g., severe binaural diplacusis, may not be very debilitating impairments with respect to the perception of music.

From a physiological point of view it seems almost certain that noise-induced pitch changes for pure tones are place effects. It is not difficult to imagine a mechanism in which the center of gravity of tone response activity changes with tone intensity or in the presence of other stimuli. On the other hand, auditory nerve fibers whose tone responses are found to be phase-locked to the stimulus tone will remain phase-locked to the tone if masking noise is introduced unless, of course, the noise is so intense that it disturbs the synchrony. In any case, there is no systematic change in the frequency to which unit responses are synchronized with increasing intensity of masking noise. The apparent fact that complex tone pitch is far less dependent on the presence of masking noise than pure tone pitch suggests the existence of two parallel pitch processing mechanisms from the periphery inward, one for pure tone pitch based on place encoding, the other for complex tone pitch based on temporal information. If no systematic pitch changes at all were observed in the partially masked complex tone conditions, the argument for two separate and independent pitch mechanisms would have been rather simple and clear cut. Our finding that there is a noticeable positive pitch shift for complex tones under masking conditions, even though it is considerably smaller than the shift observed with pure tones, suggests that the two pitch mechanisms are not entirely independent.

All three major pitch theories are affected by our results in some way. The explicit assertion of Terhardt's "virtual pitch theory" (1972b, 1974b) that virtual pitch is derived from spectral pitch cues which, in turn, are subject to the loudness and masking effects discussed in this study, is inconsistent with our data. The significance for the "pattern transformation theory" (Wightman, 1973) is that its "peripheral activity pattern" evoked by spectral components of a complex tone, which mediates the complex tone sensation, cannot be the same peripheral activity pattern that would mediate pure tone pitch sensations. For the "optimal processor theory" of Goldstein (1973), our findings simply underscore the fact that the processor inputs, which are noisy representations of stimulus frequency components, should not be identified or confused with internal representations of pure tone pitches (Green, 1976).

The author is indebted to Rhona Freeman and John Stautner for their patience and endurance throughout the experiments. H.S. Colburn provided valuable assistance. This work was supported by the National Institutes of Health, Grant NS11680-03.

REFERENCES

Goldstein, J.L. (1973). An optimum processor theory for the central formation of the pitch of complex tones. *J. Acoust. Soc. Am.* 54, 1496-1516.

Green, D. (1976). Pitch perception. In: *The Nervous System*. Vol 3 (D.B. Tower, ed). pp 147-155. Raven Press, New York.

Harris, J.D. (1947). Studies on pitch discrimination in masking II: the effect of signal/noise differential. *J. Acoust. Soc. Am.* 19, 816-819.

Henning, G.B. (1967). Frequency discrimination in noise, *J. Acoust. Soc. Am.* 41, 774-777.

Houtsma, A.J.M. (1979). Musical pitch of two-tone complexes and predictions by modern pitch theories. *J. Acoust. Soc. Am.* 66, 87-99.

Terhardt, E. and Fastl, H. (1971). Zum Einfluss von Störtönen und Störgeräuschen auf die Tonhöhe von Sinustönen. *Acustica* 25, 53-61.

Terhardt, E. (1972a). Zur Tonhöhenwahrnehmung von Klängen I. Psychoakustische Grundlagen. *Acustica* 26, 173-186.

Terhardt, E. (1972b). Zur Tonhöhenwahrnehmung von Klängen II. Ein Funktionsschema. *Acustica* 26, 187-199.

Terhardt, E. (1974a). Pitch of pure tones: its relation to intensity. In: *Facts and Models in Hearing* (E. Zwicker and E. Terhardt, eds). pp 353-360. Springer Verlag, Heidelberg.

Terhardt, E. (1974b). Pitch, consonance and harmony. *J. Acoust. Soc. Am.* 55, 1061-1069.

Van den Brink, G. (1970). Experiments on binaural diplacusis and tone perception. In: *Frequency Analysis and Periodicity Detection in Hearing*. (R. Plomp and G.F. Smoorenburg, eds). pp 362-373. Sijthoff, Leiden.

Van den Brink, G. (1972). The influence of fatigue upon the pitch of pure tones and complex tones. In: *Proc. Symp. on Hearing Theory*. Institute for Perception Research, Eindhoven.

Van den Brink, G. (1974). Monotic and dichotic pitch matchings with complex sounds. In: *Facts and Models in Hearing* (E. Zwicker and E. Terhardt, eds), pp 178-188. Springer Verlag, Heidelberg.

Van den Brink, G. (1975). The relation between binaural diplacusis for pure tones and for complex sounds under normal conditions and with induced monaural pitch shift. *Acustica* 32, 159-165.

Walliser, K. (1969). Zusammenhänge zwischen dem Schallreiz und der Periodentonhöhe. *Acustica* 21, 319-328.

Wightman, F.L. (1973). The pattern transformation model of pitch. *J. Acoust. Soc. Am.* 54, 407-416.

COMMENT ON "Influence of masking noise on the pitch of complex tones"
(A.J.M. Houtsma).

E. Terhardt
Institute of Electroacoustics, Technical University, München, FRG.

Houtsma's conclusion, which asserts inconsistency of the virtual-pitch
theory with the described experimental data, is untenable. In fact those data
are highly compatible with the virtual-pitch theory.

Although Houtsma obviously is aware that (in the monaural experiment) the
pitch-shifting effect of the low-pass noise on each of the two simultaneous
components may be different from the effect on each component presented individually, he does not draw appropriate conclusions. In fact it is highly probable that the individual spectral pitches of the 600 Hz- and 800 Hz-components
are affected significantly less in the case of simultaneous presentation than
in the case of individual presentation. The dichotic experiment does not provide a safe solution to this problem since it has been shown that interaural
pitch shift effects do exist (Terhardt, 1977). Thus, even in the dichotic condition, the spectral pitches of the two components may be affected differently
by the low-pass noise as compared to the single-tone experiment. Nevertheless,
Fig.3 of Houtsma's paper shows that for subject R.F., the noise-induced pitch
shift of the individually-presented 600 Hz component is practically identical
to the fundamental-pitch shift of the two-tone complex (i.e., maximally about
1%; compare diagrams on right top and bottom). Actually the virtual-pitch theory would predict that the spectral pitch of the 600 Hz-component is determining the fundamental pitch (virtual pitch) of the dichotic two-tone complex.
Hence in this particular case Houtsma's assertion that *"complex tone pitch is
far less dependent on the presence of masking noise than pure tone pitch"* is
inconsistent with his data which, on the other hand, are presented as *"typical
dichotic matching results"*.

The question of whether or not the fundamental pitch of a two-tone complex is affected by a low-pass noise in the same way as one or both of the
spectral pitches can be investigated directly by measuring *the individual spectral pitches of the simultaneous two tones* instead of the isolated tones. This
type of experiment is actually relevant to the question raised by Houtsma, and
can be readily carried out either monotically or dichotically. Unfortunately
Houtsma does not report anything about such an experiment.

With regard to tone perception in general, Houtsma mentions quite correctly *"that induced pure tone pitch changes are not reflected to the same extent
in complex tone pitch"*, and that this is consistent with musical experience.
In fact, this has already been recognized and discussed several years ago (cf.
e.g. Terhardt, 1972; 1975). It is one of the specific advantages of the virtual-pitch theory that the latter takes explicit account of pure tone pitch
shifts *and* complex tone pitch shifts, reconciling them with each other.

REFERENCES

Terhardt, E. (1972). Zur Tonhöhenwahrnehmung von Klängen. I. Psychoakustische
    Grundlagen. *Acustica* 26, 173-186.
Terhardt, E. (1975). Influence of intensity on the pitch of complex tones.
    Acustica 33, 344-348.
Terhardt, E. (1977). Pitch shifts of monaural pure tones caused by contralate-
    ral sounds. *Acustica* 37, 56-57.

REPLY TO COMMENT OF E. TERHARDT

A.J.M. Houtsma
Research Lab. of Electronics, Massachusetts Inst. of Technology, Cambridge, U.S.A.

I fail to see how my data support the virtual pitch theory. The data in Fig. 3 are merely an illustrative example of many observations which are all shown in Fig. 4. From this figure one can see that even in the case cited by Terhardt the slopes of the pure-tone pitch functions are .03 and .045 respectively, where the slope of the corresponding two-tone pitch function is about .02. Generally it seems quite clear from Fig. 4 that there is a sizable overall difference between noise-induced pitch shifts in pure and complex tones. According to the virtual pitch theory, the solid, dash-dotted, and dashed curves in Fig. 4 should be identical.

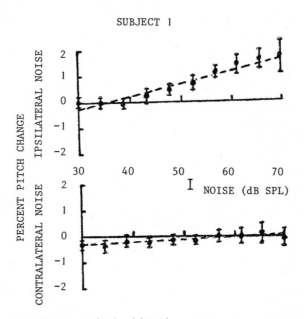

Percentage pitch shift in a 600 Hz pure tone induced by ipsilateral (top) and contralateral (bottom) 600 Hz low pass noise.

Preliminary data on controlaterally induced pitch shift for pure tones are shown for two subjects. It appears that the amount of contralateral shift is insufficient to "undo" the ipsilateral shift in order to explain the relatively small complex tone effects. Nevertheless, the experiment of measuring pure tone pitches of the simultaneous complex as suggested by Terhardt should definitely be performed.

COMMENT ON "Influence of masking noise on the pitch of complex tones"
(A.J.M. Houtsma).

G. van den Brink
*Dept. of Biological & Medical Physics, Erasmus University Rotterdam,
The Netherlands.*

Pitch of periodic pulse trains

The apparent discrepancy between Houtsma's findings and my results may not
be due at all to the type of percept, either a residue pitch or an analytical
percept of the separate components. Since all results of my experiments indicate
that residue pitch is determined by the pitches of the separate components, I
doubt whether the type of percept would make any difference anyway. Unfortunately, we were not able to check this with the signals as used, because none of the
subjects involved was able to have anything else but a residue percept, when
trying this out in conflict situations (800, 1000, 1200 Hz versus 900, 1080,
1260 Hz). Although to different extents, the criterion could be switched without
too many problems, using two-component signals, so that the certainty with regard to the type of percept is, indeed, considerably less in that case.

It is hard to judge what procedure is preferable, having no absolute built-
in pitch reference. I am, of course, inclined to prefer a situation in which
either of the signals involved is being matched with signals that are as much
alike as possible. So, pure tones with pure tones, residues with residues consisting of the same harmonics, etc. One advantage is, that both signals then
undergo the same influences, in case unforeseen factors affect the pitches.

Having testsignal and matching signal in different ears, gives the extra
advantage that the pitch of the matching signal is not being affected by signals
that are meant to influence that of the testsignal. In Houtsma's procedure, an
increasing pitch shift for the components of the matching signal can be expected
with increasing masking level, due to after-effects of the noise. These shifts
neutralize at least partly the effect of noise upon the pitch of the testsignal
that, therefore, will be underestimated with increasing noise level. Since
Houtsma's two components are near the dominant area of their fundamental, the
weight of their contributions to periodic pulse pitch may even be relatively
strong. Higher harmonics play a role in the pitch of periodic pulse trains, as
is clear from the results of Terhardt and of myself.

It seemed worthwhile to compare the signals involved as a function of the
frequency in my own experimental set up: In part A of the figure, the results of
a matching experiment of a pure tone with a periodic pulse train (duty cycle
1/7) as a function of the frequency is given for either ear between 500 and 3000
Hz. Part B shows the same for frequencies between 170 and 1500 Hz. A constant
duty cycle is to be preferred above constant pulse duration because the spectrum,
relative to the fundamental, does not change with the repetition rate. The fact
that the pitch of periodic pulse trains differs from that of pure tones points
to an influence of harmonics. This influence decreases with increasing fundamental frequency because of the sensitivity of the ear. Note that the results of
the left and the right ear show a clear resemblance, but are not identical. This
not being identical must be due to the left-right differences that cause binaural diplacusis as well.

Houtsma used periodic pulse trains with constant duration (0.1 ms) so that
below 1430 Hz the spectra of his signals contain more and increasingly stronger
harmonics than constant duty cycle signals, with decreasing frequency. In order
to judge their importance, I matched periodic pulse trains having constant duty
cycle (1/7) with signals having constant pulse duration (0.1 ms). The result is
shown in C: The frequency difference needed for equal pitches depends evidently
on the spectral contents. The equal trends in the curves B and C points to a
common source of influence. This might be due to the same components, probably
around the 4th harmonic. These harmonics are present in both spectra, having

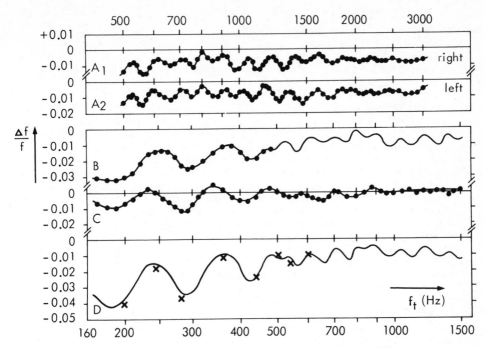

Relative frequency difference, necessary for equal pitch. Subject GB.
A. testsignal: periodical pulses; duty cycle 1/7. reference: pure tones.
B. the same as A, same frequency range as C and D (right ear).
C. testsignal: periodical pulses; pulse duration 0.1 ms.
   reference: periodical pulses; duty cycle 1/7 (right).
D. testsignal: periodical pulse; pulse duration 0.1 ms. reference: pure tones.
   solid line: sum of curves B and C; crosses: experimental values (right).

different amplitudes, so that they affect the pitches in the same qualitative way but to different extents. This difference decreases with increasing frequency up to around 1430 Hz where both signals are the same.

When pure tones are being matched with 0.1 ms periodic pulses instead of pulses with a constant duty cycle of 1/7, the effect in C comes on top of the effect in B. The sum of both is given in part D, together with results of a few actual matchings, indicated with crosses. This curve represents the controversy between Houtsma's and my findings. This result can easily account for the discrepancy of a few percents as found by Houtsma.

It must be concluded that the pitch of a periodic pulse signal is subject to contributions of more than only the first harmonic, and, therefore, depends on its spectrum. The rule that pitch of a complex sound is determined by weighted contributions of separate pitches of the components seems to hold for periodic pulse signals as well. A periodic pulse train is, therefore, not reliable as a reference signal for pitch. In fact it is the most complex tone of all.

REFERENCES

Van den Brink, G. (1975). The relation between binaural diplacusis under normal conditions and with induced monaural pitch shift. *Acustica* 32, 139-165.
Houtsma, A.J.M. (1980). Influence of masking on the pitch of complex tones. *Symp. Noordwijkerhout.*
Terhardt, E. (1974). Pitch, consonance and harmony. *J.Acoust.Soc.Am.* 55, 1061-1069.

COMMENT

REPLY TO COMMENT OF G. VAN DEN BRINK

A.J.M. Houtsma
Research Lab. of Electronics, Massachusetts Inst. of Technology, Cambridge, U.S.A.

Although it may be quite true that the pitch of the pulse-train reference signal is influenced by preceding noise exposure or by slight variations in its duty cycle, our experimental results should not be affected since the *same* reference signal is used to match partially masked pure tones *and* complex tones. All we assume is that when A is matched to C and B is matched to C, than A can be considered to be matched to B, which does not seem unreasonable as long as we stay within one psychophysical dimension. For example, if the complex tone pitch is increasingly underestimated with increasing noise due to noise after effects, as van den Brink points out, the same thing will happen with the pure tone component pitch matches. Therefore, the ratio of the pure-tone and complex-tone pitch functions, which is the quantity we are really interested in, is unaffected by such unknown pitch effects on the reference signal. Such a ratio function is a constant for van den Brink's (1975) experiment, consistent with the virtual pitch theory, but a distinctly sloping line in just about every case in our experiments.

Since our pure tone results are quite consistent with other results reported in the literature, the controversy focuses on the complex tone results. In that case, the apparent pitch was always somewhere between 198 and 202 Hz, which translates into a range of duty cycles from .019 to .021. This seems hardly significant.

Ritsma (1966) also found that pure tones could be shifted in pitch by applying low pass noise, but found no such shifts in residues. We are trying to duplicate van den Brink's (1975) results with his paradigm, but so far we have been unsuccessful. Therefore our experimental discrepancy still remains to be resolved.

REFERENCES

Ritsma, R.J. (1966). The pitch of Sinusoids and Complex Signals as Affected by masking noise. *Annual Progress Report*. Inst. for Perception Research. No. 1, 27–28.

TOWARD UNDERSTANDING PITCH PERCEPTION:
PROBLEMS, CONCEPTS, AND SOLUTIONS

Ernst Terhardt

Institute of Electroacoustics, Technical University
München, Federal Republic of Germany

1. INTRODUCTION

There is fair agreement that the past decade brought significant progress in the understanding of pitch perception. It is, however, not easy to survey the present status of our understanding. Since it is supposed that considerable obstacles of understanding are on the conceptual rather than the phenomenological side, the author's personal concept will be briefly sketched as a basis of discussion. To illustrate how that concept is applied in our research group,the present status of our work on the quantitative evaluation of the pitch percepts evoked by complex, ambiguous tonal signals will be sketched.

2. CONCEPTUAL ASPECTS OF UNDERSTANDING PITCH PERCEPTION

The whole domain of pitch perception may be characterized by three basic problems which concern (1) the qualitative and quantitative relationships of signal parameters to pitch; (2) the origin of tonal affinity and the laws governing it; and (3) the memory for absolute pitch and the laws governing it. Several crucial aspects of these problems will be briefly discussed in the following sections. Due to space limitations only very few references can be given. The reader's attention is drawn to the surveys given by Wilson (1974), Plomp (1976), and de Boer (1976).

a) *Signal parameters and pitch*

While physical stimulus parameters are solidly defined, the definition of pitch invokes some problems. Essentially, three basic concepts may be considered:
(1) The *one-dimensional* concept. Pitch is defined as "that attribute of auditory sensation in terms of which sounds may be ordered on a scale extending from low to high" (Amer. Nat. Standard Terminology). This seems to be the most neutral and safe definition, and has been the basis of most psychoacoustical experiments on pitch.
(2) The *bi-dimensional* concept. Pitch is defined as being composed of the components (dimensions) *height* and *chroma*, the latter representing the feature of "musical identity" of tones being one or more octaves apart. This definition probably is conceptually inadequate, since there is no evidence that would require the sensory attribute of height and that of octave affinity both to be attached to one sensory quality called pitch.
(3) The *bi-modal* concept. The one-dimensionality of pitch does not imply that only one type (mode) of pitch would exist. Yet pitch theorizing was impaired for a long time by the (more or less implicit) assumption that there was just one type of pitch to be explained. This inadequate conception caused considerable problems in finding the pitch-determinant parameters of complex stimuli. Systematic consideration of the variety of significant pitch phenomena revealed convincing evidence for a bi-modal concept, and an explicit definition of the two pitch modes, i.e. *spectral pitch* and *virtual pitch*, was achieved (Ter-

hardt, 1972a, b). It is the bi-modal pitch concept which logically opens the way to the current "pattern-recognition approach" to the pitch of complex signals.

Probably the most appropriate conceptual definition of pitch is provided by a combination of the one-dimensional concept (1) with the bi-modal concept (3).

A large and important part of understanding the stimulus-to-sensation-relationship is the problem of finding those physical parameters which determine the perceived pitch. This problem is considered separately for steady, deterministic signals such as pure and complex tones, and quasi-random signals such as amplitude-modulated, chopped, or repeated noise.

In the case of *deterministic signals* this problem is closely related to the concept of frequency which is not strictly regarded in all cases. The term "frequency", meaning "periods per second", may be either attached to the real acoustic signal (referring to its oscillations per second) or to any particular Fourier-component, which is a mathematically- rather than physically-defined entity. For the vast majority of tonal stimuli occuring in everyday experience it is true that pitch is monotonically related to *oscillation frequency* (the latter term is used as opposed to *spectral frequency*). Thus on first sight oscillation frequency (or its reciprocal, "periodicity") seems definitely to provide the pitch-determinant physical clue. Yet Helmholtz (1863) destroyed this concept by attaching pitch to *spectral frequency*. This was actually an excellent principle to explain the pitch of *pure* tones, but it caused serious problems in understanding the pitch of *complex* tones. Helmholtz apparently was satisfied by his idea that in complex tones the fundamental was physically so strong as to determine pitch, in spite of the presence (and aural resolution) of many other harmonics. Schouten and his colleagues, after having demonstrated experimentally that Helmholtz was wrong in the latter respect, concluded that in fact *oscillation frequency* would provide the most promising approach to a solution. However, this approach was not successful either. Rather, evidence accumulated that the pitch of complex tones is largely dependent on *spectral frequency*, though not in the way Helmholtz had supposed (cf. Terhardt, 1970; 1972a, b; Whitfield, 1970; Wightman, 1973; Goldstein, 1973; Wilson, 1974). It was this evidence that forced a conceptual re-definition of pitch, i.e. the bi-modal concept. The particular phenomenon of "central summation" of dichotically distributed spectral components in musical-interval recognition (Houtsma & Goldstein, 1972), though adding just another hint to many others, provided a sort of trigger for the new conceptual approach to quickly become popular.

Thus full compatibility of phenomenological evidence and conceptual approach has been achieved. There can hardly be any doubt that with deterministic signals *spectral frequency* should be considered the pitch-determinant clue. It should be noted that this does not imply any decision on how the auditory system actually accomplishes that frequency analysis, i.e. whether this is done in the "place-" or "periodicity- domain".

In the case of *quasi-random signals* the pitch-determining clues are not so well established. These signals evoke pitch sensations of very different strengths, being either of the spectral-pitch or virtual-pitch type. While in some cases it is rather obvious that spectral clues are pitch-determinant (e.g. band limited noise; repetition noise), in other cases temporal periodicity appears to be the only relevant physical clue (e.g. periodically amplitude-modulated white noise). On evaluating the latter phenomenon, the following aspects should be noted:
(1) The case of "pure periodicity pitch" is rare and rather hard to verify experimentally. The pitch sensation is very faint (cf. Fastl & Stoll, 1979).
(2) The signals by which "pure periodicity pitch" is evoked are not really periodic but "quasi-periodic", i.e. the periodicity exists only in the signal's envelope. This reduces the significance of that type of evidence considerably, since experiments with complex tones have convincingly established that the en-

velope of *deterministic signals* is *not* pitch-determinant.

(3) Since in the "periodicity pitch" case the pitch sensation is so faint, the possibility cannot be excluded that certain specific spectral clues which are not existent in the long-term power spectrum are detected by the auditory system and provide a source of pitch sensation (cf. Pierce et al., 1977).

Thus the vast majority of pitch phenomena suggest that spectral clues are pitch-determinant, while there is only rare and weak evidence of periodicity analysis.

b) *The origin of tonal affinity*

Essentially there are two competing hypotheses, namely (1) that the sense of harmonic intervals is an inherent feature of the auditory system and is dependent on the temporal structure of the stimulus-synchronized nerve-impulse patterns; and (2) that the sense of harmonic intervals is acquired by auditory analysis and processing of harmonic complex tones, in particular the voiced speech sounds. At present, psychophysical evidence favors the latter hypothesis (cf. Terhardt, 1972a, b; 1974; 1976). It cannot, however, be excluded that an explanation of pitch perception as such and of the harmonic sense along the line of the first hypothesis may be achievable. Significant approaches of this type do exist (e.g. Ohgushi, 1978), but a comprehensive theory covering the variety of phenomenological evidence is still lacking.

Hence the current status of psychophysical knowledge in fact supports the validity of the second of the aforementioned principles.

c) *Absolute pitch memory*

According to a widely-accepted viewpoint, the sense of musical intervals (i.e. tonal affinity, also called "relative pitch") is a basic, natural feature of the auditory system, possessed by almost every individual, while "absolute pitch" is considered as an unusual gift because it is available only to very few. However, there are significant phenomenological and theoretical indications that the conceptual approach behind that viewpoint may be inadequate. On the phenomenological side it is not established that "relative pitch" is considerably more pronounced than "absolute pitch". In an experiment with a limited number of musical tones and intervals we found that subjects not possessing absolute pitch did not perform much better in the absolute recognition of *intervals* than of *tones*. Hence, at least with respect to a limited set of items to be recognized, the actual ability of most individuals to absolutely designate musical tones seems to be basically the same as the ability to designate musical intervals. Moreover, many musically-trained individuals possess the ability, with a reliability significantly higher than chance, to identify isolated musical tones and the key in which a piece of music is performed. Thus a sort of absolute pitch may exist as a "potential" rather than readily-applicable faculty, which is common to many individuals.

This view is well in line with certain consequences of the present approach, in particular the virtual-pitch theory. According to that theory, virtual pitch of complex signals is established by matching certain pitch cues which are subharmonic to the resolved spectral components. The harmonic pitch intervals used in that process must be in the system's memory. Since the width of those intervals, in terms of pitch, will be dependent on the absolute height of the components, it follows that the absolute pitch must be "decoded" by the system: "relative pitch" presupposes the existence of "absolute pitch". Since virtual-pitch extraction is an unconscious process, it can be concluded that the memory for both absolute pitch and harmonic intervals reside at an unconscious level and are not easily accessible from the conscious and verbal level.

These arguments provide a speculative approach rather than a basis of understanding. "Absolute pitch" is still poorly understood.

3. VARIOUS PITCH PERCEPTS WITH COMPLEX STIMULI: QUANTITATIVE EVALUATION

The pitch percepts evoked by complex stimuli normally are ambiguous, i.e. more than one pitch may be assigned to one and the same stimulus. That ambiguity is rather restricted in the case of most usual musical instruments and the human voice. It may, however, become quite obvious e.g. with the sounds of carrillons and church bells. It is particularly the latter type of tonal sounds which provides a challenge to any pitch-predicting system, and the extent to which such predictions can be made correctly may be considered as another measure of the understanding of pitch perception. Basically, the entire tonal percept evoked by a complex signal may be represented by a pattern of pitch values to each of which is assigned a weight which indicates its relative salience. This pattern will comprise both spectral and virtual pitches. A procedure for the evaluation of that salience vs. pitch pattern was recently worked out by our group. Its features are briefly outlined as follows (for a complete description see Terhardt et al., 1980).

a) *Outline of the procedure*

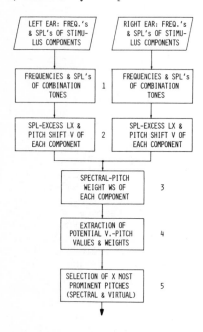

Fig.1. Flow-chart of the pitch-evaluation system

Fig.1 shows the block diagram (flow-chart). It operates on the frequencies and SPL's of the stimulus components, i.e., spectral analysis of the respective stimuli of the right and left ear is assumed to have been accomplished. The separate steps of processing are the following (numbering as in Fig.1).

i) *Addition of combination tones to the spectrum*. In complex signals comprising more than two components, aural combination tones hardly affect pitch. They do, however, with two-component stimuli, produce the so-called second effect of pitch shift (Smoorenburg, 1970). In order to account for that effect, the frequencies and SPL's of the 3rd- and 5th-order combination tones may be deduced from the stimulus data, thus obtaining a sort of effective spectrum. Recently Zwicker (1980) has suggested a formalism for quantitative evaluation of the odd-order combination tones.

ii) *Evaluation of mutual masking and pitch shifts of components*. Only those spectral components which are resolved (i.e. produce individual spectral pitches) may contribute to the tonal percept, either "directly" as spectral pitches, or "indirectly" as virtual pitches. The degree of spectral resolution of any particular spectral component is depicted by the *sound-pressure-level excess* LX, which has been defined on the basis of auditory-frequency resolution as represented by masking patterns (Terhardt, 1979). The pattern of LX-values which usually is obtained with a complex signal comprising several components, is called the *spectral-pitch pattern*. As an example the calculated spectral-pitch pattern of the synthetic vowel /a/, realized with 200 Hz fundamental frequency, is shown in Fig.2 (upper diagram, vertical lines). The physical spectrum is represented by circles. Also shown is a calculated representation of the excitation level L_E. In the present context only the LX-pattern is relevant, as it is used to

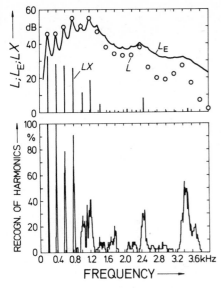

Fig.2. Amplitude spectrum (circles), calculated excitation level L_E, and calculated spectral-pitch pattern (LX) of a synthetic /a/ (upper diagram). Bottom: Relat. no. of pure-tone matches to the pitches of individual harmonics (3 S's). From Stoll (1980)

represent the relative pitch salience of every component.

The position of the vertical lines in the LX-pattern denotes the precise spectral pitches assigned to the individual components. These pitches numerically depart somewhat from the corresponding frequencies (which in this example are 200 Hz times an integer) due to the effect of pitch shift by masking. The calculation procedure has already been described elsewhere (Terhardt, 1979).

In the lower diagram an experimental spectral-pitch pattern is shown, i.e. the relative number of probe-tone matches to individual harmonics (3 S's; the same stimulus; for details see Stoll, 1980). Obviously there is a high correlation to the calculated LX-pattern, thus confirming its auditory relevance and justifying consideration of LX as an appropriate measure of the "salience" of the spectral pitches of individual components. It should further be noted that in the experimental histogram the maxima corresponding to individual harmonics are somewhat shifted horizontally, thus indicating the predicted spectral-pitch shifts.

In the pitch evaluation only those components with LX-values greater than 0 play a role. These are called "determinant components".

iii) *Assigning a weight to every spectral pitch.* The relative salience of every spectral pitch as such and its relative contribution to the formation of virtual pitch are represented by one numerical value per component, i.e. the "spectral-pitch weight". It has been defined as a function of LX and component frequency so that in particular the phenomenon of spectral dominance is taken into account (for details see Terhardt et al., 1980).

iv) *Extraction of virtual pitches and weights.* The various potential virtual pitches are extracted basically by the same algorithm as described elsewhere (Terhardt, 1979). By additional quantification and implementation of corresponding principles of the virtual-pitch theory, the calculation of virtual-pitch weights was also achieved. The implemented principles may be qualitatively listed as follows.
(1) Virtual pitch is ambiguous.
(2) Any potential virtual pitch is subharmonic to at least one stimulus component.
(3) When a particular virtual pitch is specified by a group of stimulus components, only the most salient of them will finally determine the magnitude of that virtual pitch.
(4) The salience of a particular virtual pitch is dependent on the number of determinant spectral pitches; the salience (weight) of the determinant spectral pitches; the subharmonic numbers which specify the relationship between virtual pitch and determinant spectral pitches; and the degree of harmonicity, i.e. the extent to which the determinant spectral pitches are true harmonics of the considered virtual pitch.

v) *Selection of the most prominent pitches*. As the number of potential pitches provided by steps 3 and 4 may be considerable, the main function of step 5 is to reduce the final data to a reasonable number X of most-salient pitches. Within the group of spectral pitches (provided by the 3rd processing step) the salience of a particular pitch is defined to be directly dependent on the corresponding spectral-pitch weight. Likewise, the salience of a particular virtual pitch within the group of virtual pitches (provided by step 4) is specified by the corresponding virtual-pitch weight. Thus finally only the relationship of weights between the two groups had to be specified to enable description of the salience of any pitch, i.e. without regard of whether it is spectral or virtual. This was accomplished particularly by optimizing the calculated data of a number of church bells to the corresponding psychoacoustic results (cf. the following section).

b) *Results*

A variety of harmonic and inharmonic complex tones which have been used in research on pitch perception (e.g. full harmonic complex tones; harmonic and inharmonic residue tones) have been used to test the procedure. In all cases reasonable results were obtained, i.e., the resulting salience vs. pitch distributions appeared to be highly compatible with the available psychoacoustic data. Thus the procedure was extensively tested and optimized with the sounds of several church bells which were available on tape records.

By pitch-matching experiments with 18 subjects the "targets" of the predictions were obtained (cf. Seewann & Terhardt, 1980), i.e. histograms of pitch-matches for each bell sound. The input data of the procedure were established by FFT-analysis starting 40 ms after the moment of strike. The digital spectrum data of the B&K 2031 FFT-analyzer (400 samples; bandwidth 5 kHz) were directly transferred to a HP 9830 desk computer programmed for extraction of precise component frequencies and SPL's, and for carrying out the pitch-prediction. Fig.3 depicts the FFT-spectra of two church bells, as examples. The corresponding histograms of pitch matches as obtained in the psychoacoustic experiment are shown in Fig.4. For each of the two bells the existence of relatively pronounced maxima indicates that the pitch ambiguity of these parti-

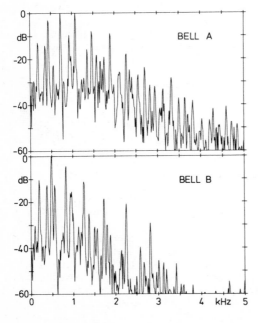

Fig.3. FFT-spectra of two church bells. The frequencies of the most prominent peaks are: 194, 446, 733, 1085, 1480, 1980 Hz for Bell A; 204, 494, 835, 1260, 1736, 2266 Hz for Bell B.

cular bells is limited. In fact, these are two examples of relatively pleasant and "musical" bell sounds. Inspection of the upper diagrams in Figs. 3 and 4 reveals that in the case of bell A the most prominent peak in the pitch histogram (around 370 pitch units) does not correspond to any prominent spectral component. That pitch value is entirely of the virtual type. With bell B the most salient pitch value (around 204 pitch units) coincides with a spectral component. In fact that component can readily be "heard out". Nevertheless, that pitch must be con-

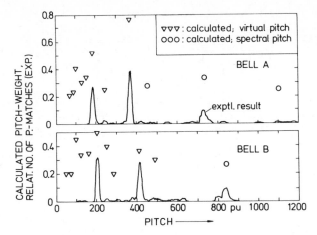

Fig.4. Predicted salience vs. pitch patterns (triangles for virtual pitch, circles for spectral pitch), and experimental pitch matching histograms (18 S's; cf. Seewann & Terhardt, 1980) for the two church bells. Only those calculated pitches are displayed the weight of which exceeds 0.2. SPL 70 dB.

sidered as being essentially a virtual pitch as well, because the virtual pitch of 204 pitch units which is conveyed by several components (one of which is the 204 Hz component) has a higher weight than the 204 pitch units spectral pitch. This is illustrated by the calculated results in Fig.4. These are represented by triangles (virtual pitches) and circles (spectral pitches), respectively, the weights of which exceed the value 0.2. The absolute weight has not yet been put into a defined relationship to the relative number of pitch matches of the psychoacoustic experiment; thus only the variation of weights along the abscissa should be compared with the maximum-minimum configuration of the pitch matching histogram. For each of the two church bells, the most prominent peak of the histogram is correctly predicted by the evaluation procedure (370 pitch units for bell A, and 204 pitch units for bell B). In the case of Bell A the second-order pitch (185 pitch units) is also correctly predicted.

As the pitch matches of minor order are regarded, these are correctly predicted with respect to pitch as such, but not so well with respect to their relative salience. In particular there is a tendency of the algorithm to predict rather low virtual pitches which are hardly found in the experimental histograms.

We investigated in the described way 17 bell sounds which had been selected by aural evaluation from a great number of tape records with the aim to get a typical representation, including sounds with low and high quality. From this sample 8 bells, i.e. about 50%, were aurally found to have agreeable or high quality. The relationship between experimental and predicted data as depicted by Fig.4 is quite typical of these 8 bells. Thus one may consider the depicted data as typical of church bells with an agreeable sound quality in general. In the case of bells with poor sound quality the experimental pitch histograms revealed extremely ambiguous pitches and the correlation to the predicted data was poor, in some cases even zero.

Summarizing it can be concluded that the pitch and pitch-salience predictions provided by the described procedure coincide well with experimental data, provided that the pitch ambiguity of the stimulus is not extremely high such that the signal is almost atonal.

Acknowledgements. Many thanks are expressed to my colleages M. Seewann and G. Stoll for their efficient assistance on working out the spectral-analysis and pitch-evaluation procedures. I am also grateful to G. Manley, E. Zwicker, and H. Fastl for providing several highly valuable comments. This work was carried out in the Sonderforschungsbereich 50 "Kybernetik", München, supported by the Deutsche Forschungsgemeinschaft.

REFERENCES

de Boer, E. (1976). On the "Residue" and auditory pitch perception. In: *Handbook of Sensory Physiol*. Vol. V, part 3. (W.D. Keidel and W.D. Neff, eds). pp 479-583. Springer, Heidelberg.

Fastl, H. and Stoll, G. (1979). Scaling of pitch strength. *Hearing Research* 1, 293-301.

Goldstein, J.L. (1973). An optimum processor theory for the central formation of the pitch of complex tones. *J. acoust. Soc. Am.* 54, 1496-1516.

Helmholtz, H.L.F. (1863). Die Lehre von den Tonempfindungen als physiologische Grundlage für die Theorie der Musik. Vieweg, Braunschweig.

Houtsma, A.J.M. and Goldstein, J.L. (1972). The central origin of the pitch of complex tones: evidence from musical interval recognition. *J. acoust. Soc. Am.* 51, 520-529.

Ohgushi, K. (1978). On the role of spatial and temporal cues in the perception of the pitch of complex tones. *J. acoust. Soc. Am.* 64, 764-771.

Pierce, J.R., Lipes, R. and Cheetham, C. (1977). Uncertainty concerning the direct use of time information in hearing: place clues in white-spectra stimuli. *J. acoust. Soc. Am.* 61, 1609-1621.

Plomp, R. (1976). Aspects of tone sensation. Academic Press, London.

Seewann, M. and Terhardt, E. (1980). Messungen der wahrgenommenen Tonhöhe von Glocken. Preprint of DAGA '80, München, March 11-13.

Smoorenburg, G.F. (1970). Pitch perception of two-frequency stimuli. *J. acoust. Soc. Am.* 48, 924-942.

Stoll, G. (1980). Psychoakustische Messungen der Spektraltonhöhenmuster von Vokalen. Preprint of DAGA '80, München, March 11-13.

Terhardt, E. (1970). Frequency analysis and periodicity detection in the sensations of roughness and periodicity pitch. In: *Frequency Analysis and Periodicity Detection in Hearing*. (R. Plomp and G.F. Smoorenburg, eds). pp 278-287. Sijthoff, Leiden.

Terhardt, E. (1972a). Zur Tonhöhenwahrnehmung von Klängen: Psychoakustische Grundlagen. *Acustica* 26, 173-186.

Terhardt, E. (1972b). Zur Tonhöhenwahrnehmung von Klängen: Ein Funktionsschema. *Acustica* 26, 187-199.

Terhardt, E. (1974). Pitch, consonance, and harmony. *J. acoust. Soc. Am.* 55, 1061-1069.

Terhardt, E. (1976). Ein psychoakustisch begründetes Konzept der Musikalischen Konsonanz. *Acustica* 36, 121-137.

Terhardt, E. (1979). Calculating virtual pitch. *Hearing Research* 1, 155-182.

Terhardt, E., Stoll, G. and Seewann, M. (1980). Quantitative evaluation of pitch and its salience for complex tonal signals. In preparation.

Whitfield, I.C. (1970). Central nervous processing in relation to spatio-temporal discrimination of auditory patterns. In: *Frequency Analysis and Periodicity Detection in Hearing*. (R. Plomp and G.F. Smoorenburg, eds). pp 136-147. Sijthoff, Leiden.

Wightman, F.L. (1973). The pattern-transformation model of pitch. *J. acoust. Soc. Am.* 54, 407-416.

Wilson, J.P. (1974). Psychoacoustical and neurophysiological aspects of auditory pattern recognition. In: *The Neurosciences: Third Study Program*. (Schmitt and Worden, eds). pp 147-153. MIT Press, Cambridge.

Zwicker, E. (1980). Simple procedure for calculating odd order aural difference tones. In preparation.

THE RELATION BETWEEN PITCH AND FREQUENCY
IN COMPLEX TONES

I. C. Whitfield

Neurocommunications Research Unit, Medical School,
University of Birmingham, England

1. INTRODUCTION

In the realm of vision we can refer to yellow or green, and are not
forced into talking of a colour of 580 mu or 520 mu. It is unfortunate
that we have no such everyday words to describe pitch. The mel, instituted
by S. S. Stevens (Stevens et al, 1937) in an attempt to produce a scale of
pitch, was concerned more with the size of intervals than with pitch identification and has never achieved currency. We are thrown back therefore on
matching the pitch of a sound to that of a simple tone, and describing the
pitch as 'n' Hertz. That necessity has led to the expectation that the
frequency 'n' ought somehow to exist in the original signal that was matched.
There is actually no more foundation for such an expectation than for the
expectation that frequencies of 475×10^{12} Hz (red) or 575×10^{12} Hz (green)
should exist in a pure spectral yellow.

I pointed out in 1969 at a previous symposium held not far from here
(Whitfield, 1970a), and again in Sandefjord (Whitfield, 1970b), that it
seems highly probable that pitch is a property of a complex of harmonics, of
which not all have to be present to establish the pitch; in particular, the
fundamental (1st harmonic) is not uniquely necessary in the establishment of
this pitch (fig 1). The single tone is then, of course, to be seen merely
as one special case of a whole family of harmonic combinations with the
same pitch. I proposed, too, that the pitch of anharmonic complexes is
derived in a similar way on a 'best fit' basis.

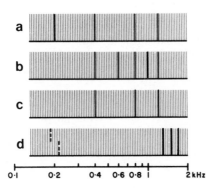

Fig. 1. (a) 1st, 2nd, 4th & 6th harmonics of 200 Hz.
(b) 2nd, 3rd, 4th, 5th & 6th harmonics of 200 Hz.
(c) 2nd, 4th & 6th harmonics of 200 Hz.
(a) and (b) have the same pitch, but (c) is an octave higher. The
'schedo-harmonics' (Whitfield, 1980) of (d) approximate equally
closely to either of two series based on the two dashed frequencies
(after Whitfield, 1970b).

361

Experiments on the pitch of an acoustic signal consisting of pulses with alternating groups of intervals of say 4.7 and 5.3 msec (Whitfield, 1979a) also suggest that pitch is a spectral phenomenon rather than a function of individual pulse intervals in nerve fibres. Models of the way in which the total power spectrum might be related to pitch have been proposed by Goldstein (1973), by Wightman (1973) and by de Boer (1977).

The basic idea that pitch is a global property, that can be established when a suitable fraction of some ensemble of inputs is present, provides a link with many other phenomena where the percept remains constant even though the actual sensory input varies. Thus the size of an object commonly remains constant with change of distance, a chair remains a chair as we walk around it, and the position of a sound source in space does not move as we move our head, even though Δt and Δf will certainly do so. There is reason to associate many of these phenomena with the cerebral cortex (Whitfield, 1979b), and it is of interest to know what effect cortical removal might have on the perception of pitch.

It is well established that although the ability of a cat to discriminate between two single tones is lost on bilateral removal of auditory cortex, the discrimination is very rapidly relearned. However, as noted above, it is not possible in such a signal to distinguish between pitch and frequency, and so we cannot say if it is indeed pitch that is being discriminated. In the case of complex tones the situation is easier, because it is possible to set up harmonic (or indeed anharmonic) complexes that have the same (to man) pitch but are composed of different frequency elements.

Because pitch is a subjective phenomenon, it is first necessary to establish that the experimental animal chosen (in this case the cat) does in fact respond to pitch in a similar manner to man. That this is the case was established in some experiments by Heffner and Whitfield (1976). The demonstration was based on the use of signals where the frequencies of the components of the complex tones moved in one direction while the pitch moved in the opposite direction. It was thus possible to distinguish between a response to frequency change and a response to pitch change.

2. EXPERIMENT

Cats were presented with a 'safe' signal consisting of a falling pair of simple tones, (say) 400 Hz → 350 Hz (A), presented once a second for 10 seconds, the sequence being repeated with a 5-second gap between 10-second periods. At random intervals one of these 10-second 'safe' signals would be replaced by a warning sequence consisting of 400 Hz → 450 Hz (B) (see note 1). The animal was trained to lick fluid continuously from a small saucer but to stop licking within 3 seconds when the warning signal appeared.

Having been trained to discriminate between a rising and a falling sequence, the cats were then presented with complex tone pairs of approximately the same pitch pattern, namely 1600 + 2000 + 2400 Hz → 1600 + 1950 + 2300 Hz (falling pitch, safe) (C) and 1600 + 2000 + 2400 Hz → 1600 + 2050 + 2500 Hz (rising pitch, warning) (D). The animals transferred rapidly, and treated these signals as they did the pure tone sequences. They were, however, then overtrained on them before the test signals were presented.

3. TEST SIGNALS

In the training series of triads just discussed it can be seen that when the pitch went up the frequencies of the components also went up (or remained the same). In the test series it was arranged that when the pitch fell, the component frequencies *rose* or remained the same, thus:

1600 + 2000 + 2400 Hz → 1700 + 2050 + 2400 Hz

Conversely, when the pitch rose, the frequencies fell:

$$1600 + 2000 + 2400 \text{ Hz} \longrightarrow 1500 + 1950 + 2400 \text{ Hz.}$$

These signals formed a test of whether the animal was responding to the component frequencies. Let us call them E and F, respectively.

E and F were inserted randomly into a series of C and D signals, without reinforcement.

The result was that E was treated like C (safe) and F was treated like D (warning) (Table 1). Thus it appears that cats hear the pitch of these complexes much like man, at least as measured by their responses.

Table I

Stimulus	Pre-op	Post-op	
C(f↓p↓)	9.1	9.2	} Training Signals
D(f↑p↑)	2.9	3.4*	
E(f↑p↓)	8.9	6.1	} Test Signals
F(f↓p↑)	3.8	7.2*	

*Average licking time (seconds) for one cat before and after bilateral removal of auditory cortex. f = frequency change; pitch = pitch change. * Scores differ $p < 001$; Mann-Whitney U test.*

4. EFFECTS OF DECORTICATION

After extensive removal of both auditory cortices (Fig 2) it was found (Whitfield, 1980), as expected, that the response to all signals, including the initial pure tone sequences, was lost. Again as expected the response to the latter was very rapidly recovered with retraining. However, this retraining on simple tones did *not* restore performance on the complex tones. There was no longer transfer. Nevertheless the animals could be trained to discriminate the complex signals C and D in the same way that they had before the operation. The question is: were they still responding to the *pitch* of these signals, or to the individual components? The E and F signals should throw light on the point. As can be seen from Table 1, not only were E and F not treated like C and D, respectively, in regard to their pitch, but neither were they in regard to their individual frequencies. Indeed, they seemed to be treated as entirely strange signals. Not only was there no constancy of pitch, but there appeared also to be no generalization for the direction of movement of the component frequencies, where E would have been expected to be like D and F like C.

To confirm this suspicion two further test sequences were presented. These were very similar to C,D, but the whole series was moved down by 100 Hz, i.e.:

$$1500 + 1900 + 2300 \text{ Hz} \longrightarrow 1500 + 1950 + 2400 \text{ Hz}$$

or up by 200 Hz, i.e.:

$$1800 + 2200 + 2600 \text{ Hz} \longrightarrow 1800 + 2250 + 2700 \text{ Hz.}$$

Neither of these signals was treated as warning, scores averaging 8.7 sec.

The tentative conclusion from this experiment is that the cat without auditory cortex is capable of learning to discriminate one frequency from another but each problem must be learned *de novo*; there is no generalization.

A fortiori, such animals do not extract a common pitch from signals, that for the normal animal have this property.

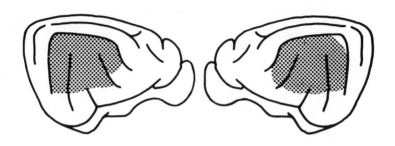

Fig. 2.   The cortical lesion.

5. DISCUSSION

The phenomenon I have been describing seems to be one of a class of phenomena that distinguishes cortical from sub-cortical behaviour (Whitfield, 1979b). As long ago as 1960 Neff attempted to account for the difference in the ability of corticate and decorticate cats to discriminate between patterns of simple tones on the basis of whether or not the 'warning' signal activated additional fibres in the brainstem.

This idea seems to be of more general application. It appears to be possible for animals to make a simple discriminatory response - such as withholding licking, or changing sides in a shuttle box - on the basis of signal pairs drawn from a very wide range of stimuli. Thus, not only can the decorticate cat detect the change from tone A to tone B or a change from a signal in the left ear to one in the right ear; it can also be trained to respond when a dichotic click train is changed from left-ear to right-ear leading (Masterton and Diamond, 1964). At a slightly more complex level, a decorticate animal - opossum (Ravizza and Masterton, 1972) - can be trained to withhold a lick response when a (freefield) sound source on the left changes to one on the right.

In the majority of such experiments the two neural patterns to be compared are presented within a second or two of each other, but that is not always a necessary condition. An example can be drawn from localization experiments, where the sound is presented each time without any comparison source. Whitfield et al (1972) showed that the unidecorticate cat usually has its localizing responses to the precedence effect disrupted for signals originating on the side opposite the lesion; however, some cats (though a minority) are able to 'localize' these signals correctly *in a Y-maze* (Whitfield et al 1978). If instead of being placed in the Y-maze, these animals are placed in an unconfined space with multiple goal boxes they then fail (Whitfield, 1979c). The Y-maze, although often used as such, is not a true localization task, but rather another two-choice situation and it looks as though these cats have learned the discrimination on the basis of two different neural patterns rather than on the identification of the position of the sound source.

I have suggested elsewhere (Whitfield, 1979b) that this is the essential difference between the intact and decorticate animal. The decorticate animal is able to learn to respond to differences between different neural patterns generated by physically different stimuli - and some of the distinctions that can be made involve quite sophisticated analysis. The sensory cortex on the other hand appears to be concerned with identifying some common relationship between different neural patterns - not features of the patterns themselves, but something common to their origin. The identities then result in, for example, the perception of a sound source as having a fixed position in space irrespective of the changes of neural pattern produced by movements of the animal's head, and in similar perceptual constancies.

On the basis of these experiments, it could well be that pitch too is a percept of this type and is dependent on auditory cortex in the same sort of way. In the decorticate animal, a whole range of physical stimuli (frequencies) can be used as a substrate for simple behavioural discriminations and (as with localization phenomena) some of these patterns can be quite complex yet still be discriminable. In the intact animal, the overriding property of periodic stimuli is membership or non-membership of a set of terms belonging to a particular harmonic series. It is that membership that determines the pitch, and the auditory cortex appears to be where the transformation occurs.

Note 1. For practical reasons the frequencies actually used were slightly different from these (e.g., 458 rather than 450 Hz), and they were randomly varied over about 10% between presentations to ensure that the animal responded to change *rather than absolute frequency. The figures have here been rounded for simplicity.*

REFERENCES

deBoer, E. (1977) Pitch theories unified. In: *Psychophysics and Physiology of Hearing*. (E.F. Evans and J.P. Wilson, eds). pp 323-335. Academic, London.

Goldstein, J.L. (1973). An optimum processor theory for the central formation of the pitch of complex tones. *J. acoust. Soc. Am.* 54, 1496-1516.

Heffner, H.H. and Whitfield, I.C. (1976). Perception of the missing fundamental by cats. *J. Neurophysiol.* 59, 915-919.

Masterton, R.B. and Diamond, I.T. (1964). Effects of auditory cortex ablation on discrimination of small binaural time differences. *J. Neurophysiol.* 27, 15-36.

Neff, W.D. (1961). Neural mechanisms of auditory discrimination. In: *Sensory Communication*. (W.A. Rosenblith, ed). pp. 259-279. Wiley and MIT Press, New York.

Ravizza, R.S. and Masterton, R.B. (1972). Contribution of neocortex to sound localization in opossum (Didelphis virginiana). *J. Neurophysiol.* 35, 344-356.

Stevens, S.S., Volkmann, J. and Newman, E.F. (1937). A scale for the measurement of the psychological magnitude of pitch. *J. acoust. Soc. Am.* 8, 185-190.

Whitfield, I.C. (1970a). Central nervous processing in relation to spatio-temporal discrimination of auditory patterns. In: *Frequency Analysis and Periodicity Detection in Hearing*. (R. Plomp and G.F. Smoorenburg, eds). pp 136-147. Sijthoff, Leiden.

Whitfield, I.C. (1970b). Neural integration and pitch perception. In: *Excitatory Synaptic Mechanisms*. (P. Andersen and J.K. Jansen, eds). pp 277-285. Universitets Forlaget, Oslo.

Whitfield, I.C., Cranford, J., Ravizza, R. and Diamond, I.T. (1972). Effects of unilateral ablation of auditory cortex in cat on complex sound localization. *J. Neurophysiol.* 37, 718-731.

Whitfield, I.C., Diamond, I.T., Chiveralls, K. and Williamson, T.G. (1978). Some further observations on the effects of unilateral cortical ablation on sound localization in the cat. *Exp. Brain Res.* 31, 221-234.

Whitfield, I.C. (1979a). Periodicity, pulse interval and pitch. *Audiology* 18, 507-512.

Whitfield, I.C. (1979b). The object of the sensory cortex. *Brain Behav. Evol.* 16, 129-154.

Whitfield, I.C. (1979c). Auditory cortical lesions and the precedence effect in a four-choice situation. *J. Physiol.* 289, 81P.

Whitfield, I.C. (1980). Auditory cortex and the pitch of complex tones. *J. acoust. Soc. Am.* 67, 644-647.

Wightman, F.L. (1973). The pattern-transformation model of pitch. *J. acoust. Soc. Am.* 54, 407-416.

This work was supported by the Science and Medical Research Councils.

TEMPORAL PROPERTIES OF THE PITCH AND
PITCH STRENGTH OF RIPPLE NOISE

W.A. Yost

Parmly Hearing Institute and Psychology Dept.,
Loyola University of Chicago, Chicago, Illinois, U.S.A.

A broadband signal when delayed (T) and added back to itself, produces a stimulus with a rippled, comb-filtered, or cosine spectrum, $|H(f)|^2 = 1 + g^2 + 2g\cos2\pi fT$, which is called the cos+ stimulus. When the signal is delayed, inverted and then added back to itself its power spectrum, $|H(f)|^2 = 1 + g^2 - 2g\cos2\pi fT$, which is called the cos- stimulus, where g(0<g<1) is the gain of the delayed waveform, f is frequency, and T is the delay in ms.

Ripple noise stimuli produce a repetition pitch with the cos+ pitch equal to 1/T and the cos- pitches equal to either 1.14/T, .88/T or both (see Bilsen, 1977 and Yost *et al*, 1978). The matched pitch, pitch discrimination (Yost *et al*, 1978), pitch stength as measured by varying g (Bilsen and Ritsma, 1970 and Yost and Hill, 1978), dichotic pitch (Bilsen and Goldstein, 1974) and an after image pitch (Wilson, 1970) have all been measured using ripple noise. In the present study we have investigated the matched pitch and pitch strength of ripple noise as a function of the duration of the stimulus. Our motivation for these studies stems from some informal observations regarding subjects' difficulty in making pitch matches for short duration stimuli and from observations concerning the peripheral-weighting model (Yost and Hill, 1979) for the pitch and pitch strength of ripple noise. The peripheral-weighting model makes use of a weighting function similar to the psychophysical-suppression function (Houtgast, 1974 and Shannon, 1976) to generate a processed, ripple-noise spectrum with a bandpass characteristic that reflects the dominance region for the pitch of ripple noise (see Bilsen, 1977 and Yost and Hill, 1979). It is the suppression of high frequencies on lower frequencies in the weighting function which is responsible for the bandpass characteristic given to the processed, ripple-noise spectrum. This bandpass characteristic centered at the dominance region yields for the cos- stimulus a spectrum which can be analyzed (by autocorrelation, for instance) to produce the two pitches at 1.14/T and .88/T. Without the bandpass characteristic (e.g., without suppression) the pitches for the cos- stimulus would be predicted (using autocorrelation, for instance) to be at values greater than 1.14/T and less than .88/T. Weber and Green (1978) have generated stimulus conditions which argue that psychophysical suppression may in fact take time to form. Thus, short-duration, ripple-noise stimuli might not (if the peripheral-weighting model is assumed) be on long enough for the suppression aspects of the weighting function to influence the processed spectrum. Without suppression for the short-duration, ripple-noise stimuli there would not be a bandpass characteristic to the processed spectrum, resulting in the pitch of the cos- stimulus being either greater than 1.14/T, less than .88/T, or both. We were interested to see if this result occurred.

The spectrum of a short duration ripple-noise stimulus will be "whitened" due to the convolution of the rippled spectrum with the spectrum of the time window associated with the short presentation. This "whitening" is similar to that obtained when the gain in the delayed network (g) is decreased towards zero. That is, the peak-to-valley changes in the spectrum are decreased. Since this is known to weaken the pitch of ripple noise (see Bilsen and Ritsma, 1970 and Yost and Hill, 1978), it is important to know if the results obtained from our experiments on shortening duration are due only to the "whitening" of the spectrum.

1. METHODS AND PITCH DISCRIMINATION RESULTS

The procedure and stimulus generation methods described by Yost and Hill (1978) were used to obtain the value of g in decibels of attenuation which was required for subjects (four subjects with varying degrees of musical training) to just barely discriminate a difference between two values of T. Values of T for both the cos+ and cos- stimuli were 3.5 ms, 4.0 ms, 4.5 ms and 5 ms. These values were chosen since both Bilsen and Ritsma (1970) and Yost and Hill (1978) have shown that pitch strength is strongest for T between 2 and 5 ms. Table I shows the results from a series of discriminations between pairs of the four values of T. This study was conducted to establish that the

Table 1. Threshold attenuation values for pair-wise discrimination between the cos+ and cos- ripple noise stimuli for the four durations and for each subject. Each row for each duration indicates the results from a comparison between the values of T shown. The cos+ matched pitches (1/T) of the four signals would be 200 Hz (5 ms), 222 Hz (4.5 ms), 250 Hz (4 ms), and 286 Hz (3.5 ms).

		S1		S2		S3		S4	
500 ms		cos+	cos-	cos+	cos-	cos+	cos-	cos+	cos-
5.0 ms vs 4.5 ms		21 dB	16 dB	23 dB	15 dB	19 dB	13 dB	18 dB	14 dB
4.5	vs 4.0	20	14	22	17	18	14	17	13
4.0	vs 3.5	21	16	21	16	20	16	18	11
200 ms									
5.0 ms vs 4.5 ms		19 dB	15 dB	21 dB	15 dB	21 dB	15 dB	19 dB	10 dB
4.5	vs 4.0	20	13	20	17	19	12	20	13
4.0	3.5	22	11	21	16	17	14	18	11
100 ms									
5.0 ms vs 4.5 ms		18 dB	14 dB	19 dB	11 dB	20 dB	12 dB	18 dB	11 dB
4.5	4.0	19	13	18	14	18	13	20	9
4.0	3.5	19	11	17	15	16	14	18	10
50 ms									
5.0 ms vs 4.5 ms		17 dB	11 dB	14 dB	8 dB	15 dB	11 dB	16 dB	8 dB
4.5	vs 4.0	15	10	15	12	14	10	15	7
4.0	vs 3.5	16	8	17	13	15	9	14	8

four ripple-noise stimuli were somewhat equivalent in terms of discriminability as measured by the amount of attenuation required for threshold discrimination (threshold attenuation) between two ripple-noise stimuli (see Yost and Hill, 1978). As can be seen, all discriminations for either the cos+ or cos- stimuli yielded essentially the same value of threshold attenuation, establishing a type of equivalency among the four stimuli.[1] As reported by Yost and Hill (1978) the cos- stimuli have weaker pitches (lower threshold attenuation) than the cos+ stimuli. As can also be seen in Table I, the discriminability of the stimuli were slightly affected by duration, with the shorter durations requiring less attenuation for threshold discrimination than the longer durations,

[1]*As in past studies, (Yost et al, 1978 and Yost and Hill, 1978) the overall level of the stimuli throughout this entire study was varied randomly over a ±4 dB range to help reduce the possibility that the subject could use local spectral changes as cues for detection.*

indicating weaker pitches. Although the subjects showed that they could make the pair-wise discriminations, the pitch quality or pitch strength of the short duration stimuli was reported as reduced compared to the longer duration stimuli.

2. METHODS AND PITCH IDENTIFICATION

This experiment was conducted in the hope that the subjects would respond more on the basis of pitch strength than they had in the discrimination experiment. One of the four ripple noise stimuli was presented on any one trial and the subject indicated without feedback which of the four had occurred. The results in Fig. 1 indicated the overall percent correct (P(C)) for each subject as a function of duration. The experiment was repeated with three different amounts of attenuation of the delayed waveform (g) at each duration. For each duration a three point psychometric function of P(C) vs. attenuation was obtained. The value of attenuation obtained at a P(C) = .57 from a linear fit to the psychometric functions was used as the dependent variable.[2] As such, this value of attenuation is intended to reflect threshold attenuation or pitch strength as suggested by Bilsen and Ritsma (1970) and Yost and Hill (1978) and as was used in Table 1. Figure 2 shows the value of threshold attenuation as a function of duration for each subject in the identification task. As can be seen from both Figs. 1 and 2 there is a fairly large decrease in identification performance and pitch strength as duration is decreased. In addition, there is much larger between-subject variability then was seen in Table 1. Performance in both identification tasks (Figs. 1 and 2) was perfectly correlated with the musical ability of the subjects, with the subject with the most musical ability showing the best performances.

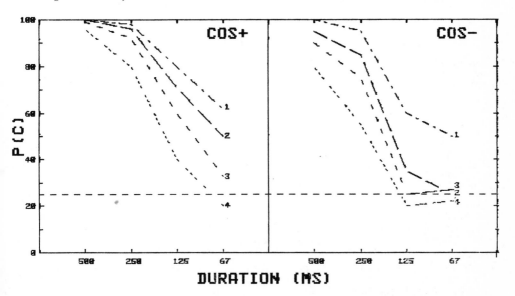

Fig. 1. Percent correct identification of the pitch of the cos+ and cos- stimuli as a function of duration. Each function represents a different subject. The dotted line at 25% represents chance performance in the four-choice identification task.

[2]*In a four-choice task a P(C) of 57% is approximately the same as a P(C) of 70.7% in a two-choice task, which was the value used in the discrimination experiment of Table 1.*

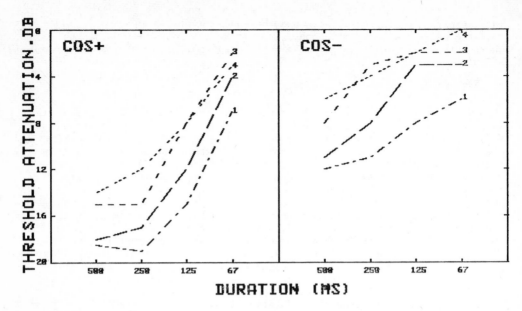

Fig. 2. The value of threshold attenuation (g) obtained in the four-choice identification task is shown for the cos+ and cos- stimuli as a function of duration. Each function represents a different subject.

The change in the depth of modulation in the spectrum due to shortening the duration is negligible at 500 and 200 ms. At 100 ms the depth of modulation is equivalent to approximately 1.5 dB of attenuation of the delayed waveform, while at 50 msec the depth of modulation is equivalent to approximately 3.5 dB of attenuation in the delayed waveform. Thus, the change in performance shown in Figs. 1 and 2 cannot be attributed entirely to this "whitening" of the spectrum due to shortening the duration.

3. DISCUSSION

The results of Figs. 1 and 2 imply that the pitch strength of ripple noise does decrease as a function of shortening duration. The stimuli, as shown in Table 1, can be discriminated when they are compared in a two-alternative, forced choice task, but identification is more difficult. That is, the stimuli can be differentiated one from another at short durations, but other aspects of the stimulus (perhaps some local spectral changes) provide cues in the discrimination task which the subjects could not use in the identification task. It is also possible that if the pitch of the stimuli changed as a function of duration then pitch identification would be poorer at these durations. To check this notion and to pursue the aspect of the peripheral-weighting model described earlier, a pitch matching experiment was conducted.

4. METHOD AND PITCH MATCHING RESULTS

A variety of matching stimuli were used in an attempt to obtain pitch matches to the cos+ and cos- stimuli at the four durations. Although the two observers were highly trained, most of our efforts, especially for the cos-stimulus, failed. That is, the pitch matches were too variable at the shorter durations (100 and 50 ms) to establish any pitch matches. We were able to obtain some useable results when the matching stimulus was a 500 ms, cos+ stimulus when matching to cos+ stimuli or a 500 ms, cos- stimulus when matching to cos- stimulus. For the cos+ stimuli the results reflected quite accurate pitch matches even when the matched stimulus was 50 ms. At all durations of the stimulus to be matched, the 500 ms, cos+ matching stimulus was adjusted to have the same delay as the cos+ matched stimulus. In other words, there appeared to be no change in the pitch of the cos+ stimuli as a function of shortening duration. The results for the cos- stimulus with T = 4 ms are shown in Fig. 3. At each duration of the cos- stimulus to be matched, the number of

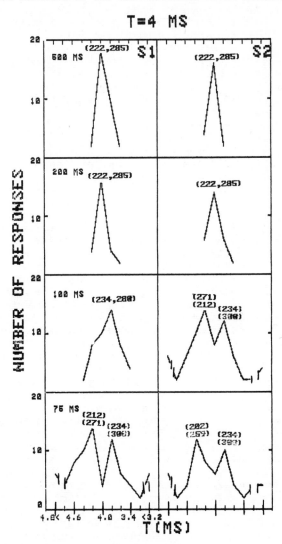

Fig. 3. *Histograms of the number of pitch matches for each value of delay (T) of the matching cos- stimulus when the cos- stimuli to be matched was presented at one of four durations (four panels). The delay (T) for the stimuli to be matched was 4 ms. The data from both observers are shown. The number in parenthesis above each maximum represents an estimate of the values in Hertz of the matched pitch.*

times each subject indicated a pitch match is shown as a function of the delay

(T) in the delayed waveform for the 500 ms, cos- matching stimulus. At 500 and 200 ms most of the responses indicated that the matching stimulus had the same pitch as the stimulus to be matched (e.g., both stimuli had the same delay, T). According to other pitch matching results (some obtained on S1 in an earlier study) the pitch of these cos- stimuli would be either 222, 285 Hz or both (see Yost *et al*, 1978). These values are shown in the parenthesis above each histogram. The match pitches, to some extent at 100 ms and even more at 75 ms (we were able to obtain reliable pitch matches at 50 ms), do not occur when the two stimuli have the same delay. This implies that the pitch of the shorter duration cos - stimuli are not the same as that of the 500 ms, cos - matching stimulus. If we assume that the subject is attempting to match one of the two pitches of the 500 ms, cos- matching stimulus to the short duration stimulus to be matched, then the numbers in parenthesis above the peaks in the functions at 100 and 75 ms indicate these matched pitches. As can be seen, the matched pitches at 100 and 75 ms are different than those obtained at 200 and 500 ms. With the present procedures we cannot be sure which pair of pitches the subjects are attempting to match. However, since pitch matches for the cos- stimuli have never been measured at values greater than .88/T or less than 1.14/T (see Bilsen, 1977), we might assume that the values of the match pitches greater than 285 and less than 222 Hz were the matched pitches for the short duration cos- stimuli.

5. DISCUSSION

Although the results of Fig. 3 at the shorter duration are still highly variable, they do indicate a possibility that the pitches at the shorter durations are different than at the longer durations. Since a great deal of effort was spent attempting to obtain a procedure for estimating pitch matches under these conditions, some other procedure (musical interval naming, for instance) will probably have to be employed to further investigate this effect. The results of Fig. 3 are somewhat consistent with the peripheral-weighting model (Yost and Hill, 1978) as explained earlier, if one assumes that psychophysical, two-tone suppression is time dependent such that short duration stimuli might not exhibit suppression.

In order to determine if this change in the pitch of the cos- stimulus was unique to ripple noise stimuli we conducted a similar experiment using a 6-tone complex as the stimulus to be matched. In this experiment the matching stimulus was a 500 ms, cos+ stimulus and its delayed waveform was varied to match either a cos- stimulus, at 500 ms or an inharmonic 6-tone complex with the 6 tones placed at the same spectral locations as the peaks in the cos- stimuli (that is, a 6-tone complex with the lowest component at 375 Hz and a 250 Hz spacing between the components). The ripple noise stimuli were filtered so that only six spectral peaks were present. As can be seen in Table 2, there

Table 2. The match pitches (1/T) using the cos+ ripple noise stimulus as the matching stimulus and a stimulus to be matched of either a 6-tone complex with the lowest component at 375 Hz and 250 Hz spacing between components, or a 500 ms, cos- ripple noise stimulus with a delay of 4 ms (1/T = 250 Hz). The number in parenthesis besides each matched pitch represents the number of times the subject indicated that pitch as the matched pitch (in each case there were 35 trials).

S1

duration	6-Tones	cos-
500 ms	256 Hz (18), 217 Hz (5)	285 Hz (19), 222 (10)
200 ms	256 Hz (19), 217 Hz (4)	–
100 ms	263 Hz (20), 225 Hz (5)	–
50 ms	263 Hz (12), 227 Hz (8)	–

S2

duration	6-Tones		cos-
500 ms	256 Hz (5),	217 Hz (18)	285 Hz (11), 222 Hz (21)
200 ms	263 Hz (6),	217 Hz (19)	–
100 ms	277 Hz (8),	217 Hz (17)	–
50 ms	263 Hz (5),	222 Hz (18)	–

was no appreciable change in the pitch of 6-tone complex as a functions of its duration. This task was relatively easy for the observers, especially compared to those used in our attempts to obtain the data shown in Fig. 3. Also, as can be seen in Table 2, the pitches of the 6-tone complex and the cos- ripple noise stimuli do not appear to be the same. Again, further experimentation is required to determine the extent of this difference. The results do seem to imply that if there is a pitch change in the cos- stimulus as a function of duration, then it is perhaps unique to the ripple noise stimulus.

In general then, the results of the present study indicate that the duration of ripple noise affects the strength of the repetition pitch and perhaps the matched pitch. As such, the results may be seen as consistent with certain assumptions pertaining to the peripheral-weighting model as proposed by Yost and Hill (1979).

This research was partially supported by a grant from the National Science Foundation. The author would like to thank Wes Grantham, Richard Fay, and Robert Lutfi for their valuable suggestions.

REFERENCES

Bilsen, F.A. (1977). Pitch of noise signals: Evidence for a "Central Spectrum". *J. Acoust. Soc. Am.* 61, 150–159.

Bilsen, F.A., and Goldstein, J.L. (1974). Pitch of dichotically delayed noise and its possible spectral basis. *J. Acoust. Soc. Am.* 55, 292–297.

Bilsen, F.A., and Ritsma, R.J. (1970). Some parameters influencing the perceptibility of pitch. *J Acoust. Soc. Am.* 47, 469–476.

Houtgast, T. (1974). Masking patterns and lateral inhibition. In: *Facts and Models in Hearing.* (E. Zwicker and E. Terhardt, eds). Springer-Verlag, New York.

Shannon, R.V. (1976). Two-tone unmasking and suppression in a forward-masking situation. *J. Acoust. Soc. Am.* 59, 1460–1471.

Weber, D.L., and Green, D.M. (1978). Temporal factors and suppression effects in backward and forward masking. *J. Acoust. Soc. Am.* 65(S), 1392–1398.

Wilson, J.P. (1970). Auditory after image. In: *Frequency Analysis and Periodicity.* (Plomp and Smoorenburg, eds). A.W. Sijthoff.

Yost, W.A., and Hill, R. (1978). Strength of the pitches associated with ripple noise. *J. Acoust. Soc. Am.* 64, 485–492.

Yost, W.A., Hill, R., and Perez-Falcon, T. (1978). Pitch and pitch discrimination of broadband signals with rippled power spectra. *J. Acoust. Soc. Am.* 63, 1166–1173.

Yost, W.A., and Hill, R. (1979). Models of the pitch and pitch strength of ripple noise. *J. Acoust. Soc. Am.* 66, 400–411.

THE EFFECT OF STIMULUS DURATION ON THE PROMINENCE OF PITCH

T.J.F. Buunen

*Applied Physics Department, University of Technology,
Delft, The Netherlands*

1. INTRODUCTION

One of the most prominent properties of the human auditory system is the
capability to attribute a specific pitch to an acoustic signal. Insight in the
functioning of the pitch extraction mechanisms is essential for the understanding of speech and music perception. In view of this importance it is readily
understood why the mechanisms of pitch perception received so much attention in
auditory psychophysics. Plomp (1976) gives a comprehensive overview of recent
developments in this field. The "state of the art" on pitch theories will therefore not be presented here. All theories have in common that they consider the
pitch of stationary signals. In natural sounds however the signals are hardly
ever stationary. Speech and musical sounds have a continuously changing short-
term spectrum and therefore it is relevant to investigate non-stationary signals in order to find out about the dynamic properties of the ear in relation
to pitch perception. The experiments reported in this paper represent a first
step in that direction and were performed to gather information about the effect of stimulus duration on prominence of pitch.

2. SIGNAL DESCRIPTION

The basic signal used in the experiments was noise added to its delayed
repetition. The long term power spectrum of this signal is a sinusoidal function of frequency of the form:

$$p(f) = 1 + m \cos 2\pi f \tau \qquad (1)$$

where τ is the value of the delay time. Because of this spectral shape the signal is sometimes called "cosine noise". The spectral modulation depth m depends
upon the level difference between the original noise and its delayed replica.
When they have equal amplitudes m is equal to 1. This particular stimulus was
chosen for several reasons. First, by changing the value of m it is relatively
easy to manipulate the strength of the spectral clue and thus the prominence of
the pitch. Second, by varying τ one can investigate the effect of different
spectral clues because for small values of τ the spectrum contains widely
spread peaks and for large values the peaks come closer together. Besides, this
signal has been investigated quite extensively (Bilsen and Ritsma (1970), Yost
et al. (1978), Houtgast (1971)) as far as its pitch and "internal" spectrum are
concerned in the stationary case. Its psychoacoustic properties are therefore
relatively well known.

The actual pitch of cosine noise depends upon the sign of m. For positive
values of m the pitch corresponds to the pitch of a pure tone with frequency
$1/\tau$ for τ values roughly between 1 and 20 ms. The sound has an ambiguous pitch
for negative values of m corresponding to a frequency of $0.88/\tau$ and $1.14/\tau$, see
Bilsen and Ritsma (1970). The signal sounds like white noise when $m = 0$.

3. PROCEDURE

Cosine noise was generated by adding analog Gaussian noise to its delayed repetition. An observer was presented with pairs of stimuli consisting of two bursts, each with duration Δt. One burst was just white noise, the other cosine noise with delaytime τ. In a two alternative forced choice procedure the observer was asked to differentiate between a pair of identical white noise bursts and two bursts consisting of one burst of white noise followed by a burst of cosine noise. In a computer controlled procedure the modulation depth m was varied for 75%-correct discrimination as a function of Δt. The signals were presented through TDH-39 headphones and electrically filtered by a low pass filter at 10kHz. The overall level of the stimuli was individually set for each observer at 50dB SL.

4. RESULTS AND DISCUSSION

The results for three subjects are presented in Fig.1. Each datapoint is the average of 3 independent sessions. The absciss gives the burst duration in milliseconds and the ordinate the attenuation of the delayed noise, equivalent to spectral modulation depth (see formula (1)).

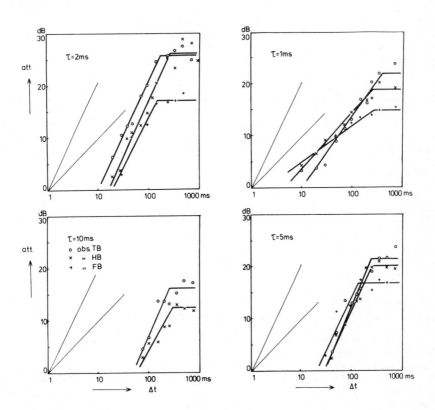

Fig.1. Results for three observers. The absciss gives the duration of the stimulus. The ordinate represents the attenuation of the delayed noise. Roughly this attenuation is equal to 20 log m.

Depending on τ it turns out that the minimum presentation time for pitch detection for signals with maximal spectral modulation (m = 1) lies between 10 and 50 ms. For larger presentation the prominence of the pitch apparently increases since the modulation depth needed to discriminate is less. This increase levels off around 200 ms showing that presentation times beyond this value give the same prominence of pitch as infinitely long stimuli. The minimal values of the modulation depth in that case correspond very well with the data by Yost et al. (1978). The fact that there is a minimal presentation time of 10-50 ms required for the perception of this pitch, can be understood in view of the short term spectrum of the stimulus. Although its long term power spectrum is perfectly sinusoidal it is evident that a spectrum based on a finite duration sample will be different from the cosine function. The effects of sample duration on the short term spectrum of a signal have been calculated theoretically by Blackman and Tukey (1958). There appear to be two major effects of sample duration on the shape of the short term power spectrum. First, the shape of this spectrum can be derived by convolution of the long term spectrum with the Fourier transform of the time window. This means that any spectral information leading to pitch sensation in the long-term spectrum of the stimulus is smoothed out when it covers a frequency range comparable to or smaller than the width of the transformed time window. Applied to the stimulus in the experiment in this paper this means that the sinusoidal function of equation (1) is smoothed out as soon as its period in the frequency domain ($1/\tau$) is of the same order of magnitude as $1/\Delta t$ where Δt is the duration of the sound. In this reasoning one can understand that for presentation times smaller than a specific value of Δt no spectral information is available in the signal. So it follows that this time Δt depends on the peak distance of the cosine noise. One expects that for large values of τ the mimimum presentation time should be larger than for small values. This is in agreement with the results of Fig.1.

The second effect of the finite stimulus duration on the power spectrum is caused by stochastic fluctuations inherent to the noisy character of the stimulus. Blackman and Tukey (1958) show that the energy of a filtered Gaussian noise burst of duration Δt is a stochastic variable described by a chi-squared distribution with a relative deviation (S) depending on the width of the analyzing filter W and the effective duration Δt of the signal according to formula (2):

$$S = \frac{1}{\sqrt{W\Delta t}}$$ (2)

The effect of these stochastic fluctuations on the shape of the short term power spectrum therefore decreases for increasing values of Δt according to a $1\sqrt{\Delta t}$ relationship. In this view the prominence of the sinusoidal shape of the spectrum of a cosine noise burst with duration Δt increases with a $\sqrt{\Delta t}$ relationship. In Fig.1 lines are drawn with a slope corresponding to Δt and $\sqrt{\Delta t}$. The slope of the experimental results is equal to the Δt-line for τ = 2, 5 and 10 ms, while for τ = 1 ms the $\sqrt{\Delta t}$-slope gives a better description. In all cases a platform is reached for Δt = 200 ms. This leads to the conclusion that an integration time around 200 ms describes the time window of the auditory system in the evaluation of the short time spectrum coded in the peripheral ear. This agrees rather well with the large integration of their duration of Plomp and Bouman (1959), Penner (1978).

The integration of spectral information following a Δt relationship applies only for τ = 10, 5 and 2 ms. For all observers the slope of the results for τ = 1 ms is different. There is no obvious explanation for this known to the author at this moment. One might speculate that the concept of spectral dominance has some bearing on it. It says that pitch information in a wide-band-sound is extracted from the frequency region roughly equal to $3/\tau$ - $4/\tau$ for cosine noise (see Bilsen and Ritsma (1970)). For τ = 10, 5 and 2 ms their regions are .35, .7 and 1.75 kHz respectively, for τ = 1 ms the dominant region lies around 3.5 kHz. The results of Fig.1 might be reformulated in stating that apparently the processing of stochastic temporal variations in the output of auditory peripheral bandpass filters occurs in two different ways depending on the frequency region. This view gives an interesting parallel with that from Terhardt (1967) on the processing of amplitude modulated sounds. Below 2 kHz

the properties of the ear in the processing of temporal fluctuations are due to
the filtering properties of the bandpass filters in the peripheral ear. Beyond
2 kHz some other mechanism is responsible. Applied to our experiments this
statement means that the stochastic fluctuations in the output of the bandpass
filters below 2 kHz can be described by simple filter theory because these determine, in Terhardts view, the processing by the ear. This explains that a
theory of increasing pitch prominence with increasing duration based on linear
filter theory works well in this region. For frequencies beyond 2 kHz however
the stochastic fluctuations in the bandpass filters are modified by the limited
time resolving properties of the ear and therefore simple linear network theory
might not work.

Although this reasoning does not give any explanations it might provide
directions for future research.

REFERENCES

Bilsen, F.A. and R.J. Ritsma (1970). Some parameters influencing the perceptibility of pitch. *J.Acoust.Soc.Am.* 47, 469-475.

Blackman, R.B. and J.W. Tukey (1958). *The Measurement of power spectra.*
Dover Publications, Inc. New York.

Houtgast, T. (1971). Psychophysical evidence for lateral inhibition in hearing.
J.Acoust.Soc.Am. 51, 1885-1894.

Penner, M.J. (1978). A power law transformation resulting in a class of short
term integrators that produce time-intensity tracks for noise bursts.
J.Acoust.Soc.Am. 63, 195-201.

Plomp, R. and M. Bouman (1959). Relation between hearing threshold and duration
for tone pulses. *J.Acoust.Soc.Am.* 31, 749-758.

Plomp, R. (1976). *Aspects of tone sensation.* Academic Press, London, New York,
San Francisco.

Terhardt, E. (1967). *Beitrag zur Ermittlung der informationstragenden Markmale
von Schallen mit Hilfe der Hörempfindungen,* Doctoral dissertation,
Technische Hochschule, Stuttgart.

Yost, W.A., Hill, R. and T. Perez-Falcar (1978). Pitch and pitch discrimination
of broadband signals with rippled power spectra. *J.Acoust.Soc.Am.* 63,
1166-1173.

COMMENT

COMMENT ON: "The effect of stimulus duration on the prominence of pitch"
(T.J.F. Buunen)

J.P. Wilson
Dept. of Communication and Neuroscience, University of Keele, U.K.

A very similar experiment was reported at the Driebergen symposium (Wilson, 1970). This also showed a discontinuity at about 250 msec, although for both 1.43 msec and 11.4 msec delays, the threshold relative amplitude between the delayed and undelayed component noises was inversely proportional to the duration of the stimulus.

It should, however, be emphasized that both these experiments may refer to *colouration* rather than *pitch strength*. In particular the threshold relative amplitudes for normal (cos+) and inverted (cos-) spectra are similar (Wilson, 1967) whereas Yost (this symposium) shows clear differences between thresholds for the two signals when delay interval rather than detectability is used as criterion. Although one could still argue about whether Yost's measure of "pitch discrimination" relates to "pitch strength", this experiment appears to be a move in the right direction.

REFERENCES

Wilson, J.P. (1967). Psychoacoustics of obstacle detection using ambient or self-generated noise. In: *Animal Sonar Systems* (Ed. R.G. Russel). Jony-en-Josas, pp. 89-114.

Wilson, J.P. (1970). An auditory after-image. In: *Frequency Analysis and Periodicity Detection in Hearing*. (R. Plomp and G.F. Smoorenburg, eds.), Sijthoff, Leiden. pp. 303-318.

ATONAL PERIODICITY SENSATION FOR COMB FILTERED NOISE SIGNALS

F.A. Bilsen and J.L. Wieman

Applied Physics Department, University of Technology, Delft, The Netherlands.

1. INTRODUCTION

One of the important issues in auditory research is the question to what extent temporal information in acoustical signals, and more specifically: the temporal coding observed in the auditory nervous system, is actually used by the auditory system in performing its main perceptive functions. For the pitch of complex tones, rather than the temporal coding the spectral coding has been shown to be essential. In one way or another, periodicity pitch is derived from the configuration of spectrally resolved frequency components. Nevertheless, the question is still open what type of processing, e.g. spectral or temporal or both, is involved in the processing and evaluation of these individual components. Moreover, it is evident that temporal processing is necessary a.o. for some forms of binaural hearing, and for the detection of low-frequency amplitude variations in monaural stimuli.

In the present paper, we use comb-filtered noise to study the way the auditory system handles temporal information. Comb filtered noise essentially consists of noise added to its single or multiple delayed version(s) (delay time τ). Perceptually, comb noise is characterized by a sensation of tonality (Repetition Pitch) for small τ-values (see e.g. Bilsen, 1966) and a "periodicity sensation" for large values of τ, which can be described as "motorboating", "rattling" or "periodic roughness". The actual trigger to the present study was the observation that the visual inspection of signal fragments in the time domain does not reveal any clear periodicity corresponding to the delay time τ. So, it is not immediately clear whether classical models handling periodic amplitude fluctuations (see e.g. Terhardt, 1974) can explain the periodicity sensation. On the other hand, the long-term autocorrelation function of course shows a relative maximum at τ. The auditory system being able only to perform a short-time analysis, the question arises whether an autocorrelation or averaging analysis performed on the temporal fine-structure or rather the temporal envelope could cope with the subjective data. In the following sections different comb filtered noise signals are investigated and compared with sinusoidally amplitude modulated (SAM) noise, especially concerning the periodicity sensation. The latter stimulus was chosen especially because of its periodic envelope and the lack of spectral information in the long-term (white) power spectrum.

2. SIGNAL DESCRIPTION

The signals used are shortly indicated here by their long-term power spectra. For further details see e.g. Bilsen (1966).

a) *Comb-filtered noise*

This signal was realized with a digital delay line (Eventide 1745 M) producing a delay τ. The input was fed with analog gaussian white noise. By feeding back the output to the input with an attenuation factor of 0.79 (corresponding to -2 dB), an infinite number of delayed versions of the input noise is obtained.

The complex Fourier-spectrum of the resulting signal is given by

$$H(j\omega) = 1+g.\exp(-j\omega\tau)+g^2.\exp(-2j\omega\tau)+\ldots\ldots, \text{ with } g = 0.79.$$

The (comb like) power spectrum $|H(j\omega)|^2$ has rather sharp peaks at n/τ ($n = 0,1,2,\ldots$). The "fundamental" is defined as $F_0= 1/\tau$.

b) *Cosine noise*

This signal is characterized by a single delayed version instead of an infinite number. The complex Fourier spectrum is given by $H(j\omega)=1+g.\exp(-j\omega\tau)$, with $g=1$. The + sign is valid for *harmonic* cosine noise (delayed version added) of which the power spectrum is a cosine function with maxima at n/τ ($n=0,1,2.$). The −sign is valid for *anharmonic* cosine noise. Then, the cosine spectrum has maxima at $(2n+1)/2\tau$.

3. PERIODICITY SENSATION OF COMB-FILTERED NOISE

In order to establish the periodicity sensation of comb noise quantitatively, it was compared with SAM noise (100% amplitude modulation). Subjects were asked to adjust the modulation frequency F_m of SAM noise such that its periodicity sensation matched the periodicity sensation of comb noise of which $F_0(=1/\tau)$ was set by the experimenter. The subject could switch at will between a continuous presentation of both stimuli, presented at a sensation level of about 40 dB SL. For each value of F_0 about 10 adjustments were made. The average value of F_m thus obtained, divided by F_0 is expressed as a measured point in Fig.1. The standard deviation (SD) is given below in the same figure. Three subjects participated in the experiment.

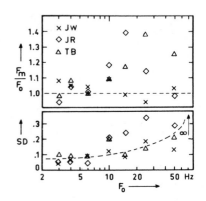

Fig.1. Matchings and standard deviation (SD) of the periodicity sensation for comb and SAM noise.

The horizontal dashed line $F_m/F_0=1$ in Fig.1 indicates perfect equality of the periodicity sensation of comb noise and SAM noise. This appears to be the case for F_0 below about 10 Hz. For F_0 above 50 Hz subjects were unable to perform the task. This is in accordance with the sharp increase in SD in this region (see dashed line indicating the trend). For these higher values of F_0, contrary to SAM noise comb noise no longer produces a periodicity sensation, but its pitch sensation takes over.

4. JUST NOTICEABLE DIFFERENCE IN PERIODICITY SENSATION

In order to obtain further insight in the processes underlying periodicity sensation, a series of measurements was dedicated to the just noticeable difference (JND) in "fundamental" F_0 of comb noise and cosine noise, especially in comparison with the JND in F_m for SAM noise.

Stimuli of 2 sec duration were presented in pairs in a 2AFC method with AX-procedure, i.e. one stimulus of a pair with delay τ and the other with τ or $\tau+\Delta\tau$ randomly. The inter stimulus interval was 800 ms. Subjects were asked to decide whether they heard any difference whatsoever between the two stimuli of a pair. The JND was expressed as $\Delta\tau/\tau$ where $\Delta\tau$ is the increment in delay that is discriminated 75% correct. The results of four subjects are given in Figs. 2 and 3 for cosine noise and comb noise respectively. Fig. 4 gives the JND ($=\Delta F_m/F_m$) for SAM noise.

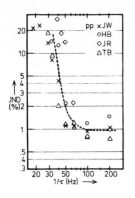

For cosine noise and comb noise a rather sudden transition can be observed around 40 Hz. Above that frequency a plateau exists equal to .3% for comb noise, and to 1% for cosine noise. This JND, obviously in the frequency range for pitch perception, may be compared to the JND of narrow noise bands (Moore, 1973). For fundamentals F_0 below 20 Hz, a JND of 10% and 20% for comb noise and cosine noise respectively is obtained. This is of the same order of magnitude as the JND for SAM noise in that region (see Fig. 4; compare also Ritsma and Hoekstra, 1974). The large increase in JND of SAM noise for higher F_m shows the decreasing effectiveness of the periodicity detection mechanism. (By the way, this might be difficult to reconcile with the finding that musically trained subjects show correct musical interval recognition in a restricted range of F_m (Burns and Viemeister, 1976)).

Fig.2. The just noticeable difference (JND) in periodicity sensation for cosine noise.

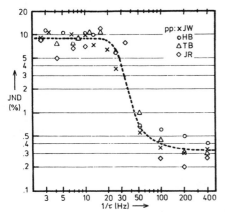

Fig.3. The JND in periodicity sensation for comb filtered noise.

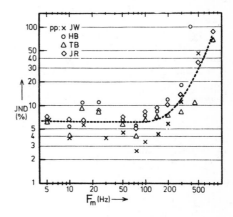

Fig.4. The JND in periodicity sensation for SAM noise.

5. LOWER LIMITS OF PITCH PERCEPTION

In the foregoing sections a transition from periodicity sensation to pitch sensation with increasing F_0 was reported for comb and cosine noise. This is understandable on the basis of the power spectrum. For low values of F_0, the peaks in the spectrum are closely spaced, and, thus, are no longer resolved by the peripheral system. This explains the lack of pitch sensation, in accordance with modern pitch theories. To obtain a further confirmation for this explanation of the transition region, the lower limit of pitch sensation was determined in an independent way.

From the literature (e.g. Bilsen, 1966) it is known that the Repetition Pitch of cosine noise is subject to a change from $1/\tau$ for harmonic cosine noise into $1.14/\tau$ and $0.88/\tau$ for anharmonic cosine noise. Here, we use this pitch change as a subjective criterion for the detectability of pitch. Subjects were presented alternately with harmonic and anharmonic cosine noise. Stimuli of 1 sec duration were presented in pairs with random order, at about 40 dB SL. Subjects had to decide whether they heard any difference whatsoever between the two stimuli of a pair. Oral reports afterwards confirmed that they used pitch as a criterion. Using a 2AFC-method, the threshold value of the delay τ was de-

Table 1.

	τ (ms)	F_0 (Hz)
JW	22.9 ± 1.9	43.7
HB	19.9 ± 1.8	50.3
TB	29.8 ± 1.8	33.6
JR	16.5 ± 1.5	60.6
average	22.3	47.0

termined for which subjects showed 75% correct discrimination between the two stimuli of a pair.

In table I these threshold values together with the standard deviation are given for four subjects. In the second column these τ-values are expressed in the fundamental frequency F_0. Apparently, the average value of 47 Hz corresponds with the transition region in Figs 2 and 3.

6. CONCLUSIONS AND DISCUSSION

a) For low fundamentals (F_0<50 Hz), the periodicity sensation of comb filtered noise and SAM noise can be matched. This is in agreement with the correspondance of the JND's (see Fig.5) in this region. Also, the SD of the matchings is of the same order of magnitude (Fig.1).

b) For cosine noise, a transition region between pitch and periodicity sensation has been found at 47 Hz (see hatched column in Fig.5). At this region the JND jumps to a different plateau.

c) The autocorrelation function of harmonic cosine noise after a hypothetical (peripheral) band filtering shows a relative maximum at τ. For anharmonic cosine noise this maximum splits up into two maxima at either side of τ., thus indicating two different periodicities. The subjective indiscriminability of both type of signals in the τ-range of periodicity sensation thus indicates the inadequacy of a description on the basis of autocorrelation performed on the temporal fine structure.

d) Autocorrelation or averaging performed on the signal envelope needs further consideration as a possibility for the system to extract time information. The perceptual similarity with SAM noise suggests this.

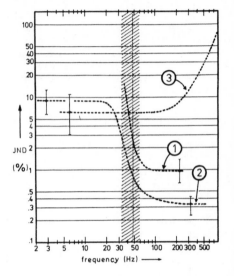

Fig.5. Summary of the measurements
Curve 1: JND of cosine noise
Curve 2: JND of comb noise
Curve 3: JND of SAM noise
hatched column: lower limit of
pitch sensation.

REFERENCES

Bilsen, F.A.(1966). Repetition Pitch; monaural interaction of a sound with the repetition of the same, but phase shifted sound. *Acustica* 17, 295-300.

Burns, E.M. and N.F. Viemeister (1976). Nonspectral pitch. *J.Acoust.Soc.Am.* 60, 863-869.

Moore, B.C.J.(1973). Frequency difference limens for narrow bands of noise. *J.Acoust.Soc.Am.* 54, 888-896.

Ritsma, R.J. and A. Hoekstra (1974). Frequency selectivity and the tonal residue. In: *Facts and models in hearing* (Zwicker and Terhardt Eds), 156-163, Springer, Berlin.

Terhardt, E.(1974). On the perception of periodic sound fluctuations (roughness). *Acustica* 30, 201-213.

COMMENT ON: "Atonal periodicity sensation for comb filtered noise signals".
(F.A. Bilsen and J.L. Wieman).

N.F. Viemeister
Department of Psychology, University of Minnesota, Minneapolis, Minnesota 55455, U.S.A.

The large increase in the JND for SAM noise noted by Bilsen and Wieman (see Fig.4) for modulation frequencies above 200-400 Hz is in agreement with the existence region for the pitch of SAM noise shown by Burns and Viemeister (1976). Our subjects show a fairly rapid deterioration in musical interval recognition for modulation frequencies above 400 Hz, for two subjects, and above 150 Hz for the third. Since these two sets of data are in reasonable agreement, the data shown by Bilsen and Wieman in Fig.4 present no difficulty for our finding that over the range of modulation frequencies within the existence region, SAM noise can convey melodic information and, in this sense possesses pitch.

REFERENCES

Burns, E.M. and N.F. Viemeister (1976). Nonspectral pitch. *J.Acoust.Soc.Am.* <u>60</u>, 863-869.

COMMENT ON: "Atonal periodicity sensation for comb filtered noise signals".
(F.A. Bilsen and J.L. Wieman)

J.P. Wilson
Dept. of Communication & Neuroscience, University of Keele, U.K.

A number of people, including ourselves, have used the term "comb-filtered" noise synonymously with "cosine" and "rippled" noise as it is an appropriate descriptor when the spectrum is plotted in dB. It is therefore confusing now to use the term differently.

Although the periodicity in comb-filtered noise may not be obvious in the waveform of a single short sample, it can be readily observed with repetitive traces or an oscilloscope triggered either by a waveform peak or a zero crossing. Such information can in principle be analysed by the nervous system.

Section VI
Binaural Hearing

Binaural hearing deals, generally speaking, with all the possible psychophysical and physiological phenomena that occur when both ears of a listener are simultaneously stimulated, either with identical, or with different, information. It deals with phenomena such as lateralization, binaural masked level differences (BMLD's), dichotic pitch and so on. In this section, special attention is paid to lateralization from interaural time differences and intensity differences and for low frequency as well as for high frequency signals. Also discussed is how lateralization and BMLD's can be used in a paradigm to establish monaural effects like lateral suppression. Alternative models that pay attention either to processing of temporal and/or of spectral information are presented. Physiological evidence and results of experiments with listeners with impaired hearing provide substantial material to verify these models.

LATERALIZATION OF COMPLEX WAVEFORMS.

G. Bruce Henning.

*Department of Experimental Psychology, South Parks Road,
Oxford.*

Leakey, Sayers, and Cherry (1958) and David, Guttman, and van Bergeijk (1959) suggested that human observers might be sensitive to interaural delays in the envelopes of complex, high-frequency waveforms. Both studies used random signals whose long-term interaural correlation was zero. Subsequent studies with simpler, deterministic signals also showed that observers can detect interaural delays in the sinusoidal envelope of an amplitude-modulated carrier whose frequency was much higher than the highest frequency at which interaural delays can be detected in pure tones (Henning, 1974; McFadden and Pasanen, 1976; Nuetzel and Hafter, 1976). It has also been shown that interaural delays in the carriers of the same amplitude-modulated signals are not detectable and it is of some interest to determine the characteristics of an envelope extractor that would preserve information about interaural delay in the envelope, but not the carrier, of such stimuli (Henning, 1980).

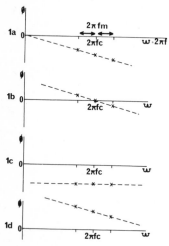

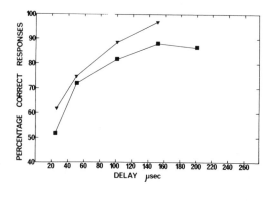

Fig. 1. shows the phase spectra for several sorts of "delay" as a function of the frequency of the components of an AM wave-form. Fig 1a. shows the effect of delaying the entire waveform; 1b. that of delaying the envel-ope; 1c that of delaying the carrier; and 1d that of delaying the envelope and advancing the carrier. All delays have the same magnitude.

Fig. 2. shows the percentage of correct responses obtained by two Observers detecting interaural delays of the entire waveform as a function of interaural delay in microseconds.

Consider the familar three component waveform produced by sinusoidally modulating the amplitude of a sinusoidal carrier to some depth m:

$$y(t) = (1+m \cdot \cos 2\pi f_m t) \sin 2\pi f_c t, \qquad\qquad 1.$$

where f_m is the modulation frequency and f_c is the carrier frequency. When m, the depth of modulation, is one, this stimulus will have a power spectrum comrising three components- the carrier (at frequency f_c Hz) and two sidebands each 6 dB less intense than the carrier at frequencies f_m Hz below and above that of the carrier. (Provided that precautions are taken in experiments to turn the signals on and off sufficiently slowly, no important information is lost in treating the spectrum as discrete.) If the signal of Equation 1. is presented to one ear and a "delayed" version of it to the other, the power spectra of the stimuli to the two ears remain identical whether the entire waveform, the envelope, the carrier, or any combination of these is delayed. Information about different delays is carried in the phase spectra which are shown in Fig. 1.

If phase is specified relative to the point when t in Equation 1 is zero, then the three sinusoidal components of y(t) each have zero phase and the ordinate in Fig. 1 can be treated as an interaural phase difference. Fig. 1a shows the effect on interaural phase of delaying the entire waveform; the interaural delays at each frequency lie on a straight line that passes through the origin (at zero frequency) and which, on these linear co-ordinates, has a slope equal to the delay-- a delay relative to y(t) produces negative slopes, an advance would produce a positive slope. Delaying the envelope has the effect, shown in Fig. 1b, of altering both the slope and intercept of the line joining the phases of the components-- the slope of the line is equal to the delay but the interaural phase is zero at the frequency of the carrier. The local slope of a continuous phase spectrum is sometimes called the group delay (Papoulis, 1962) and it is convenient to describe the slope of the line connecting the interaural phase of the discrete components of Fig. 1 as group delay. An interaural delay of the carrier (Fig. 1c) produces no group delay; all three components have the same interaural phase difference and the slope of the line joining the phases is zero. Papoulis calls the slope of the line joining the phase at each frequency to origin the phase delay. Thus each component in Fig. 1c has a slightly different phase delay.

The phase spectra resulting from delaying either the envelope or the carrier (or both) always result in co-linear interaural phase shifts; interaural envelope delays affect the slope of the line about the carrier frequency (the group delay); interaural delays of the carrier affect only the intercept of the line at the carrier frequency (phase delay); delaying the entire waveform affects both the group and the phase delay.

Since observers[1] are equally sensitive to delays in high frequency, complex waveforms that produce interaural phase spectra like those of Figs. 1a and 1b but are insensitive to delays that produce spectra like that of 1c, it is clear that we must find a model of the binaural system that is sensitive to group delay and insensitive to phase delay-- at least in its response to high-frequency amplitude-modulated signals. (Fig. 1d shows a phase spectrum produced by delaying the envelope but advancing the carrier by the same amount; this stimulus will be considered subsequently.)

1.   *The same Observers were used in all the experiments described here and the same symbols used to indicate their data. The Observer whose data are shown as a square in the author.*

The next three figures illustrate the lateralization performance of several Observers   attempting to detect interaural delays in a standard two-interval forced-choice task (Henning, 1980). On each trial the waveform of Equation 1 was presented to one ear (and a "delayed"version of it to the other ear) in the first observation interval. In the second observation interval of the trial the signals to the ears were interchanged and the Observers' task was to indicate the interval in which the signal to the right ear had been delayed. The signals were presented for 200 msec and were turned on and off with linear ramps lasting 50 msec; the sinusoidal carrier had a frequency of about 4 kHz and an intensity of 50 dB SPL; the depth of modulation was 100% and the modulation frequency was about 300 Hz and harmonically related to the carrier. A low-pass filtered noise at 44 dB Spectrum Level was continuously present.

Fig. 2 shows the percentage of correct responses in 100 trials for two different Observers as a function of interaural delay (in microseconds) obtained when the entire waveform was delayed.

Fig. 3a shows the performance that is obtained when the envelope of the waveform is delayed. The two Observers in common to the Figs show similar results and achieve 75% correct lateralization with delays of between 50 and 70 microseconds. The results of the two other Observers are shown in Fig. 3a there is considerable variability among Observers.

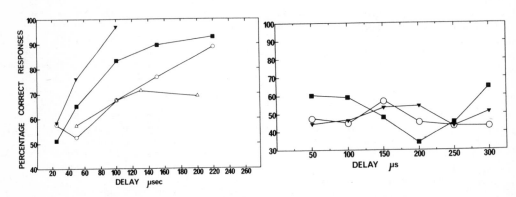

Figs. 3a and 3b show the percentage of correct responses obtained in 100 trials as a function of interaural delay in microseconds. Results for several different Observers are shown. Data shown in Fig. 3a (on the left) were obtained when the envelope was delayed-those in 3b when the carrier was delayed. The carrier frequency was about 4 kHz and the modulation frequency about 300 Hz.

Fig. 3b shows the percentage of correct judgments as a function of interaural delay in the carrier--Observers are unable reliably to detect the phase delays that result from interaural delays in the carrier. These are the usual sort of results obtained with high frequency signals (Henning, 1980).

The results obtained with low frequencies are quite different.
Figs. 4a and 4b show the lateralization performance obtained when the carrier frequency was lowered from 4 kHz to 600 Hz. The modulation frequency was again 300 Hz but now the (same three) Observers are unable to lateralize interaural delay in the envelope (Fig 4a) and readily lateralize carrier delays (Fig 4b). In this experiment the Observers, although informed by lights which interval had contained the waveforms in which the stimulus to the right ear had been delayed, were not required to maximize the number of correct responses. Rather they used the information about correct responses merely to be consistent; that is to make their performance as different from 50% correct as possible while at the same time still indicating the interval in which the leftmost signal occurred.

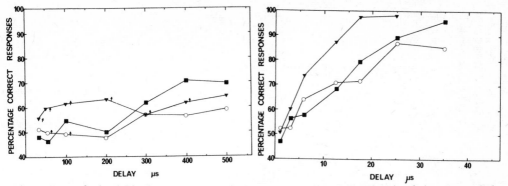

Figs. 4a and 4b show the percentage of correct responses obtained in 100 trials as a function of interaural delay in microseconds. Results for three different Observers are shown. Data shown in Fig 4a (on the left) were obtained when the envelope was delayed—those in 4b when the carrier was delayed. The carrier frequency was about 600Hz and the modulation frequency about 300Hz.

The Observers' performance with envelope delays (Fig 4a) did not differ much from 50% and the small arrows indicate points that have been reflected about the 50% correct level.

The differences in Observers' performance at high and low frequencies suggested that it might be appropriate to study the way in which both carrier and modulation frequency affected the detectability of both carrier (phase) and envelope (group) delays. To this end waveforms with interaural phase spectra like that of Fig. 1d were generated. In these waveforms the carrier was advanced by 200 microseconds (and the envelope delayed by 200 microseconds) relative to the waveform of Equation 1 so that the two cues, group and phase delay, operated in the opposite sense. In a similar two-interval forced choice task the Observers were again required to perform consistently and to report the interval in which the signal appeared to be farther to the left. It was arranged by arbitrary convention that if the Observer could reliably perform the task and if his decision were based on envelope or group delay he would achieve 100% "correct" responses. Reliable performance based on carrier or phase delay would lead to 0% correct responses (Henning and Ashton, 1980).

Carriers ranging from 500 Hz to 5kHz and modulation frequencies ranging from 50 to 800 Hz were used; the same three Observers participated.

At carrier frequencies below about 1500 Hz virtually errorless performance was possible with any modulation frequency (barring those, of course, in which the frequency of the modulation exceeded that of the carrier) and lateralization in this low-frequency region was based on phase delay. At carrier frequencies greater than 1500 Hz the Observers' ability to judge interaural delay depended on both the frequency of the carrier and that of the modulation. Whenever lateralization was possible in the high frequency region it was based on group or envelope delay.

Figs. 5a and 5b illustrate two typical sets of results.

Fig. 5a shows lateralization as a function of carrier frequency with a modulation frequency of 50 Hz; Fig 5b shows the performance with a 300 Hz modulation frequency. The transistion region near 1500 Hz is apparent in both graphs; the 50% correct performance level in that region is an indication that neither cue is effective and does not represent a region in which the opposed cues are equally effective and cancel each other's effect; it is not a region of balance in a group delay/phase delay trade. This is also the case in the low-frequency region. Increasing the group or envelope delay with carriers below 1500 Hz does not alter the level of performance; the Observers appear to be sensitive only to phase or carrier delay at low frequencies (Henning and Ashton, 1980).

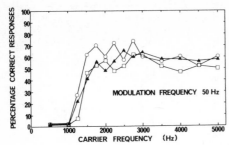

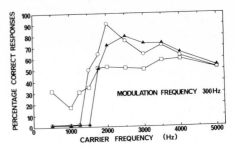

Figs. 5a and 5b show the percentage of "correct" lateralization of waveforms in which the carrier was advanced (and the envelope delayed) by 200 microseconds. Reliable performance based on envelope or group delay yields 100% correct-reliable performance based on carrier or phase delay yields 0% correct. The abscissae show carrier frequency (in Hz). Fig 5a shows the results with a 50 Hz modulation frequency-Fig 5b those with a 300 Hz modulation frequency. Results for three different observers are shown.

The detectability of interaural envelope delay appears to be a high-frequency phenomenon but the correspondence between the region in which Observers are able to use envelope delays and the region in which the tonal residue for corresponding waveforms exist (Ritsma, 1962) is far from perfect as Fig. 6a shows.

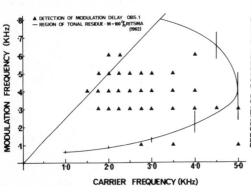

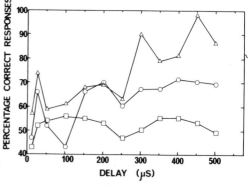

Fig 6a indicates, by filled symbols, those combinations of carrier frequency (abscissa) and modulation frequency (ordinate) at which the best Observer is able to detect envelope delay with fewer than 29% errors. The solid shows the existence region of the tonal residue (after Ritsma 1962) and the vertical lines indicate the range for Ritsma's three Observers.

Fig. 6b shows the percentage of correct lateralization judgments as a function of interaural delay. The waveform was a frequency modulated signal with a carrier of 4 k Hz, a modulation frequency of 300 Hz and a modulation index of 1.9.

The simplest envelope extractor (or group delay detector for they are equivalent with amplitude modulated waveforms) consists of two monaural devices receiving only high frequency input and each comprising an identical non-linearity and a band pass filter. The non-linearity might be a simple square-law device and the band pass filter might pass signals between 200 and 500 Hz. The monaural output of each device would contain components at both the modulation frequency, f_m, and twice that frequency. The low-frequency components in response to an input of the form y(t) would both be in cosine phase. A delay in either the entire waveform or the envelope would be reflected as delay of the same size in the component at f_m Hz and a delay of twice the size at $2f_m$ Hz. (The latter component is 12 dB below the level of the component at f_m Hz.) Carrier delays produce no delay in the output of the square-law device at either frequency. An interaural comparison of the signals at f_m Hz, then, would produce behaviour similar to that of the Observers.

A simple test of this model has been made by asking the Observers to detect interaural delays in a three component stimulus when the components are in quasi-frequency modulated phase (for example, the side-bands in sine phase and the carrier in cosine phase). Under these conditions the quadratic non-linearity produces no output at frequency f_m and on this basis it might be expected that lateralization of high-frequency complexes based on interaural delay would be impossible. However, although lateralization performance is at least a factor of two worse with this waveform, Observers' can achieve better than 75% correct responses. Moreover even with a true frequency modulated waveform (Fig 6b) observers exhibit reliable lateralization provided the interaural delay is made large.

REFERENCES.

David, E.E., Guttman, N. and van Bergeijk, W.A. (1959). Binaural interaction of high-frequency stimuli. *J. Acoust. Soc. Am.* **31**, 774-782.

Henning, G.B. (1974). Detectability of Interaural delay in high-frequency complex waveforms. *J. Acoust. Soc Am.* **55**, 84-90.

Henning, G.B. (1980). Some observations on the lateralization of complex wave forms. submitted to *J. Acoust. Soc Am.*

Henning, G.B. and Ashton, J. The effect of carrier and modulation frequency on lateralization based on interaural phase and interaural group delay. submitted to *J. Acoust. Soc Am.*

Leakey, D.M., Sayers, B. McA., and Cherry, C. (1958). Binaural fusion of low and high-frequency sounds. *J. Acoust. Soc. Am.* 30, 222 (L).

McFadden, D., and Pasanen, E.G. (1976). Lateralization at high frequencies based on interaural time differences. *J. Acoust. Soc. Am.* **59**, 634-639.

Nuetzel, J.M. and Hafter, E.R. (1976). Lateralization of complex waveforms: effects of fine structure, amplitude and duration. *J. Acoust. Soc. Am.* **60**, 1339-1346.

Papoulis, A. (1962). *The Fourier Integral and Its Applications*. McGraw-Hill, New York.

Ritsma, R.J. (1962). Existence region of the tonal residue. *J. Acoust. Soc. Am.* **34**, 1224-1229.

ACKNOWLEDGEMENT.
This research was supported by the Medical Research Council.

COMMENT

COMMENT ON: "Lateralization of complex waveforms" (G. B. Henning)

J. Blauert
Ruhr-Universität, Bochum, Fed.Rep. of Germany

The data presented in this paper fit nicely to results that have been obtained by Boerger (1965) with Gaussian shaped tone bursts. They also confirm the concept of the role of interaural fine structure delay and envelope delay respectively interaural phase delay and group delay as presented by Blauert (1974). This book gives further references to related work.

REFERENCES

Boerger, G. (1965). Die Lokalisation von Gausstönen. *Dissertation Techn. Universität Berlin.*
Blauert, J. (1974). *Räumliches Hören.* S. Hirzel Verlag Stuttgart.

LATERALIZATION OF HIGH-FREQUENCY STIMULI ON THE BASIS OF TIME AND INTENSITY

E.R. Hafter, R.H. Dye, Jr. and J.M. Nuetzel

Department of Psychology, University of California, Berkeley, California 94720, U.S.A.

1. INTRODUCTION

For nearly a hundred years, the prevailing view has been that the localization of high-frequency tones is based on Interaural Differences of Intensity (IDIs) derived from the sound-shadow cast by the head on the distal ear, while the localization of low-frequency tones is based on Interaural Differences of Time (IDTs) between sounds arriving at the two ears. This duplex theory of localization has been used to explain the fact that errors of localization are lowest for tones of low and high frequency and greatest for those in the mid range. One version of the duplex model suggests that the auditory system is insensitive to both IDIs at low frequencies and to IDTs at high; but that is incorrect. By using headphones to present the cues separately, the detectability of IDIs can be shown to be relatively constant across frequency. Thus the reduction in the sound-shadow of long wavelengths is the only limit to the usefulness of the cue for localization, making the intensity half of duplex theory seem more a matter of acoustics than of biology. The same is not true, however, for IDTs. In the free field, the interaural time-of-arrival is relatively constant above 1000 Hz though a bit less than at low frequencies (Kuhn, 1977), but when listeners are presented dichotic tones through headphones, they are essentially "phase-blind" for frequencies above about 1200 Hz.

Although it is clear that there is no sensitivity to IDTs in high-frequency sinusoids, this is not necessarily the case if the high-frequency stimuli have complex waveforms. Listeners can detect differences of time, for example, in high-frequency clicks (Harris, 1960; Yost, 1976; Hafter & DeMaio, 1975), in amplitude-modulated (AM) sinusoids with a high-frequency carrier (Leakey *et al*, 1958; Henning, 1974; Nuetzel & Hafter, 1976) and in high-frequency AM with the carrier suppressed (McFadden & Passanen, 1976). Similarly, Colburn and Esquissaud (1976) and Hafter (1977) have suggested that sensitivity to differences of time between corresponding portions of the envelopes of signals-plus-maskers can account for the Masking-level Differences (MLDs) seen at high frequencies. The conclusion must then be that the inability to lateralize high frequencies on the basis of time is a special case, true only for tones or for "near" tones such as sinusoidal AM with a very low modulation frequency (see the left hand segment of Fig. 1).

Insensitivity to IDTs in high-frequency tones is not surprising since it protects against false perceptions of delays which exceed 180° of phase. In addition, sensitivity to IDTs in transients allows the listener to use valuable information carried in stimulus onsets. That the binaural system enhances the importance of initial transients is evident in the so-called "precedence" effect where an interaural delay in the onset generally dominates the perception of laterality, regardless of IDTs in the continuing portions of the stimulus (Wallach *et al*, 1949; Tobias & Schubert, 1959). One cannot, however, completely ignore differences of time in ongoing stimuli. Listeners can extract some interaural differences from the entire stimulus, though the amount varies with the type of signal. This is seen for the lateralization of noise (Tobias & Zerlin, 1959), low-frequency tones in noise (Houtgast & Plomp, 1968), low-frequency tones without noise (Ricard & Hafter, 1973) and various types of AM (McFadden & Pasanen, 1976; Nuetzel & Hafter, 1976), where increasing the duration of the stimulus lowers the interaural thresholds. Also, Hafter *et al.* (1979a) have shown that 500-Hz tones can be lateralized even with the onsets completely masked by noise.

The research to be discussed here began with an interest in the transition from those cases, where interaural timing can be extracted from the whole stimulus, to those where only the transient information is important. As in Henning (1974), Colburn and Esquissaud (1976) and McFadden & Pasanen (1976), it rejects the spectrally determined insensitivity of the duplex model in favor of a modified onset model in which peaks in the stimulus envelope may be treated as separable onsets, with fluctuations in the envelope transducing temporal markers regardless of the carrier frequency. Thus the emphasis shifts from spectral region to the rate of modulation.

2. MODULATION FREQUENCY AND SAM

One would like to examine the limitations of rate directly. Some results from such an attempt are shown in Fig. 1. There, following Henning (1974), we (Nuetzel & Hafter, 1979) asked listeners to lateralize a sinusoidal SAM whose carrier frequency remained in-phase, interaurally, but whose modulation envelope was delayed to one ear. The effects of rate were tested by varying the

Fig. 1. Lateralization thresholds for interaural delay of a sinusoidal AM in the presence of a 1600-Hz low-pass noise. Each stimulus was gated "on" for 200 msec with a 30-msec rise-decay time. The data are averages from three subjects.

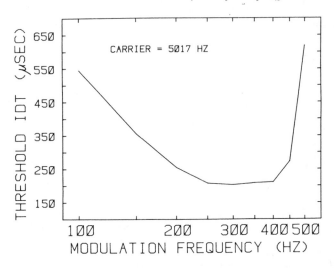

frequency of modulation. The ordinate is the threshold for interaural delay (Δt). The data plotted here are for a carrier frequency of 5017 Hz, though the forms of the functions are similar for carriers of 3017 and 4017 Hz. Also, despite considerable individual differences in the interaural thresholds, the forms of the functions relative to modulation frequency were similar. Thus, the results are given as averages from three listeners. Thresholds represent 76%-correct performance in a two-alternative, forced choice (2AFC). Because the two alternatives were created by commutating the inputs to the two headphones, the given Δts are twice the actual interaural delay. A statement in the Introduction spoke of insensitivity to IDTs in "near" tones. We see that for envelope fluctuations below 150 Hz, performance with SAM is increasingly similar to that with a 5-kHz tone, from which timing in the fine-structure cannot be extracted. It is in the right-hand segment that one would expect to see the limitations of rate. What happens though is that the thresholds began to rise in the vicinity of 350 Hz, and by 550 Hz, no listener lateralized reliably above chance for any of the carriers tested. This is well below the 1200-Hz region where sensitivity to IDTs in tones breaks down, suggesting that perhaps something other than an ability to code time was responsible for the decline in performance. A reasonable explanation is that binaural interaction disappeared as the sidebands moved increasingly outside of the critical bands of the carrier, leading to a shallower depth of modulation. If so, then, both skirts of this function show the difficulty of extracting a temporal code when the envelope of the modulation varies with too shallow a slope. An alternative hypothesis is that while neurons might follow the envelope fluctuations at higher rates, close temporal proximity would not allow for independent usage of the information in each sample.

3. PULSE MODULATION

Because SAM seemed inadequate for studying rate, at least at low frequencies, we moved instead to trains of high-frequency dichotic clicks, from which listeners would be asked to lateralize on the basis of interaural differences presented in each dichotic pair. Rate would be controlled by varying the Inter-click Intervals (ICIs), and the ability to accept and use interaural information in the individual clicks would be assessed by varying the number of clicks in the train. Yost (1976) had tested for lateralization using trains of up to 12 clicks and ICIs as small as 2.2 msec. But the spectra of his clicks contained many low frequencies, and we wished to work only in high-frequency regions, where lateralization based on waveform "fine" structure would be unlikely. Also we were hopeful of differentiating between some competing models of the rate limitation on timing, and to do so would require longer trains. Finally, high-frequency clicks would allow for shorter ICIs (higher rates), without physical interaction between successive clicks in the trains.

Clicks were generated by stimulating Krohn-Hite filters with 20-μsec rectangular pulses. There were n clicks in each train, where n = 1, 2, 4, 8, 16 or 32. The nominal ICIs were 1, 2, 5 and 10 msec. As with AM, a mirror image of the delay was presented in the two halves of a 2AFC and listeners responded to the direction of movement of the perceived intracranial image. We were worried that the subjects might compare the lagging click in each dichotic pair to the leading click in the next and thus base their answers on some kind of dichotic pitch (Bilsen & Goldstein, 1974). To prevent this, a random variation of up to ± 10% was added to each ICI.

The filters were set to bandpass at 4000 Hz; Krohn-Hite filters have a 24 dB/octave rejection rate. With each click set to a total sound pressure of 40 dB SPL we felt assured that energy in the "normal" low-frequency region of binaural interaction was negligible. Because of the relatively wide bandwidth of the filters it was not necessary to worry about interclick interactions in the electronics, even for the shortest ICI used. It is less certain that we can ignore interaction due to ringing by the basilar membrane. Kiang's (1965) report of units which time-locked to clicks of even several thousand/sec led us to treat the individual clicks as punctate stimuli whose spectra was restricted to the high-frequency region (in binaural terms) and whose rate could be varied from 100 Hz to 1000 Hz. Clearly though, at high rates where spectral components of the click trains become increasingly spread, reductions in the depths of modulation by the auditory filters occur as with SAM.

The logic used to examine the limitations of rate is similar to that suggested by Houtgast & Plomp (1968) to study the effects of duration. The notion is one of statistical summation. It says that if all of the information in a stimulus is used, an increase in its duration (in this case an increase in n) produces a proportional decrease in the variance of the noise process that limits detection. The result should be a square root decrement in threshold. Since our listeners' thresholds were orders of magnitude greater than temporal jitter in the stimulus-generating apparatus, all of the "noise" in the experiment was internal to the subjects. Therefore, if the nervous system treated each dichotic pair in the train as an independent event and if it could remember and use the information in each pair, the threshold for a train of n clicks would be:

$$\Delta t_n = \Delta t_1/\sqrt{n} \qquad \text{and,} \qquad \log(\Delta t_n) = \log(\Delta t_1) - .5 \log(n) \qquad (1)$$

4. TWO POSSIBLE LIMITATIONS OF RATE ON NEURAL CODING

Two models that will be considered here differ in the way that they respond to high rates of stimulation. Each poses the response of hypothetical neural elements and asks what happens to the probability that each click will elicit a neural event as the ICI is shortened. The first attributes the limitations of rate to refraction. It postulates that the refractory period after

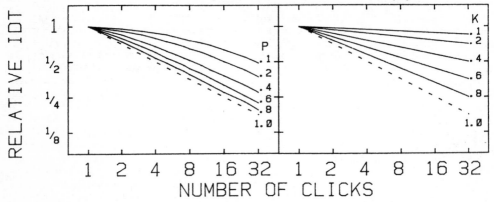

Fig. 2. *Logarithmic plots from two different models for the limitations imposed by stimulus rate on the use of interaural differences of time.*
a. *The left half computes the thresholds for n clicks (Δt_n) as:*   b. *The right computes the thresholds as:*

$$\Delta t_n = \Delta t_1/[1 + p(n-1)]^{.5} \qquad\qquad \Delta t_n = \Delta t_1/[n^k]^{.5}$$

each neural event is drawn from a stationary population and that the mean period does not vary throughout the stimulus train. It is the sort of renewal process used by Luce & Green (1974) to model long term ISI histograms taken from the 8th nerve. If the ICI is so short that a click is presented while some neurons have not yet recovered from a previous firing, the probability of firing, p, is decreased. But, for a given ICI, p is fixed. A simple statement of this model as it applies to our experiment is that the number of neural events (N) elicited by n clicks should be:

$$N = pn \qquad 0.0 \le p \le 1.0 \qquad p = f(ICI) \qquad (2)$$

If applied to equation 1, it becomes

$$\log(\Delta t_n) = \log(\Delta t_1) - .5 \log(p) - .5 \log(n) \qquad (3)$$

Note that the slope is -0.5, regardless of p. A version of this model as p grows smaller is plotted in Fig. 2a. It is unreasonable to expect rate to affect the first click in the train. Thus for the drawing, Eq. 3 was modified to read N = 1 + p(n-1). For small n's, this makes a difference, but as n grows the slopes quickly approach -0.5.

The second model to be considered asserts that the probabilities of eliciting a neural event may decline throughout the course of a train. The equation to be fit is the compressive power function that one might expect with saturation. Thus

$$N = n^k \qquad 0.0 \le k \le 1.0 \qquad k = f(ICI) \qquad (4)$$

and

$$\log(\Delta t_n) = \log(\Delta t_1) - .5k \log(n) \tag{5}$$

Here we see that the slope is not constant, but is proportional to k. Idealizations of this model as k becomes smaller are shown in Fig. 2b.

Fig. 3. Laterali-
zation thresholds
for interaural
delay in trains of
4000-Hz bandpass
clicks. Before
averaging, data
from the four sub-
jects were scaled
so that the thresh-
olds for n = 1
would be 1.0.

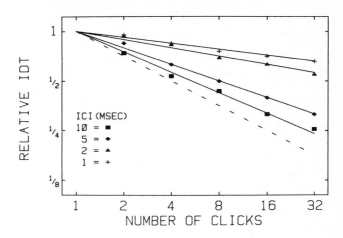

Figure 3 shows experimental results (Hafter & Dye, 1978), drawn with curves fitted from Eq. 5. The four subjects were not equally sensitive to IDTs but since the relation of interest is between the log thresholds and log n, the obtained Δts were scaled geometrically to produce identical Δts for 1 click for all subjects. They were then averaged before the logarithms were computed. An analysis of the two models was conducted by computing best fitting values of p and k for each ICI and for the data for 4, 8, 16 and 32 clicks. Because the two models are essentially inseparable for small n's, the data for 2 clicks were not included in the computations. The sums of squared differences between the data and the best fits by the first model averaged 41 times those for the second. The solid lines depict best fitting k's.[1] The dashed line is the complete summation line with slope = -0.5. In one respect, averaging across subjects is misleading; for three of the four subjects, an ICI of 10 msec produced best fitting slopes of -0.5. These individual differences and their possible meanings are discussed elsewhere (Hafter & Dye, 1980).

These data show not only that stimuli of high spectral content could carry interaural temporal cues but also that the information was transmitted and accumulated across periods of as long as 1/3 second, if the envelope frequency was sufficiently low. In this regard, the individual clicks acted somewhat like the fine structure of low-frequency sinusoids, though interestingly, the slopes that one obtains with such tones are more shallow (Houtgast & Plomp, 1968; Ricard & Hafter, 1973). Finally, the data show that the transition to an essentially transient mechanism was graded, with the effectiveness of later clicks in the train being described by a compressive power function with an exponent related to the stimulus rate. While the data do not select between bandwidth and rate hypotheses, the increasingly shallow slopes between 16 clicks and 32, stimuli which have roughly the same spectra, are supportive of the latter.

For very small k's the kind of compression implied by Eq. 4 describes the responses of phasic neurons, that is, neurons which are active only at the onsets of stimuli. For intermediate values, it probably describes the early portions of the PST histograms of even those tonic neurons whose steady-state response are modeled by Luce & Green.

1. *For the data in Fig. 3, the best fitting k's for ICIs of 10, 5, 2 and 1 msec respectively were .82, .67, .34 and .24. For the data in Fig. 4, they were .76, .85, .61 and .34.*

5. RATE AND THE DETECTION OF INTERAURAL INTENSITY

In succeeding experiments, we have tried to determine whether the compression implied above is in the binaural centers or in the monaural channels which feed them. In one of those tests, (Hafter *et al*, 1979b) listeners were asked to detect an IDI rather than an IDT. One might expect that accurate evaluations of intensity would require long time constants; thus we reasoned that if tonic information were available, the binaural system would use it.

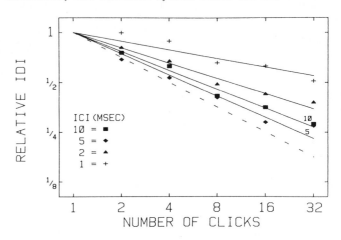

Fig. 4. Lateralization thresholds for an interaural difference in power (R - L) in trains of 4000-Hz bandpass clicks. Before averaging, data from the four subjects were scaled so that the thresholds for n = 1 would be 1.0.

All other aspects of the experiment were the same. The measure used to describe the IDI was the difference of sound-power between the right channel and the left. As such, the addition of extra information with n was akin to increasing duration in the computation of a signal-to-noise ratio, and statistical summation should again predict a slope of -0.5. The results are shown in Fig. 4. As before, the data were scaled so that subjects would have the same value for n = 1 before logarithms were computed. What we see is that the effects of rate on the ΔIs were virtually the same as those on the Δts.[1] Thus it would seem that the kinds of onset enhancement and rate limitation that affect the detection of interaural time also affect interaural intensity.

One possible explanation for this result is that the rate limitation of binaural stimuli takes place in the monaural nervous system which must handle the information prior to binaural interaction. It has often been suggested that differences of interaural intensity in clicks are coded as interaural delay by intensity-related shifts in neural latency (Deatherage & Hirsh, 1959), and the similarity between Figs. 3 and 4 once more brings that question into focus. In order to look more closely into the notion, we (Hafter *et al*, 1979c) have obtained d's from trains of clicks which contain both IDTs and IDIs. Thus far, we have presented the cues only in conjunction with both time and intensity favoring the same ear. Some results of that experiment are shown in Fig. 5. The paradigm was essentially the same as that used above; the data shown here are for n = 8 and the ICI = 10 msec. These data are from one subject, but the relative effects of IDT and IDI held across subjects and for an n of 1 and an ICI of 2 as well. The abscissa plots IDT and the parameter is IDI. The slopes of the parallel lines were computed from IDI = 0 and then fitted separately to the points for each ICI. What the parallel lines show is that the d' for both cues equaled the sum of the d's for the two taken individually. Thus the effects of time and intensity were completely additive, with no additional internal noise. Again, one interpretation of this fact is that both cues share a common code, right from the beginning. It is not proven, but it is an intriguing idea.

Fig. 5. Detecta-
bility of simul-
taneous values of
interaural delay
and interaural in-
tensity presented
in trains of eight
4000-Hz bandpass
clicks with an
ICI of 10 msec.
The data are from
one subject. Lines
are fit individ-
ually to the data
for IDIs of .2, .3
and .5 dB, using
slopes derived
from IDI = 0 dB.

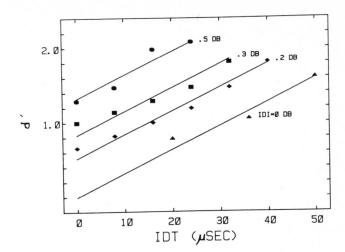

6. SUMMARY

At this stage in the progress of our work, we feel confident about some factors and have speculations about others. First, it is clear that for the lateralization of trains of high-frequency transients, the transition from a relatively slow rate of presentation to a fast one is well described by a compressive power function which reduces the effectiveness of the train as it progresses. Moreover, the fact that the magnitude of the compression is tied directly to rate suggests a form of saturation in which later clicks in the train have successively smaller probabilities of eliciting neural activity.

Interestingly, we have also seen that the compressive effects of rate act whether the interaural cue is time or intensity and that these two types of information add completely without additional noise. This points to the possibility that the effects of rate are in the more peripheral (monaural) nervous system and that the codes for IDT and IDI may even be the same.

Finally, the fact that higher rates had similar effects on interaural time and intensity suggests that an inability of neurons to follow later clicks in the train may have limited performance and not just the reduction in the depth of modulation that comes from moving spectral components of the train outside of the critical band.

Acknowledgements

We are grateful to our colleagues Beth Wenzel and Kitty Knecht for their valuable contributions to this research. Also, thanks to Brian Shelton for his comments on the manuscript and to the NIH for support.

REFERENCES

Bilsen, F.A. & Goldstein, J.L.(1974) Pitch of dichotically delayed noise and its possible spectral basis. *J. Acoust. Soc. Am.* <u>55</u>, 292-296.

Colburn, H.S. & Esquissaud, P.(1976) An auditory nerve model for interaural time discrimination of high-frequency complex stimuli. *J. Acoust. Soc. Am.* <u>59</u>, S23.

Deatherage, B.H. & Hirsh, I.J.(1959) Auditory localization of clicks. *J. Acoust. Soc. Am.* <u>31</u>, 486-492.

Hafter, E.R.(1977) Lateralization model and the role of time-intensity tradings in binaural masking: Can the data be explained by a time-only hypothesis? *J. Acoust. Soc. Am.* <u>62</u>, 633-635.

Hafter, E.R. & DeMaio, J.(1975) Difference thresholds for interaural delay. *J. Acoust. Soc. Am.* <u>57</u>, 181–187.

Hafter, E.R. & Dye, R.H.,Jr.(1978) Lateralization of clicks presented at a rapid rate. *J. Acoust. Soc. Am.* 64, S35(A).

Hafter, E.R. & Dye, R.H.,Jr.(1980) Lateralization of trains of clicks as a function of rate of presentation: Interaural time. *J. Acoust. Soc. Am.* (submitted for publication).

Hafter, E.R., Dye, R.H.,Jr. & Gilkey, R.H.(1979a) Lateralization of tonal signals which have neither onsets or offsets. *J. Acoust. Soc. Am.* <u>65</u>,471–477.

Hafter, E.R., Dye, R.H.,Jr. & Wenzel, E.(1979b) Lateralization of clicks presented at a rapid rate based on interaural differences of intensity. *J. Acoust. Soc. Am.* S121(A).

Hafter, E.R., Dye, R.H.,Jr., Wenzel, E. & Knecht, K.(1979c) Additivity of the binaural auditory cues: Interaural differences of time and interaural differences of intensity. *Bull. Psychonom. Soc.* 242(A).

Harris, G.G.(1960) Binaural interactions of impulsive and pure tones. *J. Acoust. Soc. Am.* <u>32</u>, 685–692.

Henning, G.B.(1974) Detectability of interaural delay in high-frequency complex waveforms. *J. Acoust. Soc. Am.* <u>55</u>, 84–90.

Houtgast, T. & Plomp, R.(1968) Lateralization threshold of a signal in noise. *J. Acoust. Soc. Am.* <u>44</u>, 807–812.

Kiang, N.Y-S.(1965) *Discharge Patterns of Single Fibers in the Cat's Auditory Nerve*. Cambridge, MA: MIT Press.

Kuhn, G.F.(1977) Model for the interaural time differences in the azimuthal plane. *J. Acoust. Soc. Am.* <u>62</u>, 157–167.

Leakey, D.M., Sayers, B.McA. & Cherry, C.(1958) Binaural fusion of low- and high-frequency sounds. *J. Acoust. Soc. Am.* <u>30</u>, 222(L).

Luce, R.D. & Green, D.M.(1974) Neural coding and psychophysical discrimination data. *J. Acoust. Soc. Am.* <u>56</u>, 1554–1564.

McFadden, D. & Pasanen, E.G.(1976) Lateralization at high frequencies based on interaural time differences. *J. Acoust. Soc. Am.* <u>59</u>, 634–639.

Nuetzel, J.M. & Hafter, E.R.(1976) Lateralization of complex waveforms: Effects of fine structure, amplitude and duration. *J. Acoust. Soc. Am.* <u>60</u>, 1339–1346.

Nuetzel, J.M. & Hafter, E.R.(1979) Lateralization of complex waveforms: Spectral effects. *J. Acoust. Soc. Am.* (submitted for publication).

Ricard, G.L. & Hafter, E.R. (1973) Detection of interaural time differences in short-duration, low-frequency tones. *J. Acoust. Soc. Am.* <u>53</u>, 334(A).

Tobias, J.V. & Schubert, E.D.(1959) Effective onset duration of auditory stimuli. *J. Acoust. Soc. Am.* <u>31</u>, 1595–1605.

Tobias, J.V. & Zerlin, S.(1959) Lateralization threshold as a function of stimulus duration. *J. Acoust. Soc. Am.* <u>31</u>, 1591–1594.

Wallach, H., Newman, E.B. & Rosenzweig, M.R.(1949) The precedence effect in sound localization. *Amer. J. Psychol.* <u>62</u>, 315–336.

Yost, W.A.(1976) Lateralization of repeated filtered transients. *J. Acoust. Soc. Am.* <u>60</u>, 178–181.

BINAURAL INTERACTION IN THE CAT INFERIOR COLLICULUS:
PHYSIOLOGY AND ANATOMY

S. Kuwada, T.C.T. Yin, L.B. Haberly, and R.E. Wickesberg

*Department of Neurophysiology, University of Wisconsin Medical School
Madison, Wisconsin, 53706.*

1. INTRODUCTION

Many inferior colliculus (IC) neurons are sensitive to the time of arrival of sound at the ears (Altman, 1968; Moushegian *et al.* 1964; Rose *et al.* 1966). Consequently, these neurons have been hypothesized to play a role in sound localization. For low frequency sinusoids, the response of many IC neurons is a cyclic function of the interaural delay (see Fig. 1C). This repetitive cycling, even at interaural delays beyond those that can occur naturally, indicates that these cells are sensitive to differences in the interaural phase. Variations in interaural phase can also be produced by a 'binaural beat stimulus', in which the frequency of the stimulus to one ear differs slightly from that delivered to the other ear (see Fig. 1A). Such a stimulus evokes the sensation of binaural beats in humans. It also provides the opportunity to study the sensitivity of neurons to the rate and direction of interaural phase change. A primary goal of the present paper is to compare the response of IC neurons to interaural delay and binaural beat stimuli as well as to describe their response to varying the rates and direction of interaural phase change. Some of these results have been presented (Kuwada *et al.* 1979).

A second aspect of this paper concerns the relationship between the physiological and anatomical properties of IC neurons. Several studies have reported on the diversity of neural responses found in the IC (e.g. Rose *et al.* 1963). Furthermore, studies employing the Golgi technique have described several morphological cell types in this structure (e.g. Rockel and Jones, 1973). Whether the cells sensitive to changes in interaural phase are related to a distinct morphological class of neurons is an intriguing question. In order to directly address this issue, we have employed the technique of intracellular recording followed by Horse Radish Peroxidase(HRP) marking of the impaled neuron.

2. METHODS

Cats with clean external ears were barbiturate anesthetized and both external meati were dissected free, permitting the insertion of a metal ear probe 1-3 mm from each tympanic membrane. A Telex-140 earphone was connected via a plastic tube to each ear probe. For each experiment, the sound delivery system was calibrated for intensity and phase from 60 - 30,000 Hz. Rise-fall time of all stimuli was 3.9 ms.

The dorsal surface of the right IC was exposed by aspirating the overlying visual cortex and removing the bony tentorium. A plastic chamber was cemented to the skull, filled with mineral oil and sealed with a glass plate to which a hydraulic micro-drive was attached. Indium-filled micro-pipette electrodes with gold-platinum tips were used for extracellular recording. Intracellular recordings employed bevelled glass micropipettes filled with a buffered 4% HRP solution(pH 8.6, 0.5M KCl; Z = 30 - 100 megohms).   HRP was ejected by applying a   pulsed positive current (100 ms on, 100 ms off, 1-3 min. duration, 10-20 na).

The   locations   of   all   extracellular   electrode   penetrations   were histologically verified. In the intracellular   experiments, cats were perfused intracardially with physiological   saline followed by a   1% paraformaldehyde – 1.25% glutaraldehyde buffered fixative. Tissue   was   sagittally   sectioned (80μm) and a $CoCl_2$ – DAB procedure was used   to react and intensify the HRP.

3. RESULTS AND DISCUSSION

a) *Extracellular recording*

Figure 1A is a schematic of a binaural beat stimulus. For illustrative purposes, the amplitudes of the two sine waves are different and the primary frequencies are much lower than those actually employed. In this example the stimulus to the contralateral ear (re: recording site) is higher in frequency by f_b. At ϕ = 0.0, the two sinusoids are exactly in phase but the contra-lateral signal immediately begins to lead in phase. The signals are 180 degrees out of phase at ϕ =   0.5 but shortly thereafter the ipsilateral signal leads in phase and progressively diminishes its lead until the two signals are again in phase at ϕ = 1.0 or 0.0. This cycle is repeated for each cycle of f_b. The direction of interaural phase change can be reversed by interchanging the frequencies to the two ears.

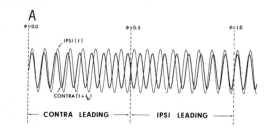

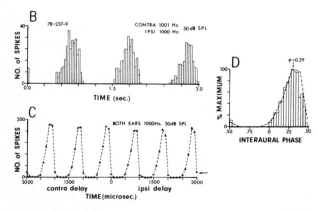

The response of an IC neuron to a binaural beat stimulus is illustrated by the   peristimulus   time histogram (PSTH) in Figure 1B.   The stimuli to the ipsi and contralateral ear were 1000 and   1001 Hz respectively, at 50 dB SPL (re: 0.0002 dyne/cm^2), 5 presentations, each 3 sec in duration. The neuron discharges   with   three distinct bursts during the duration of the stimulus. This response is consis-tent with a neuron that is sensitive to a particular range of interaural phase difference. This inter-aural phase sensitivity is shown   by   the   period histograms derived   from the PSTH by folding it on the period of the beat frequency (Fig. 1D). The interaural phase corre-sponding to the peak of maximal discharge was de-rived by   computing the phase of the first Fourier coefficient and was found to be 0.29 cycle. Figure 1C depicts the   response of the same neuron to ma-nipulations of interaural

Fig. 1. (A) Schematic of the binaural beat stimu-lus. (B) Peristimulus time histogram of the re-sponse of an IC cell to a binaural beat stimulus. (C) Interaural time delay curve for the same cell. (D) Period histogram derived from (B), and the averaged delay curve (dotted line) from (C), nor-malized so that the shapes of the curves can be compared. Copyright (1979) by the AAAS.

delay. The stimulus to both ears was a 1 sec, 1000 Hz, 50 dB SPL tone. The stimulus to first one and then the other ear was delayed in 100 μs steps to a maximum of 3000 μs. There is a cyclic discharge at the period of the stimulating frequency that is modulated above and below the level of the response to monaural (contra) stimulation (see arrow). This is evident when the delay curve is folded on the period of 1000 Hz and averaged as shown by the dotted curve in Figure 1D. The peak phase angle of this averaged delay curve (0.30) and its shape closely approximate the period histogram of the binaural beat response. In general, a cell's interaural phase sensitivity can be predicted using either type of stimulus.

The rate of interaural phase change can be increased by increasing f_b. Figure 2A is a latency dot display depicting the neural discharge pattern for different values of f_b. A 300 Hz sinusoid is delivered to the ipsilateral ear while the contralateral frequency is varied from 301 - 361 Hz. Each dot represents the time of occurrence of a spike and each row of dots depicts a single presentation of the stimulus. For illustrative purposes, we show only the response to the last 2 sec of the 3 sec stimulus. At f_b = 1 Hz, i.e. contra = 301 Hz, the cell responds with 2 bursts during the 2 sec sampling period; at f_b = 11 Hz, 22 bursts; etc. At higher f_b's, the discharge follows a precise temporal pattern, illustrating this neuron's interaural phase sensitivity. Even when a discharge does not occur, the subsequent discharge occurs at the expected temporal position. The period histograms (Fig. 2B) illustrate that the neural discharge is phase-locked, even for the highest f_b. Also evident is a systematic shift in the interaural phase of maximal discharge as a function of f_b. For most cells this shift was a linear function of f_b, suggesting that it resulted from a time delay. Due to this phase shift, the optimal interaural phase sensitivity of a neuron is best estimated from the responses to the lowest beat frequency. In our sample there are marked variations in the ability of neurons to follow high rates of interaural phase change. Some neurons cannot follow rates beyond 6 Hz whereas others show clear locking to f_b's as high as 80 Hz. In terms of primary frequencies, we have observed interaural phase sensitivity at frequencies as high as 2500 Hz.

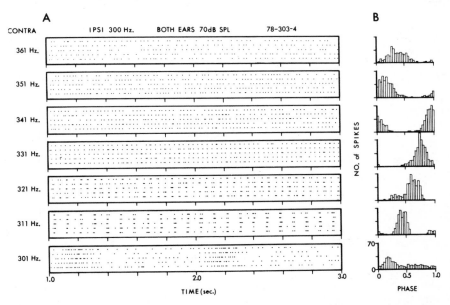

Fig. 2. (A) Latency dot rasters of an IC neuron at different beat frequencies. (B) Period histograms of the responses shown in (A).

Figure 3 shows the period histograms of three neurons for different rates and direction of interaural phase change. The left and right columns in each figure represent the two directions of phase change, and the histograms are arranged from top to bottom in order of decreasing rate. Since the direction of interaural phase is reversed in the left-hand columns relative to the right-hand ones, the abscissas have also been reversed. The results shown in Figure 3A illustrate the most common type of response seen in our sample. The number of spikes per unit time is similar for all histograms suggesting that the level of discharge is independent of rate or direction of interaural phase change. Figure 3B depicts a response pattern seen less commonly. When the signal to the ipsilateral ear is higher in frequency (right column), the cell responds to f_b's up to 10 Hz. However, when the direction of interaural phase change is reversed (left column), there is a marked reduction in the response at all f_b's. The behavior of this neuron suggests a sensitivity to the direction of interaural phase change. Figure 3C illustrates the response of a neuron that is sensitive to the rate of phase change. As f_b increases from 1 - 7 Hz there is approximately a six-fold increase in the discharge level while the responses to the two directions of interaural phase change are almost equal. All of the cells in Figure 3 respond to the static interaural phase as evidenced by their phase-locked response, but they differ in their sensitivity to dynamic phase changes.

Whether the different response patterns to binaural beat stimuli have a functional significance is not known. However, if we assume that this stimulus simulates a free-field sound source, the parameters of direction and

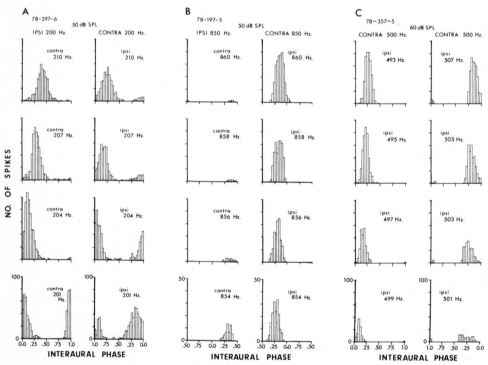

Fig. 3. Period histograms of three cells illustrating their responses as the direction of interaural phase change is reversed (left and right columns) and the rate of change is increased (bottom to top row). (A) Cell with little sensitivity to direction or rate. (B) Cell sensitive to the direction of phase change. (C) Cell sensitive to the rate of phase change. Copyright (1979) by the American Association for the Advancement of Science.

rate of interaural phase change translate to direction and speed of a sound source moving along the azimuth. Figure 4 is a schematic diagram of the assumed movement simulated by the beat stimulus illustrated in Figure 1A. Under dichotic conditions the sound is perceived to be within the head but for illustrative purposes we have projected the sound into space. The sound source is perceived to be at the midline when the two sinusoids are in phase (ϕ = 0.0), moves toward the contralateral ear as it begins to lead in phase (0.0 < ϕ < 0.5), lateralizes completely when they are 180 degrees out of phase, jumps to the ipsilateral ear as that ear begins to lead (0.5 < ϕ < 1.0), and finally returns to the midline as the two signals come back in phase. This reflects one cycle of f_b and simulates a sound moving from right to left, i.e., ipsi to contralateral ear. Interchanging the frequencies to each ear results in a contra to ipsilateral movement. Increasing the speed of the moving sound source is simulated by employing higher f_b's. The transition from contra to ipsi leading at ϕ = 0.5 will be instantaneous only at a particular frequency, which is a function of the interaural distance (Yost and Neilsen, 1977). Assuming that the binaural beat stimulus simulates the movement of sound illustrated in Figure 4, the

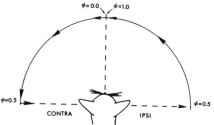

neuron described in Figure 3A will discharge when a sound source is located in a restricted zone along the azimuth such that it creates a particular range of interaural phase differences. The discharge rate is not significantly affected by the speed or direction of the sound source. The cell in Figure 3B exhibits directional sensitivity since it discharges when the sound source is located in a zone along the azimuth but its response is much greater when the sound moves from left to right than from right to left. The neuron illustrated in Figure 3C suggests a sensitivity to the speed of a moving sound source since it responds more vigorously at high rates of change of phase.

Fig. 4. Schematic of the assumed movement of the sound source during the binaural beat stimulus. Copyright (1979) by the AAAS.

In sum, we have shown that the interaural phase sensitivity of IC neurons can be studied using binaural beat stimuli and that this method yields results similar to those found using the interaural delay method. Furthermore, the sensitivity of these neurons to changes in the rate and direction of interaural phase can be studied with the beat stimuli. Although many neurons in our sample were insensitive to changes in these parameters, the responses of some neurons were clearly altered by changes in direction and/or rate. If we view the beat stimulus as simulating a moving sound source, the results suggest that some IC neurons are sensitive to the direction and/or the speed of the sound. Using click stimuli, previous studies have described directionally sensitive cells in the cat IC (Altman, 1968). The periodic response of these neurons at the rate of the beat frequency provides a possible neural correlate of the sensation of binaural beats reported by humans in a dichotic listening situation. At very low beat frequencies (f_b < 2 Hz), human listeners report the sensation of a tone rotating from ear to ear at the rate of f_b (Perrot and Musicant, 1977) which is in accord with our interpretation that the binaural beat stimulus can simulate a moving sound source.

b) *Intracellular recording*

Figure 5A is a drawing of the axonal arborization and dendritic tree of an HRP stained neuron which was reconstructed through serial sagittal sections with the aid of a drawing tube. This neuron was located in the central nucleus of the IC. The soma is approximately 20 µm in diameter. The dendrites have many spines and their general orientation (Fig. 5B) appears to follow the anatomical laminae seen in Golgi material (Rockel and Jones, 1973). Based on these morphological criteria, this cell conforms to Rockel and Jones' fusiform type of principal cell. The main axon gives off many collaterals, each of which has many terminal-like swellings. The axon could be traced over 0.9 mm in the medial-lateral dimension and appeared to be directed towards the brachium of the IC. Figure 5C shows the intracellular response of this cell to a binaural beat stimulus (f_b = 3 Hz) to both directions of interaural phase change. During stimulation there is a sustained 15 mV depolarization in the membrane potential with a superimposed modulation at the frequency of the binaural beat stimulus. Bursts of action potentials tend to be associated with the depolarizing fluctuations, thereby causing the spikes to be phase-locked to the beat frequency. This response pattern demonstrates the cell's sensitivity to changes in interaural phase. There is no clear preference for a particular direction of phase change. Between stimulus presentations the resting membrane potential was approximately –70 mV with spontaneous EPSPs and occasional associated spikes (Fig. 5C).

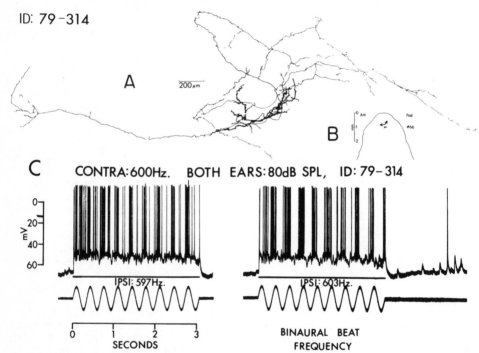

Fig. 5. (A) Camera lucida drawing of a phase sensitive IC neuron. (B) Diagram of a parasagittal section through the IC showing location of the labeled cell. Curved arrow indicates orientation of laminae described by Rockel and Jones (1973). (C) Intracellular record of the cell to a binaural beat stimulus (f_b = 3 Hz) for both directions of phase change.

Figure 6 shows the soma-dendritic (Fig. 6A) and axonal arborizations (Fig. 6B) of another HRP stained neuron in the IC. A salient feature of this cell is its extensive axonal arborization. The main axon first follows a very tortuous course while giving off many collaterals, then curves antero-laterally into the brachium of the IC. The total axonal arborization was reconstructed from thirty 80 µm thick sections, thus covering a total expanse of 2.4 mm mediolaterally. We have identified over 2000 terminal-like swellings on the collaterals of this axon. The soma was considerably larger than that

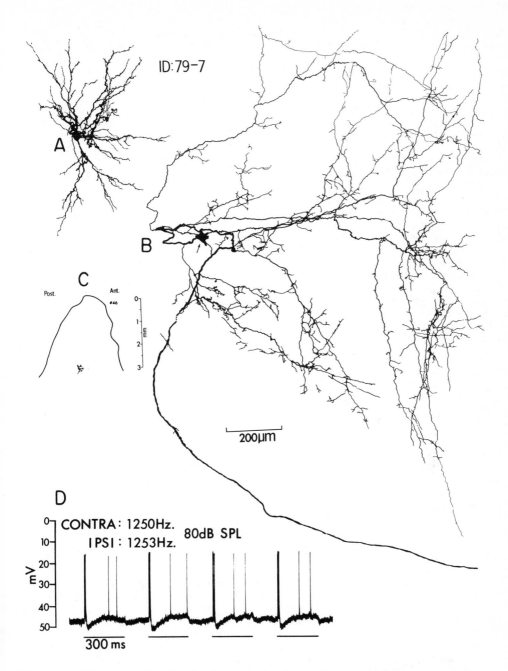

ID:79-7

A

B

C

Post.   Ant.

200μm

D

CONTRA: 1250Hz.
IPSI: 1253Hz.   80dB SPL

mV

300 ms

Fig. 6. (A) Camera lucida drawing of the dendritic tree of an onset, non-phase sensitive cell. (B) Drawing of the axonal arborization of this cell. Arrow points to the location of the soma. 200 μm scale applies to both A and B. (C) Inset diagram of parasagittal section showing location of the cell deep within the central nucleus. (D) Intracellular records of this cell showing the onset burst followed by hyperpolarization.

of the neuron in Figure 5. The dendrites are varicose with very few spines and it appears to conform to Rockel and Jones' "large multipolar" classification. An example of an intracellular record from this cell is shown in Figure 6D. In contrast to the cell illustrated in Figure 5, this cell was not sensitive to interaural phase differences. Shortly after stimulus onset, there is a burst of spikes, followed by a period of hyperpolarization, which gives way to a low amplitude sustained depolarization with 1 or 2 spikes. This response pattern resembles the commonly seen "pauser" pattern seen at many levels of the auditory system.

The ability to follow processes through many brain sections (a difficult or impossible task in Golgi-impregnated material) has revealed that most or all neurons give rise to local axon collateral systems, some of which are extremely extensive (e.g., Fig. 6), even when the primary axon is directed to higher centers. The nature of the local interactions mediated by these collaterals is presently unknown, but would appear to play an important role in integrative processing within the colliculus. As yet we have not been able to follow the main axon to its termination. Another potentially significant finding is the presence of marked varicosities on dendrites of many neurons in the IC. The fact that these varicosities are also seen in Golgi material indicates that they are probably not artifactual. However, their physiological role is not known.

The two neurons we have presented represent extremes in the spectrum of physiological and morphological types found in our sample. While a correlation between response and cell type seems to be emerging, our sample is too small at present to draw any reliable conclusions.

Acknowledgements

We thank T.J.F. Buunen for suggesting the binaural beat stimulus to simulate a moving sound source and S.T. Kitai, R.J. Preston, and G.A. Bishop for their helpful tutoring in the intracellular HRP technique. This work was supported by NIH grants NS12732 and EY02606.

REFERENCES

Altman, J.A. (1968). Are there neurons detecting the direction of sound source motion? *Experimental Neurology* 22, 13-25.

Kuwada, S., Yin, T.C.T., and Wickesberg, R.E. (1979). Responses of cat inferior colliculus neurons to binaural beat stimuli: Possible mechanisms for sound localization. *Science* 206, 585-588.

Moushegian, G.A., Rupert, A.L., and Whitcomb, M.A. (1964) Brainstem neuronal response patterns to monaural and binaural tones. *Journal of Neurophysiology* 27, 1174-1191.

Perrot, D.R. and Musicant, A.D. (1977). Rotating tones and binaural beats. *Journal of the Acoustical Society of America* 61, 1288-1292.

Rockel, A.J., and Jones, E.G. (1973). The neuronal organization of the inferior colliculus of the adult cat. I. The central nucleus. *Journal of Comparative Neurology* 147, 11-60.

Rose, J.E., Greenwood, D.D., Goldberg, J.M., and Hind, J.E. (1963). Some discharge characteristics of single neurons in the inferior colliculus of the cat I. Tonotopic organization, relation of spike counts to tone intensity, and firing pattern of single elements. *Journal of Neurophysiology* 26, 294-320.

Rose, J.E., Gross, N.B., Geisler, C.D., and Hind, J.E. (1966). Some neural mechanisms in the inferior colliculus of the cat which may be relevant to the localization of a sound source. *Journal of Neurophysiology* 29, 288-314.

Yost, W.A. and Neilsen, D.W. (1977). *Fundamentals of Hearing*. Holt, Rinehart, and Winston. pp. 155-163.

COMMENT ON : "Binaural interaction in the cat inferior colliculus: Physiology and Anatomy" (S. Kuwada, T.C.T. Yin, L.B. Haberly and R.E. Wickesberg).

D. McFadden
Department of Psychology, University of Texas, Austin, Texas 78712, U.S.A.

May I say on the behalf of the psychophysicists concerned with the binaural system that we are delighted to see a neurophysiologist at work on binaural processing again. Perhaps the neglect we have felt in recent years is at an end. Having said that, I would like to offer some constructive comments in an attempt to enhance achievement of our common goal of understanding binaural processing.

You appear to share the belief of many of us that there exist in the auditory nervous system cells "tuned" to respond maximally to sound sources located at particular points in space, and also possibly to different rates and directions of movement of those sources. In order to confirm these expectations, it seems to me imperative that one establish that cells such as those in your Figs. 1 and 3 are in fact maximally sensitive to sources located at one and only one point in space, or rate or direction of movement, and this requires in part demonstrating appropriate responses to a wide range of stimuli within the cell's response area. By "appropriate" I mean that the cell be similarly activated by the same value of interaural time difference (or rate of direction of movement) no matter how it is produced in the stimulus (let us ignore for the moment the additional complexity introduced when there is both an interaural time difference and an interaural intensity difference present). So, for example, one needs to know how each of the cells in Figs. 1 and 3 responds to other tonal and complex stimuli over a range of interaural time delays. Only with information of this sort can we reach a confident conclusion about the organization of the binaural system. I understand that you have such data; can you give us a brief summary of it?

Related to this point is a second one. While I understand that the format of your data presentation in Fig. 3 is a natural one given the stimulus you used, I would suggest that more insight into the cell's behaviour is gained by thinking in terms of interaural time, not phase. Across stimulus frequency, it is the time difference we expect to control the cell's behaviour, whereas the phase relation required to produce it changes. Phase only muddies the waters.

Also in regard to format, I must say again that I regard data presentations like that in your Fig. 1C to be potentially misleading, particularly for the outsider to the binaural literature. The figure implies that the cell has equal sensitivity to sound sources located at number of points in auditory space. But careful attention to the values along the abscissa reveals this not to be true. The cat's head is about 200-250 µsec wide. Thus, if one wants to achieve some insight into this cell's behaviour with real-world stimuli, he should ignore all of the data beyond about ± 250 µsec on either side of zero, for such extreme values of interaural time difference cannot arise naturally. All that the sections of the figure beyond ± 250 µsec reveal is that a tonal stimulus repeats when it is delayed by integral multiples of its period.

A minor philosophical point is that we should expect an animal to have at best only a *relative* map of auditory space based on interaural time differences, not an absolute one. The normal range of variation in the speed of sound prevents a particular point in space from invariably corresponding to a particular value of time difference.

Finally, a personal hope of mine is that you will consider working with some cells with high characteristic frequency. Psychophysical research indicates that you will find cells sensitive to interaural time differences in the envelopes of complex, high-frequency waveforms, much like the cells you find at low frequencies sensitive to time differences in the fine structure.

COMMENT

RFERENCES

McFadden, D. (1973). A note on auditory neurons having periodic response
    functions to time-delayed, binaural stimuli. *Physiological Psychology* 1,
    265-266.
McFadden, D. (1973). Precedence effects and auditory cells with long character-
    istic delays. *Journal of the Acoustical Society of America* 54, 528-530.
McFadden, D. and Pasanen, E.G. (1975). Binaural beats at high frequencies.
    Science 190, 394-396.

REPLY TO COMMENT OF D. MCFADDEN.

S. Kuwada
Dept. of Neurophysiology, University of Wisconsin Medical School, Madison, USA.

Many neurons in the cat inferior colliculus respond in a cyclic pattern
as a function of interaural delay. However, within this population there are
marked variations in this cycling pattern. Although we find as others have
found, neurons that exhibit "characteristic delay", we also find neurons that
do not. At present we have no basis to exclude the latter type from the sound
localization process. The role of cyclically responding inferior colliculus
neurons in localization is yet to be elucidated. Thus McFadden's criteria for
the behaviour of a cell may or may not apply.

Concerning the comments re: data presentation, I reply that the data are
presented in the manner in which they were collected. To present only the range
calculated from estimations of head size could lead the reader to believe that
at longer "unphysiologic" delays no cycling exists. Furthermore, we find neurons
that cycle only within a particular range of interaural delays, thus precluding
a standard format presentation as McFadden suggests.

Concerning the suggestions in the last paragraph, we are currently engaged
in such research. Our preliminary results indicate that cells with high best
frequency are sensitive to interaural delays in the signals envelope in a
manner similar to their low frequency counterparts.

COMMENT ON: "Binaural interaction in the cat inferior colliculus: Physiology
and Anatomy" (S. Kuwada, T.C.T. Yin, L.B. Haberly and R.E. Wickesberg).

E.F. Evans
Dept. of Communication & Neuroscience, University of Keele, U.K.

Have you any information on the question whether the delays exhibited by
the so-called "characteristic delay" cells are commonly encountered in nature,
and therefore whether these cells could serve the purpose often imputed to
them ?

REPLY TO COMMENT OF E.F. EVANS.

S. Kuwada
Dept. of Neurophysiology, University of Wisconsin Medical School, Madison, USA.

We do find some neurons that peak or minimize outside the estimated
physiological range. This may not preclude their role in localization since
other aspects other than a maximum or minimum may be the significant feature.

COMMENT ON: "Binaural interaction in the cat inferior colliculus: Physiology and Anatomy" (S. Kuwada, T.C.T. Yin, L.B. Haberly and R.E. Wickesberg).

R.M. Stern
Department of Electrical Engineering and Biomedical Engineering Program
Carnegie-Mellon University, Pittsburgh, Pennsylvania 15213 U.S.A.

I am not disturbed when physiologists report binaural units that appear to respond to interaural time delays that are larger than what could be presented to the animal by a point source in a free field. First, I would expect to find a gradual rather than abrupt decrease in the relative number of interaural time sensitive units as one examines units with characteristic delays that are larger than the limit implied by the "headwidth constraint". Second, many recent theories of binaural perception are based on the amount of information available in displays related to interaural correlation, which could be obtained from populations of units similar to some of those that Dr. Kuwada has described. It appears that at least some units with large characteristic delays are needed to account for observed psychoacoustical performance in binaural detection experiments using maskers that are presented with long interaural time delays. In other words, these "physiologically unreasonable" units may be used in performing psychoacoustical tasks involving "physically impossible" stimuli.

NOTE ON THE MODELING OF
BINAURAL INTERACTION IN IMPAIRED AUDITORY SYSTEMS

H. Steven Colburn and Rudolf Hausler[*]

*Research Laboratory of Electronics, Massachusetts
Institute of Technology, Cambridge, Mass. 02139
and
Eaton-Peabody Laboratory of Auditory Physiology,
Massachusetts Eye and Ear Infirmary, Boston, Mass.*

1. INTRODUCTION

Impaired auditory systems are receiving increased attention from physiologists and psychophysicists. In spite of this attention, the relation between
physiological pathologies and behavioral abnormalities is neither describable
nor understood at present. Further, since most clinical cases of impairments
are not understood in terms of underlying physiological pathologies, it is not
possible to relate the abnormal psychoacoustic performance of impaired listeners directly to physiological mechanisms. One theoretical approach to the
understanding of this relation is to consider the behavior expected from idealized pathologies. This requires a model for the mechanisms underlying the
psychoacoustic phenomena as well as a specification of the idealized pathologies. In this paper, we discuss expected effects on binaural hearing abilities from several idealized pathologies. Binaural phenomena have two advantages: they have been modeled extensively for normal listeners, often in
terms of neural mechanisms, and they probe different aspects of the coding relatively directly. The binaural hearing abilities we consider are: the just-
noticeable differences (JNDs) in interaural time delay, interaural correlation,
and interaural intensity difference; the binaural masking-level differences
(MLDs) for tones masked by noise; and free-field localization abilities (particularly angle discrimination in the horizontal and vertical planes). Effects
on these abilities are predicted from a simplified model of binaural interaction that was developed primarily on the basis of the binaural abilities of
normal-hearing subjects. The following types of pathologies are considered:
unilateral dead-ear (only one functioning ear), conductive hearing losses,
losses of auditory-nerve fibers, changes in tuning curves, scrambled auditory-
nerve firing patterns, and lesions in auditory nuclei central to the auditory
nerve. We believe this choice is a useful starting point, even though realistic modeling of impairments would require combinations and modifications of
these idealizations as well as more complex possibilities, such as structural
changes in the central nuclei consequent to peripheral losses.

The model underlying our considerations is illustrated by the block diagram in Fig. 1. Several properties of the model should be kept in mind as
the pathologies are considered. First, the inputs to the cochlea include not
only the usual pathways through the external and middle ears but also bone-
conduction pathways. This elaboration is usually and appropriately neglected
in models of the normal auditory system but becomes important in some circumstances, including several situations with impaired auditory systems as described below. Similar comments apply to effects of acoustic crosstalk in
earphone experiments (included in the air-conduction pathway in the figure).
Second, the nerve fibers leaving the cochlea are processed through several

★ Present Address: Hôpital Cantonal, 1211 Geneve 4, Switzerland.

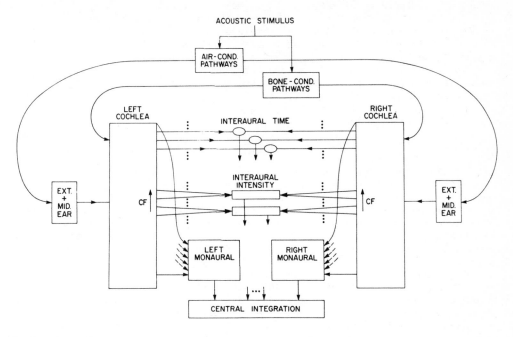

Fig.1. Block diagram of binaural interaction model.

distinct systems: an interaural time system, an interaural intensity system, and monaural systems that can process spectral (and overall level) information from each cochlea alone. Although the assumption of separate peripheral loci for interaural time and intensity processing was made on the basis of psycho-acoustic data (e.g., Hafter and Carrier, 1972), it is consistent with several behavioral-ablation, anatomical, and electrophysiological studies in animals (e.g., Masterton *et al.*, 1967; Goldberg and Brown, 1968, 1969) and with com-bined electrophysiological-behavioral studies in human subjects with multiple sclerosis (Hausler and Levine, 1980). The interaural time system comprises coincidence counters, each of which receives a single input fiber from each ear. The two fibers of a pair have a common characteristic frequency (CF) and a relative (interaural) internal time delay that is fixed for each pair and chosen from a distribution with a width of about ±1 msec. [An interaural time processor of this form is discussed and specified quantitatively in Colburn and Latimer (1978).] The interaural intensity system is also organized in terms of CF: each comparator receives inputs from a limited band of CFs and includes convergence in time as well as space so that, roughly speaking, an estimate of interaural intensity difference is made on the basis of differ-ences in the numbers of firings from each side. The monaural processing sys-tems represent the ability to use information available at a single ear with-out binaural comparisons. (We draw the monaural systems separately from the interaural systems to emphasize the importance of monaural abilities, even though the monaural information is redundant with the set of interaural time or interaural intensity outputs in many circumstances.) Third, the basic structures of these systems are independent of the CFs of the input fibers, which are conceptualized as auditory-nerve fibers for our purposes. Changes in performance with frequency are assumed to be primarily determined by changes in the auditory-nerve firing patterns and not by changes in the processing structures. Fourth, decisions about stimuli are made in more central regions in the brain, where (we postulate) the outputs of these systems (including outputs at all CFs for the time and intensity processors) are combined with memory stores and inputs from other sensory modalities. We do not assume that the central processing combines this information optimally nor that the information from each system is available independent of the other systems. Fifth, note that the information processing in this general model is consistent with many specific models that have been proposed for binaural phenomena. For discussion of this point, see Colburn and Durlach (1978), Stern and Colburn (1978), and Bilsen (1977).

2. IDEALIZED PATHOLOGIES

a) *Unilateral Dead Ear*

In the first type of pathology we consider, one ear is normal and the other is completely destroyed (the "unilateral dead ear" case) so that there is no activity related to the stimulus on fibers coming from the dead ear. The resulting lack of binaural interaction has several immediate and obvious consequences. Specifically, the interaural time and correlation JNDs would be extremely large relative to normal values and MLDs would be near zero in most cases. (The size of the JNDs and MLDs would be determined by the ability to make use of interactions between the two stimulus waveforms mediated by acoustic cross-talk or bone conduction).

For the interaural intensity JND, since interaural intensity differences require intensity changes at individual ears (and since monaural level differences, in contrast to monaural time delays, are sensitively detected by a single ear), predictions are dependent on the procedures used to define it. In some procedures (e.g., symmetrical intensity variations), substantial information is available at the normal ear, and in other procedures (e.g., random variation of overall level and spectrum), no information is available. [A similar sensitivity to paradigm is seen in normal subjects in some circumstances, e.g., when the reference intensities are imbalanced (Leshowitz *et al.*, 1974; and Hausler *et al.*, 1979)]. In the rest of this paper, we define the interaural intensity JND to be measured in such a way as to eliminate monaural information.

For localization experiments, performance predicted for a truly monaural listener depends critically upon a priori information about the stimulus. When the source spectrum is completely unconstrained, it is easy to show that monaural performance above chance is impossible. On the other hand, the spectral shape and overall level of the received signal would be a reliable source of information in most cases (e.g., a white noise stimulus at constant average or even a fixed tone stimulus). For example, Hausler *et al.*, (1979) report on a subject with one dead ear who obtained performance within the normal range for vertical and horizontal angle discrimination at all reference angles tested with a white noise stimulus (except for the angle directly to the side of the dead ear).

Localization by subjects with a unilateral dead ear provides a useful reference for the information provided monaurally. This condition is not easily simulated with a normal listener (nor with any listener with two functioning ears) since presentation of useful information to only one ear in this case requires unnatural stimuli so that the test is contaminated by misleading binaural information. Long-term real-world training makes the case of a unilateral-dead-ear subject basically different than a "dead ear" created by the stimulus. Finally, in considering performance with a unilateral dead ear, note the obvious fact that localization by subjects in whom the only functioning ear is impaired could be significantly worse than localization with one

normal ear, since the ability to use spectral information could be destroyed
by the impairment.

b) Conductive Losses

The second type of pathology considered is a conductive loss. In this
case, we might, to a first approximation, imagine a simple attenuation of the
signal at the impaired ear or ears. With this approximation, we would predict
performance by impaired listeners equal to performance of normal listeners at
equal sensation levels. For bilaterally symmetric conductive losses, this is
simply changing the overall level and, since most measures of binaural interaction are relatively independent of level (once levels are clearly above the
threshold region), we would expect small effects on binaural abilities. In
the unilateral or asymmetric conductive loss cases, even though many abilities
are affected by the resulting level imbalance, our simple approximation would
predict that interaurally balancing sensation levels in the two ears (at all
frequencies) returns performance to normal levels.

Although the simple attenuation model may be appropriate for small losses
(say less than 30 dB HL), when the loss is large (say greater than 40 dB HL),
this analysis is inadequate. As Hausler *et al.*, (1979) have suggested, stimulation of the cochlea by bone-conduction pathways is significant relative to
stimulation by the normal pathway through the external and middle ear with a
large conductive loss. When this is taken into account, predicted performance
with conductive losses is significantly different than that predicted by the
simple attenuation model. The basic limitation is that the stimulation of an
impaired cochlea is no longer specified by the pressure in the appropriate ear
canal; rather, the effective stimulus to an impaired cochlea is determined by
a combination of the stimuli presented to the two earphones in a localization
experiment and by some integrated result of the pressure distribution around
the skull in localization experiments. Thus, the bone-conducted stimulus is
only slightly different at the two cochleas so that interaural differences in
the cochlea outputs are much smaller than in the normal listener for the same
stimulus. Also, since a significant fraction of the stimulation bypasses the
external ear, the spectral pattern at the cochlea is less developed and less
dependent on source position. Further, in contrast to predictions of the
simple attenuation model, there should be no benefit from overall level
changes since both air and bone components would increase together with level.

Our general prediction is for clearly impaired interaural discrimination
and no spectral localization information at an impaired ear; however, specific
predictions for performance depend critically on the assumed phase and amplitude relations of various components and have not been completed. In unilateral conductive loss cases with one normal ear, complete monaural information
would be available at that ear (since the air-conducted components would
determine the stimulation of the cochlea on the normal side); however, the
extent to which performance could be achieved that was comparable to unilateral dead-ear cases would depend upon the ability of the central structures
to ignore the information from the interaural time and intensity systems and
from the monaural processing of the impaired side. These considerations are
consistent with the many reports in the literature of poor localization performance by subjects with conductive hearing losses (cf. Durlach *et al.*, (1980).

c) Nerve Fiber Losses

In the third type of pathology considered, a subset of nerve fibers are
eliminated or show no response to sound, while the remaining fibers function
normally. The essence of these cases is that some of the fibers are unable to
provide useful information about any stimulus, and whether this is a consequence of actual fiber losses or of hair cell damage is unimportant for the

present. We focus on the case of scattered losses; in the case of a complete loss with all fibers with CFs in a significant range eliminated, the consequences are substantial but reasonably obvious.

In the case of scattered fiber losses without complete loss in a significant frequency interval (no empty critical bands, for example), it is useful to distinguish among several effects. First, the number of independent information-carrying channels is reduced, and this alone would be expected to reduce overall performance. Rough calculations indicate that this is a relatively small effect; for example, a threshold shift of only 5 dB when 90% of the fibers are eliminated. (This follows from the usual assumption that the sensitivity index d' is proportional to the signal power and to the number of independent channels). The same reasoning applies to binaural performance so that a 90% loss of channels would increase the interaural time JND by a factor of only $\sqrt{10}$, which could be within normal intersubject scatter when subjects are not preselected. Second, since each fiber is restricted to a single, fixed, interaural delay in our model, a reduced number of fibers implies a reduced number of internal delays. As fiber losses become significant, some values of delay are eliminated in local frequency bands, even though there are fibers with CFs in this band. It is therefore possible that the dependence of performance on the reference interaural delay in this case would be clearly abnormal (e.g., selected reference delays for which very good or very poor performance results for a narrowband stimulus in a particular frequency band). This interference with performance would apply only to narrowband binaural phenomena that are clearly dependent on the interaural time system (like interaural time JNDs and MLDs) since the interaural intensity system includes convergence over many fibers in each comparator. Empirical observations of narrowband interaural time JNDs that depend dramatically on the reference delay are reported for subjects with unilateral losses (Meniere's syndrome) by Hawkins and Wightman (1978); they measured the subject's ability to distinguish a delayed stimulus from a diotic stimulus and found clear differences between the two directions of delay. Third, in cases of bilateral scattered losses of 90% of the fibers in each ear, in addition to the first two effects, the one-to-one fiber connections in the interaural time system results in an effective loss of 99% of the coincidence outputs (and therefore of the internal delays). In this case dramatic impairments in interaural time and correlation comparison would be expected, including abnormal or asymmetric dependence on reference delay for narrowband stimuli, even though interaural intensity and monaural processing, including many localization situations, could be only mildly effected (e.g., a 5 dB audiometric loss on each side as noted above).

More specific predictions of these effects are needed; however, they will be sensitive to the detailed distribution of the losses and to the detailed assumptions about the extent to which the information from pathological channels is processed or ignored. For example, if the firings on some fibers are not related to the stimulus waveform and if this set of fibers (i.e., the loss pattern) fluctuates in time, it would be difficult to ignore these fibers and greater interference would be expected.

d) Abnormal Tuning Curves

In the fourth type of idealized pathology, the normal complement of fibers is present, but the fibers have abnormal tuning curves. We further assume that the rate-intensity functions and the temporal patterns of firing are normal (except for the obvious changes in thresholds and peripheral filtering implied by the abnormal tuning curve). There are again several different cases to consider.

First, if the tuning curves are simply transported upward a constant distance on a decibel scale, the result is equivalent to a simple attenuation of the stimulus at the affected ear and the consequences for lateralization discrimination are predictable from normal listeners with appropriate stimulus levels. For example, when the loss is interaurally asymmetric, we expect reduced MLDs and impaired performance in interaural time and intensity discrimination (as observed in normal-hearing subjects with unbalanced levels). In addition to these resolution effects, we may also see changes in bias, even though the ear adapts to a longstanding loss (Florentine, 1976). Even this simple case illustrates that care must be exercised in localization-identification experiments to separate resolution from bias effects: mean absolute error or percent correct may not be an informative statistic, for example.

Second, suppose that the fibers in some CF bands have translated tuning curves and those in other bands are normal and that the pattern of translation versus CF is somewhat irregular. Note that this condition cannot be simulated or corrected by linear filtering of the stimulus since the effective stimulus from a given frequency component is not necessarily strongest for fibers with CFs at the frequency of the component. Further, the patterns of excitation in this case are unnatural and behave differently as a function of level for different stimulus frequencies. Predicted performance in many binaural or monaural experiments would depend upon the ability of the central auditory structures to interpret this unnatural recoding. For example, it would not be surprising in these circumstances to find significantly deteriorated spectral pattern resolution and therefore poor localization performance in some cases. However, if we consider interaural temporal information with stimuli at levels high enough to stimulate fibers on both sides, there is no loss of timing information and essentially normal performance in interaural time or correlation discrimination would be possible. Interaural intensity discrimination ability should be close to normal and the MLD would depend on the details of the differences from side to side.

Third, suppose that the tuning curves, in addition to CF-dependent vertical translations, have distorted shapes relative to normal, say w-shaped or broadly tuned. In this case, the ability to resolve spectral patterns would be even more severely limited. In contrast, the temporal patterns in this case would again be preserved on individual fibers for narrowband stimuli, and the interaural time and correlation JNDs would be relatively well preserved as would binaural detection thresholds with narrowband maskers. For wideband stimuli, interaural timing abilities depend upon the similarity of the shapes of the tuning curves on the two sides. If the shapes are dramatically different, it is possible that uncorrelated frequency bands of the wideband stimulus may be stimulating the right and left fibers of a pair, resulting in no useful information in the coincidence patterns for any delay, and the resulting interaural time and correlation JNDs would be very poor. Alternatively, if the shapes of the tuning curves are similar on the two sides, wideband stimuli would also lead to relatively good time and correlation JNDs, even though spectral processing would be poor in both cases. Hausler *et al.*, (1979) have reported a category of impaired subjects that is consistent with this pattern: moderate-to-severe bilateral sensorineural losses (greater than 75 dB HL at all frequencies tested for one of the subjects) with no vertical localization ability, but with interaural time and intensity JNDs very close to the normal range.

e) Distorted Firing Patterns

In the fifth type of idealized pathology, we assume abnormal patterns of firings on auditory-nerve fibers with normal tuning curves. If the timing patterns are distorted with no change in the numbers of firings (and if the distortion is unilateral or independent at the two sides), the interaural timing information is lost and the interaural time and correlation JNDs as well as the MLDs would be very poor, although some intensity and spectral

417

information would be preserved in the numbers of firings. If, in addition to the timing distortion, the average rates of firings were severly limited, all interaural processing would be significantly impaired even though thresholds could be close to normal on both sides. In the unilaterally impaired case, spectral information would be available at the good ear although its use in lateralization would depend on ignoring other distorted factors that normally contribute to good performance. In a series of psychoacoustic tests on a subject with a vestibular schwannoma, Florentine *et al.*, (1979) found no binaural abilities (in interaural time, intensity, and correlation discrimination) even though the subject's hearing loss was only 20 to 40 dB HL in the affected ear.

f) Brainstem or Central Lesions

In the last type of pathology we consider, lesions are located in the brainstem or more centrally. Lesions in individual nuclei that mediate the factors isolated in Fig. 1 could independently effect performance in the appropriate discrimination tasks or in the localization conditions that depend strongly on these factors. This notion is directly supported by the results of Masterton *et al.*, (1967) from cats with brainstem lesions and by results of Hausler and Levine (1980) and Hausler *et al.* (1979) from human subjects with multiple sclerosis. As increasingly central lesions are considered, we expect more restricted spatial regions and more integrated functions to be involved, like the ability to combine information from eyes, kinesthesis, and other nonauditory factors to a unitary perception of the world.

3. COMMENTS

We close with several comments. First, almost any combination of binaural psychophysical impairments and audiograms can be predicted assuming relatively straightforward pathological conditions in the auditory periphery. It follows that the observed complexity of the psychoacoustic data is to be expected over a population of impaired subjects. Second, although the idealized pathologies of the present study are clearly oversimplified, the treatment of these cases illustrates our approach and provides useful, if limited, insights. Present uncertainties about the actual pathologies prohibit accurate models, although some realistic studies in which the physiological data from impaired animals are explicitly described should soon be possible. Third, in any analysis of this type, there are also major uncertainties about how well the central nervous system adapts to selective losses of information and unnatural recoding of information. Evidence that this is not a simple problem comes from the observation (Hausler *et al.*, 1979) that some impaired subjects perform better in vertical angle discrimination when one ear is plugged, even though these subjects may have lived with their impairments for years in a natural environment. Fourth, the most helpful empirical projects in the context of the present paper are detailed studies of individual impaired subjects with loss etiologies for which animal models can be studied as well, like losses induced by acoustic trauma or ototoxic drugs. Finally, the serious pursuit of the approach suggested here will require careful attention to detailed information from several areas of study, including neuroanatomy, electrophysiology, and psychoacoustics, as well as clinical studies.

Acknowledgements

This work was supported by Public Health Service Grants Nos. 2 ROl NSl09l6 and 5 POl NSl3l26 and by Hôpital Cantonal's support of Dr. Hausler.

418

REFERENCES

Bilsen, F.A. (1977). Pitch of Noise Signals: Evidence for a "Central Spectrum".
   J.Acoust.Soc.Am. 61, 150-161.
Colburn, H.S. and Durlach, N.I. (1978). Models of Binaural Interaction. In:
   Hearing. Vol. IV of *Handbook of Perception*. (E.C. Carterette and M.P.
   Friedman, eds), pp. 467-518. Academic Press, N.Y.
Colburn, H.S. and Latimer, J.S. (1978). Theory of Binaural Interaction Based
   on Auditory-Nerve Data. III. Joint Dependence on Interaural Time and
   Amplitude Differences of Discrimination and Detection. *J.Acoust.Soc.Am.*
   64, 95-106.
Durlach, N.I., Thompson, C.L. and Colburn, H.S. (1980). Binaural Interaction
   in Impaired Listeners--A Review of Past Research. About to be submitted.
Florentine, M. (1976). Relation Between Lateralization and Loudness in Asym-
   metrical Hearing Losses. *J.Am.Audiol.Soc.* 1, 243-251.
Florentine, M., Thompson, C.L., Colburn, H.S. and Durlach, N.I. (1979).
   An In-Depth Psychoacoustical Study of a Patient with Vestibular
   Schwannoma. *J.Acoust.Soc.Am.* 65, S134.
Goldberg, J.M. and Brown, P.B. (1968). Functional Organization of the Dog
   Superior Olivary Complex: An Anatomical and Electrophysiological Study.
   J.Neurophys. 31, 639-656.
Goldberg, J.M. and Brown, P.B. (1969). Response of Binaural Neurons of Dog
   Superior Olivary Complex to Dichotic Tonal Stimuli: Some Physiological
   Mechanisms of Sound Localization. *J.Neurophys.* 32, 613-636.
Hafter, E.R. and Carrier, S.C. (1972). Binaural Interaction in Low-Frequency
   Stimuli: The inability to Trade Time and Intensity Completely.
   J.Acoust.Soc.Am. 51, 1852-1862.
Hausler, R., Marr, E.M. and Colburn, H.S. (1979). Sound Localization with
   Impaired Hearing. *J.Acoust.Soc.Am.* 65, S133.
Hausler, R. and Levine, R.A. (1980). Brainstem Auditory Evoked Potentials are
   Related to Interaural Time Discrimination in Patients with Multiple
   Sclerosis. *Int.Brain Research*. In press.
Hawkins, D.B. and Wightman, F.L. (1978). Interaural Time Discrimination in
   Cochlear-Impaired Listeners. *J.Acoust.Soc.Am.* 63, S52.
Leshowitz, B., Zurek, P. and Ricard, G. (1974). Measurement of the Interaural
   Amplitude Threshold for a 500-Hz Tone. *J.Acoust.Soc.Am.* 56, S56.
Masterton, B., Jane, J.A. and Diamond, I.T. (1967). Role of Brainstem Auditory
   Structures in Sound Localization. I. Trapezoid Body, Superior Olive, and
   Lateral Lemniscus. *J.Neurophys.* 30, 341-359.
Stern, R.M. Jr. and Colburn, H.S. (1978). Theory of Binaural Interaction
   Based on Auditory-Nerve Data. IV. A Model for Subjective Lateral
   Position. *J.Acoust.Soc.Am.* 64, 127-140.

COMMENT

COMMENT ON: "Note on the modelling of binaural interaction in impaired auditory systems (H.S. Colburn and R. Hausler)

E.F. Evans
Dept. of Communication & Neuroscience, University of Keele, England.

On the question of strategy, an alternative approach seems valid and possibly more cost-effective. That is to look for generalizations and convergences among patients with as carefully selected common aetiologies as possible. For example, do you consider that the successful finding of reduced behavioural frequency resolution in carefully selected patients by several laboratories, as predicted by physiological studies of appropriate animal models, is as useless as is implied by the second sentence of your paper ! ?

REPLY TO COMMENT OF E.F. EVANS

H.S. Colburn
Research Laboratory of Electronics, Massachusetts Institute of Technology, Cambridge, U.S.A.

No ! I'm afraid I overstated my position. I am fundamentally arguing in favor of the approach outlined in the paper, not at all against the work that you cite (Pick *et al.*, 1977; Hoekstra and Ritsma, 1977; Wightman *et al.*, 1977). In fact, the most important aspect of my proposed approach, the meaningful interrelation of peripheral physiological knowledge with behavioural investigations, is exemplified by this work. The second sentence of my paper was directed toward the majority of past studies especially in the area of binaural interaction.

REFERENCES

Hoekstra, A. and Ritsma, R.J. (1977). Perceptive hearing loss and frequency selectivity. In: *Psychophysics and Physiology of Hearing*. (E.F. Evans and J.P. Wilson, eds.). Academic Press, London.
Pick, G.F., Evans, E.F. and Wilson, J.P. (1977). Frequency resolution in patients with hearing loss of cochlear origin. In: *Psychophysics and Physiology of Hearing*. (E.F. Evans and J.P. Wilson, eds.). Academic Press, London.
Wightman, F.L., McGee, T. and Kramer, M. (1977). Factors influencing frequency selectivity in normal and hearing-impaired listeners. In: *Psychophysics and Physiology of Hearing*. (E.F. Evans and J.P. Wilson, eds.). Academic Press, London.

MODELLING OF INTERAURAL TIME AND INTENSITY
DIFFERENCE DISCRIMINATION

Jens Blauert

*Lehrstuhl für allgemeine Elektrotechnik und Akustik, Ruhr-Universität
Bochum, Fed. Rep. of Germany*

1. INTRODUCTION

In binaural hearing the lateral positions of the sound images are governed by interaural arrival time and level differences of the acoustical signals
at the two ears. Two classes of binaural processor models have been proposed
to explain these phenomena (for a review see Colburn and Durlach, 1978). The
first class of these models (count-comparison models) is based on an idea of
v. Békésy (1930). However, these models have never taken into account the more
complicated psychoacoustical effects, e.g. multiple and spread images. The second class of the models (coincidence or correlation models) originates from
Jeffress(1948). Up to now these models, though promising, could only explain
the processing of arrival time differences.

In a recent article Stern and Colburn (1978) proposed an extension of the
Jeffress-model in order to include level difference processing by multiplying
the probability distribution of coincidences by an appropriate level-diffe-
rence-dependent weighting function. Nevertheless they could not imagine any
physiological structure to perform such a transformation.

The purpose of this paper is to introduce a new model of binaural processing that can handle arrival time as well as level differences and is not unlikely on the ground of physiological evidence.

It is not that the existence of a physiological mechanism - similar to
our model - has already been established. However, the model has been constructed using elements which behave like physiological elements that have already been found in the auditory pathway. We do not think of our model in
terms of a general mechanism that accounts for all interaural signal processing but rather in terms of a processor that works in parallel with further
processors of different structure, each evaluating different attributes of the
ear signals.

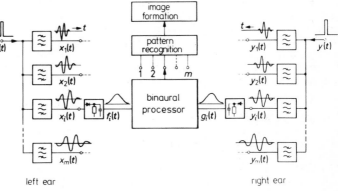

*Fig. 1. Outline of
the complete model:
The peripheral parts
are modelled by a
band pass filter
bank, followed by
half wave recti-
fiers and first
order low passes
with a cut-off fre-
quency of 800 Hz*

2. DESCRIPTION OF THE STRUCTURE OF THE MODEL

The model of the binaural processor element is embedded in a larger model that also includes peripheral signal processing. In its simplest form (Fig. 1), the frequency selectivity of the inner ear is modelled by a set of band pass filters. Every output signal of each bandpass is half-wave rectified and fed through a first order low pass with a time constant of 1.25 ms. This is done because hair cells only respond to the upper half-waves of cochlear wave-forms and because the synchrony of firings, with respect to the fine structure of the signals, is lost for frequencies above 1.6 kHz. The output signals of the low passes are used as input to the binaural processor elements which will be described in detail in the next paragraph. There is one binaural processor element for each frequency band under consideration.

The task of the set of binaural processor elements is to perform a running (discrete) interaural cross correlation in bands on the two sets of input signals. Each of the correlation functions is weighted by a function which depends on the interaural level difference in the specific frequency band. The result is a set of weighted cross correlation functions ψ_{xy} (f,τ,t) that can be plotted in a f, τ-plane. We assume that the central nervous system performs some kind of a pattern-recognition process in this f, τ-plane in order to evaluate the number, lateral position and spatial extension of the sound images.

In Fig. 2 the principal structure of the binaural processor element is shown. There is a number of fibers at each input which is stimulated simultaneously by the same input signal. At the present state of the model, we assume proportionality between the input signal and the firing probability at each instant (Duifhuis 1972). Up to now spontaneous activity and saturation effects have been omitted to restrict the number of free parameters at this point of the development of our model. Spikes coming from each fiber travel along tapped delay lines like in Jeffress's model.

However, there are two fundamental assumptions in addition to Jeffress's: (i) The number of paths with short delays is greater than the number of paths with long delays. (ii) Spikes that have been delayed by - nearly - the same amount of time are aggregated by means of "refractory" or-cells. These or-cells fire when a spike arrives at any of their inputs but are blocked within a refractory interval after each firing.

The output spikes of each or-cell are combined with the output spikes of complementary or-cells from the other ear, as shown in Fig. 2. in agreement with the original model of Jeffress. The coincidence cells respond when receiving a spike at both of the two inputs - each within a short coincidence interval. The number of spikes per interval at the output of each of the coincidence cells can be taken as an estimate of one point of a weighted interaural running cross correlation function.

The operation of the model on interaural level differences depends on the effect that the output rate of the or-cells is limited by the refractory interval. Once the spike rate at one of the inputs of a coincidence cell has reached its maximum, the rate of coincidences is governed by the spike rate at the second input. In general the effect of an increment of the spike rate at one input of a coincidence cell nonlinearly depends on the instant values of the spike rates at both inputs. This causes an asymmetry of the coincidences as a function of interaural time difference when an interaural level difference is applied.

3. SAMPLE RESULTS AND DISCUSSION

Figs. 3 and 4 show resulting coincidence functions of one binaural processor element. Two typical input functions have been chosen: (i) Sinusoidal signals with a frequency well above 1.6 kHz. These lead to DC signals at the binaural processor inputs. (ii) Sinusoidal signals with a frequency below 1.6 kHz.

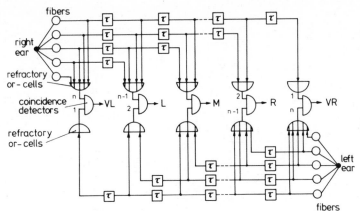

Fig. 2. Structure of the binaural processor element. The complete model provides one binaural processor element for each frequency band under consideration, e.g. for each critical band.

In this case the processor input signals are half-wave rectified, pure tones.

According to Jeffress's original ideas, each place on the abscissa corresponds to a certain lateral position of the image. In Fig. 3, a shift of the maximum of the coincidence function with respect to L_Δ can be clearly observed. In Fig. 4, the relative heights of the maxima change as a function of interaural level difference. Additionally, an evaluation with a finer resolution than 21 points on a 4 ms scale would display a slight shifting of each of the maxima.

Fig. 3. Interaural coincidence functions for three interaural level differences L_Δ as stimulated by DC input signals. This type of stimulation occurs when high frequency pure tone acoustical signals are presented to the two ears. Model parameters: 21 taps delay lines. Refractory intervals of or-cells: 0.1 ms. Coincidence intervals: 0.1 ms. Right ear signal level unchanged.

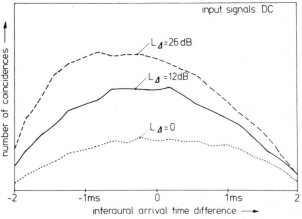

Due to the relatively large number of free parameters, the model is capable of being adapted to a variety of psychoacoustical results. For example, it elucidates an association of the center of gravity of the coincidence function with the "intensity-image" and of the peak region of the highest maximum with the "time-image" (Whitworth and Jeffress, 1961). This is in accordance with the expected trading ratios. Note that the operation of the model is dependent on the overall level. This can account for the dependence of trading-ratios on the overall level.

Double images - as observed when the two ears are fed on pure tones with 180° interaural phase shift - can be explained by the occurrence of two peaks of equal height in the coincidence function. Image broadening due to incoherence of the two ear signals is understood on the basis of broadening and continuous, stochastic shifting of the regions of maxima and the center of gravity of the coincidence curve. After spontaneous activity will be included in the model, it will also be possible to explain the decrease of the accuracy of lateralization with increasing interaural arrival time differences.

Fig. 4. Interaural coincidence functions for three interaural level differences L_Λ as stimulated by rectified 1 kHz pure tones. Model parameters as in Fig.3. Modelling with a finer resolution than 21 points would reveal a slight shift of the maxima as a funtion of level difference.

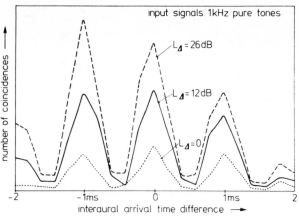

The effect of interaural level differences within our model can be described analytically by means of weighting the coincidence function for L_Λ = 0 dB. The weighting function can be approximated by a straight line with a slope depending on the amount of L_Λ. Instead in their model, Stern and Colburn (1978) proposed a rather flat, bell-shaped weighting function whose center is shifted as a function of L_Λ. This does not need to contradict our model.

Stern and Colburn were aware of the fact that generally the number of coincidences must decline with rising interaural arrival time difference. They considered that by assuming a suitable weighting function for the number of coincidences. Other authors tried to explain the same effect by supposing delay paths with a time jitter that is proportional to the delay interval. However, these assumptions did not suffice to explain the effect of interaural level differences.

In our present simple model we took a linear function to describe the dependence of the available number of delay paths on the delay interval. Other functions will be tested in the future. We also want to note that instead of tapped delay lines, a suitable ensemble of untapped delay lines with different delay intervals can be used to implement the basic assumption of the model.

We plan to further develop and refine our model in order to use it as a tool for the prediction of spatial qualities of the sound images in room- and electroacoustics.

REFERENCES

Békésy, G. von (1930). Zur Theorie des Hörens. *Phys. Z.* **31**, 857–868

Colburn, H.S. and Durlach, N.I. (1978). Models of binaural interaction. In: *Hdb. Perception*. Vol. 4. (E.C. Carterette and M.P. Friedman, eds). pp 467–518. Academic Press, New York, London, San Francisco.

Duifhuis, H. (1972). *Perceptual analysis of sound*. Diss. Techn. Hogeschool Eindhoven.

Jeffress, L.A. (1948). A place theory of sound localization. *J. Comp. Physiol. Psychol.* **41**, 35–39.

Stern, R.M.Jr. and Colburn, H.S. (1978). Theory of binaural interaction based on auditory-nerve data. IV. A model for subjective lateral position. *J. Acoust. Soc. Am.* **64**, 127–140.

Whitworth, R.H. and Jeffress, L.A. (1961). Time versus intensity in the localization of tones. *J. Acoust. Soc. Am.* **33**, 925–929.

The author gratefully acknowledges the assistance of W. Lindemann, implementing and testing the model on a HP-21 MX laboratory computer.

BINAURAL TIME PROCESSING AND TIME-INTENSITY TRADING

J. Raatgever

Applied Physics Department, University of Technology, Delft, The Netherlands.

1. INTRODUCTION

Directional hearing is generally assumed to be purely the consequence of interaural differences in time and intensity. For low frequency signals the interaural time differences between oscillations of the temporal fine structure are thought to be important, while interaural intensity differences seem to play a less pronunciated role, especially for those frequencies where the dimensions of the head are small compared to the wavelength. For high frequencies, the internal temporal fine structure not being preserved any longer, interaural differences between the signal envelopes are believed to take over, while here intensity differences definitely play an important role. For common daily sounds the different localization clues in general do not supply contradictory directional information. The uncoupling of time and intensity differences however, by using headphones for instance, leads to confusion in the perception of the true direction and distance. The resulting lateralization or localization within the head is still influenced by the different interaural parameters. Many lateralization studies in the past dealt with the question whether it is possible to compensate for an interaural time difference with respect to the perceived lateralization, by changing the interaural intensity difference. This so called time-intensity trading for lateralization appears to be possible, but is very much influenced by the experimental circumstances. Different ways to account for these trading effects have been suggested in the various theories describing binaural interaction; see e.g. the extensive literature survey given by Blauert (1974). In this respect the findings of Whitworth and Jeffress (1961) and Hafter and Jeffress (1968) are of particular interest, since for some signals containing low frequencies they reported the simultaneous existence of two different lateralization images: an "intensity image" that leads to substantial trading effects and a "time image" that can hardly be traded at all. These results may point at a separate processing of time and intensity differences, at least up to a certain level in the auditory system.

In this paper we will identify the binaural processing mechanism for low frequencies that is able to generate such time images, with the mechanism suggested by Raatgever and Bilsen (1977) accounting for lateralization and dichotic pitch. This model, summarized in the next section, predicts clear time images for various dichotic pitch phenomena. Experiments on the lateralization of such dichotic pitches will be reported and the role of interaural intensity differences will be discussed.

2. MODEL

The model can be described as follows. After sharp peripheral filtering, band-limited signals from corresponding filters at both ears pass delaying elements under preservation of the temporal structure. For every set of corresponding filters the momentary local activity along a contralateral and ipsilateral delay line will be added. This leads to internally projected two-dimensional activity patterns characteristic for the dichotic way of signal presentation. Herein the local activity (or power in a linear power evaluation) de-

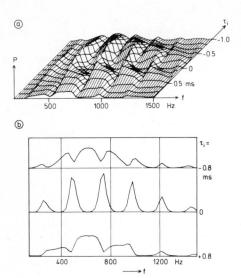

Fig.1. *Binaural activity patterns*
for MPS
a: 3-dimensional representation
b: spectra at τ_i=0 and $\pm$ 0.8 ms

pends on frequency and interaural delay. Physiologically, such a network of delaying elements corresponds with the neural network suggested by Jeffress (1948). The local addition is thought to take place by means of coincidence detecting cells (EE-cells) probably located in the SOC. The theory proceeds from the idea that the activity patterns can be scanned by the central auditory system in such a way that place (internal delay) dependent frequency spectra will be recognized and selected. In this way of thinking dichotic pitch perception is a matter of spectral pattern recognition, making use of spectral clues like depth of modulation, equal spacing of maxima, harmonicity etc.. The existence of spectral patterns optimal for pitch perception at particular internal delays implies that the sensation of dichotic pitch involves a specific lateralization.

In fig.1 calculated patterns are presented for multiple phase shifted noise (MPS) i.e. the noise is offered dichotically, filtered at one ear in such a way that the amplitude spectrum remains the same, but for all frequencies a phase difference of 180° is introduced, except for small areas around a series of harmonically related frequencies (n.250 Hz), where the phase shift is n.360° (n=0,1,2...). Fig.1a shows the 3-dimensional representation of the activity pattern while in fig.1b the spectral patterns at three internal delays are separated. For interaural delay zero, the pattern in the centre is characterized by peaks at harmonic frequencies (here: 250,500, 750 Hz etc.) resulting in the perception of a periodicity pitch corresponding to 250 Hz that is centrally localized. At other places deteriorated patterns arise, not giving rise to the perception of pitch in general. Introducing an extra interaural delay τ will lead to a shift over τ of the whole activity pattern in the direction along the τ_i axis. This means that MPS lateralization behaviour can be compared with that of dichotically delayed white noise for instance (Raatgever and Bilsen, 1977). Would we apply a phase transition of 360° at one particular frequency instead of a series harmonically related frequencies, then a dichotic stimulus arises that is characteristic for the dichotic pitch sensation first reported by Huggins (1958). In general, Huggins pitch (HP) can be considered as a special case of MPS.

3. EXPERIMENTS

Lateralization experiments have been carried out investigating the role of interaural intensity differences in the lateralization of HP and MPS. In the first instance classical time-intensity trading experiments have been performed: A HP stimulus configuration was presented with a particular interaural intensity level difference ΔL and an adjustable ex-

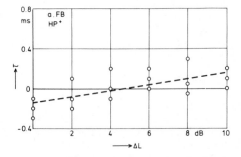

Fig.2. *Time-intensity trading*
of HP for one observer

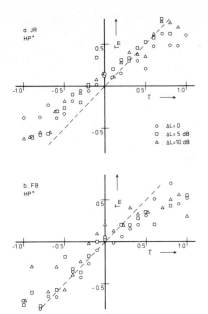

Fig.3. Lateralization of HP (interaural delay τ, level difference ΔL) compared to white noise (interaural delay $τ_m$) for 2 observers

tra interaural delay τ. The observer had to adjust the HP pitch image by means of this interaural delay in such a way that it was localized in the centre of the head. The experiments were controlled by a computer that randomized the signal presentations. Two observers took part in the experiments. One of them did not show any sifnificant trading at all, while the other had a small trading with a trading ratio of about 30 μs/dB (fig.2).

The technique applied, however, has the disadvantage to be based on the lateralization in the centre only. A more complete and accurate picture may be obtained, applying a matching procedure as follows: The lateralization of the pitch image in a dichotic pitch stimulus configuration with a given additional interaural delay τ has been matched with the lateralization of white noise with equal level at both ears and an adjustable interaural delay $τ_m$. In this way the lateralization behaviour of dichotic pitch can be compared to that of white noise over the whole possible range of image locations. Introducing an interaural intensity difference as well in the dichotic stimulus, will provide information on the time-intensity trading for lateralization. The experimental procedure was controlled by a computer that randomized the signal presentations. The same two observers were involved in the experiments. The results of the experiments

with the HP stimulus are given in fig.3. The data points represent the average lateralization judgements of HP with level differences ΔL=0, 5 and 10 dB. An upward shift of the curve would be expected if positive time-intensity trading would occur. No systematic trading can be seen. A linear regression analysis however results in a slight systematic trading with trading ratio's always less than 20 μs/dB, and about 10 μs/dB on the average for both observers.

For MPS, analogous experiments have been carried out. The results are plotted in fig.4. Here level differences of ΔL=0 and 6 dB have been applied under the same conditions used in the HP experiments. The corresponding measured points are expected to shift upwards. Besides, level differences of ΔL=-6 and -12 dB have been introduced, leading to an expected downwards shift. No systematic shifts can be seen, but a linear regression results in minor trading ratio's of about 10 μs/dB if the level difference operates in the same direction as the delay and no trading whatsoever if the effects of delay and level difference are opposite.

These ratio's, small

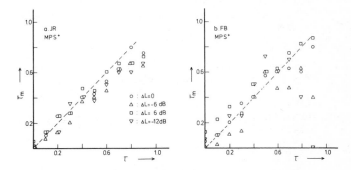

Fig.4. Lateralization of MPS (interaural delay τ, level difference ΔL) compared to white noise (interaural delay $τ_m$) for 2 observers.

427

as they are, consolidate the conclusion for HP and MPS to have time-images only.

4. DISCUSSION

The lateralization matching experiments once again demonstrated the analogy between the lateralization of dichotic pitch and the lateralization of e.g. dichotically delayed white noise (compare Raatgever and Bilsen, 1977). This is not self-evident since the stimulus configurations characteristic for HP and MPS for instance, consist of dichotic noise that has opposite phases at both ears for the major part of the frequency spectrum. Consequently, the noisy part of the stimulus is perceived as a more or less diffuse noise image that is quite differently located, compared to white cophasic noise with the same interaural delay. The character of the dichotic pitch however, is that of a weak (HP) or stronger (MPS) pitch sensation within the noise, that can be localized separately. This is a crucial point in the underlying theory, implying for the place (i.e. internal delay) where the effective spectral information is found leading to the dichotic pitch sensation, that it correlates with the lateralization of that pitch.

Interaural intensity differences are expected to cause a decreasing modulation in the internal spectral information, thus weakening the perceived phenomena coupled herewith. Dichotic pitch for instance becomes inaudible for interaural level differences more than about 20 dB. Consequently, binaural percepts like dichotic pitch, that are the results of the binaural time processing system exclusively, will not show substantial time-intensity trading. Only minor trading effects will be expected, due to latency shifts in the neurons involved. Illustrative in this respect are the findings of Crow et al. (1978) of time-intensity trading ratio's up to 40 μs/dB and 8 μs/dB on the average for neurons in the SOC. The lateralization of dichotic pitch images is expected to behave typically as found for a time image. The trading experiments presented here for HP and MPS, have confirmed this point. The trading ratio's found are significantly below the upper limit of 40 μs/dB specified for time images by Blauert (1974). The considerable time-intensity trading for the lateralization of signals having intensity images as well, is probably achieved at a different level in the binaural system.

REFERENCES

Blauert, J. (1974). *Räumliches Hören*. S. Hirzel Verlag, Stuttgart.

Cramer, E.M. and Huggins, W.M. (1958). Creation of pitch through binaural interaction. *J.Acoust.Soc.Am.* 30, 413-417.

Crow, G., Rupert, A.L. and G. Moushegian (1978). Phase locking in monaural and binaural medullary neurons: Implications for binaural phenomena. *J.Acoust. Soc.Am.* 64, 493-501.

Hafter, E.R. and L.A. Jeffress (1968). Two image lateralization of tones and clicks. *J.Acoust.Soc.Am.* 44, 563-569.

Jeffress, L.A. (1948). A place theory of sound localization. *J.Comp.Physiol. Psychol.* 41, 35-39.

Raatgever, J. and F.A. Bilsen (1977). Lateralization and dichotic pitch as a result of spectral pattern recognition. In: *Psychophysics and Physiology of Hearing* (E.F. Evans and J.P. Wilson eds.), 443-453, Academic Press, London.

Whitworth, R.H. and L.A. Jeffress (1961). Time versus intensity in the localization of tones. *J.Acoust.Soc.Am.* 33, 925-929.

ROLE OF FREQUENCY SELECTIVITY IN LOCALIZATION AND LATERALIZATION

B. Scharf   *and*   G. Canévet
Auditory Perception Lab., North-   *Laboratoire de Mécanique et d'Acous-*
eastern U., Boston, MA 02115 USA   *tique, CNRS, 13274 Marseille, France*

1. INTRODUCTION

Exemplified by the critical band, frequency selectivity has been demonstrated in detection, masking, loudness summation, phase perception, consonance judgments, and so forth (Scharf, 1970). The critical band also is a dominant feature in the lateralization of tone bursts which have a different frequency at each ear. The interaural onset time difference (ΔT) needed to lateralize a dichotic tone burst toward the leading ear is constant so long as
the frequency separation (ΔF) between the tone in the left ear and the tone in
the right ear is less than a critical band (Scharf et al, 1976). Beyond the
critical band, the lateralization threshold increases with ΔF. In short, dichotic tone bursts in the same critical band are easier to lateralize than are
tone bursts in different critical bands, and the more critical bands separa-
ting the two tones, the harder they are to lateralize. One interpretation of
these data is that a tone in one critical band is channeled along a different
neural pathway than a tone in another critical band (cf. Franssen, 1960).
Arriving at an array of "binaural comparators," neural signals in corresponding channels, i.e., originating in the same critical band in each ear, are
more easily compared for relevant interaural time differences than are signals
in non-corresponding channels. The farther apart the channels, the more uncertainty is introduced at the comparison stage, and the larger the ΔT required for lateralization. (An alternate interpretation is that the grouping
by critical bands occurs centrally, at the binaural comparator. This interpretation implies a retrocochlear basis for the critical band.)
    The dichotic lateralization data lead to the prediction that lateraliza-
tion and, by extension, localization of one sound in the presence of another
depends upon the spectral relations between the two sounds. Thus, localizing
one tone burst in the presence of another will be most difficult when the two
tones are within the same critical band and become progressively easier as
their frequency separation increases. In this paper, we first present data on
lateralization under masking and then on localization.

2. LATERALIZATION

a) *Problem and Procedures*

How large a ΔT is needed to lateralize a tone burst--the target--toward
the leading ear when a binaural burst--the masker--is presented in close temporal proximity? Presented through earphones, the target had the same frequency at the two ears and so did the masker, but target and masker differed
in frequency from each other. Lateralization threshold was measured as a
function of the frequency separation, ΔF, between target and masker. Measurements were made with several different time intervals between the onsets of
the target and masker, but most data were collected with the masker preceding
by 15 ms. The target's SPL was 60 dB, the masker's 40 dB. Target duration
was 30 ms, measured from the beginning of the burst's exponential rise to the
beginning of its fall; masker duration was 25 ms. Rise-fall times were 10 ms.
An adaptive two-alternative, forced-choice (2AFC) procedure was used in which

the observer, O, reported on each trial whether the target was more to the left or more to the right.

b) *Results and Discussion*

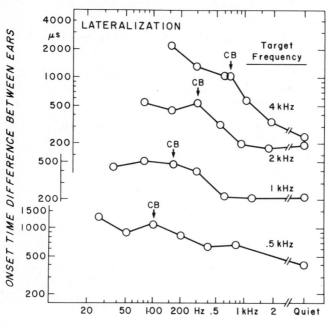

Fig. 1. Lateralization threshold as a function of the frequency difference between the masker at 40 dB SPL and the target at 60 dB.

Figure 1 shows the results for target frequencies from .5 to 4 kHz. The ordinate gives the interaural ΔT required for approximately 75% correct lateralization. The abscissa gives the ΔF. Masker frequency was always higher than target frequency. Each point is the median of 170 to 300 judgments by three trained Os. (The targets at .5 and 1 kHz were 180° out of phase in the two ears while the masker was in phase. At 2 and 4 kHz, tone and masker were in phase.) The arrows indicate the critical bandwidth as measured monaurally and in dual-frequency lateralization.

Except at 2 kHz, the data do not show a clear break in the vicinity of the critical band. Measurements at the lower frequencies are probably confounded by the absence of interaural phase cues. Nevertheless, average lateralization thresholds are always higher at subcritical ΔFs than at supercritical ΔFs. It is noteworthy that the masker, 20 dB below the level of the target, is able to grossly disrupt the lateralization of a target close in frequency. That such a weak masker can have so strong an effect on the target suggests that much of the interference occurs at target onset when the preceding masker is more intense than the target. Turning on a masker 300 ms before target onset and leaving it on for 430 ms resulted in as much interference with lateralization as turning the masker on 15 ms before the target. Turning *off* the masker just prior to signal onset reduced interference.

3. LOCALIZATION

a) *Problem and Procedures*

From the results on lateralization, we should expect that localizing one tone burst in the presence of another is poorest when the two bursts are within the same critical band. Despite technical difficulties that precluded the use of a criterion-free, sensitive measure, this general prediction is borne out reasonably well by the following experiment on localization.

Measurements were carried out in a large anechoic room with three loudspeakers 3.7 m from O. The masker came from a loudspeaker at 0° azimuth, directly in front of O who sat with his head against a rear head rest. Target signals came from two speakers located on either side of the masking speaker, one 15° to O's left and the other 15° to his right. Each burst of a series of four 30-ms tone bursts from the middle speaker was accompanied by a target signal from one of the side speakers, a signal that lagged by 20 ms (onset to onset). The first two targets were from the left speaker, and the second two from the right. Usually, O heard each combination of masker and target as a single, chord-like sound from the vicinity of the middle speaker, or in back of his head.

Since the locus of the loudspeakers was fixed, we could not vary interaural differences. Instead we used a method of limits to determine the level of the target at which O just perceived a difference between the loci of the first two sounds (masker plus left target, presented twice) and the second two sounds (masker plus right target). We also measured threshold for the detection of the lagging burst whether or not it influenced the apparent locus of the combination. The main variable was the frequency separation between target and masker.

b) *Results and Discussion*

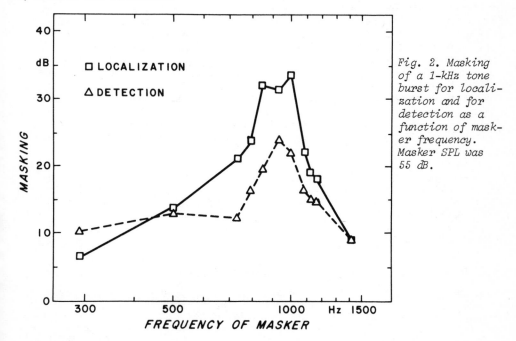

Fig. 2. Masking of a 1-kHz tone burst for localization and for detection as a function of masker frequency. Masker SPL was 55 dB.

Figure 2 shows the masking of a 1-kHz target by a 55-dB burst whose frequency is given on the abscissa. Each point is the mean of six measures from
three Os. Squares indicate the amount of masking in decibels when the Os attempted to detect displacement and triangles when they attempted to detect the
presence of the target. Masking is the increase from the level in the quiet
caused by the presence of the masker. In the quiet, mean target level required for localization was 15 dB SPL, and for detection it was 12 dB.

Frequency selectivity is evident for both localization and detection.
Over a range of about 150 Hz, nearly one critical band, masking of locus is
maximal. Outside that range, the locus of even weak lagging bursts is perceived. Selectivity is finer for detection than for localization so that detection masking is considerably less in the vicinity of the critical band.
Similar, but more variable, results have been obtained with a target at 4 kHz.
Data at 2 kHz, where localization is generally poor, were too variable to permit any conclusions.

4. GENERAL DISCUSSION AND CONCLUSIONS

Despite the limitations of our procedure for measuring localization under
masking, we have demonstrated similar frequency selectivity under masking for
both localization and lateralization. However, the two sets of data differ
with respect to the distribution of masking over frequency. The lateralization data revealed about as much interference from a frequency above the tone
as from one below (latter data not shown). But the localization data show
little masking from a higher-frequency tone. Accordingly, interference in
lateralization extends over two critical bands, whereas masking in localization seems to extend over only one critical band located below the target.
This discrepancy may stem from procedural differences and from the redundancy
of localization cues, which may include interaural intensity and phase differences as well as onset time differences.

We conclude that frequency selectivity plays a decisive role in the lateralization and localization of one sound in the presence of another. Interference with the lateralization of a tone burst is greatest from a masker in
the same critical band as the target. Similarly, perceiving the locus of a
tone burst is most difficult when the target is preceded by a lower- or equal-
frequency masking burst in the same critical band.

These findings may be related to speech perception in a noisy environment. Incoming signals from different sources and directions normally differ
in their momentary spectra. These differences permit a spatial segregation,
selective attention, and finally, comprehension of the selected speech signal.
The difficulty of persons with sensorineural hearing impairment to understand
speech in noise may be caused, in part, by widened critical bands (Florentine
et al, in press) that preclude good spatial segregation among incoming sounds.

*The authors thank R. Germain, A. Marchioni, and C. Meiselman for help in
carrying out these experiments. Research supported by CNRS and NIH. Part of
this paper was presented at the 97th meeting of the Acoustical Society of
America, June, 1979.*

REFERENCES

Florentine, M., Buus, S., Scharf, B. & Zwicker, E. (in press). Frequency se-
    lectivity in normally-hearing and hearing-impaired observers. *Journal
    of Speech and Hearing Research*.
Franssen, N.V. (1960). *Some considerations on the mechanism of directional
    hearing*. Dissertation. University of Delft, Holland.
Scharf, B. (1970). Critical bands. In: *Foundations of Modern Auditory The-
    ory*. Vol 1. (J.V. Tobias, ed). pp 157-202. Academic Press, New York.
Scharf, B., Florentine, M. & Meiselman, C.H. (1976). Critical band in audi-
    tory lateralization. *Sensory Processes 1*, 109-126.

INTERACTIONS BETWEEN TWO-TONE COMPLEXES AND MASKING NOISE

U. Sieben and R.E. Gerlach

Drittes Physikalisches Institut
Universität Göttingen, Germany

INTRODUCTION

To investigate the phase dependent interaction of the components of a harmonic two-tone complex, in the accompanying paper of Nasse and Gerlach (1980) a binaural masking threshold experiment is described. In a diotic noise situation a two-tone complex is presented to the right ear and a test tone with a small frequency difference relative to the examined component of the two-tone complex is presented to the left ear. It is assumed that this spatial separation avoids interactions of the test tone and the tone complex in the part of the peripheral auditory pathway, where the nonlinear interactions of the complex components are supposed to reside. The subjects task is to indicate the beginning and the end of the binaural beat sensation. Provided that the relative phase and amplitude of the test tone are known, the internal amplitude and phase of the examined component of the two-tone complex can be calculated with the help of a modified "equalization and cancellation" (EC-) model. On the other hand, there is the problem of whether nonlinear interactions of a strong second tone in the complex and the noise occur. Such interactions would reduce the internal cross-correlation of the noise, resulting in a less effective EC-subtraction. It is necessary to discriminate this nonlinear effect from the additional masking of the second tone in the complex.

EXPERIMENTAL RESULTS

First, we performed an experiment to determine the summation of masking effects in the monaural case, when the masker consists of a low-frequency tone (200 Hz - 700 Hz) and a uniform masking noise, low-pass filtered at 3 kHz. For constant level and frequency of the pure-tone masker, the masked threshold of a test tone depends on the masking-level of the noise. The frequency of the test-tone is chosen in such a way that phase-dependent variations of its masked threshold are avoided. Though the summation of masking-effects in general cannot be described by intensity summation (Zwicker and Herla, 1975), this is possible in our case (tone and uniform masking noise). However, when the noise masker is diotic, this simple model fails to describe the data. This is shown in Fig. 1 where the monaural data (circles) are compared with the diotic-noise data (crosses) and the predictions of an intensity-summation model (lines). Though the data in the diotic-noise situation are taken from experiments with different frequencies and levels of the pure-tone masker, they look similar if they are plotted in an appropriate coordinate system. In Fig. 2 the abscissa is the difference of the masking-levels of the noise and the pure-tone masker, i.e. of the masked threshold-levels of the test tone in dB SL when masked with the noise and the tone only, respectively. The ordinate is the difference of the actual test tone level at the masked threshold and the masking-level of the pure-tone masker. At $L_N - L_T = 5$ dB the diotic-noise data deviate from the theoretical curve about 3 dB. We interpret this deviation of the measured data from the intensity-summation-model (dotted line) as a consequence of the interaction of the tone-masker with the noise. If L_T and L_N denote the masking-levels of the tone-masker and the noise, we write in an EC-model compatibel notation:

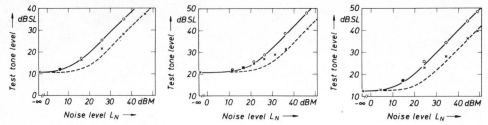

Fig.1. Masked threshold of a test-tone masked with an ipsilateral pure-tone masker and an additional ipsilateral noise (circles) or with a diotic noise (crosses). The level of the test-tone at the masked threshold is plotted versus the masking-level of the noise. The prediction of an intensity-summation model (dashed and solid lines) are compared with the data. a) Test-tone 500 Hz, pure-tone masker 200 Hz, 45 dB SL. b) Test-tone 350 Hz, pure-tone masker 200 Hz, 42 db SL. c) Test-tone 500 Hz, pure-tone masker 600 Hz, 43 dB SL.

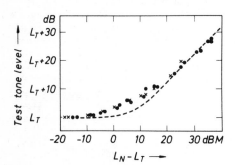

Fig.2. Comparison of the masked thresholds of a test-tone with different frequencies. The masker is an ipsilateral pure-tone and a diotic noise. The difference of the actual test-tone level at the masked threshold and the masking-level of the pure tone is plotted versus the difference of the masking-levels of the noise masker and the pure-tone masker. (Filled circles from Fig.1).

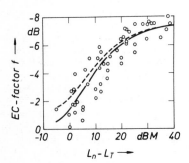

Fig.3. Comparison of the EC-factor f according with eq. 1 from our data (circles) is compared with the predictions of the half-wave rectifier model (eq. 5). The model prediction is calculated under the assumption that the EC-mechanism equalizes the internal noise intensities before subtraction (solid line) and under the assumption that the EC-mechanism maximizes the signal-to-noise ratio at the output of the cancellation mechanism (dashed line). The EC-factor is plotted versus the difference of the masking-levels of the noise and the pure-tone masker.

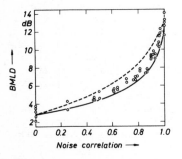

Fig.4. Measured $N_0 S_\pi$-BMLD (circles) plotted versus the interaural normalized cross-correlation coefficient ρ of the dichotic masking noise. The data are compared with the prediction of the EC-model (dashed line) and with a modified EC-model (solid line) which takes into account the half-wave rectifying in the mechanical-to-neural transduction of the signal (solid line).

$$\Delta = 10 \cdot \text{Log}\left(10^{L_T/10} + 10^{L_N/10}\right) - 10 \, \text{Log}\left(10^{L_T/10} + f \cdot 10^{L_N/10}\right) \qquad (1)$$

where Δ is the BMLD in the case of composed maskers and f is a modification of Durlach's EC-factor (Durlach, 1972). In our experiment f is a function of L_N and L_T and describes the masking-level of the noise at the output of the cancellation mechanism. With eq. 1 (solved for f), f can be calculated for the composed-masker situation from the measured data and depends on $L_N - L_T$ as shown in Fig. 3.

INTERPRETATION

There are some indications, that the neural activity of the 8-th nerve responds to something like the half-wave rectified acoustical waveform of the signal (Rose *et al*, 1971). This concept, in a simplified form, implies that in a composite-masker situation a sufficiently strong pure-tone masker can "switch off" the masking noise during time intervals for which the noise amplitude at the contralateral ear is, say, positive. On the other hand, the tone can "switch on" the noise when the contralateral noise is negative. If no other disturbances are assumed in the channel of the noise, it can be shown that the normalized cross-correlation coefficient ρ of the interaural noise equals the probability θ that the contralateral noise signals are simultaneously "switched on". However, the EC-theory supposes an additional disturbance in the auditory pathway, namely a certain internal noise in form of a stochastic time and amplitude jitter of the time structure of the signals (Durlach, 1972). This causes an additional decrease of the internal noise correlation. Durlach (1972) described the effect of this time and amplitude jitter by a single constant k. It is possible to write the EC-model in a way that this constant k is replaced by the internal cross-correlation coefficient $\rho = k^{-1}$ of the diotic noise. Since the two mechanisms of decorrelation (jitter and half-wave rectifying) are independent, the total internal cross-correlation coefficient is:

$$\rho = \theta \cdot k^{-1} \qquad (2)$$

From eq. 2 the modified EC-theory gives an expression for the EC-factor in the tone masker - $N_0 S_M$ case. The mean power of the difference of the noises in the EC-channels $n_1(t)$ of the left and $n_r(t)$ of the right ear is given by:

$$\overline{|n_1(t) - n_r(t)|^2} \, / \, \overline{n(t)^2} = 2 - 2\rho \qquad (3)$$

and for the EC-factor we get the expression:

$$f = 2/(2 - 2\rho) \qquad (4)$$

Since the constant k can be determined from the $N_0 S_\pi$ threshold (Durlach, 1972), it is necessary to calculate the simultaneous "switch on" - probability θ of the internal noise. If γ is the ratio of the masking intensities of the tone and the noise, we can show:

$$\theta = \frac{1}{2} + \frac{1}{\sqrt{\pi}} \int_{\gamma\sqrt{2}}^{\infty} e^{-\frac{v^2}{2}} \, dv + \frac{\sqrt{2}}{\pi\sqrt{\pi}} \cdot \int_{0}^{\gamma\sqrt{2}} e^{-\frac{z^2}{2}} \cdot \arcsin\left(\frac{z}{\gamma\sqrt{2}}\right) dz \qquad (5)$$

From eq. 2, 4 and 5, the prediction of the model for f is calculated. Figure 3 compares the theoretical prediction (solid line) with the data. Calculations even with this simple model are in good agreement with the data. The data are collected from two subjects with a $N_0 S_\pi$-BMLD of about 13 dB. Fig. 3 shows a nonlinear interaction of the pure tone masker and the noise even if the noise-masking level is more than 20 dB higher than that of the tone. To describe the experimental data from Durlach (1972), it is not necessary to distinguish between a cancellation model which equalizes the noise intensities before subtraction (Durlach, 1972) and a model which chooses an interaural amplifying factor in a way that the signal-noise ratio after the cancellation mechanism becomes maximal. In some asymmetric masker situations this distinction becomes necessary. Therefore, the dotted line in Fig. 3 shows the models prediction for the case that the signal-noise ratio is maximized. The difference of these two calculations is less than 1 dB at $L_T=L_N$. For lower noise levels the variance of the experimental data becomes too large to allow a reasonable estimation of f.

DISCUSSION

It was shown that in the case of composite maskers the binaural masked threshold shows other characteristics than the masked threshold in the case of monaural noise. This can be interpreted as a consequence of the assumed half-wave rectifying mechanism in the peripheral auditory pathway. The proposed model does not take into account the special shape of the excitation pattern of the masking tone or the critical band concept. However, preliminary calculations based on improved models did not result in very different predictions.

If the half-wave rectifier model represents a real process in the peripheral auditory system, we expect a decorrelation effect, particularly in the case of a masker consisting of two independent noises. Figure 4 shows the N_0S_π-BMLD plotted over the interaural crosscorrelation coefficient ρ of the dichotic masking noise. The dashed line represents the prediction of the EC-model. Obviously the slope of this curve is too flat for $\rho > 0.7$ and too steep for $\rho < 0.4$. If the half-wave rectifying mechanism is taken into account (solid line) the slopes of the models prediction follow the measurement more closely. Because in the described experiment the tone masker and the test-tone were presented ipsilaterally, the ears capability to maximize the signal to noise ratio at the output of the cancellation mechanism has only small effects on the measured BMLD's. If the test-tone is presented contralaterally to the tone masker, this effect becomes more pronounced. For the calculation of the amplitude and phase of the octave tone in the complex, which is described in the accompanying paper (Nasse and Gerlach, 1980), it is necessary to consider both effects: the decorrelation of the diotic noise by the tonal masker and the optimization of the central subtraction.

REFERENCES

Durlach, N.I. (1972). Binaural Signal Detection: Equalization and Cancellation Theory. In: *Foundations of Modern Auditory Theory*. Vol. 2. (J.V. Tobias, ed). pp 369-462. Academic Press, New York.

Nasse, H., Gerlach, R.E. (1980). Investigation of Monaural Phase Effects by Measuring Binaural Masking Thresholds. *This volume*.

Rose, J.E. *et al* (1971). Some Effects of Stimulus Intensity on the Response of Auditory Nerve Fibers in the Squirrel Monkey. *J. Neurophysiol.* 34, 685-699.

Zwicker, E., Herla, S. (1975). Über die Addition von Verdeckungseffekten. *Acustica* 34, 89-97.

SUBJECTIVE LATERALITY OF NOISE-MASKED BINAURAL TARGETS

Richard M. Stern and Eliot M. Rubinov

Department of Electrical Engineering and Biomedical Engineering Program
Carnegie-Mellon University
Pittsburgh, Pennsylvania 15213 U.S.A.

1. INTRODUCTION

While many studies have investigated the subjective lateral position of simple binaural stimuli such as pure tones, clicks, and random noise, relatively little is known about the mechanisms by which one can separately lateralize spectrally-overlapping components of more complex stimuli. The subjective lateral positions of separate components of multiple-tone complexes and click trains have previously been reported by Sayers and Cherry (1957), Sayers (1964), and Toole and Sayers (1965), but these authors do not discuss the effect of the presence of one component on the perception of the others, and the stimulus components themselves occupy adjacent rather than overlapping frequency bands. Butler and Naunton (1962, 1964) have reported that an intense masker presented to one ear through a headphone could cause the perceived location of a concealed loudspeaker to shift in azimuth, but the results of these experiments are difficult to interpret because the stimuli received by the subjects were neither specified in detail nor completely controlled.

In this study we have attempted to obtain a more quantitative measure of the effect of a broadband noise masker on the subjective lateral position of a diotic target tone. Estimates of target laterality in the presence of several different types of maskers were obtained as a function of target-to-masker ratio.

2. PROCEDURE

Our experimental procedure evolved from a lengthy series of pilot experiments. Initially we attempted to estimate the position of the masked tonal targets using several laterality-matching methods with acoustical pointers, as well as other techniques based on left-right laterality comparisons. In general, we found that the spatial image of a noise-masked binaural target is not nearly as well defined as that of a target presented in quiet, and lateralization estimates of a tone in noise are far more variable. The procedure that we ultimately adopted was designed to reduce two sources of this variability. First, it appeared that lateralization judgements were affected in part by adaptation of the noise masker in a manner similar to the phenomena reported by Bertrand (1972) and Thurlow and Jack (1973). We randomly alternated the ear to which the masker was more intense or leading in time to reduce the significance of this effect. Second, multiple target images were perceived for some stimulus configurations, and some variability in the data would be introduced if observers responded according to different images on successive trials. We used a cue tone in the main experiments to direct the observers' attention to a portion of their auditory space, one side of the head.

In our final procedure a cue tone, the target-masker complex, and a pointer tone were presented in succession during each experimental trial, with the timing shown in Fig. 1. The cue, target, and pointer were all 500-Hz tones, while the masker noise was bandpass filtered between 100 and 1000 Hz. The cue was presented monaurally to one of the two ears, the target was diotic, and the pointer tone was presented with an interaural intensity difference that was

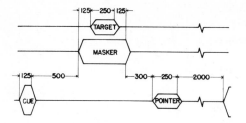

Fig.1. Stimulus timing sequence for a single experimental trial. All times are in msec. Rise/fall times are 50 msec.

randomly selected from a previously-defined set. The cue was presented at 75 dB SPL, the target was presented at 65 dB SPL, and the overall intensity of the pointer tone was adjusted to maintain a binaural loudness approximately equal to that of the target. The masker was presented in one of four configurations: (a) monaurally, (b) with an interaural intensity difference (IID) of 10 dB, (c) interaurally uncorrelated with an IID of 10 dB, and also (d) with an interaural time delay (ITD) of 500 μsec.

The observer was instructed to direct his or her attention to the side of the head to which the cue tone was presented, and to indicate whether the component of the masked target image in that region was perceived to the left or to the right of the pointer tone. The percentage of target-right judgements was plotted as a function of the IID of the pointer, and the pointer IID producing 50 percent comparisons in each direction was taken as an estimate of the subjective position of the target. The target-to-masker ratio E/N_0 and masker configuration were held fixed for each block of trials, but the masker signals to the two ears were randomly commuted from ear to ear to avoid adaptation effects. The cue was presented to the ear toward which the masker was perceived during half the blocks of trials, and to the opposite ear during the remaining blocks. Results were tabulated separately according to the polarity of the interaural differences of the masker, and transformed and averaged according to assumptions that the observers' auditory systems were left-right symmetric.

3. RESULTS

Estimates of the lateral position of the masked target are plotted in Fig. 2 as a function of E/N_0 for each of the four masker configurations. Filled symbols represented laterality estimates obtained from blocks of trials when the cue was presented to the ear toward which the masker was perceived, while the open symbols indicate results obtained when the cue was presented to the opposite ear. Each data point was obtained from the results of 250 to 400 trials. The most conspicious attribute of these data is the striking contrast between the results generated by the two cue conditions. The target image tends to be perceived near the center of the head at high values of E/N_0. As E/N_0 is decreased, this image decomposes into at least two components with positions that approach the two ears. We refer to these separate target images that appear displaced from and attracted toward the masker image as "masker-opposed" and "masker-bound" images respectively. Data were not obtained from all subjects for all conditions in part because of the inability of some subjects to consistently hear both target images. In general, the data for the masker-opposed image were considerably less variable than the masker-bound data. Surprisingly, we found considerable intersubject variability for the masker-opposed image at high values of E/N_0. LD, and to a lesser extent RR, perceived a significantly displaced target image in contrast to the more central one indicated by ER's data. As noted above, the polarity of the masker ITD or IID was randomly al-

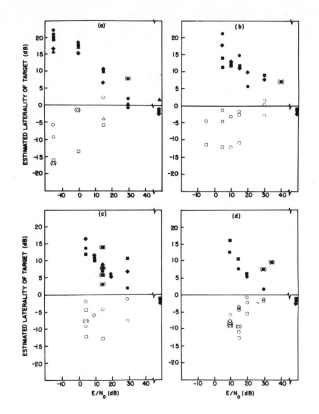

Fig.2. Estimates of the sub-jective lateral position of a diotic target in noise are plotted as a function of target-to-masker ratio E/N_0 for four masker configura-tions. During each block of trials a monaural cue tone was presented to either the ear toward which the masker was perceived (open symbols) or to the opposite ear (fil-led symbols). The data points at the far right of each panel indicate lateral-ity estimates obtained in quiet. Masker configurations were (a) monaural, (b) IID of 10 dB, (c) interaurally un-correlated with IID of 10 dB, and (d) ITD of 500 µsec. Subjects were AP ($\blacktriangle$), ER ($\bullet$), RR ($\blacklozenge$), and LD ($\blacksquare$).

ternated to reduce adaptation effects. While the data points of Fig. 2 were obtained by averaging across the masker-left and masker-right trials, the later-ality estimates in some cases would differ by more than 10 dB if these sets of trials were considered separately. These data points are enclosed by paren-theses and indicate an additional source of response variability and/or bias that we do not understand at present.

Throughout the experiment we encouraged the observers to comment on their perceptions and the difficulty of the task at hand. The laterality-comparison task was most easily accomplished when either the monaural or correlated ampli-tude-shifted masker was presented, and the masker-opposed target images for these masker configurations were particularly robust and consistently perceived. Observer ER found that the masker-bound image was somewhat more difficult to perceive for these two masker configurations, and RR could not perceive this image at all.

In general, the experimental task was more difficult when the uncorrelated or time-delayed masker were presented. Observers ER and RR could attend to two separate target images simultaneously in some of these cases. With the uncor-related masker they perceived an additional central image while listening for the masker-bound image, while for the time-delayed masker two images could be perceived simultaneously on either side of the midline.

For several masker conditions LD's data showed a highly lateralized masker-opposed image even for very large values of E/N_0. In an informal experiment using correlated amplitude-shifted maskers he reported that he could simulta-neously perceive two images, one highly displaced away from the ear toward which the masker is perceived, and a second more central image. As E/N_0 was increased, the central image would begin to dominate his perceptual space. The displaced image tended to fade away, but did not move toward the midline as E/N_0 increased.

4. DISCUSSION AND SUMMARY

We found that the image of a masked diotic tonal target is perceived near the center of the head at large values of E/N_0, and splits into at least two components that approach each ear as E/N_0 is decreased. Nevertheless, the psychophysical task is a rather difficult one, and the data are highly variable within and across subjects. It is not known whether these variations indicate that a given image manifests itself differently for different subjects (or the same subject during repeated runs) or whether variability in the data results from an additional multiplicity of images, with different ones attended to by different subjects. Similarly, the data may reflect the changes in loci of a pair of isolated target images that move toward the two ears as E/N_0 is decreased, or they may represent a perceptually-averaged composite of more fundamental components that are fixed in space but vary in strength as a function of E/N_0. We also cannot be sure that additional target images could not be isolated with additional training or an improved experimental paradigm. The data trends and subjective comments by the observers indicate that the target images with various masker types are perceived qualitatively differently, and quite possibly may be generated by different perceptual processes. We believe that the complex nature of the perceptual images of a tone in noise revealed by our experiments may provide at least a partial explanation for some of the ambiguities and contradictions of previous experimental results.

REFERENCES

Bertrand, M.P.(1972). Aspects of Binaural Experimentation. *Proc. Roy. Soc. of Medicine* 65, 807-812.
Butler, R.A. and Naunton, R.F.(1962). Some Effects of Unilateral Auditory Masking Upon the Localization of Sound in Space. *J. Acoust. Soc. Amer.* 34, 1100-1107.
Butler, R.A. and Naunton, R.F.(1964). Role of Stimulus Frequency and Duration in the Phenomenon of Localization Shifts. *J. Acoust. Soc. Amer.* 36, 917-922.
Sayers, B. McA.(1964). Acoustic-Image Lateralization Judgements with Binaural Tones. *J. Acoust. Soc. Amer.* 36, 923-926.
Sayers, B. McA. and Cherry, E.C.(1957). Mechanism of Binaural Fusion in the Hearing of Speech. *J. Acoust. Soc. Amer.* 29, 973-987.
Thurlow, W.R. and Jack, C.E.(1973). Some Determinants of Localization-Adaptation Effects for Successive Auditory Stimuli. *J. Acoust. Soc. Amer.* 53, 1573-1577.
Toole, F.E. and Sayers, B.McA.(1965). Lateralization Judgments and the Nature of Binaural Acoustic Images. *J. Acoust. Soc. Amer.* 37, 319-324.

Acknowledgements

This research was partially supported by NIH Grants 5 R01 NS14908 and 1 T32 GM07477.

A NEW "LOOK" AT AUDITORY SPACE PERCEPTION

F.L. Wightman and D.J. Kistler

Auditory Research Laboratory, Northwestern University
Evanston, Illinois U.S.A.

1. HISTORY

It is well established that localization, or auditory space perception as we call it, is heavily dependent on interaural time and intensity differences. Early research on localization was almost exclusively focussed on these two areas. However, in the last two decades, there has been considerable research on localization cues other than interaural time and intensity differences. Studies of the cues provided by a listener's pinnae have been most prevalent. The convolutions of the pinnae constitute a complex acoustical network, and impose a direction-dependent filtering on an incoming stimulus. It is now well established that this spectral shaping is important for localization (see Butler, 1975, for a review of this work). It also appears that the interaural difference cues provided by the asymmetry of a listener's pinnae may be important (Searle *et al.*, 1975). Other recent experiments have considered the role of head movements (Thurlow and Runge, 1967), visual cues (Gardner, 1968) and a-priori knowledge of stimulus properties (Coleman, 1962) in localization. The specific contributions of all these factors to auditory space perception are not well understood.

a) *Limitations of Previous Work*

There are large gaps in our understanding of auditory space perception. In fact, it might be argued that the most basic issues are the least well understood. For example, while a great deal has been learned about how certain stimulus variables influence the accuracy of localization, it is still not entirely clear what it is about everyday sounds that leads to their externalization. That sounds are nearly always "out there" is a fundamental property of our auditory environment.

Most localization experiments do not test whether or not a given stimulus appears to be "out there." In fact, very few of the data from classical studies are relevant to this issue. For example, that a subject listening over headphones can discriminate or detect "simulated" azimuth or elevation changes with the same precision as a listener in free space says nothing about whether the headphone-transduced sounds actually appeared to be "out there."

Another problem with previous work on localization is its limited scope. By virtue of the stimuli used, the listener's task, the type of data collected, and the way those data have been presented, the emphasis of nearly all previous studies has been on the accuracy or precision of localization. Data of this sort are obviously important, and lead quite naturally to development of mathematical models of localization performance (e.g., Searle *et al.*, 1976). However, experiments which measure only localization accuracy may miss or obscure other important aspects of auditory space perception. For example, two sounds may be judged as originating from the same direction (azimuth and elevation), but one may actually appear to be close to the listener (or inside his head) and the other far away. Or, sounds may be judged to have the same azimuth, (e.g., in experiments on azimuth discrimination), but the fact that they may appear to have quite different elevations is never recorded.

2. OUR RESEARCH

The research described here represents an attempt to overcome some of the limitations of previous work, by treating auditory space perception as a whole, rather than as a sum of constituent processes. Thus, our experiments have been designed not merely to measure horizontal or vertical localization accuracy, but to quantify certain features of the "shape" of auditory space, and the distortions of that space that result from various stimulus manipulations. The procedures we have developed to assess the shape of auditory space are based on multidimensional scaling (MDS) techniques.

The central assumption which underlies the application of multidimensional scaling (MDS) models to the study of perception is that stimuli are represented in an observer's experience by continuous parameters or dimensions. The aim of MDS is usually to reveal the number of dimensions relevant to the perception of interstimulus relationships, and to determine the relative positions of the stimuli on each perceptual dimension. Thus, MDS provides a model for the perceptual configuration of stimuli. Interpretation of this configuration generally involves associating the dimensions of the scaling solution with psychological or physical variables which are presumed to have affected a subject's perception.

The input data for the MDS algorithms are contained in a matrix of empirically-determined similarities (dissimilarities) between pairs of stimuli. By iteratively transforming the similarities, MDS provides a geometric representation of the stimuli by mapping them into a set of points such that the distance between any two points reflects the empirically-determined similarity of the stimuli.

Exploratory applications of MDS frequently yield dimensions which are difficult to interpret, since the final configuration of stimuli and its interpretation can be heavily influenced by the investigator's expectations and biases. As a result of this interpretation problem, many researchers are unwilling to use MDS techniques. Confirmatory (as opposed to exploratory) applications of MDS avoid many of the interpretation problems, since they use a theory or physical model to predict the dimensionality and the structure of the stimulus configuration. Thus some objective measure of the goodness of fit of the scaling solution to the theory or model can be computed. We are using MDS in a confirmatory sense to investigate auditory space perception.

a) *Simulations*

We felt it would be useful, before testing actual listeners, to carry out a number of simulations in order to evaluate the potential utility of applying MDS procedures to the study of auditory space perception. The aim of the simulations was to determine 1) the degree to which we might expect scaling solutions obtained from listeners' distance judgments to "look like" the actual physical arrangement of the sound sources; 2) the effect on the scaling solution of a listener's uncertainty (error) regarding source locations; 3) the effect of front-back confusions, which could conceivably lead to violations of the "triangle inequality"; 4) the influence of the number of sources on the "goodness of fit" between the scaling solution and the actual physical arrangement of sources.

The simulations were carried out by means of a simple computer program. Given a triad of stimuli (each stimulus is defined by its spatial coordinates), the program first derives what we call the "perceptual" coordinates of each member of the triad. These "perceptual" coordinates are computed by adding a gaussian error to the actual source coordinates. This error has a zero mean and location-specific variance. In accord with classical localization data, the error is greater for source positions above the listener than for source positions in front or on the side. The actual error-variances used were extrapolated from estimates of the normal human jnd for azimuth, elevation, and distance taken from existing literature. Once the "perceptual" coordinates are established, the program computes the three inter-source distances, and makes the two triadic-comparison decisions (longest distance and shortest distance) without error. In case of tie (two equal distances), a random choice is made with equal a-priori probability. The data are then transformed into a half-matrix of dissimilarities, and analyzed (by the KYST algorithm) exactly as if they were actual data from a listener.

The results of the simulations were encouraging. With zero source-position variance (i.e., an errorless subject) the scaling solution nearly perfectly fit the physical "space" of sources (a perfect fit is not to be expected due to the occurrence of ties) regardless of exactly how the sources were spatially arranged. Moreover, the goodness of fit (as measured by the correlation between the solution's coordinates and the actual source coordinates) was not affected by the number of stimuli (for 12-22 sources). In "no-variance" conditions the goodness of fit (correlation) was always greater than .996. The same general finding held for the simulations in which the variance of the "perceptual" coordinates was non-zero, although when the variance was four times our estimated "normal" variance, the fit was relatively poor (r=.68 in the worst case). Figure 1 shows the scaling solution obtained from a typical simulation.

Simulation of "front-back confusions", of the type normally reported in localization experiments, had no untoward effect on the

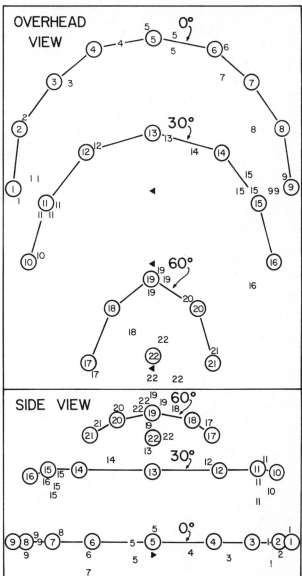

Fig. 1. Results of Multidimensional Scaling analysis of simulated triadic comparison data. The numbers represent sound sources. Circled numbers are from the "no-variance" condition. Lines connect sources at equal elevation (in the "Top View", the two lower sets of data have been displaced downward for convenience). The solid triangles indicate the listener's position and his direction of view.

443

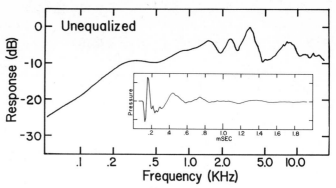

Fig. 2. Amplitude response of a typical loudspeaker, before equalization. The inset shows the loudspeaker's impulse-response.

scaling solution. For the most part, front-back confusions appeared simply as added variance in the positions of the confused points. Only when five times the "normal" number of front-back confusions were simulated, was the scaling solution unreasonably distorted.

In summary, we could find nothing in the results of our simulations that would lead us to be more than normally cautious in applying MDS procedures to localization judgments.

b) *Listeners*

The aim of our first experiment with actual listeners was to establish a baseline, or control level of performance, with which future results could be compared. In MDS terms, we wanted to obtain the closest match possible between the space revealed by the scaling solution and the physical space as defined by the location of sound sources. For this reason, we chose stimulus and response parameters that could be expected to optimize performance.

i) Stimuli. The stimuli were 200 msec bursts of white noise, presented in an anechoic room at about 70 dB SPL. The noise bursts were transduced by matched and digitally-equalized miniature loudspeakers.

ii) Loudspeaker placement and equalization. After testing several small loudspeakers, the Realistic "Minimus 0.7" (4"x3"x7") was chosen due to its relatively uniform response and its low price. Out of 30 originally purchased the 22 with the best matching amplitude responses were selected. Loudspeaker responses were measured digitally by taking the Fourier Transform of the averaged response of the speaker to a 20 microsecond unipolar impulse, recorded by a B & K 1/2" free-field condenser microphone placed 2 meters away from and on-axis to the speaker. Figure 2 shows a typical averaged impulse response, along with the amplitude response of the same speaker. The amplitude responses of all 22 fell within 5 dB of the response shown in this figure. The 22 speakers were hung from thin wires in an anechoic chamber and were arranged as if on a surface of a 1/4-sphere, roughly 2 meters in radius, with the position of the listener's head at the center. Table I gives the actual coordinates of each speaker (estimated error of placement is less than 2° azimuth or elevation and less than 1 cm distance). This arrangement was the result of several compromises. First, we wanted the speakers more or less evenly distributed over the surface of the 1/4 sphere; thus, more speakers were placed at 0° elevation than at higher elevations. Second, to minimize acoustic affects due to the separation of the two driver elements in each speaker, we wanted the sources as far as possible from the listener. Overhead, the maximum possible distance was 1.4 meters, while in front, on the sides, and behind we could accommodate a distance of 2 meters. Figure 3 shows the loudspeaker arrangement with a listener in place. Note that the speakers are all on the listener's right

Table I. Coordinates of the 22 loudspeakers used in the localization experiment. The listener's head is assumed to be at the origin, with 0° azimuth straight ahead and 90° azimuth on the right. The azimuth and elevation entries are degrees, and the distance entries are meters. Note that seven speakers were common to all three stimulus groups.

SPEAKER	AZIMUTH	ELEVATION	DISTANCE	GROUP
1	0.0	0.0	2.00	A,B,C
2	22.5	0.0	2.00	C
3	45.0	0.0	2.00	A
4	67.5	0.0	2.00	B
5	90.0	0.0	2.00	A,B,C
6	112.5	0.0	2.00	C
7	135.0	0.0	2.00	A
8	157.5	0.0	2.00	B
9	180.0	0.0	2.00	A,B,C
10	0.0	30.0	1.82	B
11	30.0	30.0	1.82	A,B,C
12	60.0	30.0	1.82	C
13	90.0	30.0	1.82	A
14	120.0	30.0	1.82	B
15	150.0	30.0	1.82	A,B,C,
16	180.0	30.0	1.82	C
17	0.0	60.0	1.60	A
18	45.0	60.0	1.60	B
19	90.0	60.0	1.60	A,B,C
20	135.0	60.0	1.60	C
21	180.0	60.0	1.60	A
22	0.0	90.0	1.40	A,B,C

side. We assumed, for the purposes of this study, that localization on the two sides is symmetric. After the speakers were in place, their responses were again measured, at a point where the center of a listener's head would be. An "equalizing" impulse response was computed for each speaker, by taking the inverse transform of the reciprocal of the speaker's transfer function (approximately). All stimuli to be presented to a listener were first convolved with the appropriate "equalizing" impulse response. The purpose of the equalization was to minimize the inter-speaker differences, and maximize the uniformity of each speaker's response in the range 200 Hz – 20 kHz. Figure 4 shows an example of an equalized speaker's impulse response and its amplitude response.

iii) Procedure. Listeners were seated in such a way that their heads were at the center of the speaker array, with all the speakers at ear-level or above (0° elevation is ear-level), and on the right side (0° azimuth is straight ahead). Since the chamber was nearly dark at all times, listeners were not well aware of the positions of the speakers. They were told to sit quite still, not moving the head at all if possible (the head was not restrained). (Note: All five subjects tested thus far have spontaneously commented that their task is facilitated if 1) the head is held motionless, and 2) eyes are shut.) On each trial of the triadic-comparison task, computer-equalized noise bursts are presented to each of three speakers, one at a time. Listeners control the presentation of the sounds (with pushbuttons) until they make a judgment of which two sounds appear closest together in space and which two appear furthest apart. After the two responses, another triad of stimuli is made available. The listeners continue in this way until all possible triads have been heard. With 22 speakers taken in triads, more than 1500 trials would be required (about 15 hours of subject time) per condition. Since this is obviously too heavy a burden on the listener, the sources were presented in three groups of

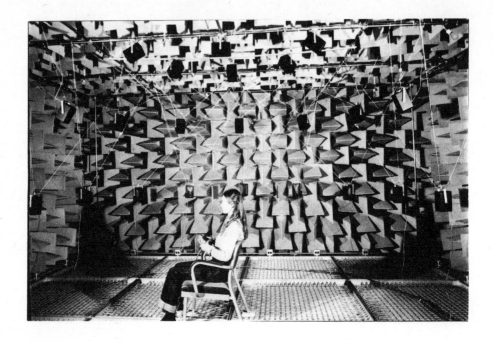

Fig. 3. The anechoic chamber with a listener in position. The loudspeakers are the small black boxes above and on the listener's right side.

12 (220 trials, or about 2 hours of subject time per group); seven speakers were common to all three groups, and the remaining 15 were distributed uniformly across the three groups, 5 per group. Table I identifies which speakers formed groups A, B, and C. Each of five normal-hearing subjects listened to all three stimulus configurations.

iv) Data analysis. The judgments from the triadic comparison task were transformed according to conventional practice into a half-matrix of dissimilarities. This matrix was then subject to multidimensional scaling analysis via the familiar KYST routine. In order to have a convenient basis for comparing one solution to another, and for comparing each to the physical space, each solution (a matrix of 12 points specified in three dimensions) was rotated orthog-

Fig. 4. Amplitude response of a typical loudspeaker, after equalization. The inset shows the equalized loudspeaker's impulse-response.

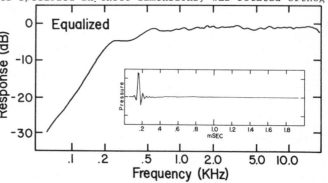

onally to maximum congru-
ence with the matrix of actual physical coordinates
of the sources. This transformation of course changes
only the aspect of view of
the solution; it does not
affect the interrelation-
ships among the points.

v) Results. Figure 5 shows
a two-dimensional representation of the MDS solution
obtained from one of our
subjects' triadic comparison data. The solutions
from the other four sub-
jects were indistinguish-
able. In general the con-
gruence between the experimental solutions and the
real space is quite good.
The "poorest" subject, listening to configuration A,
produced a "goodness of fit"
(Pearson correlation) of
0.955, while the "best"
subject produced a goodness
of fit of 0.987. This con-
firms our expectation that
in this listening condi-
tion localization would be
quite accurate. The regions
of the space in which the
fit is not as good (above
and behind the listener)
are just those where prior
data suggest localization
accuracy is reduced. In
addition the distortions of
the space (as revealed by
the solutions) are qualitatively and quantitatively
consistent with our simu-
lations (cf. Fig. 1). Note
also that the seven stimuli
common to the three stimulus
groups are located (by the
analysis) in roughly the
same positions in the three
separate scalings. This
gives us added confidence
in the robust nature of
the task and the analysis.

The five subjects
produced quite similar
MDS solutions for the three
stimulus groups. Mean
stress values for condi-

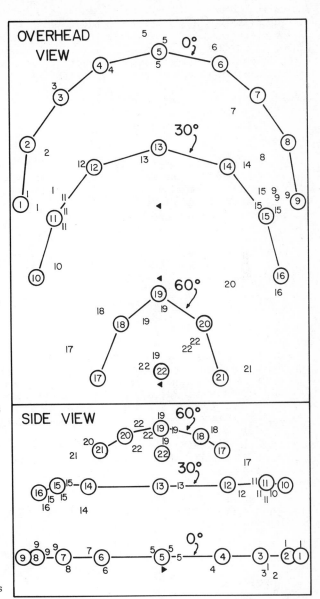

*Fig. 5. Results of Multidimensional Scaling
analysis of actual triadic comparison data.
The numbers represent sound sources. Circled
numbers are from the "no-variance" condition.
Lines connect sources at equal elevation (in
the "Top View", the two lower sets of data
have been displaced downward for convenience).
The solid triangles indicate the listener's
position and his direction of view.*

tions A, B, and C were .03, .027, and .019, respectively. Mean r values, indicating goodness of fit, were .965, .967, and .969 for conditions A, B, and C, respectively. A condition X subjects analysis of variance indicated significant differences in stress as a function of stimulus configuration ($F_{2,8}$= 6.236, p<.02) but no significant differences among subjects ($F_{4,8}$=1.16, p>.05). A condition X subjects analysis of variance of transformed r values ($\tanh^{-1}r$) yielded nonsignificant effects for conditions ($F_{2,8}$=.185, p>.05) and subjects ($F_{4,8}$=2.24, p>.05). Tukey's test for nonadditivity indicated nonsignificant condition X subjects interactions for stress ($F_{1,7}$=.008, p>.25) and goodness of fit ($F_{1,7}$=.634, p>.25).

C. CONCLUSION

We believe that MDS techniques can indeed provide a new "look" at auditory space perception. These are the only procedures we know of that can evaluate auditory space perception as an integrated process rather than as simply a sum of constituent subprocesses. Of course, the simple experiment we have described here is only a beginning. The real utility of the procedure can be measured only by what new insights it provides and what new knowledge it brings. We are hopeful, and are currently applying the new procedures to a number of basic questions about auditory space perception.

Acknowledgment

This work was supported by NSF.

REFERENCES

Butler, R.A. (1975). The influence of the external and middle ear on auditory discriminations. In: *Handbook of Sensory Physiology*, Vol. V/2: Auditory System(W.Keidel and W. Neff, eds). pp 247-260. Springer-Verlag, New York.
Coleman, P.D. (1962). Failure to localize the source distance of an unfamiliar sound. *J. Acoust. Soc. Am.* 34, 345-346.
Gardner, M.B. (1968). Proximity image effect in sound localization. *J. Acoust Soc. Am.* 43, 163.
Searle, C.L., Braida, L.D., Cuddy, D.R. and Davis, M.F. (1975). Binaural pinna disparity: Another auditory localization cue. *J. Acoust. Soc. Am.* 57, 448-455.
Searle, C.L., Braida, L.D., David, M.F., and Colburn, H.S. (1976). Model of auditory localization. *J. Acoust. Soc. Am.* 60,, 1164-1175.
Thurlow, W.R. and Runge, P.S. (1967). Effect of induced head movements on localization of direction of sounds. *J. Acoust. Soc. Am.* 42, 480-488.

Section VII
Psychoacoustical and Phonetical Interrelations

Over the last decade an increasing number of studies is devoted to clinical applications of fundamental auditory research. It has been realized, for instance, that traditional pure-tone audiograms provide very limited information with regard to a person's hearing capacity. The importance of diagnosing frequency resolution has been recognized especially. The relation between psychophysical tuning curves and hearing impairment has been dealt with in several of the sections during the meeting. In the concluding section, special attention is paid to the relation between frequency resolution and speech intelligibility. The interrelationships between different auditory functions and between psychophysical concepts are also being investigated systematically. This relatively young branch of the auditory tree promises to increase our knowledge of unimpaired auditory functions as well.

RELATIONS BETWEEN AUDITORY FUNCTIONS

J.M. Festen

Faculty of Medicine, Free University,
1007 MC Amsterdam, The Netherlands

1. INTRODUCTION

In psychophysics the characteristics of human hearing are described by
auditory functions representing properties of sensation as a function of physical parameters of the stimulus. Subsequently these functions are combined in
hearing theory to elaborate an understandable model of the hearing mechanism.
Often the connections between the auditory functions originate from theoretical considerations or physiological knowledge. To prove relations among auditory functions it would be ideal to have the possibility to control at will
the physical and physiological properties of the ear. The effects on the auditory functions would be very informative concerning the minimum number of
parameters by which the mechanism can be described. Not having this control,
we can try to use the interindividual differences in a similar way. The success of this approach depends upon the nature of the interindividual differences: they have to reflect differences in basic auditory functions rather
than being only accidental differences of a derived function, and, on top of
that, they should be free of bias caused by differences in e.g. training and
alertness. Furthermore, as the differences among subjects are only small, it
is of vital importance to reduce measurement error as far as possible (cf.
Festen *et al*, 1977).

In the literature our point of view has received very little attention.
For hearing impairment there are a number of studies devoted to the relation
between speech perception and other auditory parameters, but with respect to
peripheral auditory processes in normal hearing only a study by Elliott *et al*
(1966) was found. They studied discrimination of frequency, intensity, and
duration together with the absolute threshold and speech discrimination and
concluded that these auditory abilities are relatively independent of each
other.

In this study we wanted to include three important properties of the peripheral hearing organ, namely: frequency resolution, time resolution, and
nonlinearity. Our hypothesis is that these three are basic auditory functions
which are reflected in a number of auditory tests. To check this hypothesis it
is mandatory to include several tests related to each of the hypothetical
underlying factors. As tests related to frequency resolution we chose the auditory bandwidth measured with comb-filtered noise and the slopes of the psychophysical tuning curve, measured both in direct masking and in forward masking. Three tests related to temporal resolution were adopted. First the width
of a temporal window was determined, which is the time-domain analogue of the
auditory filter, and, additionally, the slopes of the forward and backward-
masking curves were measured. As regards nonlinearity the strength of the cubic difference tone was measured for an optimum frequency ratio between the
primaries and the degree of lateral suppression was determined for one
suppressor condition. Because the auditory functions may vary essentially with
signal frequency, all tests were administered for the same frequency (1000 Hz).

2. EXPERIMENTS

The twelve experiments which make up this study are schematicly represented in Fig. 1. The right column gives the temporal structure of the signals and the left column the spectral structure. The probe signals are dashed and the maskers are fully drawn. All experiments were carried out in test and retest and we used an adaptive 2AFC to obtain the threshold. Here the experiments will be indicated only briefly.

1) *Absolute threshold*. Each session started with the determination of the absolute threshold at 1000 Hz in three runs of 2AFC trials. The observation periods were indicated visually.

2) *Bandwidth in simultaneous masking*. With a 40-dB-SPL probe and a variable masker, threshold levels were measured for peak and trough of comb-filtered noise with peak spacings of 1000, 667, and 500 Hz. In test and retest all conditions were measured twice.

3) *Bandwidth in nonsimultaneous masking*. As Experiment 2, but in forward masking with a probe signal of 35 dB SPL and for peak spacings of 333, 250, and 167 Hz.

4) *Shallow edge in simultaneous masking*. The slope of the shallow edge of the psychophysical tuning curve was estimated by determining the masked thresholds for masker frequencies of 950 and 550 Hz (three runs per condition). A low-pass noise was added in order to mask distortion products.

5) *Shallow edge in nonsimultaneous masking*. As Experiment 4, but in forward masking for masker frequencies of 950 and 750 Hz and without noise.

6) *Steep edge in simultaneous masking*. The steep edge of the psychophysical tuning curve was estimated from the threshold frequencies for two masker intensities, 70 and 90 dB SPL (again three runs per condition). A low-pass noise was added in order to mask distortion products.

7) *Steep edge in nonsimultaneous masking*. As Experiment 6, but in forward masking and without noise.

8) *Temporal window*. With octave-filtered clicks of constant level threshold intensities were measured for intensity-modulated noise in peak and trough conditions and for modulation frequencies of 10, 15 and 20 Hz. In the test and the retest all conditions were measured twice.

9) *Forward masking*. The slope of the forward-masking curve was determined by measuring the time interval required to detect an octave-filtered click after termination of a noise masker for masker levels of 35 and 55 dB/Hz. Each condition was measured three times in test and retest. The signal was presented two times in both observation periods of the 2AFC in order to give a more accurate discrimination between the probe and the random fluctuations of the noise at the end of the masker.

10) *Backward masking*. As Experiment 9, but here the probe preceded the masker.

11) *Cubic difference tone*. The strength of the CDT was measured in two stages. First, the forward-masking-threshold level A of a 1000-Hz probe was measured for a two-tone masker generating a CDT at the probe frequency, and secondly, the level of an acoustic component of frequency $2f_1-f_2$ necessary to mask this probe was measured. The outcome of the second stage was defined as the CDT level.

12) *Suppression*. The strength of lateral suppression was measured for a multi-component suppressor using the same procedure as in Experiment 11. The multi-component suppressor was used to introduce strong suppression effects, but a drawback of this signal is the generation of combination tones influencing the measured suppression.

The stimuli were gated with cosine-squared onset and termination, having rise and fall times of 15 msec, with the exception of the Experiments 9 and 10, and the signals were presented monaurally via electro-dynamic earphones (Beyer DT 48).

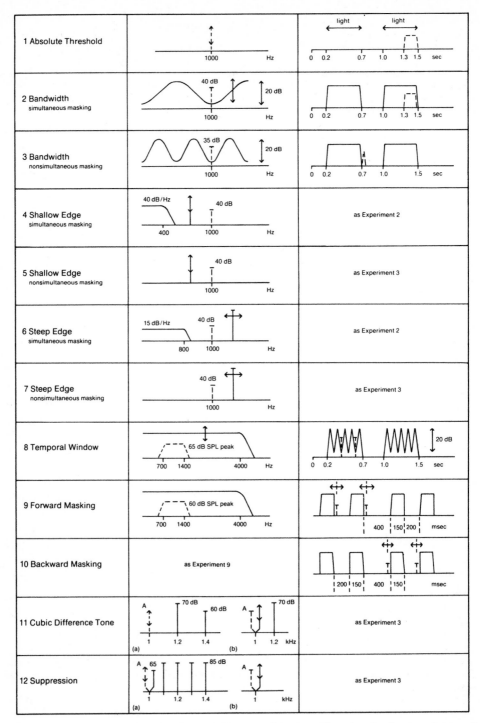

Fig.1. Schematic representation of 12 experiments. The spectral structure of the signals is given in the left column and the temporal structure in the rigth column. The probe signals are dashed and the maskers are fully drawn.

3. PROCEDURE

In the various tests different signal parameters were used to reach the threshold, for instance: probe-signal intensity, masker frequency, and time delay between masker and probe. As an example we describe the measuring procedure for an experiment with a constant probe signal and a variable masker intensity. Each run of 2AFC trials consisted of three stages. The first stage started well above threshold and after each correct response the masker level was raised by a fixed amount untill the first false response. In the second stage the masker intensity was decreased after each false response and raised after two successive correct responses. This stage was introduced to provide a good starting point for the last stage and was terminated after the fourth false response. Stage three consisted of a constant number of trials (20 for the simultaneous-masking experiments and 30 for nonsimultaneous masking) and the mean level of the successive trials was adopted as the final estimate of the threshold. In this stage the masker level was raised after three successive correct responses which procedure converges to a detectability chance of 79%. After each correct response the subject was provided with a visual feedback.

To remove unwanted variance from the data we determined difference scores wherever possible. In these scores interindividual differences in training and alertness are cancelled, provided that these factors exert the same influence upon the two masked thresholds which constitute the difference score. For this reason these two measurements always succeeded each other immediately. A disadvantage of difference scores is the increase of error variance by a factor two with respect to the raw scores.

Finally, the sequence of tests in the whole experiment may contribute to the reduction of measurement error. A randomization of the test sequence over subjects eliminates systematic errors in the mean test results but causes error variance in the interindividual differences as a consequence of sequence effects. However, in this study we were not in the first place interested in optimum average test results but rather in optimum interindividual differences, and for this reason all subjects were tested according to the same schedule.

Testing took place in four morning sessions on four successive days. Half of the tests was carried out in the first session and the other half in the second session. The third and the fourth session were a replication of the first two sessions and provided a retest by which for each test the reliability could be calculated. For each four-day period two subjects participated in the experiments. On the average a test block lasted for a quarter of an hour, after which the subject had a break of the same duration. In the breaks for one subject the other subject was tested. Altogether 50 normal hearing subjects were tested.

4. RESULTS AND DISCUSSION

a) *Correlations*

The results of the individual tests will not be given here; they are discussed in detail elsewhere (Festen and Plomp, 1980). Instead, as we were interested in the first place in the relations among the tests, we will focus our attention on the matrix of correlations (Table I). As can be seen in the table most of the correlations are very low (for 50 subjects $|r| > 0.36$ is significant at a level of 1% and $|r| > 0.28$ at a level of 5%). However, a number of correlations should have our attention. For instance, there is a significant correlation ($r = -0.29$) between the steepness of the shallow edge of the tuning curve and the width of the auditory filter, both measured in simultaneous masking. This correlation may be interpreted as a causal relation in which the shallow edge is one of the determinants of the bandwidth. There is a positive correlation ($r = 0.28$) between the strength of the cubic difference tone and

experiment	kind of score	2	3	4	5	6	7	8	9	10	11	12
1 absolute threshold	*level*	.23	.17	-.04	-.36	.27	-.38	.08	.37	.12	.26	.00
2 bandwidth simult.	*width*		.17	-.29	-.23	-.08	-.18	-.09	-.06	-.06	.28	.27
3 bandwidth nonsimult.	*width*			-.05	-.07	.16	.08	-.08	.07	.01	-.09	-.13
4 shallow edge simult.	*slope*				.09	-.13	-.07	.39	.12	.08	.03	-.16
5 shallow edge nonsimult.	*slope*					-.15	-.02	-.22	-.12	-.09	-.06	.33
6 steep edge simult.	$(slope)^{-1}$						-.12	-.14	.05	-.03	-.11	-.17
7 steep edge nonsimult.	$(slope)^{-1}$							.14	-.12	.12	-.09	-.08
8 temporal window	*width*								.19	.35	-.02	-.22
9 forward masking	$(slope)^{-1}$									.08	.13	.05
10 backward masking	$(slope)^{-1}$										-.17	-.16
11 cubic difference tone	*strength*											-.03
12 suppression	*strength*											

Table I. Matrix of correlations between the difference scores (including the absolute threshold). With each of the experiments the kind of score is indicated for a correct interpretation of the sign of the correlations.

the auditory bandwidth, which is in line with the general finding that the generation of combination tones is favoured by a strong interaction between the primaries. This relation is illustrated in Fig.2 by the results of the bandwidth experiment for three subgroups differing in the strength of their CDT.

Regarding nonlinearity, there is also a positive correlation (r = 0.33) between the strength of lateral suppression and the steepness of the shallow edge of the tuning curve measured in nonsimultaneous masking, suggesting a sharpening of the frequency selectivity due to suppression.

With respect to temporal resolution, there are a few significant correlations. There is a positive correlation (r = 0.39) between the width of the temporal window and the steepness of the shallow edge of the tuning curve. Furthermore, there is also a positive correlation (r = 0.35) between the

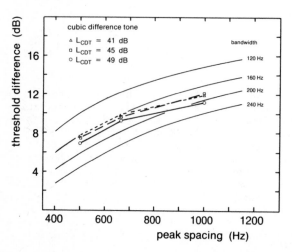

Fig.2. Threshold-level difference for a 1000-Hz probe tone between peak and trough of comb-filtered noise as a function of peak spacing. Different symbols represent three subgroups with different mean CDT level (16, 18, and 16 subjects, respectively). The smooth curves show calculated threshold differences for a gaussian-shaped filter.

reciprocal of the slope of the backward-masking curve and the width of the temporal window, which means that a steep slope goes with a narrow window. Finally, there are a few significant correlations of the absolute threshold: one with the forward-masking slope and one with each of the slopes of the tuning curve in nonsimultaneous masking. For these correlations we have no simple explanation.

b) *Reliability of the tests*

Since most correlations in Table I are very low, the question arises whether these correlations are truely low or only obscured by measurement error. To answer this question the results of the test and the retest for each experiment were used to calculate the test reliability. Subsequently an estimation of the true correlation could be given according to the equation

$$r_\infty = r_{xy} / (r_{xx} r_{yy})^{0.5}, \qquad (1)$$

where r_∞ is the correlation coefficient between the true components in the tests X and Y, or between the average result of the tests X and Y if both were repeated infinite times, r_{xy} is the actually obtained correlation coefficient and r_{xx} and r_{yy} are the coefficients of reliability of X and Y, respectively (cf. Guilford, 1954). The reduction of correlation coefficients due to measurement error, given by the denominator in Eq.1 is called *attenuation*. Fig.3(a) gives the attenuation for each pair of tests. Now that we know the attenuation and the obtained correlation coefficient we can calculate the estimated true correlation by means of Eq.1. The result is shown in Fig.3(b), were the parameter of the curved lines is the absolute value of the estimated true correlation. Here we see that even after a correction for attenuation most correlations are still very low; none of the corrected correlations is

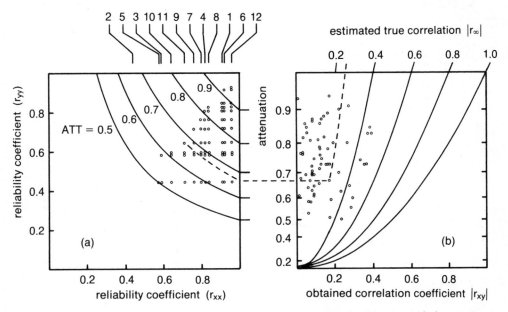

Fig.3. Correction for attenuation applied to 66 correlation coefficients from Table I. Panel (a) gives the attenuation for each pair of tests as a function of their individual reliabilities. The test reliabilities are indicated at the top by the No. of the experiment. Panel (b) gives a scatter diagram of the attenuation found in panel (a) versus the obtained correlations. Different values of the estimated true correlation are represented by curved lines.

greater than 0.5, and thus the low correlations between the tests are not caused by poor test relialibity.

c) *Additional scores*

Apart from the scores already discussed, a number of experiments, or combinations of experiments, give rise to interesting additional scores. The following new scores were introduced:
1) For the tuning curve in simultaneous masking the mean threshold level for the two masker frequencies on the shallow edge (score 4a) and the mean threshold frequency for the two masker levels on the steep edge (score 6a) were introduced.
2) For the tuning curves in simultaneous and in nonsimultaneous masking the Q_{10dB} was calculated (score 4,6 and 5,7 , respectively).
3) For the backward-masking and the forward-masking curves the mean Δt between probe and masker was calculated (score 10a and 9a, respectively).
The correlations introduced by the additional scores are combined in the matrix of Table II. The scores representing parallel shifts (4a, 6a, 9a, and 10a) are confounded with differences in training and alertness among the subjects. These effects have no influence on the correlations between "shift" scores and difference scores, but if the correlations among "shift" scores mutually are high this may be the result of effects of training and alertness in both tests.

The additional scores introduced a number of interesting correlations. In simultaneous masking the bandwidth of the auditory filter measured with comb-filtered noise correlates with Q_{10dB} (r = -0.26) and with the shift of the steep edge away from the probe frequency (r = 0.38).

The possible relation between suppression and the shift of the steep edge of the tuning curve, as proposed by Vogten (1978), could not be demonstrated. With respect to suppression, however, there appears to be a rather high correlation with Q_{10dB} in nonsimultaneous masking (r = 0.48) and a correlation with

	experiment	kind of score	4a	6a	9a	10a	4,6	5,7
1	absolute threshold	*level*	-.06	.29	.23	.06	-.06	-.16
2	bandwidth simult.	*width*	-.25	.38	.03	-.03	-.26	-.05
3	bandwidth nonsimult.	*width*	.01	.14	-.07	.02	-.08	-.12
4	shallow edge simult.	*slope*	xxx	.06	.24	.50	xxx	.11
5	shallow edge nonsimult.	*slope*	.22	-.33	.00	.00	.11	xxx
6	steep edge simult.	$(slope)^{-1}$	-.03	xxx	-.09	-.23	xxx	-.20
7	steep edge nonsimult.	$(slope)^{-1}$	.08	-.22	-.08	-.03	-.04	xxx
8	temporal window	*width*	.11	.18	.49	.53	.39	-.36
9	forward masking	$(slope)^{-1}$	.00	.10	xxx	.17	.13	-.02
10	backward masking	$(slope)^{-1}$	.05	-.05	.28	xxx	.08	-.22
11	cubic difference tone	*strength*	.13	.19	.04	-.05	.07	-.03
12	suppression	*strength*	.07	-.22	-.21	-.09	-.11	.48
4a	shallow edge simult.	*mean level*		-.30	-.25	.07	xxx	.26
6a	steep edge simult.	*mean freq.*			.50	.34	xxx	-.27
9a	forward masking	*mean Δt*				.50	.23	-.19
10a	backward masking	*mean Δt*					.52	-.09
4,6	Q_{10dB} simult.	*sharpness*						.15
5,7	Q_{10dB} nonsimult.	*sharpness*						

Table II. Matrix of correlation coefficients introduced by the additional scores. Correlations between scores obtained from the same data are omitted.

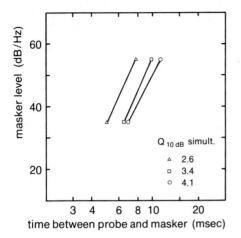

Fig.4. Level of wide-band noise just masking an octave-filtered click probe (1000 Hz) preceeding the masker, as a function of the time between probe and masker. Different symbols represent three subgroups with different tuning-curve sharpness (16, 18, and 16 subjects, respectively).

the slope of the shallow edge of the tuning curve, also in nonsimultaneous masking (r = 0.33). These correlations may be understood as a sharpening of the tuning due to lateral suppression (cf. Houtgast, 1973).

Finally, there is a number of high correlations which are all related to temporal resolution. The width of the temporal window is correlated with the parallel shift away from the masker in both the forward-masking curve (r = 0.49) and in the backward-masking curve (r = 0.53). Additionally, this shift of the backward-masking curve away from the masker is correlated with a good frequency resolution via the slope of the shallow edge in simultaneous masking (r = 0.50) and also via Q_{10dB} in simultaneous masking (r = 0.52). These relations show a trade-off between temporal resolution on one hand and frequency resolution on the other hand, which is in agreement with a theory proposed by Duifhuis (1973). The latter relation is illustrated in Fig.4 by the backward-masking results for three subgroups with different tuning-curve sharpness.

REFERENCES

Duifhuis, H. (1973). "Consequences of peripheral frequency selectivity for nonsimultaneous masking", *J. Acoust. Soc. Am.* 54, 1471-1488.

Elliott, D.N., Riach, W.D., Sheposh, J.P. and Trahiotis, C. (1966). "Discrimination performance of high school sophomores on a battery of auditory tests", *Acta Oto-Laryngol.*, suppl. 216.

Festen, J.M., Houtgast, T., Plomp, R., and Smoorenburg, G.F. (1977). "Relations between interindividual differences of auditory functions", In: *Psychophysics and Physiology of Hearing*, (E.F. Evans and J.P. Wilson, eds). pp 311-319. Academic Press, London.

Festen, J.M. and Plomp, R. (1980). "Relations between auditory functions in normal hearing", submitted to *J. Acoust. Soc. Am.*

Guilford, J.P. (1954). *Psychometric Methods.* McGraw-Hill, New York.

Houtgast, T. (1973). "Psychophysical experiments on 'tuning curves' and 'two-tone suppression'", *Acustica* 29, 168-179.

Vogten, L.L.M. (1978). "Low-level pure-tone masking: a comparison of 'tuning curves' obtained with simultaneous and forward masking", *J. Acoust. Soc. Am.* 63, 1520-1527.

Acknowledgements

The author is much indebted to Prof. R. Plomp for supervising the project.

PSYCHOACOUSTICAL AND PHONETIC MEASURES
OF TEMPORAL PROCESSING IN NORMAL
AND HEARING-IMPAIRED LISTENERS

Richard S. Tyler and A. Quentin Summerfield

*MRC Institute of Hearing Research, University of Nottingham,
Nottingham NG7 2RD, United Kingdom*

1. INTRODUCTION

It is now well established that cochlear pathology typically results in a degradation of frequency analysis and that this can be related to poor speech intelligibility (Tyler, 1979; Bonding, 1979; Tyler, Fernandes and Wood, 1980). The effect of cochlear pathology on temporal processing is less clear. Our aim in the present study is to examine several psychoacoustical measures of temporal processing (temporal integration, gap detection, temporal DL, and gap DL) and to relate these indices to measures of frequency resolution [(psychoacoustical tuning curves (PTC)], speech-intelligibility in noise, and the identification and discrimination of synthetic voiced and voiceless stop consonants distinguished by differences in voice onset time (VOT).

2. METHOD

Sixteen normal and eight hearing-impaired listeners were tested. All listeners were given a minimum of 20 minutes practice. In the psychoacoustical tasks, each threshold was obtained twice, and a third time if the first two values differed by more than 6 dB or 8 ms. Stimuli were presented monaurally to the ear with the least pure-tone threshold loss. When appropriate, a contralateral 1/3 octave narrow-band noise (NBN) was used to mask the non-test ear.

Thresholds were estimated with a three-interval, forced-choice procedure using an adaptive three-up one-down strategy (estimating the 79.4% threshold). In the psychoacoustical tasks, the run was terminated when the same level had been visted four times. The threshold was calculated as the average of all the levels that were revisted more than twice. The intervals were demarcated with a 1-s warning light and three 1-s interval lights, each separated by a 0.5-s pause. This sequence was terminated by a vote light. Feedback was provided by illuminating the correct interval light. We find the 3-interval forced-choice method preferable to the more widely used 2-interval method, because naive listeners can select the interval that sounds different, regardless of the parameters under test.

In the *Temporal Integration* condition, listeners were required to select which of the three intervals contained the signal. Thresholds were obtained for tones of 10- and 1000-ms durations. The initial 8-dB step size was reduced to 2 dB after 3 reversals in direction. The task was performed with pure-tone stimuli of 500 and 4000 Hz.

PTCs were obtained at 500 and 4000 Hz. Listeners were required to select which of three intervals contained both signal and masker, when the other two intervals contained only the masker. Masker intensity was varied with an ini-

458

tial 8-dB step size which was reduced to 2 dB after 3 reversals. For the 500-Hz signal (at 10 dB SL), masker frequencies were 350, 450, 550 and 650 Hz. For the 4000-Hz signal, masker frequencies were 2500, 3500 and 4200 and 5000 Hz.

In the *Gap-Detection* condition, listeners were required to select which of three, 1-s noise bursts contained a silent gap. The initial gap of 80 ms was varied with an 8-ms step size, which was reduced to 2 ms after 3 reversals. The gap occured 500 ms after the noise onset, and the duration of the gap was subtracted from the duration of the following noise, keeping the total duration of the noise at 1 s. The task was performed with NBN stimuli of 500 Hz and 4000 Hz.

In the *Gap-DL* condition, listeners were required to select which of three 1-s noise bursts contained the longest silent gap. The standard stimulus was a noise burst of 500 ms, followed by a *30-ms* silent gap, followed by a 470-ms noise burst. (The duration of the gap increment was always subtracted from this later 470 ms.) The initial increment in the gap was 100 ms and was varied using a step size of 8 ms, which was reduced to 2 ms after 3 reversals. The task was performed with NBN stimuli of 500 and 4000 Hz. A second Gap-DL condition was implemented in which the standard gap duration was *100 ms* and the initial increment in the gap was 120 ms.

In the *Temporal-DL* condition, listeners were required to select which of three noise bursts (which began 500 ms after the interval-light onset) was the longer. The standard duration was *30 ms* and the initial increment of 100 ms was varied with an 8-ms step size, which was reduced to 2 ms after 3 reversals. The task was performed with NBN stimuli of 500 and 4000 Hz.

The -3 dB points of the NBN stimuli were 450 and 550 Hz for the 500-Hz signal, and 3700 and 4300 Hz for the 4000-Hz signal. The noise skirts dropped off at 96 dB/octave and the noise floor was at least 50 dB below energy within the pass band. The normal listeners received the 500-Hz NBN stimuli at 62 dB SPL and 102 dB SPL, and the 4000-Hz stimuli at 49 dB SPL and 89 dB SPL. The hearing-impaired listeners were only tested at the higher intensities. All durations (gaps included) are specified between 50% points on the envelope. All rise-fall times were 6 ms, between 10 and 90% points on the envelope.

Speech intelligibility in noise was assessed with the FAAF test (Foster and Haggard, 1979) presented at 98 dB SPL (ANSI, 53.6- 1969)in the presence of a continuous, speech-spectrum shaped noise of 78 dB A (as measured in a Bruel and Kjaer 4153 artificial ear).

Listeners identified and discriminated two sets of *synthetic speech syllables*. For the identification test, two 7-member continua of 5-formant consonant-vowel syllables ranging in VOT from 0 to +60 ms in steps of 10 ms were created with an OVE IIIb serial resonance speech synthesiser. Formant bandwidths and relative intensities were determined according to Fant (1960). One continuum ranged from /ba/ to /pa/, the other from /bi/ to /pi/. For the vowel /a/, the first formant (F1) was set to 760 Hz and the second formant (F2) to 1050 Hz. For /i/, F1 was set to 270 Hz and F2 to 2050 Hz. Inclusion of both vowels would allow examination of spectral influences on temporal processing in a phonetic task. Following practice trials, listeners heard separate randomisations containing ten instances of each member of each continuum and identified the initial consonant as either /b/ or /p/. In the discrimination task a three-up, one-down adaptive procedure was used to determine the 79.4% DL for VOT increments with standards of +15 ms and +30 ms. The initial increment was 30 ms and the initial step size was 8 ms. The step size was reduced to 2 ms after four reversals, and the DL was computed as the mean of the VOTs at the next four reversals. The stimuli were presented in a three-interval forced-choice format. The intensity of the VOT stimuli varied both with the vowel and with VOT. They were presented to the normal listeners at two levels, one 40 dB down relative to the other, and to the hearing-impaired listeners only at the higher level which was /ba/:VOT = 0, 96.5 dB SPL; /pa/:VOT = 60, 95.0 dB SPL; /bi/:VOT = 0, 88.0 dB SPL, /pi/:VOT = 60, 86.5 dB SPL (ANSI, S3.6-,1969).

3. RESULTS

a) *Psychoacoustics*

i) *Normal listeners*   Table I shows the results of the psychoacoustical tasks. Stimulus frequency had little effect on the temporal-processing tasks. The only exception was the gap-detection task, where it was easier to detect the gap in the 4000-Hz NBN rather than the 500-Hz NBN. There was a tendency for poorer temporal resolution in the low-intensity conditions. This effect is apparent with gap-detection at 500 Hz, but is reduced or nonexistent with gap detection at 4000 Hz and gap DL (100 ms). Note the large intersubject variability with the gap-DL conditions. This was not evident in either the gap-detection or temporal-DL condition.

ii) *Hearing-impaired listeners*   The lower section of Table I displays results for the hearing-impaired listeners whose average thresholds at 500 and 4000 Hz were elevated by about 26 and 59 dB compared to the normals. PTC tuning was generally poorer for the hearing-impaired listeners, particularly at 4000 Hz where their pure-tone thresholds were higher. Temporal integration at 500 Hz was similar for the hearing impaired and the normals, but at 4000 Hz was reduced for the hearing-impaired listeners. On the remaining psychoacoustical tasks, the hearing-impaired listeners generally performed more poorly than the normals. However there were large *individual* differences among the hearing-impaired group, with normal performance on some tasks.

b) *Speech tasks*

Table II shows the results of the speech tasks. For the VOT tasks, four scores have been tabulated for each vocalic context. The first is an estimate of the VOT corresponding to the phoneme BOUNDARY, (the 50% crossover on the identification function). It was computed by totalling the number of 'B' responses and subtracting five. Our primary interest is to use this measure as an indicant of any *change* in the balance of voiced and voiceless percepts between conditions, for which it is as sensitive as are phoneme boundaries estimated by more sophisticated curve-fitting procedures (Miller and Morse, 1979). The second measure is an estimate of the SLOPE of the identification function in the region of the phoneme boundary. It was computed as the difference between the number of 'B' responses made to the pair of stimuli spanning the phoneme boundary divided by the number of milliseconds of VOT distinguishing them. Consistency across listeners was high for both the BOUNDARY and SLOPE measures. However, this was not true of the VOT DLs where greater variability among listeners occurred.

i) *Normal listeners*   The average /ba-pa/ phoneme boundary at the higher intensity, 22.4 ms, corresponds almost exactly to the value of 23 ms reported by Lisker and Abramson (1970) for speakers of Americal English. In the present study, boundaries increased with the change in vocalic context from /a/ to /i/ and with the reduction in intensity. VOT DLs were larger in /i/ context than /a/, and with standards of 30 compared to 15 ms, but did not vary with presentation level. (The apparent exception for the 15-ms standard with the vowel /i/ is largely due to two listeners who produced atypically large DLs at the higher intensity.)

ii) *Hearing-impaired listeners*   Neither the phoneme boundaries nor the boundary slopes produced by the hearing-impaired listeners differed systematically from those of the normals. There is a trend in the averaged data for DLs to be longer for the impaired group. Like normals, the impaired listeners tended to produce larger DLs with /i/ compared to /a/, and with the 30-ms compared to the 15-ms standard.

Table I: Results for the psychoacoustical tasks. Average data for 16 normal listeners are shown for high- and low-intensity stimuli in rows one and two. This is followed by individual data from hearing-impaired listeners for high-intensity stimuli. Average data for hearing-impaired listeners are shown in the bottom row. Standard deviations are given in brackets. The first data column displays pure-tone thresholds. The PTC TUNING was determined by subtracting the slope on the low-frequency side of the signal frequency from the slope on the high-frequency side. A sharply tuned PTC will be represented by a large value while flattened or w-shaped PTCs will be represented by small or negative numbers. The PTC Tuning for the normals was averaged from 12 and 15 listeners, for the 500- and 4000-Hz PTC, respectively. Temporal-integration values represent the relative differences between the thresholds of the 1-s and 10-ms tones. [CNT =could not test]

LISTENER TYPE	THRESHOLD (dB SPL)		PTC TUNING (dB/Hz)		TEMP INTEG (dB)		GAP DETECT (ms)		GAP DL (30) (ms)		GAP DL (100) (ms)		TEMP DL (30) (ms)	
	500	4000	500	4000	500	4000	500	4000	500	4000	500	4000	500	4000
NORMAL														
High Intensity	20.0 (4.8)	16.5 (4.8)	.10 (.06)	.017 (.01)	12.5 (4.7)	11.2 (3.0)	13.3 (4.2)	7.43 (1.6)	53.1 (17.7)	51.2 (14.4)	75.7 (29.5)	71.2 (23.2)	18.8 (4.8)	17.9 (5.1)
Low Intensity							23.0 (6.7)	7.68 (1.7)	66.2 (14.1)	60.7 (16.9)	74.3 (28.8)	67.6 (29.5)	23.5 (6.1)	23.2 (6.6)
HEARING IMPAIRED														
1	56	79	.05	.002	28.0	7.8	17.7	13.4	108.3	71.5	108.0	84.8	60.4	33.0
2	44	68	.11	0	2.0	5.7	11.2	8.5	77.3	67.3	92.0	100.0	53.3	47.2
3	28	82	-.01	CNT	22.0	5.3	19.8	10.0	63.0	62.4	98.0	97.8	36.0	50.8
4	42	79	.17	.004	10.0	14.3	21.0	13.5	140.0	144.3	128.0	146.3	86.0	63.5
5	32	50	.12	.008	20.0	7.0	23.3	6.3	110.8	104.8	120.8	123.0	52.0	33.3
6	24	74	.17	.001	25.6	4.0	20.6	8.5	65.3	56.0	64.5	68.0	38.6	37.0
7	73	80	.03	-.002	9.2	3.5	24.5	19.0	54.0	44.0	57.1	56.1	20.0	24.0
8	72	90	-.16	CNT	4.5	2.0	79.7	20.0	101.5	98.0	108.0	120.0	74.0	84.7
Average	46.4 (19.0)	75.3 (11.9)	.060 (.1)	.002 (.003)	15.1 (9.9)	6.2 (3.7)	27.2 (21.6)	12.4 (5.0)	90.0 (29.7)	80.9 (32.6)	97.0 (25.2)	99.5 (29.9)	52.5 (21.2)	46.7 (19.7)

Table II: Results for the FAAF and VOT tasks. Average data from normals are shown for high- and low-intensity stimuli in rows one and two above individual data from hearing-impaired listeners for high intensity stimuli. Average data from hearing-impaired listeners are tabulated in the bottom row. Standard deviations have been bracketed. The results of the VOT ta s are summarised by four scores for each vocalic context. The first (PB) is an estimate of the VOT corresponding to the phoneme boundary (the 50% crossover) on the identification function. The second measure (SL) is an estimate of the slope of the identification function in the region of the phoneme boundary. The third and fourth measures (DL(15) and DL(30)) are the difference limens for VOT increments above standards of 15 and 30 ms, respectively.

LISTENER TYPE	SPEECH INTELLIGIBILITY FAAF (% correct)	VOT CONTINUUM /ba/-/pa/				VOT CONTINUUM /bi/-/pi/			
		BOUNDARY (ms)	SLOPE (%B/ms)	DL(15) (ms)	DL(30) (ms)	BOUNDARY (ms)	SLOPE (%B/ms)	DL(15) (ms)	DL(30) (ms)
NORMAL									
High Intensity	83.6 (2.9)	22.4 (5.0)	7.1 (1.5)	11.0 (11.7)	30.1 (20.7)	24.8 (5.5)	6.3 (1.9)	23.1 (19.1)	34.5 (22.5)
Low Intensity		27.9 (3.9)	5.6 (2.3)	11.1 (2.7)	30.4 (18.3)	29.5 (3.9)	5.9 (2.1)	15.7 (11.6)	34.6 (18.0)
HEARING IMPAIRED									
1	73	24	9	9	30	27	6	62	85
2	80	24	7	9	35.5	27	8	59	51
3	65	21	6	10	58	25	10	34	27.5
4	63	18	4	8	31	19	7	32	61
5	59	23	8	6.5	46	22	5	53.5	67
6	70	21	6	42	42.5	28	8	62.5	52
7	61	26	10	5	29	29	6	40.5	76.5
8	37	39	5	85	85	32	1.5	12	85
Average	63.5 (12.7)	24.5 (6.3)	6.9 (2.0)	21.8 (28.2)	44.6 (19.1)	26.1 (4.1)	6.4 (2.5)	44.4 (18.0)	63.1 (19.6)

4. DISCUSSION

Our results suggest that temporal processing can be appreciably impaired with hearing loss. These findings co-exist with reduced frequency analysis, poor speech intelligibility in noise, and a reduction in the sensitivity to VOT differences. However, *identification* of voiced and voiceless stop consonants appears to be normal.

a) *Psychoacoustics·*

i) *Normal listeners*   Our listeners were inexperienced and received only limited practice compared to those in typical psychoacoustical experiments. Thus, our measurements are somewhat inflated compared to those obtained from more practiced listeners, but we feel that comparisons among groups and parametric variations are still meaningful.

Plomp (1964) has suggested that gap detection is related to the decay of sensation of the preceding noise burst that bounds the gap. His data obtained with white noise indicate little effect of level, except that gap detection becomes poorer for levels less than 20 dB SL. Our results show no intensity effect for the 4000-Hz NBN, and poorer gap detection at the lower intensity (about 20-25 dB SL) for the 500-Hz NBN. Comparing our data obtained at 500 and 4000 Hz, the better gap detection at 4000 Hz implies a greater decay of sensation at that frequency. The shorter time constants and larger bandwidths associated with higher-frequency auditory filters are consistent with these findings.

Our larger gap DL at lower intensities and with longer standards is compatible with the results of Abel (1972b). Our temporal DL tasks showed little dependence on frequency, which agrees with the results of Small and Campbell (1962) under similar conditions. Creelman (1962) and Abel (1972a) suggest there is no intensity effect, provided that the stimulus is clearly audible. We show a slight increase in temporal DL at low intensities, where our stimuli were about 20-25 SL (500 Hz) and 25-35 dB SL (4000 Hz).

It is interesting to examine the gap-DL (30 ms) and temporal-DL (30 ms) results. They allow a direct comparison between temporal discrimination of unfilled (gap DL) and filled (temporal DL) intervals. Our data indicate that filled intervals are about three times easier to discriminate than unfilled intervals.

ii) *Hearing-impaired listeners*   If auditory-filter bandwidths are *larger* in hearing-impaired than in normal listeners, then a simple physical realisation of the filter would predict shorter time constants. This might imply *better* temporal resolution in the impaired group. Our findings do not support such a straightforward analogy. It may be that such an effect does exist, but is obscured by other abnormalities.

Our results are consistent with previous research showing poorer gap detection in hearing-impaired listeners (Boothroyd, 1973; Fitzgibbons and Wightman, 1979), but disagree with the conclusions of Rhum *et al*, who reported normal temporal DL in listeners with noise-induced hearing loss. However Rhum *et al* used longer standards (300, 500 and 1000 ms) than our 30-ms standard. They reported that the averaged hearing-impaired temporal DL (300-ms, 4000-Hz tonal standard) was 15.2 ms at 10 dB SL. Their normal DLs averaged 11.9 ms at 10 dB SL and 7.9 ms at 50 dB SL. Therefore, our results do not conflict with those of Rhum *et al*.

Jestadt *et al* (1976) reported that temporal resolution (as measured with Huffman sequences) in normal listeners is poorer at low stimulus intensities. Most of their hearing-impaired listeners were better than normals when compared at similar SLs, but were poorer than normals when compared at similar SPLs. In our data, several hearing-impaired listeners fall within normal limits when compared with the low-intensity stimuli (notably, gap detection at 500 Hz). However, most of our hearing-impaired listeners performed more poorly than normals, regardless of whether they are compared with the high- or low-intensity stimuli.

b. *Speech tasks*

i) *Normal listeners*   The tendency for phoneme boundaries to fall at longer VOTs in /i/ context compared to /a/ has been observed before. In general boundaries fall at progressively longer VOTs as the frequency of the first formant at the onset of periodicity is lowered. It is not known whether the effect should be attributed directly to psychoacoustic factors or to perceptual compensation for the co-variation of F1 onset frequency and VOT that occurs in speech production (Summerfield and Haggard, 1977). A difference in boundary location with absolute intensity has not been reported before. Repp (1979) showed that the boundary on a /da-ta/ VOT continuum shifted by about 10 ms towards longer VOTs as the *relative* intensity of the periodic compared to the aperiodic portions of the stimuli increased over a 24-dB range. Repp found that the boundary did not shift as the overall intensity of the stimuli was reduced from 80 to 69 dB SPL. In the present study, a lower intensity was employed at which the onset of aperiodicity may have been less well defined.

It is not possible to isolate the factors which gave rise to larger VOT DLs in /i/ compared to /a/ context. The aperiodically-excited second and third formants traversed higher frequencies with /i/, and the spectral energy at the onset of periodicity was lower and more diffuse with this vowel. However, the absense of any increase in DLs as overall intensity was lowered, renders explanations in terms of energy relations suspect.

ii) *Hearing-impaired listeners*   Hearing-impaired listeners identified the members of the two VOT continua almost identically to the normals (as measured by their phoneme boundaries and boundary slopes) but they discriminated VOT differences more poorly, particularly with the vowel /i/. Parady *et al* (1979) also examined the abilities of hearing impaired listeners to identify and discriminate synthetic CV stimuli differing in VOT. They reported congruence of identification *and* discrimination data between normal, moderately-impaired and most severely-impaired listeners. Our adaptive procedure would be expected to provide a more sensitive index of discriminative ability than would their procedure which required listeners to discriminate fixed 30-ms differences in VOT. Our result supports Parady *et al*'s contention that speech identification and discrimination tasks may tap different auditory/phonetic processes.

c. *Correlations among measures*

We have examined the correlations among our various measures across the combined group of normal and hearing-impaired listeners. In comparing VOT DLs with other measures, it is important to note that different perceptual strategies could be employed in the VOT DL task with the two different standards. With the 15-ms standard which was heard as /b/, the task could be performed *phonetically* so long as the VOT of the comparison was greater than about 25 ms causing it to be heard as /p/. With the 30-ms standard the task could only be performed *acoustically*, since both the standard and the comparison were heard as /p/. Thus, different patterns of correlations might be expected at the two standards. This is most clearly the case when a comparison is made with the GAP DLs, where sizeable correlations emerged predominantly with the 30-ms VOT DLs. An analogy to the GAP-DL task could be the detection of increments in the relative absence of energy between the broad-band burst of energy at syllable onset and the subsequent onset of energy in the first formant. It remains to be determined why this may be a significant component of the VOT DL task at 30 ms, but not at 15 ms. The *absense* of a correlation with the 15-ms standard, may result from listeners adopting a *phonetic* strategy; or alternatively, a 'GAP-DL' strategy may have been *psychoacoustically* inappropriate due to difficulties in detecting the "gap". Other psychoacoustical DLs correlate with both the 30-ms *and* the 15-ms VOT DLs. The most consistent pattern occurred for the Temporal DLs, confirming expectations that the detection of differences in the energy or duration of aperiodicity in F2 and F3 is an important component of VOT discrimination.

Measures of PTC tuning correlate well with speech intelligibility, consistent with the notion that frequency selectivity, as portrayed by PTCs, reflects an important aspect of speech perception. The results of the gap detection task also display high correlations with speech intelligibility suggesting that gap detection may be an informative measure of temporal resolution. However, these analyses do not allow for the effects of other variables (eg age, pure-tone threshold), which may mediate the above correlations. As more data become available such effects will be tested.

Acknowledgement

We wish to thank A. Davis, M. Fernandes and E. Wood for their assistance with data collection and analysis, and M. Haggard for comments on this paper.

REFERENCES

Abel, S.M.(1972a). Discrimination of temporal gaps. *J.Acoust.Soc.Am.*52,519-524

Abel, S.M.(1972b). Duration of discrimination of noise and tone bursts. *J. Acoust. Soc. Am.* 51, 1219-1223.

Bonding, P.(1979). Frequency selectivity and speech discrimination in sensorineural hearing loss. *Audiology* 8, 205-216.

Boothroyd, A.(1973). Detection of temporal gaps by deaf and hearing children. S.A.R.P. 12, Clarke School for the Deaf.

Creelman, S.D.(1962). Human discrimination of auditory duration. *J.Acoust. Soc. Am.* 34, 582-593.

Fitzgibbons, P.J. and Wightman, F.L.(1979). Temporal resolution in normal and hearing-impaired listeners. *J.Acoust.Soc.Am.* 65, Suppl 1, S133.

Foster, J.R. and Haggard, M.P.(1979). FAAF - An efficient test of speech perception. *Proceedings of the Institute of Acoustics.* Nov 4-6,1979.

Jestadt, W., Bilger, R.C., Green, D.M., Patterson, J.H. (1976). Temporal acuity in listeners with sensorineural hearing loss. *J.Speech Hear.Res.*10, 357-370.

Lisker, L. and Abramson,A.S.(1970). The voicing dimension: some experiments in comparative phonetics. In: *Proceedings of VI International Congress of Phonetic Sciences.* Prague, Academia.

Miller, C.L. and Morse, P.A.(1979). Selective adaptation effects in infant speech perception paradigms. *J.Acoust.Soc.Am.* 65, 789-798.

Parady, S., Dorman, M.F., Whaley,P. and Raphael,L.J.(1979). Identification and discrimination of VOT by listeners with moderate, severe and profound sensorineural hearing loss. *J.Acoust.Soc.Am.* Suppl. 1, 66, S89.

Plomp, R.(1964). Rate of decay of auditory sensation.*J.Acoust.Soc.Am.*36,277-282

Repp,B.H.(1979). Relative amplitude of aspiration noises as a voicing cue for syllable-initial stop consonants. *Language and Speech.*

Ruhm, H.B., Mencke, E.O.,Milburn,B.,Cooper, W.A.,Rose, D.(1966).Differential sensitivity to duration of acoustic signals. *J.Speech Hear.Res.*9,371-384.

Small, A.M. and Campbell, R.A.(1962). Temporal differential sensitivity for auditory stimuli. *Am.J. of Psychol.* 75, 401-410.

Summerfield, A.Q. and Haggard, M.P.(1977). On the dissociation of spectral and temporal cues to the voicing distinction in initial stop consonants. *J. Acoust. Soc. Am.* 62, 435-448.

Tyler,R.S.(1979). Measuring hearing loss in the future. *British J.of Audiology* Suppl. 2,13, 29-40.

Tyler, R.S., Fernandes, M. and Wood, E.J.(1980). Masking, temporal integration and speech intelligibility in individuals with noise-induced hearing loss. In: *Disorders of Auditory Function III.* (I.G.Taylor,ed).Academic Press.

REDUCED SPEECH INTELLIGIBILITY AND ITS PSYCHOPHYSICAL CORRELATES
IN HEARING-IMPAIRED SUBJECTS

W.A. Dreschler

Faculty of Medicine, Free University,
1007 MC Amsterdam, The Netherlands

1. INTRODUCTION

In assessing the consequences of hearing impairment, an important question
is which auditory properties are responsible for the reduction in speech intelligibility. Primarily, of course, the pure-tone audiogram is at issue, but particularly in subjects with sensorineural losses the relation between audiogram
and speech intelligibility is only poor (cf. Noble, 1973). Therefore, it has
been assumed that other auditory properties are involved too. In the first
place, the frequency resolving power of the ear may be an explanatory factor
(Evans, 1978; Scharf, 1978), but there is scarcely experimental evidence for
this assumption. Secondly, speech intelligibility can be affected by a reduced
sound discrimination ability due to suprathreshold distortions, which may be
independent of the audiogram or of the frequency resolving power (for instance,
loudness recruitment). Thirdly, but probably with important practical consequences, there are indications, that speech perception in noise depends on other auditory properties than speech perception in quiet, corresponding to the
distinction Plomp (1978) made for speech-reception thresholds in quiet and in
noise. In this study these three aspects are investigated further in subjects
with sensorineural hearing impairment.

2. SUBJECTS, TESTS AND PROCEDURES

In a preliminary stage a very heterogeneous group of 10 hearing-impaired
adolescents was tested (Dreschler and Plomp, 1980). In a second stage the number of tests was extended and applied to 25 sensorineurally impaired adolescents. Regarding only the common tests of both stages and ignoring in the first
group the two subjects with a conductive loss, a total of 33 sensorineurally
impaired subjects has been subjected to the following experiments:
1) The audiogram was measured at octaves from 250 to 4000 Hz in a 2AFC procedure, using an adaptive up-down strategy.
2) The critical ratio at 1000 Hz was determined by measuring the masked threshold of a 1000-Hz tone in white noise with a spectral density of 60 dB/Hz, using
the same adaptive 2AFC procedure.
3) The discrimination ability was tested by investigating the perception of i-
solated vowel segments, generated by repeating one period by the computer. Using the method of triadic comparisons, dissimilarity matrices for a set of 8
vowels were obtained.
4) The speech-reception threshold for sentences was measured in quiet and at
four levels of interfering noise by means of the accurate test developed by
Plomp and Mimpen (1979).

All tests were performed monaurally with headphones, and, for the estimation of the accuracy, in test and in retest. In the following the mean values
of test and retest are used. For ease of survey, data-reduction techniques
were applied.

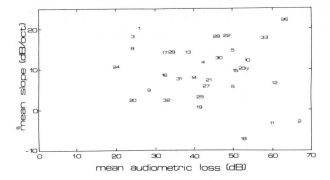

Fig.1. Representation of the individual audiograms in terms of two parameters: the mean audiometric loss and the mean audiometric slope.

3. RESULTS

The audiometric data of all subjects were subjected to a principal-components analysis to achieve data reduction with a minimum loss of information about inter-individual differences. In two dimensions, 84% of the total variance could be explained (53% by the first and 31% by the second dimension). In this plane the direction of the mean audiometric loss was approximately at right angles to the direction of the mean audiometric slope, corresponding to the results of the preliminary study. Therefore, inter-individual differences could be described also in terms of mean loss and mean slope of the audiogram, as done in Fig.1 (the slope of audiograms with a progressive loss towards higher frequencies is defined as positive).

The critical ratio, expressed as tone threshold in dB relative to noise spectral density in dB/Hz ranged from 21.6 to 36.2 dB with a mean value of 29.9 dB and an inter-individual standard deviation of 3.0 dB.

The dissimilarity matrices of all subjects were analysed by Carroll and Chang's INDSCAL, performed in two dimensions. An assumption in INDSCAL is that all subjects use the same fundamental dimensions in their judgement of the stimuli. The plot of all stimuli as a function of these dimensions, called the

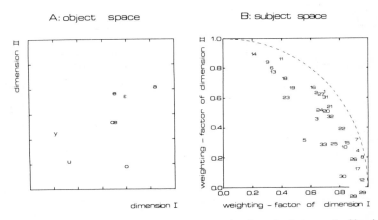

Fig.2. Results of a two-dimensional INDSCAL analysis of the vowel-dissimilarity matrices. In panel A the object space is given for the 8 vowels, indicated with IPA symbols. Panel B presents the subject space with the individual weightings.

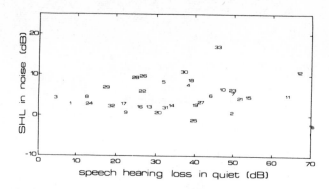

Fig.3. The calculated values of speech hearing loss (SHL) in noise (D), plotted versus the calculated values of SHL in quiet (A+D).

object space, is given in Fig.2(a). Because of the close correspondence with the well known F1-F2 representation of vowel spectra (correlation coefficients between the factor loadings and the formant positions are 0.92 and 0.87, respectively), the fundamental dimensions in vowel perception may be assumed to be the positions of the first and second formant of the vowels. However, the subjects differ with respect to the weight in which each dimension contributes to the final decision. The plot of these individual weightings, called the subject space, is presented in Fig.2(b). The quarter of a circle represents the extreme position of the individual points, reached if all variance is explained by the first two dimensions. On the average, the F1-information accounts for 51% of the total variance, the F2-information for 27%.

For each subject the speech-reception thresholds as a function of the interfering noise level were fitted according to a model by Plomp (1978). From the fitted curves two parameters emerged: (1) the D-parameter, representing the elevation of the speech-reception threshold in noise, relative to the noise level, interpreted as a distortion term; (2) the (A+D)-parameter, representing the threshold elevation in quiet, interpreted as resulting from attenuation (A) and distortion (D) together. In Fig.3 the individual results are plotted.

The correlations between the parameters mentioned are given in Table I. The significance is indicated by underlining.

	2	3	4	5	6	7
1. *mean audiometric loss*	-0.15	0.47	0.03	-0.11	0.79	0.53
2. *mean audiometric slope*		-0.29	0.43	-0.52	-0.46	0.41
3. *critical ratio*			-0.09	0.04	0.33	0.05
4. *F1-weighting*				-0.88	-0.08	0.30
5. *F2-weighting*					0.08	-0.51
6. *SHL in quiet (A+D)*						0.28
7. *SHL in noise (D)*						

Table I: Matrix of correlation coefficients for the parameters extracted. The underlined values are significant at the 1% level, the dashed lines indicate values, which are significant at the 10% level. (n=33).

4. DISCUSSION AND CONCLUSIONS

From the separate tests and their correlations points of interest are:
1) From the pure-tone thresholds of this group of sensorineurally impaired subjects about 84% of the total variance could be explained by a description of the audiograms in terms of mean audiometric loss and mean audiometric slope.
2) The fundamental dimensions involved in vowel perception are the positions of the first and second formant of the vowels. The individual weightings of these two dimensions show a trade-off between the F1- and F2-information.
3) Speech-reception thresholds in quiet and noise are only weakly correlated.
4) The critical ratio is related to the mean audiometric loss. Considered in more detail, especially the low-frequency thresholds were responsible for this relation, which explains the weak negative correlation with the mean slope.
5) In vowel perception the trade-off between the F1- and F2-weighting is only influenced by the mean slope of the audiogram, in such a way that a sloping audiogram stimulates a high F1-weighting and a low F2-weighting.
6) The relation between the audiogram and the speech-hearing loss in quiet and noise is a complex one: both parameters are positively correlated with the mean audiometric loss, but for descending audiograms the D-parameter is favoured at the cost of the (A+D)-parameter. From Fig.1 and Fig.3 it can be seen, that the D-parameter is relatively low for flat audiograms and high for sloping ones.
7) Speech perception in noise is also correlated with the distortions in vowel perception, but in view of the common underlying dependence of both on the mean audiometric slope it is doubtful whether this is an independent effect.

These conclusions are in fair agreement with the results of the first group of 10 subjects (Dreschler and Plomp, 1980). However, compared with the total group, the first group was dominated by descending audiograms (88% of the total variance could be explained by one factor, interpreted as the high-frequency loss). The critical ratio was strongly correlated to this high-frequency loss factor (r=0.91), resulting in the difficulty to ascribe deteriorations in vowel and speech perception to either the audiogram or the critical ratio.

From the total group it can be seen, that the effect of the critical ratio on the speech-hearing loss is only weak, although the critical-ratio values in this group are clearly higher than in normal-hearing subjects. Therefore, the question which auditory properties are together with the audiogram responsible for the reduced speech intelligibility has not been answered thus far. To investigate the role of consonants in this matter, consonant confusions in quiet and in noise were determined in the second group and are studied now.

REFERENCES

Dreschler, W.A. and Plomp, R. (1980). "Relation between psychophysical data and speech perception for hearing-impaired subjects", submitted to *J.A.S.A.*
Evans, E.F. (1978). "Peripheral auditory processing in normal and abnormal ears", *Scand. Audiol.*, suppl. 6, 9-47.
Noble, W.G. (1973). "Pure-tone acuity, speech-hearing ability and deafness in acoustic trauma", *Audiology* 12, 291-315.
Plomp, R. (1978). "Auditory handicap of hearing impairment and the limited benefit of hearing aids", *J.A.S.A.* 63, 533-549.
Plomp, R. and Mimpen, A.M. (1979). "Improving the reliability of testing the speech-reception threshold for sentences", *Audiology* 18, 43-52.
Scharf, B. (1978). "Comparison of normal and impaired hearing II: frequency analysis, speech perception", *Scand. Audiol.*, suppl. 6, 81-106.

Acknowledgements

This research was granted by the Netherlands Organization for the Advancement of Pure Research. The author wishes to thank Prof. R. Plomp for his stimulating support of this study.

COMMENT ON "Reduced speech intelligibility and its psychophysical correlates in hearing-impaired subjects" (W.A. Dreschler).

G.F. Pick
Department of Communication & Neuroscience, University of Keele, Keele, Staffordshire, ST5 5BG, England.

Pick, Evans, and Wilson (unpublished experiments) have investigated the relationship between speech intelligibility and frequency resolution. Speech audiograms from a sub-group of the patients described in Pick *et al.* (1977) were measured in the quiet and in the presence of 79 dB SPL white noise masker (an adequate suprathreshold masker in the frequency range 0.5 to 4 kHz for the patients chosen). A correlation greater than that reported by Dreschler was found between the 1 kHz critical ratio and the speech reception threshold (SRT) both in the quiet (r=0.73, n=16), and in the presence of the masking noise (r=0.40, n=11). A higher correlation was also found between mean audiometric threshold (averaged at 0.5, 1 and 2 kHz) and SRT (r=0.91, n=21 in quiet, and r=0.41, n=17 in masking noise). The reasons for these differences are not clear, but might be related to the use by Pick, *et al.* of patients with fairly flat losses, and the use of free-response, CVC-word tests.

Pick, *et al.* (1977) investigated the relationship between critical ratio and pure-tone threshold. Table one shows a partial matrix of correlations between pure-tone threshold and critical ratio. The table indicates that some

critical ratio frequency (kHz)	Pure tone threshold frequency (kHz)					number of ears
	0.5	1	2	4	Mean for frequencies	
0.5	0.74	0.61				19
1	0.65	0.75			0.69	26
2		0.50	0.51	0.48		21
4			0.38	0.46		18

Table 1. Correlation coefficients

correlation is lost when audiometric thresholds are averaged and that the best correlation is obtained between tone threshold and critical ratio at the same frequency. It also appears that critical ratios are slightly better correlated with pure tone threshold at an octave lower than at an octave higher in frequency.

REFERENCES

Pick, G.F., Evans, E.F., and Wilson, J.P. (1977). Frequency resolution in patients with hearing loss of cochlear origin. In: *Psychophysics and Physiology of Hearing.* (E.F. Evans and J.P. Wilson, eds.). Academic Press, London.

COMMENT ON: "Reduced speech intelligibility and its psychophysical correlates in hearing-impaired subjects" (W.A. Dreschler)

R.S. Tyler
M.R.C. Institute of Hearing Research,
University Park,   University of Nottingham, U.K.

The correlation obtained by Dreschler between critical ratio and mean audiometric loss are consistent with some of our own findings.   We have measured tonal thresholds in broad-band noise in 10 normal and 16 cochlear-impaired listeners at 4 signal frequencies and 4 masker levels (Tyler, Fernandes and Wood, 1980).   With a 60 dB/Hz noise level, the correlation coefficients between thresholds in noise and thresholds on quiet were r = 0.36, 0.44, 0.63 and 0.64 for signal frequencies of 0.5, 1.0, 2.0 and 4.0 kHz respectively.   A few hearing-imparied listeners display pronounced masking effects with low noise levels, but normal masking effects with high noise levels.   In other words, the critical ratio can depend upon the noise level at which they are tested. Under some stimulus conditions, we find a significant correlation between masked thresholds and speech intelligibility.   However, both are also related to absolute thresholds, and we are not able to establish any causal relationships.

Tyler, R.S., Fernandes, M. and Wood, E.J. (1980).   Masking of Pure tones by broad-band noise in cochlear-impaired listeners: *submitted for publication.*

RELATIONS BETWEEN HEARING LOSS, MAXIMAL WORD DISCRIMINATION SCORE AND WIDTH OF PSYCHOPHYSICAL TUNING CURVES

R.J.Ritsma, H.P.Wit and W.P.van der Lans

Institute of Audiology, University Hospital Groningen, The Netherlands.

1. INTRODUCTION

In clinical practice it is a well known fact that a sensorineural hearing loss affects the absolute hearing threshold as well as the speech-sound discrimination. The loss in speech-sound discrimination is thought to be due in part to a widening of the auditory filter. The aim of this study is to compare the filter bandwidths for the frequencies 500, 1000, 2000 and 4000 Hz with the hearing loss and with the maximal word discrimination score; the latter being a measure of speech-sound discrimination.
Pick et al. (1977) measured the frequency resolution using Békésy threshold tracings under masking by comb-filtered noise. Correlationcoëfficients of +.60 and +.72 were found between the patients' bandwidths and hearing levels (0 to 80 dB loss) at four different probe frequencies (500, 1000, 2000,and 4000 Hz). At losses up to about 20 dB the indicated frequency-resolving bandwidths were normal, but above 30 dB loss the bandwidths tended to be larger with larger losses. Zwicker et al.(1978) developed a clinical method for determining psychophysical tuning curves with the two-tone masking procedure, using only a few (6) masker tones at frequencies above and below each of two probe tones (500 and 4000 Hz). Groups of subjects with different types of impaired hearing were compared with normal in sharpness of tuning as seen in the frequency slopes of the masker levels. The 10 dB-bandwidth could not be determined because with this procedure measuring of the tip of the tuning curve is impossible.
As we were interested in the filter-bandwidths for speech frequencies of every patient, a new clinical method for determining psychophysical tuning curves has been developed.

2. METHOD

Psychophysical tuning curves were obtained by determining the minimum level of a narrow-band noise needed to mask a pure tone signal of fixed level and frequency as a function of the center frequency of the masker. Due to its fluctuating amplitude a narrow-band noise masker obscures beats produced when the center frequency is close to the signal frequency and thus makes it possible to measure the tip of the tuning curve (Johnson-Davies et al., 1979). The signal was a sine wave with a level of 15 dB SL. switched on and off smoothly with an on-duration of 220 msec and an off-duration of 280 msec. The narrow-band noise was generated by a sine-random-generator (B&K, type 1024). This generator produces band noise with steep skirts (36 dB/100 Hz). For a signal of 500 and 1000 Hz the band noise had a width of 100 Hz; for a signal of 2000 and 4000 Hz a width of 300 Hz. The stimuli were presented monaurally via TDH-39 headphones. For the determination of the tuning curves 7 masker frequencies were taken, three below, one equal to, and three above each of the four signal frequencies. The experiment employed normal Békésy threshold tracing for determination of both the hearing level in quiet and the masker levels at the various frequencies.

3. SUBJECTS

13 Subjects with normal hearing and 45 patients with rather flat hearing losses up to 60 dB in the range of 250-6000 Hz participated in the experiment. The hearing losses were of cochlear origin. The restriction of hearing losses up to 60 dB was made because for higher losses the psychophysical tuning curve tends to deteriorate into a W-shape, making a 10 dB-bandwidth determination meaningless (Leshowitz, et al., 1977; Hoekstra, et al., 1977). From these 45 patients 15 ears possessed an audiogram with a slope less than 10 dB per octave below 2000 Hz and a slope less than 20 dB per octave above 2000 Hz. For these 15 ears the mean hearing loss with the SD is given in fig. 1.

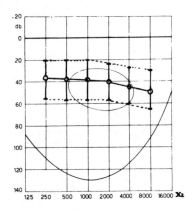

Fig. 1 Mean hearing loss with SD as a function of frequency for 15 selected ears.

4. RESULTS AND DISCUSSION

All subjects gave reliable results as could be checked by comparison of their hearing level in quiet and the masker level of the narrow-band noise centered to the probe frequency (SD=2.5 dB). Fig. 2 shows a representative result of psychophysical tuning curves at 2000 Hz, obtained from three subjects: (A) with normal hearing, (B) a hearing loss of 25 dB and (C) a hearing loss of 54 dB . The Q_{10}-values (center frequency/10 dB-bandwidth) are given.
The mean Q_{10}-values found for the 13 subjects with normal hearing, are at the frequencies 500, 1000, 2000 and 4000 Hz: 3.0 ± 0.5, 5.0 ± 0.7, 4.6 ± 0.7 and 5.8 ± 1.0, resp. Variation of these mean Q_{10}-values has been caused by the width of the narrow-band noise at the various frequencies, 100 Hz at 500 and 1000 Hz and 300 Hz at 2000 and 4000 Hz. For reason of comparison the Q-values for the subjects with normal hearing have been normalized on the averaged value of 4.6, giving correction factors of 1.53, 0.91, 1.01 and 0.79 for the signal frequencies 500, 1000, 2000 and 4000 Hz.
For the 15 selected ears the normalized Q_{10}-values for the various frequencies are plotted as a function of the hearing loss in fig. 3. The correlation coefficient is -.80. Extrapolation down to a hearing loss of 0 dB gives a Q_{10}-value of 5.5. As subjects with normal hearing have a normalized Q_{10}-value of 4.6 it seems likely to assume that the Q_{10}-value is constant for hearing losses up to 15 dB (Pick et al., 1977). In the range of 15-65 dB hearing loss the Q_{10}-value decreases linearly from 4.6 to 1.0, i.e. the Q_{10}-value of the mechanical filter as can be derived from Békésy's curves (von Békésy, 1960).

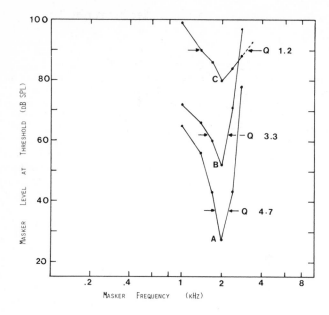

Fig.2 *Psychophysical tuning curves obtained from three subjects: (A) with normal hearing, (B) a hearing loss of 25 dB and (C) a hearing loss of 54 dB.*

The maximal word discrimination score was taken as a measure for speech-sound discrimination. It has been derived from ordinary speechaudiometry using PB-

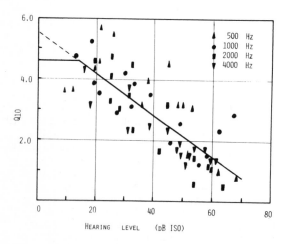

Fig.3 *The normalized Q_{10}-values for various frequencies as a function of the hearing loss for 15 selected ears. (The sloping straight line is the linear regression line fit to all 60 points).*

word lists. In fig. 4 the maximal word discrimination score has been plotted as a function of the $\overline{Q}_{10}$-values for all patients. The $\overline{Q}_{10}$-value is the mean of the individual Q_{10}-values for the frequencies 500, 1000, 2000 and 4000 Hz. For $\overline{Q}_{10}$-values larger than 3.0 the spread in the maximal word discrimination score is rather small. For $\overline{Q}_{10}$-values less than 3.0 the spread is tremendous. For a $\overline{Q}_{10}$-value of 2.0 the maximal word discrimination score varies between 25 and 100 per cent.

Hoekstra, et al. (1977) did not find a one-to one relationship between tuning curve and frequency discrimination with bandfiltered periodic pulse trains. In general they found that a bad tuning curve did not imply bad frequency discrimination. From this study we conclude that widening of the auditory filter may have influence on speech-sound discrimination, but if so, it is not the only decisive factor.

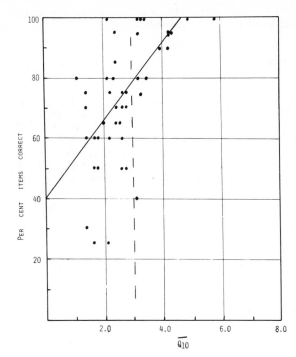

Fig. 4 *The maximal word discrimination score as a function of the mean 10 dB-bandwidth $(\overline{Q}_{10})$ for all 45 patients.*

REFERENCES

von Békésy, G.(1960). Experiments in hearing. Mc Graw–Hill, New York, pp 454.

Hoekstra, A. and Ritsma, R.J. (1977). Perceptive hearing loss and frequency selectivity. In: *Psychophysics and Physiology in hearing.* (E.F.Evans and J.P.Wilson, eds.), pp 263-271. Ac.Press.London.

Johnson-Davies, D. and Patterson, R.D. (1979). Psychophysical tuning curves: Restricting the listening band to the signal region. In: *J.Acoust. Soc.Am.* 65, 765-770.

Leshowitz, B. and Lindstrom, R. (1977). Measurement of nonlinearities in listeners with sensorineural hearing loss. In: *Psychophysics and Physiology in hearing.* (E.F.Evans and J.P.Wilson, eds.). pp 283-292. Ac.Press. London.

Pick, G.F., Evans,E.F. and Wilson, J.P. (1977). Frequency resolution in patients with hearing loss of cochlear origin. In:*Psychophysics and Physiology in hearing.* (E.F.Evans and J.P. Wilson, eds.), pp 273-281. Ac.Press.London.

Zwicker, E. and Schorn, K. (1978). Psychoacoustical tuning curves in audiology. In: *Audiology,* 17, 120-140.

COMMENT ON "Relations between hearing loss, maximal word discrimination score and width of psychophysical tuning curves" (R.J. Ritsma, *et al.*)

G.F. Pick,
Department of Communication & Neuroscience, University of Keele, Keele, Staffs. ST5 5BG, U.K.

Ritsma *et al.* suggest that frequency resolution bandwidth remains normal for hearing losses of less than 20dB. I believe that this statement is not unequivocably proven by the results of Ritsma, *et al.* or by those of Pick *et al.* (1977), because of the large intersubject differences in frequency resolution at any hearing loss. Evidence against the idea was obtained after I received a fairly large, inadvertent, left-ear temporary threshold shift. Fig. 1 (lower) shows threshold recovery as a function of time at three tone frequencies (1kHz – dotted, 2kHz-dashed, and 4kHz-continuous). Threshold had recovered to within 10dB of normal after about three days. The upper part of Fig. 1 shows the recovery of frequency resolution bandwidth as a function of time for the same three frequencies. This bandwidth was obtained using a variant of the method described in Pick *et al.* (1977), using a comb-filtered noise masker with mean spectrum level of 35.7dB SPL. Frequency resolution appears to be impaired at 4kHz until about 30 days after exposure to the noise.

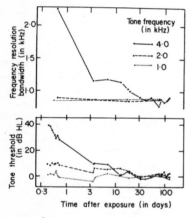

Fig. 1 (Note that upper ordinate should be divided by two for the 2 kHz data, and by four for the 1 kHz data).

(See also comment to paper by Dreschler (this volume))

REFERENCE

Pick, G.F., Evans, E.F. & Wilson, J.P. (1977). Frequency resolution in patients with hearing loss of cochlear origin. In: *Psychophysics and Physiology of Hearing*. (E.F. Evans & J.P. Wilson, eds), pp273-281. Academic Press, London.